BRITISH NORTH AMERICA

N O R T H

A M E R I C A

WESTERN
INTERIOR
PROVINCES

•Santa Fe

EASTERN
INTERIOR
PROVINCES

UNITED STATES

WEST
FLORIDA

A T L A N T I C

VICEROYALTY
OF NEW SPAIN

St. Augustine

EAST FLORIDA

GULF OF MEXICO

TROPIC OF CANCER

Mexico City
(Tenochtitlan)
Cholula⊙
Acapulco

Vera
Cruz

Mérida

Havana

BAHAMA
ISLANDS

O C E A N

CUBA

SANTO
DOMINGO

San Juan

JAMAICA

PUERTO
RICO

Granada⊙

Santa Marta

Cartagena

CARIBBEAN SEA

San José

Portobelo

Caracas

TRINIDAD

Panamá

Bogotá

Orinoco R.

DUTCH
GUIANA

FRENCH
GUIANA

P A C I F I C

VICEROYALTY OF
NEW GRANADA

EQUATOR

GALAPAGOS IS.

Isla Española

Quito⊙

Guayaquil

Barro do
Rio Negro

Amazon R.

Belém

São Luís de
Maranhao

S O U T H

Fortaleza

Cajamarca

VICEROYALTY OF BRAZIL

Pernambuco
(Recife)

Trujillo

VICEROYALTY

Bahia

O C E A N

Callao⊙Lima

Cuzco

A M E R I C A

São Francisco

OF PERU

L. Titicaca

La Paz

Ouro Prêto

TROPIC OF CAPRICORN

Potosí

Paraguay

Rio de Janeiro

São Paulo

VICEROYALTY

Asunción

OF

São Vicente

Tucumán

Pôrto Alegre

Aztec Confederation

RÍO DE LA PLATA

BANDA
ORIENTAL

Rio Grande

Maya Kingdom

Valparaiso
Santiago
de Chile

•Mendoza

Montevideo

Inca Confederation

Concepción•

Bueno Aires

Rio de la Plata

Non-Latin America

Valdivia

Miles

0   500   1000   1500

PATAGONIA

COLONIAL PERIOD

TIERRA
DEL FUEGO

Cape Horn

LATIN AMERICA

LATIN AMERICA

A Historical Reader

Edited by

LEWIS HANKE
University of Massachusetts, Amherst

Little, Brown and Company
Boston

Library of Congress Catalog Card No. 73-2825

SECOND PRINTING

*Published simultaneously in Canada
by Little, Brown & Company (Canada) Limited*

Printed in the United States of America

The photographs in the text are reproduced courtesy of the
following sources:
p. 2, Library of Congress; p. 38, Library of Congress;
p. 92, Foto C. Reyes-Valerio; p. 122, Instituto Nacional de
Anthropologia e Historia, Mexico; p. 164, Library of Congress;
p. 224, Library of Congress; p. 254, Pedro Grases; p. 286, Historical
Pictures Service, Chicago; p. 318, Instituto Nacional de Anthropologia
e Historia, Mexico; p. 374, Historical Pictures Service, Chicago;
p. 446, Hispanic Society of America; p. 484, United Press International;
p. 538, John W. F. Dulles; p. 582, Sra. Gertrude Duby Blom.

*To all teachers
wherever they may be
in schools, community colleges,
and universities with or without walls,
who are helping students
to gain fuller understanding of
the complexities, varieties, and values
of Latin American civilizations*

PREFACE

The selections in this volume come from the second, revised edition of my two-volume set of readings entitled "History of Latin American Civilization: Sources and Interpretations," and are designed particularly for one-semester courses. Both works are intended to provide students with a representative collection of historical documents and views on the civilization of that enormous and variegated area to the south that we call Latin America. Many significant publications have appeared during the last five years, which accounts for the fact that about half of the items in this volume were not included in the first edition of the two-volume edition.

Publications on Latin America, especially on its recent history and particularly on such key figures as Fidel Castro, Che Guevara, and Salvador Allende, are being produced in such numbers that it is difficult if not impossible to select material. Inasmuch as teachers may be expected to follow this literature as it appears, these readings do not attempt to include much on such topics because writings on current Latin American economic and political affairs often become out of date rapidly.

Moreover, it has always seemed to me that we must depend upon the teachers to give tone and direction to the courses they offer. Readings can be useful, but it is teachers in the classroom who have the opportunity, and the responsibility, to include in their courses the results of their own experience, their own readings, their own approaches to the study of Latin America. Likewise, as more and more general students are attracted to Latin America because of the excellence of the teachers and in order to learn about this remarkable continent, teachers will discover a considerable variety in motivation and interest among their students. They need, and deserve, some personal attention to bring to their attention readings of special connection to their individual concerns. Only an alert teacher can adequately perform this essential part of the learning process.

ACKNOWLEDGMENTS

Though I accept full responsibility for the planning and execution of this volume, I have been given much help by my colleagues and students in the preparation of the first and second editions of the two-volume edition which have served as the basis for this work. In the difficult task of drawing upon these volumes for the one-volume edition, I have been fortunate in having available the advice of Dorothy T. Scanlon. Other teachers who made valuable contributions with their insights and experience were Gerald F. Burroni, Wayne M. Clegern, Robert Dodds, Francis A. Dutra, Thomas O. Flickema, Benjamin A. Frankel, Donna Guy, Embert J. Hendrickson, Karen Kennelly, Dawn Keremitsis, Robert Keith, Richard Kornweibel, David T. Leary, Theodore E. Nichols, L. M. Renzulli, Jr., John David Rice, F. Rivera, Peter Rodríguez, William F. Sater, Richard E. Sharpless, Harold Sims, William B. Taylor, and Bernard D. Williams.

In the selection of illustrations for this volume I have benefitted from the advice and assistance of Ignacio Bernal, Theodore S. Beardsley, Jr., Susan Shattuck Benson, John W. F. Dulles, Diane Edwards LaVoy, Robert C. Smith, Kenneth C. Turner, and the staff of the Land Tenure Center of the University of Wisconsin.

To all who helped prepare this volume, I offer my grateful thanks.

Lewis Hanke

CONTENTS

THE COLONIAL EXPERIENCE *1*

SECTION XII

SECTION XIII

SECTION XIV

SECTION XV

Twentieth-Century Revolutionary Changes   583

THE
COLONIAL
EXPERIENCE

An Indian Experiment to Determine Whether Spaniards Were Mortal. Many strange and wondrous fantasies were held by Spaniards as they conquered America (Reading 3). In the early years, they attempted to find out whether Indians "could live like Spanish farmers" by a series of sociological experiments.

Indians also experimented on Spaniards, and in 1508 some Puerto Rican Indians decided to find out whether the Spaniards were mortal or not. If immortal, as was suspected, why bother to war against them? So the Indians held several conquistadores under water in the river to see whether they would be drowned. Then they hauled the lifeless Spaniards to the bank, explaining it was all a joke — for they apparently were convinced the Spaniards were really immortal. But after three days, "when the bodies began to stink," the Indians realized the truth, declared war, and almost wiped the Spaniards out.

The Flemish engraver and book publisher Theodore de Bry (1528–1598) depicted this remarkable experiment.

The Transit
of Civilization

THE INFLUENCE OF EUROPE

Why have so little effort and imagination been spent on determining what ideas, institutions, values, and ways of life the Portuguese and Spaniards carried to America during their more than three centuries of colonial rule? More particularly, why has such minor attention usually been given in Latin American history courses to the European scene, the background from which the conquerors and colonists came?

One answer can be given easily: there is simply too much material on Spanish and Portuguese history, and what interest historians have displayed in the subject has been too narrowly focused on the specific ethnic, cultural, and institutional elements the mother countries transplanted across the Atlantic from 1492 on. Charles Julian Bishko of the University of Virginia, who has been a major figure in enlarging our views of Iberian background studies, would emphasize the period from 711 when the Arabs first swept into the Iberian peninsula until the death of Philip II in 1598, which marks the end of "the basic epoch of the discovery, conquest, and colonization of the Spanish and Portuguese Indies." But he also states: "broadly speaking, from the chronological standpoint, the Background stretches from the first human habitation of the Peninsula right down to present-day Spanish and Portuguese influence upon Latin America."

To this enormous chronological scope, Professor Bishko would join an equally all-embracing approach:

First, the subject should be studied not merely in terms of politico-mili-

3

tary history and biography, but as broadly as modern historians treat Latin America itself, in its social, religious, economic, cultural and juridical aspects. Second, the overworked mechanical formula of tracing Ibero-American ideas or institutions to their metropolitan ancestors should be expanded to include the larger problem of why, how, and from what general context these and not other forms were adopted for use in the Indies. Third, interpretations of the Background should recognize in medieval and early modern Spain and Portugal highly complex, unstable societies moving, in the midst of violent internal change and conflict, from an original dynamic diversity towards the more static ethnic, religious and constitutional uniformity and centralization of the arteriosclerotic seventeenth century, to which, not to earlier periods, so many of our glib generalizations about Spain and Portugal really apply.[1]

Given the size of the task, is it any wonder that Latin Americanists, pressed to cover a large New World history in a short time, have tended to devote scant attention to the Old? Fortunately for students who wish to pursue Iberian background studies further, there has recently appeared a valuable one-volume survey that for the first time provides a solid basis of readings in English.[2]

Another explanation of the special problem faced by Iberian background studies is the influence that present politics sometimes exert on the writing of history. Since the sixteenth century, arguments have been loud and bitter on the correct interpretation of the role of Portugal and Spain in the New World. Grand generalizations still flourish.[3] For some, these Iberian nations redeemed a wilderness of savages and brought them into a Christian, Western way of life; for others the institutions and ways of life brought from Europe were largely destructive and were almost wholly responsible for all the ills Latin America has suffered from 1492 to today. The historical study of these important and enduring influences in the lives of Latin Americans has been hampered by the passion and dogmatism engendered all too often by political considerations.

[1] Charles Julian Bishko, "The Iberian Background of Latin American History: Recent Progress and Continuing Problems," *Hispanic American Historical Review,* 36 (1965), pp. 50–80. The quotations from this article appear on pp. 53–55.

[2] H. B. Johnson, Jr., ed., *From Reconquest to Empire: The Iberian Background of Latin American History,* Borzoi Books on Latin America (New York: Knopf, 1970).

[3] See the author's "A Modest Proposal for a Moratorium on Grand Generalizations: Some Thoughts on the Black Legend," *Hispanic American Historical Review,* 51 (1971), pp. 112–127. For a rebuttal see Benjamin Keen's article, ibid., pp. 336–355.

THE IBERIAN BACKGROUND

We must remember that conquest and colonization was not a simple process, for it varied somewhat from region to region. Moreover, early modern Europe in the era of the Renaissance and Reformation carried medieval elements as well as some modern ideas into an already populated continent whose cultures had been evolving for centuries with few outside contacts. There were also differences between the history and life styles of the Portuguese and Spanish peoples, even though they shared the same peninsula, cherished the same faith, and had much in common. Less has been written on the Portuguese background, but the veteran social historian Gilberto Freyre briefly describes his interpretation of the mobility, miscibility, and adaptability of the Portuguese as significant elements in their character (Reading 1).

Spanish precedents for institutional developments have been studied,[4] but the subject of specific medieval survivals in the New World has received less attention. Ideas are sometimes underestimated by "practical" historians, but no one can ignore the influence of the fancies and speculations as the Spaniards came into contact with an unknown continent and its puzzling people (Reading 3).

Plants and animals are also an integral part of history, and James A. Robertson has compiled one of the few general descriptions of Spanish contributions in this field (Reading 2). Here indeed is an important topic worthy of further study, for the early chroniclers recorded remarkably sharp and detailed observations of flora and fauna. Carl Sauer stated that perhaps no other part of the world has an equal wealth of such data for that time.[5] A recently discovered Aztec map now in the Library of Congress indicates that the Indian leader Don Carlos Chichimecatecotl as early as 1536 began to develop orchards in Mexico, both by introducing Spanish apple, pear, and quince trees and by grafting them onto native stocks.[6]

[4] See Robert S. Chamberlain's *Castilian Backgrounds of the Repartimiento-Encomienda* (Washington, D.C.: Carnegie Institute of Washington, 1939) and "The *Corregidor* in Castile in the Sixteenth Century and the Residencia as Applied to the *Corregidor*," *Hispanic American Historical Review,* 23 (1943), pp. 222–257.

[5] *Handbook of South American Indians,* vol. 6 (Washington, D.C.: Government Printing Office, 1950), p. 487.

[6] Howard F. Cline, "The Oztoticpac Lands Map of Texcoco, 1540," *Quarterly Journal of the Library of Congress,* 23, no. 2 (Washington, D.C., 1966), p. 106. Indians were knowledgeable about plants, as may be seen from Margaret A. Towle's *The Ethnobotany of Pre-Columbian Peru* (Chicago: Aldine Publishing Co., 1961), an excellently

Spaniards embarked upon their conquests in America at the very moment when Antonio de Nebrija had produced the first modern grammar of any European language, the *Gramática Española* (1492), and they raced over the great stretches of the New World while the printing press was being intensely developed in Spain. The books that Spaniards brought to their colonies for pleasure or instruction, or for converting the Indians, are an impressive tribute to their love of the printed page and their conviction of the need to communicate through books. Their record of printing in America, as the Chilean scholar José Toribio Medina has abundantly shown, is most impressive. The sheer quantity of research on printing and books in the Spanish colonies makes it impossible to present a brief selection that will do justice to this aspect of Iberian culture transfer. Many good works exist for the interested student.[7]

NEW WORLD INFLUENCE ON THE OLD

The effect of America on Europe has been even less thoroughly investigated than the transit of civilization westward across the Atlantic. The most immediate and dramatic effect was to be seen in Sevilla, the Andalusian port town that was converted into a thriving international metropolis. The discovery of America doubled its population within fifty years to make it the largest city in Spain, and the fabulous riches that arrived from the New World attracted such a horde of wealth seekers that Lope de Vega generally referred to Sevilla as a "new Babylonia." Professor Ruth Pike eloquently describes the change in the city's tone and values:

> In the sixteenth century Sevillian society underwent a profound transformation. New and economic values were created and old ones discarded as a result of the city's new position as chief port for the Indies. Traditional beliefs emphasizing virtue and valor as the basis for no-

---

documented account of the utilization of wild and domesticated plants in the prehistoric culture of the Andes. See also Pedro Armillas, "Gardens on Swamps: Archeological Research Verifies Historical Data on Aztec Land Reclamation in the Valley of Mexico," *Science,* 174, no. 4010 (November 12, 1971), pp. 653–661. "The material foundations for Aztec imperialism were established by the farmers who had conquered the swamps." Ibid., p. 660.

[7] On one important development see Lawrence S. Thompson, "The Libraries of Colonial Spanish America," *Bibliotheca Docet: Festgabe für Carl Wehmer* (Amsterdam: Verlag der Erasmuss-Buchhandlung, 1963), pp. 257–266. For a more general view see Irving A. Leonard, *Books of the Brave: Being an Account of Books and Men in the Spanish Conquest and Settlement of the Sixteenth-Century New World* (Cambridge, Mass.: Harvard University Press, 1949).

bility fell into disuse. An acquisitive society was emerging, and a spirit of gain overwhelmed the city. Greed for money and dissatisfaction with social and economic status became the common affliction of all Sevillians. The riches from the New World cast a spell over the whole town.[8]

Another obvious and significant effect was the inflation caused by the great influx of minerals, especially silver, which Professor John Lynch has competently analyzed. Spain was primarily an exporter of raw materials and an importer of manufactured goods, and she used American silver to make up for her unfavorable trade balance. Spain also "lavished more and more on foreign enterprise," and the result was a sharp increase in prices, which raised the cost of living for all Spaniards.[9] Since the classic work on Spanish prices by Earl J. Hamilton a generation ago, much attention and some criticism have been directed toward his explanation that American silver caused the price revolution. Recently a Hungarian historian, Tibor Wittmann, has suggested that internal conditions in Spain were perhaps even more influential than the influx of American silver.[10] But another survey of the enormous literature on Spain's decline confirms that her economy was indeed adversely affected by riches from the New World.[11]

Except for treasure, the influence of the New World on the Old has had an uncertain effect, which Professor John H. Elliott sets forth in a persuasive way (Reading 4). Since the sixteenth century the question has been raised in Europe whether the discovery of America was a boon or bane for mankind. In the eighteenth century, prize contests were organized in France for the best essay on the subject, and generalizations pro and con flourished among the Enlightenment philosophers.

The Pacific Ocean as well as the Atlantic was a highway that moved ideas, plants, silks, and spices back and forth between Spanish America and the Orient. There is much documentation, mostly in rare printed chronicles and

[8] Ruth Pike, *Aristocrats and Traders: Sevillian Society in the Sixteenth Century* (Ithaca: Cornell University Press, 1972), pp. 1, 21.

[9] Earl J. Hamilton, *American Treasure and the Price Revolution in Spain, 1501–1650* (Cambridge, Mass.: Harvard University Press, 1934).

[10] Tibor Wittmann, "Apuntes sobre los métodos de investigación de la decadencia castellana (siglos XVI–XVII)," *Nouvelles Études Historiques publiées à l'occasion du XIIe Congrès International des Sciences Historiques par la Commission Nationale des Historiens Hongrois* (Budapest: Académie des Sciences de Hongrie, 1965), pp. 243–259.

[11] John H. Elliott, "The Decline of Spain," *Past and Present* (London), no. 26 (November 1961), pp. 52–75. For a more general view see Elliott's brilliant *The Old World and the New, 1492–1650* (Cambridge, England: Cambridge University Press, 1970), and "The Discovery of America and the Discovery of Man," *Proceedings of the British Academy*, 58 (1972), pp. 3–27.

manuscripts, on trans-Pacific influences, but only a beginning has been made toward telling the full story.[12] Another study requiring more attention is the influence of America on Africa. We must not forget the migration of food plants to Africa. As Philip D. Curtin has emphasized, "at least two new-world crops were introduced into Africa in the sixteenth century: manioc and maize spread very widely and came to be two of the most important sources of food on that continent."[13]

Did colonial Brazil exert an influence on Portugal? Professor James Duffy of Brandeis University has been working on this interesting but little-known subject and has reached some tentative conclusions:

> Portugal's overseas enterprise left a distinctive impression on the small nation's personality. As a result of Portugal's dramatic thrust into new and distant lands — Africa, America, India and beyond — cultural values were changed and then crystallized in the sixteenth and seventeenth centuries. . . .
>
> I believe that the pattern of Portuguese culture, certainly more than that of any other European nation, has been shaped by the consciousness of expansion. . . . A large part of Portuguese historical and artistic writing has concerned itself with overseas themes. Portuguese art and architecture reflect the same preoccupation. The Portuguese Catholic Church has long seen itself as a militant missionary force. Portuguese folklore has been enriched by motifs from one part of the remote world or another. Even Portuguese science has more often centered its attention on colonial phenomena than on those of the metropolis. This constant interest in the overseas world has contributed to the formation of the unique Portuguese personality.[14]

A FINAL QUESTION

Why were some Iberian customs, ideas, and institutions accepted or modified in America and others rejected? As the anthropologist George Foster emphasizes, Spanish forms were welcomed by Indians in the field of material culture and techniques when they were recognized by the Indians as useful, and when there were no indigenous counterparts or where Spanish forms represented a significant extension of their indigenous forms. But in the broad field of folk

---

[12] Pablo Guzmán-Rivas, "Geographic Influences of the Galleon Trade in New Spain," *Revista Geográfica* (Rio de Janeiro), 27, no. 53 (July–December 1960), pp. 5–81.

[13] *The Atlantic Slave Trade: A Census* (Madison, Wis.: 1969), p. 270.

[14] Statement by Professor Duffy, March 3, 1960.

culture — dietary patterns, superstitions, folk medicine, folklore, and music — "Spanish traits found themselves in competition with indigenous traits, and often with no clear advantage." [15] As George Kubler described the process in Peru:

> Indian populations under colonial pressure retained powers of selective choice, accepting certain European subsistence activities, and rejecting others. In Peru, these patterns of selective choice were governed, on the whole, by environmental limitations and by antecedent Indian needs and habits. Most interesting are these latter. Once a European food plant, for instance, had weathered the transportation to an American climate, that import was doomed to failure unless it found Indian acceptance. Examples in Peru during the sixteenth century were European squashes and gourds and beans; rice, and gardening vegetables; grapes and orchard fruits; barley and rye. If cultivated, these species were grown only for European use, and never came to dominate Indian subsistence. On the other hand, Indians accepted and exploited horse- and cattle-breeding, pigs, sheep, and goats, as well as cats; chickens; sugarcane, mustard, garlic, and alfalfa. In the absence of specially intense pressures, therefore, the Indian communities could pick and choose among the new subsistence activities. Their choices were governed by certain simple considerations. They were not interested in European species that closely resembled their own or provided analogous satisfactions. European squashes illustrate the point: a plantfood insufficiently distinguished from Indian varieties. Indians were also disinclined to cultivate plants from which few by-products were available, or which required large amounts of land: orchards and vineyards are examples. They also refused species whose cultivation entailed radical changes in the ceremonial organization of labor. Thus wheat, barley, and rye, which require careful, continuous cultivation, cannot be grown by the traditional, easy-going communal methods of Andean corn-agriculture. The Indians long avoided these crops, even in favorable climatic and geographical conditions.
>
> But horses and cattle, unlike the native livestock (llama, alpaca, vicuña), could be used as draft animals, and their hides and fats were useful by-products. The Indians accepted them, even at the expense of giving over arable land to alfalfa and other fodder crops. Sugarcane, to take another case, yielded a prized sweetening, a welcome addition to Indian diet, as well as fuel from the discarded fiber. Mustard and garlic

[15] George M. Foster, *Culture and Conquest: America's Spanish Heritage* (Chicago: Quadrangle Books, 1960), p. 229.

finally, competed successfully as condiments with Indian peppers, and entailed no basic changes in the methods of agriculture.[16]

It also appears that "cultural crystallization" took place in the early years of the conquest: "The early decades in America were decades of decision, a time when new adjustments and colonial cultures were roughed out and the basic outlines set." [17]

The readings in this section will indicate some important and constant flow of ideas and materials back and forth across the Atlantic Ocean between the Iberian motherlands and their American colonies. Much more research must be undertaken, but enough is known to suggest the extent of this reciprocity in the history of Latin America.

[16] George Kubler, *Mexican Architecture of the Sixteenth Century,* vol. 2 (New Haven: Yale University Press, 1948), p. 419.

[17] Foster, *Culture and Conquest,* p. 234. For a valuable comparison of Spanish American culture traits by a veteran scholar, see Foster's "Report on an Ethnological Reconnaissance in Spain," *American Anthropologist,* 53 (1951), pp. 311–325.

1. Portugal Won an Enormous Empire with a Ridiculously Small Number of Men

GILBERTO FREYRE

No course on Latin American history would be complete without a selection from the writings of Gilberto Freyre, the most copious and influential Brazilian historian of the twentieth century. With the publication of *The Masters and the Slaves* in 1933 Freyre began his long campaign to convince his countrymen, and the world, that the Portuguese had created a unique civilization in the New World, based on a peaceful intermingling of races. His interpretation has been increasingly challenged, but he had a way with words and with concepts that at least provides a good basis for useful discussion. The present selection exhibits one of his fundamental convictions — the power and influence of sex in history, in this case the way in which a small number of Portuguese men were able to establish an empire because of their impressive procreative abilities. This virility, plus Portuguese mobility and adaptability, for Freyre explains the astonishing success of the Portuguese as colonizers.

The singular predisposition of the Portuguese to the hybrid, slave-exploiting colonization of the tropics is to be explained in large part by the ethnic or, better, the cultural past of a people existing indeterminately between Europe and Africa and belonging uncompromisingly to neither one nor the other of the two continents; with the African influence seething beneath the European and giving a sharp relish to sexual life, to alimentation, and to religion; with Moorish or Negro blood running throughout a great light-skinned mulatto population, when it is not the predominant strain, in regions that to this day are inhabited by a dark-skinned people; and with the hot and oleous air of Africa mitigating the Germanic harshness of institutions and cultural forms, corrupting the doctrinal and moral rigidity of the medieval Church, drawing the bones from Christianity, feudalism, Gothic architecture, canonic discipline, Visigoth law, the Latin tongue, and the very character of the people. It was Europe reigning without governing it: it was Africa that governed. . . .

Within this antecedent factor of a general nature — the bi-continentalism or, better, the dualism of culture and of race — there are other, subordinate factors that call for our special attention. One of these is the presence among the elements that united to form the Portuguese nation of individuals of Semitic origin, or stock, individuals endowed with a mobility, a plasticity, and adaptability social as well as physical that are easily to be made out in the Portuguese navigator and cosmopolitan of the fifteenth century. Hereditarily predisposed to a life in the tropics by a long tropical habitat, it was the Semitic element, mobile and adaptable as no other, that was to confer upon the Portuguese colonizer of Brazil some of the chief physical and psychic conditions for success and for resistance — including that economic realism which from an early date tended to correct the excesses of the military and religious spirit in the formation of Brazilian society.

This mobility was one of the secrets of the Portuguese victory. Without it, it is not to be explained how a country that was practically uninhabited, with a population that was numerically insignificant as a result of all the epidemics, famines, and especially wars that had afflicted the peninsula in the Middle Ages, should have succeeded in virilely besprinkling with what was left of its blood and culture populations so diverse and at so great a distance from one another: in Asia, in Africa, in America, and in the numerous islands and archipelagoes. The scarcity of man-power was made up for by the Portuguese through mobility and miscibility, by dominating enormous spaces and, wherever they might settle, in Africa or in America, taking wives and begetting offspring with a procreative fervor that was due as much to violent instinct on the part of the individual as it was to a calculated policy stimulated by the State for obvious economic and political reasons.

Individuals of worth, warriors, administrators, technicians, were shifted about by the colonial administration in Lisbon like pieces on a backgammon board: from Asia to America and from there to Africa, depending upon the exigencies of the moment or of the region. To Duarte Coelho, grown rich from his stay in India, John III intrusts the new *capitânia* of Pernambuco. His sons, trained in fighting the American Indians, are summoned to the more difficult wars in Africa. From Madeira technicians in the manufacture of sugar are sent to the plantations of northern Brazil. Ships employed in trade with the Indies are made use of for commerce with the American colony. From Africa whole nations, almost, of Negroes are transported for agricultural labor in Brazil. An astounding mobility. An imperial domain achieved by an all but ridiculous number of Europeans running from one end to another of the known world as in a formidable game of puss-in-the-corner.

As to their miscibility, no colonizing people in modern times has exceeded or so much as equaled the Portuguese in this regard. From their first contact with women of color, they mingled with them and procreated mestizo sons;

and the result was that a few thousand daring males succeeded in establishing themselves firmly in possession of a vast territory and were able to compete with great and numerous peoples in the extension of their colonial domain and in the efficiency of their colonizing activity. Miscibility rather than mobility was the process by which the Portuguese made up for their deficiency in human mass or volume in the large-scale colonization of extensive areas. For this they had been prepared by the intimate terms of social and sexual intercourse on which they had lived with the colored races that had invaded their peninsula or were close neighbors to it, one of which, of the Mohammedan faith, was technically more highly skilled and possessed an intellectual and artistic culture superior to that of the blond Christians.

Long contact with the Saracens had left with the Portuguese the idealized figure of the "enchanted Moorish woman," a charming type, brown-skinned, black-eyed, enveloped in sexual mysticism, roseate in hue, and always engaged in combing out her hair or bathing in rivers or in the waters of haunted fountains; and the Brazilian colonizers were to encounter practically a counterpart of this type in the naked Indian women with their loose-flowing hair. These latter also had dark tresses and dark eyes and bodies painted red, and, like the Moorish Nereids, were extravagantly fond of a river bath to refresh their ardent nudity, and were fond, too, of combing their hair. What was more, they were fat like the Moorish women. . . .

In opposition to the legend of the "enchanted Moorish woman," although it never attained the same prestige, there evolved that of the "Moorish hag," representing, it may be, an outlet for the blonde woman's sexual jealousy toward her colored sister. Then, there were outbreaks of religious hatred, with the blond Christians from the north pitted against the dark-skinned infidels, a hatred that was later to result in the idealization throughout Europe of the blond type as identified with angelic and divine personages, to the detriment of the brunet type, which was associated with evil and fallen angels, with the wicked, and with traitors. One thing we know is that in the fifteenth century, when ambassadors were sent by the Republic of Venice to the two Spains, bearing greetings to King Philip II, the envoys noted that in Portugal certain women of the upper classes were in the habit of dyeing their hair a "blond color," while both there and in Spain a number of them "painted their faces a white and red tint" by way of "rendering their skin, which is a trifle swarthy — which is, indeed, quite swarthy — more fair and rosy, being persuaded that all swarthy-skinned women are ugly."

Meanwhile, it may be stated that the brown-skinned woman was preferred by the Portuguese for purposes of love, at least for purposes of physical love. The fashions of the blonde woman — limited, for that matter, to the upper classes — were the reflection of influences coming from abroad rather than a genuine expression of the national taste. . . . Moreover, in our national lyricism there is no tendency more clearly revealed than one toward a glorification of the mulatto woman, the *cabocla* or Indian woman, the brown-skin or brunette type, celebrated for the beauty of her eyes, the whiteness of her teeth, for her wiles and languishments and witching ways, far more than are the "pale virgins" and the "blonde damsels." These latter, it is true, appear here and there in a sonnet or popular song (*modinha*) of the eighteenth or nineteenth century, but they do not stand out as the others do.

Another circumstance or condition that favored the Portuguese as much as did miscibility and mobility in the conquest of the land and the domination of the tropical peoples was their acclimatability. With respect to physical conditions of soil and temperature, Portugal is Africa rather than Europe. The so-called "Portuguese climate" of Martonne, unique in Europe, is one that approximates the African. Thus, the Portuguese was predisposed by his own mesology to a victorious encounter with the tropics; his removal to the torrid regions of America was not to bring with it the grave disturbances associated with adaptation nor the profound difficulties of acclimatization that were experienced by colonizers coming from cold climates.

2. *Spaniards Brought Animals, Fruits, Vegetables, and All Manner of Plants*

JAMES A. ROBERTSON

The late James A. Robertson, the first editor of the *Hispanic American Historical Review* and a pioneer in developing the study of Latin American history in the United States, here describes the fundamental contributions of Spain in introducing plants and animals to America. This was the peaceful side of the conquest, not yet fully understood.

"Very extraordinary," says the good Jesuit father, Bernabé Cobo, writing in 1652, "is the abundance of the increase in this New World of all the animals fruits, vegetables, and all manner of plants which the Spaniards have taken

"Some Notes on the Transfer by Spain of Plants and Animals to Its Colonies Overseas" by James A. Robertson, *James Sprunt Historical Studies,* 19 (Chapel Hill: University of North Carolina Press, 1927), pp. 7–21, passim. Reprinted by permission.

to it since they discovered and settled it." So true was this, continues the same author, that some people doubted that certain things had been transferred from Spain at all, but declared them native to the new lands. A residence of forty years in America, however, and an acquaintance with old men who remembered when certain European animals and plants were not to be found in the Indies, or who remembered, even, when some of them were first brought over, gave Cobo a right to speak with a certain authority on the matter. Induced by friends or officials, the observant Jesuit had the pre-science to write down what he knew of the bringing of new forms of life to the Indies, and his chapters on the subject are valuable testimony.

But Cobo, although he will be used largely in this paper, is not the only authority on this phase of Spain's constructive labors in the colonies. Others — and some much earlier than he — left partial records of animal and plant transfers to and from the Indies, among them Cortés, the conqueror, Oviedo, the official, Acosta, the Jesuit (whose books have run into many editions), Herrera, the chronologist, Solórzano, the jurist, and many others. . . . Even a slight study shows that Spaniards thought of other things beside gold and precious stones, and that among the early explorers, discoverers, officials, and others, were persons with a large outlook and some with a scientific type of mind — largely untrained though they may have been in the exact tenets of science. Thus we find the great pioneer Cortés writing:

> I assure your Caesarian Majesty that, could we but obtain plants and seeds from Spain, and if Your Highness would be pleased to order them sent to us . . . the ability of these natives in cultivating the soil and making plantations would very shortly produce such abundance that great profit would accrue to the Imperial Crown of your Highness. . . .

Cobo's evidence is especially interesting and valuable. He states that he does not know in all instances by whom introductions were made into each province; yet he remarks the problem is not a very difficult one, for most products were taken first to Isla Española, whence they were transferred to other regions. It is true, however, as he says, that some products were taken to other parts without passing through Isla Española first. Since his acquaintance was more intimate with Peru than any other region, it is not surprising that he confines himself more especially to that country.

On his very first voyage, Columbus noted the lack of European fruits, vegetables, grains, and animals. Accordingly, on his second voyage, he carried animals for breeding purposes, besides seeds and slips of plants. Later expeditions did the same thing, so that, says Cobo, "there are very few plants of all the kinds grown in Europe which have not been transferred to this land." And he makes the same observation that the transfer of animals and plants has been more advantageous to the New World than the immense wealth of gold and silver sent thence to Spain. One may predict, he continues, that every Spanish plant will thrive in the New World. One potent cause for the great increase in plants and trees has been the destruction and change of site of many Spanish and Indian settlements. Abandoned by their inhabitants, gardens have run riot, while cattle reverting to a wild state, have continued to breed and have formed immense herds. Soldiers on entering a ruined city in Chile found veritable groves of various kinds of fruit trees, which bore excellent fruit. The Indians once destroyed a Spanish settlement in the valley of Neyva, situated between Peru and the Nuevo Reino de Granada. They left some of the cattle behind, which continued to breed and within a short time had formed immense wild herds.

On their part the Indians, recognizing the benefits to be derived from the new animals and plants, ere long began to pay their tributes in wheat and cattle. The immensity of excellent grazing lands was a potent aid in the breeding and dissemination of animals; while plants, in addition to human agency (both of Spaniards and natives) were often spread by birds and in other ways.

TRANSFER AND SPREAD OF ANIMALS

The American Indies were astonishingly bare of domestic animals. Dogs of questionable breeds, and cats, were not rare, and there were some wild pigs. The wild buffalo or American bison roamed the plains of North America; in South America, the Indians had tamed the vicuña and llama. But horses and domestic cattle were unknown. Columbus, himself, took the first horses to Isla Española in 1493. Ponce de León, Narváez, Soto, and Luna y Arrelano had horses in their expeditions to Florida. Cortés took this friend of man to Mexico, where the awestruck natives thought it some sort of powerful god; Pizarro, to Peru; and Coronado, into the southwest. There is no doubt that horses aided very materially in the conquest.

In the first years of the conquest, it was common to pay from 3,000 to 4,000 pesos for a horse, but they bred so rapidly in the New World that the price dropped very materially within a comparatively short time. Very soon also some horses escaped into the wilds where they quickly reverted to a wild state forming as seen above immense herds. Wild herds were no uncommon sight in Isla Española, and they rose to uncommon proportions in the colonies of Paraguay and Tucumán. The immense herds that roamed through our own western country are too well known to need more than mention. These also were often the descendants of horses that escaped from the conquistadores.

In Cobo's time the best horses came from Chile, where they had been introduced from Peru.

Shortly after their permanent entrance into the Philippines (1565), the Spaniards also took horses thither, but the sturdy Chinese horse had been there for many years. The small ponies that are capable of drawing such extraordinarily large loads are descended from the Spanish horses (often Arabs or mixed with Arab) and the Chinese horse.

The first cattle were taken to Isla Española at the beginning of the conquest, and to Peru three or four years after Pizarro's entrance. Like the horse, some of them escaped into the wilds and before long they too were formed into large herds in various regions. Indeed, wild cattle were so numerous in Isla Española and other West Indian islands, that it was found profitable to kill them for their flesh and hides. The men who made this their business, most frequently English, Dutch, or French, though the scourings of many other nations gradually drifted into the seas of the Indies, were known as *boucaniers,* a word derived from an old Indian term, *boucan* or *buccan,* meaning the method of drying or smoking the meat; and since the piratical crews which scurried along the Spanish main during the sixteenth and seventeenth centuries were usually recruited from these men, the term "buccaneer," meaning pirate came into the English language. Acosta notes that in 1587, a single fleet carried over 64,000 hides to Spain. The pirate Esquemelin noted the large number of wild cattle in Isla Española and says that the bulls found there were of huge bulk.

The first asses in the New World were taken to Isla Española, whence they spread into other regions, being taken to Peru by Captain Diego Maldonado, who obtained them in Jamaica. But most likely because of the abundance of horses throughout the Indies, neither asses nor their hybrid offspring, the mules, were very abundant in America in Cobo's time. However, asses could be procured in Lima for prices ranging from 10 to 15 pesos; while mules, which were very dear in early days, could be had at reasonable figures in Cobo's time, working mules fetching only 30 to 40 pesos, riding mules, 60 to 100 pesos, and choice animals, 200 to 300 pesos.

The New World had various kinds of wild, but no domesticated pigs. Because of their food value, the early conquistadores were accustomed to take large droves of European swine with them on their explorations and *entradas,* as, for instance, did Pizarro to Peru in 1531 and slightly later, Soto to Florida. Only four years after Pizarro's entrance into Peru, a slaughter house was erected in Lima, the first meat to be sold therein being pork. A decree of the cabildo of Lima, dated August 14, 1536, ordered that a pig be killed daily and the meat sold for twenty reals per *arroba,* and that no other animals were to be killed. In the middle of the seventeenth century pigs could be bought for eighteen pesos in Lima and even more cheaply in other places. Lard had a steady sale and the rendering of it was a fairly profitable business.

Sheep, when transferred from Spain to the warm regions of America (and the same was true of the transfer to the Philippine Islands), did not thrive well. Later, however, it was found that those reared in the highlands of Peru and in Chile fared better, and in those localities it was not long after their introduction before the woolen goods made from their fleece were able to compete with those of Spain. The Spaniards also early took goats and rabbits to the new lands, as well as dogs, although the Indians had plenty of the latter, albeit of poor breeds. The European dogs were used in tracking the poor Indians who fled before the cruelty of their self-appointed masters, and many a victim fell before the ferocity of the great hunting mastiffs and bloodhounds. The classic example of the dog in the early days of American colonization was the animal used by Juan Ponce de León in his conquest of Porto Rico, which shared like and like with the soldiers in all booty and wages. Pizarro took dogs to Peru, and Soto to Florida. Las Casas, the Apostle to the Indians, speaks in scathing terms of the cruelty of the dogs and the curious reader will find many interesting pictures of the dog in the great works published by Theodore de Bry in the latter part of the sixteenth century. There were instances of the dog's reverting to a wild state, and Esquemelin mentions the great, wild dogs of Isla Española descended from those brought in by the Spaniards. . . .

INTRODUCTION OF PLANT LIFE

It was quite natural for the Spaniards on coming to their new lands to look for the plant life to which they had been accustomed; and not finding it, to attempt to introduce it, both to remind them of the land of their birth and to serve as food and for other uses. It was also quite natural for them to transfer the plant life of the colonies to Spain or from one colony to another, but with this phase of transfer we have no concern in the present article. In bringing seeds, roots, and slips from the mother country, it is not surprising that many difficulties were encountered, for methods of packing were generally crude, and in the long voyages in their insecure ships, it was not uncommon for everything to be drenched with seawater, while the intense heat as they entered the tropics caused many of the seeds to rot. The story of the transfer of wheat, for instance, is a thrilling one. Various attempts to bring seed had failed, and it seemed impossible to bring the seed alive to America. At last, however, what it seemed impossible to accomplish by design was brought about by pure accident. It is recounted that a Negro slave of Cortés, while preparing rice for the expeditionaries one day, discovered several grains of good wheat. These were planted in New Spain and grew, and the resultant grains were also planted. In due time, the harvest was sufficient for use. A similar story is told of the introduction of wheat into Peru. Doña Inez Muñoz, wife of Martín de Alcántara — one of the conquistadores who had come to Peru with Pizarro — one day in 1535 while cleaning rice to make some soup for the family meal, found a few grains of good wheat in the rice barrel. Since she was much interested in transferring Spanish products to the new possessions, she recognized the value of her discovery. Accordingly, she planted the grains in her garden. What a gala day that must have been when the first shoots appeared above the ground, for the wheat grew rapidly and yielded abundantly. For several generations the harvest was in turn planted and in 1539 the first flour mill was erected in Peru. Next year, the cabildo of Lima regulated the sale of flour, and on November 19, 1541, bread was sold at one real for two and one-half *libras* (pounds). Other grains, including barley and rice, were early planted in Peru and flourished. . . .

The first cultivated seed or slip of the vine was taken to Lima by Hernando de Montenegro, and so rapid was the development that by 1551 grapes were being gathered in abundance. In that year, being placed on sale, under the auspices of Licentiate Rodrigo Niño, they brought half a *peso oro* or 225 *maravedis* per *libra*. However, Montenegro, to whom the grapes belonged, considered this price too low and appealed to the audiencia of Lima asking that he be permitted to sell at a higher rate. So greatly were the first plants esteemed, says Cobo, that it was necessary to have them guarded by armed men, so that the shoots should not be stolen. The first vines taken from Peru to Chile sold at 3,000 pesos, and the shoots at 100 pesos each. In Cobo's time there was an annual export from Peru of more than 100 shiploads of grapes. The price of the wine made from the grapes dropped to as low as three to four pesos per *arroba*. As time passed most of the Spanish varieties of grapes were transferred to Peru and flourished; and as might be expected, found favor not only with the whites but with the Indians as well. The Jesuit Joseph de Acosta, writing much earlier than Cobo, bears similar testimony of the vine, but says that this most useful product did not thrive in Tierra Firme or in the islands. The vines bore well in New Spain, however, but the grapes were there used only for eating, no wine being made, because as Acosta conjectures, the grapes did not ripen thoroughly on account of the rains of July and August. On the other hand, he says, excellent wine was made in Peru and Chile; and so great was the increase in those regions that the tithes of the church increased five or six times within twenty years.

The olive was first brought to Peru by Antonio de Ribera, one of the principal settlers of that country. Having been sent to Spain as procurator for the new colony, on his return in 1560, he brought many olive plants from Seville, but only two or three survived the voyage. Planting these in his garden he had them carefully guarded against theft by Indians and dogs. Notwithstanding his care, however, all the plants except one were stolen one night, and taken to Chile where being planted they throve exceedingly. The one left to Ribera became the parent of all the trees in Peru, and in Cobo's time was still living although the garden in which it had been planted had been transferred to a community of nuns. . . .

Sugarcane was first brought to the West Indies by Pedro de Atienza, an inhabitant of Concepción de la Vega in Isla Española, and from this place it spread all over the tropical Indies redeeming much territory that had been considered as only waste. The product was larger than in its former home, and grew so abundantly that sugar was made in great quantities and soon became very cheap, costing only four or five pesos per *arroba*. In Peru, notwithstanding the heavy consumption of sugar, there was a considerable export to Spain.

The first sugar in the Indies is said to have been made by Gonzalo de Vibora, who brought over sugar experts to Isla Española, and who erected a horse mill for expressing the juice. "To him alone," says Oviedo, "are due thanks for the first manufacture of sugar in America." So rapid was the development of sugar growing that despite the heavy capital needed to run a mill because slave labor only was employed, many sugar mills were early established, among mill owners being Luis Colón, Cristóbal de Tapía, Miguel de Pasamonte, Lucas Vasquez de Ayllón, and many others whose names are familiar. Until sugar became an object of export, ships had to return to Spain in ballast. In 1553, so much sugar was made in Mexico that heavy exports were made from Vera Cruz and Acapulco to Spain and Peru. One shipment of sugar to Spain before 1590 amounted to 898 boxes, each presumably of 8 *arrobas'* weight, and this notwithstanding the heavy consumption in the Indies. Sugar, indeed, became the chief product of the West Indian islands, and its abundance created a great demand for confections of various kinds. . . .

Oranges and lemons spread so rapidly that it early became not uncommon to see them growing wild in Isla Española. Acosta, indeed, says that whole forests of wild oranges were found growing in many localities. The first oranges (both sweet and sour varieties) were taken to Isla Española from Spain, and throve wonderfully both inside the city of Santo Domingo and in other parts of the island, and spread very soon to the other islands. The first oranges were taken to Peru by Baltasar Gogo and planted in a garden not far from Lima. Lemons were unknown in Peru when Cobo first went there, but when he wrote they had been flourishing for a score of years.

The mulberry was introduced into the New World by Hernando Cortés, who tried to establish the silk industry in New Spain. The first bananas in the New World, according to Oviedo, were planted in Isla Española in 1516 by Tomás Berlanga, a Dominican priest, who is said to have brought them from the Canary Islands; but Acosta says that they had been known in America before the arrival of the Spaniards. Cobo is probably in error in his assertion that the first bananas were planted in Tierra Firme, but probably correct when he says that the first ones were taken to Peru by a lady of Panama who went to that country.

With regard to the plant life of the New World, Candolle says that of 247 plants cultivated in America, 199 originated in the Old World, 45 in America, 1 in Australia, while the native habitat of 2 can not be determined. It might be well in this connection to repeat Humboldt's warning, lest we get to believing that the New World was poorer in useful plant life than was really the case. He says:

> In general, if one considers the garden plants of the Aztecs and the great number of farinaceous and sugar roots cultivated in Mexico and in Peru, he will see that America was not nearly so poor in food plants as would appear from the untrustworthy evidence advanced by certain savants, who know the new continent only through the works of Herrera and Solis.

And he notes further that, before the arrival of the Spaniards in America, Mexico and the Cordilleras of South America produced several fruits quite similar to those of the temperate climate of the old continent.

On the other side of the globe, the Spaniards transferred various products to the Philippine Islands, both from the American Indies and from Spain. This story may not be taken up in any detail in this paper. Suffice it to say that Miguel López de Legazpi, who made the first permanent Spanish settlement in the Philippines (that at Cebu), in writing his official report of 1565, states that the soil was so fertile that four days after the Spanish forces had taken the native town of Cebu, "the Castilian seeds had already sprouted."

Whatever mistakes the Spaniards made in their colonization of their new possessions, whether in the western or eastern hemisphere, one can indorse much of what Claudio Gay says, namely:

> Never has a nation carried the colonizing spirit to a degree as high as the Spaniards. Although many of them expatriated themselves with the

sole object of enriching themselves at any price, the majority had the firm resolution to contribute to the civilizing and evangelizing of semi-barbaric peoples. With this object they carried with them, not only the principal elements of civilization, such as domestic animals, wheat, beans, vegetables, etc., but also a force of goodwill and of perseverance truly wonderful which naught could change.

3. *The New World Was a Place of Wonder and Enchantment Populated with Mysterious and Bewildering People*

LEWIS HANKE

Fantasy has often exercised a subtle and persistent influence in the lives of men and women. The conquest of America afforded Spaniards a rich opportunity to use their imagination, and also to speculate about the wondrous lands and mysterious people the conquistadors found there. Some classical doctrines, such as Aristotle's views on the natural slavery of certain peoples, were dusted off and applied to the Indians to justify the claims of those who considered them inferior beings fit only to serve the superior Spaniards.

The Spaniards who actually saw America not only became tremendously excited and stimulated but they tended to look at the New World through medieval spectacles. The wealth of ideas and legends developed with such luxuriance during the Middle Ages was transferred at once to America; this medieval influence was especially marked during the early years of the discovery and conquest. . . .

Spanish captains went forth to their conquest expecting to encounter many kinds of mythical beings and monsters depicted in medieval literature: giants, pygmies, dragons, griffins, white-haired boys, bearded ladies, human beings adorned with tails, headless creatures with eyes in their stomachs or breasts, and other fabulous folk. For a thousand years a great reservoir of curious ideas on man and semi-men had been forming in Europe, and was now freely

From *Aristotle and the American Indians* by Lewis Hanke (Chicago: Henry Regnery Co., 1959), pp. 3–11, passim. Reprinted by permission of Henry Regnery Company and The Bodley Head, Ltd.

drawn upon in America. St. Augustine in his *City of God* had a whole chapter on "Whether the descendants of Adam or of the sons of Noah produced monstrous races of men," and by the end of the fifteenth century a rich body of fantastic ideas was ready for use in America. Trumpet-blowing apes, for example, "formed parts of a loosely defined pictorial cycle combining subjects from the world of fable with the exotic beasts of the Bestiaries and the Marvels of the East." It is not surprising, therefore, to find that the early historian Gonzalo Fernández de Oviedo had heard of a Peruvian monkey that "was no less extraordinary than the griffins," for it had a long tail, with the upper half of its body covered with many-hued feathers and the lower half with smooth, reddish fur. It could sing, "when it felt like it," in the same dulcet tones as a nightingale or a lark.

Wild men also had captured popular imagination during the Middle Ages. They were depicted on the façades of churches, as decorations for manuscripts, and in tapestries, as ferocious beings of wild mien rending lions barehanded or smashing their skulls with trees or mighty clubs. Wild men served as jamb figures on the façade of the fifteenth-century San Gregorio monastery in Valladolid in which Las Casas lived during the 1550 disputation with Sepúlveda. The wildman motif was much used in Spain, crossed the Atlantic with Spanish workmen, and is seen on the façade of the Casa del Montejo in Yucatan, built in 1549. Wild men also supported the arms of Charles V in Tlaxcala. Given this medieval mélange of man, beast, and mythical creature, we are not surprised to find that a 1498 edition of John of Holywood's *Sphaera Mundi* describes the inhabitants of the New World as being "blue in colour and with square heads." One of the earliest pictures of American natives, printed as a wood engraving about 1505, showed the same fantastic spirit. The caption read as follows:

They go naked, both men and women; they have well-shaped bodies, and in colour nearly red; they bore holes in their cheeks, lips, noses and ears, and stuff these holes with blue stones, crystals, marble and alabaster, very fine and beautiful. This custom is followed alone by the men. They have no personal property, but all things are in common. They all live together without a king and without a government, and every one is his own master. They take for wives whom they first meet, and in all this they have no rule. They also war with each other, and without art or rule. And they eat one another, and those they slay are eaten, for human flesh is a common food. In the houses salted human flesh is hung up to dry. They live to be a hundred and fifty years old, and are seldom sick. . . .

Fifteenth-century Europeans had assumed their knowledge of the world to be exact, and the appearance of a vast unknown continent across the seas shook their confidence in themselves. Ingenious attempts were made to demonstrate that the early Christian authorities foreshadowed that shattering event, the discovery of America. If the new lands could be related somehow to the world they knew, a bridge could be built between the known and the unknown. The natives of this marvellous new world were, of course, at the centre of speculation. Even before the first decade had passed, these plumed and painted peoples — so inevitably and so erroneously called Indians — had become the principal mystery which perplexed the Spanish nation, con-quistadores, ecclesiastics, crown, and common citizens alike. Who were they? Whence came they? What was their nature, their capacity for Christianity and European civilization? Most important of all, what relationship would be the right one for the Spaniards to establish with them?

The popular image, in the first feverish months, of a terrestrial paradise was soon succeeded by that of a hostile continent peopled with armed war-riors rushing out of the tropical forests or strange cities to resist the advance of the Spanish soldiers and the missionary efforts of their companion friars. The early suppositions that the lost Ten Tribes of Israel were the progenitors of the Indian — held by more than one serious writer of the day — or even the later idea that in some mysterious way the Welsh nation had sent out these strange shoots — failed to answer satisfactorily the urgent basic questions: Who and what are these creatures? How shall we treat them? Can they be Christianized and brought to a civilized way of life? How shall this be attempted, by war or by peaceful persuasion? The conquistadores tended to ask rather pointedly: When may just war be waged to compel the Indians to serve God and the king and us? And the ecclesiastics asked eagerly: How can the natives be made to change from what they are to what they ought to be?

Two circumstances were responsible for these questions, which were asked by no other European colonizing nation with such general and genuine con-cern. The first was the nature of the Spanish people themselves, a people legal-istic, passionate, given to extremes, and fervently Catholic. Three events of the year 1492 reflect some of the most fundamental characteristics of Span-iards and their history. Granada, the last of the Moorish kingdoms, fell to the Catholic Kings Ferdinand and Isabella on January 2, the Jews were next expelled, and on August 3 Columbus set sail. The final conquest of Granada was the climax of a long national effort to establish Christian hege-mony in Spain. This long travail had helped to prepare the nation for larger tasks. Isabella herself discovered this in that same year, 1492, when she bluntly asked the scholar Antonio de Nebrija, as he presented to her his Spanish *Gramática,* the first grammar of a European modern language ever written: "What is it for?", and the Bishop of Avila, speaking on behalf of the scholar, replied: "Your Majesty, language is the perfect instrument of empire."

The second circumstance was the nature of the dominion exercised by the Spanish crown in America, by which the Spaniards felt themselves responsible for the conversion of the natives. The decrees of Pope Alexander VI, the famous bulls of donation of 1493, which were used at first to justify the exertion of Spanish power in the new lands, specifically entrusted to the crown of Castile the Christianization of these lands. Without becoming embroiled, as the Spaniards themselves became, in the legal and moral implications of these papal pronouncements, we may be clear that the Spaniards had, logically, to determine Indian nature and capacity before they could legitimately pursue either conquest or Christianization.

Most Spaniards, no matter what attitude they developed towards the Indians, were usually profoundly stirred by them. Kings and the Council of the Indies instituted prolonged and formal enquiries in both Spain and America on their nature. Few significant figures of the conquest failed to deliver themselves of opinions on the Indian's capacity for Christianity, ability to work, and general aptitude for European civilization. Among the documents which remain to us are not only opinions but also numerous and curious proposals for the protection and welfare of the Indians. Early in his career Las Casas proposed the introduction of Negro slaves to the islands, in order to spare Indians the heavy labour which was destroying them, but later repented and opposed Negro slavery as well as Indian slavery, "and for the same reasons." Spaniards never fought, however, as hard or as consistently against Negro slavery as they did on behalf of the Indians, not even Las Casas. Despite his final rejection of Negro slavery, as late as 1544 he owned several Negro slaves and no document has come to light which reveals any concerted opposition to Negro slavery during the sixteenth century. Why did the consciences of Spaniards twinge more easily for Indians than for Negroes? Perhaps Iberian peoples had become accustomed to having Moslem Negro slaves, and Indians were not only new to them but had never had an opportunity to hear the faith before. The Jesuits Alonso de Sandoval and Pedro Claver were to work on behalf of Negroes in the seventeenth century but the moral conscience of the modern world was first roused by the plight of the American Indian.

Many men and many methods were engaged in the attempt to help the American Indians. In the same month (May, 1550) that saw the beginning of the famous discussion on the nature of the Indian, a Sevillan named Cristóbal Muñoz obtained a contract from the king to introduce 100 camels into Peru. Why? To spare the Indians the bearing of heavy burdens up and down the Andes. The archives of Spain and America are full of absorbing documentation on what the conquerors thought of the conquered people in this first widespread meeting of races in modern times. The amount and quality of the information available is unparalleled in the records of any other colonizing nation, and constitutes a wealth of material not yet fully exploited by anthropologists.

As the conquerors and clerics moved forward into America in the uneasy partnership which the crown's double purpose of political dominion and religious conversion enjoined upon them, stubborn facts and theological convictions clashed resoundingly. The voices of individuals and of different factions — ecclesiastics, soldiers, colonists, and royal officials in America as well as of men of action and thought in Spain — rose continually during the sixteenth century in a loud chorus of conflicting advice to the Spanish kings and the Council of the Indies. Each man, each faction, held a profound conviction about the nature of the Indians and all generalized about them as though they were a single race. Each made his own views on the Indians the basis of a recommendation for a government policy which he urged upon the powers in Spain as the one true solution which would once and for all set the enterprise of the Indies on a firm and unassailable foundation. The crown considered all these recommendations and ruled above all individuals and all factions, jealous of its prerogatives and determined to prevent the growth of a powerful and turbulent aristocracy such as had just been broken in Spain by the unremitting efforts of Ferdinand and Isabella. It was the Emperor Charles V and his counsellors, therefore, who had to decide eventually what doctrine should be applied to the American Indians. In the feverish days of the early conquest, when even hard-bitten conquistadores suffered strange dreams and the New World was to some men a place of wonder and enchantment populated with mysterious and bewildering people, it is not surprising that even the ancient theory of Aristotle, that some men are born to be slaves, was borrowed from antiquity and found conveniently applicable to the Indians from the coasts of Florida to far-distant Chile.

4. The Impact of America on Europe Was Complex and Uncertain

J. H. ELLIOTT

Though still a relatively young man, Professor Elliott of King's College, London, has already made notable contributions to Spanish and Spanish-American history through *The Revolt of the Catalans* (1963) and *Imperial Spain, 1469–1716* (1963). Recently he has turned his wit and his scholarship to assessing the reasons why America puzzled Europeans who found it so difficult to understand the alien civilization across the ocean. In this selection he explains "the uncertain impact" of the New World on the Old. Perhaps this uncertainty may be explained, in part at least, by the fertility of European imagination concerning America. As late as 1774 Pedro Alonso O'Crouley wrote a work on Mexico that included a chapter, "Remarkable Curiosities," on the wonders of the New World, "which ranged from a woman who had borne forty-eight children to the leashing of fleas with minute gold chains, an accomplishment of the Indians of Mexico."*

Nearly three hundred years after Columbus's first voyage of discovery, the Abbé Raynal, that eager inquirer after other men's truths, offered a prize for the essay which would best answer the following questions. Has the discovery of America been useful or harmful to mankind? If useful, how can its usefulness be enhanced? If harmful, how can the harm be diminished? Cornelius De Pauw had recently described the discovery of the New World as the most calamitous event in human history, and Raynal was taking no chances. "No event," he had cautiously begun his vast and laborious *Philosophical and Political History of the Settlements and Trade of the Europeans in the East and West Indies,* "has been so interesting to mankind in general, and to the inhabitants of Europe in particular, as the discovery of the new world, and the passage to India by the Cape of Good Hope." It took the robust Scottish forthrightness of Adam Smith, whose view of the impact of the discoveries was generally favourable, to turn this non-committal passage into an *ex cathedra* historical pronouncement: "the discovery of America, and that of a passage

From *The Old World and the New, 1492–1650* by J. H. Elliott (Cambridge, England: Cambridge University Press, 1970), pp. 1–27 passim. Reprinted by permission.
    * *A Description of the Kingdom of New Spain, by Señor Don Pedro Alonso O'Crouley,* trans. and ed. Seán Galvin (San Francisco: John Howell, 1972), p. 110.

to the East Indies by the Cape of Good Hope, are the two greatest and most important events recorded in the history of mankind.". . .

Raynal's formulation of his questions no doubt tended to prompt philosophical speculation and dogmatic assertion, rather than rigorous historical inquiry. But this was less easily evaded in 1792, when the Académie Française asked competitors to examine the influence of America on the "politics, commerce and customs of Europe." It is difficult not to sympathize with the sentiments of the anonymous prize-winner. "What a vast and inexhaustible subject," he sighed. "The more one studies it, the more it grows." Nevertheless, he succeeded in covering a great deal of ground in his eighty-six pages. As might have been expected, he was happier with America's political and economic influence on Europe than with its moral influence, which he regarded as pernicious. But he showed himself aware of the concealed danger in this enterprise — the danger of attributing all the major changes in modern European history to the discovery of America. He also made a genuine attempt, in language which may not sound totally unfamiliar to our own generation, to weigh up the profits and the losses of discovery and settlement. "If those Europeans who devoted their lives to developing the resources of America had instead been employed in Europe in clearing forests, and building roads, bridges and canals, would not Europe have found in its own bosom the most important objects which it derives from the other world, or their equivalent? And what innumerable products would the soil of Europe not have yielded, if it had been brought to the degree of cultivation of which it is capable?". . .

For all the interest and importance of the theme, the historiography of the impact of America on Europe has enjoyed a distinctly chequered career. The eighteenth-century debate was conducted in terms which suggest that the participants were more concerned to confirm and defend their personal prejudices about the nature of man and society than to obtain a careful historical perspective on the contribution of the New World to Europe's economic and cultural development. It was not until Humboldt published his *Cosmos* in 1845 that the reactions of the first Europeans, and especially of the Spaniards, to the alien environment of America assumed their proper place in a great geographical and historical synthesis, which made some attempt to consider what the revelation of the New World had meant to the Old.

Nineteenth-century historiography did not show any great interest in pursuing Humboldt's more original lines of inquiry. The discovery and settlement of the New World were incorporated into an essentially Europocentric conception of history, where they were depicted as part of that epic process by which the Renaissance European first became conscious of the world and of man, and then by degrees imposed his own dominion over the newly-discovered races of a newly-discovered world. In this particular story of European history — which was all too easily identified with universal history — there was a tendency to place the principal emphasis on the motives, methods and achievements of the explorers and conquerors. The impact of Europe on the world (which was regarded as a transforming, and ultimately beneficial, impact) seemed a subject of greater interest and concern than the impact of the world on Europe.

Twentieth-century European historiography has tended to pursue a similar theme, although from a very different standpoint. The retreat of European imperialism has led to a reassessment — often very harsh — of the European legacy. At the same time the development of anthropology and archaeology has led to a reassessment — sometimes very favourable — of the pre-European past of former colonial societies. Where European historians once wrote with the confidence born of an innate sense of European superiority, they now write burdened with the consciousness of European guilt.

It is no accident that some of the most important historical work of our own age — preoccupied as it is with the problem of European and non-European, of black and white — should have been devoted to the study of the social, demographic and psychological consequences for non-European societies of Europe's overseas expansion. Perhaps future generations will detect in our concern with these themes some affinity between the historians of the eighteenth and twentieth centuries. For Raynal and his friends were similarly consumed by guilt and by doubt. Their hesitancy in evaluating the consequences of the discovery and conquest of America sprang precisely from the dilemma involved in attempting to reconcile the record of economic and technical progress since the end of the fifteenth century with the record of the sufferings endured by the defeated societies. The very extent of their preoccupation with the great moral issue of their own times, the issue of slavery, helped to create a situation not without its parallels today. For if their preoccupation stimulated them to ask historical questions, it also tempted them to reply with unhistorical answers. . . .

From 1492 the New World was always present in European history, although its presence made itself felt in different ways at different times. It is for this reason that America and Europe should not be subjected to a historiographical divorce, however shadowy their partnership may often appear before the late seventeenth century. Properly, their histories should constitute a continuous interplay of two distinctive themes.

One theme is represented by the attempt of Europe to impose its own image, its own aspirations, and its own values, on a newly-discovered world, together with the consequences for that world of its actions. The other treats of the way in which a growing awareness of the character, the opportunities and the challenges represented by the New World of America helped to shape and transform an Old World which was itself striving to shape and transform the New. . . .

Gold and conversion — these were the two most immediate and obvious connotations of America, and those most likely to be associated with the name of its discoverer. It was only by slow degrees that Columbus began to acquire the status of a hero. He figured as the central protagonist in a number of Italian epic poems written in the last two decades of the sixteenth century, and in 1614 he at last appeared as the hero of a Spanish drama, with the publication of Lope de Vega's extraordinary play, *El Nuevo Mundo descubierto por Cristóbal Colón*. Lope shows a genuine historical appreciation of the significance of Columbus's achievement when he puts into the mouth of Ferdinand the Catholic a speech affirming the traditional cosmography of a tripartite globe, and scoffing at the possibility that there might exist a portion of the world still to be discovered. At the same time, his Columbus, as a dreamer mocked by the world, has already started on his career as the romantic hero who becomes the symbol of man's unquenchable spirit of discovery.

There were already intimations of this romanticization of Columbus during the sixteenth century. But more commonly he was set within the framework of a providential interpretation of history, which depicted him as a divinely appointed instrument for the spreading of the gospel — and even here he was likely to find himself relegated to second place by the more obviously heroic figure of Hernán Cortés. But not even the mass-conversion of hitherto unknown peoples was sufficient of itself to ensure a firm place for Columbus, or Cortés, or for the New World, in the European consciousness. In some circles — especially certain humanist and religious circles, and in the merchant communities of some of Europe's leading cities — the interest was intense, although partial, and often specialized, in character. But it seems that the European reading public displayed no overwhelming interest in the newly-discovered world of America. . . .

It is difficult not to be impressed by the strange lacunae and the resounding silences in many places where references to the New World could reasonably be expected. How are we to explain the absence of any mention of the New World in so many memoirs and chronicles, including the memoirs of Charles V himself? How are we to explain the continuing determination, right up to the last two or three decades of the sixteenth century, to describe the world as if it were still the world as known to Strabo, Ptolemy and Pomponius Mela? How are we to explain the persistent reprinting by publishers, and the continuing use by schools, of classical cosmographies which were known to be outdated by the discoveries? How are we to explain that a man as widely read and as curious as Bodin should have made so little use of the considerable information available to him about the peoples of the New World in the writing of his political and social philosophy?

The reluctance of cosmographers or of social philosophers to incorporate into their work the new information made available to them by the discovery of America provides an example of the wider problems arising from the revelation of the New World to the Old. Whether it is a question of the geography of America, its flora and fauna, or the nature of its inhabitants, the same kind of pattern seems constantly to recur in the European response. It is as if, at a certain point, the mental shutters come down; as if, with so much to see and absorb and understand, the effort suddenly becomes too much for them, and Europeans retreat to the half-light of their traditional mental world. . . .

How can we expect a Europe so conscious of its own infallibility — of its unique status and position in God's providential design — even to make the effort to come to terms with a world other than its own? But this Europe was not the closed Europe of an "age of ignorance." Instead, it was Renaissance Europe — the Europe of "the discovery of the world and of man." If Renaissance ideas and attitudes played an important part — however elusive it may be to determine exactly *what* part — in prompting Europeans to set out on voyages of discovery and to extend their mental as well as their geographical horizons, might we not expect a new kind of readiness to respond to fresh information and fresh stimuli from a newly-discovered world?

The conclusion does not necessarily follow. In some respects the Renaissance involved, at least in its earlier stages, a closing rather than an opening of the mind. The veneration of antiquity became more slavish; authority staked fresh claims against experience. Both the boundaries and the content of traditional disciplines such as cosmography or social philosophy had been clearly determined by reference to the texts of classical antiquity, which acquired an extra degree of definitiveness when for the first time they were fixed on the printed page. Fresh information from alien sources was therefore liable to seem at worst incredible, at best irrelevant, when set against the accumulated knowledge of the centuries. Given this deference to authority, there was unlikely to be any undue precipitation, least of all in academic circles, to accept the New World into consciousness.

It is also possible that a society which is wrestling — as late medieval Christendom was wrestling — with great spiritual, intellectual and political problems, is too preoccupied with its internal upheavals to devote more than fitful attention to phenomena located on the periphery of its interests. It may be too much to expect such a society to make a further radical adjustment — and one which this time involves the assimilation of an entirely new range of alien experiences. Against this, however, it could be argued that a society which is in movement, and displays symptoms of dissatisfaction, is more likely to show itself capable of absorbing new impressions and experiences than a static society, satisfied with itself, and secure in the assurance of its own superiority. . . .

The obstacles to the incorporation of the New World within Europe's intellectual horizon were formidable. There were obstacles of time and space, of inheritance, environment and language; and efforts would be required at many different levels before they were removed. At least four different processes were involved, each of which raised peculiar difficulties of its own. First of all there was the process of observation, as defined by Humboldt when he wrote: "To see . . . is not to observe; that is, to compare and classify." The second process was description — depicting the unfamiliar in such a way that it could be grasped by those who had not seen it. The third was dissemination — the diffusion of new information, new images and new ideas, so that they became part of the accepted stock of mental furniture. And the fourth was comprehension — the ability to come to terms with the unexpected and the unfamiliar, to see them as phenomena existing in their own right, and (hardest of all) to shift the accepted boundaries of thought in order to include them.

If one asks *what* Europeans saw on arriving on the far side of the Atlantic, and *how* they saw it, much will inevitably depend on the kind of Europeans involved. The range of vision is bound to be affected both by background, and by professional interests. Soldiers, clerics, merchants, and officials trained in the law — these are the classes of men on whom we are dependent for most of our first-hand observation of the New World and its inhabitants. Each class had its own bias and its own limitations; and it would be interesting to have a systematic survey of the extent and nature of the bias for each professional group, and of the way in which it was mitigated or altered, in individual cases, by a humanist education.

One Spanish official in the Indies who transcended many of the limitations of his class, and achieved an unusual degree of insight into Quechua society by dint of learning the language, was Juan de Betanzos. In the dedication to his History of the Incas, written in 1551, he spoke of the difficulties he had met in composing the work. There was such a quantity of conflicting information, and he was concerned to find how differently the *conquistadores* speak about these things, and how far removed they are from Indian practice. "And this I believe to be due to the fact that at that time they were not so much concerned with finding things out as with subjecting and acquiring the land. It was also because, coming new to the Indians, they did not know how to ask questions and find things out, for they lacked knowledge of the language; while the Indians, for their part, were too frightened to give them a full account."

The professional preoccupations of the conquistadores, and the difficulties of conducting any form of effective dialogue with the Indians, are more than enough to account for the deficiencies of their reports as descriptions of the New World and its inhabitants; and it is a piece of unusual good fortune that the conquest of Mexico should have thrown up two soldier-chroniclers as shrewd in their observation and as vivid in their powers of description as Cortés and Bernal Díaz. In Cortés's letters of relation it is possible to see at work the process of observation, in Humboldt's sense of the word, as he attempts to bring the exotic into the range of the familiar by writing of Aztec temples as mosques, or by comparing the marketplace of Tenochtitlán with that of Salamanca. But there are obvious limits to Cortés's capacity of an observer, particularly when it comes to depicting the extraordinary landscape through which his invading army marched. . . .

Even where Europeans in the New World had the desire to look, and the eyes to see, there is no guarantee that the image which presented itself to them — whether of peoples or of places — necessarily accorded with the reality. Tradition, experience and expectation were the determinants of vision. Even a presumably sober official of the Spanish Crown, Alonso de Zuazo, manages to transmute Hispaniola in 1518 into an enchanted island where the fountains play and the streams are lined with gold, and where nature yields her fruits in marvellous abundance. Bernal Díaz, in many ways so down-to-earth and perceptive an observer, still looks at the conquest of Mexico through the haze of romances of chivalry. . . .

It is hard to escape the impression that sixteenth-century Europeans . . . all too often saw what they expected to see. This should not really be a cause for surprise or mockery, for it may well be that the human mind has an inherent need to fall back on the familiar object and the standard image, in order to come to terms with the shock of the unfamiliar. The real test comes later, with the capacity to abandon the life-belt which links the unknown to the known. Some Europeans, and especially those who spent a long time in the Indies, did successfully pass this test. Their own dawning realization of the wide divergence between the image and the reality, gradually forced them to abandon their standard images and their inherited preconceptions. For America was a *new* world and a *different* world; and it was this fact of difference which was overwhelmingly borne in upon those who came to know it.

"Everything is very different," wrote Fray Tomás de Mercado in his book of advice to the merchants of Seville; "the talent of the natives, the disposition of the republic, the method of government and even the capacity to be governed."

But how to convey this fact of difference, the uniqueness of America, to those who had not seen it? The problem of description reduced writers and chroniclers to despair. There was too much diversity, too many new things to be described, as Fernández de Oviedo constantly complained. "Of all the things I have seen," he wrote of a bird of brilliant plumage, "this is the one which has most left me without hope of being able to describe it in words." Or again of a strange tree — "it needs to be painted by the hand of a Berruguete or some other excellent painter like him, or by Leonardo da Vinci or Andrea Mantegna, famous painters whom I knew in Italy." But the sheer impossibility of the task itself represented a challenge which could extend the boundaries of perception. Forcing themselves to communicate something of their own delight in what they saw around them, the Spanish chroniclers of the Indies occasionally achieved a pen-picture of startling intimacy and brilliance. What could be more vivid than Las Casas's description of himself reading matins "in a breviary with tiny print" by the light of the Hispaniola fireflies? . . .

Even where the observer depicted a scene with some success, either in paint or in prose, there was no guarantee that his work would reach the European public in an accurate form, or in any form at all. The caprice of publishers and the obsession of governments with secrecy, meant that much information about the New World, which might have helped to broaden Europe's mental horizons, failed to find its way into print. Illustrations had to run further hazards peculiar to themselves. The European reader was hardly in a position to obtain a reliable picture of life among the Tupinambá savages of Brazil when the illustrations in his book included scenes of Turkish life, because the publisher happened to have them in stock. Nor was the technique of woodcuts sufficiently advanced, at least until the second half of the sixteenth century, to allow a very faithful reproduction of the original drawing. . . .

In spite of all the problems involved in the dissemination of accurate information about America, the greatest problem of all, however, remained that of comprehension. The expectations of the European reader, and hence of the European traveller, were formed out of the accumulated images of a society which had been nurtured for generations on tales of the fantastic and the marvellous. . . . The temptation was almost overpoweringly strong to see the newly-discovered lands in terms of the enchanted isles of medieval fantasy. But it was not only the fantastic that tended to obtrude itself between the European and reality. If the unfamiliar were to be approached as anything other than the extraordinary and the monstrous, then the approach must be conducted by reference to the most firmly established elements in Europe's cultural inheritance. Between them, therefore, the Christian and the classical traditions were likely to prove the obvious points of departure for any evaluation of the New World and its inhabitants. . . .

The reverence of late medieval Europeans for their Christian and classical traditions had salutary consequences for their approach to the New World, in that it enabled them to set it into some kind of perspective in relation to themselves, and to examine it with a measure of tolerant interest. But against these possible advantages must be set certain obvious disadvantages, which in some ways made the task of assimilation appreciably harder. Fifteenth-century Christendom's own sense of self-dissatisfaction found expression in the longing for a return to a better state of things. The return might be to the lost Christian paradise, or to the Golden Age of the ancients, or to some elusive combination of both these imagined worlds. With the discovery of the Indies and their inhabitants, who went around naked and yet — in defiance of the Biblical tradition — mysteriously unashamed, it was all too easy to transpose the ideal world from a world remote in time to a world remote in space. Arcadia and Eden could now be located on the far shores of the Atlantic.

The process of transposition began from the very moment that Columbus first set eyes on the Caribbean Islands. The various connotations of paradise and the Golden Age were present from the first. Innocence, simplicity, fertility and abundance — all of them qualities for which Renaissance Europe hankered, and which seemed so unattainable — made their appearance in the reports of Columbus and Vespucci, and were eagerly seized upon by their enthusiastic readers. In particular, they struck an answering chord in two worlds, the religious and the humanist. Despairing of the corruption of Europe and its ways, it was natural that certain members of the religious orders should have seen an opportunity for reestablishing the primitive church of the apostles in a New World as yet uncorrupted by European vices. In the revivalist and apocalyptic tradition of the friars, the twin themes of the new world and the end of the world harmoniously blended in the great task of evangelizing the uncounted millions who knew nothing of the Faith.

The humanists, like the friars, projected onto America their disappointed dreams. In the *Decades* of Peter Martyr, the first popularizer of America and its myth, the Indies have already undergone their subtle transmutation. Here were a people who lived without weights and measures and "pestiferous moneye, the seed of innumerable myscheves. So that if we shall not be ashamed to confesse the truthe, they seem to lyve in the goulden worlde of the

which owlde wryters speake so much: wherin men lyved simplye and inno-
centlye without inforcement of lawes, without quarrelling Iudges and libelles,
contente onely to satisfie nature, without further vexation for knowledge of
thinges to come."

It was an idyllic picture, and the humanists made the most of it, for it
enabled them to express their deep dissatisfaction with European society, and
to criticize it by implication. America and Europe became antitheses — the
antitheses of innocence and corruption. And the corrupt was destroying the
innocent.

But by treating the New World in this way, the humanists were closing the
door to understanding an alien civilization. America was not as they imagined
it; and even the most enthusiastic of them had to accept from an early stage
that the inhabitants of this idyllic world could also be vicious and bellicose,
and sometimes ate each other. This of itself was not necessarily sufficient to
quench utopianism, for it was always possible to build Utopia on the far side
of the Atlantic if it did not already exist. For a moment it seemed as if the
dream of the friars and the humanists would find its realization in Vasco de
Quiroga's villages of Santa Fe in Mexico. But the dream was a European
dream, which had little to do with the American reality. As that reality came
to impinge at an increasing number of points, so the dream began to fade.

The Battle Waged by Francisco Pizarro Against Atahualpa. When Pizarro and his men captured the Emperor Atahualpa at Cajamarca in 1532, Inca power began to fail and soon the conquistadores were able to defeat the Indians at Cuzco and other strategic centers in Peru. Thereafter the "Men of Cajamarca" were marked men who played a large role in the Spanish empire in Peru (Reading 9).

This is another example of the art of Theodore de Bry (1528–1598) who has recreated so many scenes of early American history.

Relations between Indians and Spaniards

THE STRUGGLE FOR JUSTICE

So large a part of the history of Spanish America involves the relations between the conquering Spaniards and the conquered Indians that this whole volume might be devoted to it. So much controversy has revolved around the subject from 1492 until today that selecting representative material is a difficult task.

No great champions of the Indians came to the fore in Brazil comparable to such figures as Bartolomé de Las Casas in Spanish America except the Jesuit António Vieira. This fact, combined with the condition of the Indians in Brazil, who were much more primitive than the Aztecs, Mayas, and Incas, resulted in a much less dramatic cultural clash between the Portuguese and the indigenous peoples they encountered during the colonial period in Brazil. We therefore limit this section to the Spanish experience in America, although interesting parallels may be drawn by consulting such works as Dr. Mathias Kiemen's writings.[1]

The struggle for justice for the Indians began in the conquest's earliest years, although the sermons of Antonio de Montesinos marked the first sharp, public confrontation of colonists and friars on how the Indians were to be treated justly, according to Christian doctrine (Reading 5). The struggle

[1] Mathias Kiemen, "The Indian Policy of Portugal in America, with Special Reference to the Old State of Maranhão, 1500–1755," *The Americas*, 5 (1948), pp. 131–171, and *The Indian Policy of Portugal in the Amazon Region, 1614–1693* (Washington, D.C.: Catholic University of America Press, 1954).

39

for justice occurred because the crown, ecclesiastics, and even some soldiers wanted the conquest to be conducted justly, for one of the principal aims of Spain was to Christianize the Indians. What constituted justice and how it could be achieved were thorny questions; they were raised frequently during the discovery, colonization, and administration of the new dominions. One immediate problem the Spanish captains faced in the New World was how to conduct a just war against the Indians. The Requirement, drawn up in 1513 to be read before hostilities began, was the answer of Dr. Palacios Rubios (Reading 6). This document rests upon principles accepted for many years by the crown.

FUNDAMENTAL LAWS

The Requirement was only one of the many ordinances devised by Spain in its attempt to regulate relations with the Indians. The Spaniards were very legalistically minded and within twenty years after Columbus first landed in America had worked out the Laws of Burgos. In 1526 the Requirement was incorporated into the basic law governing conquests, which was first followed during the conquest of Yucatán by Francisco de Montejo. In 1542 the Council of the Indies hammered out the New Laws, after terrific disputes in Spain. The hot controversies continued between those who would protect the Indians and those who would exploit them. By 1573 the principal conquests were over, and a law on discoveries was promulgated that lasted for a long time. Each of these fundamental laws had a long and complicated history, and the controversies surrounding their interpretation reveal much of the spirit and practice peculiar to Spanish legislation. The most important question, of course, was to what extent were they actually obeyed, and no one has yet been able to answer this question in a way satisfactory to all historians.

THE SHOCK OF CONQUEST

However important the legal issues involved in the conquest, at least on the part of the Spaniards, the confrontation between the New World natives and the invading Europeans was also a great dramatic event. Both peoples expressed wonder at the actions and achievements of their adversaries. Bernal Díaz del Castillo, the foot soldier in the little band of warriors with which Cortez toppled the Aztec empire, describes in his classic *True History of the Conquest of New Spain* their first battle with the Indians, and their first view of the great City of Mexico and of Montezuma and his court in awestruck tones (Reading 7). History is usually written by the winners, and Indian records of the conquest are scanty. But a Mexican anthropologist, Miguel León Portilla, has skillfully pieced together the fragments of Indian documentation recording their reaction to the Spaniards and the conquest, which is a moving statement with true poetic power (Reading 8). But the decisive fact was the military superiority of the Spaniards, well exemplified in the analysis John Hemming gives of the final battle for Cuzco as Pizarro's men strove to complete their work by capturing the Inca stronghold (Reading 9).

INDIAN WOMEN AND THE CONQUEST

Although "the Spanish Conquest was a conquest of women" according to one authority, we know very little about this fundamental part of Latin American history. A useful generalized picture has been given (Reading 10), but this can provide only a slight understanding of the intimate drama that must have often occurred when a European married or had relations with an Indian. Fortunately sixteenth-century Spanish chroniclers have preserved for us two remarkable anecdotes that reveal at least samples of the kind of human problems that developed during the mixing of races that went on all over the Iberian empires. In the first (Reading 11) an Inca princess balks at marrying a Spanish commoner because of his low birth, and in the second a famous conquistador in Florida clearly preferred the pretty wife of a cacique, but in the interest of friendly relations with the Indians finally bit the nail and accepted the cacique's plain elder sister.[2]

A Swedish anthropologist has recently pointed out that the Aztec women lost even more than their men as a result of the triumph of Cortez, "for the women lost their social position and became servants to the new masters." Moreover, some Aztec women were economically independent through careers as weavers or midwives and even as merchants. After the conquest "the general situation of the women deteriorated, so that such activities as were formerly performed by a servant group fell to them, and this often without the social appreciation that the professional groups had enjoyed." The Catholic Church further restrained Indian women's "possibilities of extending their activities and thus their cultural participation beyond the traditional home-sphere." [3]

[2] See *Pedro Menéndez de Avilés: Memorial by Gonzalo Solís de Merás,* translated from the Spanish with notes by Jeanette Thurber Connor, introduction by Lyle N. McAlister (Gainesville: University of Florida Press, 1964), pp. 144–151.

[3] Anna-Britta Hellborn, *La participación cultural de las mujeres: Indias y mestizas en el México precortesiano y postrevolucionario* (Stockholm: The Ethnographical Museum, 1967), pp. 300–301.

Though the details of the process of "the conquest of women" are far from clear, the results are obvious. Mestizaje, the mixing of the races (Indian, Negro, and White) for some qualified observers constitutes the main theme in Latin America's entire history.

THE MANY DIFFERENT INTERPRETATIONS

Interpretations of Spanish rule in America began in the sixteenth century and have continued until today. Here we see a variety of views, sometimes contradictory, by two Americans — a historian who has written an outstanding work on colonial Mexico, and another historian who has concerned himself with the struggle for justice (Readings 12–13). These contrasting perspectives on the essential contribution of Spain offer students an excellent opportunity to exercise critical judgment on what they read. This, after all, is one of the principal reasons we study history.

5. *The Sermons of Friar Antonio de Montesinos, 1511*

It is symbolic that the struggle for justice was touched off by an almost unknown friar. No writings of Montesinos have come down to us, nor any picture of him, and of his life after his famous sermons on the Caribbean island of Hispaniola we know little, except that he spoke once at court in Spain on behalf of the Indians and met his death while protecting them in Venezuela. Millions of Americans have never heard his name or been aware of his first cry on behalf of human liberty in the New World, which Pedro Henríquez Ureña termed one of the great events in the spiritual history of mankind. Our only records of his great moment in history appear in the royal instruction ordering him to be silent and in the *History of the Indies* by Bartolomé de Las Casas, whose description, written over four hundred years ago, conveys to us vividly the passion and the force of this first dramatic blow struck for freedom in the New World.

On the Sunday before Christmas in 1511 a Dominican friar named Antonio de Montesinos preached a revolutionary sermon in a straw-thatched church on the island of Hispaniola. Speaking on the text "I am a voice crying in the wilderness," Montesinos delivered the first important and deliberate public protest against the kind of treatment being accorded the Indians by his Spanish countrymen. This first cry on behalf of human liberty in the New World was a turning point in the history of America and, as Pedro Henríquez Ureña termed it, one of the great events in the spiritual history of mankind.

The sermon, preached before the "best people" of the first Spanish town established in the New World, was designed to shock and terrify its hearers. Montesinos thundered, according to Las Casas:

> In order to make your sins against the Indians known to you I have come up on this pulpit, I who am a voice of Christ crying in the wilderness of this island, and therefore it behooves you to listen, not with careless attention, but with all your heart and senses, so that you may hear it; for this is going to be the strangest voice that ever you heard, the harshest and hardest and most awful and most dangerous that ever you expected to hear. . . . This voice says that you are in mortal sin, that you live and die in it, for the cruelty and tyranny you use in dealing

From *The Spanish Struggle for Justice in the Conquest of America* by Lewis Hanke, (Boston: Little, Brown and Company 1965), pp. 17–18. Copyright 1949, American Historical Association; Copyright © 1965, Little, Brown and Company. Reprinted by permission of Little, Brown and Company and the University of Pennsylvania Press.

with these innocent people. Tell me, by what right or justice do you keep these Indians in such a cruel and horrible servitude? On what authority have you waged a detestable war against these people, who dwelt quietly and peacefully on their own land? . . . Why do you keep them so oppressed and weary, not giving them enough to eat nor taking care of them in their illness? For with the excessive work you demand of them they fall ill and die, or rather you kill them with your desire to extract and acquire gold every day. And what care do you take that they should be instructed in religion? . . . Are these not men? Have they not rational souls? Are you not bound to love them as you love yourselves? . . . Be certain that, in such a state as this, you can no more be saved than the Moors or Turks.

Montesinos thereupon strode out of the church with head high, leaving a muttering crowd of colonists and officials behind him, who were astounded, but not one was converted. He had come as near to convincing his hearers of their wrongdoing as would a theological student in our day who delivered a soapbox philippic in Wall Street on the biblical text "Sell that which thou hast and give to the poor, and thou shalt have treasure in heaven."

The colonists gathered at the house of the Governor, Diego Columbus, protested against the sermon as a scandalous denial of the lordship of the king in the Indies, and delegated a group which went indignantly to the monastery to exact an apology and disavowal. The vicar, Pedro de Córdoba, unimpressed by the delegation's threat to expel the offensive friar, assured them that Montesinos had spoken for the Dominican group. He promised, however, that Montesinos would preach the next Sunday on the same topic. The colonists thereupon retired, believing they had won their point.

Word of the expected retreat spread quickly, and the following Sunday most of the leading Spaniards crowded into the church. Montesinos mounted the pulpit and announced the disquieting text "Suffer me a little, and I will show thee that I have yet to speak on God's behalf." Rather than explaining away his previous sermon with dialectic subtleties, he proceeded to belabor the colonists anew, with even more passion than before, warning them that the friars would no more receive them for confession and absolution than if they were so many highway robbers. And they might write home what they pleased, to whom they pleased.

These words were soon heard in Spain, even by the King. On March 20, 1512, Ferdinand ordered Governor Diego Columbus to reason with Montesinos. If the Dominican and his brothers persisted in their error, previously condemned by the canonists, theologians, and learned men gathered to deliberate on the problem ten years before, the Governor was instructed to send them to Spain by the first ship so that their Superior might punish them "because every hour that they remain in the islands holding such wrong ideas they will do much harm."

Three days later on March 23, 1512, the Dominican Superior in Spain, Alonso de Loaysa, reproved Montesinos in an official communication to the Dominican Provincial in Hispaniola and ordered him to prevail upon the friars to stop preaching such scandalous doctrine. The Provincial was warned that no more friars would be sent if such preaching were permitted to continue.

Thus began the first great struggle for justice in the New World.

6. The Requirement, 1513, a Most Remarkable Document

One of the most dramatic and most debated documents in the history of Spanish America has been the Requirement or manifesto drawn up by jurists and theologians in Valladolid in 1513. It was designed to be read to Indians before hostilities could be legally launched, and was first employed in 1514 by the aged and vitriolic conquistador Pedrarias Dávila near Santa Marta. Later it was made part of the baggage that every conquistador carried to America, and it was used in a number of curious circumstances:

> The Requirement was read to trees and empty huts when no Indians were to be found. Captains muttered its theological phrases into their beards on the edge of sleeping Indian settlements, or even a league away before starting the formal attack, and at times some leather-lunged Spanish notary hurled its sonorous phrases after the Indians as they fled into the mountains. Once it was read in camp before the soldiers to the beat of the drum. Ship captains would sometimes have the document read from the deck as they approached an island, and at night would send out enslaving expeditions, whose leaders would shout the traditional Castilian war cry "Santiago!" rather than read the Requirement before they attacked the near-by villages.*

Modern historians have usually treated the Requirement in a derisive or ironical spirit. Spaniards themselves, when describing this document, have often shared the dilemma of Las Casas, who confessed on reading it that he could not decide whether to laugh or to weep. He roundly denounced it on

* Lewis Hanke, *The Spanish Struggle for Justice in the Conquest of America* (Boston: Little, Brown and Company, 1965), p. 34.

practical as well as theoretical grounds. Even its author, the jurist Palacio Rubios, "laughed often" when he was told of how it was applied in the New World, though the learned doctor still believed that it satisfied the demands of Christian conscience when executed in the manner originally intended.

On the part of the King, don Fernando, and of doña Juana, his daughter, Queen of Castille and Leon, subduers of the barbarous nations, we their servants notify and make known to you, as best we can, that the Lord our God, Living and Eternal, created the Heaven and the Earth, and one man and one woman, of whom you and I, and all the men of the world, were and are descendants, and all those who come after us. But, on account of the multitude which has sprung from this man and woman in the five thousand years since the world was created, it was necessary that some men should go one way and some another, and that they should be divided into many kingdoms and provinces, for in one alone they could not be sustained.

Of all these nations God our Lord gave charge to one man, called St. Peter, that he should be Lord and Superior of all the men in the world, that all should obey him, and that he should be head of the whole human race, wherever men should live, and under whatever law, sect, or belief they should be; and he gave him the world for his kingdom and jurisdiction.

And he commanded him to place his seat in Rome, as the spot most fitting to rule the world from; but also he permitted him to have his seat in any other part of the world, and to judge and govern all Christians, Moors, Jews, Gentiles, and all other sects. This man was called Pope, as if to say, Admirable Great Father and Governor of men. The men who lived in that time obeyed that St. Peter, and took him for Lord, King, and Superior of the universe; so also have they regarded the others who after him have been elected to the Pontificate, and so it has been continued even until now, and will continue until the end of the world.

One of these Pontiffs, who succeeded that St. Peter as Lord of the world, in the dignity and seat which I have before mentioned, made donation of these isles and Terra-firme to the aforesaid King and Queen and to their successors, our lords, with all that there are in these territories, as is contained in certain writings which passed upon the subject as aforesaid, which you can see if you wish.

So their Highnesses are kings and lords of these islands and land of Terra-firme by virtue of this donation; and some islands, and indeed almost all those

Based upon the translation given in Arthur Helps, *The Spanish Conquest in America and Its Relation to the History of Slavery and to the Government of the Colonies,* vol. 1 (London, 1900), pp. 264–267.

to whom this has been notified, have received and served their Highnesses, as lords and kings, in the way that subjects ought to do, with good will, without any resistance, immediately, without delay, when they were informed of the aforesaid facts. And also they received and obeyed the priests whom their Highnesses sent to preach to them and to teach them our Holy Faith; and all these, of their own free will, without any reward or condition, have become Christians, and are so, and their Highnesses have joyfully and benignantly received them, and also have commanded them to be treated as their subjects and vassals; and you too are held and obliged to do the same. Wherefore as best we can, we ask and require you that you consider what we have said to you, and that you take the time that shall be necessary to understand and deliberate upon it, and that you acknowledge the Church as the Ruler and Superior of the whole world and the high priest called Pope, and in his name the King and Queen doña Juana our lords, in his place, as superiors and lords and kings of these islands and this Terra-firme by virtue of the said donation, and that you consent and give place that these religious fathers should declare and preach to you the aforesaid.

If you do so, you will do well, and that which you are obliged to do to their Highnesses, and we in their name shall receive you in all love and charity, and shall leave you your wives, and your children, and your lands, free without servitude, that you may do with them and with yourselves freely that which you like and think best, and they shall not compel you to turn Christians, unless you yourselves, when informed of the truth, should wish to be converted to our Holy Catholic Faith, as almost all the inhabitants of the rest of the islands have done. And besides this, their Highnesses award you many privileges and exceptions and will grant you many benefits.

But if you do not do this, and wickedly and intentionally delay to do so, I certify to you that, with the help of God, we shall forcibly enter into your country and shall make war against you in all ways and manners that we can, and shall subject you to the yoke and obedience of the Church and of their Highnesses; we shall take you and your wives and your children, and shall make slaves of them, and as such shall sell and dispose of them as their Highnesses may command; and we shall take away your goods, and shall do all the harm and damage that we can, as to vassals who do not obey, and refuse to receive their lord, and resist and contradict him; and we protest that the deaths and losses which shall accrue from this are your fault, and not that of their Highnesses, or ours, nor of these cavaliers who come with us. And that we have said this to you and made this Requirement, we request the notary here present to give us his testimony in writing, and we ask the rest who are present that they should be witnesses of this Requirement.

7. *The True History of the Conquest of Mexico*

BERNAL DÍAZ DEL CASTILLO

One of the classics of the conquest is *The True History of the Conquest of New Spain,* written down long after the events by Bernal Díaz del Castillo, one of the small number of conquistadors who fought under Ferdinand Cortez in the conquest of Mexico. His honest and forthright account gives us a lifelike picture of how it all really happened. A more official account may be found in the letters Cortez sent back to Spain to impress the king and court of his great deeds in the New World.* The foot soldier's story is in a more familiar tone; Bernal Díaz was blunt, too, for he was responsible for that pithy explanation of why Spaniards went to America: "We came to serve God, and also to get rich."

Bernal Díaz throughout his detailed *True History* displayed a respect and admiration for many aspects of Indian culture. But like practically all Spaniards the human sacrifices practiced by the Indians revolted him from the first time he heard of them:

> Thirty of us soldiers, well armed, went in two boats to the Island [of San Juan de Ulúa] and we found there a temple where there was a very large and ugly idol which was called Tescatepuca and in charge of it were four Indians with very large black cloaks and hoods, such as the Dominicans or canons wear. . . .
>
> They had this day sacrificed two boys and cut open their chests, and offered the blood and hearts to that cursed Idol. The priests came towards us to fumigate us with the incense with which they had fumigated their Tescatepuca, for when we approached them they were burning something which had the scent of incense, but we would not allow them to fumigate us, for we felt much pity at seeing those two boys who had just been killed and at beholding such great cruelty.†

The Indian prisons also brought stern condemnation by Bernal Díaz: "In Tlaxcala we found wooden houses furnished with gratings, full of Indian men and women imprisoned in them, being fed up until they were fat enough to be sacrificed and eaten. These prisons we broke open and destroyed, and set free the prisoners who were in them, and these poor Indians did not dare to go in any direction, only to stay there with us and thus

---

* *Hernando Cortés: Five Letters, 1519–1526* (New York: Norton, 1962). The most recent and best edition is *Hernán Cortés: Letters from Mexico,* trans. and ed. A. R. Pagden (New York: Grossman, 1971).

† *The True History of the Conquest of New Spain, by Bernal Díaz de Castillo,* trans. and ed. Alfred Percival Maudslay (London: The Hakluyt Society, 1908), vol. 1, pp. 55–56.

escape with their lives. From now on, in all the towns that we entered, the first thing our Captain ordered us to do was to break open these prisons and set free the prisoners."‡

The True History deserves to be read in its entirety, and good paperback editions are available.§ Here are a few selections in which Bernal Díaz records their early impressions of Mexico and the Mexican Indians.

1. *How all the Caciques of Tabasco and its dependencies attacked us, and what came of it*

I have already said how we were marching along when we met all the forces of the enemy which were moving in search of us, and all of the men wore great feather crests and they carried drums and trumpets, and their faces were coloured black and white, and they were armed with large bows and arrows, lances and shields and swords shaped like our two-handed swords, and many slings and stones and fire-hardened javelins, and all wore quilted cotton armour. As they approached us their squadrons were so numerous that they covered the whole plain, and they rushed on us like mad dogs completely surrounding us, and they let fly such a cloud of arrows, javelins and stones that on the first assault they wounded over seventy of us, and fighting hand to hand they did us great damage with their lances, and one soldier fell dead at once from an arrow wound in the ear, and they kept on shooting and wounding us. With our muskets and crossbows and with good sword play we did not fail as stout fighters, and when they came to feel the edge of our swords little by little they fell back, but it was only so as to shoot at us in greater safety. Mesa, our artilleryman, killed many of them with his cannon, for they were formed in great squadrons and they did not open out so that he could fire at them as he pleased, but with all the hurts and wounds which we gave them, we could not drive them off. I said to Diego de Ordás "it seems to me that we ought to close up and charge them," for in truth they suffered greatly from the strokes and thrusts of our swords, and that was why they fell away from us,

‡ Ibid., pp. 288–289.
§ Bernal Díaz, *The Conquest of New Spain,* trans. J. M. Cohen (Baltimore: Penguin Books, 1967), and *The Discovery and Conquest of Mexico by Bernal Díaz del Castillo,* trans. with notes by A. P. Maudslay, Intro. by Irving A. Leonard (New York: Grove Press, 1958).
From *The True History of the Conquest of New Spain, by Bernal Díaz del Castillo,* trans. and ed. Alfred Percival Maudslay (London: The Hakluyt Society, 1908–1910), vol. 1, pp. 118–121; vol. 2, pp. 34–63, passim.

both from fear of these swords, and the better to shoot their arrows and hurl their javelins and the hail of stones. Ordás replied that it was not good advice, for there were three hundred Indians to every one of us, and that we could not hold out against such a multitude, — so there we stood enduring their attack. However, we did agree to get as near as we could to them, as I had advised Ordás, so as to give them a bad time with our swordsmanship, and they suffered so much from it that they retreated towards a swamp.

During all this time Cortés and his horsemen failed to appear, although we greatly longed for him, and we feared that by chance some disaster had befallen him.

I remember that when we fired shots the Indians gave great shouts and whistles and threw dust and rubbish into the air so that we should not see the damage done to them, and they sounded their trumpets and drums and shouted and whistled and cried "Alala! alala!"

Just at this time we caught sight of our horsemen, and as the great Indian host was crazed with its attack on us, it did not at once perceive them coming up behind their backs, and as the plain was level ground and the horsemen were good riders, and many of the horses were very handy and fine gallopers, they came quickly on the enemy and speared them as they chose. As soon as we saw the horsemen we fell on the Indians with such energy that with us attacking on one side and the horsemen on the other, they soon turned tail. The Indians thought that the horse and its rider was all one animal, for they had never seen horses up to this time.

The savannas and fields were crowded with Indians running to take refuge in the thick woods near by.

After we had defeated the enemy Cortés told us that he had not been able to come to us sooner as there was a swamp in the way, and he had to fight his way through another force of warriors before he could reach us, and three horsemen and five horses had been wounded.

As soon as the horsemen had dismounted under some trees and houses, we returned thanks to God for giving us so complete a victory.

As it was Lady day we gave to the town which was afterwards founded here the name of Santa Maria de la Victoria, on account of this great victory being won on Our Lady's day. This was the first battle that we fought under Cortés in New Spain.

After this we bound up the hurts of the wounded with cloths, for we had nothing else, and we doctored the horses by searing their wounds with the fat from the body of a dead Indian which we cut up to get out the fat, and we went to look at the dead lying on the plain and there were more than eight hundred of them, the greater number killed by thrusts, the others by the cannon, muskets and crossbows, and many were stretched on the ground half dead. Where the horsemen had passed, numbers of them lay dead or groaning from their wounds. The battle lasted over an hour, and the Indians fought all the time like brave warriors, until the horsemen came up.

We took five prisoners, two of them Captains. As it was late and we had had enough of fighting, and we had not eaten anything, we returned to our camp. Then we buried the two soldiers who had been killed, one by a wound in the ear, and the other by a wound in the throat, and we smeared the wounds of the others and of the horses with the fat of the Indian, and after posting sentinels and guards, we had supper and rested.

2. [*The Great City of Mexico*]

As soon as the messengers had been despatched, we set out for Mexico, and as the people of Huexotzingo and Chalco had told us that Montezuma had held consultations with his Idols and priests whether he should allow us to enter Mexico, or whether he should attack us, and all the priests had answered that his Huichilobos had said he was to allow us to enter and that then he could kill us, as I have already related in the chapter that deals with the subject, and as we are but human and feared death, we never ceased thinking about it. As that country is very thickly peopled we made short marches, and commended ourselves to God and to Our Lady his blessed Mother, and talked about how and by what means we could enter [the City], and it put courage into our hearts to think that as our Lord Jesus Christ had vouchsafed us protection through past dangers, he would likewise guard us from the power of the Mexicans.

We went to sleep at a town called Iztapalatengo where half the houses are in the water and the other half on dry land, where there is a small mountain (and now there is an Inn there) and there they gave us a good supper. . . .

The next day, in the morning, we arrived at a broad Causeway, and continued our march towards Iztapalapa, and when we saw so many cities and villages built in the water and other great towns on dry land and that straight and level causeway going towards Mexico, we were amazed and said that it was like the enchantments they tell of in the legend of Amadis, on account of the great towers and cues and buildings rising from the water, and all built of masonry. And some of our soldiers even asked whether the things that we saw were not a dream? It is not to be wondered at that I here write it down in this manner, for there is so much to think over that I do not know how to describe it, seeing things as we did that had never been heard of or seen before, not even dreamed about.

Thus, we arrived near Iztapalapa, to behold the splendour of the other Caciques who came out to meet us, who were the Lord of the town named Cuitlahuac, and the Lord of Culuacan, both of them near relations of Montezuma. And then when we entered that city of Iztapalapa, the appearance of the palaces in which they lodged us! How spacious and well built they were, of beautiful stone work and cedar wood, and the wood of other sweet scented trees, with great rooms and courts, wonderful to behold, covered with awnings of cotton cloth.

When we had looked well at all of this, we went to the orchard and garden, which was such a wonderful thing to see and walk in, that I was never tired of looking at the diversity of the trees, and noting the scent which each one had, and the paths full of roses and flowers, and the many fruit trees and native roses, and the pond of fresh water. There was another thing to observe, that great canoes were able to pass into the garden from the lake through an opening that had been made so that there was no need for their occupants to land. And all was cemented and very splendid with many kinds of stone [monuments] with pictures on them, which gave much to think about. Then the birds of many kinds and breeds which came into the pond. I say again that I stood looking at it and thought that never in the world would there be discovered other lands such as these, for at that time there was no Peru, nor any thought of it. [Of all these wonders that I then beheld] to-day all is overthrown and lost, nothing left standing. . . .

Early next day we left Iztapalapa with a large escort of those great Caciques whom I have already mentioned. We proceeded along the Causeway which is here eight paces in width and runs so straight to the City of Mexico that it does not seem to me to turn either much or little, but, broad as it is, it was so crowded with people that there was hardly room for them all, some of them going to and others returning from Mexico, besides those who had come out to see us, so that we were hardly able to pass by the crowds of them that came; and the towers and cues were full of people as well as the canoes from all parts of the lake. It was not to be wondered at, for they had never before seen horses or men such as we are.

Gazing on such wonderful sights, we did not know what to say, or whether what appeared before us was real, for on one side, on the land, there were great cities, and in the lake ever so many more, and the lake itself was crowded with canoes, and in the Causeway were many bridges at intervals, and in front of us stood the great City of Mexico, and we, — we did not even number four hundred soldiers! and we well remembered the words and warnings given us by the people of Huexotzingo and Tlaxcala and Tlamanalco, and the many other warnings that had been given that we should beware of entering Mexico, where they would kill us, as soon as they had us inside.

Let the curious readers consider whether there is not much to ponder over in this that I am writing. What men have there been in the world who have shown such daring? But let us get on, and march along the Causeway. When we arrived where another small causeway branches off (leading to Coyoacan, which is another city) where there were some buildings like towers, which are their oratories, many more chieftains and Caciques approached clad in very rich mantles, the brilliant liveries of one chieftain differing from those of another, and the causeways were crowded with them. The Great Montezuma had sent these great Caciques in advance to receive us, and when they came before Cortés they bade us welcome in their language, and as a sign of peace, they touched their hands against the ground, and kissed the ground with the hand. . . .

3. [*Montezuma and His Splendid Court*]

The Great Montezuma was about forty years old, of good height and well proportioned, slender, and spare of flesh, not very swarthy, but of the natural colour and shade of an Indian. He did not wear his hair long, but so as just to cover his ears, his scanty black beard was well shaped and thin. His face was somewhat long, but cheerful, and he had good eyes and showed in his appearance and manner both tenderness and, when necessary, gravity. He was very neat and clean and bathed once every day in the afternoon. He had many women as mistresses, daughters of Chieftains, and he had two great Cacicas as his legitimate wives, and when he had intercourse with them it was so secretly that no one knew anything about it, except some of his servants. He was free from unnatural offences. The clothes that he wore one day, he did not put on again until four days later. He had over two hundred chieftains in his guard, in other rooms close to his own, not that all were meant to converse with him, but only one or another, and when they went to speak to him they were obliged to take off their rich mantles and put on others of little worth, but they had to be clean, and they had to enter barefoot with their eyes lowered to the ground, and not to look up in his face. And they made him three obeisances, and said: "Lord, my Lord, my Great Lord," before they came up to him, and then they made their report and with a few words he dismissed them, and on taking leave they did not turn their backs, but kept their faces toward him with their eyes to the ground, and they did not turn their backs until they left the room. I noticed another thing, that when other great chiefs came from distant lands about disputes or business, when they reached the apartments of the Great Montezuma, they had to come barefoot and with poor mantles, and they might not enter directly into the Palace, but had to loiter about a little on one side of the Palace door, for to enter hurriedly was considered to be disrespectful.

For each meal, over thirty different dishes were prepared by his cooks according to their ways and usage, and they placed small pottery brasiers beneath the dishes so that they should not get cold. They prepared more than three hundred plates of the food that Montezuma was going to eat, and more than a thousand for the guard. When he was going to eat, Montezuma would sometimes go out with his chiefs and stewards, and they would point out to him which dish was best, and of what birds and other things it was composed, and as they advised him, so he would eat, but it was not often that he would go out to see the food, and then merely as a pastime.

I have heard it said that they were wont to cook for him the flesh of young boys, but as he had such a variety of dishes, made of so many things, we could not succeed in seeing if they were of human flesh or of other things, for they daily cooked fowls, turkeys, pheasants, native partridges, quail, tame and wild ducks, venison, wild boar, reed birds, pigeons, hares and rabbits, and many sorts of birds and other things which are bred in this country, and they are so numerous that I cannot finish naming them in a hurry; so we had no insight into it, but I know for certain that after our Captain censured the sacrifice of human beings, and the eating of their flesh, he ordered that such food should not be prepared for him thenceforth.

Let us cease speaking of this and return to the way things were served to him at meal times. It was in this way: if it was cold they made up a large fire of live coals of a firewood made from the bark of trees which did not give off any smoke, and the scent of the bark from which the fire was made was very fragrant, and so that it should not give off more heat than he required, they placed in front of it a sort of screen adorned with figures of idols worked in gold. He was seated on a low stool, soft and richly worked, and the table, which was also low, was made in the same style as the seats, and on it they placed the table cloths of white cloth and some rather long napkins of the same material. Four very beautiful cleanly women brought water for his hands in a sort of deep basin which they call "xicales," and they held others like plates below to catch the water, and they brought him towels. And two other women brought him tortilla bread, and as soon as he began to eat they placed before him a sort of wooden screen painted over with gold, so that no one should watch him eating. Then the four women stood aside, and four great chieftains who were old men came and stood beside them, and with these Montezuma now and then conversed, and asked them questions, and as a great favour he would give to each of these elders a dish of what to him tasted best. They say that these elders were his near relations, and were his counsellors and judges of law suits, and the dishes and food which Montezuma gave them they ate standing up with much reverence and without looking at his face. He was served on Cholula earthenware either red or black. While he was at his meal the men of his guard who were in the rooms near to that of Montezuma, never dreamed of making any noise or speaking aloud. They brought him fruit of all the different kinds that the land produced, but he ate very little of it. From time to time they brought him, in cup-shaped vessels of pure gold, a certain drink made from cacao which they said he took when he was going to visit his wives, and at the time he took no heed of it, but what I did see was that they brought over fifty great jugs of good cacao frothed up, and he drank of that, and the women served this drink to him with great reverence.

Sometimes at meal-times there were present some very ugly humpbacks, very small of stature and their bodies almost broken in half, who are their jesters, and other Indians, who must have been buffoons, who told him witty sayings, and others who sang and danced, for Montezuma was fond of pleasure and song, and to these he ordered to be given what was left of the food and jugs of cacao. Then the same four women removed the table cloths, and with much ceremony they brought water for his hands. And Montezuma talked with those four old chieftains about things that interested him, and they took leave of him with the great reverence in which they held him, and he remained to repose. . . .

8. *The Grief of the Conquered: "Broken Spears Lie in the Roads"*

MIGUEL LEÓN PORTILLA

Spanish chronicles present only one side of the story, that of the conquerors. The Mexican anthropologist Miguel León Portilla was the first to bring together a selection of the accounts by the Indians, some written as early as 1528, only seven years after the fall of Mexico City. These writings give a brief history of the dramatic confrontation of Indians and Spaniards as told by the victims, and include reports by native priests and wise men who managed to survive the persecution and death that took place during the final struggle.

The selection begins with the story of how frightened Montezuma was by the reports of the messengers he had sent to see Cortez and his soldiers.

MOTECUHZOMA GOES OUT
TO MEET CORTES

The Spaniards arrived in Xoloco, near the entrance to Tenochtitlan. That was the end of the march, for they had reached their goal.

Motecuhzoma now arrayed himself in his finery, preparing to go out to meet them. The other great princes also adorned their persons, as did the nobles and their chieftains and knights. They all went out together to meet the strangers.

They brought trays heaped with the finest flowers — the flower that resembles a shield; the flower shaped like a heart; in the center, the flower with the sweetest aroma; and the fragrant yellow flower, the most precious of all. They also brought garlands of flowers, and ornaments for the breast, and necklaces of gold, necklaces hung with rich stones, necklaces fashioned in the petatillo style.

Thus Motecuhzoma went out to meet them, there in Huitzillan. He presented many gifts to the Captain and his commanders, those who had come to make war. He showered gifts upon them and hung flowers around their necks; he gave them necklaces of flowers and bands of flowers to adorn their breasts; he set garlands of flowers upon their heads. Then he hung the gold necklaces around their necks and gave them presents of every sort as gifts of welcome. . . .

MOTECUHZOMA AWAITS WORD
FROM THE MESSENGERS

While the messengers were away, Motecuhzoma could neither sleep nor eat, and no one could speak with him. He thought that everything he did was in vain, and he sighed almost every moment. He was lost in despair, in the deepest gloom and sorrow. Nothing could comfort him, nothing could calm him, nothing could give him any pleasure.

He said: "What will happen to us? Who will outlive it? Ah, in other times I was contented, but now I have death in my heart! My heart burns and suffers, as if it were drowned in spices . . . ! But will our lord come here?"

Then he gave orders to the watchmen, to the men who guarded the palace:

From *The Broken Spears: The Aztec Account of the Conquest of Mexico,* ed. Miguel León Portilla (Boston: Beacon Press, 1962), pp. 29–149, passim. Copyright © 1962 by Beacon Press; originally published in Spanish under the title of *Vision de los Vencidos:* copyright © 1959 by Universidad Nacional Autónoma de México. Reprinted by permission of Beacon Press.

"Tell me, even if I am sleeping: 'The messengers have come back from the sea.' " But when they went to tell him, he immediately said: "They are not to report to me here. I will receive them in the House of the Serpent. Tell them to go there." And he gave this order: "Two captives are to be painted with chalk."

The messengers went to the House of the Serpent, and Motecuhzoma arrived. The two captives were then sacrificed before his eyes: their breasts were torn open, and the messengers were sprinkled with their blood. This was done because the messengers had completed a difficult mission: they had seen the gods, their eyes had looked on their faces. They had even conversed with the gods!

THE MESSENGERS' REPORT

When the sacrifice was finished, the messengers reported to the king. They told him how they had made the journey, and what they had seen, and what food the strangers ate. Motecuhzoma was astonished and terrified by their report, and the description of the strangers' food astonished him above all else.

He was also terrified to learn how the cannon roared, how its noise resounded, how it caused one to faint and grow deaf. The messengers told him: "A thing like a ball of stone comes out of its entrails: it comes out shooting sparks and raining fire. The smoke that comes out with it has a pestilent odor, like that of rotten mud. This odor penetrates even to the brain and causes the greatest discomfort. If the cannon is aimed against a mountain, the mountain splits and cracks open. If it is aimed against a tree, it shatters the tree into splinters. This is a most unnatural sight, as if the tree had exploded from within."

The messengers also said: "Their trappings and arms are all made of iron. They dress in iron and wear iron casques on their heads. Their swords are iron; their bows are iron; their shields are iron; their spears are iron. Their deer carry them on their backs wherever they wish to go. These deer, our lord, are as tall as the roof of a house.

"The strangers' bodies are completely covered, so that only their faces can be seen. Their skin is white, as if it were made of lime. They have yellow hair, though some of them have black. Their beards are long and yellow, and their moustaches are also yellow. Their hair is curly, with very fine strands.

"As for their food, it is like human food. It is large and white, and not heavy. It is something like straw, but with the taste of a cornstalk, of the pith of a cornstalk. It is a little sweet, as if it were flavored with honey; it tastes of honey, it is sweet-tasting food.

"Their dogs are enormous, with flat ears and long, dangling tongues. The color of their eyes is a burning yellow; their eyes flash fire and shoot off sparks. Their bellies are hollow, their flanks long and narrow. They are tireless and very powerful. They bound here and there, panting, with their tongues hanging out. And they are spotted like an ocelot."

When Motecuhzoma heard this report, he was filled with terror. It was as if his heart had fainted, as if it had shriveled. It was as if he were conquered by despair. . . .

THE SPANIARDS TAKE POSSESSION OF THE CITY

When the Spaniards entered the Royal House, they placed Motecuhzoma under guard and kept him under their vigilance. They also placed a guard over Itzcuauhtzin, but the other lords were permitted to depart.

Then the Spaniards fired one of their cannons, and this caused great confusion in the city. The people scattered in every direction; they fled without rhyme or reason; they ran off as if they were being pursued. It was as if they had eaten the mushrooms that confuse the mind, or had seen some dreadful apparition. They were all overcome by terror, as if their hearts had fainted. And when night fell, the panic spread through the city and their fears would not let them sleep.

In the morning the Spaniards told Motecuhzoma what they needed in the way of supplies: tortillas, fried chickens, hens' eggs, pure water, firewood and charcoal. Also: large, clean cooking pots, water jars, pitchers, dishes and other pottery. Motecuhzoma ordered that it be sent to them. The chiefs who received this order were angry with the king and no longer revered or respected him. But they furnished the Spaniards with all the provisions they needed — food, beverages and water, and fodder for the horses.

THE SPANIARDS REVEAL THEIR GREED

When the Spaniards were installed in the palace, they asked Motecuhzoma about the city's resources and reserves and about the warriors' ensigns and shields. They questioned him closely and then demanded gold.

Motecuhzoma guided them to it. They surrounded him and crowded close with their weapons. He walked in the center, while they formed a circle around him.

When they arrived at the treasure house called Teucalco, the riches of gold and feathers were brought out to them: ornaments made of quetzal feathers, richly worked shields, disks of gold, the necklaces of the idols, gold nose plugs, gold greaves and bracelets and crowns.

The Spaniards immediately stripped the feathers from the gold shields and ensigns. They gathered all the gold into a great mound and set fire to everything else, regardless of its value. Then they melted down the gold into ingots. As for the precious green stones, they took only the best of them; the rest were snatched up by the Tlaxcaltecas. The Spaniards searched through the whole treasure house, questioning and quarreling, and seized every object they thought was beautiful.

THE SEIZURE OF MOTECUHZOMA'S TREASURES

Next they went to Motecuhzoma's storehouse, in the place called Totocalco [Place of the Palace of the Birds], where his personal treasures were kept. The Spaniards grinned like little beasts and patted each other with delight.

When they entered the hall of treasures, it was as if they had arrived in Paradise. They searched everywhere and coveted everything; they were slaves to their own greed. All of Motecuhzoma's possessions were brought out: fine bracelets, necklaces with large stones, ankle rings with little gold bells, the royal crowns and all the royal finery — everything that belonged to the king and was reserved to him only. They seized these treasures as if they were their own, as if this plunder were merely a stroke of good luck. And when they had taken all the gold, they heaped up everything else in the middle of the patio.

La Malinche called the nobles together. She climbed up to the palace roof and cried: "Mexicanos, come forward! The Spaniards need your help! Bring them food and pure water. They are tired and hungry; they are almost fainting from exhaustion! Why do you not come forward? Are you angry with them?"

The Mexicans were too frightened to approach. They were crushed by terror and would not risk coming forward. They shied away as if the Spaniards were wild beasts, as if the hour were midnight on the blackest night of the year. Yet they did not abandon the Spaniards to hunger and thirst. They brought them whatever they needed, but shook with fear as they did so. They delivered the supplies to the Spaniards with trembling hands, then turned and hurried away. . . .

THE MASSACRE IN THE MAIN TEMPLE
DURING THE FIESTA OF TOXCATL

At this moment in the fiesta, when the dance was loveliest and when song was linked to song, the Spaniards were seized with an urge to kill the celebrants. They all ran forward, armed as if for battle. They closed the entrances and passageways, all the gates of the patio: the Eagle Gate in the lesser palace, the

Gate of the Canestalk and the Gate of the Serpent of Mirrors. They posted guards so that no one could escape, and then rushed into the Sacred Patio to slaughter the celebrants. They came on foot, carrying their swords and their wooden or metal shields.

They ran in among the dancers, forcing their way to the place where the drums were played. They attacked the man who was drumming and cut off his arms. Then they cut off his head, and it rolled across the floor.

They attacked all the celebrants, stabbing them, spearing them, striking them with their swords. They attacked some of them from behind, and these fell instantly to the ground with their entrails hanging out. Others they beheaded: they cut off their heads, or split their heads to pieces.

They struck others in the shoulders, and their arms were torn from their bodies. They wounded some in the thigh and some in the calf. They slashed others in the abdomen, and their entrails all spilled to the ground. Some attempted to run away, but their intestines dragged as they ran; they seemed to tangle their feet in their own entrails. No matter how they tried to save themselves, they could find no escape.

Some attempted to force their way out, but the Spaniards murdered them at the gates. Others climbed the walls, but they could not save themselves. Those who ran into the communal houses were safe there for a while; so were those who lay down among the victims and pretended to be dead. But if they stood up again, the Spaniards saw them and killed them.

The blood of the warriors flowed like water and gathered into pools. The pools widened, and the stench of blood and entrails filled the air. The Spaniards ran into the communal houses to kill those who were hiding. They ran everywhere and searched everywhere; they invaded every room, hunting and killing.

THE SIEGE OF TENOCHTITLAN

Now the Spaniards began to wage war against us. They attacked us by land for ten days, and then their ships appeared. Twenty days later, they gathered all their ships together near Nonohualco, off the place called Mazatzintamalco. The allies from Tlaxcala and Huexotzinco set up camp on either side of the road.

Our warriors from Tlatelolco immediately leaped into their canoes and set out for Mazatzintamalco and the Nonohualco road. But no one set out from Tenochtitlan to assist us: only the Tlatelolcas were ready when the Spaniards arrived in their ships. On the following day, the ships sailed to Xoloco.

The fighting at Xoloco and Huitzillan lasted for two days. While the battle was under way, the warriors from Tenochtitlan began to mutiny. They said: "Where are our chiefs? They have fired scarcely a single arrow! Do they think they have fought like men?" Then they seized four of their own leaders and put them to death. The victims were two captains, Cuauhnochtli and Cuapan, and the priests of Amantlan and Tlalocan. This was the second time that the people of Tenochtitlan killed their own leaders. . . .

THE FIGHTING IS RENEWED

The Spaniards made ready to attack us, and the war broke out again. They assembled their forces in Cuepopan and Cozcacuahco. A vast number of our warriors were killed by their metal darts. Their ships sailed to Texopan, and the battle there lasted three days. When they had forced us to retreat, they entered the Sacred Patio, where there was a four-day battle. Then they reached Yacacolco.

The Tlatelolcas set up three racks of heads in three different places. The first rack was in the Sacred Patio of Tlilancalco [Black House], where we strung up the heads of our lords the Spaniards. The second was in Acacolco, where we strung up Spanish heads and the heads of two of their horses. The third was in Zacatla, in front of the temple of the earth-goddess Cihuacoatl, where we strung up the heads of Tlaxcaltecas.

The women of Tlatelolco joined in the fighting. They struck at the enemy and shot arrows at them; they tucked up their skirts and dressed in the regalia of war.

The Spaniards forced us to retreat. Then they occupied the market place. The Tlatelolcas — the Jaguar Knights, the Eagle Knights, the great warriors — were defeated, and this was the end of the battle. It had lasted five days, and two thousand Tlatelolcas were killed in action. During the battle, the Spaniards set up a canopy for the Captain in the market place. They also mounted a catapult on the temple platform.

EPIC DESCRIPTION OF THE BESIEGED CITY

And all these misfortunes befell us. We saw them and wondered at them; we suffered this unhappy fate.

> Broken spears lie in the roads;
> we have torn our hair in our grief.

The houses are roofless now, and their walls
are red with blood.

Worms are swarming in the streets and plazas,
and the walls are splattered with gore.
The water has turned red, as if it were dyed,
and when we drink it,
it has the taste of brine.

We have pounded our hands in despair
against the adobe walls,
for our inheritance, our city, is lost and dead.
The shields of our warriors were its defense,
but they could not save it.

We have chewed dry twigs and salt grasses;
we have filled our mouths with dust and bits of adobe;
we have eaten lizards, rats and worms. . . .

When we had meat, we ate it almost raw. It was scarcely on the fire before
we snatched it and gobbled it down.

They set a price on all of us: on the young men, the priests, the boys and
girls. The price of a poor man was only two handfuls of corn, or ten cakes
made from mosses or twenty cakes of salty couch-grass. Gold, jade, rich
cloths, quetzal feathers — everything that once was precious was now considered worthless.

The captains delivered several prisoners of war to Cuauhtemoc to be sacrificed. He performed the sacrifices in person, cutting them open with a stone
knife. . . .

ELEGIES ON THE FALL OF THE CITY

INTRODUCTION.   By way of conclusion, we present three "songs of sorrow,"
true elegies written by the post-Conquest Aztec poets. The first song, from the
collection of *Cantares mexicanos* in the National Library of Mexico, was
probably composed in 1523. The second is part of a whole series of poems
recounting the Conquest from the arrival of the Spaniards in Tenochtitlan to
the ultimate defeat of the Aztecs. We have selected only the most dramatic
moments from the last section of this series. The third song, also from the
Cantares mexicanos, recalls the traditional symbolism of "flowers and songs."
It laments that only grief and suffering remain in the once proud capital.

These elegies are among the first and most poignant expressions of what Dr. Garibay has called "the trauma of the Conquest." They reveal, with greater eloquence than the other texts, the deep emotional wound inflicted on the Indians by the defeat. (Introductory note by Miguel León Portilla.)

The Fall of Tenochtitlan

Our cries of grief rise up
and our tears rain down,
for Tlatelolco is lost.
The Aztecs are fleeing across the lake;
they are running away like women.

How can we save our homes, my people?
The Aztecs are deserting the city:
the city is in flames, and all
is darkness and destruction.

Motelchiuhtzin the Huiznahuacatl,
Tlacotzin the Tlailotlacatl,
Oquitzin the Tlacatecuhtli
are greeted with tears.

Weep, my people:
know that with these disasters
we have lost the Mexican nation.
The water has turned bitter,
our food is bitter!
These are the acts of the Giver of Life. . . .

The Imprisonment of Cuauhtemoc

The Aztecs are besieged in the city;
the Tlatelolcas are besieged in the city!

The walls are black,
the air is black with smoke,
the guns flash in the darkness.
They have captured Cuauhtemoc;
they have captured the princes of Mexico.

The Aztecs are besieged in the city;
the Tlatelolcas are besieged in the city!

After nine days, they were taken to Coyoacan:
Cuauhtemoc, Coanacoch, Tetlepanquetzaltzin.
The kings are prisoners now.

Tlacotzin consoled them:
"Oh my nephews, take heart!
The kings are prisoners now;
they are bound with chains."

The king Cuauhtemoc replied:
"Oh my nephew, you are a prisoner;
they have bound you in irons.

"But who is that at the side of the Captain-General?
Ah, it is Dona Isabel, my little niece!
Ah, it is true: the kings are prisoners now!

"You will be a slave and belong to another:
the collar will be fashioned in Coyoacan,
where the quetzal feathers will be woven.

"Who is that at the side of the Captain-General?
Ah, it is Dona Isabel, my little niece!
Ah, it is true: the kings are prisoners now!"

Flowers and Songs of Sorrow

Nothing but flowers and songs of sorrow
are left in Mexico and Tlatelolco,
where once we saw warriors and wise men.

We know it is true
that we must perish,
for we are mortal men.
You, the Giver of Life,
you have ordained it.

We wander here and there
in our desolate poverty.
We are mortal men.
We have seen bloodshed and pain
where once we saw beauty and valor.

We are crushed to the ground;

we lie in ruins.
There is nothing but grief and suffering
in Mexico and Tlatelolco,
where once we saw beauty and valor.

Have you grown weary of your servants?
Are you angry with your servants,
O Giver of Life?

9. *Francisco Pizarro and His Men on the Road to Cuzco, 1533*

JOHN HEMMING

The conquest of Peru was not as sudden or dramatic as the downfall of the Aztec empire, but it was dramatic enough. John Hemming, a young British businessman, has demonstrated that the writing of history cannot be left exclusively to the professional historian, for his solid and well-written volume, *The Conquest of the Incas,* is the first satisfying and sound general work on the conquest of Peru that has appeared in a generation.

The following selection brings out clearly the military aspects of the clashes between European-trained soldiers and the Inca warriors.

The four battles on the road to Cuzco — Jauja, Vilcashuaman, Vilcaconga, and the pass above Cuzco — had demonstrated the immense superiority of mounted, armoured Spaniards over native warriors. The Inca empire did not, as is sometimes supposed, go under without a struggle. Whenever the native armies were led by a determined commander they fought with fatalistic bravery. In the course of the Conquest the Incas, who were themselves formidable conquerors against other Andean tribes, tried to adapt their fighting methods to meet the extraordinary challenges of invasion by a more advanced civilisation. The mounted knight had dominated European military history since Roman times. This formidable figure could be stopped only by other horsemen using similar equipment, by archers, pikemen or elaborate defences. His domination of the battlefield ended only with the evolution of rapid-firing firearms.

Whenever American natives had time to assimilate European weapons they were able to mount an effective resistance — for instance the natives of southern Chile, who acquired pikes and horses, or those of North America who adopted horses and firearms. But the Incas did not have time to make these adaptations to their fighting techniques, and their bare mountainous country did not possess suitable wood for pikes or bows.

The Inca armies were now confronting the finest soldiers in the world. Spanish tercios were considered the best in Europe throughout the sixteenth century. They had behind them the successful expulsion of the Moors from Spain, and many who now fought in Peru had participated in the defeat of Francis I at Pavia or of the Aztecs in Mexico. The men who were attracted to the American conquests were the most adventurous — as tough, brave and ruthless as the members of any gold rush. In addition to greed they possessed the religious fervour and unshakeable self-confidence of a crusading people which had been fighting the infidel for centuries and was still on the advance. Whatever one may think of their motives, it is impossible not to admire their bravery. In skirmish after skirmish their first reaction — almost a reflex — was to charge straight into the thick of the enemy. Such aggressiveness was intended as a psychological shock-tactic, and its effect was heightened by the invaders' reputation for success, invincibility, almost divinity.

Atahualpa's nephew Titu Cusi tried to describe the awe felt by his people in the face of these strangers. "They seemed like viracochas, which was our ancient name for the universal creator. [My people] gave this name to the men they had seen, partly because they were very different from us in clothing and appearance, and also because we saw that they rode on enormous animals that had feet of silver — we said 'silver' because of the shine of the horses' shoes. We also called them this because we had seen them expressing themselves on to white sheets, just as one person talks to another — this referred to their reading books and letters. We called them viracochas because of their magnificent appearance and physique; because of the great differences between them — some had black beards and others red ones; because we saw them eat off silver; and also because they possessed yllapas (our name for thunder) — we said this to describe the arquebuses which we thought to be thunder from heaven."

During the actual fighting of the Conquest, the Spaniards owed everything to their horses. On the march their horses gave them a mobility that continually took the natives by surprise. Even when the Indians had posted pickets, the Spanish cavalry could ride past them faster than the sentries could run back to warn of danger. And in battle a mounted man has an overwhelming advantage over a man on foot, using his horse as a weapon to ride down the enemy, more manoeuvrable, less exhausted, inaccessible and continually striking downwards from his greater height.

At the time of the Conquest there was a revolution in the method of riding. The pike and arquebus had made the fully armoured knight too vulnerable. He was now replaced by the trooper, jinete, on a lighter, faster horse. Instead of riding "a la brida" with legs stretched out to take the shock of jousting, the riders of the Conquest adopted a new style called "a la jineta." This method had the rider in "the position of the Moors, with short stirrups and the legs bent backwards so as to give the appearance of almost kneeling on the horse's back. . . . With the high Moorish saddle, the rider used the powerful Moorish bit, a single rein, and always rode with rather a high hand. The reason was that the horses were all bitted on the neck, that is to say they turned by pressure on the neck and not by pulling at the corners of the mouth. . . . As the bit had a high port, and often a long branch, the raising of the hand pressed the port into the palate . . . and a horse turned far more rapidly and suffered less [than under] the modern system."

Both Spaniards and Indians attached immense importance to horses, the tanks of the Conquest. To Spaniards the possession of a horse elevated a man, entitling him to a horseman's share of conquered treasure. During the months of waiting at Cajamarca, Spaniards had paid fantastic prices for the few available horses. Francisco de Xerez described these prices "even though some people may find them unbelievably high. One horse was bought for 1,500 pesos de oro and others for 3,300. The average price for horses was 2,500, but there were none to be found at this price." This was sixty times the price being paid for a sword at Cajamarca at the same time, and the inflated values of Peru of course represented small fortunes in contemporary Spain. Many deeds of sale that have survived from the period confirm them.

For the Indians, their enemies' great horses assumed a terrible value. They thought little of a Spaniard on foot, cumbersome in armour and breathless from the altitude; but the horses filled them with dread. "They thought more of killing one of these animals that persecuted them so than they did of killing ten men, and they always placed [the horses'] heads afterwards somewhere that the Christians could see them, decked in flowers and branches as a sign of victory."

The Spanish conquistadores wore armour and steel helmets. Some of the infantry wore a simple steel cap called a salade, of which the barbute type was still common at the time of the Conquest. It looked like a steel Balaclava helmet, similar to a modern steel helmet, but lower over the forehead and nape of the neck. The cabasset was another simple helmet. Its high domed crown resembled a 1920s cloche, and it often had a small apical peak like a French revolutionary liberty cap. But the most famous helmet was the morion. This was a bowl-like chapel-de-fer to which an elongated brim had been added. This brim swept along the sides in an elegant upward curve, rising to a point at the front and rear. The crown was often protected by a steel crest running from front to rear like that on the helmet of a French poilu of the 1914–18 War.

All Spanish soldiers wore armour, but this varied in elaboration. Many of the wealthy leaders wore full armour, which came in a wide variety of styles ranging from heavy gothic suits to the Maximilian suits of the 1530s and 1540s. The period of the Conquest was the high point of the art of making armour. Plates covering exposed areas of the body were brilliantly jointed with articulated lames and hinges to permit freedom of movement to every limb. Special protective plates covered the shoulders, elbows and knees; but the steel of the breastplates and leg and arm protections was as light as possible. A full suit of armour weighed only about sixty pounds, and this weight was quite tolerable, being evenly distributed over the entire body. In the latter half of the century some parts of the body were less thoroughly protected, in order to economise weight. Instead of head-to-foot armour, soldiers adopted a half-suit extending only to the jointed lames, called tassets, that formed a skirt below the breastplate, or a three-quarter suit extending to the knees. Suits of armour had their own helmets. A solid crown covered the head and extended over the neck where it joined a series of overlapping plates called a gorget. The cheeks and chin were defended by a piece called bevor, and a hinged visor covered the face. This helmet also became lighter, with the visor being replaced by a peak across the forehead and a series of protective bars across the face itself.

Although most of the rich men in the Conquest owned full armour or acquired it when they received shares of treasure, they often used lighter substitutes when fighting Indians. Some wore china mail shirts, which weighed between fourteen and thirty pounds. These varied according to the size of their links, but most could withstand a normal thrust. Some suits had thicker or flattened wire at vulnerable places to reduce the size of the holes. Other conquistadores abandoned even chain mail in favour of padded cloth armour called escaupil, which they adopted from the Aztecs. Escaupil normally consisted of canvas stuffed with cotton. Spanish soldiers also defended themselves with small shields, generally oval bucklers of wood or iron covered in leather.

The most effective Spanish weapon was a sword: either the double-edged cutting sword, or the rapier, which over the years gradually lost its cutting edge and became thinner and more rigid for thrusting. These were the weapons that slaughtered thinly protected Indians. Sword manufacture had reached perfection by the sixteenth century, and Toledo was one of the most famous centres for the craft. Strict regulations and apprenticeships ensured that high standards were maintained. A blade had to survive rigorous testing before being decorated and mounted in its hilt: it was bent in a semicircle and in an s-bend, and then struck with full force against a steel helmet before being passed. The sword was often decorated with a motto: "never unsheathed in vain"; "por mi dama y mi rey, es mi ley" ("for my lady and my King, this is my law"); or more blatant advertising such as "Toledan quality, the soldier's dream." The blade, some three feet long, light, flexible and extremely strong and sharp, was a deadly weapon in the hands of skilled swordsmen. And the Spanish conquistadores, acknowledged as the finest fighting men in Europe, made it their business to be supreme in this art. Throughout the century swords, like horses, were rigorously forbidden to Indians under any circumstances whatsoever.

In addition to his sword, and to supporting daggers and poniards, the cavalryman's favourite weapon was his lance. Along with the crouching, highly mobile jineta method of riding, came the "lanza jineta." This was ten to fourteen feet long, but light and thin, with a metal tip shaped like a diamond or olive leaf. The rider could charge with the shaft resting against his chest; he could hold it down level with his thigh, parallel to the galloping horse, with his thumb pointed forwards in the direction of the blow; or he could stab downwards with it. Each method was enough to penetrate Indian padded armour.

It has sometimes been said that the Spanish triumph was due to their firearms. This was not so. Arquebuses were sometimes fired during the Conquest, but there were very few of them, and they played no significant role beyond producing a great psychological effect when they did go off. It was not surprising that few arquebuses were used. The cavalry despised them as an ungentlemanly arm, and the Conquest was largely the work of horsemen. They were unwieldy, from three to five feet long, and often needing a support at the end of the barrel. They were difficult to load: a measured charge of powder had to be pushed down the muzzle, followed by the ball. And they were even more difficult to fire: fine powder led through a hole to the main charge, and this had to be lit by a wick. Arquebusiers carried the long rope-like wick coiled around themselves or around the weapon; they lit it by striking a flint and tinder; and they had to blow on the lighted end before applying it to the powder. Later innovations produced an s-curved piece of metal that slightly accelerated the process by pressing the wick on to the powder. But it was almost a century before the flintlock was introduced.

Crossbows were used in the Conquest, but again with limited effect. This weapon had been invented to shoot a missile with sufficient velocity to penetrate armour, but the thrust was gained at the expense of ease or speed. The steel bow had to be bent back mechanically, either by heaving on a system of pulleys or by winding back along a series of ratchets with the help of a wheel called a cranequin. All this involved a laborious process of upending the weapon, treading the head against the ground, and heaving up the bow-string. The metal bolt, once fired, killed any Indian it struck, but the natives were not impressed by this cumbersome device, which often misfired or suffered mechanical breakages.

What could Quisquis's men offer against this armoury? They were still fighting in the bronze age, and their use of metal was unimaginative. They simply copied shapes that had been developed in stone, and their bronze was sadly blunt when matched against Spanish steel. They used a variety of clubs and maces, massive, heavy clubs of some hard jungle palm, and smaller hand-axes or head-breakers called champis. These had stone or bronze heads, shaped either as simple circles or adorned with star-shaped spikes — such heads litter museums and collection of Inca artefacts. Some of the larger clubs had blades like butchers' choppers. Almost all the Spanish soldiers and horses were battered and wounded by these clubs. But it was all too rare for one of these biblical weapons actually to kill a mounted, armoured, slashing Spaniard.

The natives had more success with their missiles. A favourite among the highland tribes was the sling, a belt of wool or fibre some two to four feet long. This was doubled over the projectile, generally a stone the size of an apple, and twirled about the head before one end was released. The sling-shot then spun off to its target with deadly force and accuracy. Coastal tribes used palm throwing-sticks to fire javelins with fire-hardened points. The most effective weapon against cavalry was the long bow, but this was rarely used in Inca armies. Forest Indians used bows and arrows, just as they do today — their forests produced the necessary springy woods for their manufacture, and the dense conditions made arrows ideal weapons for shooting forest game. Whenever Inca armies fought near the Amazonian forests they could enlist jungle tribes with deadly contingents of archers, but they failed to exploit this fine weapon in the highlands.

An Inca warrior was a splendid figure. He wore the normal male dress of a knee-length tunic and resembled a Roman or Greek soldier or a medieval page. His tunic was often adorned with a patterned border and a gold or bronze disc called canipu in the centre of the chest and back. He had bright woollen fringes around his legs, below the knee and at the ankle, and often a plumed crest across the top of his helmet. The helmets themselves were thick woollen caps or were made of plaited cane or wood. Many soldiers wore quilted armour similar to the escaupil of the Aztecs. Beyond this the only protection was a round shield of hard chonta-palm slats worn on the back, and a small shield carried on the arms. These shields added further colour to the Inca battle line, for their wooden bases were covered with cloth or feather-cloth and had a hanging apron, all of which was decorated with magical patterns and devices.

After their defeat in the fierce fight above Cuzco, Quisquis's men lost heart. While the Spaniards spent an anxious night on the hill above the city, the natives left their campfires burning and slipped away in the darkness. When dawn broke Quisquis's army had vanished. "The Governor drew up the infantry and cavalry at the first light of dawn the following morning, and marched off to enter Cuzco. They were in careful battle order, and on the alert, for they were certain that the enemy would launch an attack on them along the road. But no one appeared. In this way the Governor and his men entered the great city of Cuzco, with no further resistance or fighting, at the hour of high mass, on Saturday, 15 November 1533."

10. *The Conquest of Women*

MAGNUS MÖRNER

The Swedish historian Magnus Mörner has been the leader in this generation in the study of the large and complicated subject of race relations in Latin America. During the last decade he has published widely on various aspects of the problem and has stimulated other scholars to enter the field. The following selection comes from one of his recent studies, which, though brief, is the best single volume on the subject with an excellent guide to widely scattered publications.

THE CONQUEST OF WOMEN

When they went ashore, Columbus and his men found that often the Indians of the Antilles tried to hide their women from the white strangers. On other occasions the Indian women showed themselves and were even importune in their admiration for the newcomers. Naturally enough, the discoverers thought that the first attitude was due to the jealousy of the Indian husbands,

From *Race Mixture in the History of Latin America* by Magnus Mörner (Boston: Little, Brown and Company, 1967), pp. 21–27, passim. Reprinted by permission.

whereas the women, of course, were only expressing their love. Such a romantic interpretation of the first meeting of the races can also be found in the accounts of contemporary chroniclers and later historians. But in 1924 a Spanish historian made the sobering observation that the Indian attitudes would be better explained by their animist belief. At first they had to resist the alien spirits. When this was no longer possible, they had to surrender entirely. In addition, the Arawaks were not aware of any relationship between copulation and pregnancy. The latter was explained merely in an animistic way. However true this may be, perhaps the boldness of the alien spirits at last succeeded in arousing the jealousy of the Indian husbands — when Columbus returned to Hispaniola on his second voyage, he found that the men he had left there had been killed. The Indians explained, an eyewitness reports, that one of the Spaniards "had taken three women to himself, and another four; from whence we drew the inference that jealousy was the cause of the misfortune that had occurred."

From the very beginning, Spanish and Portuguese eyewitnesses and chroniclers devoted enthusiastic accounts to the beauty of the Indian girls. Also, a tough German mercenary, Ulrich Schmidel, who took part in the conquest of Río de la Plata, sounds inspired when talking about the Jarayes women: "Very handsome and great lovers, affectionate and with ardent bodies, in my opinion." I would be the last to deny that such expressions in the otherwise not overly romantic chronicles might sometimes be sincere and based on experience. In fact, the female type of the forest tribes is rather close to the feminine ideal in Europe during the Renaissance and later. But I suspect that the sixteenth-century authors sometimes dwelt on the beauty and enchantment of the Indian women in order to satisfy the literary taste of the times. Therefore there is little reason to take these accounts very seriously, or to refer to them, as some historians do, as explaining the rapidity and character of the process of race mixture. Above all it would, as I see it, be absurd to consider them an evidence of a lack of prejudice on the part of the conquistadores. The basic explanation of the rapidity with which race mixture proceeded after the first contact is undoubtedly to be found in the lack of white women at the time of the first expeditions, and the months of abstention during the passage. The satisfaction of a natural instinct should not be confused with social and esthetic attitudes. . . .

In a way, the Spanish Conquest of the Americas was a conquest of women. The Spaniards obtained the Indian girls both by force and by peaceful means. The seizure of women was simply one element in the general enslavement of Indians that took place in the New World during the first decades of the sixteenth century. Indian slavery was finally prohibited categorically in the

New Laws of 1542. It then gradually disappeared, at least in most areas of Spanish America. . . .

Bernal Díaz, that remarkable eyewitness of the conquest of Mexico, presents a lively account of the actual enslavement of women. Cortés had decided that all the slaves taken by the soldiers should be branded, so that the Royal fifth (the Crown's share) and his own share of the human booty could be taken. When the soldiers returned the following day to recover the remaining slaves, they discovered to their dismay that Cortés and his officers had "hidden and taken away the best looking slaves so that there was not a single pretty one left. The ones we received were old and ugly. There was much grumbling against Cortés on this account. . . ." Military campaigns have no doubt always been accompanied by rape and other brutalities against the defenseless. . . .

The Spaniards also obtained women in the form of gifts and as tokens of friendship from the Indian *caciques*. This kind of hospitality has existed in many other environments and ages. Bernal Díaz tells us how the Cacique Xicotenga offered Cortés his virgin daughter and four other pretty girls to his captains. Similar episodes abound in the chronicles of the times. From Paraguay, Rui Díaz de Guzmán reports that the Guaraní caciques considered the gift of women to be an excellent means of allying themselves with the Spaniards. "They called all of them brothers-in-law. This is the origin of the existing custom of calling the Indians entrusted to you *Tobayá* which means brother-in-law. And it so happened that the Spaniards had many sons and daughters with the Indian women they received." Once confirmed by the gift of women, the alliances between Spaniards and Indians were likely to be strong and lasting. This could very well be of greatest importance for the success of a small group of conquistadores. As Inca Garcilaso de la Vega puts it, "as soon as the Indians saw that a woman had been begotten by a Spaniard, all the kinsfolk rallied to pay homage to the Spaniard as their idol and to serve him because they were now related to him. Such Indians were of great help during the Conquest of the Indies.

Another way of obtaining women was provided by the *encomienda,* the famous institution by which Indians were distributed among Spaniards who were granted their tribute. In his turn, the recipient of an encomienda was supposed to protect and civilize his Indians and see to it that they were Christianized. At least until the New Laws (1542), the Indians usually paid their tributes to the *encomendero* in days of work. It is not surprising that the encomenderos often asked for female domestic servants. As Bishop Juan de Zumárraga of Mexico observed, in his well-known letter to Emperor Charles in 1529, such servants were used as concubines more often than not.

Near Cuenca in present Ecuador, Cieza de León reports, the Indians sent their wives and daughters to carry the Spaniards' luggage, while they stayed at home. The chronicler remarks that these women were "beautiful, and not a little lascivious, and fond of the Spaniards." . . .

However the Spaniard and the Portuguese of the early sixteenth century had obtained them, by force, purchase, or gift, he lived surrounded by Indian women. Sometimes they were his slaves or the kind of serfs called *naborías* in the Caribbean and *yanaconas* in Peru; sometimes they were, theoretically, free servants. This way of life often produced the impression of a real harem, though some accounts of contemporary observers seem exaggerated, perhaps because they were shocked or too enthusiastic. We should not take as a statistically verified fact the report that in Paraguay, called the Paradise of Mohammed, every Spaniard had an average of twenty to thirty women.

The Church, of course, by no means approved of this situation, but it was certainly not easy to do anything about it. The Bishop of Santo Domingo wrote to the Emperor in 1529 that when his Spanish parishioners were living in sin the concubines were their own Indian servants "and nothing can be found out about it." Furthermore, the results of such unions were often born in faraway places. As another report from Santo Domingo during the same period put it: "there are a great many mestizos here, sons of Spaniards and Indian women who are usually born in *estancias* and uninhabited places." The civil authorities during the Conquest were often satisfied with having the Indian women baptized prior to coition. Thus, the commander of an expedition in Cartagena in 1538 was instructed that he should see to it that "no soldier slept with any Indian who was not a Christian." The conquistadores themselves seem to have taken the reproaches for being promiscuous very lightly, whether they were aware of fulfilling a "civilizing" mission or not. Accused by the Inquisition of a great many blasphemous utterances, the old conquistador Francisco de Aguirre, governor of Tucumán, confessed among other things to having declared that "the service rendered to God in producing mestizos is greater than the sin committed by the same act." . . .

There can be no doubt that casual intercourse and concubinage accounted for most of the crossing during the Conquest. And polygyny was more than frequent. But it should not be forgotten that marriage also brought about race mixture. Intermarriage was explicitly permitted by the monarch in 1501. Two years later Governor Ovando of Santo Domingo was instructed to see to it that "some Christians [i.e., Spaniards] marry some Indian women and some Christian women marry some Indian men, so that both parties can communicate and teach each other and the Indians become men and women of reason.". . . The colonial authorities were far from enthusiastic about it, but there were always some churchmen around who put pressure on them to permit or even promote intermarriage. Spanish-Indian couples living in concubinage should be persuaded to marry. According to a chronicler, Governor Ovando ordered the Spaniards in Santo Domingo either to marry their Indian partners or to part company: "In order not to lose their authority over the Indian women and their services they married them.". . .

It seems fair to draw two conclusions on the basis of what we know about race mixture during the Conquest. In the first place, the color of the sexual partner was of no importance, as well stated by Juan de Carvajal, a conquistador of Venezuela. When accused of promiscuity he flatly replied: "No one in these parts who has a homestead can live without women, Spanish *or* Indian." Second, it is obvious that the Spaniards preferred to marry Spanish women, above all, probably because of their desire to provide their descendants with a good lineage.

To the Indian women, association with the conquistadores offered many advantages, even though they were not allowed to marry. But many seem to have become aware of their inferiority to their white rivals. Chronicler Gonzalo Fernández de Oviedo tells a pathetic story of how Indian girls tried to bleach their skin. The Indian women could hope that the children they had with the whites would be accepted as free "Spaniards.". . .

11. *Would the Inca Princess Marry a Common Spanish Soldier? Maybe "Yes," Maybe "No"!*

GARCILASO DE LA VEGA

Indians and Spaniards had a number of traits in common, especially a love of litigation and a highly developed class system. The Aztecs, Incas, and the Mayas all had hierarchical societies that influenced their relations with the conquerors. In Peru, particularly, the strength of the Inca empire and the dissensions among the Spaniards led some of the conquerors to seek marriage with Inca princesses as a possible hedge against contingencies. But at least one Inca princess, a daughter of the famous Inca Huaina Cápoc, was choosy and did not relish the idea of marrying a former Spanish tailor, even though he was a captain. She finally gave in, but her response to the priest's question whether she really wanted to marry him — "Maybe I will, maybe I won't" — has been interpreted as a possible key to understanding the ambivalent attitudes in Latin America today toward the acceptance of European civilization and values.

This story comes from the *Royal Commentaries on the Laws of the Incas,* written in the early seventeenth century by the Peruvian historian "the Inca" Garcilaso de la Vega, himself the son of an Inca princess and a Spanish captain of noble lineage who refused to marry the princess and arranged to marry her off to a Spanish soldier.

. . . Many of the colonists who had Indians had been killed in the later wars, and their widows had duly inherited the Indians. In order that they should not make second marriages among those who had not served His Majesty, the governors arranged marriages for them. This occurred throughout Peru, and many widows were so treated. Moreover many were the losers, since they found themselves wedded to husbands much older than the ones they had lost. The former wife of Alonso de Toro, Gonzalo Pizarro's commander, who had a great allocation of Indians, was married to Pedro López Cazalla, President La Gasca's secretary.

Martín de Bustincia's wife, who was the daughter of Huaina Cápac and herself (not her husband) the owner of the Indians, was married to a very good soldier called Diego Hernández, a very worthy man, who was said in his youth to have been a tailor — though it is more likely that this was false than true. The princess learned this and refused the match, saying that it was unjust to wed the daughter of Huaina Cápac with a *ciracamayo,* meaning tailor. Although the bishop of Cuzco and Captain Diego Centeno, as well as other personages who went to attend the ceremony of betrothal, begged and pleaded with her, it was all to no purpose. They then sent to fetch her brother Don Cristóbal Paullu, whom we have already mentioned. When he came, he took his sister into a corner of the room and told her privately that it was impolitic for her to refuse the match, for by so doing she would render the whole of the royal line odious in the eyes of the Spaniards, who would consider them mortal enemies and never accept their friendship again. She agreed, though reluctantly, to her brother's demands, and so appeared before the bishop, who wished to honor the betrothed by officiating at the ceremony.

When the bride was asked through an Indian interpreter if she consented to become the bride and spouse of the aforesaid, the interpreter said "did she want to be that man's wife?" for the Indian language had no verb for consent or for spouse, and he could therefore not have asked anything else.

The bride replied in her own tongue: *"Ichach munani, ichach mana-*

From *Royal Commentaries of the Incas and General History of Peru* by Garcilaso de la Vega, El Inca, trans. with intro. by Harold V. Livermore (Austin and London, 1965), vol. 2, pp. 1229–1230. Reprinted by permission.

munani," meaning: "Maybe I will, maybe I won't." Whereupon the ceremony continued. It was held in the house of Diego de los Ríos, a *vecino* of Cuzco. They were still alive and living as man and wife when I left Cuzco.

Other marriages of this kind took place throughout the empire, and were arranged so as to give allocations of Indians to claimants and reward them with other people's properties. Many, however, were dissatisfied, some because their income was small and others because their wives were ugly: there is no perfect satisfaction in this world. . . .

12. *Spanish Exploitation of Indians in Central Mexico*

CHARLES GIBSON

Every student of Latin American history must at some time tackle the problem of how to handle the Black Legend of Spanish cruelty and oppression in America. The literature on the subject is enormous, and the emotions involved are sometimes considerable. Here we see how one of the veteran scholars in the field judges Spain's work in Mexico. Professor Gibson's meticulous research, published in *The Aztecs under Spanish Rule,* has given him an excellent background for the task.

The Black Legend provides a gross but essentially accurate interpretation of relations between Spaniards and Indians. The Legend builds upon the record of deliberate sadism. It flourishes in an atmosphere of indignation, which removes the issue from the category of objective understanding. It is insufficient in its awareness of the institutions of colonial history. But the substantive content of the Black Legend asserts that Indians were exploited by Spaniards, and in empirical fact they were.

We have not commented in detail on the conquest itself, a separate subject, already much studied. The conquest has a bearing here not for its military events but for its consequences, and the over-all consequence of conquest was the condition of Spanish domination and Indian subjugation. Aztec peoples could not confront Spaniards as a unified nation, with diplomacy and negotia-

Reprinted from *The Aztecs under Spanish Rule: A History of the Indians of the Valley of Mexico, 1519–1810* by Charles Gibson with the permission of the publishers, Stanford University Press. © 1964 by the Board of Trustees of the Leland Stanford Junior University. pp. 403–409.

tion. Conquest destroyed Aztec nationalism and fixed adjustments at a local level. Nearly everything that could be called imperial in Aztec affairs came to an end. If Aztec society be thought of as a graduated complex of progressively more inclusive units, from the family and calpulli at one end to the total empire at the other, it becomes evident that conquest eliminated all the more comprehensive structures while it permitted the local and less comprehensive ones to survive.

The demarcation or cut-off point was the jurisdiction of the tlatoani. This became the cabecera, the essential unit of the early colonial period, on which encomienda, the missionary church, cacicazgo, and tribute and labor exactions directly depended. The cabecera won out over alternative organizing principles of greater or lesser range. One may suppose that this followed in part from the role of the tlatoani in Indian society, a role than was repeatedly affirmed in the events of pre-conquest history. But it was the consequence also of relations between Spaniards and Indians. Conceivably a differently ordered Spanish rule might have made the tribe rather than the cabecera the essential colonial unit. An opposite type of Spanish power might have settled on the calpulli. We can glimpse some such alternative forces at work in the various readjustments and modifications made upon the standard cabecera, as when repartimiento reinvoked the tribal groups or when nontlatoani towns were granted in encomienda and allowed to become cabeceras.

The most evident changes in Indian society occurred during the first forty or fifty years. This was the time when Indian peoples, or some of them, met the Spanish influence part way and reached positive degrees of cultural accord. The mid-sixteenth century has a special interest in the history of humanistic tutelage, with the community of Santa Fe, the Gante school, and above all the Colegio of Santa Cruz in Tlatelolco. One can speak here of a cultural florescence for upper-class Indians, and we may cite again the remarkable Badianus Herbal, a systematic catalogue of plants, classified in a European tradition, painted in an Indian style, its glosses written in Nahuatl by one learned native commentator and translated into Latin by another. The herbal was composed in 1552, and it seemed to give promise, thirty years after the conquest, of a combined culture, with enduring Indian values enriched by a European admixture.

The total possible range of Indian reaction at this time was relatively extensive. Because two complicated societies were intermeshing, opportunities for new combinations continually arose. It is in the sixteenth century that we find the most diverse individual incidents and the most unsettled conditions in both societies. But the long-term tendencies were toward the solutions of the seventeenth and eighteenth centuries, and the scope of Indian response became more limited. As the Indian population was reduced in size, Spanish controls became fixed and the traditional leaders lost power. Colonial law only partially reacted to what occurred, and local customs acquired a greater force than law. After the sixteenth century few individuals stand out in either society, and the history becomes one of localized groups. The seventeenth and eighteenth centuries have a peculiarly leaderless quality, as if all alternative solutions had been discarded.

Neither society was at first unified in its response to the conditions proffered by the other. Indians were at first divided between those who cooperated and those who resisted, and between the upper class and the maceguales. Both lines of division tended to disappear. But the geographical divisions in Indian society remained. The patterns of subordination, however uniform in their abstract characteristics, were locally bounded. Cabecera jurisdictions, encomiendas, and haciendas were discrete manifestations of localism effectively preventing a consolidation of Indian interests. All native conduct was so confined. No two towns were ever capable of uniting in organized resistance. The common qualities of Indian towns were insufficient bases for concerted action.

In Spanish society friars and encomenderos were the main conflicting parties of the early period. The friars, almost alone among Spaniards, were guided by principles of Christian humanitarianism. It could be argued that even they exploited native peoples in their coercive indoctrination and their extirpation of pagan practices. Yet their effort as a whole may be distinguished from that of other Spaniards. What happened was that the spiritual component of Hispanic imperialism disappeared or concentrated its energies elsewhere. Its effect for Indians was confined to the early period. The church ceased to be active in Indian defense as ecclesiastics adopted the methods and attitudes of civilian colonists. Churchmen could oppose encomienda in part because they were prohibited from becoming encomenderos, but ecclesiastical condemnation of latifundium would have meant condemnation of an institution that was essential to ecclesiastical wealth and power. There were many other divisions, of course, within Spanish society, but none of them bore directly upon Indian life or livelihood. Thus the creoles despised the peninsulares, but the issue between them was not native welfare, and in some degree what they were disputing over was Indian spoils.

Tribute, labor, and land were the most clearly defined categories of Spanish demand. The three were differentiated in the colonial period, and the legal instruments were different in each case. Tribute and labor were state-controlled after the mid-sixteenth century, and their consequences for Indian society, however serious, were less severe than in the case of land. Tribute and labor were periodically adjusted to population changes, and the extreme Spanish requirements were confined to the earliest times. Moreover, tribute and labor were already familiar types of pre-conquest exaction, and the degree of change between the one period and the other has often been overstated by critics of the Spanish regime.

Spanish usurpation of land has received less attention, probably because it followed the conquest by some years and did not occupy a major position among the Las Casas accusations. It occurred gradually, through many individual events over a long period, and phenomena that take place in this way lack the dramatic appeal of cataclysms like conquest. So deficient is the Black Legend with regard to land that until recently historians were interpreting hacienda as a direct outgrowth of encomienda. Only in our own time has this fundamental error been corrected, most effectively through the work of Silvio Zavala.

It is often said, with an implication of significance, that the lands of America were the property of the crown of Castile. But the point is at best legalistic, and for Indian history it is immaterial. The crown played an insignificant role either in fostering or in inhibiting latifundia. Legal possession of land by the crown did not mean that land usurpation, too, was a state-controlled enterprise. It was private and frequently illegal, though the state came to tolerate it and to profit from it through the devices of denuncia and composición. That it did not occur immediately is probably less the result of legal restriction than of sheer numbers of Indian people and the universality of Indian occupation of land. A prerequisite was available land, and this was not present when the Spaniards first came. Encomienda was therefore an appropriate institution for the early years. But with Indian depopulation, land became accessible, and when it became accessible, it was usurped.

One consequence of the historical concern with selected Black Legend themes is a weakness in our knowledge of hacienda history. The sections of this book that deal with hacienda make some contribution to the subject, but they suffer from inadequate information and lack a secure conceptual frame. Hacienda, perhaps more than any other single colonial topic, still needs systematic investigation, not alone in the Valley of Mexico but in all areas. We cannot now confidently compare our documented examples of Valley of Mexico hacienda with the institution in other regions, and until we can the Valley conditions will remain imperfectly defined. . . . My own feeling is that the hacienda is a crucial institution, that for various reasons its study has been slighted, and that we would be well advised to make a concerted effort toward solving the historical problems that it raises.

With respect to land there can be no doubt that the hacienda came to be the dominant mode of control. In the tempo of its history it contrasts with tribute and labor. The extreme Spanish demands for tribute and labor occurred early, before much land was transferred to Spanish possession. This transfer, on the other hand, took place on a large scale only in the late sixteenth century and after, when private exploitation of tribute and labor had already been brought under state control. In a sense, land represented a new avenue of exploitation for Spaniards, after other avenues were blocked. But the hacienda combined its essential control of land with secondary controls over labor and tribute, and the result was the most comprehensive institution yet devised for Spanish mastery and Indian subordination. If there appeared, as we have thought, some benign features of hacienda, these are explicable in terms of the total matrix within which hacienda developed. Human character tends toward benevolence as well as toward cruelty, and the hacienda could afford certain kinds of benevolence that would have been incongruous with the harsher, more superficial, less subtle coercions of encomienda. Thus the hacendado could appear as the protector and advocate of his Indians against outside pressures. The encomendero was intended by law to play this same role, but he never did.

That land was important to Indians is obvious. Some of the most intimate and revealing documents of all Indian history are the native títulos for community land possession. The títulos were an Indian response to Spanish usurpation and Spanish legalism. Their purpose was to integrate community opposition against alienation. They speak only sparingly, or not at all, of conquest, tribute, and labor. They see the essential treat to community existence where in fact it lay, in Spanish seizures of land.

There had been seizures of land before the conquest, as in the "lands of Montezuma," but these had been accommodated within Indian practices of land disposition. The difference is one of degree. Moreover, the pre-conquest period, so far as we know, offers no comparable situation of population change. When Indian society seemed headed for extinction, in the late sixteenth and early seventeenth centuries, its practical need for land likewise diminished, and Indian gobernadores and others became the accomplices of Spaniards in the transfer of titles. When the population began to increase in the late seventeenth and eighteenth centuries the need for land correspondingly increased. But by then it was too late. Land transfer was cumulative in a way that tribute and labor exactions were not. Every increase in Indian population in the late colonial period meant an additional number that could not be incorporated in the traditional calpulli tenure, or could be incorporated only with a corresponding strain on other community institutions. The available land was hacienda land, and the new population could now be incorporated within colonial society only through the mediation of hacienda. When the hacendado authorized the towns to rent some of his lands or gave permission to individuals to occupy huts on the hacienda properties, both the hacendado and the Indian beneficiaries could regard the act as one of benevolence. All surrounding conditions were accepted as normal. An aristocracy had been created through innumerable acts over generations of time. Even if there had been an inclination to assign blame, there was no one to accuse, for no one was responsible. The institution and the ethos of the institution dominated all its members. A conquistador who killed or an encomendero who overcharged could be convincingly criticized on moral grounds, but similar criticism appeared excessive when turned against the hacendado, who had inherited most of his lands and played a paternalistic role in a society he had not created. . . .

The Indian community was further beset by a series of demands not comprehended in the three classifications of tribute, labor, and land. Most of these were designed to extract from its economy the increment remaining beyond minimum subsistence. Ecclesiastical fees fall in this category, as do the forced sales in corregimiento and the usurpations of produce. The political officials' handbook of 1777 openly declared the corregimiento of Chalco to be worth thirty times the corregidor's salary, a statement that suggests the extent of precedented extra-legal exploitation by officials appointed to uphold the law.

Variations occurred from area to area in the timing and intensity of these processes. Tacuba was an early victim. Xaltocan prospered for a time and yielded in the seventeenth century. Tepetlaoztoc made a late recovery based not on land but on a pack-train commerce. Chalco province attracted powerful hacendados and became an area of extreme land pressures. By contrast, Xochimilco lacked the kind of land that attracted hacendados and by a coincidence of circumstances maintained its craft economy and chinampa agriculture throughout the colonial period. Tenochtitlan and Tlatelolco, which lacked land from the start, remained virtually immune from the struggle against the hacienda. But Tenochtitlan made a more viable economic adjustment than Tlatelolco, which suffered progressively from drought, emigration, and neglect.

What we have studied is the deterioration of a native empire and civilization. The empire collapsed first, and the civilization was fragmented in individual communities. Some creativity appeared in the early stages of change, but the process as a whole could not be called a creative one for Indians. The community proved to be the largest Indian social unit capable of survival, and it survived in spite of manifold and severe stresses. The cofradía and the fiesta were enlisted to support it. Indians in general yielded to Spanish demands, protesting only in rare instances of community resistance. The civilization became infused with Hispanic traits at many points, but it retained an essential Indian character, partly through the conviction of its members, partly because it was depressed to a social status so low that it was given no opportunities for change. One of the earliest and most persistent individual reponses was drink. If our sources may be believed, few people in the whole of history were more prone to drunkenness than the Indians of the Spanish colony.

13. *The Dawn of Conscience in America*

LEWIS HANKE

Generalizations are often dangerous because it is almost always difficult or even impossible to summarize in a few words a complicated historical event. Yet most of us concerned with the history of Spain in America sometimes indulge in generalizations, as they stimulate us to think about our work in large terms. Here are mine!

The image many English-speaking people have of Spanish action in America is one of almost unrelieved cruelty to the Indians, and many unfavorable judgments have been made on Spanish action in the New World in comparison with English colonization. Spaniards naturally resented these judgments, and a "war of the myths" has resulted. One myth makes the Spaniards the heroes, the English the villains, and the Indians the victims and the opposing myth makes the Spaniards into villains, the English into heroes, but still casts the Indians in the role of victims. My aim is to present some relatively little-known aspects of Spanish-Indian relations, not to present a well-rounded comparison of European colonial practices, and certainly not to engage in the war of the myths.

　　All European explorers and colonists who came to the New World encountered native peoples. But only the Spaniards met so many millions of natives, whom they called Indians, in the vast stretches of their empire which eventu-

From "The Dawn of Conscience in America: Spanish Experiments and Experiences with Indians in the New World" by Lewis Hanke, *Proceedings of the American Philosophical Society*, 107, no. 2 (April 1963), pp. 83–92, passim. Reprinted by permission of the American Philosophical Society.

ally reached from California to Patagonia. The very fact of large numbers of natives settled under the control of the Aztec, Inca, and Maya empires required the Spaniards to devise a different method of treating them from that worked out by the English, French, and Portuguese for the largely nomadic and much smaller number of natives they found sparsely scattered in their territories. . . .

In the effort to govern the mass of Indians in their great empire the Spaniards adapted some institutions from their own medieval experience of long fighting against the Moslems and created others to meet the needs of New World conditions. The determination of the Crown and the Church to Christianize the Indians, the imperious demand of Spaniards for labor forces to exploit the new lands for revenue for the Crown and for themselves, and the attempts of some Spaniards to protect the Indians resulted in a very remarkable complex of relations, laws, and institutions which even today leads historians to contradictory conclusions on the reality of Spanish rule in America. The encomienda system, by which groups of Indians were assigned to Spaniards, a device to provide both labor and goods to the Spaniard and protection and religious instruction for the Indians, was both stoutly defended as necessary and bitterly attacked as un-Christian throughout the sixteenth century by Spaniards themselves. The Spanish imperial policy of attempting to civilize the Indians by urbanizing them led to many curious experiments and experiences, and in the end was fatal for large numbers of natives. George Kubler has pointed out in his substantial work on Mexican architecture:

> no building could be achieved without the prior urbanization of the participants. To urbanize the Indian populations was to dislocate and destroy the patterns of indigenous culture. Such cultural extirpation brought about, in turn, the biological decrease of the Indian race. . . . Each building, and each colonial artifact, was nourished by the destruction of of a culture and the decline of a race.

Spain made many efforts to mitigate the lot of the Indians by appointing official "Protectors," setting up special courts to try cases involving them, and sending out numerous investigating groups to discover what might be done to help them. She tried many stratagems in the sixteenth century particularly to ensure that Indians would be brought under Spanish rule by peaceful means alone, and be persuaded to accept Christianity by reason instead of by force. To achieve this end the Dominican Bartolomé de Las Casas and his brother Dominicans attempted to preach the faith without the backing of the sword in Chiapas, and Vasco de Quiroga established his Utopian communities in Michoacan. In many places a system of Indian segregation was worked out by friars and royal officials to protect them from other Spaniards who would exploit them, and this practice was followed throughout the colonial period, culminating in the famous Jesuit missions in eighteenth-century Paraguay. The difficult, indeed impossible, double purpose of the Crown to secure revenue and also to Christianize the Indians inevitably led in fact to a series of angry disputes, evil compromises, and some glorious episodes throughout the more than three centuries of Spanish rule in America.

Today, in looking back on the total encounter of Spaniards and Indians, two developments hold special interest for us, living as we do in a world society whose multiplicity and variety of cultures become daily more evident and more significant. For the first time in history one people — the Spaniards — paid serious attention to the nature of the culture of the peoples they met; and, perhaps most striking of all, the controversies which developed in sixteenth-century Spain and America over the just method of treating the Indians led to a fundamental consideration of the nature of man himself. This "dawn of conscience in America" was only a faint daybreak; indeed, who can say that in the twentieth century we have reached high noon? The fact that we are still struggling ourselves to discover how to live justly in a world of many races and many cultures give the Spanish struggles of the sixteenth century a poignant and familiar ring. . . .

It was the friars, looking for souls to win, rather than the conquistadores, who first began to study Indian customs, history, and religion. The missionaries needed to know the names and attributes of Indian gods, the sacrifices made to them, and as accurately as possible the mentality of the Indians in order to lead them away from their pagan rites toward Christianity. The founder of American anthropology was Friar Ramón Pané, who accompanied Columbus on his second voyage for the express purpose of observing the natives and reporting on their ways and who was the first European to learn an Indian language.

The Crown encouraged ecclesiastics throughout the sixteenth century to study the Indians, and numerous volumes on their cultures were in fact prepared. Administration officials such as Alonso de Zurita also compiled reports, and the questionnaires sent out regularly to all Spanish governors in the New World by the Council of the Indies included a number of items on Indians. The result of all this enquiry is a magnificent body of linguistic, archaeological, and ethnographical material which is both contradictory at times and difficult to assess because so much remains in manuscript and even the printed editions available are often poor, lacking indexes and proper notes. . . .

Closely linked with these anthropological studies and with Spain's struggle to work out a just Indian policy was the much disputed question of the nature of the Indians. The first twinge of official conscience was expressed by Ferdinand and Isabella in 1495 when they learned that a shipload of Indians Columbus had sent back from Hispaniola had been sold as slaves because they had been taken in rebellion. The monarchs thereupon instructed Bishop Fonseca, who managed Indian affairs, that the money from this sale should not be accepted until their Highnesses could inform themselves from men learned in law whether these Indians could be sold with good conscience. No document that I know of has recorded the answer the sovereigns requested. A dramatic public protest in America against Indian slavery was made by a Dominican friar named Antonio de Montesinos, who in a revolutionary sermon preached in 1511 on the island of Hispaniola thundered:

> Tell me, by what right or justice do you keep these Indians in cruel servitude? On what authority have you waged a detestable war against these people, who dwelt quietly and peacefully on their own land? . . . Are these not men? Have they not rational souls?

This sermon led to serious disputes and discussions in Spain, out of which came the 1512 Laws of Burgos to govern relations between Spaniards and Indians as well as juridical treatises on the basis for Spanish dominion in the New World.

The legalistic and religious nature of the Spaniards led both to their intense preoccupation with the just basis for their newly discovered overseas territory and with the nature of the Indians whom they were attempting to draw into the Christian world. Francisco de Vitoria, a Dominican professor at the University of Salamanca, discussed these matters with great vision and clarity in his lectures and many of his students later went to America with their attitudes determined by his teachings. Vitoria remarked in one treatise, *De Indis:* "The Indians are stupid only because they are uneducated and, if they live like beasts, so for the same reason do many Spanish peasants." He also asserted that discovery alone gave Spaniards no more right to American territory than the Indians would have acquired had they "discovered" Spain. Vitoria and other Spanish political theorists of the time addressed themselves to the fundamental legal questions raised when Europe invaded America and, long before Grotius, laid down an enduring basis for international law.

Most significant of all, the Spanish inquiry into the nature of the Indians and their capacity for entering into the Christian commonwealth led Spaniards to grapple with that ultimate problem — the nature of man himself. Of all the ideas churned up during the early tumultuous years of American history, none had more dramatic implications than the attempts made to apply to the natives there the Aristotelian doctrine of natural slavery: that one part of mankind is set aside by nature to be slaves in the service of masters born for a life of virtue free of manual labor. Learned authorities such as the Spanish scholar Sepúlveda not only sustained this view with great tenacity and erudition but also concluded, without having visited America, that the Indians were in fact such rude and brutal beings that war against them to make possible their forcible Christianization was not only expedient but lawful. Many ecclesiastics, especially Las Casas, opposed this idea scornfully, with appeals to divine and natural laws as well as to their own experience in America. The controversy became so heated and the emperor's conscience so troubled over the question of how to carry on the conquest of the Indies in a Christian way that Charles V actually ordered the suspension of all expeditions to America while a junta of foremost theologians, jurists, and officials was convoked in the royal capital of Valladolid to listen to the arguments of Las Casas and Sepúlveda. All this occurred in 1550, after Cortez had conquered Mexico, Francisco Pizarro had shattered the Inca empire, and many other lesser-known captains had carried the Spanish banners to far corners of the New World.

Las Casas and Sepúlveda duly fought their great battle of ideas before the junta in Valladolid. The details of their arguments cannot be indicated here. The foundation on which Las Casas based his argument was that the Indians were truly men capable of becoming Christians. Drawing upon the information he had brought together in his massive anthropological work the *Apologetic History,* he documented his contention that the Indians had many skills and accomplishments and in fact possessed a culture worthy of respect. He cited their agricultural methods as well as their irrigation systems; illustrated their ingenuity by the way they derived twenty-two products from the maguey tree, contrived delicate ornamental collars of fish bones, and created remarkable gold jewelry. He drew special attention to their extraordinary capacity to learn the Old World crafts which the Spaniards had brought with them, giving a careful account of the way the Indians made knives and rubber balls. He also described the cleverness of their painters, their feather work, their silver making with few tools, and, after little training, their competence in fashioning musical instruments, their work as carpenters, and their hand lettering so fine that it could sometimes not be distinguished from printing. The only thing he found an Indian could not do as well as a Spaniard was to shoe a horse. He described the Indian mining methods and included an account of their ball games. Above all, however, he claimed, the Indians excelled in the dramatic arts and demonstrated this with various illustrations. He described the military organization of both the Mexican Indians and the Incas of Peru, a topic on which relatively few data are provided by other works, and gave much information on their coca chewing and tobacco smoking, together with an excellent description of the great teeming market in Mexico City.

He devoted many pages to the religion of the Indians, and the most strik-

ing aspect of this section is his attitude toward Indian sacrifices. He considered
that the most religious peoples were those which offered to God the most
magnificent sacrifice, and those who offered human beings had — in his opinion — a very noble concept indeed of their God. The Indian fasts, mortifica-
tions of the body, sacrifices of animals and men, were clearly superior to the
sacrifices of the ancient peoples. Under the horrible and bloody aspects of
these rites Las Casas discerned a commendable spirit of religious devotion
which could be directed to higher ends and enlisted in the service of the only
true God.

Las Casas was deeply convinced of the importance of education and therefore was particularly impressed by the meticulous attention paid by the Mexican Indians to the education of their children in the ways of chastity, honesty,
fortitude, obedience, and sobriety. He cried:

> Did Plato, Socrates, Pythagoras, or even Aristotle leave us better or
> more natural or more necessary exhortations to the virtuous life than
> these barbarians delivered to their children? Does the Christian religion
> teach us more, save the faith and what it teaches us of invisible and su-
> pernatural matters? Therefore, no one may deny that these people are
> fully capable of governing themselves and of living like men of good
> intelligence and that they are more than others well ordered, sensible,
> prudent, and rational.

Las Casas believed firmly in the capacity of all people for civilization; he
emphatically rejected a static and hopeless barbarism. "All the peoples of the
world are men," he insisted, and declared that God would not allow any nation to exist, "no matter how barbarous, fierce, or depraved its customs"
which might not be "persuaded and brought to a good order and way of life"
provided the persuasion was peaceful. To practical conquistadores and administrators, men aiming at immediate worldly goals and faced with different kinds
of Indians, and perhaps to the Crown as well, jealous of all royal prerogatives,
Las Casas' reiteration that the only justification for the presence of Spaniards
in the New World was the Christianization of Indians by peaceful means alone
must have seemed dangerous nonsense. One can imagine with what contempt
and horror his announcement was received that Spain ought to abandon
America, with all its Indians un-Christianized, rather than to bring them into
the fold by forcible and — to him — profoundly un-Christian methods. The
important fact to us today is that Sepúlveda's doctrine did not triumph at
Valladolid in 1550 and that his treatise was not approved for publication until
late in the eighteenth century.

Since the Valladolid debate the problem of how to treat peoples unlike ourselves in color, race, religion, or customs has given rise in every century to the

most diverse and inflammatory opinions. In general the idea of the inferiority of natives to Europeans appeared in whatever far corners of the world Europeans reached. In the English colonies, for example, only Roger Williams had any respect for Indian culture and small attention was given the theories about Indians.

The battle waged by Las Casas and all the other Spaniards of his opinion to win recognition of the humanity of the Indians and to understand their culture is far from won. But today those who believe that "all the peoples of the world are men" have powerful allies. Anthropologists have gone on record that "the basic principles of opportunity and equality before the law are compatible with all that is known of human biology. All races possess the abilities needed to participate fully in the democratic way of life and in modern technological civilization." The United Nations Universal Declaration of Human Rights, adopted four centuries after the Valladolid controversy, announced: "All human beings are born free and equal in dignity and rights. They are endowed with reason and conscience and should act towards one another in a spirit of brotherhood." The Ecumenical Council, now in session at the Vatican, with members "from every nation under heaven" expressed the thought even more succinctly in its Message to Humanity: "We proclaim that all men are brothers, irrespective of the race or nation to which they belong."

Only a partisan in the "war of the myths" would dare to claim that the ideals announced by the Spanish crown were generally followed in the American territory under Spanish rule. Nor should anyone claim that the Spaniards fully accomplished their purpose: to incorporate the mass of New World Indians into a Christian and a European world.

For we know in the twentieth century that the Spaniards faced impossible problems: the clash of cultures complicated by the great area in which they operated, the tremendous diversity of the Indians encountered, and the small number of Spaniards available for conversion and education of the millions of Indians. One important doctrinal question remains. Why did Negroes never receive the same solicitous attention as Indians, and why did the conscience of Spaniards twinge so much more easily for Indians than for Negroes?

The Jesuit Alonso de Sandoval did indeed write a treatise in the seventeenth century on the culture of the different tribes of Negroes brought to Cartagena and may therefore be called the first Africanist in America. But neither Sandoval nor his disciple Pedro Claver ever denounced Negro slavery as an un-Christian institution, and the moral conscience of Europe was first roused in modern times by the plight of the Indians of America. The difference between the Spanish attitude toward Indians and Negroes has not yet been satisfactorily explained, and remains an important problem for investigation.

Is it not remarkable enough, however, that some sixteenth-century Span-

iards studied Indian cultures and that a whole school of powerful and articu-
ate members of this intensely nationalistic people fought stoutly for the rights
of the Indians? During the early years of expansion which eventually carried
European ideas and goods to almost every corner of the earth, Spain produced, it is true, an aggressive advocate of Aristotle's doctrine of natural slavery. But she also produced the powerful champion of Indians as men, whose
voice along with many other Spanish voices proclaimed the dawn of conscience in America. No matter how far rockets may reach into outer space,
will any more significant problems be discovered than those which agitated
many Spaniards during the conquest of America? When the story is told of
man's attempts in history to grapple with this most difficult problem — how
to relate to other men of unfamiliar cultures — will not this become clear:
that when the Spanish Crown and Council of the Indies refrained from stig-
matizing the natives of the New World as natural slaves they placed an important milestone on the long road, still under construction, which winds all too
slowly toward civilizations which respect the dignity of man, that is to say of
all men?

The Acolman Convent in Mexico. This large and imposing convent was one of the many religious structures built in Mexico during the first generation or so after Cortez defeated Montezuma. Its enormous walls and artistic facade are eloquent testimony of the great contribution by Indians and Spaniards alike to the architecture of sixteenth-century Mexico which George Kubler has described so well (Reading 15).

SECTION III

Population Questions

HOW MANY INDIANS?

A lively controversy has been under way for a long time on how many Indians inhabited America in 1492 and how many were in Mexico in 1519 on the eve of the Spanish conquest.[1] These are important questions, but difficult to handle in brief selections. Bailey W. Diffie and Ángel Rosenblat have tended to discount the early very high estimates, while Woodrow W. Borah and Sherburne F. Cook have concluded that central Mexico at least had a very dense population with perhaps as many as 25 million in 1519, and that about only 1 million survived by 1600.[2] Rosenblat estimates that the aboriginal population of both Mexico and Peru in 1492 was only about 13 million, while Borah conjectures that there may have been about 100 million Indians in the New World. Another scholar has arrived at a figure even higher than that of Borah.

[1] For excellent treatments of the enormous and complicated literature, see Henry F. Dobyns, "Estimating Aboriginal American Population: An Appraisal of Techniques with a New Hemispheric Estimate," *Current Anthropology,* 7 (1966), pp. 395–416; Woodrow W. Borah, *The Historical Demography of "Aboriginal and Colonial Latin America: An Attempt at Perspective"* (a paper delivered at the XXXVII International Congress of Americanists, Mar del Plata, 1966); and "The Historical Demography of Latin America: Sources, Techniques, Controversies, Yields," in *Population and Economics. Proceedings of Section V of the Fourth Congress of the International Economic History Association, 1968,* ed. Paul Deprez (Winnipeg, Canada: University of Manitoba Press, 1969[?]).

[2] Woodrow Borah and Sherburne F. Cook, *The Aboriginal Population of Central Mexico on the Eve of the Spanish Conquest* (Berkeley and Los Angeles: University of California Press, 1963), p. 89, and Woodrow W. Borah, "La despoblación del México Central en el siglo XVI," *Historia Mexicana,* 12 (1962), p. 179. Ángel Rosenblat presents his latest views in *La población de América en 1492 — viejos y nuevos cálculos* (Mexico: El Colegio de México, 1967).

93

Doubtless further research will resolve some of the present doubts, but no matter what the figure arrived at it is clear that the demographic disaster that took place in Mexico after 1492 was one of the most severe known to history. This demographic revolution varied in intensity from region to region of the Spanish empire, and the decline appears to have been generally less in South America than in Mexico. For example, "the remarkable fact about the Indians of the Ecuadoran highlands during the three centuries of colonial rule was that their numbers did not diminish appreciably." [3]

THE DISASTROUS EFFECTS OF DISEASE

On the causes for the startling decline of the Indian population, no one doubts that disease was a decisive influence (Reading 14). Closely allied to disease and overwork was the traumatic shock of conquest on the Indians, which Professor George Kubler expertly explores (Reading 15). Though Professor Kubler's interests are largely in the field of art history, he is at home in a number of social science disciplines and has read widely in the copious literature on the conquest. Thus his writing reflects an unusual sensitivity to the complex problems involved in a study of the demographic disaster in Mexico. Notice his analysis of the astonishing development of large-scale ecclesiastical building campaigns at the same time as the periods of severe population loss. Notice also that Kubler cites the *Relaciones geográficas* to show that Indian informants, responding to this official query on why the Indian population declined, testified that their diet, clothing, and living conditions were better before the Spaniards came. This point has previously been emphasized by the anthropologist Zelia Nuttall. [4]

Nor was disease limited to the sixteenth century. In one of the few monographs on the history of medicine in Latin America, Professor Donald B. Cooper of Ohio State University shows how epidemics troubled Spanish ad-

[3] John L. Phelan, *The Kingdom of Quito in the Seventeenth Century* (Madison: University of Wisconsin Press, 1967), p. 44.

[4] Zelia Nuttall, "The Causes of the Physical Degeneracy of Mexican Indians after the Spanish Conquest as Set Forth by Mexican Informants in 1580," *Journal of Hygiene,* 27 (1927), pp. 40–43. This was reported from the pueblo of Ocelotepec: "In olden times the natives lived a hundred years or more and now they die young and what they say and explain and communicate to each other on the subject is that the reason for this is: that anciently the children were put to work at the age of six or seven. As there were so many wars there was no time to cultivate much and so they ate little, slept in the open and were fitted to live in constant labour. After the Spaniards came they wore clothes, slept in houses, ate and drank and indulged themselves much. In those days an Indian married at forty and now at twelve or fifteen. . . ."

ministrators in Mexico during the later part of the colonial period.[5] And the veteran scholar Sherburne F. Cook gives an interesting description of the round-the-world voyage of Dr. Francisco Xavier Balmis to vaccinate the Spanish colonial population against smallpox. "Seldom, perhaps never," wrote Professor Cook, "in the history of medicine has there embarked an expedition so grandly conceived, so well executed, so uniformly successful as that of Balmis. . . . Through this one act on the part of the corrupt and decadent government of Spain more lives probably were saved than were lost in all the battles of Napoleon." [6]

THE EFFECTS OF THE DEMOGRAPHIC DISASTER

Grave economic and social consequences resulted from the immense loss of Indian life, though the precise figures are still in doubt. Professor Borah has been a pioneer here, too, and has presented a challenging hypothesis of a century-long depression in Mexico beginning in the 1570s, with significant results:

> The sharp and long-continued decrease of Mexico's Indians from the Conquest until the beginning of the eighteenth century must be accounted one of the most important factors in Mexican history. Had the aboriginal populations of central Mexico borne the impact of Conquest with little demographic loss, there would have been scant room for their conquerors except as administrators and receivers of tribute. Mexico today would be an Indian area from which, in the process of achieving independence from Spain, a white upper stratum holding itself apart, like the British in India, could easily have been expelled. In Haiti, expulsion and massacre at the time of the great slave uprisings disposed rather easily of a similar group of owners and administrators. . . . At the end of the seventeenth century, the distinctively Mexican economy was already organized on the basis of latifundia and debt peonage, the twin aspects of Mexican life which continued nearly to our day and which helped provoke the Revolution of 1910–1917.[7]

The "Berkeley School" has produced many detailed and technical studies to make known their research findings. Here is a recent overview by Borah

[5] Donald B. Cooper, *Epidemic Disease in Mexico City, 1761–1813* (Austin: University of Texas Press, 1965).

[6] Sherburne F. Cook, "Balmis and the Introduction of Vaccination to Spanish America," *Bulletin of the History of Medicine,* 11 (1941), p. 543.

[7] Woodrow W. Borah, *New Spain's Century of Depression* (Berkeley and Los Angeles: University of California Press, 1951), p. 44.

and Cook, giving a résumé of the more important conclusions in their population studies for the economic and social history of Mexico (Reading 16).

SPECIAL PROBLEMS

Much new material has been made known in recent years on the history of the Negro in the New World, as Professor Frederick P. Bowser has recently demonstrated in a valuable survey article.[8] Relatively little has been published on the population of Brazil, but Professor Dauril Alden of the University of Washington has recently revealed that there is much to be learned.[9]

The coming generation of students will benefit from the increasing interest and competence of historians in population questions. Problems of interpretation will still remain. For example, disease certainly helped Cortez win over Montezuma, but other elements were involved such as the assistance of Indian allies who had long opposed the Aztecs. The army that captured Tenochtitlán was really an army of Indians captained by a few Spaniards.

And despite the growing interest in medical history much remains to be done. The situation has not greatly changed from the description made by John Tate Lanning some years ago:

> In the history of the transition from medico-astrological texts and such drugs as crawfish eyes, tapir claws, livers of the pelican, gallbladder, calcined frogs, spirit of earthworms, and lizard oil to modern chemistry and pharmacy there is ample latitude for work. . . . From the quacks and midwives to the experimenting Dr. Hipólito Unánue; from the time that a disguised obstetrician was executed for practicing his art to the establishment of obstetrical hospitals; for the search for symptoms in the stars to their location in the patient, is also a long, uncharted course. As late as the eighteenth century, the primary medical question about a two-headed child was: Do such creatures have souls, and if so, one or two? As late as 1785, patients' blood was taken alternately from the right and left arms to maintain the equilibrium of the patient.[10]

One further thought. Unless the Latin American statistical sources upon which historians depend greatly improve, calculations are bound to be tenta-

---

[8] Frederick P. Bowser, "The African in Colonial Spanish America: Reflections on Research Achievements and Priorities," *Latin American Research Review,* 7 (1972), pp. 77–94.

[9] Dauril Alden, "The Population of Brazil in the Late Eighteenth Century: A Preliminary Survey," *Hispanic American Historical Review,* 43 (May 1963), pp. 173–201.

[10] John Tate Lanning, "Research Possibilities in the Cultural History of Spain in America," *Hispanic American Historical Review,* 16 (1936), p. 156.

tive and subject to revision. In France, for example, such detailed information is extant that historians know that in a given small community "there was a marked increase in the numbers of both illegitimate births and pregnant brides, and that from 1789 to 1839 the latter represented 24 percent of all brides." [11] It is doubtful that sources will be available to this extent for any period of Latin American history.

[11] *Times Literary Supplement* (London), March 3, 1972, p. 243. The book reviewed was Marcel Lachiver, *La Population de Meulan du XVIIᵉ au XIXᵉ Siècle* (Paris: Sevpen, 1971).

14. *The Disastrous Effects of Disease*

ALFRED W. CROSBY

Historians have been very slow to recognize how formidable an ally the Spaniards had in disease, which goes far to explain some of the stunning victories of the conquistadors. Much remains to be discovered about the medical history of Latin America, but at least we have here one detailed statement on the ravages of various diseases during the conquest, by Professor Alfred W. Crosby of Washington State University.

The most sensational military conquests in all history are probably those of the Spanish conquistadores over the Aztec and Incan empires. Cortés and Pizarro toppled the highest civilizations of the New World in a few months each. A few hundred Spaniards defeated populations containing thousands of dedicated warriors, armed with a wide assembly of weapons from the stone and early metal ages. Societies which had created huge empires through generations of fierce fighting collapsed at the touch of the Castilian.

After four hundred years the Spanish feat still seems incredible. Many explanations suggest themselves: the advantage of steel over stone, of cannon and firearms over bows and arrows and slings; the terrorizing effect of horses on foot-soldiers who had never seen such beasts before; the lack of unity in the Aztec and Incan empires; the prophecies in Indian mythology about the arrival of white gods. . . .

For all of that, one might have expected the highly organized, militaristic societies of Mexico and the Andean highlands to survive at least the initial contact with European societies. Thousands of Indian warriors, even if confused and frightened and wielding only obsidian-studded war clubs, should have been able to repel at least the first few hundred Spaniards to arrive.

The Spaniards had a formidable ally to which neither he nor the historian has given sufficient credit — disease. The arrival of Columbus in the New World brought about one of the greatest population disasters in history. After

From "Conquistador y Pestilencia: The First New World Pandemic and the Fall of the Great Indian Empires" by Alfred W. Crosby, *Hispanic American Historical Review,* 47 (1967), pp. 321–337, passim. Reprinted by permission of Duke University press.

the Spanish conquest an Indian of Yucatán wrote of his people in the happier days before the advent of the Spaniard:

> There was then no sickness; they had no aching bones; they had then no high fever; they had then no smallpox; they had then no burning chest; they had then no abdominal pain; they had then no consumption; they had then no headache. At that time the course of humanity was orderly. The foreigners made it otherwise when they arrived here.

It would be easy to attribute this lamentation to the nostalgia that the conquered always feel for the time before the conqueror appeared, but the statement is probably in part true. During the millennia before the European brought together the compass and the three-masted vessel to revolutionize world history, men at sea moved slowly, seldom over long distances, and across the great oceans hardly at all. Men lived at least in the same continents where their greatgrandfathers had lived and rarely caused violent and rapid changes in the delicate balance between themselves and their environments. Diseases tended to be endemic rather than epidemic. . . .

Migration of man and his maladies is the chief cause of epidemics. And when migration takes place, those creatures who have been longest in isolation suffer most, for their genetic material has been least tempered by the variety of world diseases. Among the major subdivisions of the species *homo sapiens* the American Indian probably had the dangerous privilege of longest isolation from the rest of mankind. The Indians appear to have lived, died, and bred without extra-American contacts for generation after generation, developing unique cultures and working out tolerances for a limited, native American selection of pathological micro-life. Medical historians guess that few of the first rank killers among the diseases are native to the Americas. (A possible exception is syphilis. It may be true, as Gonzalo Fernández Oviedo maintained four hundred years ago, that syphilis should not be called *mal francés* or *mal de Nápoles,* but *mal de las Indias.*)

When the isolation of the Americas was broken, and Columbus brought the two halves of this planet together, the American Indian met for the first time his most hideous enemy — not the white man or his black servant, but the invisible killers which these men brought in their blood and breath. The fatal diseases of the Old World killed more effectively in the New, and comparatively benign diseases of the Old World turned killers in the New. There is little exaggeration in the statement of a German missionary in 1699 that "the Indians die so easily that the bare look and smell of a Spaniard causes them to give up the ghost." The process is still going on in the twentieth century, as the last jungle tribes of South America lose their shield of isolation.

The most spectacular period of mortality among the American Indians occurred during the first century of contact with the Europeans and Africans. Almost all contemporary historians of the early settlements from Bartolomé de las Casas to William Bradford of Plymouth Plantation were awed by the ravages of epidemic disease among the native populations of America. We know that the most deadly of the early epidemics in the New World were those of the eruptive fevers — smallpox, measles, plague, typhus, etc. The first to arrive and the deadliest, said contemporaries, was smallpox.

At this point the reader should be forewarned against too easy credulity. Even today smallpox is occasionally misdiagnosed as influenza, pneumonia, measles, scarlet fever, syphilis, or chicken pox, for example. Four hundred years ago such mistakes were even more common, and writers of the accounts upon which we must base our examination of the early history of smallpox in America did not have any special interest in accurate diagnosis. The early historians were much more likely to cast their eyes skywards and comment on the sinfulness that had called down such obvious evidences of God's wrath as epidemics than to describe in any detail the diseases involved. It should also be noted that conditions which facilitate the spread of one disease will usually encourage the spread of others, and that "very rarely is there a pure epidemic of a single malady." Pneumonia and pleurisy, for instance, often follow after smallpox, smothering those whom it has weakened. . . .

Smallpox has been so successfully controlled by vaccination and quarantine in the industrialized nations of the twentieth century that few North Americans or Europeans have ever seen it. But it is an old companion of humanity, and for most of the last millennium it was among the commonest diseases in Europe. With reason it was long thought one of the most infectious of maladies. Smallpox is usually communicated through the air by means of droplets or dust particles, and its virus enters the new host through the respiratory tract. There are many cases of hospital visitors who have contracted the disease simply by breathing for a moment the air of a room in which someone lies ill with the pox. . . .

Where smallpox has been endemic, it has been a steady, dependable killer, taking every year from three to ten percent of those who die. Where it has struck isolated groups, the death rate has been awesome. Analysis of figures for some twenty outbreaks shows that the case mortality among an unvaccinated population is about thirty percent. Presumably, in people who have had no contact whatever with smallpox, the disease will infect nearly every single individual it touches. When in 1707 smallpox first appeared in Iceland, it is said that in two years 18,000 out of the island's 50,000 inhabitants died of it.

The first people of the New World to meet the white and black races and their diseases were Indians of the Taino culture who spoke the Arawak language and lived on the islands of the Greater Antilles and the Bahamas. On the very first day of landfall in 1492 Columbus noted that the Tainos "are very unskilled with arms . . ." and "could all be subjected and made to do all that one wished." These Tainos lived long enough to provide the Spaniard with his first generation of slaves in America, and Old World disease with its first beachhead in the New World.

Oviedo, one of the earliest historians of the Americas, estimated that a million Indians lived on Santo Domingo when the European arrived to plant his first permanent colony in the New World. "Of all those," Oviedo wrote, "and of all those born afterwards, there are not now believed to be at the present time in this year of 1548 five hundred persons, children and adults, who are natives and are the progeny or lineage of those first."

The destruction of the Tainos has been largely blamed on the Spanish cruelty, not only by the later Protestant historians of the "Black Legend" school but also by such contemporary Spanish writers as Oviedo and Bartolomé de las Casas. Without doubt the early Spaniard brutally exploited the Indians. But it was obviously not in order to kill them off, for the early colonist had to deal with a chronic labor shortage and needed the Indians. Disease would seem to be a more logical explanation for the disappearance of the Tainos, because they, like other Indians, had little immunity to Old World diseases. At the same time, one may concede that the effects of Spanish exploitation undoubtedly weakened their resistance to disease.

Yet it is interesting to note that there is no record of any massive smallpox epidemic among the Indians of the Antilles for a quarter of a century after the first voyage of Columbus. Indians apparently suffered a steady decline in numbers, which was probably due to extreme overwork, other diseases, and a general lack of will to live after their whole culture had been shattered by alien invasion. How can the evident absence of smallpox he explained, if the American Indian was so susceptible, and if ships carrying Europeans and Africans from the pestilential Old World were constantly arriving in Santo Domingo? The answer lies in the nature of the disease. It is a deadly malady, but it lasts only a brief time in each patient. After an incubation period of twelve days or so, the patient suffers from high fever and vomiting followed three or four days later by the characteristic skin eruptions. For those who do not die, these pustules dry up in a week or ten days and form scabs which soon fall off, leaving the disfiguring pocks that give the disease its name. The whole process takes a month or less, and after that time the patient is either dead or immune, at least for a period of years. Also there is no non-human carrier of smallpox, such as the flea of typhus or the mosquito of malaria; it must pass from man to man. Nor are there any long-term human carriers of smallpox, as, for instance, with typhoid and syphilis. It is not an over-simplification to say that one either has smallpox and can transmit it, or one has not and cannot transmit it.

Consider that, except for children, most Europeans and their slaves had had smallpox and were at least partially immune, and that few but adults sailed from Europe to America in the first decades after discovery. Consider that the voyage was one of several weeks, so that, even if an immigrant or sailor contracted smallpox on the day of embarkation, he would most likely be dead or rid of its virus before he arrived in Santo Domingo. Consider that moist heat and strong sunlight, characteristic of a tropical sea voyage, are particularly deadly to the smallpox virus. The lack of any rapid means of crossing the Atlantic in the sixteenth century delayed the delivery of the Old World's worst gift to the New.

It was delayed; that was all. An especially fast passage from Spain to the New World; the presence on a vessel of several nonimmune persons who could transmit the disease from one to the other until arrival in the Indies; the presence of smallpox scabs, in which the virus can live for weeks, accidentally packed into a bale of textiles — by any of these means smallpox could have been brought to Spanish America.

In December 1518 or January 1516 a disease identified as smallpox appeared among the Indians of Santo Domingo, brought, said Las Casas, from Castile. It touched few Spaniards, and none of them died, but it devasted the Indians. The Spaniards reported that it killed one-third to one-half of the Indians. Las Casas, never one to understate the appalling, said that it left no more than one thousand alive "of that immensity of people that was on this island and which we have seen with our own eyes." . . .

Thus began the first recorded pandemic in the New World, which was "in all likelihood the most severe single loss of aboriginal population that ever occurred." In a matter of days after smallpox appeared in Santo Domingo, it leaped the channel to Puerto Rico. Before long, Tainos were dying a hideous and unfamiliar death in all the islands of the Greater Antilles. Crushed by a quarter-century of exploitation, they now performed their last function on earth: to act as a reserve of pestilence in the New World from which the conquistador drew invisible biological allies for his assault on the mainland. . . .

The melodrama of Cortés and the conquest of Mexico need no retelling.

After occupying Tenochtitlán and defeating the army of his rival, Narváez, he and his troops had to fight their way out of the city to sanctuary in Tlaxcala. Even as the Spanish withdrew, an ally more formidable than Tlaxcala appeared. Years later Francisco de Aguilar, once a follower of Cortés and now a Dominican friar, recalled the terrible retreat of the *Noche Triste*. "When the Christians were exhausted from war," he wrote, "God saw fit to send the Indians smallpox, and there was a great pestilence in the city. . . ."

With the men of Narváez had come a Negro sick with the smallpox, "and he infected the household in Cempoala where he was quartered; and it spread from one Indian to another, and they, being so numerous and eating and sleeping together, quickly infected the whole country." The Mexicans had never seen smallpox before and did not have even the European's meager knowledge of how to deal with it. The old soldier-chronicler, Bernal Díaz del Castillo, called the Negro "a very black dose" for Mexico, "for it was because of him that the whole country was stricken, with a great many deaths."

Probably, several diseases were at work. Shortly after the retreat from Tenochtitlán Bernal Díaz, immune to smallpox like most of the Spaniards, "was very sick with fever and was vomiting blood." The Aztec sources mention the racking cough of those who had smallpox, which suggests a respiratory complication such as pneumonia or a streptococcal infection, both common among smallpox victims. Great numbers of the Cakchiquel people of Guatemala were felled by a devastating epidemic in 1520 and 1521, having as its most prominent symptom fearsome nosebleeds. Whatever this disease was, it may have been present in central Mexico along with the pox.

The triumphant Aztecs had not expected the Spaniards to return after their expulsion from Tenochtitlán. The sixty days during which the epidemic lasted in the city, however, gave Cortés and his troops a desperately needed respite to reorganize and prepare a counterattack. When the epidemic subsided, the siege of the Aztec capital began. Had there been no epidemic, the Aztecs, their war-making potential unimpaired and their warriors fired with victory, could have pursued the Spaniards, and Cortés might have ended his life spread-eagled beneath the obsidian blade of a priest of Huitzilopochtli. Clearly the epidemic sapped the endurance of Tenochtitlán to survive the Spanish assault. As it was, the siege went on for seventy-five days, until the deaths within the city from combat, starvation, and disease — probably not smallpox now — numbered many thousands. When the city fell "the streets, squares, houses, and courts were filled with bodies, so that it was almost impossible to pass. Even Cortés was sick from the stench in his nostrils." . . .

If we attempt to describe the first coming of Old World disease to the areas south of Panama, we shall have to deal with ambiguity, equivocation, and simple guesswork, for eruptive fever, now operating from continental bases, apparently outstripped the Spaniards and sped south from the isthmus into the Incan Empire before Pizarro's invasion. Long before the invasion, the Inca Huayna Capac was aware that the Spaniards — "monstrous marine animals, bearded men who moved upon the sea in large houses — were pushing down the coast from Panama. Such is the communicability of smallpox and the other eruptive fevers that any Indian who received news of the Spaniards could also have easily received the infection of the European diseases. The biologically defenseless Indians made vastly more efficient carriers of such pestilence than the Spaniards.

Our evidence for the first post-Columbian epidemic in Incan lands is entirely hearsay, because the Incan people had no system of writing. Therefore, we must depend on secondary accounts by Spaniards and by mestizos or Indians born after the conquest, accounts based on Indian memory and written years and even decades after the epidemic of the 1520s. The few accounts we have of the great epidemic are associated with the death of Huayna Capac. He spent the last years of his life campaigning against the people of what is today northern Peru and Ecuador. There, in the province of Quito, he first received news of an epidemic raging in his empire, and there he himself was stricken. Huayna Capac and his captains died with shocking rapidity, "their faces being covered with scabs."

Of what did the Inca and his captains die? One of the most generally reliable of our sources, that of Garcilaso de la Vega, describes Huayna Capac's death as the result of "a trembling chill . . . , which the Indians call *chucchu,* and a fever, called by the Indians *rupu.* . . ." We dare not, four hundred years later, unequivocally state that the disease was not one native to the Americas. Most accounts call it smallpox, or suggest that it was either smallpox or measles. Smallpox seems the best guess because the epidemic struck in that period when the Spaniards, operating from bases where smallpox was killing multitudes, were first coasting along the shores of Incan lands.

The impact of the smallpox pandemic on the Aztec and Incan Empires is easy for us of the twentieth century to underestimate. We have so long been hypnotized by the derring-do of the conquistador that we have overlooked the importance of his biological allies. Because of the achievements of medical science in our day we find it hard to accept statements from the conquest period that the pandemic killed one-third to one-half of the populations struck by it. Toribio Motolinía claimed that in most provinces of Mexico "more than one half of the population died; in others the proportion was little less." "They died in heaps," he said, "like bedbugs."

The proportion may be exaggerated, but perhaps not as much as we might think. The Mexicans had no natural resistance to the disease at all. Other diseases were probably operating quietly and efficiently behind the screen of smallpox. Add too the factors of food shortage and the lack of even minimal care for the sick. Motolinía wrote: "Many others died of starvation, because as they were all taken sick at once, they could not care for each other, nor was there anyone to give them bread or anything else." We shall never be certain what the death rate was, but, from all evidence, it must have been immense. . . .

In Peru the epidemic of the 1520s was a stunning blow to the very nerve center of Incan society, throwing that society into a self-destructive convulsion. The government of the Incan Empire was an absolute autocracy with a demigod, the Child of the Sun, as its emperor. The loss of the emperor could do enormous damage to the whole society, as Pizarro proved by his capture of Atahualpa. Presumably the damage was greater if the Inca were much esteemed, as was Huayna Capac. When he died, said Cieza de León, the mourning "was such that the lamentation and shrieks rose to the skies, causing the birds to fall to the ground. The news traveled far and wide, and nowhere did it not evoke great sorrow." Pedro Pizarro, one of the first to record what the Indians told of the last days before the conquest, judged that had "this Huayna Capac been alive when we Spaniards entered this land, it would have been impossible for us to win it, for he was much beloved by all his vassals."

Not only the Inca but many others in key positions in Incan society died in the epidemic. The general Mihcnaca Mayta and many other military leaders, the governors Apu Hilaquito and Auqui Tupac (uncle and brother to the Inca), the Inca's sister, Mama Coca, and many others of the royal family all perished of the disease. The deaths of these important persons must have robbed the empire of much resiliency. Most ominous loss of all was the Inca's son and heir Ninan Cuyoche.

In an autocracy no problem is more dangerous or more chronic than that of succession. One crude but workable solution is to have the autocrat, himself, choose his successor. The Inca named one of his sons, Ninan Cuyoche, as next wearer of "the fringe" or crown, on the condition that the *calpa,* a ceremony of divination, show this to be an auspicious choice. The first *calpa* indicated that the gods did not favor Ninan Cuyoche, the second that Huascar was no better candidate. The high nobles returned to the Inca for another choice, and found him dead. Suddenly a terrible gap had opened in Incan society: the autocrat had died, and there was no one to take his place. One of the nobles moved to close the gap. "Take care of the body," he said, "for I go to Tumipampa to give the fringe to Ninan Cuyoche." But it was too late. When he arrived at Tumipampa, he found that Ninan Cuyoche had also succumbed to smallpox pestilence.

Among the several varying accounts of the Inca's death the one just related best fits the thesis of this paper. And while these accounts may differ on many points, they all agree that confusion over the succession followed the unexpected death of Huayna Capac. War broke out between Huascar and Atahualpa, a war which devastated the empire and prepared the way for a quick Spanish conquest. "Had the land not been divided between Huascar and Atahualpa," Pedro Pizarro wrote, "we would not have been able to enter or win the land unless we could gather a thousand Spaniards for the task, and at that time it was impossible to get together even five hundred Spaniards. . . ."

The psychological effect of epidemic disease is enormous, especially of an unknown disfiguring disease which strikes swiftly. Within a few days smallpox can transform a healthy man into a pustuled, oozing horror, whom his closest relatives can barely recognize. The impact can be sensed in the following terse, stoic account, drawn from Indian testimony, of Tenochtitlán during the epidemic.

> It was [the month of] Tepeilhuitl when it began, and it spread over the people as great destruction. Some it quite covered [with pustules] on all parts — their faces, their heads, their breasts, etc. There was a great havoc. Very many died of it. They could not walk; they only lay in their resting places and beds. They could not move; they could not stir; they could not change position, nor lie on one side; nor face down, nor on their backs. And if they stirred, much did they cry out. Great was its [smallpox'] destruction. Covered, mantled with pustles, very many people died of them.

. . . For those who survived, the horror was only diminished, for smallpox is a disease which marks its victims for the rest of their lives. The Spanish recalled that the Indians who survived, having scratched themselves, "were left in such a condition that they frightened the others with the many deep pits on their faces, hands, and bodies." "And on some," an Indian said, "the pustules were widely separated; they suffered not greatly, neither did many [of them] die. Yet many people were marred by them on their faces; one's face or nose was pitted." Some lost their sight — a fairly common aftereffect of smallpox.

The contrast between the Indians' extreme susceptibility to the new disease and the Spaniards' almost universal immunity, acquired in Spain and reinforced in pestilential Cuba, must have deeply impressed the native Americans. The Indian, of course, soon realized that there was little relationship between

Cortés and Quetzalcóatl, and that the Spaniards had all the vices and weaknesses of ordinary men, but he must have kept a lingering suspicion that the Spaniards were some kind of supermen. Their steel swords and arquebuses, their marvelously agile galleys, and, above all, their horses could only be the tools and servants of supermen. And their invulnerability to the pox — surely this was a shield of the gods themselves!

One can only imagine the psychological impact of smallpox on the Incan peoples. It must have been less than in Mexico, because the disease and the Spaniards did not arrive simultaneously, but epidemic disease is terrifying under any circumstances and must have shaken the confidence of the Incan people that they still enjoyed the esteem of their gods. Then came the long, ferocious civil war, confusing a people accustomed to the autocracy of the true Child of the Sun. And then the final disaster, the coming of the Spaniards.

The Mayan peoples, probably the most sensitive and brilliant of all American aborigines, expressed more poignantly than any other Indians the overwhelming effect of epidemic. Some disease struck into Guatemala in 1520 and 1521, clearing the way for the invasion shortly thereafter by Pedro de Alvarado, one of Cortés' captains. It was apparently not smallpox, for the accounts do not mention pustules but emphasize nosebleeds, cough, and illness of the bladder as the prominent symptoms. It may have been influenza; whatever it was, the Cakchiquel Mayas who kept a chronicle of the tragedy for their posterity, were helpless to deal with it. Their words speak for all the Indians touched by Old World disease in the sixteenth century:

> Great was the stench of the dead. After our fathers and grandfathers succumbed, half of the people fled to the fields. The dogs and vultures devoured the bodies. The mortality was terrible. Your grandfathers died, and with them died the son of the king and his brothers and kinsmen. So it was that we became orphans, oh, my sons! So we became when we were young. All of us were thus. We were born to die!

15. *Why So Many Indians Died in Mexico and What Effects This Had upon Their Life and upon the Building of Churches*

GEORGE KUBLER

The two-volume contribution by Professor George Kubler of Yale, *Mexican Architecture in the Sixteenth Century,* is impressive not merely because of the splendidly detailed description of the great burst of Spanish building activity but also because of his broad approach to the problems involved. His is no narrowly technical architectural work but includes valuable information and insights into labor questions, religious influences, and culture shock that make these volumes one of the outstanding cross-disciplinary studies in Latin American studies.

An appalling mortality among the Indians marked the first century of Spanish colonization. The sources are unanimous about the fact. Even the hyperbolic statements of interested parties could only suggest a reality that defied any exhaustive statistical approach. Measurement and tabulation were incapable of keeping pace with the successive population disasters that struck New Spain, New Galicia, and the other territories of what is today the republic of Mexico. The diction of the historians of the time is replete with allusions to calamity; Motolinía, for instance, enlarged upon the ten various "plagues" that had beset the affairs of the colony, Mendieta dedicated an entire chapter to the problem of depopulation, and Domingo de Betanzos, the eminent Dominican missionary, prophesied the total extinction of the Indian race if the disasters were to continue without abatement.

On the other hand, during these troubled years of the sixteenth century, a great colonial state was brought into being, with its administrative and spiritual center in Mexico. The foundation of hundreds of new urban settlements took place. A stable and highly productive colonial economy was established. Many specialized institutions came into being, and the tangible economic returns from the colony soared to a peak at the end of the century. In other words, more and more of the equipment of civilization was being produced

From *Mexican Architecture of the Sixteenth Century* by George Kubler, 2 vols. (New Haven: Yale University Press, 1948), vol. 1, pp. 30–67, passim; vol. 2, pp. 417–418. Reprinted by permission of the author.

among a race that simultaneously underwent a diminution of numbers rarely equalled in the history of mankind. . . .

The nearly constant presence of disease naturally perturbed the white colonists, although epidemic was no novelty for Europeans of the sixteenth century. . . . A nation, such as Spain or England, suddenly fell ill, agonized, and recovered, but meanwhile the disease had swept communities bare, sometimes taking the children, sometimes the old people, or only the women, but more generally leaving an exhausted fraction of the population to bury the dead and renew the life of the community. The phenomenon was therefore not unfamiliar to the colonists, and they accepted it as an ineradicable condition of communal existence. Many remedial measures were taken to abate the severity of disaster, but on the whole, the colonists were far more agitated about the social causes of loss than about disease itself.

The other great primary cause of elimination has evoked much controversy. In brief, it may be designated as the "homicidal theory" of loss, and its best-known publicist was the Dominican Bishop of Chiapas, fray Bartolomé de las Casas. The title of Las Casas' famous tract, *Breve relación de la destrucción de las Indias occidentales,* is an epitome of the homicidal theory, which attempts to assign all losses of population to direct action — to the bestial cruelty of the Spanish colonists, and their systematic slaughter of enormous masses of the Indian population. Torture and overwork and massacre were the chief instruments of mass homicide, with the result that the *Breve relación* is a catalogue of horrors, containing no mention of disease. Las Casas' attention was devoted mainly to conditions in the Antilles, where, in his opinion, in 1552, of three million Indians on Española at the time of the Discovery, only two hundred remained alive. Las Casas felt that the situation was less incriminating in Mexico, but he insisted that between 1518 and 1530, four millions had been slaughtered there, and in 1519, thirty thousands were massacred in Cholula alone. Two facts should be kept in mind. Las Casas never experienced the fury of any of the great epidemics. In 1520–21, he was engaged in the foundation of the ill-starred colony of the Knights of the Golden Spur on the Pearl Coast of Venezuela, while in 1531, he resided in Española and in Nicaragua. . . .

The homicidal theory nevertheless bears some relation to a reality that we may reconstruct from other sources. As we have seen, torture, overwork, and murder were the means employed by the Spaniards, in Las Casas' theory, to destroy the Indian populations. In this form, it was a massive and undifferentiated theory, which assigned effects of an unknown magnitude to direct, malevolent action. The encomendero lashed his Indians to death, buried them alive, loaded their bodies to the breaking point, or else he murdered them with knife and gun. Las Casas admitted no indirect causes that might lie beyond the control of the indicted party. Later in the century, however, it is of the greatest interest to behold this blunt doctrine analyzed, refined, and made accurately descriptive in the hands of civil servants, whose commissions probably derived in part from the agitation aroused in Spain by Las Casas' writings.

The treatment of the question by the learned and intelligent Auditor, Alonso de Zorita, is worth close attention. In general, Zorita interpreted excessive mortality as a function of economic extortion. For the concept of direct homicide, he substituted a far richer social interpretation. Thus he catalogued the examples of extravagant forced labor conducive to a high death rate. Among these were the great public works; an excessive rate of tribute; heavy labor in the mines, in personal services, in the cultivation of certain crops, such as cacao and sugar-cane; and in military duty. Zorita even assigned pestilence to these various causes, and he was perhaps not far from the mark. For instance, reform legislation upon forced labor (the Nuevas Leyes) preceded the longest recess from epidemic during the century, from 1546 to 1573. . . .

In addition to the obvious check or hindrance to increase — a high incidence of epidemic disease that is possibly related to homicidal forms of economic exploitation — other determinants worked towards depopulation. Such causes are of two distinct kinds; those deriving from the dislocation of Indian culture, with attendant cultural shock, and those deriving from the reorientation of Indian culture — into the channels of a Christian society, an absolute State, and a mercantile economy. Both were powerful agents for depopulation, acting in rather different ways.

The effects of reorientation are fairly obvious. It should be emphasized that such effects occurred, not directly because of the greed and ill-will of the colonists, but as part of the price of any cultural reorganization, however benevolent in intention.

We must look to the Indians themselves for some account of the effects of reorientation. About 1580, after the great epidemic losses, the Crown was sufficiently concerned to inquire through its agents what interpretation the natives themselves placed upon the fact of their decline. The answers are recorded in the *Relaciones geográficas,* and although the full series has not been published, the available documents of this class yield most interesting clues to the problem. In these cosmographic questionnaires, it was asked of the natives in each community why the Indian race displayed greater longevity in antiquity. The answers came from many regions, and they display surprising acuity. Their general drift pertains to the superiority of indigenous culture over that of the Europeans. The ancient ways are always portrayed as more austere and less luxurious. Nearly all the declarants who pronounced upon the matter asserted that the Indians took less food in antiquity, and therefore enjoyed better health. The taking of much salt and hot food were particularly blamed. Only one settlement claimed that the diet did not differ as to quantity. The ancient restrictions upon alcoholic beverages, the practice of ceremonial warfare with its limited mortality, and the observance of the ancient pieties are also very frequently catalogued among the reasons for the superior health of the Indians before the Conquest. In many communities it was significantly reported that general hygiene and medication were much better in antiquity. The Indians especially approved the pre-Conquest costume, which involved fewer clothes and greater immunity to weather. They also noted that their ancestors had been more addicted to bathing; that they slept upon hard beds; that their herb-doctors were better than the colonial practitioners; and that the European custom of bloodletting was harmful. Finally, the ancient cleanly method of disposing of the dead by cremation was preferred to the Christian burial enforced by the whites. An allusion to the deleterious effects of a mercantile economy dependent upon transportation by human carriers is contained in the numerous assertions that the Indians were formerly more healthy and long-lived because they travelled less. Finally, direct reference to the central problems of fertility and the sex-ratio between males and females is carried by the many protests against the abolition of polygamy and against the practice of youthful marriages enforced by the Christians. Here the Indians touched upon the heart of the problem: the most delicate mechanisms of the culture, its rituals and customs of procreation, had been tampered with by the whites. The complaints are registered from all the main areas of New Spain, and they are among the few verbal expressions from Indian sources attesting to the essential lesions effected by the reorientation of Indian life into a colonial pattern.

As to losses deriving from the dislocation of Indian culture, no quantitative measure of any kind is suggested by the texts. But one set of replies from Indian informants, contained in the *Relaciones geográficas* cited above, bears upon the question, and it yields an important clue. It was supposed by the Indians that their reduced longevity was partly to be explained by the amount of work they were doing. A peculiar difference of opinion was expressed: in some communities, the view was advanced that the Indians did *less* work in antiquity than in colonial life, and in others, it was stated that the Indians did *more* work in antiquity and therefore lived longer. The number of communities in which the latter view was voiced is double the number of those in which the Indians were represented as doing less work before the Conquest.

The prevalent opinion in 1580 was therefore that the Indians were not working so hard as before the Conquest.

A sixteenth-century text explicitly mentions this situation. In 1545, a colonist writing to the Emperor said that great orderliness had prevailed in Motecuzoma's time: "Each man followed his calling. . . . There were inspectors . . . and now all are vagabonds and idlers." The white settlers naturally shared this official opinion. But it may be pointed out that there allegations did not always benefit their interests. To assever that the Indians were not working hard enough was needed to undermine the pro-Indian, humanitarian legislation on forced labor. The tax-collector, however, took it to signify that the tribute-burden was inadequate. The encomendero, in turn, knew that increase in the tribute-burden entailed some decrease in his own profit from Indian labor.

The most articulate opinion upon this question came from the pen of the learned and experienced Alonso de Zorita. He pointed out, after 1565, that the Europeans were mistaken in believing that the Indians were not working hard. But most of their work was being done for Europeans, and very little work was being done by the Indians for themselves. Hence it was perfectly true that the work of self-sustenance done by Indians was less in colonial times and more in antiquity; in the total labor-burden, however, the Indians were giving most of their time to the service of the whites.

To return to the Indians' own views upon the matter, it is to be emphasized that any proper interpretation of the proposition that the Indians worked harder in antiquity depends upon the meaning of the term, "work," to Indians. Their allegations make sense only when "work" is interpreted as "occupation," that is, as the entire routine of a ritual life that includes subsistence activities. To the pre-Conquest highland Indians, few differences were apparent between the work of producing ceremonial, and the ceremonial of doing work. All communal activities were ritual in character, and the year was filled with an intricate succession of ceremonial occasions, among which subsistence activities played a cardinal role. But in colonial life, when physical labor without ceremonial adornment was forced on the Indians, they became, so to speak, psychologically unemployed. In the absence of ceremonial, a dissipated indolence between moments of forced economic labor was inevitable. What would have been "leisure" to a modern community was complete absence of "occupation" to the Indians, only partly filled by the ritual and service of the church. Thus an extravagant economic exploitation may quite rightly have been regarded by the Indians as insufficient "work." An unoccupied leisure, filled with idling, drunkenness, and a minor ritual obligation to the church, would also be regarded as insufficient. In brief, the European secularization of all labor was antithetic to the Indian concept of "work." For the pre-Conquest Indian, all work was ultimately a ritual: for the European, work was almost exclusively a profane necessity, and to the Indians, the metamorphosis of work from ritual into an unadorned necessity must have been among the most disturbing and revolutionary aspects of their contact with Europeans.

Now the ritual life of Indian culture, with its rich and intricate form of esthetic experience, may have been far from ideal. It was punctuated by human sacrifice and by rites of great cruelty. Yet its psychic values must have been more satisfying to Indians than the drab and incomprehensible life of partial labor for economic ends imposed by the Spaniards. The Mendicant missionaries realized these deficiencies in colonial life, and sought to compensate for them with an abundant ceremonial which was unusual even by contemporary European standards. In an admirable chapter, Robert Ricard commented upon the extraordinary frequency and complexity of the ceremonial instituted by Mendicants. Sumptuous decorations filled the churches for the many important festivals; each community prepared musical offerings of voices and instruments; pilgrimages were encouraged to holy sites; each week processions, public dances, and theatrical performances of religious character were arranged; the needs of organized sociability were supplied by the intricate system of the sodalities, or *cofradías,* in each settlement. All these ceremonial activities, Ricard implies, were continuous, occupying the various groups and classes during the entire year, replacing the elaborate pre-Conquest calendar, and bringing Christianity a little closer to the Indians. Yet all this could be true only for the great Mendicant communities, in which friars were constantly resident, always available to supervise and encourage the new festivities. Where there were no friars, and where the secular clergy held control, little of the substitute or surrogate ceremonial could be supplied. In effect, a majority of the Indian population of Mexico was not provided with such relief from labor.

Hence it is reasonable to suggest that the Indians of Mexico were psychologically unemployed during the first century following the Conquest. Their situation in the sixteenth century is closely comparable to that of the natives of Polynesia and Melanesia and other island groups of the Pacific during the nineteenth century. The dislocation and reorientation of an antecedent culture entail a decrease in the rate of replacement among the bearers of that culture. An observable depopulation of the area is apparent. As the reorientation and dislocation of Indian life went on, numerous symptoms of a state of shock among the affected peoples became evident. These symptoms usually took the form either of violently destructive action, or of a lowered vitality and will to survive.

Systematic abortion and infanticide, as well as mass suicides, were reported from several areas. In Michoacan, for instance, a certain sorcerer was said to have induced crowds of bewitched Indians to kill themselves. Alonso de Zorita knew of many cases of Indian suicide to escape the payment of an impossible tribute, and he also cited the numerous abortions and the general refusal to procreate among the Mixe and Chontal Indians. In western Mexico as well, Lebrón de Quiñones found that the Indian women had been ordered not to conceive, that many refrained from intercourse, and that abortion was regularly practised, to ensure the rapid disappearance of the tribe. These are perhaps no more than isolated and sporadic instances, but they bespeak a general disintegration of the vital forces of the Indian race that also took much less radical forms. Drunkenness, for example, became alarmingly common, as reported by the Indian informants of 1579–81, and it appears to have been the drunkenness of despair and frustration.

The history of the many Indian revolts during the century may also be construed as a phenomenon of cultural shock. Such revolts were severely punished, and the rate of elimination in certain areas may reasonably be attributed to Spanish reprisals. The uprisings were especially common at the periphery of the colony. . . .

Hence all approaches to the problem appear to yield the same answer: increased elimination and decreased replacement are the results of colonization, constantly reducing the spread and density of the native populations. . . . At every point the two processes of increased elimination and decreased replacement are closely related. It is hard to believe that great epidemic losses are not registered in some decreases of the birth-rate, for an epidemic reducing the numbers of young women involves losses in fecundity which cannot immediately be recovered. . . .

Every available line of evidence returns us to the correlation between decline and the building activity of the religious orders. This activity does not mean simply the building of churches; it signifies the layout and construction of entire settlements according to rudimentary concepts of regional planning. The greatest number of urban projects was in progress at the time of the most severe losses of population. Was such activity a cause, or an effect of decline in number? The correct answer depends upon how we assess the intentions of the building friars. It is certain that the friars regarded a well regulated community life as essential to the health of the inhabitants. Such a community life could develop only in well planned, well built towns.

The urbanizing work of the Mendicants was both cause and effect, disease and cure, reason and consequence, at least in part, for the high mortality suffered by the Indians. The heavy burden of labor, and the unhygienic conditions of work in new and improperly equipped settlements gave epidemic disease a rich harvest. And yet the same work, continued through and beyond the epoch of contagion, helped to protect and shelter the town-dwellers from new incursions.

As with other significant fragments of colonial life, the construction of any one of the buildings studied in this book is a process enmeshed in most intricate relationships. It has been demonstrated that no building could be achieved in Mexico without prior urbanization of the participants. To urbanize the Indian populations was to dislocate and destroy the patterns of indigenous culture. Such cultural extirpation, in turn, brought about the biological decrease of the Indian race. Hence the architecture that is the subject of this study was built at the expense of one of the great historical configurations of human society. Each building, and each colonial artifact was nourished by the destruction of a culture, and the decline of a race. . . .

.   .   .

The amount and quality of building in Mexico between the Conquest and 1600 may now be evaluated. In terms of quantity alone it probably exceeded by many times the total volume of monumental building in all Mexico during Aztec history (1250–1520). The Mexican landscape was basically altered by urban reconcentration, by hydrostatic works, by the profiles of the immense churches rearing high above the Indian pyramids. Not only was volume of construction increased, but the demands upon human skill were vastly greater than in pre-Conquest building.

How can we explain so much activity? How did it happen that three and a half million Indians accepted the material culture of so few colonists? Why is this architecture so various in structure and style, and so excellent in form? Why did so few pre-Conquest traits of technique, iconography, and style survive in early colonial art? In general, why did the Indians of Mexico, unlike the Pueblos of New Mexico, accept and reduplicate nearly the entire range of European building techniques, without essential loss or deformation?

The form of the questions, as they are written here, suggests a preliminary answer. The conventional interpretation, that the Indian peoples were coerced and exploited to these ends, against their will, and under conditions of slavery, is unsatisfactory in face of the evidence of texts and buildings. It is as if we were to say that the growth of a prize crop of corn results only from the farmer's bellicose design against nature; his merciless exploitation of water, sun, and soil; his ruthless tyranny in depriving the seed of the natural conditions of growth. But anyone will agree that the seed is essential, and that without it, the farmer's pains are for nothing. The conventional view appears in another form of statement: had the Indian peoples been left to their own devices, their cultural achievement would have been far richer and more valuable. This again amounts to saying that the farmer is at fault for subjecting plants to any kind of cultivation, good or bad, or that the finest fruits will grow from the least tended plants. However these things may be, such conventional views either overestimate or underestimate the rôle of an autonomous response to colonization from indigenous peoples.

The simple empirical fact is that the Indians were not exterminated by colonization in Mexico, and that their labor produced an intricate, abundant, and qualitative material culture. That their absolute productive capacity increased during the sixteenth century cannot be questioned, in spite of the loss of numbers through epidemic disease. The phenomenon of reduced populations attaining a more complex civilization in the span of fifty years suggests intimate participation and eager acquiescence by those numbers in the work at hand. The occasional withdrawals or resistances to colonization have already been noted; they were sporadic and peripheral: events in the metropolitan regions indicate the avidity of the Indians for European ceremonial and technology. No one will deny that the initial conquest meant coercion of Indians by Europeans. No one will deny that coercion continued throughout the sixteenth century. But the kind and degree of coercion changed between the conquest and the early stages of colonization: from military coercion to the forms of social compulsion without which society cannot persist. There is good reason to believe that sixteenth-century colonial compulsions upon Indian society were less onerous and less destructive of human resources than those applied by the Aztec confederacy during the fifteenth century. . . .

16. *Why Population Estimates Are Important in the Interpretation of Mexican History*

WOODROW BORAH and SHERBURNE F. COOK

For some twenty years Professors Borah and Cook have been studying the records of population in Mexico, and have produced a literature which is remarkable for its scope and depth. The methods they have developed are somewhat complicated and require more mathematical knowledge than most historians possess. Their conclusions on the meaning of their calculations for the interpretation of Mexican history are clearly of importance, even though they have not been universely accepted. Here is one of their most recent condensed statements on their findings.

A long series of questions comes to focus on the debate over the size of the population of central Mexico on the eve of the Spanish conquest, say A.D. 1518. Scholars who hold to the view that there was a dense aboriginal population also find that there was a complex society with very extensive division of labor, highly elaborate social stratification even to hereditary rulers and nobility, and that a numerous peasantry very much like that of pharaonic Egypt supported the elaborate superstructure. . . .

Scholars who hold to the opposing view that there was a relatively sparse population would find that pre-Conquest Meso-American society consisted of a series of chiefdoms somewhat more elaborate than those of the Iroquois. . . . The positions have remained strangely fixed since the eighteenth century and even earlier. Additional questions are (1) whether the Spanish conquest brought about a drastic decrease in Indian numbers, and (2) whether over the course of millennia since the beginnings of the Classical (Teotihuacán) Period in the first centuries of the Christian Era, Indian population has shown fairly steady increase until the explosion of our century or whether population in central Mexico has been characterized by an essentially cyclical movement. If this last interpretation is correct, after the nadir of the early seventeenth century Mexican numbers may now be nearing the climax of another upswing.

The debate has been able to continue for centuries because so much of the information available consisted of reports and chronicles of an essentially qualitative character. The relatively few statements of number could be declared moot or discredited by resort to techniques of literary and textual criticism. The discussion itself was essentially literary, characterized by the well-turned phrase heaping scorn upon opponents.

An essentially new approach to the debate has become possible in recent years through the uncovering in archives of substantial masses of quantitative data. Most materials are fiscal, but can be used for estimating population. . . .

Our results . . . strongly support the view that there was in central Mexico when Cortés landed on the coast of Veracruz a very dense population. The two hundred thousand square miles of central Mexico had an average population density of one hundred twenty-five persons per square mile. A peasantry, using digging stick methods of cultivation, with stone and wooden implements, with no large domesticated animals for power or food, but profit-

From "Conquest and Population: A Demographic Approach to Mexican History" by Woodrow Borah and Sherburne F. Cook, *Proceedings of the American Philosophical Society,* 113, no. 2 (April 1969), pp. 177–183, passim. Reprinted by permission.

ing from the highly productive maize-beans-squash complex, provided support for a superstructure of artisans, merchants, priesthood, nobility, and rulers. The surplus from each family was small but the peasantry was enormous and the superstructure accordingly elaborate. It was most elaborate in the seats of empire on the Mexican plateau, which drew huge stocks of foodstuffs and other products as tribute and levied on the lowlands for prized cotton, cacao, and feathers. Around the lakes of the Valley of Mexico and Lake Pátzcuaro, where canoe traffic meant a considerable advantage over transportation by human bearer, there grew up substantial metropolitan concentrations.

The vast population of early sixteenth-century central Mexico developed because of an unusually productive agriculture and relative isolation which shielded it from the epidemics of the Old World. Population density probably had passed the long-term carrying power of the land at the then level of technology as is evident from the widespread erosion that was taking place even under relatively benign cultivation by digging stick. The vast extension of human sacrifice in the middle of the fifteenth century looks remarkably like a response to population pressure. To an already overextended population the Spanish conquest came as catastrophe. Destruction of war and the dislocation of productive and distributive systems were greatly compounded by the unwitting introduction within a few years and in rapid succession of the temperate and tropical diseases of the Old World. Within less than a century the population of central Mexico shrank from approximately twenty-five millions to under two millions; the tropical coasts became the disease-ridden wastes that they have remained until recent decades.

Had the Spanish conquest taken place without catastrophic shrinkage of population, the history of Mexico might have been more nearly parallel to that of Indian or China, the superimposition of a numerically small ruling stratum that at a later date could be expelled by a reorganized native society. As events actually occurred in Mexico, the disappearance of the Indians made room for the addition of substantial contingents of Europeans and Negroes, who contributed the increasingly important and now numerically predominant group of mixed-bloods, mostly the Indian-European mixture known as mestizos. Culturally, the shrinkage of the Indian population permitted the entrance of European elements on a scale and with a thoroughness that would otherwise have been difficult, if not impossible.

The reorganization of social and political structures paralleled the decline in native numbers. In the first decades after the conquest, the Spaniards tended to preserve native forms and systems, except for the replacement of native religion by Christianity, the Europeans entering as a small uppermost class that attempted to draw support through tribute and other forms of taxation with the minimum of change needed to adjust native forms to European wants. The Spaniards, for example, wanted gold but had little use for the prized featherwork that was an important component of Aztec levies. By the middle of the sixteenth century, the native population shrank to a point at which it could no longer support both native and Spanish superstructures. At the mid-century the growing arrears in payments and complaints of too harsh levy led to a prolonged series of investigations by the royal government, and the investigations in turn into a struggle among the recipients of support to preserve their shares. In the end, the native rulers, nobility, and community governments and the Christian church lost very substantially whereas the Crown and the small group of Spanish who received tributes as its surrogates (the encomenderos) actually increased their shares. The native nobility and native officials were held to tribute; all exemption of their servants and serfs was ended; and a moderate, uniform tribute based on a uniform classification was instituted. In the same years, the burden on the Indian peasantry through levy by nobility and church for community expenditures was severely limited, and the exaction of labor put under a system of viceregal license (in effect, a kind of rationing). By the closing decades of the sixteenth century, although the reformed tribute system continued to function well, the native population shrank to so low a level that it could not furnish labor and goods to the Europeans under the existing forms of levy. A more radical solution was slowly put into effect, namely, that much of food for the Europeans, especially wheat and meat, was raised on their own estates, that the Europeans carried on much of their own production, and that labor was provided increasingly by Indians working for wages but tied to the Spaniard by debt. The system had the vast advantage for the Spaniards that the debt peons were available for all or substantial portions of their time. It had the further effect of withdrawing large numbers of Indians from their towns and placing them in Spanish towns, mines, and on Spanish estates, where tribal and community linkage was lost and the Indians merged into the new mixed-blood, Hispanized population. The Indian communities, beyond the losses through deaths, lost members further through recruitment of debt peons, migration to the economically more active Spanish settlements, and interbreeding. Accordingly, demographic recovery, when it began in the early and middle seventeenth century, was marked by the slower rate of increase of the Indians relative to the Europeans and Hispanized segments. Today the population of central Mexico is larger than it was in the reign of Montezuma the Younger, but Mexico is essentially a European state, with European language and European culture.

We may look at Mexican history in yet another way. Professor Cook has found in the Teotlalpan, the region northwest of Mexico City that was once the seat of the Toltec Empire (ninth to twelve centuries A.D.), a series of cyclical movements of population, the cycles covering from four to five centuries each. The upward movements within the cycles coincided with the dominance of the societies of Teotihuacán, the Toltecs, and the Aztecs. The downward movements have coincided with the breakdown of political systems. That breakdown has been marked by the successful invasion of central Mexico by invaders from outside the region. In all cycles before the coming of the Spaniards, the invaders were nomads from the arid regions to the north (Chichemecs) who became the dominant stratum in a reorganized society. One may hold that the coming of the Spaniards ended such cyclical movements, or that it has continued the movements save for the fact that the invaders came from across the ocean. Concomitantly with the coming of the Spaniards there has taken place the decline of population that in other cycles either preceded or accompanied invasion. The Spaniards more thoroughly reorganized society and technology than previous invaders. The state that they established eventually covered a far larger territory that included much of the old Chichemec domain. During their domination, as in other cycles, the population reached a low point and began an upswing that has continued with little interruption for over three centuries, the change from Spanish colony to independent but Europeanized state in 1821 having little effect. Today Mexico has the largest human population it has ever had. The Teotlalpan is again heavily populated. Whether or not Mexico has freed itself from a cyclical pattern may be tested in the coming century.

Juana Inés de la Cruz, Poetess and Scholar in Seventeenth-Century Mexico. This famous nun and outstanding poet of the Hispanic world in the seventeenth century is portrayed, quietly seated, in the only painting that has come down to us. But she was an independent thinker, too, whose life was one great struggle to develop her immense talent in the conservative society of her time (Reading 19). She did not disdain manual labor and found inspiration in everyday concerns, for she once remarked that if Aristotle had been a cook and had observed what went on in a kitchen he would have had many more ideas.

SECTION IV

Science and Education

Spaniards born in the New World cherished strong resentments against those who came from Spain to occupy the honorific and well-paid jobs in colonial administration. They were also humiliated to see that hard-working peninsulares were economically superior, too. On top of all this, the intellectuals in the colonies were depreciated by many Europeans who held the curious belief that the children of Spanish parents in the colonies declined prematurely in their mental faculties. American-born scholars resented the tolerant condescension and even outright contempt that their supercilious cousins across the Atlantic exhibited, and they reacted strongly. Carlos Sigüenza y Góngora, an outstanding scientist of seventeenth-century Mexico, once sourly remarked that his mathematical computations were not acknowledged or accepted by European professors because they were not "made in Germany." [1]

European condescension continued throughout the colonial period, and later. Perhaps some readers will be surprised to find in this volume a section on "Science and Education," for most accounts in English on the Iberian colonies pay little attention to these subjects since there still exists some doubt that the intellectual aspects of Latin American history are worth writing about. The readings given here were selected from the large bibliography, mostly in Spanish and Portuguese, which when fully known should alter somewhat the world's view of these developments in the Iberian colonies.

The interest displayed in Spain for more information on the New World was practical as well as scientific. Spaniards were alert to the possible medical properties of plants; as early as 1528 a druggist named Antonio de Villasante

[1] Irving A. Leonard, *Don Carlos de Sigüenza y Góngora: A Mexican Savant of the Seventeenth Century* (Berkeley: University of California Press, 1929), p. 63.

123

signed a contract with the crown that permitted him to produce and sell medicines, especially balsam, which he had discovered on the island of Hispaniola. The first notable expedition was sent by Philip II in 1570, when he dispatched Dr. Francisco Hernández to Mexico to investigate the medicinal value of plants there. He traveled throughout Mexico for six years, collected much scientific data, and participated actively in the attempts to stop the epidemic of 1576. He also compiled much information on the native foods, for he was an adventurous gourmet: he lavished praise on corn and cacao; he sampled the flesh of most animals, finding the rabbit "less tasty and tougher" than those in Spain, but he was enthusiastic about turkeys.[2]

A few years later Philip II ordered a Valencian mathematician to make astronomical observations in Mexico and the Philippines. From the earliest days of the conquest the vast regions and variegated peoples of the New World attracted the attention of many thoughtful priests and writers, which led to much useful speculation by such thinkers as the Jesuit José de Acosta, who is now recognized as having an important place in the history of scientific thought (Reading 17).

Many Spaniards studied and wrote about the languages and cultures of the Indians, and the Franciscan Bernardino de Sahagún has been recognized as one of the first modern anthropologists. The collection of Aztec poetry and history taken down by Sahagún with the help of his Aztec pupils and learned Indians conversant with the literature of the pre-Conquest Mexican society has been called "the most remarkable collection of oral literature ever made." Selections from his history help us to understand the nature of Indian life as do the selections from Aztec poetry (Reading 18).

Seventeenth-century Spanish America is often described as given over to soporific and arid theological disputes, suppression of thought, and general stagnation. But we also find such able jurists and royal officials as Juan Solórzano y Pereyra, such noted scholars as Antonio de León Pinelo, such historians as Antonio Vázquez de Espinosa and Bernabé Cobo, to name only a a few of the eminent intellectual figures of this supposedly dull period. One of the greatest creative writers was the Mexican nun Juana Inés de la Cruz, who has been called "the supreme poet of her time in Castilian," and whose life tells us much of the handicaps that women suffered in the colonial society (Reading 19).

Some writers of the time *were* dull, such as Pedro de Peralta of Peru, but

---

[2] Germán Somolinos D'Ardois, "Vida y obra de Francisco Hernández," in Francisco Hernández, *Obras,* 1 (Mexico: Universidad Nacional Autónoma de México, 1960), pp. 194–224.

even his life helps us to understand the intellectual spirit of the times.[3] There were some innovators. The Jesuit Alonso de Sandoval, for example, first proposed that the culture of the Negro slaves be seriously studied in order to Christianize them more effectively (Reading 20).

Another entirely different kind of scholar from the plodding Peralta was to be found in Spanish America, Carlos Sigüenza y Góngora, whose learning was much more scientific, as Professor Leonard explains in his biography of this notable figure. This Mexican man of letters was also an antiquarian, cosmographer, cartographer, engineer, explorer, historian, and counselor of viceroys. His scientific spirit is best shown by his actions and attitude during the eclipse of the sun on August 21, 1691:

> For almost a quarter of an hour the land was buried in Stygian darkness. An eerie chill descended abruptly with the pall of night, both of which phenomena caused the dogs to howl dismally and the women and children to shriek in terror. Indians hastily deserted their fruit and vegetable stands on the central square of Mexico City and fled, stumbling and falling as they ran, to the refuge of the Cathedral where they offered up their frightened prayers. The church bells added their loud, discordant note to the general confusion.
>
> "In the meantime [stated Sigüenza], I stood with my quadrant and telescope viewing the sun, extremely happy and repeatedly thanking God for having granted that I might behold what so rarely happens in a given place and about which there are so few observations in the books." [4]

And Professor Leonard concludes: This incident, perhaps better than any other, epitomizes the man and his times. While the superstitious populace flees in dread and terror from natural phenomena which it does not try to understand, the zealous — and pious — scientist stands with his instruments in his hand joyfully scanning the heavens amidst the unnatural obscurity and eagerly searching for data which may add to the sum of human knowledge and happiness." [5]

At the end of a busy and productive life (1645–1700) his worldly possessions consisted of two shirts and a large library that he bequeathed to the Jesuit college. His will specified that his body should be dissected after his

---

[3] Irving A. Leonard, "A Great Savant of Colonial Peru: Don Pedro de Peralta" *Philological Quarterly,* 12 (January 1933), pp. 54–72.

[4] Irving A. Leonard, *Baroque Times in Old Mexico* (Ann Arbor: University of Michigan Press, 1959), p. 175.

[5] Leonard, *Don Carlos de Sigüenza y Góngora,* p. 55.

death, so that physicians and surgeons might learn more about disease and thus help other sufferers.[6]

Universities are often considered strongholds of conservatism, and sometimes they have been. The strength of tradition may usually be seen in the way professors get their positions, and in Spanish America the method was open competition. Fortunately there has been preserved a full account of the presentation one eager contestant made for a professorship at the University of Mexico.[7] But to appreciate university life fully one must know about student life: how they were admitted, what they did while students, and what entitled them to a degree.

The Portuguese showed less concern than the Spaniards for scientific matters, but historians of science may discover in Brazilian and Portuguese archives activities that will change the picture. It was the explorer-naturalists of the eighteenth century who opened up America scientifically to the world:

> They dispelled legends, they uncovered facts. They rediscovered rubber, studied quinine, and coca leaf. They measured the earth's surface, entered the jungle and collected plants, studied the animals, measured the tides and developed the science of meteorology. The natural phenomena of America were investigated, codified, and embodied in literature — a literature that freed the continent from the fantasies which had persisted for some three hundred years.[8]

The story of the many scientific expeditions Spain sent to the New World has yet to be fully told. The Balmis round-the-world smallpox vaccinating operation has been studied,[9] and the outstanding labors of José Celestino Mutis are at last being recognized. Spain's prime concern with botany has long been noted, for Alexander von Humboldt stated: "No European government has laid out greater sums to advance the knowledge of plants than the Spanish government." Why this was so has been explained by Professor Arthur Robert Steele of the University of Toledo in his account of one of the outstanding scientific expeditions to Peru. The study of plants raised no religious problems, as other branches of science might, and the economic value of New World plants was attractive, too, to the Spanish government.[10]

[6] Ibid., p. 181.

[7] George Robert Graham Conway ed., *Friar Francisco Naranjo and the Old University of Mexico* (Mexico: Privately printed at Gante Press, 1939).

[8] Philip Louis Astuto, "Scientific Expeditions and Colonial Hispanic America," *Thought Patterns,* 6 (Brooklyn: St. John's University Press, 1959), p. 1.

[9] S. F. Cook, "Francisco Xavier Balmis and the Introduction of Vaccine to Latin America," *Bulletin of the History of Medicine,* vol. II, pp. 543–557, vol. 12, pp. 70–89.

[10] *Flowers for the King: The Expedition of Ruiz and Pavón and the Flora of Peru* (Durham, N.C.: Duke University Press, 1964).

17. *The Scientific Ideas of José de Acosta*

THEODORE HORNBERGER

The Jesuit historian José de Acosta well represents the effect of the New World on the educated Spaniards. He was astonished by the number of plants unknown in Europe; he listed dozens in his work on the Indies and concluded by writing "and a hundred other plants the names of which I do not remember." He also commented on the Aztec system of government, on the land systems of the Incas and their tribute arrangements, on the numerous cattle on the Caribbean islands, on the wealth of the silver mines at Potosí, where he served for a time as priest, on the reasons for Indian ready acceptance of Christianity, and on many other things.

But his most important contribution was as a scientific theorist. As Professor Theodore Hornberger of the University of Pennsylvania emphasizes, Acosta was "curious about the puzzles presented by the phenomena he had observed" in his travels in America, and "is the best available guide to the source and growth of the colonial scientific tradition," for no one in the English colonies "produced such a sweeping view of the problems posed by the observed facts of the New World."

By the rights of discovery and of conquest, the New World belonged in the sixteenth century to the Spaniards. They were the first to report upon the geography of the new-found western lands; their voyagers were the first to describe the strange inhabitants, animals, and plants of the Americas, and to point out in glowing terms the economic possibilities across the Atlantic. So swiftly did the Spaniards take advantage of their opportunities, intellectual as well as economic, that only thirty-four years after the first voyage of Columbus there appeared a systematic treatise on the natural history of the new world: *De la Natural Hystoria de las Indias* (Toledo, 1526), by Gonzalo Fernández de Oviedo y Valdés. By the end of the century Spanish knowledge of America had been brilliantly summarized by José de Acosta, sometimes known as the American Pliny. Although Acosta's *Historia Natural y Moral de las Indias* (Seville, 1590) has been recognized as the most useful and the most

From "Acosta's *Historia Natural y Moral de las Indias:* A Guide to the Source and Growth of the American Scientific Tradition" by Theodore Hornberger, *Studies in English* (Austin: University of Texas Press, no. 19, 1939), pp. 139–162, passim. Reprinted by permission of the author and the University of Texas Press.

learned of the early commentaries, one cannot say that its truly central place in American cultural history has been widely appreciated. . . .

Acosta's book reveals, more clearly than any other single work, two important facts: (1) that the intellectual conquest of the New World owed more to the ancients than is generally suspected, and (2) that new hypotheses developed along lines determined by certain puzzling questions which grew out of men's actual experience in America.

Most of the meagre outline of Acosta's life is derived from his own books. He was born in 1540 at Medina del Campo, between Valladolid and Salamanca in northwestern Spain. At the age of thirteen he joined the Society of Jesus, and was presumably educated in one of the colleges of that order. His work leaves no question of his profound learning, much of it doubtless acquired before 1570, when he left Spain to go to the Jesuit college at Juli, near the western shore of Lake Titicaca, in what is now southern Peru. . . .

Acosta was in Peru for about fifteen years, first in Juli and then in Lima. Besides taking an active part in the Jesuit work and in the third Council of Lima, he found time to write a number of books, which he took with him in manuscript when he returned to Spain in 1587. In the course of that homeward journey he stopped for a good part of 1586 in Mexico, where he continued to amass information on the natural history and civilization of the new colonies, the activity which had shared his attention with theology in Peru. Back in Spain, he quickly published the result of his labors, those of a scientific nature appearing at Salamanca in 1588, as *De Natura Novi Orbis Libri Duo.* Two years later, at Seville, there was published a translation of the two books of the *De Natura,* together with five additional books, under the title of *Historia Natural y Moral de las Indias.* Before his death in 1600 at Salamanca, where he was head of the Jesuit college, he had published, in addition, six theological treatises. . . .

In Book I Acosta deals with five questions of physical geography which had already, by 1590, led to marked disagreement among the learned: (1) What is the shape of the heavens and the earth? (2) Do the antipodes actually exist? (3) Are the torrid zones inhabitable? (4) Did the ancients have any knowledge of the New World? (5) How was the New World populated with men and beasts? No better illustration can be found of the way in which actualities forced men in Acosta's age to devise better working hypotheses than their traditional learning supplied.

With Aristotle, Acosta holds that both the heaven and the earth are round. Against this opinion, and in support of the alternative that the earth is flat and the heaven like a roof over it, were Chrysostom, Theodoret, Theophilus, Lactantius, Procopius, Jerome, and even Augustine. Acosta does not wish to belittle the church fathers, who may perhaps have "well imployed their studies in causes of greater waight," but he concludes that

> there is no doubt but the opinion which Aristotle and the other Peripateticks held with the Stoicks (that the figure of Heaven was round, and did moove circularly in his course), is so perfectly true, as we which doe now live in Peru see it visibly. Wherin experience should be of more force then all Philosophicall demonstrations, being sufficient to proove that the Heaven is round, and comprehends and contaynes the earth within it of al parts.

Nevertheless, Acosta marshals his arguments carefully: Heaven is round because it is the most perfect body, demanding the most perfect figure; in Peru, moreover, dark spots in the Milky Way can be seen circling continually about the earth, always relatively in the same position to certain fixed stars, "alwaies of one forme and bignes, as we haue noted by infallible observation." . . . We must conclude, says Acosta, "that in the holy scriptures we ought not to follow the letter which killes, but the spirit which quickeneth, as saith S. Paul." Yet Acosta, as Andrew Dickson White long ago pointed out, was still among the conservatives, since he left the earth in the midst of a round and finite universe, failing even to mention the Copernican astronomy.

Acosta is likewise on the side of experience as against authority in his remarks upon the distribution of land and sea; one could not well live in Peru and deny that in the antipodes, although the greater part be sea, "there is likewise land, so as in all parts of the world, the earth and water imbrace one another, which truely is a thing to make vs admire and glorifie the Arte of the soveraigne Creator." Yet the belief that the known world was surrounded by an encircling ocean had been held by Aristotle and most other ancient philosophers, the great exceptions being Crates of Mallos and Ptolemy, whom Acosta does not mention. . . . But "although he were a great Philosopher," Aristotle was deceived on this matter, as were Pliny, Virgil, and Ovid. Their reasons, Acosta admits, were good, and would seem so still "if visible experience did not vnfold this doubt."

In his discussion of the fourth question, Acosta's patriotism comes to the fore; he is disturbed that "some at this day, seeking to obscure the felicitie of this age and the Glory of our Nation, strive to proove that the new-found world was knowne to the Ancients." He is at pains, therefore, to discount the stories of extraordinary voyages in Pliny, the allusions in Seneca's *Medea,* the "great Atlanticke Iland" of Plato, and the suggestions of Arias Montano and Josephus that the Biblical Ophir and Tharsis (or Tarshish) are references to Peru. Nor can he accept the twentieth verse of Obadiah as a prophecy "that

this new worlde should be converted to Iesus Christ by the Spanish nation."
He is, in fact, constrained to doubt

> that the Ancients had knowledge in the Art of Navigation, whereby men
> at this day passe the Ocean, . . . I find not that in ancient bookes there
> is any mention made of the vse of the Iman or Loadstone, nor of the
> Compasse to saile by; yea, I beleeve they had no knowledge thereof.

How, then, did men and animals come to the New World? On this problem
Acosta's authorities afford no theories; he will write, therefore, "what I have
conceived, and what comes presently into my minde, seeing that testimonies
faile mee whom I might follow, suffering myselfe to be guided by the rule of
reason, although it be very subtill." Men must have come to Peru either by
sea or by land. If they came by sea, it must have been by accident, since they
lacked the modern aids to navigation, in particular the compass needle mag-
netized by the loadstone. Acosta is well-informed about the compass, even to
the extent of knowing about magnetic variation. Yet, admitting that men may
have come by accident, there remains the puzzle of how wild beasts got to the
Indies, after the Deluge had destroyed all except those in Noah's ark. Acosta's
conclusion after considering the possibilities of their swimming or flying
hither, is

> that the new world, which we call Indies, is not altogether severed and
> disioyned from the other world; . . . no man knowes how farre the
> land runnes beyond the Cape of Mendozino in the South sea, . . . no
> man knowes the lands on the other part of the Straight of Magellan. . . .

Book II consists of discussion of why the equatorial zone is not only habit-
able, to the confounding of Aristotle and Pliny, but also sometimes actually
more comfortable than the regions just outside the tropics. Acosta finds this
problem so fascinating that he is moved "to search out the causes, not moved
therevnto so much by the doctrine of ancient Philosophers, as by reason and
certaine experience." There are difficulties, of course, in accounting by a
single rule for all the diversities of climate under the line: what is true of Peru
is not true of Ethiopia; what is true of some parts of Peru is not true of others.
In general, however, the first thing to remember is Aristotle's error in thinking
that where the sun is nearest the earth the climate will necessarily be most hot
and dry. On the contrary, it is when the sun is most directly overhead that
Peru has most rain and humidity. The reason, Acosta thinks, is that the sun
draws from the ocean a great abundance of vapors, which dissolve into rain,
usually in the afternoon. In the other zones there is on the other hand, most
moisture when the sun is farthest away. . . . Other things contribute to the

comfort of living in Peru: the longer nights, the nearness of the ocean, the highness of the land, and, most important of all, the freshness of the winds which commonly come up in the afternoon. Each of these Acosta treats briefly, but he leaves the particular "discourse of windes, waters, landes, mettalls, plants, and beasts (whereof there is great aboundance at the Indies)" to Books III and IV. . . .

Acosta's scheme in Books III and IV is roughly Aristotelian or Scholastic, although he does not attempt to write of natural history in full. Book III treats of the simple bodies, or elements: air, water, earth, and fire — the subject of such Aristotelian writings as the *De Mundo,* the *De Generatione et Corruptione,* and the *Meterologica.* Book IV deals with the mixed bodies, both inanimate and animate: metals, plants, and beasts. These divisions are among the most ancient in natural philosophy, going back, in the case of the four elements, at least as far as Empedocles, who lived in the fifth century B.C. . . .

By far the largest portion of Acosta's third book deals with the air, or winds. A deep dissatisfaction with Aristotle's explanations is again apparent, as Acosta notes the great diversities in the winds, and concludes that

> it is needefull to seeke further to knowe the true and originall cause of these so strange differences which we see in the windes. I cannot conceive any other, but that the same efficient cause which bringeth foorth and maketh the winds to grow dooth withall give them this originall qualitie, for in trueth the matter whereon the windes are made, which is no other thing (according to Aristotle) but the exhalation of the interior Elements, may well cause in effect a great parte of this diversitie, being more grosse, more subtile, more drie, and more moist. But yet this is no pertinent reason, seeing that we see in one region, where the vapours and exhalations are of one sorte and qualitie, that there rise windes and effects quite contrary. We must therefore referre the cause to the higher and celestiall efficient, which must be the Sunne, and to the motion and influence of the heavens, the which by their contrary motions give and cause divers influences.

Thus Acosta takes up, with marked intelligence, the problem of the trade winds, or Brizes (as they were called in the sixteenth and seventeenth centuries). He recognizes their importance to navigation, since they make possible an easy voyage from east to west, and he describes them meticulously. Unfortunately, although he approximates the true explanation of their cause, he falls short of stating it because of his ignorance or rejection of the Copernican demonstration of the motion of the earth. "The earth," he insists, "is not moved," nor is the element of water, "for that it is united to the earth and makes one sphere, so as the earth keeps it from all circular motion." . . .

The relatively large amount of space devoted by Acosta to meteorology and climatology has a significance which is not wholly obvious. From the first, colonial Americans appear to have been keenly interested in the weather, in part, no doubt, because of economic reasons and an understandable curiosity. . . .

The greater part of Acosta's discussion of the element of water is actually descriptive geography. He indicates the position of the North and South Seas (the Atlantic and Pacific Oceans), of the Strait of Magellan, of the supposed Northwest Passage, of lakes in Peru and Mexico, of unusual springs and fountains, and of the Amazon and Plata Rivers. There are inserted chapters on tides and on Indian methods of fishing. These pages reveal a fairly good grasp of the geographical knowledge of his day, when the western world had absorbed the information derived from Magellan's voyage. . . .

Acosta's discussion of the element of earth is largely a description of the topography of Peru and Mexico, with comments on the economic possibilities of the various regions. Like almost all Americans of the colonial era, he is keenly conscious of how much of the New World remains unexplored and anxious to estimate the extent of the continents. Relevant to the element of fire, he sees "no special matter at the Indies which is not in other regions." Volcanoes he explains as "places that have the propertie to draw vnto them hote exhalations, and to convert them into fire and smoke which, by their force and violence, cast out other thicke matter which dissolves into ashes, into pumico stone, or such like substance." This is mere acceptance of certain basic theories of the *Meteorologica*. Acosta is sure that volcanic flames are not hell fire, as Basil and others taught, because hell fire is without light. . . .

Acosta's fourth book is divided fairly evenly among his three "mixtures and compounds": metals, plants, and animals. From the point of view of the history of technology and biology, this section is probably the most important of the work, because of its full account of Spanish-American mining processes, and its descriptions of the more unusual American plants and animals. . . .

Besides accounts of the gold, silver, and mercury mines of Peru, and the methods used to find and refine these metals, Acosta has brief chapters on emeralds and pearls. Throughout these sections he is heavily indebted to the twenty-third book of Pliny's *Historia Naturalis*. His material on plants is divided into comment on those "proper and peculiar to the Indies" and briefer mention of "the rest that are common to the Indies and Europe." He speaks of the planting and the uses of maize, or Indian corn. . . . The general impression conveyed is that plant life flourishes abundantly in the New World, although Acosta admits that some importations, such as cherries, have not done well, "the which I do not impute to want of temperature, for that there is of all sorts, but to carelessness, or that they have not well observed the temperature." His remarks, in short, are an invaluable source of knowledge of Spanish-American agriculture at the end of the sixteenth century, and have been used extensively by commentators on that subject. . . .

Last of all, Acosta describes the animals of the New World, those "carried from Spaine," those "of the same kinde we have in Europe, and yet not carried by the Spaniardes," and those "proper to the Indies, whereof there are none in Spaine." The first class has increased enormously; Acosta hints that fortunes are still being made in hides and wool, almost without exertion. The second class he has spoken of before; that there are lions, tigers, bears, boars, foxes, and other wild beasts in the New World is good evidence that there is some connection by land with the Old, "being impossible to swimme the ocean: and it were a follie to imagine that men had imbarked them with them." Many of these wild beasts, he points out, are slightly unlike the European varieties. The birds, he conceives, might more easily have passed to America. The real problem falls under his third heading:

> It were a matter more difficult to shew and prove, what beginning many and sundry sorts of beasts had, which are found at the Indies, of whose kindes we have none in this continent. For if the Creator had made them there, wee may not then alleadge nor flie to Noahs Arke, neither was it then necessary to save all sorts of birds and beasts, if others were to be created anew. Moreover, wee could not affirme that the creation of the world was made and finished in six days, if there were yet other kinds to make, and specially perfit beasts, and no lesse excellent than those that are knowen vnto vs. If we say then that all these kinds of creatures were preserved in the Arke by Noah, it followes that those beasts, of whose kindes we finde not any but at the Indies, have passed thither from this continent, as we have said of other beasts that are knowne vnto vs. This supposed, I demand how it is possible that none of their kinde should remaine heere? and how they are found there, being as it were travellers and strangers. Truly it is a question that hath long held me in suspense.

As Andrew Dickson White has shown, the old theological theories of the number of species and their geographical distribution were soon to be overthrown by just evidence as this. "It may be," Acosta suggests, "God hath made a new creation of beasts." Or it may be that, although all came out of

the ark, diverse kinds dispersed themselves into the most suitable regions.
. . . The point, once more, is that the whole discussion illustrates Acosta's
astuteness in perceiving significant problems.

Like all the early travelers, Acosta was mightily impressed with the number
and strangeness of the birds and beasts of the Indies. He describes the humming bird, the condor, the turkey buzzard, the macaw, and the sea fowl whose
dung, guano, so wonderfully fattens the ground. He points out the singulari-
ties of the peccary, the tapir, the armadillo, the iguana, the chinchilla, the
guinea pig. Indian monkeys are given a whole chapter, including "the fooler-
ies, tricks, traverses, and pleasant sportes they make when they are taught,
which seem not to come from brute breasts, but from a man-like vnderstand-
ing." He deals with the various varieties of the llama at some length, distin-
guishing the vicuna, the alpaca, and the guanaco. . . .

So much for the content of Acosta's four books on the natural history of
the Indies, written, as have been said, to correct the errors of Scholastic science in the light of the new evidence from America. As has been shown, much
of his work was descriptive, and in his curiosity about strange plants and animals and their possible economic uses he is representative rather than distinctive. To be sure, he was more than ordinarily familiar with the backgrounds
of ancient and medieval science, a fact which made him discriminating in his
selection of things to be described and systematic in his treatment of them. His
unique qualities, however, derive from his having been a scientific theorist,
curious about the puzzles presented by the phenomena he had observed and
not unduly respectful of "the ancient and received Philosophy." He went beyond mere observation to develop and weigh scientific hypotheses, naive now,
perhaps, but by no means naive at the time he wrote or in the two centuries
thereafter.

One cannot but be impressed, indeed, with the way in which Acosta's speculations foreshadowed most of the main directions of colonial science. His
interest in geography, his curiosity about the aborigines, his concern with meteorology and climatology, his speculations about the number and distribution
of species — all these are characteristic of his successors in the English colonies
to the north. Nowhere else, perhaps, can one find them altogether; the English,
surely, produced no such sweeping view of the problems posed by the observed facts of the New World. It is not too much to say, therefore, that
Acosta is the best available guide to the source and the growth of the colonial
scientific tradition, a tradition thus far imperfectly understood. . . .

18. *Selections from the Writings of the First Anthropologist in America, and from Aztec Poetry*

BERNARDINO DE SAHAGÚN

Sahagún was born in 1499 in Spain, where he entered the Franciscan Order and studied at the University of Salamanca before embarking for the New World in 1529.* He was one of the first Europeans to examine Indian culture in a serious professional spirit. He considered the Mexican Indians a sinful people, marveled at their degradation in certain respects, and believed in physical punishment to make them follow the Christian path. He would rouse Indians in the night to beat them, and reported that he "lovingly propelled them towards heaven with blows."†

Yet Sahagún also respected the Indians and their culture, which he studied with such persistence and skill that he is now looked upon as the father of the Náhuatl language and culture.

Other friars made special studies of Indian cultures. The Dominican Bartolomé de Las Casas not only denounced Spanish cruelty to the Indians but also in his *Apologetic History* insisted that the Indians had developed a remarkably rich culture that must not be measured by a Spanish yardstick. Though the Franciscan Diego de Landa did not share Las Casas's enthusiasm for the Indians, nevertheless he did admire certain parts of it — their sophisticated calendar, their food, architecture, some of their moral conceptions, and the beauty of their women.

Many other Spaniards wrote about the culture of the natives they found in America, but Bernardino de Sahagún's *General History of the Things of New Spain* has generally been considered the most professional and substantial. He began to collect material on Aztec history and customs in 1547. Ten years later his Provincial ordered him to prepare a history of Indian culture on the assumption that it would aid in the then-faltering missionary effort. Between 1558 and 1560 he lived in a native village, where he systematically questioned a dozen of the oldest and most knowledgeable inhabitants he could find, using a carefully prepared list of culture elements as the basis for his investigation. His subjects also drew many pictures to explain their history. Sahagún then moved to another village to check his data by using a fresh set of informants during 1560 and 1561. The next three years were occupied in organizing his data, and only then did he begin writing. The result, completed in 1569, was a remarkable study.

* For a general view of Sahagún's life, see Fanny R. Bandelier, ed., *A History of Ancient Mexico* (Nashville: Fisk University Press, 1932). For a more recent and detailed view, see Luis Nicolau D'Olwer, *Historiadores de América: Fray Bernardino de Sahagún* (Mexico, 1952).

† Luis Villoro, *Los grandes momentos del indigenismo en México* (Mexico, 1950), p. 68.

Sahagún's manuscript suffered incredible vicissitudes after leaving his hands. They were lost or misplaced for many years, but eventually surfaced and now are to be found mostly in Florence and Madrid. He died in Mexico in 1590 without knowing the fate of the work upon which he had labored so long. At last his treatise is recognized as one of the most complete and valuable sources on practically all aspects of the life of the ancient Mexicans. He lived in an age when few persons took an interest in any culture except their own. Today when anthropologists so restlessly roam the world that there must be few Indians in even the remotest part of Brazil who have not been interrogated by some foreign scholar to learn about their social structure and cultural elements, the attitude and accomplishments of Sahagún may not seem impressive. But if we remember that Sahagún was an active member of one of the most militantly religious people of Europe, who had just emerged from a centuries-long struggle to expel the Moslems from Spain, his *History* was clearly a remarkable achievement, which approaches in philosophic insight and imagination the spirit of Claude Levi-Strauss in his already classic *Tristes Tropiques*.

The *History of the Things of New Spain* consisted of the following books: (1) Gods worshipped by Indians; (2) Their fiestas; (3) Their ideas in immortality and death ceremonies; (4) Astrology, to determine good or bad fortune; (5) Agüeros (witch doctors) to divine the future; (6) Indian rhetoric and moral philosophy; (7) Their natural philosophy; (8) Their lords and government; (9) Their merchants and mechanical arts; (10) Their vices and virtues; (11) Their animals, birds, fish, herbs, trees, fruits, flowers; (12) The conquest of Mexico.

Sahagún at times encountered much opposition to his scholarly activities. Some thought friars should spend their time converting Indians rather than studying their customs, some of which were unchristian. But Sahagún apparently felt that, like a physician, he must know their "diseases" before he could cure them. The result was a magnificently detailed description of Indian life that has never been surpassed. The following selections are merely samples from an enormous reservoir of knowledge about ways of Aztec life.

One of the outstanding works of scholarship undertaken in the United States during the last quarter century has been the translation into English by Arthur J. O. Anderson and Charles E. Dibble of the massive *General History of the Things of New Spain* by Sahagún. Originally prepared in Spanish and in Náhuatl, with about 1,850 drawings, this impressive work remains the fundamental source on Aztec culture. The editors have accomplished a monumental task, for they translated directly from the Indian text and provided a wealth of explanatory footnotes.‡

‡ *Bernardino de Sahagún, General History of the Things of New Spain: Florentine Codex,* trans. from the Aztec into English, with notes and illustrations, by A. J. O. Anderson and C. E. Dibble (Salt Lake City: University of Utah; and Santa Fe, N.M.: School of American Research, 1950–).

No. 1. Tenth Chapter, in which is told
how the rulers took their pleasure

When the ruler went forth, in his hand rested his reed stalk which he went moving in rhythm with his words. His chamberlains and his elders went before him; on both sides, on either hand, they proceeded as they went clearing the way for him. None might cross in front of him; none might come forth before him; none might look up at him; none might come face to face with him.

He sang; songs were learned; chants were intoned. They told him proverbs and pleasantries to pass the time.

They played ball. There were his ball-catchers and his ball-players. They wagered [in this game] all [manner of] costly goods — gold, golden necklaces, green stone, fine turquoise, slaves, precious capes, valuable breech clouts, cultivated fields, houses, leather leg bands, gold bracelets, arm bands of quetzal feathers, duck feather capes, bales of cacao — [these] were wagered there in the game called *tlachtli*.

On the two sides, on either hand, it was limited by walls, very well made, in that the walls and floor were smoothed. And there, in the very centre of the ball court, was a line, drawn upon the ground. And on the walls were two stone, ball court rings. He who played caused [the ball] to enter there; he caused it to go in. Then he won all the costly goods, and he won everything from all who watched there in the ball court. His equipment was the rubber ball, the leather gloves, girdles, and leather hip guards.

Patolli was played with large beans — four large beans with holes bored into the surfaces. The game was won when from their hands they scattered the four beans on a mat painted in widely spaced black [lines], with which the *patolli* mat was designed. There went to be added the counters — twelve [of them], six the property of each, the counters of each of the contenders. He who won in playing *patolli*, won all the costly goods: golden necklaces, green stone, fine turquoise, bracelets on which were round, green stones or fine turquoise, quetzal feathers, slaves, houses, fields, precious capes, mats, large capes, green stone lip plugs, golden ear plugs, duck feather capes. And he who played *patolli*, who cast the beans, if then he made one [of them] stand,

Fray Bernardino de Sahagún, General History of the Things of New Spain, ed. Arthur J. O. Anderson and Charles E. Dibble, bk. 8, *Kings and Lords* (1954), pp. 29–30. Reprinted by permission of the school of American Research and the University of Utah.

if the bean stood up there on its thicker end, it was taken as a great omen; it was regarded as a great marvel. Then he won all the costly goods. [The other] lost even though he had not yet attained the specified number of throws. Thus were all agreed; thus all came to the end [of the game].

They shot with bow and arrow — with a bow, with a shaft, with bird arrows, with darts. With this belonged a bracelet on which were large, round, green stones or fine turquoises. The ruler placed it about his wrist.

They used a sling, and cast stones with the sling. With these belonged a net for the small stones, rounded so that the small stones were polished. With these they cast stones at small birds. They hunted with a bird net; with it they captured various birds.

Flower gardens were laid out; flower beds were laid out. They put in them all the various flowers.

There were their jesters who provided them solace and gave them pleasure. And [there were those] who rolled a log with their feet thus bringing pleasure in many ways. Their deeds were laughable and marvelous; for with the soles of his feet one man [lying] below this did — he made a thick, round log dance with the soles of his feet [while] he lay upon his back and cast the log upward. With only the soles of his feet he did this.

Many things they did to bring men pleasure. There were their servants, their pages who attended them and gave them solace; dwarfs, cripples, hunchbacks, servants. They kept eagles, ocelots, wolves, mountain cats, and various birds.

No. 2. How Rulers Admonished Their Daughters When They Reached the Age of Discretion

NO. 2. EIGHTEENTH CHAPTER

Here it is related how the rulers admonished their daughters when they had already reached the age of discretion. Thus they urged them to prudence [and] virtue, public [and] private. They placed before them, revealed to them, the nobility, the government, the honor, that they should in no way blacken, dirty, discredit the lineage. Very good were the words with which they admonished them.

"Here art thou, thou who art my child, thou who art my precious necklace, thou who art my precious feather, thou who art my creation, my offspring, my blood, my color, my image. Now grasp, hear that thou hast come to life, thou wert born; that our lord of the near, of the nigh, the maker, the creator, hath sent thee to earth.

"All now that thou hast become knowledgeable, already thou observest how things are. There is no rejoicing, there is no contentment; there is torment, there is pain, there is fatigue, there is want; torment, pain dominate. Difficult is the world, a place where one is caused to weep, a place where one is caused pain. Affliction is known. And the cold wind passeth, glideth by. Most certainly on one the wind lesseneth the heat. And it is a place of thirst, it is a place of hunger. This is the way things are.

"Hear well, O my daughter, O my child, the earth is not a good place. It is not a place of joy, it is not a place of contentment. It is merely said it is a place of joy with fatigue, of joy with pain on earth; so the old men went saying. In order that we may not go weeping forever, may not die of sorrow, it is our merit that our lord gave us laughter, sleep, and our sustenance, our strength, our force, and also carnal knowledge in order that there be peopling.

"All make life gay on earth in order that no one go weeping. And although it is so, although this is the way of life on earth, is it perhaps therefore heard, is it perhaps therefore feared, is life perhaps therefore lived in weeping? For there is living on earth; there is one's becoming a lord; there is one's becoming a ruler; there is one's becoming a nobleman; there is one's becoming an eagle warrior; there is one's becoming an ocelot warrior. And who is saying that this is how it is on earth? Who is just yielding to death? For there is the doing of things; there is the providing of a livelihood; there is the building of houses; there is labor; there is the seeking of women; there is marriage; there is the marriage of women to men; there is the marriage of men to women.

"And now, O my daughter, hear it well, look at it deliberately; for behold, here is thy mother, thy noble one. From her womb, from her breast thou wert chipped, thou wert flaked. It is as if thou wert an herb, a plant which hath propagated, sprouted, blossomed. It is also as if thou hadst been asleep and hadst awakened.

"See, hear, and know it is on earth. May thou live, may thou just live, may thou continue a little. In what manner wilt thou live? In what manner wilt

Fray Bernardino de Sahagún, General History of the Things of New Spain, ed. Arthur J. O. Anderson and Charles E. Dibble, 6, *Rhetoric and Moral Philosophy* (1969), pp. 93–94. Reprinted by permission of the School of American Research and the University of Utah.

thou continue a little? They say the earth is a dangerous place, a fearsomely dangerous place, O my daughter, O dove, O little one. Know that thou comest from someone, thou art descended from someone; that thou wert born by someone's grace; that thou art the spine, the thorn, of our lords who went leaving us, the lords, the rulers who already have gone to reside beyond, those who came guarding the realm, and who came giving fame, who came giving renown to nobility.

"Hear this. Especially do I declare unto thee that thou art a noblewoman. If thou wert only to esteem thyself as a precious person! — This, even though thou art a woman. Thou art a precious green stone, thou art a precious turquoise. . . .

No. 3. How Many Kinds of Drunkards There Were

NO 3. FIFTH CHAPTER

Which telleth how many kinds of drunkards there were.

And it was said that the wine was known as Four Hundred Rabbits.

One drinker might not harm or belittle his day sign. The wine did not irritate him; it did not cause him irritation or make a fool of him. He only went to sleep, and continued to sleep. He became pale and remained pale, sitting with drooping head — remaining with head bowed; he sat rolled up like a ball, and remained coiled; he sat embracing himself, hugging himself; he rested on his shins, and remained on his shins; he squatted on his heels and remained on his heels. He was only by himself, and calmly went off by himself. Peacefully he stretched out; quietly he fell down exhausted. In no way did he offend one. He stretched out, rumbling as he slept, groaning, snoring, as if he had torn off his nose, as if he enjoyed the sleep.

And one of them only wept. He loosed tears as if bringing good to himself, sobbing as he pressed them out. Like hail stones they showered down, a great course of water simply streaming down. His tears buried him. He could not stop. Verily, that which the wine made him remember ate his heart out.

And for one of them his only joy and pleasure was in song, in singing. He wished not to talk; he neglected listening to jests, to counsel, to stories. As if

Fray Bernardino de Sahagún, General History of the Things of New Spain, ed. Arthur J. O. Anderson and Charles E. Dibble, bk. 4, *The Soothsayers* (1957), pp. 15–16. Reprinted by permission of the School of American Research and the University of Utah.

it unleashed his song, when he drank the wine, he so recalled his song, as if it engulfed him. So the wine worked on him.

And another did not sing; he did nothing but talk. Uncontrolled he talked; he spoke much. He chattered, jabbered, gibbered, and mumbled. With ill-will he eavesdropped and betrayed others. He blustered, vaunted, and sang praises of himself; he esteemed and made himself out as great. He belittled what others said, speaking deceitfully and constantly shaking his head. He pretended to be rich and reprimanded the poor; he pretended to be superior, to be one in authority. Haughtily, he thought well of himself. He did not deflate himself; he did not overcome nor chastise his tongue. No one could force him to recant. He thought himself superior, better than others.

Indistinct was his speech. What did he say? He was as if stirred, and his words bubbled up and burst forth. It was as if he argued, harangued, enforced silence, and drove all people away, put them to flight, numbed them with terror, visited them with afflictions, made them shrink with fright, and assailed them with his words.

It seemed that he disgusted others, and did not inquire what they said. Wherever they may have spoken, or undertaken something, he seemed to make little of it and kick it aside. But when he had drunk nothing, he seemed to be dumb, one who whispered, fearful of people, quite frightened.

For all this he excused himself by saying: "It is because I no longer knew what I said; for I was drunk. The wine had taken effect upon me; I was over-wrought."

And another drunkard was very suspicious. He misunderstood; not as things were did he hear them. Often he blamed his wife. If anyone only looked at her, he then said to him: "Why dost thou make eyes at my wife?" Then he gave rise to hatred, fury, and murder, etc. And all that which was spoken he took as applying to him. He suspected that when there was occasion for mirth, he was thereby being defamed, the object of ridicule. Without reason he belabored the people. The wine and drinking cursed him.

And if it were a woman, she simply went to her knees; she remained on her knees. No longer was she rational. She sat with legs outstretched; she remained with legs outstretched. And if she were much besotted, if she were much affected, her hair simply formed a mantle over her. She tumbled there, with hair streaming out, etc.

All of these kinds [of drunkenness] here mentioned, each one, showed upon and were the doing of the drunkard. It was said: "So is his rabbit. Thus was his day sign; in this way did the wine gods manifest themselves on him." And if a drunkard fell over a precipice, or else fell somewhere [else], it was said: "He was affected by the wine gods."

******

The Ancient Wisdom of the Pre-Columbian Peoples of Middle America

High on the walls of the remarkable National Anthropological Museum in Mexico City have been placed Spanish translations of some of the poetry of the Indians the Spaniards found in the New World. These Biblical sayings, together with the archaeological and ethnographical reconstructions exhibited in the Museum, provide an excellent view of the past and recent life of the Indians.

******

Must I thus depart?
As the flowers that perished?
Nothing that I have will endure?
Nothing of my fame here on earth?
Not even flowers, not even songs?

******

Let there be light!
Let the sky and the earth awake!
There will be no glory or grandeur
Until a human being exists,
The complete man.

******

These Toltecs were certainly wise
For They Were Accustomed to Carrying on a Dialogue With Their
        own Hearts.

******

They began to instruct their children
How they must live
How they were to respect other individuals
How they were to cleave to what is proper and good
How they were to avoid evil,
Fleeing resolutely from what is bad,
From Perversion and Greed.

******

Here, Tenochas, you will learn
How the Great and Famous City of Mexico Tenochtitlán began,
In the midst of the waters, in the *tular,*
In the cane breaks where we were living.
Where we were born
We, the Tenochas.

******

As long as the world shall endure
The fame and glory of
México-Tenochtitlán Will Not Perish.

******

Take care for the things of the earth
Accomplish something: cut wood, cultivate the soil,
Plant nopal trees and maguey,
You will thus have something to drink, to eat, to dress yourself with.
In this way you will stand on your own feet, you will be a true man,
Thus you will get along in life
Thus the world will take account of you, will praise you
Thus you will make yourself known.

******

May they not stumble in the ups and downs of the road
May they not encounter obstacles behind or before
Nor anything which may afflict them
Let all their paths be pleasant paths, smooth paths.

******

Every noon, every year,
Every day, every wind,
Flourishes, and also perishes,
Likewise all men finally arrive at a quiet place to rest.

******

The editor wishes to thank Dr. Ignacio Bernal, Director of the Museo Nacional de Antropología for permission to use this material. Translations by the editor.

19. *Sor Juana Inés de la Cruz:* "The Supreme Poet of Her Time in Castilian"

IRVING A. LEONARD

Professor Leonard, who was the Domingo Faustino Sarmiento Professor at the University of Michigan at the time of his retirement a few years ago, made an outstanding contribution in what might be best called cultural history. Of his many studies the best known are *Baroque Times in Old Mexico* (1959) and *Books of the Brave* (1949). His writings were always marked by a grace of style and detailed research that explain their readability and their permanent value.

The late Pedro Henríquez Ureña, probably the most distinguished Latin American literary critic of this century, termed Sor Juana's life "a prodigious tale of devotion and knowledge." * He emphasized the obstacles she faced, "the many censors who doubted the wisdom of so much learning in a woman who even succeeded once in inducing a mother superior — 'a very saintly and very foolish woman' — to forbid her the reading of books."

This prohibition lasted only three months: she faithfully gave up books, but this did not prevent her from thinking: "and so, though I did not study in books, I studied in all the things God created." This meant pondering on the many individual differences between people, even though they were of the same species. The geometrical figure of objects interested her: "She observes two girls playing with a spinning top and decides to find out what kind of curve it draws while it spins — she sprinkles flour on the floor and discovers that the curve is a spiral. In the kitchen, she remarks on the properties of sugar or eggs and adds: 'If Aristotle had known how to cook, he would have written even more than he did.'"

Henríquez Ureña also pointed out that her poetry reflects the conditions of her life in seventeenth-century Mexico:

> In a superb sonnet to the rose she draws from its brief life the traditional lesson — "thy life deceives and thy death teaches" — but in another sonnet she approves the rose's life — "happy it is to die while young and fair and not endure the insult of old age." This is an expression of her persistent fighting spirit, which led her to write the defiant lines: "If my displeasure from my pleasure comes, may heaven give me pleasure at the cost of displeasure" — lines strikingly coincident with a number of folk songs and proverbs in Mexico.

Sor Juana needed all the persistence and courage that she had. Archbishop Francisco Aguiar y Seixas (1632–1698), who was in power during the last

* All quotations in this headnote come from Pedro Henríquez Ureña, *Literary Currents in Latin America* (Cambridge, Mass.: Harvard University Press, 1945), pp. 75–82.

years of Sor Juana's life, helps us to appreciate the spirit of some of the
dominant forces of the age. Professor Leonard discreetly terms him "misogynistic," but his hatred of women led him to shun all contact with them.
He even refused to make the ceremonial visit on the Viceroy required by
protocol, because he would meet the Vicequeen at the same time. He was a
pious and hardworking prelate withal; he visited all parts of his enormous
archbishopric and founded a seminary and a colegio as well as a "House
for Demented Females" and a "House For Women Abandoned by Their
Husbands."

Even though the times were against Sor Juana, she wrote on a subject
always dangerous for women to take up: men. "Her best known poem is
the one in defense of women; . . . it is her thesis that men are irrational
in blaming women for their imperfection, since men constantly strive to
make women imperfect. It is not great poetry, but it is a polemical masterpiece."

One August day of 1667 in Mexico City an attractive, talented girl, still some
months short of her sixteenth birthday, entered the sternly ascetic Order of
Discalced Carmelites as a chorister. The convent that received her was the
one that had been the dream of those earnest nuns, Sister Inés de la Cruz and
Sister Mariana Encarnación when they plied the fickle Archbishop García
Guerra so assiduously earlier in the century with sweetmeats and seductive
music. Though immediate success had eluded these efforts, it will be recalled,
patience was triumphant in 1616, and the new religious community came into
being. The young lady who, a half century afterwards, gained admittance to
its holy precincts was Doña Juana Inés de Asbaje y Ramírez de Santillana,
better known as Sister Juana Inés de la Cruz, . . . famed as the "last great
lyric poet of Spain and the first great poet of America." Also musically gifted,
her ecclesiastical name was possibly adopted in veneration of the instrument-
playing hostess of Fray García Guerra and cofounder of the Carmelite convent, of which she was now a temporary inmate.

In an age when matrimony and religious reclusion were the sole careers open
to respectable females, the act of taking the veil was a commonplace event in
Mexican society. In most sisterhoods the discipline was not severe, and within
the cloistered walls many comforts and amenities of secular life could be enjoyed, including the services of personal slaves. Indeed, for daughters whose
matrimonial prospects were not bright, an immured existence of this sort
seemed a desirable alternative, and a young woman whose parents or relatives

From *Baroque Times in Old Mexico: Seventeenth-Century Persons, Places, and Practice*
by Irving A. Leonard (Ann Arbor: University of Michigan Press, 1959), pp. 172–191,
passim. Copyright © by the University of Michigan, 1959. Reprinted by permission.

could provide the requisite dowry was regarded as fortunate. But the case of
the adolescent Doña Juana Inés de Asbaje y Ramírez de Santillana seemed
exceptional, and strangely obscure the reasons for her decision. Here was a
maiden "that was far more beautiful than any nun should be," the darling of
the viceregal court, and the favorite maid-in-waiting of the vicereine. Her personal attractiveness, her nimble wit in penning verse for any occasion, and her
amazing knowledge of books, were all very nearly the talk of the town. In
fact, the admiring Viceroy himself, on one occasion, had arranged that a
group of the leading professors at the University of Mexico should examine
the precocious girl in various branches of learning, and when she emerged
triumphant from this ordeal, the learned gentlemen marveled at the erudition
and composure of a maiden who hardly seemed more than a child.

Her rise and renown in the courtly circle of the capital had been truly
phenomenal. A village lass, born in 1651 in a tiny hamlet called Nepantla,
"the land in between," that looked up to the snow-crested volcanoes Popo-
catepetl and Ixtacihuatl, she had begun to read at the age of three, later devouring the small library of her gandfather. When eight years old she went to
Mexico City to live with relatives. Soon this pretty child prodigy caught the
eye of the vicereine who brought her to reside amidst the luxury and splendor
of the viceregal Palace. In this sophisticated environment the young girl rapidly
acquired a maturity that quite belied her years, and in the Court she soon
found herself envied for her wit by the women and desired for her physical
charms by the men.

Social success of this sort in such aristocratic circles was all the more extraordinary in the light of her illegitimate birth, though this circumstance was,
perhaps, undisclosed to anyone save her confessor. Her mother, it was later
revealed, had had two separate trios of children by as many men, and neither
of these unions the Church had hallowed. It was not an uncommon situation
at the time, even in families of some distinction, but it was hardly a genealogi-
cal asset for any one of patrician pretensions. That this lowly origin influenced
the resolve of Juana Inés de Asbaje y Ramírez de Santillana, who thus bore
the surnames of her progenitors, to become a nun is likely but, as the sole
explanation of her choice, it is unlikely. Her deep passion for study, her stated
"total disinclination to marriage," and the promptings of her zealous confessor, the Jesuit *calificador* of the Inquisition, Antonio Núñez de Miranda, had
undoubtedly made a life of reclusion seem attractive to her troubled spirit, and
finally moved her to abandon the pomp and glitter of the Palace social whirl,
of which she was so conspicuously a part.

That this determination was attended by doubts, misgivings, and inner conflict appears evident in the fact that illness caused her to withdraw from the
Carmelite order within three months. The transition from a worldly court to

the harsh confinement of a convent proved too abrupt and severe. Early the following year, however, she took her first vows in the Jeronymite community, the milder discipline of which was better suited to the sensitive temperament and scholarly aspirations of the poetess. The remainder of her forty-three years of life she spent chiefly within the book-lined walls of her cell, to which she retreated as often as her conventual duties permitted. There she pored over her accumulating volumes, attended to an extensive correspondence within and outside of the broad realm of Old Mexico, and wrote the verses so widely known in her time and that have since won enduring fame.

Her poetry is varied in meter and theme, including love lyrics that occasionally border on the erotic, tender Christmas carols, morality plays, allegorical pieces, and even secular three-act comedies like those performed in the public theaters of Spain and Spanish America. Much of this metrical expression abounded in literary conceits and was clothed in the ornate, florid, and obscure style of prevailing Baroque fashion. Unlike most verse of her contemporaries, however, subtle meaning and profound feeling often lay hidden in the intricate foliage of words and clever figures of speech. . . . Yet many of her sonnets and shorter lyric poems have an almost limpid clarity and an exquisite beauty that mark her as the supreme poet of her time in Castilian.

As time passes the appeal of this Creole nun-poetess increases and the circle of her admirers enlarges. It is not merely the esthetic merit of so much of her verse which brings her this homage — though she is often regarded . . . as among the greatest poets in the speech of Spain — but, perhaps even more, the complex personality refracted in many of her writings. Her more intimate and spontaneous expression offers glimpses so fleeting and elusive of the inner life of an extraordinary woman that they serve to pique the reader's curiosity rather than to satisfy it. In certain lines her intention seems illumined for a bare moment, like a flash of lightning in the night, only to be followed by an obscurity more impenetrable than before. Thus it is that the enigmatic quality of Sister Juana's verses, even more than the technical perfection of the best of them, inspires a veritable cult and wins for her an expanding audience. . . .

In the multiplying criticism of the life and work of the Mexican nun-poetess there is increasing agreement that her intellectual distinction exceeds her eminence as a poet, and that her preoccupation with ideas was greater than with artistic creation. Without minimizing the deeply emotional and feminine nature of Sister Juana, she was basically a rationalist with a passion for knowledge, and the processes of analysis were stronger and more obsessive than any other of her psyche. Her extraordinary gift as a lyric poet was ancillary to her acutely rational mentality, and her supreme aspiration was the freedom of her mind to roam untrammeled and unimpeded through every realm of thought. To read, to study, to experiment ". . . just to see if, by studying, I might grow less ignorant . . ." was the consuming desire of her existence. Since earliest childhood she had experienced this powerful yearning and later she had begged her mother to permit her to attend the University of Mexico disguised in male clothing. "What is indeed the truth," she wrote in her famous *Reply to Sister Philotea,* a letter of much autobiographical significance, "and which I do not deny (in the first place because it is well known to everyone, and in the second place because, though it may be to my detriment, Heaven has bestowed upon me the blessing of a very great love of truth), is that, ever since the first glimmer of reason struck me, this inclination to learning has been so urgent and powerful. . . ." In her young innocence she had desisted from eating cheese in the belief that such food would make her unpolished and uncouth, hence ". . . the desire to know was stronger in me than the desire to eat, even though the latter is so strong in children. . . ." This "inclination" triumphed over every other urge, including the sexual — for marriage she had a "total negation" she had declared — and she candidly confesses that her decision to take the veil — her only other choice — was largely influenced by the relatively freer opportunity it promised for study. The more solitary practices of the Carmelites had induced her, perhaps, to select that Order first. She had thought to escape the tyranny of what almost seemed a vice by dedicating herself as a bride of Christ, but ". . . poor, wretched me! I merely brought myself with me, together with my worst enemy, this inclination!" Instead of extinguishing this passion for reading and cogitation she found that, once subjected to her vows, this thirst for learning ". . . exploded like a charge of powder.". . .

In the medieval atmosphere of seventeenth century Mexico where women could not dream of independent lives, where it was axiomatic that they possessed inferior intelligence, and where they were scarcely more than chattels of their fathers, brothers, and husbands, intellectual curiosity in Sister Juana's sex was not only indecorous but sinful. It might, indeed, be the workings of the Evil One and, therefore, imperil one's salvation, as her superiors in the convent more than once assured her. Though there were learned women in history, any emulation of them by a nun was not without an attendant sense of guilt. Sister Juana herself had not escaped this feeling, for she wrote: ". . . I have prayed God to subdue the light of my intelligence, leaving me only enough to keep His law, for anything more (according to some persons) is superfluous in a woman." But, even in these despairing words, one seems to detect in a parenthetical phrase, in which the masculine form is used, a veiled rancor against the man-made world of her time. But her obvious intellectual distinction also aroused the jealousy and antipathy of her companions in the convent, and over the years this hostility developed in her a persecution complex. Her brilliant, inquiring mind seemed always a source of vexation. "If my intelligence is my own," she wrote in one of her poems, "why must I always find it so dull for my ease and so sharp for my hurt?"

This avid curiosity and desire for knowledge, so at odds with her time, place, and sex, seemed only to bring down upon her head the criticism and censure of those about her:

> Why, people, do you persecute me so?
> In what do I offend, when but inclined
> with worldly beauties to adorn my mind,
> and not my mind on beauty to bestow?
> I value not a treasure trove, nor wealth;
> the greater measure of content I find
> in placing riches only in my mind,
> than setting all my intellect on wealth.
> And I esteem not beauty, for, when past
> it is the spoils of age's cruelty;
> nor faithless riches carefully amassed.
> Far better nibble, it seems to me,
> at all life's vanities unto the last
> than to consume my life in vanity.[1]

And again in one of her ballads she asks bitterly why her fondness for truth must always bring her punishment. "If this fondness I have is licit and even an obligation, why should they chastise me because I do what I must?"

These protests, indicating a sensitiveness to sharp disapproval around her, recur so frequently as to suggest a more disturbed state of mind than would result from eminence in the accepted forms of learning of her time, even after due allowance is made for the fact that such pursuits were deemed unsuitable for a woman, and particularly one bound by vows of perpetual submission. This exaggerated feeling of persecution was possibly generated in part by a growing sense of guilt engendered by the *kind* of knowledge that she was seeking and by the *kind* of methods that she was using to acquire it. In short, her learning might appear more secular than ecclesiastical — "What a pity it is that so rich a mind should so debase itself in the petty matters of this world!" the Bishop of Puebla was to chide her — and her procedures more

---

[1] Translated by Pauline Cook in *The Pathless Crook* (Prairie City, Ill.: Decher Press, 1951). Reprinted by permission [Ed.].

experimental or scientific in the modern way than scholastic and philosophic. Even more reprehensible than mundane knowledge were the unorthodox means of seeking it. "Experimentation tugged at Sister Juana from earliest childhood," comments a student of her life. Here, then, is the possibility of a conflict, intellectual in origin which, given her environment, profession, and sex, would inevitably be spiritual and emotional as well. This inner discord, with its concomitant overtones of heresy and disobedience, could well produce a brooding conviction of guilt and thus, through anxiety, accentuate a feeling of persecution. . . .

It was Sister Juana's fate to have her being in this age when, even in Old Mexico, though ever so slightly, the long accepted and sole approach to truth was beginning to be threatened by a new way, a new method. Almost imperceptibly the traditional scholastic and authoritarian concepts of revealed knowledge were yielding to the more sensate procedures of scientific observation and analysis. In the Mexico City of her time there was greater awareness of this intellectual revolution than commonly believed, and the capital had a tiny group of savants who were abreast of contemporary thought, even that of non-Catholic Europe. The comparatively free circulation of nontheological books during the sixteenth and seventeenth centuries, the frequent presence in the viceroyalty of transient men of learning from the Old World, and the personal correspondence of local scholars with thinkers abroad, had all contributed to a more vital mental climate in the New World centers than the contemporary dominance of a medieval Church was thought to permit. A small number of Creole *sabios* were already familiar with the ideas and writings of Erasmus, Copernicus, Kepler, and particularly Descartes, whose philosophies they discussed among themselves in comparative freedom and even cited in their published writings.

Most conspicuous of this intelligentsia of New Spain was Don Carlos de Sigüenza y Góngora. He was a professor of mathematics in the University of Mexico, renowned for his studies of astronomy, archaeology, history and natural philosophy, and also an intimate friend of Sister Juana. Living at the Hospital del Amor de Dios where he served as chaplain, he was a frequent visitor at the Jeronymite convent a few blocks away where the nun-poetess had her cell. It appears that these two intellectually gifted and lonely people enjoyed long discussions together in the locutory of the convent. Sigüenza, a very minor poet, was encouraged in these exercises by Sister Juana, while she in turn received his stimulation and training in scientific disciplines. It is likely that she acquired the mathematical instruments and some of the books said to have furnished her cell as a result of this association. Indeed, the attainments of these two figures working together have moved a discerning critic to comment that they were ". . . the first ones (in Mexico) in whom the modern spirit appears or manifests itself." It was Sigüenza who most often brought visiting savants to her convent, including the great mission-founder of the American Southwest, Father Eusebio Francisco Kino. And it was he who initiated the exceedingly intelligent nun into the new methodology propounded by Descartes, of which there are faint indications in her verse. Doubtless it was he who understood her enthusiasm for, and encouraged her in, the performance of such simple experiments in physics as she mentions in her *Reply to Sister Philotea*. And it was he who shared her love for the dawning Age of Enlightenment of which they both were unconscious precursors in Mexico.

The inherent critical capacity of Sister Juana, coupled with omniverous reading, moved her to welcome a more pragmatic approach to truth. Latent in her mind was a healthy skepticism regarding the effectiveness of purely verbal rationalization, and her eager curiosity was insidiously drawn to experimentation and direct observation. A scrutiny of Sister Juana's verse and prose tends to support the conviction that she felt an instinctive distrust of the scholasticism dominating the intellectual life of viceregal Mexico. Her deeper regard for observation and a more scientific analysis seems apparent when, in the *Reply,* she emphasizes the importance of varied studies and methods in throwing light on speculative learning, particularly theology, and her underlying preference is revealed when she adds: ". . . and when the expositors are like an open hand and the ecclesiastics like a closed fist." Her reactions to the specious learning and rhetorical ratiocination around her, characterized chiefly by polemical disquisitions with ostentatious displays of classical quotations and cloudy verbosity, emerge clearly in the ballad beginning with the pathetic verse "Let us pretend that I am happy." The wordy debates of bookish pedants and charlatans of the so-called intelligentsia filling the air about her with their din move her to exclaim metrically: "Everything is opinions and of such varied counsels that what one proves is black, the other proves is white.". . .

In the *Reply* she comments, with veiled scorn, on the affectation that passed as learning in the excessive number of quotations from authorities: ". . . and I add that their education is perfected (if nonsense is perfection) by having studied a little Philosophy and Theology, and by having a smattering of languages, by which means one may be stupid in numerous subjects and languages because the mother tongue alone is not room enough for a really big fool." Mindful, likewise, of the self delusion facilitated by the verbalism of scholasticism, Sister Juana believed that everyone should keep within his own mental limitations. If this were so, she tartly exclaims: "How many warped intelligences wandering about there would not be!"

Perhaps the most penetrating stanza of this same ballad is the one in which she puts her finger on the core of true wisdom, the development of sound judgment: "To know how to make varied and subtle discourses is not knowledge; rather, knowledge simply consists of making the soundest choices.". . .

Thus it appears that Sister Juana found herself not only torn between "reason" and "passion," but also between *two methodologies of reason.* The time-honored dialectics and syllogisms of scholasticism were still entrenched as the accepted means of rationalization in the Church of Christ which held her in its protective arms and to which she was irrevocably bound by vows. This great institution sheltered and loved her, and obedience to its authority and ways was her ineludible obligation. Yet, deep within, she could not reciprocate its love. Instead, she seemed possessed by a way of thinking that threatened to undermine the assumptions on which the Faith rested. On the true object of her affections, the new concept of experimentalism relying on the senses rather than on authority, her benevolent guardian, the Church, severely frowned. Such intellectual exercise might well be inimical to the divine science of theology, and it was potentially, if not actually, heretical. Adherence to such thinking could seriously jeopardize her eternal salvation, which was infinitely precious to her. In her religious play, *The Divine Narcissus,* she wrote: "Behold that what I yearn for I am powerless to enjoy, and in my anxious longing to possess it, I suffer mortal pangs.". . . But convent-bound in the medieval atmosphere of the ecclesiastical society of Mexico City she could only feel at war with it and with herself. The love and kindliness implicit in the Church's paternalism claimed her gratitude and, of course, her vows compelled obedience to it. Yet the persistent longing for a freer expression of her intuition and for another and more open avenue to truth and to God prevented complete reciprocation and submission. . . .

As the dawn of April 17, 1695 was casting a wan light over the troubled City of Mexico the wracked and broken spirit of Sister Juana quietly claimed its longed-for release from the prison of her aloneness. "See how death eludes me because I desire it," she had exclaimed in one of her poems, "for even death, when it is in demand," she had added, "will rise in price." Over the long years of her short life she had struggled against the viselike prejudices and incomprehension of her time and place. She had dreamed of a liberation from the shackles of static traditions and stultifying conventions. She had dared to rebuke the men of her society for their double standard of morality and had thus struck a first blow for women's rights.

> Which has the greater sin when burned
> by the same lawless fever:
> She who is amorously deceived,
> or he, the sly deceiver?

Or which deserves the sterner blame,
though each will be a sinner:
She who becomes a whore for pay,
Or he who pays to win her? [2]

But more than all else she had struggled for a freedom of thought for all. "There is nothing freer than the human mind," she had proclaimed to a world that could not comprehend these words, or could only hear them as subversive of a God-given truth. Against her the odds were too great and their relentless pressure brought at last a total renunciation of all effort and a complete submission of her intellect. The passionate woman in her capitulated to the devout nun and this surrender left her bereft of life. Physically she survived herself briefly.

To the unhappy nun-poetess during the last four of five years of her existence the world outside must have seemed a projection of her own inner turmoil and affliction. A series of disasters and phenomena were then plaguing the city and its environs, bringing suffering, fear and violence. Heavy rains in 1691 brought successively ruinous floods, crop destruction, famine, and pestilence, while a total eclipse of the sun stirred panic fear. Sullen discontent and mounting tensions erupted into mass riots that nearly toppled Spanish authority in the land. As these sinister events darkened the world without, the storm, so long brewing within Sister Juana Inés, broke.

In 1690 she inadvertently brought to a head the disapproval and hostility of her religious associates slowly gathering over the years. In some way she was induced to write a successful rebuttal of certain views set forth long before in a sermon by a famous Portuguese Jesuit, Father Vieira. Her skill in manipulating the methods of neo-scholasticism evidently pleased the Bishop of Puebla who took it upon himself to publish her paper. At the same time, in the guise of "Sister Philotea," he wrote her a letter chiding her alleged neglect of religious literature and her fondness for profane letters. "You have spent a lot of time studying (secular) philosophers and poets, and now it would seem reasonable to apply yourself to better things and to better books." Clearly, this was a reproof from a superior high in the hierarchy and it could not fail to distress a nun tormented by guilt feelings. Through months of declining health she brooded on a reply to the Bishop's censure. Finally, under date of March 1, 1691, it took form in her famous *Reply* in which, with many autobiographical details and with alternate humility and boldness, she defended herself from the prelate's strictures.

Obscure complications followed this epistolary exchange, chief of which

[2] Robert Graves, trans., "Against the Inconsequences of Men's Desires . . ." *Encounter*, no. 3 (December 1953). Reprinted by permission of Robert Graves [Ed.].

was the withdrawal of her confessor, Father Antonio Núñez de Miranda, who had influenced her decision to enter the convent and had counseled her over the years. Vainly he had urged her to turn from what he considered worldly matters and apply her great talents to things eternal. All her devoted supporters, it seemed to her, were falling away through absence, desertion, or death. And she had never enjoyed the favor of the misogynistic Archbishop Aguiar y Seijas, who had involved her in his frenzied almsgiving. In 1693, as if to remind everyone of her worldliness, a second edition of a volume of her poems, which the vicereine, her friend and patroness, had extracted from her, appeared in Spain, and copies doubtless reached Mexico City soon after. This intended kindness may have hastened her final surrender. On February 8, 1694, using blood from her veins as ink, she indited an abject reaffirmation of her faith and renewed her vows, which she signed: "I, Sister Juana Inés de la Cruz, the worst in the world." She renounced all her possessions, the gifts and trinkets of her admirers, the mathematical and musical instruments that she had so long studied and used, and — the most painful wrench of all — those silent and precious companions of her cell, her beloved books. All were sold and the proceeds given to charity. With this bitter deprivation, she gave herself to excessive acts of penance, self-flagellation, and mortification of the flesh. The coveted death of the body came at last during her tireless ministrations to sisters of her community decimated by a pestilence sweeping the city. . . .

20. *Alonso de Sandoval, the First Advocate of Black Studies in America*

NORMAN MEIKLEJOHN

Liberty for the Indians was strongly advocated from the time of Las Casas, but no such powerful voice was raised against the enslaving of Negroes in Africa and their dispatch to the colonists in Latin America. Las Casas once even recommended Negro slavery, in the hope of saving his beloved Indians, but he later recanted and declared that it was as unjust to enslave Negroes as Indians, "and for the same reasons." Another Dominican, Tomás de Mercado, condemned the West African slave trade in his *Tratos y Contratos* (1569), and a Portuguese Jesuit argued in a 1608 manuscript memorial that the law against Amerindian slavery should be extended to include Negroes. Nothing happened.

Another Jesuit, the Spaniard Alonso de Sandoval, also denounced the Negro slave trade in his rare treatise *De instauranda Aethiopum* (Seville, 1627). As Professor Charles R. Boxer states:

Sandoval, though with obvious reluctance, admitted the validity of Negro slavery under the conditions stipulated by canon and civil law. He also admitted that the Amerindian in his natural state was born free, and consequently felt himself to be such, whereas the Negro was used to servitude in his native habitat. Having said this, he then proceeded to denounce the Negro slave-trade even more violently than had Tomás de Mercado. He argued that Negroes were just as human as were any of the other races of mankind, although they were more shamefully abused than any, and that in the eyes of God a Negro's soul was worth just as much as that of a white man. Far from finding them bestial and unruly savages, as many slave-owners and dealers claimed that they were, he praises their candid and tractable character, providing his points with a wealth of anecdote from his own experience as rector of the Jesuit college at Cartagena de Indias.

Sandoval denounces the sophistries and abuses of the slave-traders, even going so far as to advise that they should be refused the sacraments, if they do not mend their ways. He points out that the internecine tribal wars in Africa had greatly increased as a result of the European demand for slaves, and that slaves obtained in this way could not be regarded as having been taken in a "just war." Contrary to what many modern apologists for the slave system assert, he states emphatically that most slave-owners made no efforts to look after their slaves, or to treat them as valuable property which was difficult to replace; but on the contrary the owners and planters treated their Negroes with callous and calculated brutality, careless if they died as a result of it.*

Reverend Norman Meiklejohn, A.A., of Assumption College in Worcester, Massachusetts, prepared his doctoral dissertation at Columbia University on Negro slavery in Nueva Granada. The following selection comes from this dissertation. Some day we should have an English translation of Sandoval's notable treatise. It is full of unusual detail; Professor Boxer states: "Sandoval gives a very interesting description of the tribal markings of the Guinea and Angola slaves, so that the tribes and districts from which they came could be better identified. I believe this to be the first time that such a classification was attempted, or at any rate printed." † But enough is known now to salute Sandoval for his recognition of the cultural diversity of the Negroes and the need to study their languages and customs so as better to evangelize them.

Later on, another Spanish Jesuit in Peru, Diego de Avendaño, became convinced that Negro slavery was just as wrong as Indian slavery and in his two-volume *Thesaurus Indicus* (Amberes, 1668) called for another royal

* Charles R. Boxer, *Salvador de Sá and the Struggle for Brazil and Angola, 1602–1686* (London: The Athlone Press, University of London, 1952), pp. 237–238.
† Ibid., p. 238, note 35.

investigation similar to that which provoked the disputation in 1550 between Sepúlveda and Las Casas, whose doctrine Avendaño largely was following. Nothing happened. The Spanish crown did establish in Spain in 1683 a royal commission to examine the legitimacy of African Negro enslavements and of the slave trade. The commission, on the basis of age-old custom, the toleration of these practices by the papacy and the clergy, and the economic advantage to the crown from Negro slavery, concluded that the king should entertain no scruples concerning legitimacy.

Alonso de Sandoval, the remarkable apostle to the Negroes, was born in 1576 in Seville, while his parents were en route to the Indies. Educated by the Jesuits in Lima, Peru, he entered the Jesuit Order in 1593 and was ordained a priest circa 1600. In 1604, he volunteered for service in the newly established Jesuit vice-province of Nueva Granada, and in 1605 he began to work in the Jesuit college in Cartagena. His duties there, like those of the other members of the college community, were wide-ranging. They included teaching, ministering to the spiritual needs of the white, Negro, and Indian populations, and making missionary field trips to outlying settlements along the Caribbean coast and inland. For a number of years, Sandoval served as procurator of the Cartagena community, and from 1624 to 1627 he held the post of rector of the college. Dynamic, energetic, and aggressive, Sandoval could be sharp in tongue and harsh in manner. As an administrator, his unorthodox methods earned him a rebuke from his Superior General and made him ineligible to receive the highest honors which the Order bestowed upon its most outstanding members.

Like his fellow Jesuits on the staff of the college, Sandoval ministered to the Negro slaves. But unlike them, he experienced a strong sense of mission to Christianize them. A possible explanation for this sense of mission to the Negro may be Sandoval's background in Lima.

In 1607, Martín de Funes, Procurator of the Jesuits in Nueva Granada, presented a report on the Negro slaves to the Superior General, Father Aquaviva. In this report, the physical and spiritual situation of the Negro slaves in Nueva Granada was described as utterly miserable, and the Jesuits there requested permission to assume the responsibility of serving as their *doctrineros*. Shortly afterward, the General entrusted the major responsibility for the Negro ministry of Cartagena to Sandoval. On the strength of this assignment, Sandoval later took pride in calling himself the Father of the Slaves.

From "The Observance of Negro Slave Legislation in Colonial Nueva Granada" by Norman Meiklejohn (Ph.D. dissertation, Columbia University, 1968), pp. 264–284, passim. Printed by permission of the author.

Already, in 1610, the Negro slave population of Cartagena numbered in the thousands. There were more than 5,000 residing on the surrounding estancias alone. To these numbers must be added the yearly transient population of 2,000 to 4,000 slaves who arrived fresh from Africa and who remained in Cartagena while waiting to be sold locally or to be shipped to other ports. If the spiritual destitution of the Negro slaves of Cartagena had sparked the zeal of Sandoval, the utter misery of the Negro slave cargoes set him ablaze. Many were ill with contagious diseases; some were on the point of death. All were hungry, thirsty, exhausted, and practically naked. Many entertained fantastic fears as to the dire fate which awaited them.

Sandoval made it a practice, on receiving news of the arrival of a slave ship, to hasten to the port and board the ship. There he proffered drinking water (especially to the infants), and then sought out the dying to prepare them for their final journey. Once the slave cargo had been unloaded and deposited in warehouses, Sandoval went among the slaves offering them a measure of relief and consolation, and trying to identify them as to language and tribe. Then, having called those of his Cartagena slave acquaintances who had knowledge of the languages of the newly arrived slaves to serve as interpreters, he set about examining the new arrivals in order to verify their baptism. Those who had been baptized he helped to prepare to receive the sacraments. Those who had not been baptized, or whose baptism seemed doubtfully valid, he catechized and then baptized. To all he gave words of encouragement regarding their future as slaves.

The preoccupation of Sandoval with the baptism of slaves was not merely juridical; i.e., seeing to it that all African immigrants had been baptized in accordance with the law. Rather it was apostolic. As a minister of the gospel, he considered baptism a matter of paramount importance. On their baptism depended the slaves' eternal salvation or their eternal perdition. Until Sandoval began to look into the matter of slave baptisms, the presumption had been that all Negro slaves arriving in Cartagena had been baptized in Africa. No one in Cartagena had checked into the matter, any more than had any of the priests and masters in various parts of Spanish America among whom the slaves spent the remainder of their days.

What was Sandoval's dismay when his inquiries began to reveal that many of the slaves had never been baptized, and that the baptism of an even greater number had been invalidly performed? This meant that many slaves were going through life being treated as Catholics and receiving the sacraments when in reality they were pagan. Those slaves who had to continue their voyage by land or sea were in danger of loss of life. If by chance they had not been baptized, or their baptism was invalid, those who died were, in the mind of the sixteenth-century Catholic, doomed to hell fire.

Proceeding cautiously and methodically, Sandoval looked more closely into the matter. He continued to question arriving slaves concerning the details of their baptism. He questioned the masters of slave ships, asking them what they knew of baptismal procedures at the African ports; he also wrote to priests stationed in African slave ports. His most pessimistic suspicions were verified. He found that, although some efforts had been made to correct abuses in Luanda, many baptisms were invalidly performed there, and even more so at Cabo Verde and the river ports in Guinea. The sacrament was being given mechanically and without concern for those circumstances necessary for an adult baptism to be valid. That is, the receiver of the sacrament had to know what the sacrament meant. He had to want to receive it. And the water had to touch his scalp. Sandoval learned that before sailing to America the slaves were assembled on the docks to hear a priest give a short harangue in Portuguese. Then, without making any further attempt to explain to the slaves the significance of what he was about to do, or to ask them if they wished to receive baptism, the priest sprinkled them with water and pronounced the words of baptism. . . .

Deeply concerned over this neglect in such an important matter as baptism, Sandoval submitted his findings to the Archbishop of Seville. Seville was the only Spanish port trading with both Africa and America, and many slave traders and investors resided there. It was also the port of entry for African slaves into Spain and contained a large Negro population. The prelate had his Negro faithful examined by a committee of theologians. Their conclusions agreed with those of Sandoval. Thereupon, besides sending a report to the Holy See, which apparently took no action, the Archbishop decreed that in his diocese the entire Negro population of 30,000 should be assiduously examined with regard to the validity of their baptism. The procedure which he ordered for this examination was the one proposed by Sandoval.

The work undertaken by Sandoval to examine the baptismal credentials of every slave who arrived in Cartagena was monumental. It meant that Sandoval and his assistants would have to examine the entire slave and free Negro population of Cartagena and its surroundings, as well as the many Indians whose baptism had been equally invalid because of lack of understanding and consent on their part. It meant that they would have to examine individually the thousands of Negro slaves arriving in Cartagena annually. Since, in Sandoval's estimation, any one of seventy different languages and dialects were apt to be spoken by the incoming slaves, he had to secure interpreters for all those languages. This entailed first of all identifying the slave's tribe according to his physical appearance, traits, scarifications. Then he had to identify a slave's language. After this had been done, he had to check his list of interpreters, find the proper ones, and obtain the loan of their services from their masters. It also meant working for hours on end through interpreters who were often tired, and who found the work distasteful because many of the slaves were diseased. Some time after the publication of his treatise, Sandoval's superiors were persuaded to buy seven slaves whose principal role was to serve as interpreters for Father Sandoval and his principal assistant, Father Peter Claver.

Once the interpreter was on hand, Sandoval proceeded to pose all sorts of technical questions regarding their baptism to men and women who were of an entirely different culture and at a very different level of sophistication. All this was done in the tropical heat of Cartagena, amid the human stench of the slave ships or slave depots. Once the unbaptized, the doubtfully baptized, and the invalidly baptized had been identified and set apart, there followed a lengthy instruction on the basic teachings of the Church and on the meaning of baptism. . . .

In spite of his noble intentions, and the correctness of his methods, Sandoval met with criticism and resistance. Some clerics resented the intervention of a friar into what they considered their exclusive preserve. This of course was only one of many instances of clashes in the colonies between order priests and the diocesan clergy. The latter had official jurisdiction over the faithful, whereas order priests could minister to them only as a result of privileges extended to them by the Holy See and approved by the Crown. The diocesan clergy were scandalized that Sandoval should baptize slaves in a warehouse; they insisted that, according to regulations, the ceremony should be performed in church with all the customary solemnity. To this objection, Sandoval responded that there was no way of knowing who among the slaves would stay long enough in Cartagena to be able to receive baptism in the church. Rather than risk the possibility of their departure before being baptized, it was safer to perform the rite as quickly as possible. Besides, he added, clergymen did not permit the invasion of their churches by filthy naked slaves. On the contrary, they considered it an affront to the house of God and to the dignity of the sacrament being administered. The objection regarding jurisdiction was more serious since it was made by the Bishop's Council and added the further charge that the Jesuits were deriving financial profit from their endeavor. The matter was taken to court and a legal suit followed between the Jesuits on the one hand and the Archbishop of Cartagena and his Council on the other. The Jesuits not only won their case in court; they also won the admiration of the plaintiffs as well. They did this by having the clerics accompany them for a routine day of work among the shipboard and warehouse slaves.

A further source of resistance was the slaves themselves. Many had been living as Catholics; to admit that they might have been pagans all along was a humiliation they could not bear. Thus, some of them did not cooperate with the examining priests who sought to ascertain if their baptism had been valid or not. Others suspected that their baptism had not been valid, but postponed admitting it to the priests out of shame. Another difficulty arose when the slaves who had been baptized on the ships and in the warehouses discovered that there was a more solemn form of baptism. Envious of those slaves who had been solemnly baptized in the church, they tended to conclude that their original baptism had not been valid and they sought to be baptized anew in a church ceremony.

For Sandoval it was not enough that the Negro slaves were baptized. He also wanted them to share fully with their masters the privileges of the Christian life. To this end he strove to persuade them to confess their sins and receive Holy Communion a few times a year. . . .

Success in his undertaking to have slaves share in the fullness of the Church's sacramental life depended to a great extent on the master's cooperation in facilitating the slave's recourse to the confessional and to Communion. While admitting that some masters cooperated in this, Sandoval complained gloomily that others took all sorts of devious means to impede the further catechesis of their slaves and especially their reception of the sacraments other than baptism.

Some motives for this reticence were mentioned at the beginning of this chapter. An additional motive, which might have been a mere pretext on the part of some, was the contention that Negroes, like Indians, were incapable of comprehending the Christian religion. As we have seen, many priests completely neglected their spiritual ministry to the Negroes, allegedly for that reason. No arguments, nor papal bulls could eradicate their prejudices. The priests, even the missionaries, tended to attribute to the stupidity of the Negroes what was really poor pedagogy on their part. Besides entertaining the notion that they could evangelize Indians or Negroes in a language that these latter could barely understand, if at all, they explained Christian doctrine in scholastic terms. They made little or no effort to adapt their teaching to the native capacity, the culture, and the language patterns of the Negroes. Furthermore, the priests were more comfortable with their prejudices, for the serious and thorough Christianization of the slaves would have required considerable work. The conviction that the Negroes were incapable of anything beyond baptism freed them from any obligation to further ministry.

If this reluctance was true of confessions and Communion, it was even more true of the sacrament of Extreme Unction, the ministering of which would often have entailed going about at night, bringing the viaticum and the holy oils to dying slaves in squalid and repugnant surroundings. In the same spirit, masters who were convinced of their slaves' limited capacity for Christian living did not bother to call the priest when their slaves were dying. Even if the priest came, Sandoval tells us, some masters pretended that none of their slaves was ill. Sandoval was forced to rely on doctors to inform him when slaves were in serious danger of death.

It is no wonder that, faced with the monumental task we have just described, Sandoval required assistance. Apparently he was never given more than one assistant at a time; the one who assisted him longest was Peter Claver. Less dynamic than Sandoval, Peter Claver was a humble lover and servant of the poor. Sandoval exhausted himself for the spiritual profit of the slaves. Yet he was never able to forget the slaves' crudeness, their ignorance, their dirtiness, and their smell. Throughout his treatise his disdain for the Negro slaves shows through. In his later years he even admitted to Claver that news of an arriving slave ship made him break into a cold sweat, so revolting to his nature were the conditions under which he would once again exercise his apostolic ministry. At opposite poles was Claver, who had the advantage of a mild temperament, a profound humility, an authentic affection and love for the poor, and an acquired indifference to filth and stench and festering sores. Different as they were, these two Jesuits, in a period of fifty years, affected the lives of 300,000 Negro slaves who either passed through the port of Cartagena or lived in that city, its surroundings, and in settlements along the coast and inland. There is no calculating the untold thousands of Negro slaves who received better treatment as a result of the heroic example of Sandoval and Claver.

But Sandoval was not content with the work he was doing directly with the bozales in the Port of Cartagena. He dreamed of making authentic Christians of all the Negro slaves in the Spanish empire. This he would do by writing a treatise on the subject and addressing it to the members of the Company of Ignatius Loyola. His treatise would be both a clarion call to all Jesuits to bring Christ to the most abandoned of God's children, the Negro slaves, and a handbook on methods appropriate to that end. The treatise, which was finished by 1620, represented the fruit of fifteen years of experience as well as of extensive research. Though Sandoval was successful in having it published in 1627, he continued to improve it and the first volume of an expanded second edition was published in 1647. The second volume of the expanded edition never appeared.

One finds in Sandoval's treatise much material of considerable interest, not only on the subject of Negro slaves and the Church, but on the seventeenth-century mind and on the state of knowledge of geography, anthropology, and natural science in that century. Sandoval's geography is imperfect; his anthropology is a compendium of information on Africans and Asians that could be found in contemporary sources, enriched by first-hand observation of Negroes in Cartagena. The treatise also speculates on the causes of monsters, of Negroid characteristics, and of the incidence of albinos.

In Part One of his treatise Sandoval examined Negro peoples and their customs, and various aspects of the slave trade. He considered the various groups of negroid peoples and described their location, social organization, religion, customs, and practices. Because the Negroes living in the area between Cabo Verde and Angola constituted the bulk of the Negro population brought to Nueva Granada, Sandoval described their coloring, physical characteristics, tatoos and scarifications, natural disposition, and religious attitudes.

On the basis of a study of contemporary theologians and his own investigations, Sandoval was convinced that much of the slave trade was immoral, but he accepted the opinion of the Jesuit school that purchasers in America could buy slaves in perfect good faith. The important thing for Sandoval, however, was not to complain of slavery but rather to labor to improve the lot of the slaves. He described the slaves' departure from Africa, the "middle passage," their condition as they arrived in Cartagena, and the treatment they received in the depots and slave market.

Part Two of the treatise contains descriptions of the life of slaves in Nueva Granada and of the ministry to Negro slaves. The Negro slaves suffered greatly at the hands of their masters. Indeed, some masters treated their animals better than they treated their slaves. Nevertheless, Sandoval conceded, some masters did treat their slaves well. Slaves were also made to suffer spiritually as their masters neglected their spiritual needs and opposed their full participation in church life. As a result, Sandoval claimed, slaves lived like brutes and appeared incapable of living like civilized Christians. Sandoval further accused masters of favoring concubinage and prostitution, and of seeking to prevent marriages, of making the conjugal state undesirable by restricting a married slave's movements and by separating children from their parents. Nonetheless, Sandoval encouraged the slaves to obey their masters in the spirit of the gospels. He also encouraged masters to treat their slaves with paternal care, giving them what they needed, correcting them with charity, and bearing with them patiently.

In concluding Part Two Sandoval told his Jesuit readers that the Negro ministry was an excellent school for the acquisition of holiness through the practice of all the virtues. It offered numberless occasions for exercising the corporal and spiritual works of mercy.

In the third part of his treatise, Sandoval presented his method for evangelizing the Negro slaves. This method, which we considered earlier, can be summarized in a few key phrases. The missioner should always take the initiative in seeking out slaves. He should prepare and use wisely his own corps of interpreters, and use simple language in teaching Christian doctrine. He should always check the validity of the baptism of the slaves he attends, foster frequent reception of sacraments, and the observance of the Church's precepts. . . .

Miners at Work in the Mountain of Silver in Potosí. From the time of its discovery in 1545, this mining community — The Imperial Town of Potosí, as it came to be called — attracted much attention. The conquistador Pedro Cieza de León first published in 1553 a sketch of the mountain high in the Andes which became one of the greatest silver centers in the world, and not long after a Turkish scholar reproduced this sketch to astonish his readers in far-off Constantinople. Potosí was also located on early Chinese maps.

The present engraving comes from the indefatigable Theodore de Bry (1528–1598), the Flemish artist and printer whose work has been widely used. He never went to America, so that his engravings reflect what he had been able to learn from the printed material available.

SECTION V

The Development of Society

THE POSITION OF WOMEN

The history of the women of Latin America has not yet been written or even attempted, though there is rich documentation on the subject. Apparently historians have considered women scarcely worth writing about. They were convinced that very few Iberian women went to the New World, the conquistadors mated with the Indian women to produce a mixed race, so what more was there to say? Then Richard Konetzke, the distinguished German historian who revived Latin American studies at the University of Cologne after World War II, demonstrated that there was a great deal more that could and should be said. Though few women went to America in the early, rough days of conquest, the Crown steadfastly encouraged women to migrate in order to establish a sound Spanish society. A permanent society would not develop without women to establish stable homes, and matrimony was favored in every way the Crown could think of.[1]

Professor James Lockhart has illustrated how sound were these views by publishing a pioneer work on the social history of Peru that is bound to have a powerful influence in turning the attention of students to the rich possibilities of the field. The selection on the second generation of women in Peru shows his methods and their exciting results (Reading 21). Brazilian women are even less known, but Dr. A. J. R. Russell-Wood turned up in his researches on the Misericórdia (Brotherhood) of Bahia much valuable information on dowries for women, which also reveals much of their position in colonial society (Reading 22).

[1] Richard Konetzke, "La emigración de mujeres españolas a América durante la época colonial," *Revista Internacional de Sociología* (Madrid), 3 (1945), pp. 123–150.

BIOGRAPHICAL SOURCES

One of the noticeable deficiencies of our present documentation is that so much of it is limited to official or legal sources. Some material on the life of merchants is coming to light, which should greatly enlarge our understanding because business played such a large role.[2] And at long last, private letters on family affairs are being printed to reveal more intimate aspects of colonial life.[3] But much more can and should be done to widen the documentary base.

Another important initiative has been the demonstration by Professor Lockhart of the value of biographical sources; indeed, he has stimulated the present experiment in this section to provide a variety of sources on the lives of Spaniards in America that constitute the raw material for social history. Some of these sources are statements drawn up by individuals to convince the government that they merited preferment or position, while others are remarkable vignettes carved by Professor Lockhart out of the solid rock of archival collections to tell the story of the "Men of Cajamarca," that blue-ribbon group of men who captured Atahualpa in Cajamarca on November 16, 1532. Sometime we may have an adequate biographical dictionary, whose need was recognized long ago by Marcos Jiménez de la Espada. He planned to produce such a work, but never achieved it.[4]

[2] Guillermo Lohmann Villena, *Les Espinosa: Une famille d'hommes d'affaires en Espagne et aux Indies à l'époque de la colonisation* (Paris: École Pratiques des Hautes Études, 1968); Enrique Otte, "Mercaderes burgaleses en los indicios del comercio con México," *Historia Mexicana,* 18 (1968), pp. 108–144, 258–285; "Los mercaderes vascos y los Pizarro: cartas inéditas de Gonzalo y Hernando Pizarro y su mayordomo Diego Martín," *Travaux de l'Institut d'Études Latino-Américaines de l'Université de Strasbourg,* 6 (1966), pp. 25–42; and "Mercaderes vascos en Tierra Firme a raiz del descubrimiento del Perú," *Mercurio Peruano,* nos. 443–444 (1964) (Libro Jubilar de Víctor Andrés Belaúnde), pp. 81–89.

[3] Professor Enrique Otte of the Free University of Berlin has started to publish family letters that he discovered during his long experience in the Archive of the Indies. As samples, see his "Nueve cartas de Diego de Ordás," *Historia Mexicana,* 14 (1964), pp. 102–129, 321–338; "Cartas privadas de Puebla del siglo XVI," *Jahrbuch für Geschichte von Staat Wirtschaft und Gesellschaft lateinamerikas,* 3 (Cologne, 1960), pp. 10–87; "Semblanza espiritual del poblador de Indias (siglos XVI y XVII)," *Verhandlungen des XXXVIII: Internationalen Amerikanistenkongresses,* 3 (Munich, 1970), pp. 441–449; and "La Nueva España en 1529," *Historia y sociedad en el mundo de habla española: Homenaje a José Miranda* (Mexico: El Colegio de México, 1971), pp. 95–111.

[4] Marcos Jiménez de la Espada, *Relaciones Geográficas de Indias: Peru,* 1 (Madrid, 1965), p. xxxix.

TENSIONS IN COLONIAL LIFE

The colonial centuries have often been presented as a quiet, even dull time when nothing much happened. This was largely due to the ignorance of historians, for we now know that it was a time of tensions. In Brazil, there was civil war in the mining camps, while in Mexico the relatively small number of Negro slaves nevertheless caused much concern because of their revolts. Riots resulting from economic problems sometimes occurred in Mexico City (Reading 23). Moreover, in Mexico the native-born Spaniards lost out to the men from the mother country, which led to widespread frustration (Reading 24), and in Peru rivalry between friars from Spain and those born in Peru led to bloodshed and a continuing bitterness (Reading 25). The loud cries of anguish by the *criollos* on discrimination against them may have been somewhat exaggerated, at least in Peru. A recent study shows that the judges of the Audiencia of Lima were predominantly creoles: "The creole aristocrats in Peru were no powerless political ingenues. Rather they had built up an extremely strong position combining local wealth and social prominence with high administrative and judicial position." [5] Tensions existed among all sections of society in the booming mining camp, at the Villa Imperial de Potosí, for this mountain of silver in the high Andes exemplified in gaudy colors the passion for wealth that drew many Spaniards to the New World (Reading 26).

INDIAN MOBILITY

Another element in the varied pattern of emerging society was the Indians. Some few were able to enter Spanish society, at least to some extent, while others were able to increase their wealth and power by taking advantage of the opportunities offered by the economic and administrative structure introduced by the Spaniards. So there was some mobility, at least for the men.

COLONIAL SOCIETY NOT MONOLITHIC

All of these readings tend to reinforce the idea that Iberian colonial society varied from region to region, and from century to century. We have no volume

[5] Leon G. Campbell, "A Colonial Establishment: Creole Domination of the Audiencia of Lima During the Late Eighteenth Century," *Hispanic American Historical Review,* 52 (1972), p. 20. Professor Campbell supports his interpretation with biographic sources. See his "Survey of Career, Data, Connections, and Property of the Judges of the Audiencia of Lima, 1777," ibid., pp. 21–25.

as yet comparable to Eileen Powers's *Medieval People* or S. E. Morison's *Builders of the Bay Colony*. Eventually our historians will go beyond lapidary phrases, if they follow the lead of Konetzke, Lockhart, and others. Magnus Mörner has already provided a realistic view of the eighteenth-century ruler Pombal's support for marriages in Brazil of Portuguese settlers with Indians.[6] He struck off a splendid phrase: "His Majesty does not distinguish between his vassals by their color but by their merits." But this "liberal" policy toward Indians was deeply rooted in political objectives including his relentless struggle against the Jesuits, whom he expelled in 1767, and it did not extend to Negroes in Brazil.

Similarly we probably will have to free ourselves of such easy generalizations as the famous one by Cervantes, who failed to get the job in America that he had hoped for but felt he knew enough to describe the people there in this fashion: "The refuge and haven of all the poor devils of Spain, the sanctuary of the bankrupt, the safeguard of murderers, the way out for gamblers, the pomised land for ladies of easy virtue, and a lure and disillusionment for the many, and a personal remedy for the very few." [7]

[6] Magnus Mörner, *Race Mixture in the History of Latin America* (Boston: Little, Brown and Company, 1967), pp. 50–51.

[7] As quoted by Charles R. Boxer, *Race Relations in the Portuguese Colonial Empire, 1415–1825* (Oxford: Clarendon Press, 1963), p. 86.

21. *Spanish Women of the Second Generation in Peru*

JAMES LOCKHART

Professor James Lockhart of the University of California, Los Angeles, created a social history of early Peru by mining systematically the rich notarial records there. His monograph on *Spanish Peru, 1532–1560* was a pioneering volume that revealed how promptly and how strongly Spaniards developed a stable society in Peru.

Spanish women constituted a large minority of the settlers in Peru in the conquest period, and their significance was even greater than their numbers, for although women from home were not numerous enough to give every Spaniard a wife, they sufficed to keep Spanish Peru from being truly a society without women. The analysis Gilberto Freyre made of Brazilian society, that in the absence of European women, Indian women largely determined early Brazilian culture insofar as it had to do with the household, cannot be applied to Peru. While Indian influence was important, both immediately and over time, Peru even in the first generation had enough Spanish women to preclude the simple loss of any important culture elements.

Nevertheless, assessing the role of Spanish women in conquest Peru is a delicate task. In view of the old tradition among historians of ignoring them, the cultural and biological contribution of Spanish women to the building of a European society in Peru requires emphasis. Spanish women were commonly present at almost all times and places during the early occupation of Peru, and therefore cannot be considered a rarity. On the other hand, there can be no doubt that in Spanish Peruvian society, as in any new community, women were greatly outnumbered by men. Tabulations for the Indies as a whole, based on the *Pasajeros a Indias,* have indicated a ratio of about ten to one. As suggested by Richard Konetzke, however, the actual proportion of women in the Indies must have been higher than it had been at emigration, because of the higher mortality among men. For Peru this was a factor of more than usual significance, with the major Indian rebellion, twenty years of civil wars, and innumerable expeditions of discovery into surrounding jungle areas.

A list of Spanish and apparently Spanish women in Peru during the period

From *Spanish Peru, 1532–1560* by James Lockhart (Madison: University of Wisconsin Press, © 1968 by the Regents of the University of Wisconsin), pp. 150–169, passim. Reprinted by permission.

169

of 1532–60, assembled from all sources used for the present study, reached a total of 550, but this figure is even more ambiguous raw material for arriving at an overall estimate than was the similar list of artisans, since women had little occasion to appear in notarial and official records. Therefore, it is reasonable to think that the list of 550 women, brought together from the same archival sources as the more than 800 artisans, is a much smaller fraction of the total than in the latter case; but there is no firm basis for even the rudest approximation of a statistical estimate.

A second element of uncertainty in the listing is the quite broad interpretation Spaniards were willing to give to the concept of a Spanish woman. Women were identified in legal records only as to their marital status, but Spanish women were recognizable as not being specifically called Negro, Indian, or mestizo. The Spanish secretaries were very consistent in specifying Negro and Indian women; with mestizo women, particularly daughters of prominent Spaniards, they were somewhat less so, but this group did not become important until the late 1550's. There was, however, hesitance and inconsistency, both in fact and in the matter of their explicit identification in documents, when it came to two groups who were in the process of being absorbed among the ordinary Castilian women: the *moriscas* and certain light-skinned, Spanish-speaking mulatto women. The moriscas, slave women of Muslim descent, were for the most part Caucasian, Spanish-born, and converted to Christianity, and they spoke Spanish as a native language. Fully acculturated mulatto women were also usually born in Spain or an older colony. Slave-mistresses of both types often obtained their freedom, and married Spaniards or in other ways took their places among the ranks of Spanish women, which they might well do, considering their birthplace. It is particularly hard to find reasons to deny full status as Spanish women to the moriscas who were simply undergoing a process familiar for centuries in Spain's Christian reconquest.

At any rate, one must keep in mind that Spanish women included a minority of moriscas and mulatto women with, after 1555, the addition of some mestizo women. To define the size of the minority is statistically impossible, but it can hardly have been more than a tenth of all ostensibly Spanish women. To make a rough commonsense estimate, then, of the statistical importance of Spanish women, including the women from ethnic minority groups who were accepted as Spanish, and taking into consideration the *Pasajeros a Indias,* Konetzke, and the implications of the list made for the present study, it appears probable that from the early 1540's on, Peru had one Spanish woman for every seven or eight men, in absolute numbers perhaps three or four hundred women by 1543 and a thousand by 1555.

Few Spanish women, except moriscas, took part in the actual conquest of

Peru in the years 1532–35, but followed close behind the fighting. . . . The number of Spanish women would seem to have grown quite steadily until 1548, when, with the end of the great Gonzalo Pizarro rebellion, they came into the country at a much faster rate than before. By 1548 enough time had elapsed so that a very large number of Spanish Peruvians had roots in the country, were sure they wanted to stay, and sent for female relatives, such a summons being the principal mechanism for the entry of Spanish women.

As the relatives of the male Spanish Peruvians, the women shared the social and regional origins of the rest of the population. A sampling of the regional origins of Spanish women showed all the principal regions in their usual order, and close to their usual proportions of the total. Andalusia was at the head of the list, as was to be expected, but Andalusian women had already lost the overwhelming numerical superiority they apparently had in the Caribbean area in the early years of the sixteenth century. . . .

The social quality of Spanish women in Peru was as varied as that of the men, ranging from the sisters of fishermen to the daughters of counts. Just as with men, there took place over the years a rise in average social status on the Spanish scale, as the wealth of Peru attracted people from an ever broader spectrum of Spanish society. It would be hard to say whether social origin had more or less importance among the men than among the women. On the one hand, a woman who could buy fine clothes and learn to imitate polite behavior could make herself more nearly the equal of high society than could a man, who faced the barrier of literacy. For while some ladies could read and write and play keyboard instruments, such accomplishments were far from universal even at the highest level. On the other hand, the use of the "doña" drew a sharp line down the middle of the female population, based on Spanish peninsular distinctions. . . .

Many of the encomenderos' wives in the 1530's, having been married in Spain before their husband became rich, or picked from the generally plebeian women already in the Indies at that time, did not boast the title "doña." After the 1540's, the encomenderos married practically only doñas, and the older ladies' lack of title was sorely felt, but no change was possible. It could happen that their younger sisters, brought to Peru to share the family's good fortune and to make advantageous matches, would be allowed to assume the "doña" which was denied the rich and powerful patronesses. For the second generation, the "doña" was standard for the legitimate daughter of any encomendero, whether the mother bore the title or not, and was commonly allowed to the daughters of any prominent and wealthy man. . . .

Family and regional ties were even more important for women than for men. The great majority of women either arrived as part of a family, or were sent for by male relatives already in Peru. The motive was usually to seek marriage or join a husband. If the husband died, as could happen without a moment's notice in tumultuous Peru, the woman would be thrown completely on family and compatriots, for unless she was wealthy, a widow or single woman could sustain herself only with difficulty or loss of honor.

Probably nine-tenths of all adult Spanish women were married. Previous chapters have indicated how marriage was, though not universal, the rule among encomenderos and established artisans; it was common for lawyers, doctors, notaries, and shipmasters, and not unknown among merchants. All this added up to a formidable demand for marriageable women. The natural desire to form matches was given urgency among the Spaniards by their particularly strong drive to perpetuate and enhance their lineage, and by the importance of an honorable, legitimate wife in the Spanish ideal of life. The official threat to deport all those who, having wives in Spain, failed to have them brought to the Indies, cannot be considered a major factor. Most of the time, and for most people, it was a dead letter, though governors could rid themselves of troublesome individuals by invoking it, and the royal officials could use it to extort money.

There was only one area where official policy had a strong effect in encouraging marriage, though there it was admittedly of utmost importance. While an encomendero could hope to avoid the various royal ordinances threatening to take away the encomiendas of those who did not marry, he had no chance of passing his encomienda on to his heirs unless he married and had legitimate children. At this point official policy became a serious matter, for the deadly competition to secure encomiendas would allow nothing else. Many encomenderos had their mestizo sons legitimated to inherit their property, but legitimation was never allowed to include the right to succeed in the father's encomienda, except for the children of Francisco Pizarro and one other noted captain. The encomendero's incentives to marry were increased even more by the prospect, then still very much alive, that the encomienda could be converted into a perpetual fief and family possession. With these motivations, some encomenderos began to marry or bring their wives to Peru as soon as, or even before, the first phase of the conquest was ended. Ten years after the conquest, a large minority, perhaps a third, had their wives with them; in certain more settled areas like Lima, Trujillo, and Piura the proportion was no doubt greater. By the early 1550's two-thirds of the encomenderos of highland Cuzco were married; and in 1563 there were only thirty-two encomenderos left unmarried in all Peru, of almost five hundred.

Certain aspects of marriage were the same whether the man was an encomendero or an artisan, the wife wellborn or plebeian. Practically all marriages were strategic alliances arranged with a view to improving the partners' wealth or social standing; if a few Spaniards married for love, they were exceptions not indicative of any trend for the nature of marriage to change in the Indies. Both partners were seeking the greatest wealth and the highest lineage possible in the other party; but the classic type of match in the Indies was that in which the man had acquired wealth or power and now wanted to gain matching social prestige by marrying a woman of higher birth, though often poor. In these cases the man contributed a large dowry, perhaps many thousands of pesos, reversing the traditional process. Almost always the fiction was maintained that the dowry originated with the wife or her relatives, but occasionally the man, alleging the "custom of the Indies," would grant the sum openly, in consideration of the lady's virginity and high birth. However, if the higher lineage was on the man's side, the dowry reverted to its traditional form. Some encomenderos paid princely dowries, of 20,000 pesos and over, to have their sisters or daughters marry a member of the Spanish high nobility or a magistrate of the Audiencia.

The dowry had other uses as well. At times it simply represented the total property and money which a widow or wealthy spinster brought into a marriage, and meant to keep under her control. A dowry could also be a hedge against future indebtedness; sometimes husbands acknowledged receipt of a fictional dowry far in excess of the total worth of man and wife, so that if in the future the husband's property were seized for debts, or if claims heaped up after his death, the wife could always retain this large amount in the family as dowry goods.

Spanish Peru, as has been seen elsewhere, was not a place where social mobility was easy, but there were ways a man could, within certain limits, raise his position through his own activity in war or commerce. For a woman, on the other hand, there was hardly anything she could do independently to enhance her position, and much that she could do to lower it. Women took their original status from their family, and it could be altered only through marriage. Practically the only chance for a woman of humble birth to reach the top rank of Peruvian society was to marry an obscure man who later became an encomendero. After the 1530's this was a rare occurrence.

Except for the minority who had married in Spain before leaving, encomenderos chose their wives primarily from among the female relatives of prominent people, other encomenderos or churchmen, in their own Peruvian community. Marriage in the upper levels of society was the first area of life where a new Peruvian regionalism superseded the Spanish regionalism to which the settlers remained generally faithful when choosing friends and associates. Though it would not be unheard of for an encomendero of Cuzco to seek out a bride from his home town, he would be more likely to choose a sister or cousin of the richest and most powerful of his Cuzco colleagues who would deign to consider a match, regardless of the two men's regional origin in Spain. (Such marriages were often arranged while the brides were still in Spain.) In this way, the encomendero class in each Spanish Peruvian town had by 1560 become a closely interrelated group.

Other encomenderos made matches with the wellborn, and allegedly well-born, ladies who were imported for that purpose almost as a speculative business venture. An impecunious father with three or four marriageable daughters and some claim to hidalgo status would set out from Spain to Peru with no other assets than the prospective marriages and, in some cases, royal cédulas recommending that the Peruvian governors show favor to whomever the daughters might marry.

The encomenderos' wives were the most important and influential women in Peru, their position as central in its way as that of their husbands. They were the heads of large households of dependents, servants, and slaves. (Alone of all the women in the country, some of them had the luxury of a Spanish woman head servant.) Aside from their household responsibilities, they were often left in charge of their husbands' encomiendas and general affairs. In this broader function they were not thought to perform well; there was general agreement that the most heartless, avaricious, and destructive tribute collectors were Spanish women.

Nevertheless, the encomenderos' wives, always maintaining their homes even when the encomenderos were absent at war, were an important force for social and economic continuity, a continuity which was not broken with the death of the encomendero. The mortality rate in the civil wars among prominent men was high, and one woman might retain the same house, servant staff, encomienda, and landed property through as many as three or four husbands. Because of the pressures of custom, the governors, and the dissatisfied pretenders, no woman who inherited an encomienda could stay unmarried. She might have a limited choice as to her next husband, but had to remarry almost immediately. Some governors merely implored and hinted at reprisal if compliance was not forthcoming, while others straightforwardly informed the ladies concerned that they had arranged their marriage; but all were adamant. The record for noncompliance was set by María de Escobar, a woman of immense wealth, seniority, and political power, who managed to place a three-year interval between her second and third husbands. In cases like these, the encomienda was juridically and in fact more the woman's than the man's. . . .

The wives of men who were not encomenderos, among whom artisans' wives were the largest group, could not live with as much magnificence as women in the upper rank, but they came nearer to that ideal than might be imagined. In a singular fashion, Spanish Peru preserved most of the social distinctions of the Peninsula, and even invented new ones based on seniority and the possession of encomiendas, yet at the same time, because of the fabulous wealth available to the intruders, and the presence of a large servile population, even those Spaniards who were thought of as poor and plebeian could afford things that in Spain were the perquisites of wealth. Most Spanish women dressed in fine stuffs; none were without servants. An artisan's wife could be expected to have a considerable staff, who would call her "señora" and relieve her of most of the burden of daily housekeeping. In Lima in 1546, the wife of one far from prosperous artisan was waited upon by a Negro woman slave, a freed Indian woman of Nicaragua, and a Peruvian Indian servant, aside from two slaves who aided her husband in his work. In the main, artisans' wives and encomenderos' wives lived in different circles, choosing their confidantes, *comadres,* and dining companions from among their equals. Yet there were points of contact; often a humble woman stood in a kind of client relationship to an encomendero's wife, and it could happen that the wife of an encomendero would serve as sponsor at the wedding of an artisan.

Independent economic activities of women, carried on either by married women from the base of their dowry goods, to which they retained rights, or by widows and spinsters who had to gain a living, were channeled into certain areas defined by convention. Women owned a great deal of city real estate, both for their own residences and for the purpose of renting out, but were not too often seen as the owners of agricultural land or livestock. A large proportion of Negro slave house servants were the personal property of women, and much speculative buying and selling took place. Like all other elements of Spanish Peruvian society, women who had achieved solvency invested as silent partners in merchandise and loaned money.

There were single women in Lima who over the years acquired great wealth and a solid position, though not much social prestige, through such enterprise. It was not that any stigma attached to these activities in themselves, being practiced by the most patrician of ladies, but if a woman was of humble origin, or had a less than honorable start, such facts were not subsequently forgotten.

Other fields open to women were more in the nature of feminine specialties, and had strongly lower class connotations. The baking of bread and biscuit, both for ordinary city consumption and for the provision of ships and armies, was carried out largely under the supervision of women. Spaniards spoke of the *panaderas* as if male bakers did not exist, which was not quite true, but there is no doubt that the business was mainly shared by Spanish women and free mulatto and Negro women, the bulk of the work in either case being done by Negro slaves and Indians. Women naturally monopolized the occupation of midwifery, which they combined with the general healing of ailments. Poor women, doing as they have always done, sewed and took in boarders. Hospitality by the rich was the principal method of housing and feeding transients in Peru, but some of the women who accepted boarders for a fee began, by the late 1540's and the 1550's, to evolve into regular innkeepers (who also sold odds and ends to the public), not only in Lima but as far into the highlands as La Paz. . . .

For their self-protection and for their honor, it was prudent for women who kept inns to marry, and those who could find willing husbands did so. In 1547 la Valenciana married an Antonio de Toledo, who thenceforth helped in the operation of her house. She became deeply committed to Toledo in more than a formal sense, giving him free management of her properties and supporting his relatives. But the relationship came to an end because of a difficulty that plagued marriage in the Indies. Toledo was a bigamist. Presumably la Valenciana's husband in Spain had died before the new match, but Toledo's first wife was still alive. He had succumbed to the temptation that overcame more than one Spaniard in Peru, that of forgetting a poor, distant wife in Spain for a new one who was rich and present. After a year the validity of the marriage was challenged in the ecclesiastical courts, only to be confirmed, until finally around 1554 Toledo's previous marriage was established beyond doubt, he was exiled from Peru, and his marriage with la Valenciana was invalidated.

There is no particular reason to think that la Valenciana's place was ever more than a boarding house. But it is possible; not all adventurers in the Indies were male. Already in 1537 Bishop Berlanga of Panama complained of the presence of too many single women of bad morals. There were always a certain number of women, not necessarily of the very lowest origin but certainly of low repute, who served the Spaniards as prostitutes, camp followers, and mistresses.

Full-fledged prostitutes definitely existed in Lima, the center of all amenities, and in rich Potosí, but there were not enough such women to be organized by the houseful. Nor was there anything like mass demand for the physical woman. Spanish men found Indian women attractive, and any Spaniard could have as many as he wanted. Spanish prostitutes catered more to the need of Spaniards to be near a woman who shared their language and culture. As much as anything else there were entertainers, who might, like María de

Ledesma in Potosí, have a fine vihuela or guitar and know how to play and sing well. Jokingly, half in derision, these women were commonly called "doña" by their clients, and this usage has found its way into the chronicles of the civil wars; but they were not so termed in any serious context.

Far more common than true prostitutes were adventuresses who were prepared to form loose relationships, either temporary or quite permanent, with any man who would support them well. They were not averse to an advantageous marriage, but could expect marriage only under unusual circumstances. Often such a woman served in effect as interim or replacement wife for a man whose real wife was still in Spain, or, even more characteristically, for a man who was single and desired female companionship, but did not want to marry until he was in a position to make a match with a wealthy or well-born lady who could do honor to his lineage. When that time came, if the relationship had been a meaningful one and the man was generous, he might give his former mistress a dowry and marry her to another, less ambitious Spaniard. . . .

At the opposite pole from the concubines were the feminine devotees of the church. Peru was slow to develop true convents of nuns, and the ones that began to be organized, as 1560 neared, already belonged to a new era. But they were preceded, in the late 1540's and 1550's, by the *beatas*. Beatas, a specifically Spanish phenomenon, were women living in pious retirement, sometimes individually and sometimes in groups, who wore the habit of an order with which they had some, usually formal, connection.

The Dominican beatas seem to have been the first to organize themselves; in 1548 the Dominican beata Mari Hernández de Pereda donated her house for the purpose, though she soon added the clause that a rival, Leonor del Aguilar, should not be allowed entry. Later the Dominican friars persuaded her to revoke the clause, and the formerly excluded Leonor, who had lived in her own small house with a mulatto slave girl and a mestizo child she cared for, came there to live. Discipline, one can see, was not what might be expected from regular nuns, but the Dominican effort was serious and sustained. Leonor del Aguilar remained a beata for at least ten years; the Dominican house was still in existence in 1557, and even had affiliated members in the coastal valley of Chincha, where the Dominican friars maintained a monastery.

The Dominican beatas were women of modest circumstances; another establishment started under Augustinian sponsorship around 1557 drew from a different stratum of society, its membership being prominent widows and daughters of encomenderos, all of them doñas. After some years the beatas became regular nuns and founded a convent of the same order.

Rich and poor, concubine and beata, Spanish women made their most basic contribution to the development of the country by educating those around them in the ways of the homeland. In their houses Spanish was spoken and learned. They taught their Negro and Indian maids to make beds, sew European clothes, and prepare Spanish foods in Spanish fashion. As irregular as some of their own private lives may have been, they taught religion to their slaves and servants, and encouraged them to form steady unions and marry.

But above all, this influence extended to the second generation, for whose upbringing the Spanish women were responsible, a generation which included not only their own fully Spanish children, but large numbers of mestizo children, fathered by Spanish settlers who were not content to see their offspring raised as Indians. The demand for people to care for such children was large, and any Spanish woman, whether she had children of her own or not, could expect to be importuned to raise mestizos and orphans. Once the children were taken in, personal attachment grew, whatever the original agreement had been. . . .

When it came to the wives of encomenderos, their collections of children were truly imposing. Isabel de Ovalle, twice married but childless, raised two orphaned Spanish girls, a mestizo girl who had been befriended by her first husband, and two more mestizo girls she had taken in on her own initiative (not to speak of two Negro slave orphans she meant to free). She planned to give them all substantial dowries. Childlessness was not, of course, the rule among encomenderos' wives, many of whom were notably fertile. Doña Francisca Jiménez had, by 1548, ten children alive and with her; two by her first husband, three by her second, and five by her third. She was also raising the mestizo daughter of her second husband, who acted as her maid. This was the fate of many mestizo children who were raised in Spanish homes; they received sustenance, education, and affection, but were seen in the light of servants.

There was, then, growing up in Peru during the 1540's and 1550's, a new generation whose cultural heritage was strongly Spanish, whether they were of pure Spanish blood or mestizo. For the future character of the colony, this group was of immense importance; but in the period before 1560 they remained little more than a potentiality. Hardly any representative of the second generation, either Spanish or mestizo, appeared in any kind of independent role during the whole thirty years from the time the conquering expedition set out for Peru, not even in the humbler fields of endeavor such as artisanry.

Mestizos and Spanish children were born in Peru from 1533 on, but the second generation had its true beginnings only after the Indian rebellion ended in 1537. By 1560 only a small minority of the second generation were over twenty years of age. The new generation also had to contend with the general Spanish reluctance to entrust anything important to the very young; in the Spanish legal tradition, very much in force in Peru, both men and women were minors and required guardians until their twenty-fifth birthday. Emerging into independence was rendered yet more difficult by the crushing prestige of the first generation of settlers, which kept them in command in all walks of life for an abnormally long time. . . .

There was in conquest Peru no one standard treatment or fixed social evaluation of the thousands of mestizo children born of Spanish fathers and Indian mothers. Many, never recognized, grew up with their mothers as Indians and were reabsorbed into the indigenous population. In other cases, Spaniards went to great lengths to provide for mestizo offspring. Some Spanish fathers sent for their mestizo children to join them from as far away as Mexico and Nicaragua. Many made plans to send mestizo sons and daughters to Spain, to be raised at home by their own families, and though this did not come to fruition as often as intended, it was no idle thought.

For those who were in one way or another received among the Spanish Peruvians, their condition as mestizos was a handicap, but depending on other factors, did not preclude acceptance at a fairly high level. It is hard to separate the Spaniards' feelings about racial mixture, as it affected the mestizos, from their position on illegitimacy, for ninety-five per cent of the first generation of mestizos were illegitimate. To judge by the treatment accorded the few legitimate mestizos, who were accepted fully as equals, the Spanish may have considered illegitimacy to be a more serious blemish than mixture with Indians. Legitimate mestizos could and did inherit encomiendas, and one was considered for an appointment to the city council of Lima. Moreover, there were cases of Spaniards who had both Spanish and mestizo sons out of wedlock and gave them all equal treatment. . . .

The path was easier for the girls of this class, who could hope to marry within Spanish Peruvian society, perhaps not to their fathers' equals, but to substantial Spaniards of lower degree. To a Spaniard, such a marriage offered the advantages of an alliance with the girl's father, and a large dowry, which might be enough for him to live on. If the father was exceptionally rich and powerful, his mestizo daughter might be able to marry well by any standards. A daughter of the famous captain Lorenzo de Aldana married a large encomendero of Charcas. Diego Maldonado, called the Rich, married his daughter to a Spanish don, with a dowry of 20,000 pesos. Ordinarily, however, such girls married men from the second rank: majordomos, merchants, entrepreneurs, or gentlemen pretenders without encomiendas.

The pattern seen among the mestizo children of encomenderos repeated itself at the lower levels, but with alteration. Above all, the frequent presence on the scene of the Indian mother reduced the intensity of Hispanization. Ordinary Spaniards often succeeded in marrying their daughters to juniors or inferiors; a shipmaster to one of his sailors, or a merchant to his factor. But the point was soon reached at which the size of the dowry and the prestige of the father did not suffice to attract suitors. Many Spaniards fulfilled their duty to their mestizo children (both boys and girls) by making them a "donation." If the donation was large, perhaps a thousand pesos in value, the child could be assured of a future, but usually it was much less: two or three hundred pesos, or a mare with a colt, or a few goats. A child so endowed would probably succeed in being raised by some Spanish family, but the amount was not enough for a dowry or a start in life.

By the 1550's, therefore, a major problem in Peru was what to do with the many mestizo girls who were growing up Spanish, but were not wealthy enough to find Spanish husbands. It became a favorite form of charity to donate dowries to mestizo orphans. In Cuzco and Lima, philanthropic citizens established houses to shelter them. (Hardly ever did it occur to the charitable to arrange a marriage between two mestizos, partly, no doubt, because men did not marry as young as women, and few mestizo men had come of age). Philanthropy could not, of course, take care of all the Hispanized mestizo girls; apparently very many ended in purely servile positions, or took to loose living, or were abandoned entirely. . . .

All in all, the Spaniards must be judged to have shown an unusual amount of interest in the fate of their mestizo offspring. Even if many, possibly most, mestizo children suffered neglect, there were many hundreds who were protected, and grew up inside Spanish Peruvian society.

In order to explain the relatively good treatment of mestizos it is not necessary to imagine any unusually strong parental tenderness on the part of the Spaniards, though some had such feelings (they were often struck, it appears, by how much their mestizo children resembled them). Most important was the strong Spanish feeling for lineage, which emphasized solidarity with all one's relatives near and distant, as well as the necessity of carrying on the family name. Another factor was the strict Spanish machinery for legal guardianship. Finally, there was the special sense of responsibility which the Spaniards, in the Arab tradition, felt for the protection of females. At all levels, more care was lavished on mestizo girls than boys, with the probable result that a higher proportion of them were absorbed into the Spanish population, and indeed, with men more numerous in that population than women, they were more needed.

To sum up the substance of the chapter, there were among the settlers of

Peru a large minority of Spanish women who, living in the cities, often as heads of the large households of encomenderos, were able to exert a cultural influence on the urban population out of proportion to their numbers. Even humble women had mixed servant staffs to whom they taught Spanish ways. The household of one almost indigent Spanish woman of Lima could stand as a paradigm of Spanish Peru: herself, her Negro slave, her Indian servant, and a mestizo orphan girl. Above all, the Spanish women were responsible for the existence of a second Spanish generation who were to inherit the encomiendas and other wealth of the first, and they provided the surroundings in which a generation of mestizos grew up to be primarily Spanish in language and culture.

22. Dowries Helped to Reduce Domestic Instability, Illegitimacy, and Prostitution in Bahia

A. J. R. RUSSELL-WOOD

The history of women in colonial Brazil remains largely to be written, for documentation appears to be scanty and what does exist has not been carefully organized or systematically studied. The British Brazilianist Dr. A. J. R. Russell-Wood has made skillful use of the available records of the Santa Casa de Misericórdia (The Holy House of Mercy) of Bahia to shed light on the attitudes of society toward women and their role in the life of this colonial capital. The Misericórdia was an important institution for social welfare developed in Portugal and transplanted in Brazil. As a charitable brotherhood it had an important role in connection with dowries and marriage, foundlings, prisons, hospitals, burials, and charity.

The Misericórdia of Bahia in the seventeenth and eighteenth centuries . . . maintained a hospital, a retirement house and a foundling wheel and its members visited the prison regularly. The Misericórdia also strove to assist people in modest circumstances by outright alms. Brothers were supplied with the names of needy citizens by parish priests and these were visited and assisted

From *Fidalgos and Philanthropists: The Santa Casa da Misericórdia of Bahia, 1550–1755* by A. J. R. Russell-Wood (1968), pp. 173–200 passim. Originally published by the University of California Press; reprinted by permission of the regents of the University of California and Macmillan, London and Basingstoke.

in so far as the resources of the brotherhood permitted. Dowries were granted to girls to enable them to preserve their honour and contract suitable marriages. In colonial Brazil even a girl of respectable parentage found difficulty in marrying unless she had a dowry. Without this aid from the Misericórdia there was a very real danger that she would slip into a life of prostitution. In the concession of dowries the Misericórdia was contributing on a private level to a national policy. . . . The concession of dowries had been regarded as politically expedient since the earliest days of the Portuguese expansion. . . .

The Misericórdia of Bahia played a valuable rôle in advancing the national policy of marriages and in affording some degree of protection to girls who might otherwise have been unable to marry or whose precarious financial position would have rendered them susceptible to prostitution. All records in the Misericórdia archives for the sixteenth century were destroyed by the Dutch, but for the seventeenth and eighteenth centuries the registers afford a complete record of bequests made to the brotherhood for the provision of dowries.

The dowries for which testators provided in their wills fell in three categories. First, there were dowries granted by the testator to the daughters of a relative or of a friend. In such cases the Misericórdia was merely the executor of the will and passed on the dowry to the nominee after the estate of the testator had been settled. Secondly, there were dowries left to the Misericórdia for immediate distribution to orphan girls without the brotherhood incurring any further obligation. Thirdly, there were dowries left by the testator for administration by the Misericórdia. These were financed from the interest on capital placed on loan and were granted annually. Before discussing the last two types of dowry, I wish to dwell briefly on the attitudes of mind revealed by the terms of these wills towards the position of women in colonial Brazil because frequently these attitudes show social, religious and racial preoccupations.

Wills making legacies for the allocation of dowries have certain features in common. The testator was usually of the upper class and the main beneficiaries were his nieces. In all cases the concession of a dowry, be it to a relative or not, depended on the undoubted virtue of the nominee. These aspects have implications in the wider social context of colonial ideology.

Testators who provided dowries for their relatives were not all of the landed aristocracy of Bahia. Nevertheless they were sufficiently prominent in the social life of the city to be very conscious of class distinction. This preoccupation with social standing is very apparent in the clauses of a will stipulating the terms for the concession of a dowry. Jorge Ferreira, who had died in 1641 leaving 2,450$000 to the Misericórdia for the saying of masses, was of the landowning class and had just such a preoccupation. The owner of a sugar plantation in Sergipe, a provision farm in the Serra, a smallholding in Rio Vermelho and houses in the city of Bahia, he was not one to wish that his niece should marry below her station. Thus he had bequeathed the results of his sixty-three years' labour to his niece, Jerónima Ferreira, as a dowry "so that her husband may be ennobled thereby." . . .

Preoccupation with the maintaining of social prestige and with the hazards of marrying "below one's station" led many families of Bahia to send their daughters to convents in Portugal rather than risk the possibility of their contracting socially undesirable marriages in Bahia. Young girls and boxes of currency were constant features of any fleet from Bahia to Portugal in the late seventeenth and early eighteenth centuries. Dom João de Lencastre (Governor-General, 1694–1702) told the king of the social and economic evils of this practice. No longer were there any society marriages in Bahia, and large sums of money were being sent to the convents of Lisbon, Oporto and Viana to provide for the expenses of these girls. . . .

Not only was the practice of sending girls to Portugal prejudicial to the society and economy of Bahia. Frequently the girls themselves were the victims of parents who compelled their daughters to take the veil against their will. It was this human aspect rather than the financial and social well-being of Bahia which induced Dom João V to act. In a decree of March 1732, he ordered that in future no girl should be sent from Brazil to Portugal without the royal consent having been previously obtained. Before such permission would be granted, the viceroy and governors were to hold a full enquiry to determine all the circumstances of the petition made by a girl wishing to go to Portugal. In addition to this civil enquiry, there was to be an ecclesiastical report. The archbishop or bishop was to interview the girl and ensure that the petition was born of true religious vocation and not of parental intimidation. The penalties for non-observance of this decree were severe. The captain of a ship found carrying a girl against her will was liable to a fine of 2,000 *cruzados* and two months' imprisonment. This measure effectively curtailed the traffic in girls from Bahia to the convents of Portugal because the royal consent was granted on few occasions. It could not stop the traffic in coin from Bahia to Portugal for dowries for nieces and relatives of testators in Brazil. . . .

Religious feeling may have contributed on a sub-conscious level to the decision of many families to send their daughters to the convents of Portugal. The other characteristic of the wills recorded in the registers of the Misericórdia — that legacies to relatives were frequently confined to the nieces of the testator — had a purely physical basis. Barrenness among white women and infant mortality were frequent in the tropics. On the one hand was the case of the businessman Gaspar dos Réis Pinto who had been married three times but was still without offspring. On the other was Luzia Freire, widow of a brother of the Misericórdia, who had produced eight children of whom only two had survived. In his will of 1643 Gaspar dos Réis Pinto ordered his executor to sell his plantations in Sergipe and Rio Vermelho and distribute as many dowries as possible from the proceeds. For her part Luzia Freire stipulated in her will of 1685 that monies derived from the sale of her sugar plantation in Patatiba and her cattle ranches on the S. Francisco river be applied to the saying of masses for her soul. These purely physical factors obviously led many testators to send to distant relatives in Portugal the fruits of a lifetime's labour in the tropics.

Bahians who made legacies to nieces and the daughters of relatives in Brazil were guided by a different set of reasons. All testators were obsessed by the possibility of spurious claimants challenging their wills in an attempt to inherit lands or possessions. The wills of married couples and bachelors alike often began with the categorical statement that the testators had no offspring "natural or spurious." Such was the extent of this fear that many testators adopted a matrilineal attitude when making their legacies. Two Bahian bachelors of the early seventeenth century, Francisco Dias Baião and Diogo Fernandes, stipulated that only the daughters of their relatives could benefit from their wills. In no circumstances was a male relative to inherit. The philanthropist Felippe Correia, after making numerous legacies to the Misericórdia in his will of 1650, left his plantations in Pituba to his sister on the condition that in no way was her husband to enjoy part ownership of these properties. Possibly this condition may have been the result of personal animosity; if so, there was no reference to it, and Correia gave as his reason that he wished the property to remain in the Correia family. Other testators founded trusts to be enjoyed by the distaff side only. In the event of there being no more female descendants the trust was to be administered by a brotherhood for charitable purposes.

The attitude towards what might be called the "legitimacy of the womb" and even the practice of sending daughters to Portugal may have been influenced by the multi-racial nature of Bahian society. There was always the fear that a daughter might have an affair with a coloured man. In this there was one law for males and quite another for females. It was considered rather *macho,* or masculine, for a teenage son of a white family to have a coloured mistress: if she did conceive, so much the worse for her. On the other hand, for a white girl to have a coloured *amigo,* or lover, was tantamount to demanding social ostracism. This fear on the part of parents was rarely expressed but strongly felt. When the lawyer Jerónimo de Burgos and his wife had established a trust in 1664 for the saying of masses and charitable purposes, they had stipulated that after the terms of the trust had been fulfilled any additional income should be given to their heirs provided that "they do not marry anyone tainted with the blood of the forbidden races." In an age when race and creed were often equated, such a clause effectively ruled out coloured or New Christian partners.

The attitudes of Bahians towards the distaff side of their families have shown that many of the conditions attached to legacies were prompted by racial, religious and social prejudices. Bahia was a multi-racial society and the coloured population was infinitely larger than the white population. The enthusiasm felt by the early settlers for the Amerindian girls and Negresses continued even after there had been an increase in the number of white women available for marriage. The so-called *Minas* (probably Fulahs or Ashantis) were especially favoured because of their good appearance, dignified carriage, and their fame as mistresses of the culinary skills. The attitudes shown by testators in their wills towards their coloured slaves reveal the complexity of the racial issue.

Historians and anthropologists alike have dwelt on the manner in which the white masters exploited their female slaves. It is undeniable that the girls of the *senzalas,* or slave quarters, were often the concubines of the masters, the butts for the anger of jealous wives, and the playthings of adolescent sons. But there was another side to the picture of inter-racial contact which is usually forgotten. Many slave owners appear to have taken a genuine interest in the welfare of their slaves. The receipt ledgers of the Misericórdia frequently recorded payments of up to 50$000 made by a plantation owner for the cure of a slave in the hospital of the brotherhood. João de Mattos referred in his will, with evident pride, to how he had arranged the marriage of one of his slave girls and had given her a dowry and some household possessions. Many slaves were granted their freedom as a reward for years of faithful service. A wealthy widow, Theodora de Góis, who died in 1693, granted her slave Luiza her freedom and ordered that a dowry of 100$000, clothing and gold trinkets be given her on marriage. This paternal attitude on the part of the white ruling classes towards the coloured population was not limited to slaves. Many families adopted coloured children. Pedro Viegas Giraldes and Felippe Correia, both benefactors of the Misericórdia in the seventeenth century, brought up mulatto children in their homes. The history of the relationships between masters and slaves, white and black, was not always a chronicle of cruelty and exploitation. There was often an undercurrent of Christian idealism among the authoritarian and domineering plantation owners of colonial Bahia.

On other occasions the attitude of the white man to his slaves was not paternal, but uxorious. One slave owner, Pedro Domingues, was consumed by jealousy at the prospect of his concubine marrying. In his will of 1676 he granted her her freedom, the ownership of his house, and three slaves on the condition that she should stay single. Other slave owners had had children by their slave girls and made generous provision for both mother and child. A smallholder, Diogo Fernandes, left detailed instructions in his will for the care and education of his son by a Negress: he was to be taught the Bible and trained as an apprentice in a mechanical trade. The bachelor Joseph Lopes, who had established a "chapel of masses" in the Misericórdia in 1656, also regarded his favourite crioula as more than a mere *peça de Indias* ("pieces of the Indies"). He granted the mother and her son and daughter their freedom. The little girl was to be placed in an honourable home and on marriage was to receive a dowry of 100$000 and furniture. Evidently the family of Joseph Lopes had opposed his recognition of paternity, because he stipulated that his daughter should not be boarded in the house of any of his relatives. This respect for the Negro slave was based largely on her rôle as the mother of the white man's children. The glorification of the wife in her maternal rôle still persists in Brazil and although a fickle husband may indulge in the enchantments of his concubine to the full, he will rarely leave his wife, simply because she is the "mother of my son."

Preoccupations of class, creed and colour were constant factors in the minds of Bahians of the seventeenth and eighteenth centuries. Anxiety for the preservation of class status was allied to an obsession with the maintaining of purity of blood. Members of an essentially male-dominated society were influenced by these two factors into adopting matrilineal attitudes when making their wills. The position of women in Portuguese colonial society is usually presented as insignificant. Travellers to colonial Brazil commented on the seclusion of females. The seclusion of women in colonial times has been considered by historians as indicative of the insignificant position they enjoyed, but it seems likely that the womanhood of colonial Bahia was a good deal more influential than is generally realised.

The attitudes to women and slaves illustrate to the full the almost paradoxical variety of outlook in colonial Brazil. The apparent contradiction of a male-dominated society adopting matrilineal attitudes had its counterpart in the attitude towards the coloured population. On the one hand was the brutality of the slave ships and slave markets. On the other hand was the Christian charity shown in the adoption of a coloured orphan, the emancipation of a slave, or the granting of dowries. A modern visitor to Bahia referred to the "Bay of all saints and of all devils." This would have been an accurate epigram for Bahia in colonial times when idealism and materialism, virtue and vice were so closely interwoven. . . .

The administration of dowries by the Misericórdia exemplifies all that was good and all that was bad in the brotherhood. Dowries were given to coloured girls as well as white girls, to girls of the city and to girls of the surrounding region. By so doing, the Misericórdia offered a social service without parallel in Bahia of the eighteenth century. Many girls who would otherwise not have married, or would have been degraded, were able to marry honourably. By this action the Misericórdia was to a small degree responsible for reducing the domestic instability, illegitimacy and prostitution for which Bahia was notorious. Unfortunately its powers of administration did not equal its idealism. Loans were placed on poor securities and lost. Legal disputes made others impossible to collect. Small sums were lost through the dishonesty of brothers or employees. The Misericórdia was affected by external factors: disruption of the economy; the decrease in the value of properties; lack of co-operation from the judiciary in law suits brought against debtors. It was pride which prompted the Mesas to continue granting dowries for as long as they did, without consideration for hard financial realities. Although it is easy to condemn the administrative deficiencies of the brotherhood, the important rôle played by the Misericórdia in the distribution of dowries can only command respect.

23. *Riots in Seventeenth-Century Mexico City*

CHESTER LYLE GUTHRIE

A large volume could be written on the tumults and disturbances in Mexico City from the time of Cortez until Spanish power was broken three centuries later. Here is a chapter on this subject by Dr. Chester Lyle Guthrie, one of the many scholars who received their historical training under Professor Herbert Eugene Bolton at the University of California, Berkeley.

When the Pilgrim Fathers were making their first settlement in America, indeed when Jamestown was still a struggling community, New Spain already possessed a world-famous metropolis, Mexico City. Time and two empires had established it as perhaps the greatest in the New World. Well-nigh a cen-

"Riots in Seventeenth-Century Mexico City: A Study of Social and Economic Conditions" by Chester Lyle Guthrie, *Greater America: Essays in Honor of Herbert Eugene Bolton* (1945), pp. 243–258, passim. Originally published by the University of California Press; reprinted by permission of the Regents of the University of California.

tury under Spanish control, Mexico City spoke of Hernán Cortés as a figure of the dim past, and had seen the children of the conquistadors grow white-haired.

In the aftermath of conquest, social and economic problems had arisen which were both grave and troublesome. The soldiers of fortune became less and less important, while the merchant, the artisan, the farmer, and other more stable if less romantic elements gained in influence. A man without a profession or trade, or without financial resources, was finding it harder and harder to make a living. Many were forced to accept public or private charity, or else had to depend on begging and the soup of the monasteries. Further-more, the large, conquered Indian population was still in the city and had to be absorbed into the body politic. The time had passed when the Indian prob-lem could be thrust aside by military repression, for the conquered natives had by now attained to a certain legal status. Also, free Negroes and a multi-tude of racial mixtures, each requiring a place in society, had arisen. Mestizos, mulattoes, *castizos, lobos, chinos, zambos,* to mention only a few of the blood combinations, had to be fitted into the social scale. Riots and unrest followed almost as a natural consequence from such numerous and varied social and economic stresses. The following brief discussion of the events surrounding the two major riots of the century may assist the reader to an understanding and evaluation of the underlying causes of the discontent.

The first outbreak occurred on January 15, 1624. On that day the people emerged from early morning Mass in the great cathedral of Mexico with one of the most dreaded edicts ever issued in New Spain ringing in their ears. The pronouncement had been to the effect that all churches would be closed under an order of *cessatio a divinis.* Furthermore, the viceroy, at that time the haughty and unpopular Diego Carrillo de Mendoza y Pimentel, Marqués de Gelves, had been called a heretic and excommunicated. Soon the populace were giving voice to their disapproval of the administration, which they held responsible for the course of events. Scattered at first, then from all sides, came shouts of "Long live the Church!" "Long live the Faith!" "Death to bad government!" "Death to this excommunicated heretic!"

At this unfortunate moment the viceroy's secretary, Cristóbal Osorio, drove into the square in an open carriage. He was recognized, and some urchins selling vegetables in the market raised the shout of "Heretic!" "Heretic!" Osorio ordered a halt and called to his retainers to discipline the youthful hecklers. It was a mistake. In self-defense the boys pelted the servants with stones and even directed some at the secretary himself. Soon other boys joined in hurling missiles, and before long they were assisted by their elders. Indians, mulattoes, mestizoes, and Negroes made up the mass of the first attackers. Even some poor whites joined the mob. Under such a barrage, Osorio had to make the best escape possible; there was not time then to uphold dignity and rank. Consequently, he shouted to the driver to whip the horses to a run, and the carriage thundered into the courtyard of the viceregal palace just ahead of a cloud of flying stones and debris. In haste the guards forced shut the ponderous doors in the face of the raging people.

From that moment the fury of the mob was turned against the palace. With each hour the position of the defenders grew more and more precarious, for the unrelenting pressure of thousands of milling, shouting rioters was more than the civil and military power of Mexico City could withstand. In vain did the viceroy make promise after promise to the people; in vain revoked, even, the edict which had brought about his excommunication. Vainly also did the Inquisition, the great councils, and even the influential citizens strive to calm the rioters. Not until hope of saving the palace was gone did the supporters of the viceroy, especially the audiencia, the greatest of the governing councils, withdraw its aid. By five o'clock in the evening the rioters had burned and sacked the palace. Viceroy Gelves escaped with his life only by the device of putting on servant's clothing and mingling with the crowd, shouting with the rest, "Death to this heretic viceroy!"

A series of events had contributed to this serious outbreak in Mexico City. In the first place, a critical food shortage had caused a virtual famine. Maize, which supplied the principal sustenance of most of the population, had more than quadrupled in price. The resulting misery was very great. And prices of other foodstuffs rose, thus adding to the discontent.

Perhaps second to hunger as a cause of unrest was the viceroy's unfortunate inability to make himself acceptable. By means of impolitic moves he had alienated almost every group in the society of the capital. To the official class he was an unjust and insulting taskmaster, whose arbitrary and retroactive punishments seemed quite out of proportion to the crimes for which they were inflicted. To the rich he was a dangerous reformer; to the poor, an implacable tax collector, law enforcer, and general meddler. Even in executing his reforms he allowed himself to be outmaneuvered and placed in the false position of favoring monopoly and oppression, while other men and institutions, particularly the Church, were credited with any betterments achieved.

Especially violent, however, were the viceroy's quarrels with the Church. After many disagreements, Gelves and the strong-minded archbishop, then a certain Juan Pérez de la Serna, clashed over the use of churches as asylums for fugitives from justice. Neither the archbishop nor the viceroy would give way in the matter. In the end, both parties resorted to their most potent weapons. The viceroy obtained a decree exiling the archbishop, and the archbishop in turn placed the city under an interdict and excommunicated the viceroy. Each made every effort to see his sentence imposed, with the result that the restless population improved its opportunity to riot against the government.

Thus the first riot of the century passed in violence and bloodshed, and for many years there were no great hostile outbreaks to disturb the administrative calm of the city, though other rumblings of discontent were heard from time to time. The danger of mob violence soon gave little concern to the minds of the representatives of the sovereigns of Spain. The old fundamental complaints against the colonial order remained, however, and in less than two generations the greatest riot of the century occurred in Mexico City.

Nature as well as society seemed to conspire to bring misery upon the people of the capital of New Spain. The summer of 1691 was an unusually wet season. Lake Texcoco, from which Mexico City was separated only by a dike and with which it was connected by canals, was changed from a dry, dusty plain into a large body of water. Roads became impassable; supplies ran low; pastures were flooded; and many of the adobe walls of the poorer houses melted, leaving the inhabitants wet, shivering, and hungry. To add to the general distress, the following winter was unusually severe, with snow blanketing the surrounding hills and making it impossible to bring supplies into the city. As a result of the inclement weather, the summer crops in the vicinity of Mexico City were so weakened and rotted that they fell victim to a blight, called by the Indians *chahuistle*. The winter and spring crops were failures, also. Prices began rising, as in 1624.

Under such conditions, the public granary, or *alhóndiga,* was called upon in greater and greater measure to allay the distress. At first it was an agency for stabilizing prices, but soon it became one of the most important sources of food supply. From dispensing a normal amount of six to eight hundred *fanegas* of grain a day (a *fanega* being about one and six-tenths bushels), the *alhóndiga* was soon called upon to dole out as much as six thousand *fanegas* a day. Under pressure, the government strove frantically to keep enough grain on hand, both by public means and through private initiative, but to little avail.

As famine increased, the lower class became more and more restless and intractable. Not only was food scarce, but more and more the wheat-eating, Spanish-descended part of the population was forced to turn to maize as the principal stay of its diet. This, as it happened, provided a new employment for the Indians since maize was most generally eaten by them in the form of tortillas, and they were the ones who best knew how to make that substitute for wheaten bread; and, impressed by their new importance, they became difficult to control. At the *alhóndiga* there was bedlam. Each Indian woman strove to obtain as much maize as possible before the supply should run short, in order to be the first to get her wares to market. Much of the newly found opulence, so far as the men were concerned, went for pulque, which happened to be plentiful that season. Soon in the smoke-filled, dimly lighted *pulquerías,* as the native liquor shops were called, Indians were giving vent both to their old irritations and to their new feeling of superiority. Did not the laws of the land state, said they, that the natives should be served first at the *alhóndiga?* Certainly the Spaniards had grown afraid of the noble Aztecs. Encouraging these beliefs were the mestizos, the mulattoes, and the other malcontents. As a result, to the increasing restlessness in the city, growing out of the misery and discontent of all the lower class, was further added a combative spirit on the part of what was usually the most humble of the social elements in Mexico City, the once-conquered Indian.

As the year 1692 progressed, the scarcity of food became greater and greater. The government of the viceroy looked on all sides for supplies, in a desperate effort to curb the growing discontent. Only by keeping the city quiet until the new harvest should be reaped could the crisis be passed peacefully. The attempt was a failure. An adequate food supply was nowhere to be found.

Early in the afternoon of June 6, word was given out that the maize had been exhausted, and in the ensuing disorder an Indian child was suffocated. This, of course, aroused the anger of the native population. Next day, the crowd at the grain market was sullen and quarrelsome, with the result that the viceroy appointed two of his high-ranking officials to watch over the transactions and keep order. All went well until the maize was once more exhausted and the officials had finally left the market. Then the crowd again became unmanageable; and in the uproar which followed, word flew from mouth to mouth that an Indian woman had been whipped to death by one of the *alhóndiga's* attendants. The *alhóndiga* was promptly deserted as the angry Indians and their supporters marched to the palace, there to seek redress. They were turned away by the palace guards, and consequently went to the palace of the archbishop, where again they were refused a hearing. From there they swarmed back to the government palace, where rioting began in earnest. The Indians were soon joined by Negroes, mulattoes, mestizos, and poor whites, called *saramullos.*

Even more terrible, perhaps, than the riot of 1624 was this new uprising of the lower class. With few weapons other than sticks, stones, fire, and their bare hands, the rioters laid siege to the palace. The outbreak found the administration of the viceroy unable to protect itself. The military forces of the city had become greatly reduced in man power and efficiency during the two generations of peace following 1624, and, as chance would have it, this lack of preparedness was made even more disastrous to the administration by the fact that the crisis came on a church holiday, when many of the officers and men, including even the viceroy, were absent from the palace.

"Long live the Virgen del Rosario!" "Long live the king!" "Long live pulque!" cried the mob as they strove harder and harder to break into the palace. At the same time, and with even more zest, they howled "Death to the viceroy!" "Death to his wife!" "Death to the *corregidor!*" "Death to the Spaniards!" "Down with bad government!" To these cries they added curses of such ingenuity and expressiveness that even the Spaniards were astonished. Shouts of "Death to the Gachupines who eat up all our maize!" did not reassure the onlookers, who, afraid to oppose the mob, had gathered in the streets leading into the square. It soon seemed impossible that the palace could hold out much longer. Especially was the mob successful in setting fires. Most of the palace was blazing, and some of the other government structures, such as the buildings of the *cabildo,* or town council, in which was the *alhóndiga,* were fired. Before the rioters were halted, they had even tried to burn the palace of Pedro Cortés, Marqués del Valle, heir to the title of the famous conquistador.

The mob was diverted only by the action of the clergy and — perhaps more effectively — by the opportunity offered to the rioters for looting the rich market in the Plaza Mayor. While the Indians were trying to take the palace, many of the *saramullos,* and others of the lower class, broke into the *cajones,* as the shops in the plaza were called. First, the stores containing axes, bars, swords, and knives were ransacked for arms and tools. Then the shops with weak doors or roofs were forced open. When the Indians and those besieging the palace saw what was going on, they promptly left what they were doing and joined the plundering of the market. . . .

Among the clergy, the tardily aroused archbishop was the one who took the initiative. He had at first paid little heed to threats of mob action, but once violence occurred he realized the seriousness of the situation. His first move was to call all the churchmen together to plan a course of action, but it was not until nine o'clock in the evening that the forces he organized were ready to act. Two processions, one of Jesuits and the other of friars of Our Lady of Mercy, bravely entered the square singing, praying, and carrying saintly images. . . .

Although a few stopped to listen to the Jesuits and the friars, it was one of the secular clergy who was most successful in diverting the rioters from their purpose. The treasurer of the cathedral, Manuel de Escalante y Mendoza, accompanied by two priests and a friar, took the Holy Sacrament and went into the plaza. The viceregal palace seemed to be beyond help so he forced his way to the palace of the Marqués del Valle, where the Indians had started a fire against the portals. The flames were mounting fast, but the padre was able to persuade the rioters to desist and to put out the blaze. Then the mob turned to the house of one of the important officials, with the intention of burning it, and once more the treasurer prevented them. In fact, he succeeded in keeping them from starting more fires anywhere. Other priests came to his assistance, and soon one was preaching in the native tongue, persuading the Indians to go home, and was heeded.

The destruction caused by this second riot was very great both in lives and property. Undoubtedly, scores were killed and many more were injured, though casualties were never counted since every attempt was made to keep the identity of the rioters secret from the avenging officials. As for the material losses, they were staggering. The great viceregal palace was so badly burned that it had to be rebuilt. The shops in the square had been thoroughly ransacked, and the buildings of the *cabildo* in large part demolished. In all, it was estimated that damage amounting to some three millions of pesos had been done.

For an understanding of the causes underlying the riots, one must delve into the social history of the period. There were at least three reasons for unrest in Mexico City in the seventeenth century. First, there was great social inequality, produced by sharply marked class distinctions which were mainly racial. Second, there was the precarious economic status of the largest part of the population, the part which in the main suffered most from the irritations and restrictions of differences in caste. Finally, administrative weaknesses offered an opportunity for major demonstrations to break out; for, as events showed, the viceregal government was unable to defend itself quickly and effectively against a determined domestic disturbance.

Three fundamental class divisions, based upon likenesses of interest and occupation, were discernible in colonial Mexico City. The first of these, the upper or ruling class, was composed of the rich and the nobility of Spanish extraction. Associated with them were the great merchants and others of the wealthy middle class, between whom and the nobility there was very little social differentiation. Even for a gentleman of noble birth, trading on a large scale was considered a satisfactory occupation. If any cleavage existed, it was between those born in Spain and those born in the New World.

Fallen from high estate, and now perhaps more properly to be considered as of the middle class, was a small, clannish group, the impoverished descendants of the conquistadors. Turbulent and haughty, they usually engaged in some trade or minor occupation. Sometimes, our of deference to the services rendered by their ancestors, the most needy of these were appointed to minor positions in the government.

Aping the nobility, but for the most part economically nearer to the masses, was the lower middle class, including the artisans and poorer shopkeepers. This group, however, was few in numbers and of little influence in the direction of the city's affairs. Instead of absorbing many of the masses, it kept its ranks closed by means of exclusive guild regulations, with the result that a large and restive lower class remained unaccommodated in the community. Consequently, the city's class struggle was essentially between the two extremes, and was emphasized by the great size of the lower class.

By far the most numerous and restless social group was this lower one. In an estimated population of a quarter million, its members represented from three to five times the total of those above them. Most of the viceroys had already been aware that they poverty, their vices, and the hopelessness of their position in the social scale might ripen them for crime and violence.

Among the more difficult to control were those outcast whites, together with some Indians and mixed-bloods, who were called vagabonds. Petty thievery and chicanery were their stock in trade, and any untoward disturbance would at once enlist them as rioters.

Of the non-Spanish elements which helped to form the lower class, the one which ranked the highest in the social scale was that composed of the mestizos, those who had a mixture of Indian and Spanish blood. Their number was quite large. It was admitted that they were presumptuous and almost as troublesome as the other groups among the masses, but the officials pointed out that they showed more promise of development than others of the racial mixtures.

Many and diverse were the strains which included Negro blood. The Negroes, both of mixed and of pure descent, formed a sizable part of the population of the seventeenth-century Mexico City. As a rule they were considered untrustworthy by the rest of the citizens.

Outnumbering the mestizo and Negro elements were the Indians. They were the ones upon whom fell the chief burden of manual labor in colonial society. If an aqueduct had to be repaired, Indians were promptly assigned to the job. If a load was to be moved, or any other task of similar nature was to be performed, Indians were always called upon. Consequently, their very low position in the scheme of colonial life, as well as the fact that their interests, by the same token, were so widely separated from those of the ruling class, made them especially inclined to join subversive movements. . . .

For the most part, members of the lower class depended upon wages for their livelihood. Trade and industry employed a large number in the lesser capacities, while personal service and government projects accounted for another sizable group. Ordinarily, the wages paid were just enough to meet the needs of the laborer.

In industry, the lower class suffered many restrictions. Although a large proportion was employed in the trades, the rules of the guilds were so formulated that persons of non-Spanish origin, of which the lower class was mostly composed, could never hope to rise higher than the unskilled, low-paid levels. Even the very poor whites could hope for little from the guilds, for the expense of going through the period of apprenticeship, and of paying the fees and fulfilling the requirements attendant upon examination for entrance into one of the trades, made such a course a practical impossibility. In fact, restrictions were so stringent that Viceroy Linares complained that there was a marked lack of opportunity even for Spanish youths to enter a trade.

For those who were not absorbed into industry, domestic service, or governmental activities, there was little left to do but to peddle fruit, vegetables, flowers, grass, and similar goods in the public markets. Should this fail, only begging or crime was left.

Unemployment and partial unemployment added greatly to the problems of the wage earners. Many of the Indians, especially, worked at seasonal occupations in the country. Out of season, they spent almost their entire time in idleness; or so said Viceroy Juan de Mendoza y Luna, Marqués de Montesclaros. Furthermore, the presence of so many vagabonds of all races and mixtures in the city indicated that there was a great deal of unemployment. To Giovanni Gemelli Careri, a noted Italian observer, it seemed as if almost all the Indians were idle and therefore reduced to cheating in order to make a living. Viceroy Linares complained of the great number of idlers who lived by doing occasional odd jobs and, the rest of the time, by dishonesty. . . .

Under such circumstances a fluctuation in the price of any basic commodity, such as maize, was a matter of great importance. There were a number of times when the price of maize became very high, notably in 1624 and in 1692, the years of the two riots, when it rose to four and five times its normal figure, or about ten *reales*. In several other periods of scarcity, high prices caused unrest and demonstrations among the poor — without violence, however.

To counteract the fluctuating cost of living, the government felt obliged to give some aid to the poor. This help, together with direct charity, was one of the characteristics of colonial Mexico City. It was believed that without governmental regulation the price of the fundamental necessities would rise so high that none but the well-to-do and the rich could live comfortably, or perhaps even exist at all. Besides, charity was not only a civic duty; it was an important part of the religious life of the time. The poor, the widows, and the orphans found a place in the financial budgets of the government, institutions, and private individuals. Nevertheless, in spite of these mitigating influences, the fundamental problem of a low standard of living, barely at the subsistence level, helped to keep society unstable.

Many means of price fixing were tried. Perhaps most noteworthy was the supervision and operation of the public grain market, the *alhóndiga*. For the institution the government established numerous and complicated rules, which somewhat alleviated the general situation. The difficulty was that during the years of plenty most of the rules and regulations would fall into disuse and the market would be practically abandoned as a major activity of the government. When a time of scarcity arrived, this shortsighted policy left the *alhóndiga* too badly crippled to act as efficiently as it should have done. Besides grain, almost all other commodities, such as meat, fruit, vegetables, and bread, were carefully regulated in price, in an attempt at fairness both to the consuming public and to business.

As the social and economic conditions of the era were basic factors in the development of movements of unrest, so in turn was the failure of the government to provide itself with adequate forces to suppress those outbreaks which led to rioting. When uprisings threatened the capital, three forces of protection were available to the viceroy: the regularly constituted police authority, the guard of soldiers kept in Mexico City, and the citizen militia, which was supposedly ready to answer a call to arms in case of an emergency. Twice in the seventeenth century all three of these agencies failed. . . .

There remains the question why the great tumults of the century occurred only in the years 1624 and in 1692. Two reasons present themselves. First, there was the difference in the degree to which scarcity in foodstuffs was felt. In 1624 and in 1692 the suffering was much greater, and continued over longer periods of time, than during other crises which developed in the seventeenth century. Hence the people were driven to extremes of desperation. Second, there was the difference in the administrative ability of the persons in authority. Several times the poor were so far aroused that many of them went in a body to the palace, and each time obtained satisfaction quickly and with a minimum of irritation because the viceroys proved equal to the occasion. This was not true in 1624 and in 1692, when the potentially dangerous conditions in Mexico City ended in uprisings.

The tumults achieved few permanent results, by reason of their nature. In the first place, although the riots were exceedingly violent, they lasted only for very short periods, thus quickly relieving the government from pressure for reform. Second, they were spontaneous outbreaks without plan, program, or leadership, and flared up from immediate resentment. Consequently, the riots prompted administrative reform in the city but brought about no permanent social or economic improvement. Once quiet was restored, and there was no longer any reason for the government to be alarmed, most of the new regulations were relaxed until another period of crisis arrived. The importance of the riots, then, lies in the light which they throw upon social and economic conditions under the viceroys, and not upon the reforms which followed close upon them.

24. Why Were Creoles Unable to Compete with Spanish Immigrants?

D. A. BRADING

Professor David Brading of Yale University here analyzes clearly the explanations, true and fancied, for the fact that the Spaniards born in Mexico could not compete with the immigrants from Spain. The peninsular Spaniards excelled in wealth, trade, office-holding, and in mining. His conclusions help us to understand why the American Spaniards were both weak and dissatisfied toward the end of the colonial period.

During the eighteenth century the Crown granted some 50 new titles of nobility to persons resident in New Spain. In most cases the only observable criterion of selection was the possession of great riches. The Mexican aristocracy was recruited from the financial élite, and in general can be accepted as a representative sample of the colony's wealthy classes. An analysis of its composition, therefore, will yield revealing evidence as to the formation of great fortunes in New Spain. The scheme shown in the table will best illustrate this pattern.

From "The Creole Inheritance," in *Miners and Merchants in Bourbon Mexico 1763–1810* by D. A. Brading (Cambridge, England; Cambridge University Press, 1971), pp. 208–216, passim. Reprinted by permission.

Mexican nobility of the eighteenth century (creations).

	Peninsulars	Americans	Unknown	Total
Miners	9	6	1	16
Merchants	10	—	—	10
Landowners	2	10	—	12
Officials	7	1	—	8
Unknown	1	2	—	3
Total	29	19	1	49

Two significant facts emerge from this scheme. In the first place the importance of mining and commerce as compared to landowning and office-holding. The significance of mining is increased if we note that the two younger ennobled sons of the Count of Regla are placed in the category of landowners although their estates were purchased from their father's mining profits and that one official gained his wealth and title through marriage to a daughter of the Count. The second striking phenomenon is the great quantity of peninsular Spaniards, not merely in trade and office-holding, but also in mining. They obtained 60 per cent of all new creations of nobility.

Clearly the scheme — and the arguments of previous chapters which it largely confirms — provokes the query: Why were the creoles unable to compete with the immigrant Spaniards? For here we have a society established for over two hundred years which still required — or permitted — immigrants of relatively humble extraction to seize control of commerce and a good part of mining, to assemble great fortunes, and to crown their achievements with the purchase of titles of nobility. The gachupín success rested upon the failure of the creole. Why was the creole unable to compete with his immigrant cousin, and what were the consequences of this failure?

Most contemporary observers of colonial society gave a forthright and harsh response to our query. The American Spaniard of the respectable classes, they asserted, was idle. True, the more sympathetic hastened to qualify this judgment, declaring that the creole best exercised his talents in the professions, in literature and the arts. But most agreed that he lacked all sense of business. In consequence there existed a universal tendency for the American Spaniards to consume their inherited estates. Now admittedly, evidence for these generalisations is almost entirely literary but the unanimity of both passing travellers, permanent residents, and even accounts written by creoles themselves is sufficiently striking as to demand discussion. For if we accept this testimony as reliable then we are confronted with an unexpected and indeed controversial conclusion to our study of Mexican miners and merchants.

In 1763 Father Ajofrín, an itinerant Capuchin friar, stated: "Notwith-standing that the natives or creoles are so capable and fit for letters and the professions, it has been found that they do not have the required economy for trade, the management of haciendas and the administration of their house-holds; it happens all the time that gachupín fathers leave their sons great for-tunes in commerce and haciendas, and within a short time these are consumed or diminished."

In 1809 Pedro de Fonte, later Archbishop of Mexico, made a similar but more hostile observation:

> Since their education is in opulence and comfort, they view with distaste serious occupation and fall quickly into a languid inertia which at the same time buries them in vice and misery. Most can glory in the wealth of their fathers and ancestors, but there are few who have not wasted their fortune and property, or if they retain a part, then the profit barely exceeds the interest of the mortgages with which their estates are charged. Favoured or exalted by their noble origin, they despise the Indians and mixed breeds, and ashamed of their own vices and dissipations, entertain a secret aversion to, and envy of, the Europeans, who by their toil, so-briety and energy enjoy consideration and comfort. This class, rival to all the rest, wishes to enjoy alone the advantage of this soil.

Both priests were, of course, peninsular Spaniards; they expressed the opinions and prejudices of the gachupín community resident in Mexico. But corroboration for their views can be gleaned from various declarations made by the Mexican creoles themselves. At the beginning of the eighteenth century, for example, Juan Antonio de Ahumada in an open letter to the new king, Philip V, asseverated that the American Spaniards were little better than pil-grims in their own country. They were rarely if ever appointed to high office in the Church or the royal administration. Without such reward they lacked all incentive to study or to undertake arduous achievements and in consequence they relapsed into a vicious sloth, the source of all their evils and failure.

The ayuntamiento of Mexico City, a creole stronghold, largely concurred with Ahumada's argument. In 1771 in a petition presented to the Spanish Crown they demanded that public office in New Spain should be reserved to natives of the country. They were at pains to emphasise the noble ancestry of the American Spaniards; many of the best families in the Peninsula, they asserted, had despatched their younger sons to the New World. The common gachupín insinuation that most creoles possessed Indian blood was vehemently denied. Furthermore, they affirmed that their children "are bred and educated in the same splendour [as their forefathers], enjoy delicate foods, ornate clothing, the pomp and attention of servants, sumptuous buildings and exquisite furniture . . . they are ignorant of manual work and for the most part dedicate themselves to their studies. . . . Mechanic jobs neither agree with the lustre of their birth nor offer a decent subsistence." Given this upbringing the American Spaniard depended upon public office in order to subsist. Without it, so the ayuntamiento argued, the creoles were forced to enter the priesthood or to remain bachelors. If they did risk marriage, economic necessity would drive their children into the ranks of the populace.

In effect, both Ahumada and the author of the 1771 petition agreed with the observations of Ajofrín and Fonte; they differed only in their explanation: the peninsular clerics ascribed creole failings to their character and the nature of their talents, whereas the two Mexicans explained the disastrous situation of their class by its virtual exclusion from public office. That the creole was idle and that he tended to waste his fortune no one denied.

Clearly, what we have here is a description of a colonial élite denied its birthright — the governance of the country. The American Spaniard, by reason of his family and race, was born, bred and educated within a socially privileged and materially comfortable class, demonstrably superior to the surrounding coloured population. "All creoles are born to be hidalgos," wrote Juan López de Cancelada, an acute observer. Now hidalgos, generally speaking, rarely sought to enter business; instead they expected public employment. And in the New World the American Spaniards from the sixteenth century until Independence besieged the Crown with petitions for office and complaints at their exclusion. The creole wanted to be a viceroy, a governor, a bishop, a general, a high court judge. It was from the exercise of political power that he aspired to obtain both prestige and profit. Denied access to such positions he did not, unless driven by extreme necessity, engage in economic enterprise; instead, he live off his estates, took up a profession, and consumed his inheritance.

Juan López de Cancelada wrote an amusing dialogue about the consequences of the creole's dislike of business as seen by gachupín cousin and creole son.

> *Gachupín* — I came from Spain without a penny: I received 20,000 pesos from my uncle's business in the ten years during which I worked for a third of the profits, leaving my uncle 350,000 pesos; and my cousin, who then inherited the money, has wasted it, and now wants to support himself, his wife and children, without knowing more than Latin.

> *Creole* — He came to my father's house from Spain without shoes, a brute of a fellow, and now that he is rich he wishes to be consul. These gachupines come here to be somebody and to take possession of all that our land produces: we are to be blamed for permitting it.

It was Lucas Alamán who summarised the final effect of the American Spaniard's character and ambitions:

> The result of these unhappy propensities [of creole character] was the short duration of fortunes, so that the Europeans' efforts in working to gather and leave an estate to their children can be compared to the bottomless tunnel of the Danaides which was never filled no matter how much was thrown into it. Hence in order to endure in prosperity and opulence the Spanish race in America required to be remade continuously by European families as those formed by their predecessors fell into obscurity and poverty.

Himself the son of an immigrant merchant, Alamán cited the Andaluz proverb, "Father a merchant, son a gentleman, grandson a beggar." The cycle of three generations is, of course, echoed in the proverbs of many nations. The rise and fall of wealthy families is a constant within most societies. Equally frequent is the recruitment of successful merchants into the ranks of the landed classes and the preference of their sons to enter the professions. But in one important respect New Spain differed from other such traditional societies. In Mexico it was generally immigrants who made fortunes, it was the native-born who lost them. The usual circular process of rise and fall was therefore broken. For the most part it was European Spaniards who ascended the social scale, it was American Spaniards who descended. There was small chance of upward social mobility for any creole. New Spain, therefore, possessed a peculiarly colonial society — colonial in the sense that both prestige and wealth went to immigrants rather than to the native-born. Our argument of course depends upon the assumption that the populace, by reason of its racial composition and lack of education, was unable to climb to the level of the respectable classes, so that a creole family, once submerged among the masses, could rarely hope to regain its lost status. Naturally this process of social decline did not affect families with equal rapidity: in general it was the grandsons of the successful immigrant who most felt the pinch of economic necessity. By then, the original estate had been subjected to two testamentary divisions. It was in this generation that the battle of existence began in earnest.

Our presentation of Alamán's theory has been both extreme and schematic; many exceptions to the rule can be advanced and in any case it foreshortens what was often a century-long struggle for social survival. Moreover, as so far argued, it must leave us more puzzled than convinced. For Alamán, like Ajofrín and Fonte, explained the process of social decline by appeal to the creole's education and character. Yet surely economic reasons must be adduced if we are to explain why inherited capital was consumed or dissipated. Was it just indolence and unsatisfied political ambitions that prevented the creole from accumulating wealth or maintaining his estate? Or did his financial ruin spring from his choice of occupation? What in fact could the creole do; what jobs were open to him?

Once posed in this form, the problem becomes more manageable. For the most cursory examination immediately reveals the fact that the professions — the creole's chosen field of activity — provided sustenance for remarkably few people. In 1803 an official inquiry found that New Spain possessed 386 lawyers, of whom only 210 actually practised. The great majority (over 171) lived in Mexico City. Yet even this small number found it difficult to gain a livelihood. In 1807 Carlos María de Bustamante complained that after eight years of practice, "I hardly have sufficient bread for my family." He averred that a mere handful of men monopolised litigation in the audiencia, making great fortunes while "the remainder of the lawyers groan in poverty."

Other careers were hard to seek. There were fewer doctors than lawyers; in 1793 they did not number more than 140. Notaries were similarly sparse — no more than 180. The regular army, recruited since the 1760s, formed a new but limited source of employment. By 1800 it did not have more than 200 creole officers. We can now better appreciate the importance of the royal bureaucracy. But its numbers are not easy to calculate. Whereas nearly all lawyers, doctors and notaries were creole, the bureaucracy was precisely the profession most dominated by peninsular Spaniards. Possibly there were up to a thousand posts on which were assigned salaries sufficient to maintain in comfort a family of the respectable classes. But we do not know the proportion held by creoles.

All these occupations dwindle, however, in comparison to the Church. By 1809 New Spain possessed 7,431 priests and religious, the overwhelming majority of whom were native-born Spaniards. True, many clergymen, particularly the encumbents of country parishes, were recruited from the lower levels of society — not all seven thousand were born into families of the "gente decente." Moreover, in the higher offices and the religious orders some peninsular Spaniards were to be found. But in general it was the creole who staffed the multitude of clerical institutions — the cathedral chapters, the university, the colleges, the hospitals, the monasteries and the parishes. For the Church offered both social prestige and generous stipends; the clergy were the natural leaders of Mexican society.

But of course the entrance of numerous young creoles of the upper class into a celibate priesthood abruptly terminated the course of many wealthy families. No doubt the Church offered an asylum for the impecunious — a refuge for the progeny of families descending the social scale. But many cases could be cited where the unexpected death of an elder brother brought a considerable inheritance to the surviving son who had become a priest. Nor could such estates be legally passed on to illegitimate children. The Church, therefore, was a key institution which by its insistence upon celibacy contributed to undermine the stability of the colonial élite.

Apart from the professions the impecunious creole could always enter some form of economic enterprise. But here, especially in commerce, he was confronted by the clannish confraternity of gachupín merchants who distrusted his capacity and honesty and who frequently refused to concede him necessary credit. Many American Spaniards did become traders but few attained more than a mediocre success. The conventional stereotypes about creole character — his lack of business sense and his unreliability — became self-fulfilling predictions. Moreover, as Dr Mora pointed out, whereas the gachupín was supported by an extended network of paisanos, the creole had to struggle as an individual.

If in general the slow, penny-pinching routine of shopkeeping did not attract the American Spaniard, by contrast the speculative, lucky-strike quality of silver mining exercised a perennial fascination. But silver mining tended to attract men who were either foolishly avaricious or hopelessly impoverished. It was all too easy for a creole of moderate means to lose his entire fortune in an unsuccessful mine; it was even more common for a creole of good family and no means to sink without trace amidst the rough camaraderie of the mining camp. Then again, in an industry so heavily dependent upon mercantile capital, the creole miner and refiner suffered the effects of gachupín prejudice and competition. Nevertheless, despite the industry's hazardous nature, it undoubtedly offered the American Spaniard far better opportunities for social redemption than was possible in commerce. But as a prescription it was a remedy that more often killed than cured. It certainly injected a feverish quality into colonial society.

In the last resort, neither the limited number of professional jobs, the celibacy of the clergy, the gachupín control of trade, nor the risk-laden nature of silver mining will suffice to explain the social and economic debility of New Spain's native-borne élite. For the stronghold, the basis, of the creole class was the land. The immigrant merchants, the wealthy miners, creole and gachupín alike — these men all invested their fortunes in the purchase of haciendas. In a country without joint stock companies or banks only the land offered rich entrepreneurs the prospect of a well-endowed and secure future for their descendants. Lucas Alamán's theory, therefore, stands or falls upon the economic viability of the Mexican hacienda. If these large estates were profitable then it is difficult to explain why the families which owned them should have been subject to a continuous process of social replacement. No description of the Mexican élite can be complete without a discussion of the hacienda and its problems.

Whereas the 6,680 ranchos and the 4,680 Indian villages listed in 1809 of necessity mainly lived off their own crops, New Spain's 4,945 haciendas and estancias produced for a market. A hacienda existed to provide its owner with an income. True, many were left deserted as mere parks for semi-wild herds of cattle and sheep, but in such case they served no observable purpose. For in general most landowners preferred to live in a town; they visited their estates for a few months in a year, if at all, and for the rest entrusted their property to the care of a manager. The Mexican hacendados formed an absentee land-lord class who relied upon their estates to yield an income sufficient to maintain an upper-class town-dwelling family in style and comfort. Almost no one bought a hacienda to live on it, still less to feed himself. Many large estates frequently had to support two élite families — the owner's and that of his manager.

But as a unit of production the hacienda was notoriously defective. For there was a peculiar disproportion between the number and average size of the Mexican hacienda — some covered over a hundred square miles — and the minuscule market it supplied. Travellers of the period, such as Father Morfi, lamented over the vast tracts of land left derelict by their owners. But to what point cultivation, if the crops could not be sold? Only the sparsely distributed chain of towns and mining camps offered an adequate market. True, certain regions such as the Bajío and the Valley of Mexico presented urban markets situated at an economic distance. But elsewhere most haciendas made use of but a small portion of their land, and rented out the remainder to their peons, vagrant squatters and neighbouring Indian villages. Moreover, the depressed price level of most agricultural produce did not permit landowners, even on favourably situated estates, to make much profit. For example, the one district of Chalco, with some help from Toluca, satisfied Mexico City's demand for maize; yet in 1773 it was estimated that average production per hacienda amounted to no more than 3,000 fanegas a year, which, with maize prices varying from one to two pesos a fanega, provided a return of at most 6,000 ps., from which the production costs had still to be subtracted.

In general, the Mexican hacienda yielded a poor return upon the large quantity of capital usually invested in its purchase. . . . A contributory cause for the colonial hacienda's low income was to be found in the taxes to which its produce was subject. The Crown levied an excise duty of 6 per cent, and sometimes 8 per cent, on the value of all its sales. In addition the Church collected a tithe of all its produce. The Jesuit estates mentioned above, once confiscated, paid, in both excise and tithe, over 14 per cent of their total income. The Church bore heavily upon Mexican agriculture: in the period 1779–89 its tithes in New Spain (excluding Yucatán) averaged 1,835,000 ps. a year.

Moreover, the Church also acted as the colony's land bank. By 1805 it possessed a capital of about 44 million pesos, which was mainly invested in mortgages and loans secured upon urban and, more especially, rural property. This huge sum represented the accumulated product of three centuries of pious donations, testamentary bequests and invested interest. It comprised the annuities that supported the secular clergy and the endowments that sustained hospitals, asylums, orphanages and colleges. Thus the Mexican hacienda, upon which largely fell the burden of paying the 5 per cent interest accruing from these clerical mortgages and annuities, maintained not merely the fabric and liturgy of the Church, but also the entire charitable, medical and educational establishment of the colony.

The explanation for this peculiarly heavy burden can be found in the reciprocal needs of the Church and the land-owning class. Most haciendas required credit, and hence tended to accumulate debts. A bad harvest, a drought, a mining or commercial venture, a charitable donation, a daughter's dowry, an annuity for a younger son, mere conspicuous consumption: all these expenses were met by mortgages charged upon haciendas, and although in the first instance such loans were usually only granted for five-year periods, an almost perpetual extension was common. It was not infrequent to encounter haciendas which bore inherited mortgages worth up to 50 per cent of their market value. For its part the Church — almost the only source of long-term credit open to the hacendado — clearly deemed haciendas to be far safer prospects than silver mines or an *obraje;* only urban property offered comparable advantages. Moreover, such mortgages yielded an income — at 5 per cent — without the labour that outright ownership of an estate entailed. Thus most clerical capital was charged upon the hacienda, invested in land, the colony's only tangible security which provided an income. Naturally this reciprocity of interest between Church and landowner soon led to situations where the impecunious hacendado became little more than a manager for his clerical creditors. The intendant of Puebla reported that the 38 haciendas and 17 ranchos of Cholula were worth 788,442 ps., of which value 550,504 ps. were held by the Church. Although Cholula was probably atypical, the tendency it represented was universal. By the end of the eighteenth century most haciendas bore a heavy burden of debt.

The Mexican hacienda thus constituted a weak foundation for a stable class of landed families. The cycle which Gómez de Cervantes observed at work in the seventeenth century proved to be a continuous process, equally applicable to the eighteenth century. Apart from a handful of magnates, the owners of entire provinces such as the Rincón Gallardo or the Marquises of San Miguel de Aguayo, the average hacendado family found it difficult to weather the passage of the generations. In general a contemporary student of clerical mortgages declared that few families held their estates for more than three generations. Francisco Pimentel stated that barely a hacienda existed which had not been purchased with capital acquired in mining, industry or trade. If such be the case then the Mexican hacienda was a sink through which drained without stop the surplus capital accumulated in the export economy. The fortunes created in mining and commerce were invested in land, there to be slowly dissipated or to be gradually transferred into the coffers of the Church. In consequence, a continuous replacement in the hacendado class occurred. New Spain's élite was unstable in composition precisely because its chosen economic basis, the hacienda, absorbed and wasted the greater part of the colony's accumulated capital. This instability was not to end until the Mexican Revolution.

25. *Tensions between Spanish- and Spanish-American-Born Friars in Seventeenth-Century Peru*

ANTONINE TIBESAR

Father Antonine Tibesar of the Academy of American Franciscan History has carried on research for a number of years on the ecclesiastical history of Peru. Here he describes the growing tension between friars from Spain and those born in Peru, based on a wide variety of sources.

Serious trouble eventually came, which led to fire, tumultuous scenes, and death. The long-range consequences were unfortunate for the Church: "the clergy suffered a continuing loss of both prestige and numbers. . . . The alternative seems to have been a mistake for both Church and State."

Within recent years there has been increasing interest in those aspects of Spanish American history which represent a growing political consciousness

From "The Alternativa: A Study in Spanish-Creole Relations in Seventeenth-Century Peru" by Antonine Tibesar, O.F.M., *The Americas,* 11 (1955), pp. 229–283, passim. Reprinted by permission.

among the inhabitants of those lands especially during the seventeenth and eighteenth centuries.

Perhaps nowhere can the growth of this sentiment be studied with greater ease than in the religious orders. By their development, the religious orders, the Augustinians, Dominicans, Franciscans, Jesuits, and Mercedarians, came to consist almost exclusively of *criollos* (descendants of Europeans born in America) and *Chapetones* (friars born in Europe, in particular in Spain): the two groups which were to be the leaders of the two contending parties in the wars of independence. The ultimate estrangement of these two groups developed during the colonial period in the course of which the rising creole desire to manage their own affairs encountered increasing opposition from the Spanish Crown. The encounters were not always peaceful. The participants, on both sides, in good faith held to their principles with a deep conviction of which the incidental vehemence is perhaps the clearest proof. Neither side yielded readily. This is true also of the friars.

By their constitutions, most religious orders held elections every three or four years in which the friar-delegates freely elected their provincials and his council. Of course, these elections afforded the creoles, and the Spaniards too, a perfect opportunity to voice their sentiments regarding the type of candidate which they preferred with comparative freedom and immunity. Thus the chapters of the religious orders may in a certain sense be regarded as the first forum in which the creole was able to state for the first time his preference in regard to his ruler. There was perhaps little political significance, at least in the beginning, in the decisions of these chapters. The friars were not revolutionaries seeking to overthrow Spanish authority, though they may well have wished to restrict the extent of the Spanish monopoly of positions and power. Neither were these chapters wholly without political significance. Many friars in the seventeenth century were members of powerful creole families. Their relatives, who did have political ambitions which were regularly thwarted by the royal policy of preferring *Chapetones* exclusively for the highest offices, regarded these chapters with more than passing interest. In them their unspoken protests found voice. This was realized by the royal officials and in an effort to curb creole aspirations the Crown imposed the *alternativa:* the forced alternation in the higher offices of the respective provinces of Spanish and Peruvian friars.

The first friars who arrived in Peru were, of course, almost exclusively Europeans. The bulk of these were Spaniards, though we do find Portuguese, French, and even Germans in their ranks. The Dominicans and the Mercedarians came with Pizarro in 1531 with the Franciscans following their example after a few months. The Augustinians came in 1551 and the Jesuits in

1568. From the very beginning, the Dominicans do not seem to have received any Indians or those with Indian blood in their ranks, and all available evidence today points to the conclusion that the Dominicans as a rule received only Spanish or creoles. The Mercedarians at an early date, certainly before 1548, had already established the policy of admitting Indian and mestizo boys — a fact which may help to explain the attitude of that order towards the Pizarros and also its loss of social acceptance by the Spaniards which resulted in its royal suppression in 1568. The Franciscans seem to have adopted in the beginning the Dominican attitude, although there are some indications that they may have admitted Indians as lay brothers, though not as priests. In general also the Augustinians accepted the Dominican policy and at a comparatively early date, 1571, forbade the reception of mestizos. The attitude of the first Jesuits towards the mestizos is not clear but after the arrival of Father Joseph de Acosta in 1572, the Jesuits, for a time, became the devoted protectors of the mestizos and admitted a number into their Order, among them the famous Blas de Valera. The experiment, however, did not prove happy and in 1582 the Jesuits also excluded them. From that time, until possibly the middle of the eighteenth century, the religious order in Peru with the exception of the Jesuits were to be made up almost exclusively of creoles and *Chapetones*. After their sad experiences with the mestizos, the Jesuits proceeded to limit also the numbers of creoles who might join their company. This limitation was not removed until late in the eighteenth century.

The other Orders had placed no limit on the reception of creoles and accordingly as the century advanced an ever greater proportion of the total number came to be drawn from this class. The desire to manage their own affairs grew apace with their numbers and importance and before the end of the sixteenth century encountered considerable opposition from the Spanish friars who had founded the provinces in Peru and had enjoyed a monopoly in their government for a number of decades. In particular was this true of the Dominicans who had been the first religious to organize a province in that country and apparently also the first to receive candidates. It is understandable therefore that this problem would become acute first of all among them. As early as 1565, Castro informed the Crown of the existence of factions among them. Castro did not specify the cause of the division but in 1588, Viceroy Villar reported that the desire of the creole Dominicans to govern themselves was the cause of internal difficulties. At the same time, the viceroy added that the Spanish Dominicans were few in number. By 1592, the creoles were so firmly entrenched among them that they were able to pass a law which prohibited the entrance of any Spaniard into the Dominican Lima province. The situation must have been very similar in the other Orders for by 1593, the majority of the friars in all Orders in Peru were creoles, though none of the others is known actually to have forbidden the reception of Spaniards.

The situation occasioned by the emergence of the creole friars to positions of power disturbed the royal officials both in Peru and in Spain. It would simplify the problem if we could state that this uneasiness was merely the reflection of the usual antagonism of the metropolis versus the colony. However the matter is not quite that simple. The Spanish officials and the Crown just did not feel at this time that the creole friars were quite ready to manage their own affairs and they feared that under continual creole control the state of the religious orders would decline or deteriorate. Fairness demands that this writer state that he found no responsible Spanish official whose uneasiness over creole control at this time was motivated by racial or political implications. Their opposition was based at the end of the sixteenth century not on discernible political motives but on the lack of personal qualifications by the creole class in general.

Actually it is somewhat difficult to comprehend the need for Spanish concern because at this very time when the authorities were worrying about creole competence, the Church in Peru was being or was about to be blessed with a series of men and one woman of extraordinary virtue. However that may be, the official reason for Spanish opposition to creole control at that time was the widely held belief that the creoles just were not then fit for the job. Strange to say, creole resentment against continued Spanish monopoly seems to have been based at this time on the same grounds. The creole friars felt that the Spanish friar who came to Peru or the Spanish boy in Peru who wished to be a friar were usually the misfits or the laggards from Spain and the creoles did not want them. Besides they felt that even the best Spanish friars frequently were unable to view with sympathy and equanimity the innovations which the circumstances of life in the New World had rendered necessary. Here again, therefore, the personal qualifications seem to have been the prime consideration, not the racial or political. This was to change both for the Spaniards and for the creoles in the course of the next century, as we shall see. But in the early years of the seventeenth century, the creole-Spanish problem does not seem to have been rooted in either racial or political considerations and suggestions made at that time by the viceroys and others which might have tended towards that development were either ignored or expressly prohibited, perhaps in the hope that the problem might somehow finds its own solution.

If such were indeed the desire of the Crown, it was doomed to be frustrated. The problem would not disappear and the solution which was evolved during the ensuing decades of the seventeenth century — if solution it may be called — was in essence racial. This solution was called the *alternativa*. The *alternativa* signified the forced alternate election of Spaniards and creoles to the main offices in the provinces irrespective of superior qualifications or superior numbers. The reason for selection, therefore, was primarily the place of birth. . . . Despite the great numerical superiority of the creoles, the Spanish friars maintained an almost complete monopoly of the higher offices in the Lima province down to almost 1650 with relatively little creole dissent. However, by 1630, there is evidence of an awakening creole consciousness of their power. . . . On the basis of numbers . . . the Spanish friars were receiving a fair representation in the election of the provincial — the highest office in the province filled by direct and free election of the members of the province. However, the disturbing element in the picture was the constant trend against the Spaniards, and these had little hope for improvement in the ratio. This disquieted the Europeans and rumbles of their dissatisfaction with the turn of events are discernible in their letters to the Crown beginning already in the 1640's. The ready made equalizer was the *alternativa*. . . .

The motives which led the Spanish friars to seek the *alternativa* may be reduced to three: (1) distrust of creole capabilities and perhaps also of their loyalty; (2) a feeling that the creoles owed such consideration to the Spaniards because of their services in the past; (3) a vague certainty of Spanish superiority. Nowhere do the Spanish friars assert that they seek the *alternativa* because of ambition, just as nowhere do the creoles admit that they wish to reject the *alternativa* for the same reason. It is evident that the creoles, or Americans and Peruvians as they were frequently called during the debate, could not agree completely with the views advanced by their Spanish brethren. Nor apparently was there any neutral ground upon which to base a compromise. The argument therefore would have to continue until either one side or the other was adjudged the victor. In 1666, this meant that the Peruvians would have to appeal since the 1664 decree had been adverse to their wishes. . . . [All appeals failed, and by 1680 the Americans seemed to be ready for open revolt.]

On Sunday evening, December 29, 1680, at about eleven o'clock a fire was discovered at one of the five doors leading to the private quarters of the Commissary General, Father Marcos Terán. Though both Terán and the viceroy-archbishop claim that this fire was begun by the creoles, neither of them investigated its origin. The city council of Lima which "conducted a thorough investigation uncovered nothing concerning either the authors or the origin of the fire." Their conclusion was that "it might have been started by some student friars or by others to throw blame on them." At any rate no harm was done and the remaining four doors permitted Terán free egress.

As soon as the alarm was given by a lay brother who chanced to pass on his way to bed from the convent chapel, a Spanish friar of most curious ancestry and habits and five men in lay clothes, all fully armed, rushed from the quarters of Terán and roamed the cloisters while Terán made his way to the chapel of La Soledad. When asked later what these armed men were doing in his quarters, Terán answered that he had been warned a few days before that the creoles were plotting to kill him and the Spanish friar had organized an armed guard.

At the time the alarm was first given some of the younger friars were just rising to go to church for their regular midnight prayers. Some of these began to toll the church bells to give the alarm and this was soon taken up also by the bells of the cathedral — the official sign of an enemy attack. The confusion both within San Francisco — which is three blocks long by about a block and a half wide — and in the city was indescribable. In the city itself perhaps matters were worse than in the convent because the people had just passed through a series of alarms due to the pirates along the coast and their first thought was of course that the pirates had returned.

The viceroy was informed at 11:30 P.M. of the happenings and immediately ordered the *alcaldes* and their infantry to the monastery to search for weapons and to quiet the people now gathering there. The search continued until 2 A.M. though no weapons were found anywhere except in the quarters of Terán, which in the words of the *maese de campo* were "many and good ones too." Terán was escorted by some of the soldiers to the viceregal palace while three companies patrolled the streets outside the monastery and another company was garrisoned within to control the main doors. The majority of these soldiers were Spaniards.

Monday, December 30, passed in this fashion. "It was a day of shots and confusion within and without the monastery." No friar was permitted to leave and all doors remained under the control of the soldiers. Under the circumstances, of course, tension mounted between the Spanish soldiers and the creole friars especially the young students as insults were shouted back and forth. Terán issued a statement laying all the blame on the Peruvian friars and placing all of them under excommunication. During the late afternoon about 2,400 soldiers were concentrated around the monastery in obedience to the viceroy's orders to the astonishment of the people. The *alcaldes* were again sent in to search for arms with no more success than on the preceding night, even though the entire monastery was searched room by room.

Tuesday, December 31, came with a company of soldiers still camped in the monastery and others on the outside. The viceroy had sent them into the convent on Sunday night perhaps without much thought and the problem now seemed to have been how to withdraw them without losing prestige. Some reason had to be found to justify this extreme measure. In the palace, the viceroy and some of the members of the audiencia agreed with Terán that this was the occasion to exile fifteen more friars to Chile: nine of them priests and six student friars. Among the priests was Father Cristoval de Contreras, the nominal leader of the creoles. Accordingly at 5 P.M. the *alcalde de corte,* D. Gaspar de Cuba, came to San Francisco and asked to see the nine priests. When the priests came and were informed of the purpose of the visit, they merely requested permission to return to their rooms to get some clothes. Thereupon, without protest or other difficulty, all nine were put in coaches drawn up outside the monastery and driven under guard to Callao preparatory to their shipment to Chile. After seeing the nine priests driven off, the *alcalde* returned to call for the six students. As he knocked at the door of the students' quarters, he heard a shot from within and a terrible scream. Without fulfilling his mission, the *alcalde* departed as soon as he heard that a friar deacon, Francisco Manrique, had been shot and instantly killed by a shot in the heart by a soldier of a Basque company which was on guard. What seems to have happened was that the students were panic-stricken when they heard the *alcalde* had come to take away some of their number. They tried to escape by fleeing through a *puerta falsa* which they mistakenly thought was unguarded. As they opened the gate, one of the guards fired and Manrique fell mortally wounded. The tension of three days on the guards and on the friars had reached its climax.

Pandemonium now broke loose. The people in the streets hearing the shot and the ensuing screams and shouts broke open one of the doors of the church to enter the monastery. The friars at the same time tried to get out of the monastery but the soldiers resisted their efforts until one of the priests brought the Blessed Sacrament from the students' chapel. Thereupon one of the captains, the only creole captain, ordered his men who were guarding the door to the church to permit the friars to leave. Lima now saw what was most probably the strangest procession in its entire history emerge from the church of San Francisco. A huge mulatto had picked up the body of the slain deacon and carried it cradled in his arms with the blood oozing to the ground. Most of the friars followed the Blessed Sacrament to the College of the Jesuits of San Pablo, while the mulatto carried the body across the *plaza mayor* in front of the viceregal palace to the church of the Dominicans, while the bells of the churches tolled in mourning. Only those of San Francisco were silent because the guards would not permit the few friars who remained to ring them. The viceroy issued a *bando* to clear the streets, but that was not necessary. Stunned by the happenings of the afternoon, the people dispersed rapidly, each one rather anxious to get home. . . .

It was quite evident that events had gotten out of hand. The people of Lima, submissive and rather timid, were greatly disturbed and it may well have been true, as the viceroy stated, that only good fortune prevented a bloody outbreak. Certainly a more virile race would have done something long before that. The Augustinian, Jesuit, and Mercedarian superiors in Lima protested not only against the tyranny of the viceroy and of the commissary general but against the *alternativa* as well. Among the people, aroused nationalistic loyalties divided husband from wife, parents from children. Some wives even asked to be separated from their husbands. More to be feared were the rumbles of discontent among the Indians of the sierra and of unrest among the miners. Now it was the turn of the authorities to be dismayed at the effects which their imprudent measures had provoked. With a complete lack of a sense of responsibility for the chaos to which the Franciscan Order had been reduced, Terán blithely announced that he thought that he could no longer do anything with the creoles and hence he would take the first ship to leave the country. Apparently he did so too, and from the north finally sent a letter appointing the Spaniard, Father Diego Phelipe de Cuellar to handle the situation. Liñán also suddenly decided that he had never wanted to support Terán's efforts anyway. Instead on January 1, 1681, he decided to permit the *alternativa* to lapse and to withdraw the troops from San Francisco. As he wrote to the king:

> Although the disobedience and rebellion of these creoles galls me greatly, it is almost impossible to punish it as it deserves because of the general support they receive from the entire kingdom because of family ties and because of the sympathy [por la pasión] of all the other Orders.

Liñán then passed the problem to Madrid by recommending that the Crown should punish the friars by taking away their *doctrinas* and by appointing the provincial in the future from Madrid. . . .

The tensions engendered by the *alternativa* affected both State and Church in Peru. Politically, this struggle helped to emphasize the fact that while in law the Peruvians and Spaniards were equal vassals of the same kind, in fact the Peruvians were regarded by the Crown as colonials. Hence, there is reason to agree with those who profess to see in the *alternativa* one of the factors which fostered the growth of a Peruvian national consciousness and thereby, at least indirectly, of a desire for independence. Certainly at the time when other factors rendered the decision in favor of national independence feasible, the *alternativa* would have done much to prepare the minds of the Peruvians to concur in and to favor that decision.

More pronounced, perhaps, were the effects, both direct and indirect, upon the Church itself. Directly, to judge from the records of the Franciscans, the clergy suffered a continuing loss of both prestige and numbers. During the decade, 1680–1690, relatively few Peruvians entered the Franciscan Order in Lima, while before that date the annual increase averaged nearly twenty-four. At the same time, the young men after 1690 who did become Franciscans seem definitely to have belonged to a lower social class than had those who had been received before that decade. Also the average of the annual entrants never seems to have reached the volume maintained earlier. . . .

It is possible that the Church may have suffered also indirectly from the *alternativa*. At that time, there was union of Church and State. In the earlier decades of Peruvian history, the Church had undoubtedly profited from this union. Now the State demanded its payment. At a time when Spanish prestige was declining throughout the world, the Crown needed all the support it could muster. In this effort, it forced the Church, at least in the *alternativa* affair, to identify its interests with those of the State. Perhaps any other position at that time would have been unthinkable. It would seem to be just as unthinkable, although at this time there is little concrete proof for or against this theoretical conclusion, that the later revolutionary political leaders should have cherished the Church while hating the State with which it was identified.

In the long run, therefore, the *alternativa* seems to have been a mistake for both Church and State. The creole friars tried to persuade the royal officials to adopt this belief. They had failed. Accordingly, on January 6, 1686, the *alternativa* was finally imposed on the Lima Franciscans by explicit royal order.

26. *The Imperial City of Potosí, Boom Town Supreme*

LEWIS HANKE

The history of the mining city of Potosí in colonial Peru, now part of Bolivia, might be reduced to a series of graphs recording the amount of silver produced each year. Such a statistical report would tell the economic story of Potosí, and someday when the archives have been more thoroughly searched a chart of rising and falling production to indicate the curves of prosperity and decline in Potosí's history will surely be made. The following sketch, however, emphasizes the human aspects of the vicissitudes of this legendary silver city.

No city in all of the vast territory of America won for the King of Spain — save perhaps Mexico City — has had a more interesting or more important history than Potosí, located in the Viceroyalty of Peru. The colorful story of this great mountain of silver began when the Inca Emperor Huayna Capac started digging almost a century before the Spaniards arrived. He was halted — so legend has it — by a terrible noise and a mysterious voice which commanded, in the Quechua Indian language: "Take no silver from this hill. It is destined for other owners." The *conquistadores* heard no such prohibitory voice in 1545 when they were told of the rich silver ore by Indians who had accidentally discovered it, and indeed, if they had, would doubtless have considered themselves the rightful owners. They immediately began to develop Potosí, which was to become one of the most famous mines in the history of the world.

Treasure seekers flocked from Spain and many other parts of the world to this bleak and uninviting spot high up in the Andes, to exploit the silver in the *Cerro,* or sugar-loaf mountain, which rises majestically over the plateau to a height of almost 16,000 feet above sea level. The first census, taken by Viceroy Francisco de Toledo about twenty-five years after the news of the lode first burst upon the world, showed the unbelievable total of 120,000 inhabitants. By 1650 the population had risen — we are told — to 160,000 and Potosí was incomparably the largest city in South America. At a time when Virginia and the Massachusetts Bay Colony were puling infant colonies, unsure of their next harvest, Potosí had produced such quantities of silver that its very name had become so common a symbol for untold wealth that Don Quijote quoted to it Sancho Panza. *Vale un Potosí,* the Spaniards expressed it. The phrase "as rich as Potosí" became current in English literature as well, for within a generation of its discovery the astronomical quantities of silver mined there had become known to Spain's enemies and to others in far corners of the world. Potosí was soon marked on maps by the Portuguese, always the vigilant rivals of Spain, and even on the Chinese world map of Father Ricci, where it was placed in its correct position and called Mount *Pei-tu-hsi.*

The flush times of Potosí lasted for almost two centuries, and during this period the Imperial City (as it was officially designated by the Emperor Charles V) developed a wealthy and disorderly society. The vice, the piety, the crimes, the *fiestas* of these Potosinos, all were on a vast scale. In 1556, for example, eleven years after the founding of the city, the inhabitants celebrated the accession of Philip II to the throne of Spain with a party which lasted twenty-four days and cost eight million pesos. In 1577 three million pesos were spent on water works, an improvement which ushered in a period of even greater prosperity. By the end of the sixteenth century, miners in

From *The Imperial City of Potosí: An Unwritten Chapter in the History of Spanish America* by Lewis Hanke (The Hague: Martinus Nijhoff, 1956), pp. 1–42, passim. Reprinted by permission of the publisher.

search of recreation could choose among the fourteen dance halls, the thirty-six gambling houses, and the one theater, the price of admission to which ranged from forty to fifty pesos. Later, one of the governors organized a "grandiosa fiesta," to celebrate an ecclesiastical event, which included the establishment in one plaza of a circus "with as many different kinds of animals as in Noah's Ark, as well as fountains simultaneously spouting wine, water, and the native drink *chicha."* The seventeenth-century ecclesiastical chronicler Antonio de la Calancha declared: "In Potosí the signs of Libra and Venus predominate, and thus most of those who live there incline to be covetous, friends of music and festivities, zealous in the pursuit of riches, and somewhat given to venery." The scanty literature now available emphasizes about equally the carnal pleasures obtainable in the silver-rich mining camp, and the curious, awe-inspiring, and stupendous events of its uproarious history. Our knowledge of Potosí may be said to be still in the folklore stage.

For many years Potosí was boom town supreme and full of turbulence. Treachery, assassination, and civil war flourished as the natural result of the gambling, the intrigues, the antagonism between Peninsular Spaniards and American born Creoles, and the rivalries for the favor of women. Fighting became a pastime, a recognized social activity. Even the members of the town council came to their meetings armed with swords and pistols, and wearing coats of mail. The Dominican friar Rodrigo de Loaysa described the "accursed hill of Potosí" as a sink of iniquity, but the Viceroy García Hurtado de Mendoza declared that the mine was the *nervio principal en aquel reino,* "the principal support of that realm."

At one time, in the early part of the seventeenth century, there were some 700 or 800 professional gamblers in the city and 120 prostitutes, among them the redoubtable courtesan Doña Clara, whose wealth and beauty, the chroniclers assure us, were unrivalled. The most extravagant woman in Potosí, she was able to fill her home with the luxuries of Europe and the Orient, for her salon was frequented by the richest miners, who competed enthusiastically for her favors. Vagabonds abounded, and royal officials indignantly reported that there ne'er-do-wells did nothing but dress extravagantly and eat and drink to excess. So high were the stakes that one Juan Fernández dared to start a revolution in 1583, by which he hoped to make himself king of Potosí. He and his brothers planned to seize the city and, "despite the fact that he was a married man, Fernández had selected a widow, María Alvarez, to share the throne of his kingdom-to-be." The government learned of this plot and captured Fernández before his revolution could erupt, but this was not the last time that the wealth of Potosí engendered a fever of boundless hope and all-consuming desire among the bold spirits attracted to that cold and windy city.

A thick volume could be compiled on the plots that were hatched. One was the conspiracy led by Gonzalo Luis de Cabrera and the *relator* of the Audiencia de La Plata named Juan Díaz Ortiz. They caused royal officials much trouble in 1599 because they tried to smuggle in hundreds of Englishmen through the port of Buenos Aires to help them with their plans to take over Potosí.

When other mines were discovered, particularly after 1640, production began to slacken at Potosí. It continued to decline steadily throughout the eighteenth century, despite frantic efforts to improve the methods by which the silver was exploited, and at last the glory departed. The War for Independence was a decisive influence in the final decline of Potosí under Spanish rule. During this agitated period the Indians practically stopped working in the mine, and it was difficult to obtain materials needed for its operation. Up to 1816 Potosí was lost and won by the opposing forces three times. After 1816 Upper Peru was wholly occupied by royalist forces despatched by the Viceroy in Lima, and continuous guerrilla warfare was the rule. . . .

The citizens of Potosí early felt the growing pains of greatness and from the earliest years demanded royal recognition of their city's value to the crown. The Emperor Charles V bestowed upon Potosí the title Imperial City, and placed upon its first coat of arms the words: "I am rich Potosí, the treasure of the world, and the envy of kings." His prudent son Philip II devised the scarcely less modest legend on the shield he sent them, which is used to the present day: "For the powerful Emperor, for the wise King, this lofty mountain of silver could conquer the whole world." Here was a slightly veiled royal hint that it took money to make the wheels of empire turn around. Besides the royal cut of one-fifth of all silver mined there was also the possibility of "gifts" or "loans" by individual Potosinos to a succession of ever necessitous kings whose coffers held too little for their needs. A number of documents in the archives attest to the fact that Potosinos did assist the crown in this way.

The Potosinos naturally expected some return for their assistance. As the old Spanish proverb has it: "You trim my whiskers and I'll do your topknot." Therefore the Villa Imperial regularly sent representatives to the court thousands of miles away to make known their desires. Potosí early became irked at the fact that the City of La Plata, some 150 miles away, held jurisdiction over it. The miners at Potosí struggled to throw off this yoke and by 1561 had gained their independence.

The *cabildos* or municipal councils in America were relatively weak creatures in the Spanish colonies, but not so the group that ran the affairs of rich Potosí. Their representatives enjoyed real bargaining power, and they presented their demands in well-executed and detailed documents. Antonio de León Pinelo, one of the most outstanding administrators, lawyers, and bibliographers of the seventeenth century, drew up briefs and petitions on behalf of Potosí. Sebastián de Sandoval y Guzmán was particularly active, and his *Pretensiones de la Villa Imperial de Potosí,* printed in excellent fashion in Madrid in 1634, was typical of a whole literature which might be labeled "Pretensiones de Potosí."

What did the miners want? A steady supply of Indians for the *mita,* mercury at a low price, and freedom from bureaucratic interference by royal officials were some of the demands; and loud and insistent complaints of the miners on these and other problems fill many volumes in the archives. They resisted the drawing off of miners to fight as soldiers in Chile or other threatened parts of the empire. They felt that the regulation of Viceroy Toledo, establishing that miners should never be imprisoned for debt or their property sold to satisfy debts, was a wise law which should never be revoked, because it assured a steady production upon which depended the economic health of Potosí and consequently a steady revenue to the crown. The Real Banco de San Carlos was designed to help the miners, too, and the history of this bank will doubtless provide a valuable chapter in the fiscal history of Potosí.

The Potosinos agitated for an exemption from the *alcabala,* or sales tax, and also urged the crown to see to it that merchants in Panama and Peru sent sufficient merchandise to the ever-thirsty markets of Potosí. Above all, the Potosinos wanted the royal share of silver mined cut down from one fifth to one tenth of production.

All these and other privileges and exemptions were clamored for by a city conscious of its power and aware of the king's constant need for funds. Sometimes these requests were granted in part and for limited periods, but the Potosinos were never completely satisfied. As late as 1783 we find the king decorating the Villa Imperial with the title of "Fidelísima" or "Most Faithful," in another royal attempt to assuage some of their feelings with fine words. The struggle between a succession of hard-pressed monarchs and Potosí was in fact a continuous seesaw, ending only with the successful revolution against Spain. . . .

The wealth of Potosí drew to this Andean mining center Indians from many parts of Peru, a forced migration movement of great proportions that had never before been seen in the land, for under Inca rule only Indians on royal business had moved along the Inca highways. Negroes were also brought to Potosí, despite the doubts concerning their usefulness in the cold, rarefied atmosphere of Potosí. Spaniards from most parts of the peninsula and from all walks of life participated in the rush to explore the mine, and it does not seem strange to learn that one of the miners was a descendant of Columbus.

Foreigners were so numerous that the crown became alarmed at the dangers of their presence. A document dated 1581 lists the foreigners then in the city, and many other censuses of foreigners and reports on what they were doing, and whether their presence was "inconvenient" or not, were prepared by the hard-working representatives of the crown. The Inquisition documents provide information on suspected heretics and also on various Portuguese, who seem to have prospered in Potosí.

Another concern of the crown was the large number of vagabonds and ne'er-do-wells that flourished in the city. Not only did these lazy fellows not produce silver, but they might even be potentially dangerous, as a rebel group. Orders were despatched regularly for the "vagabonds that infest the city" to be punished and summarily ejected. These measures failing, the crown suggested that they be discreetly encouraged to engage in new discoveries and colonization attempts. If not killed in the frontier battles, at least they would be drawn away from Potosí and established far away, perhaps never to return!

The whole round of social life in this ebullient community has a sort of wild-west atmosphere. It was a vast melting pot, even more so than some other parts of the empire, for few white women could stand the climate; childbirth was particularly difficult because of the altitude. By 1586 enough *mestizos* or mixed bloods were present to provoke a riot, and the history of Potosí is well laced with disturbances which probably derived, in part at least, from the tremendous mixing of peoples that went on steadily. One little-known rebellion was attempted in 1599 with the help of the English.

This mixing of racial strains produced some interesting results. From time to time legal documents are found in the archives concerning the action of an individual who wishes to be recognized legally as a *mestizo,* because otherwise he would be forced to work in the mines as an Indian. And at least one legal process relates to a person who stated that he was an Indian and did not want to be considered a *mestizo.*

Tailors went berserk in 1604 over an election of their guild officers and even Augustinian friars once had to be reproved by the government for resisting the law with swords. Some ecclesiastics engaged in commerce or led loose lives, the crown interested itself in sending married men back to their wives in Spain or in other parts of the empire, excess ostentation in funerals had to be reproved, bull fights held in holy years were frowned upon, Indians who had fancy merchandise forced upon them against their will protested, priests quarrelled about preferential places in processions, and the descendants of Diego Huallpa, the discoverer of the mountain of silver, claimed special rights and privileges they considered due them. The detail on the social life of Potosí is rich, copious, and unexploited. . . .

Even if all the thousands of pages of manuscripts on Potosí were to be organized and made available for study, and even if monographs were prepared on all the topics listed above, problems of interpretation would still remain.

One great pitfall to be avoided is that of exaggerating everything connected with the mine. Historians writing on Potosí have not infrequently fallen victims of the boom spirit so typical of the city itself. . . Américo Castro reaffirms the belief in the overriding importance of American treasure in the history of Spain in Europe, and Víctor Andrés Belaunde has remarked that the entire colonial epoch in Peru might be designated as a "vast religious and political organization for the exploitation of the mines." The Cerro was the most noted of these mines and just as the Portuguese classic seventeenth-century historian Francisco Manoel de Melo referred to that "inestimable Potosí," other writers old and new, Spanish and foreigner, beat the drum on behalf of Potosí. The belief in the opulence of Peru generally began when Atahualpa in 1532 paid over to Francisco Pizarro a roomful of gold and two more of silver. And even after New Spain began in the seventeenth century to produce more silver than Peru, the Viceroy of Peru still received a higher salary than the Viceroy of New Spain, whose position was considered an inferior one. Was this due, in part at least, to the influence of Potosí and the general belief in its supposedly inexhaustible wealth? Myths about Potosí still influence the historians who study its past.

We know that Charles V and Philip II were usually hard pressed for cash, but did Potosí really provide funds for running the empire, in the splendid way it is supposed to have done? Or were the undramatic and mundane factories in the Low Countries the solid economic base for Spain, as R. H. Tawney stated years ago? If so, was not the revenue from Potosí still a fairly steady flow which permitted the Spanish crown to act more independently than if it had to rely on Spanish revenue alone?

Did Potosí also affect the economy of the other parts of Europe? Did its cheaply produced silver cause the collapse of such mining centers as those directed by the Fuggers in Tyrol? We know, from the classic study of Earl J. Hamilton, of the influence of American treasure on prices in Spain. G. N. Clark is even more emphatic and has this to say, in commenting on the discovery of Potosí and the fact that in a few years silver was flowing to Europe in quantities that had never been imagined before: "This might in other conditions have affected silversmiths and ladies more than anyone else; but coming at this time it played a part, and perhaps a very great part, in changing the hunger for the precious metals as money into a surfeit of them. All over

Europe metallic money became easier to get; in other words there was a great rise in prices, which is called 'the price revolution.' . . . Some men became suddenly rich. All those who were entitled to fixed sums, whether as rents or as taxes or dues, could buy less with these sums than before; all those who were free to demand what prices they could exact had new and rising opportunities. So, broadly speaking, the old world of landlords and peasants found it harder to carry on; the traders and bankers found it easier, and capitalism advanced."

What was the influence of Potosí in America itself? Did mining play a progressive role, as Bailey W. Diffie believes, through which "an urban civilization came into existence, a middle class was created, the buying power of the people increased . . . and in general America was able to grow?" Or did Potosí help to fasten upon the Viceroyalty of Peru a pernicious economic and social system which exacted quick profits from the mines, and kept agriculture in such a secondary place that its growth was dangerously retarded and a feudal society prolonged for centuries? If the answer is "yes" to this last question, can one escape the conclusion that some of the present desperate problems of Bolivia constitute, in part at least, a heritage from Potosí? Or, perhaps, did the mountain of silver rather help to develop a Bolivian nationality by establishing an economic, governmental, and social nucleus around which a nation could be organized, as that energetic historian of La Paz, Humberto Vásquez Machicado, has suggested? Or is it possible that each proposition contains some measure of truth? . . .

One final observation must be made which affects all the problems of interpretation raised above. Potosí was a part, albeit a particularly important and flamboyant part, of a vast empire and functioned within the structure which Spain established in America. Its history, therefore, must be written with one eye on the rest of the empire. Potosí was necessarily influenced by the legislation, policies, and foreign entanglements of Spain just as the mountain of silver exerted an influence on other parts of America and the mother country as well. The history of Potosí is a broad and complicated story, and therefore a tale which cannot be told adequately from the vantage point of the Cerro alone. If its historians are to avoid myopia, they must always remember that Potosí, although physically isolated from most of the other New World possessions of Spain, was in fact an integral part of lands governed by the crown of Spain from its capital thousands of miles away. Potosí was unusual, of course, in some ways. The rapidity of its growth, for example, sets Potosí apart from Mexico City, whose population grew rather slowly until recent years, and from Lima, which never suffered the spectacular decline that came upon Potosí in the eighteenth century.

The truly unique aspects of Potosí, however, were its size and dramatic history. Other mining centers existed in the empire and developed somewhat similar societies and sets of institutions. But Potosí came to exhibit those common characteristics of all mining societies in such a theatrical way that it became symbolic of the process that was going on everywhere. Perhaps herein lies the real justification for assigning to Potosí a long and significant chapter in the history of Spain in America. Just as the vociferous and learned Dominican Bartolomé de Las Casas, although not the only defender of the Indians, most persistently captured the imagination of his contemporaries and later generations as The Defender, so Potosí exemplified, in the gaudiest and most memorable colors, the passion for wealth that drew many Spaniards to the New World. Bernal Díaz del Castillo, the famous and articulate foot-soldier of Cortez, exhibited the remarkable combination of *Gott und Gewinn* which characterized the Spanish conquest of America when he exclaimed: "We came here to serve God, and also to get rich." As the mountain of Potosí towers above the surrounding peaks, so will this mine, once its story is adequately told, stand as the towering symbol for the spirit of all Spaniards who came to the New World to get rich.

The Pride of Spaniards in America. Historians today looking back on the action of Spain in the New World see many problems and many crises (Readings 27–30). But Spaniards were satisfied, even complacent, about their American empire, as may be seen from the official work by Antonio de Herrera entitled "General History of the Deeds of Spaniards in the Islands and Tierra Firma of the Ocean Sea." This title page from an eighteenth-century edition, with representations of all the Inca rulers, illustrates the conviction many Spaniards had that their work of civilizing and converting the Indians and of developing a new society overseas was a worthwhile and even noble accomplishment.

SECTION VI

Crisis and Climax in the Eighteenth Century

The century before the Portuguese and Spanish colonies in America won their independence brought considerable cultural, economic, and political change. Tensions between the mother countries and the New World increased, despite or perhaps because of the many improvements in the lot of the overseas colonists. The Iberian empires were no longer so isolated from the world, and the increasingly determined attempt of Spain and Portugal to keep their American citizens more efficiently under peninsular control led to resistance rather than acquiescence. Portugal administered a shock to Brazil when she expelled the Jesuits in 1759, even before Spain took the same decisive step a few years later. The causes for what many considered a harsh and wrong attack in both Brazil and Spanish America upon this powerful order were many and complicated, as Professor Magnus Mörner has ably shown in a volume on this controversial event.[1] Whatever the real causes for the expulsion of the Jesuits, this action helped to loosen the ties that bound the colonies to the mother countries.

A different set of circumstances in Mexico created another kind of problem. Spain decided to organize a colonial militia to protect the land from foreign incursion, such as Havana and Manila had both suffered in 1762 at the hands of the British. The well-born young men in Mexico displayed no great enthusiasm for military service until granted the *fuero militar,* which conceded such privileges and immunities as to create an officer class largely exempt from civil responsibility. Thus came into being a significant inequal-

[1] Magnus Mörner, *The Expulsion of the Jesuits from Latin America,* Borzoi Books on Latin America (New York: Knopf, 1965).

ity that laid the basis for the nineteenth-century military dictators. Yet relatively speaking, Mexico appeared to be advanced. Alexander von Humboldt, in his classic overview of Mexico about 1800, lauded Mexico City: "No new city of the new continent, without even excepting those of the United States, can display such great and solid scientific achievements as the capital of Mexico." He added, however: "Mexico is the country of inequality. Nowhere does there exist such a fearful difference in the distribution of fortune, civilization, cultivation of the soil, and population" (Reading 27).

Eighteenth-century Peru was the locale of probably the most significant Indian rebellion in the whole colonial period. Led by the mestizo José Gabriel Tupac Amaru, Marquis of Oropesa but also descended from the Inca leader Tupac Amaru who had been beheaded by Viceroy Francisco de Toledo in 1572, its history "is intricate and obscure." Was the revolt primarily aimed at ending the oppression of the Indians, as many have asserted, or was it an attempt to throw off the Spanish yoke completely and achieve an independent Peruvian Indian state? Few accept this view: "The Indians wished to capture Spanish institutions, not destroy or displace them by others." [2] Whatever the true causes, and research is still going forward, the rebellion of 1780–1781 failed despite widespread support of Indians and the aid of the leader's intelligent and vigorous wife. But the bloody affair shook Spanish officialdom somewhat; in 1787 an audiencia was established in Cuzco, which was designed to afford greater protection for the Indians against exploitation by their Spanish governors and Indian chiefs alike.

One action, this time by the crown, did have considerable influence on economic, political, and religious life in Upper Peru — the expulsion of the Jesuits. Though this sudden operation struck a blow at Jesuit power throughout the Iberian colonies, the way it was carried out reveals the practically absolute power of the Spanish king even in the far corners of his vast empire in America.

Another problem in Peru was declining mineral production, upon which its economy had been based ever since the Potosí silver mines were discovered in 1545. Silver production depended upon mercury, which the Huancavelica mine had provided in great quantities since about 1570. The crown devised many plans to revive Huancavelica during the eighteenth century without much success. Stagnation and decay did not characterize the Spanish American Empire generally in the eighteenth century, however, and the late Professor C. H. Haring stated in his fundamental work that "at the end of the colonial era

[2] George Kubler, "The Quechua in the Colonial World," *Handbook of South American Indians,* 2, ed. Julian H. Steward (Washington, D.C.: Smithsonian Institution, 1946), pp. 331–410.

most of the American provinces enjoyed greater prosperity and well-being than ever before." [3]

Professor R. A. Humphreys concurs with this view and presents an excellent general analysis and description of the fall of the Spanish Empire in America, which stretched "in unbroken line from California to Cape Horn. From Stockholm to Cape Town is less distant, and within the area ruled by Spain all western Europe from Madrid to Moscow might lie and be lost" (Reading 30). But other interpretations flourish, too, as may be seen from an "essay on economic dependence in perspective" (Reading 28) by Stanley J. and Barbara H. Stein in their stimulating volume *The Colonial Heritage of Latin America,* and Professor Philip W. Powell's defense of Spanish rule in America (Reading 29).

Some Brazilian historians have reached dismal conclusions on Portuguese colonial rule. Caio Prado, Júnior, has recently written: "The panorama offered by colonial society may be summarized as follows: settlement, scattered and unstable; economy, poor and miserable; mores, dissolute; administration, both lay and ecclesiastical, inept and corrupt." A nineteenth-century Brazilian, Capistrano de Abreu, penned a famous description of the colonial family in Brazil: "Taciturn father, submissive wife, cowed children." [4]

These divergent modern interpretations point to an important aspect of the study of Latin American history — the sharp and apparently irreconcilable disagreements over the true nature of Portuguese and Spanish rule. Characteristically there is more written on Spanish America than on Brazil. The dispute goes back to the earliest part of the Conquest when Bernal Díaz del Castillo, indignant at the pro-Cortez version of the Conquest, wrote his *True History of the Conquest of Spain.* Today the questions foremost in the minds of many historians relate to the social and economic impact of conquest on the conquered Indians and enslaved Negroes. Comparative history has become a flourishing growth industry today among an ever-widening circle of historians who grapple with problems involving factual, moral, and nationalistic considerations.

Comparative cruelty and questions of comparative oppression are almost impossible to discuss in such a way as to satisfy many historians, because facts are difficult to obtain and moral indignation is often present. Alexander von Humboldt in his classic work on Mexico at the end of the colonial period believed that the condition of the Indians was not much worse than that of

[3] C. H. Haring, *The Spanish Empire in America* (New York: Harcourt, Brace, and World, 1963), p. 322.

[4] Caio Prado, Júnior, *The Colonial Background of Modern Brazil* (Berkeley and Los Angeles: University of California Press, 1969), p. 414.

the serfs of the time on the rural estates of the Baltic. Stanley J. and Barbara H. Stein acknowledged that it might be valid to state that the existence of West European peasants, craftsmen, and miners was as wretched as that of the lowest stratum of society in Spanish America in the sixteenth and seventeenth centuries. But they go on to ask: "Were West Europeans forced into mines and kept there in the seventeenth century without surfacing from Monday to Saturday? Was there in operation in western Europe an annual labor draft which forced unwilling laborers to move hundreds of miles to pit-heads along with their families, supplies, and pack animals?" [5] One wonders whether anyone can really compare the lives of the wretched, because of the inherent problems and prejudices involved. Yet the comparisons go on. In the April 1972 issue of the *American Historical Review* we find a review of a monograph by the Dutch historian J. G. Van Dillen on the economic and social history of the Dutch Republic in which Charles R. Boxer remarks: "He does not ignore the widespread poverty among many sections of the lower classes during the 'Golden Century' [1580–1650]. The textile workers of Leiden, for example, seem to have fared little better than the Amerindian laborers in the *obrajes* or textile sweatshops of colonial Spanish America." [6]

The selections (Readings 28–30) by the Steins, Powell, and Humphreys are designed to afford students an opportunity to sample representative views of historians and to encourage further meditation on these basic controversies that color much of the writing on Latin American colonial history.

Finally, in discussing Spanish American economic ills, we should not forget that there has always existed in Spanish-speaking lands a not unimportant segment of society that maintains that economic matters are of minor significance. Américo Castro has expressed it this way: "Religious faith as a basis for life and the monarchy as social horizon" are the two fundamental facts of Spanish life. "Those who attribute the troubles of Spaniards to the poverty of their land are perpetuating a myth." [7] Another eminent Spanish historian, Claudio Sánchez Albornoz, violently disagrees with Castro on many points, but both are convinced, as were many Spanish writers of Spain's Golden Age in the sixteenth century, that economic affairs were only minor determinants in Spanish history. How far Spanish Americans today are moved by these attitudes is a moot question, as is the question of to what extent those countries with large Indian populations have inherited the noneconomic attitudes of the pre-Columbian peoples. These considerations of values may be debatable, but they cannot be ignored by the historian.

---

[5] Stanley J. and Barbara H. Stein, *The Colonial Heritage of Latin America* (New York: Oxford University Press, 1971), p. viii.

[6] *American Historical Review,* 77 (1972), p. 531.

[7] Américo Castro, "The Spanish People," *Texas Quarterly,* 3 (1960).

27. *Problems and Progress in Mexico*

ALEXANDER VON HUMBOLDT

The first non-Spaniard of stature to be allowed to visit the empire in the last years of Spanish rule was the German scientist Alexander von Humboldt, whose detailed and discerning descriptions enabled the world to see what Mexico was like about 1800. He compiled much useful data on the geology, rainfall, soil, and other physical characteristics of the land, but we value him today for his honest and informative view of economic, political, and society life on the eve of the revolution.

Mexico is the country of inequality. No where does there exist such a fearful difference in the distribution of fortune, civilization, cultivation of the soil, and population. The interior of the country contains four cities, which are not more than one or two days' journey distant from one another, and possess a population of 35,000, 67,000, 70,000, and 135,000. The central table-land from la Puebla to Mexico, and from thence to Salamanca and Zelaya, is covered with villages and hamlets like the most cultivated part of Lombardy. To the east and west of this narrow strip succeed tracts of uncultivated ground, on which cannot be found ten or twelve persons to the square league. The capital and several other cities have scientific establishments, which will bear a comparison with those of Europe. The architecture of the public and private edifices, the elegance of the furniture, the equipages, the luxury and dress of the women, the tone of society, all announce a refinement to which the nakedness, ignorance, and vulgarity of the lower people form the most striking contrast. This immense inequality of fortune does not only exist among the cast of whites (Europeans or Creoles), it is even discoverable among the Indians.

The Mexican Indians, when we consider them *en masse,* offer a picture of extreme misery. Banished into the most barren districts, and indolent from nature, and more still from their political situation, the natives live only from hand to mouth. We should seek almost in vain among them for individuals who enjoy anything like a certain mediocrity of fortune. Instead, however, of a comfortable independency, we find a few families whose fortune appears so much the more colossal, as we least expect it among the lowest class of the people. In the intendancies of Oaxaca and Valladolid, in the valley of Toluca,

From *Political Essay on the Kingdom of New Spain* by Alexander von Humboldt, trans. John Black (London: Longman, Hurst, Rees, Orme, and Brown, 1811), vol. 1, pp. 134–217, passim.

and especially in the environs of the great city of la Puebla de los Angeles, we find several Indians, who under an appearance of poverty conceal considerable wealth. When I visited the small city of Cholula, an old Indian woman was buried there, who left to her children plantations of *maguey* (agave) worth more than 360,000 francs. These plantations are the vineyards and sole wealth of the country. However, there are no caciques at Cholula; and the Indians there are all tributary, and distinguished for their great sobriety, and their gentle and peaceable manners. The manners of the Cholulans exhibit a singular contrast to those of their neighbors of Tlascala, of whom a great number pretend to be the descendants of the highest titled nobility, and who increase their poverty by a litigious disposition and a restless and turbulent turn of mind. Among the most wealthy Indian families at Cholula are the Axcotlan, the Sarmientos and the Romeros; at Guaxocingo, the Sochipiltecatl; and especially the Tecuanouegues in the village de los Reyes. Each of these families possesses a capital of from 800,000 to 1,000,000 of livres. They enjoy, as we have already stated, great consideration among the tributary Indians; but they generally go barefooted, and covered with a Mexican tunic of coarse texture and a brown colour, approaching to black, in the same way as the very lowest of the Indians are usually dressed.

The Indians are exempted from every sort of indirect impost. They pay no *alcavala;* and the law allows them full liberty for the sale of their productions. The supreme council of finances of Mexico, called the *Junta superior de Real Hacienda,* endeavored from time to time, especially within these last five or six years, to subject the Indians to the alcavala. We must hope that the court of Madrid, which in all times has endeavored to protect this unfortunate race, will preserve to them their immunity so long as they shall continue subject to the direct impost of the *tributos.* This impost is a real capitation tax, paid by the male Indians between the ages of ten and fifty. The tribute is not the same in all the provinces of New Spain; and it has been diminished within the last two hundred years. In 1601, the Indian paid yearly 32 reals of plata of *tributo,* and four reals of *servicio real,* in all nearly 23 francs. It was gradually reduced in some intendancies to 15 and even to five francs. In the bishopric of Mechoacan, and in the greatest part of Mexico, the capitation amounts at present to 11 francs. Besides, the Indians pay a parochial duty (*derechos parroquiales*) of 10 francs for baptism, 20 francs for a certificate of marriage, and 20 francs for interment. We must also add to these 61 francs, which the church levies as an impost on every individual, from 25 to 30 francs for offerings which are called voluntary, and which go under the names of *cargos de cofradias, responsos* and *misàs para sacar animas.*

If the legislation of Queen Isabella and the Emperor Charles V appears to favour the Indians with regard to imposts, it has deprived them, on the other hand, of the most important rights enjoyed by the other citizens. In an age when it was formally discussed if the Indians were rational beings, it was conceived granting them a benefit to treat them like minors, to put them under the perpetual tutory of the whites, and to declare null every act signed by a native of the copper-coloured race, and every obligation which he contracted beyond the value of 15 francs. These laws are maintained in full vigour; and they place insurmountable barriers between the Indians and the other casts, with whom all intercourse is almost prohibited. Thousands of inhabitants can enter into no contract which is binding (*no pueden tratar y contratar*); and condemned to a perpetual minority, they become a charge to themselves and the state in which they live. . . .

Amongst the inhabitants of pure origin the whites would occupy the second place, considering them only in the relation of number. They are divided into whites born in Europe, and descendants of Europeans born in the Spanish colonies of America or in the Asiatic islands. The former bear the name of *Chapetones* or *Gachupines,* and the second that of *Criollos.* The natives of the Canary islands, who go under the general denomination of *Islenos* (islanders), and who are the *gerans* of the plantations, are considered as Europeans. The Spanish laws allow the same rights to all whites; but those who have the execution of the laws endeavour to destroy an equality which shocks the European pride. The government, suspicious of the Creoles, bestows the great places exclusively on the natives of Old Spain. For some years back they have disposed at Madrid even of the most trifling employments in the administration of the customs and the tobacco revenue. At an epoch when every thing tended to a uniform relaxation in the springs of the state, the system of venality made an alarming progress. For the most part it was by no means a suspicious and distrustful policy; it was pecuniary interest alone which bestowed all employments on Europeans. The result has been a jealous and perpetual hatred between the Chapetons and the Creoles. The most miserable European, without education, and without intellectual cultivation, thinks himself superior to the whites born in the new continent. He knows that, protected by his countrymen, and favored by chances common enough in a country where fortunes are as rapidly acquired as they are lost, he may one day reach places to which the access is almost interdicted to the natives, even to those of men distinguished for their talents, knowledge and moral qualities. The natives prefer the denomination of *Americans* to that of Creoles. Since the peace of Versailles, and, in particular, since the year 1789, we frequently hear proudly declared, "I am not a *Spaniard,* I am an *American!"* words which betray the workings of a long resentment. In the eye of law every white Creole is a Spaniard; but the abuse of the laws, the false measures of the colonial government, the example of the United States of America, and the influence of the opinions of the age, have relaxed the ties which formerly united more closely the Spanish Creoles to the European Spaniards. A wise administration may reestablish harmony, calm their passions and resentments, and yet preserve for a long time the union among the members of one and the same great family scattered over Europe and America, from the Patagonian coast to the north of California. . . .

The Spanish laws prohibit all entry into the American possessions to every European not born in the peninsula. The words European and Spaniard are become synonymous in Mexico and Peru. The inhabitants of the remote provinces have therefore a difficulty in conceiving that there can be Europeans who do not speak their language; and they consider this ignorance as a mark of low extraction, because, everywhere around them, all, except the very lowest class of the people, speak Spanish. Better acquainted with the history of the sixteenth century than with that of our own times, they imagine that Spain continues to possess a decided preponderance over the rest of Europe. To them the peninsula appears the very centre of European civilization. It is otherwise with the Americans of the capital. Those of them who are acquainted with the French or English literature fall easily into a contrary extreme; and have still a more unfavorable opinion of the mother country than the French had at a time when communication was less frequent between Spain and the rest of Europe. They prefer strangers from other countries to the Spaniards; and they flatter themselves with the idea that intellectual cultivation has made more rapid progress in the colonies than in the peninsula.

This progress is indeed very remarkable at the Havannah, Lima, Santa Fe, Quito, Popayan, and Caraccas. Of all these great cities the Havannah bears the greatest resemblance to those of Europe in customs, refinements of luxury, and the tone of society. At Havannah, the state of politics and their influence on commerce is best understood. However, notwithstanding the efforts of the *patriotic society of the island of Cuba,* which encourages the sciences with the most generous zeal, they prosper very slowly in a country where cultivation and the price of colonial produce engross the whole attention of the inhabitants. The study of the mathematics, chemistry, mineralogy, and botany, is more general at Mexico, Santa Fe, and Lima. We everywhere observe a great intellectual activity, and among the youth a wonderful facility of seizing the principles of science. It is said that this facility is still more remarkable among the inhabitants of Quito and Lima than at Mexico and Santa Fe. The former appear to possess more versatility of mind and a more lively imagination; while the Mexicans and the natives of Santa Fe have the reputation of greater perseverance in the studies to which they have once addicted themselves.

No city of the new continent, without even excepting those of the United States, can display such great and solid scientific establishments as the capital of Mexico. I shall content myself here with naming the School of Mines, directed by the learned Elhuyar, to which we shall return when we come to speak of the mines; the Botanic Garden; and the Academy of Painting and Sculpture. This academy bears the title of *Academia de los Nobles Artes de Mexico*. It owes its existence to the patriotism of several Mexican individuals, and the protection of the minister Galvez. The government assigned it a spacious building, in which there is a much finer and more complete collection of casts than is to be found in any part of Germany. We are astonished on seeing that the Appollo of Belvidere, the group of Laocoon, and still more colossal statues, have been conveyed through mountainous roads at least as narrow as those of St. Gothard; and we are surprised at finding these masterpieces of antiquity collected together under the torrid zone, in a table-land higher than the convent of the great St. Bernard. The collection of casts brought to Mexico cost the king 200,000 francs. The remains of the Mexican sculpture, those colossal statues of basaltes and porphyry, which are covered with Aztec hieroglyphics, and bear some relation to the Egyptian and Hindoo style, ought to be collected together in the edifice of the academy, or rather in one of the courts which belong to it. It would be curious to see these monuments of the first cultivation of our species, the works of a semibarbarous people inhabiting the Mexican Andes, placed beside the beautiful forms produced under the sky of Greece and Italy.

The revenues of the Academy of Fine Arts at Mexico amount to 125,000 francs, of which the government gives 60,000, the body of Mexican miners nearly 25,000, the *consulado,* or association of merchants of the capital, more than 1,500. It is impossible not to perceive the influence of this establishment on the taste of the nation. This influence is particularly visible in the symmetry of the buildings, in the perfection with which the hewing of stone is conducted, and in the ornaments of the capitals and stucco relievos. What a number of beautiful edifices are to be seen at Mexico! nay, even in provincial towns like Guanaxuato and Queretaro! These monuments, which frequently cost a million and a million and a half of francs, would appear to advantage in the finest streets of Paris, Berlin, and Petersburg. M. Tolsa, professor of sculpture at Mexico, was even able to cast an equestrian statue of King Charles the Fourth; a work which, with the exception of the Marcus Aurelius at Rome, surpasses in beauty and purity of style everything which remains in this way in Europe. Instruction is communicated *gratis* at the Academy of Fine Arts. It is not confined alone to the drawing of landscapes and figures; they have had the good sense to employ other means for exciting the national industry. The academy labours successfully to introduce among the artisans a taste for elegance and beautiful forms. Large rooms, well lighted by Argand's lamps, contain every evening some hundreds of young people, of whom some draw from relievo or living models, while others copy drawings of furniture, chandeliers, or other ornaments in bronze. In this assemblage (and this is very remarkable in the midst of a country where the prejudices of the nobility against the casts are so inveterate) rank, colour, and race is confounded: we see the Indian and the Mestizo sitting beside the white, and the son of a poor artisan in emulation with the children of the great lords of the country. It is a consolation to observe, that under every zone the cultivation of science and art establishes a certain equality among men, and obliterates for a time, at least, all those petty passions of which the effects are so prejudicial to social happiness.

Since the close of the reign of Charles the Third, and under that of Charles the Fourth, the study of the physical sciences has made great progress, not only in Mexico, but in general in all the Spanish colonies. No European government has sacrificed greater sums to advance the knowledge of the vegetable kingdom than the Spanish government. Three *botanical expeditions* in Peru, New Granada and New Spain, under the direction of MM. Ruiz and Pavon, Don Jose Celestino Mutis, and MM. Sesse and Mocino, have cost the state nearly two millions of francs. Moreover, botanical gardens have been established at Manila and the Canary islands. The commission destined to draw plans of the canal of *los Guines,* was also appointed to examine the vegetable productions of the island of Cuba. All these researches, conducted during twenty years in the most fertile regions of the new continent, have not only enriched science with more than four thousand new species of plants, but have also contributed much to diffuse a taste for natural history among the inhabitants of the country. The city of Mexico exhibits a very interesting botanical garden within the very precincts of the viceroy's palace. Professor Cervantes gives annual courses there, which are very well attended. This *savant* possesses, besides his herbals, a rich collection of Mexican minerals. M. Mocino, whom we just now mentioned as one of the coadjutors of M. Sesse, and who has pushed his laborious excursions from the kingdom of Guatimala to the north-west coast or island of Vancouver and Quadra; and M. Echeveria, a painter of plants and animals, whose works will bear a comparison with the most perfect productions of the kind in Europe, are both of them natives of New Spain. They had both attained a distinguished rank among *savans* and artists before quitting their country.

The principles of the new chemistry, which is known in the Spanish colonies by the equivocal appellation of new philosophy (*nueva filosofia*), are more diffused in Mexico than in many parts of the peninsula. A European traveller cannot undoubtedly but be surprised to meet in the interior of the country, on the very borders of California, with young Mexicans who reason on the decomposition of water in the process of amalgamation with free air. The School of Mines possesses a chemical laboratory; a geological collection, arranged according to the system of Werner; a physical cabinet, in which we not only find the valuable instruments of Ramsden, Adams, Le Noir, and Louis Berthoud, but also models executed in the capital, even with the greatest precision, and from the finest wood in the country. The best mineralogical work in the Spanish language was printed at Mexico, I mean the Manual of Oryctognosy, composed by M. del Rio, according to the principles of the school of Freyberg, in which the author was formed. The first Spanish translation of Lavater's Elements of Chemistry was also published at Mexico. I cite these isolated facts because they give us the measure of the ardour with which the exact sciences are begun to be studied in the capital of New Spain. This ardour is much greater than that with which they addict themselves to the study of languages and ancient literature.

28. *"The Pre-eminent Social Legacy of Colonialism Was the Degradation of the Labor Force, Indian and Negro, Everywhere in Latin America"*

STANLEY J. and BARBARA H. STEIN

The Steins are one of the few husband and wife teams writing on Latin American history. Though Professor Stein of Princeton University first established his reputation by two outstanding monographs on Brazilian nineteenth-century history, he afterward turned to investigating the roles of merchants in Mexico and Spain in the last half century of the colonial period, and with Mrs. Stein, also trained in history, has carried on prolonged archival research on this theme. The present selection is taken from a volume on *The Colonial Heritage of Latin America* and has a frankly economic and social focus in which they treat "certain basic institutions, patterns of behavior and attitudes which have had impressive continuity in Latin America: hacienda, plantation and associated social patterns, mining enclaves, the export syndrome and related trade mechanisms and mentality; elitism and racism; nepotism, clientilism, and a tradition of private right in public office."

Revolution in America occurred in 1810 because the criollo elite finally provided the leadership that the castas and the lower even more oppressed strata of colonial society had long awaited. To those who have examined the process of economic development and social change in a historical context it is clear that social systems appear to have extraordinary powers of cohesion, flexibility, adaptation. The cohesion of Latin American colonial social structures was maintained, if transformed, during three centuries largely because no viable alternative system appeared. Fidelity to Spain, sanctified by religious injunction, cemented the structure of colonial society, economy, and polity. The principle of hierarchy, of superordinate and subordinate social groups tied to the European metropolises, was accepted since it satisfied the interests and aspirations of an elite which, in effect, had the monopoly of force to maintain it.

In deciding to break with metropolitan controls, the colonial elite found natural allies in the mestizos, mulattoes, and castas in general; the Indian masses they handled gingerly. The Indians recognized their exploitation under the colonial system, but their bitterness had never successfully found effective expression. The criollo leaders now feared the masses, who often erupted in urban and rural violence, and they rationalized their repression and exploitation of them with the myth that they were inferiors. Undoubtedly some of the colonial elite believed that the Indian masses might remain inert in case of rebellion or, if mobilized intelligently, could be controlled to aid in the elimination of the handful of Spanish bureaucrats and merchants. Support by the castas strengthened the elite's position and promised assistance in controlling the Indians. With the backing of the castas, who were perhaps even more irked by the Spanish-imposed social hierarchy and by restrictions on "passing" and upon economic activity, some of the colonial elite probably saw the possibility of a rather peaceful transition toward independence. In allying with the castas, they co-opted a small but influential social group whose role was magnified by the expansion and diversification of the eighteenth-century colonial economy and by demographic growth.

From *The Colonial Heritage of Latin America: Essays on Economic Dependence in Perspective* by Stanley J. and Barbara H. Stein (New York: Oxford University Press, 1970), pp. 114–119. Copyright © 1970 by Oxford University Press, Inc. Reprinted by permission.

Put another way, one detects in eighteenth-century Latin America the transformation of the older bases of colonial hierarchy, estates and corporations, into something approximating economic classes based upon wealth and income. The castas seem to have grown proportionately faster than the other social groups, and the lighter-skinned castas moved upward into the group of what were now called American Spaniards. In a word, "passing" became easier and more widespread. Castas were accepted in the colonial militia where criollo officers predominated. The large and growing intermediate group of mestizos and mulattoes spilled over from the hacienda and the Indian communities to fill the expanding number of occupations a diversifying economy requires. They resented the social stigma a colonial regime fastened upon them because of their "inferior" social origins. They bribed local priests to register their children as Spaniards rather than as light mulattoes or light mestizos, or they later had parish records changed. European officials at the end of the eighteenth century complained of the difficulty of registering people as castas for tax purposes. Nor could castas be kept out of artisan guilds nor even kept from pursuing artisan production outside them. They became weavers who established their own weaving shops; they became shopkeepers and itinerant merchants; they entered the church in large numbers; they flowed into the lesser bureaucracy. In colonial areas of heavy slave importation in the eighteenth century the number of free Negroes and mulattoes increased proportionately. It is not that racial prejudice declined: it is simply that rigid maintenance of status based upon color and ancestry became too difficult. To some extent the sheer number and diversity of castas tended to create a new basis of hierarchy, wealth, at the end of the colonial period. Those able to break away from the status of slave, those who abandoned the Indian communities or indigenous enclaves of Amerinds, became a middle group which could survive only by ruthless pursuit of self-interest. The Hispanized Indian or ladino, the mestizo, the free Negro, became in many cases a more ruthless exploiter of his social inferiors than the White elite. This was becoming evident before the wars of independence; it was to become even clearer afterward.

If the major legacy of colonial society was degradation and social conflict, what basis exists then for the often heard view that the Iberians had a policy toward Indians and Negroes which was more humanitarian and more tolerant than that of the non-Catholic west Europeans in America? It is true that there were sensitive, articulate, and hard-headed churchmen in the colonies who perceived the deculturizing, brutalizing, and exploitative aspects of culture-contact and imperialism in the sixteenth century. Such a man was Las Casas. One must, however, recall that other clerics who left posterity detailed ethnographic accounts of the social, political, and religious history of the conquered peoples of America studied the major institutions and values of dominated peoples in order to make colonial rule enduring. They were applied anthropologists. This, after all, was the aim of Las Casas' clerical contemporaries, Landa and Sahagun. If they often admired the institutions described, the admiration was given grudgingly.

Iberian colonialism did not exterminate subject peoples. It did accept the people of miscegenation. It did tolerate a degree of slave manumission. Yet the direction of colonial rule was not toward social uplift, toward integration; colonial rule was predicated upon separation, not integration, whether one examines tax systems, access to political or military office, even the church. Limited social integration and racial toleration were by-products of special conditions, in particular, the shortage of free labor available for interstitial occupations, those between field hand and elite. Since few Europeans were available to fill these jobs, the colonial society had to supply them. Hence the number of mestizos and mulattoes accepted at certain levels of society, in certain occupational roles. The fact that access to high status and occupation was rigidly controlled permitted the absorption of some newcomers.

The pre-eminent social legacy of colonialism was the degradation of the labor force, Indian and Negro, everywhere in Latin America. This is the abiding significance of debt peonage and chattel slavery. That occasionally members of the mixed groups were incorporated into the ruling group during the colonial period or distinguished themselves in the struggle for independence is not a persuasive argument for the racial integration of either colonial or post-colonial society. To argue in this fashion is to raise random sexual activity to the level of planned parenthood and to consider the growth of a mestizo or mulatto population a reliable index of racial integration and equality. On the contrary, it might be argued that the rigor of the barriers to upward social mobility — the barriers of birth, color, and economic deprivation in both colonial and post-colonial Latin America — permitted the elite to absorb an insignificant percentage of the more aggressive mixed groups and thereby to preserve the essence of social stratification. Absorption into the elite meant that newcomers accepted the social values and aspirations of that group; in striving for higher status, they lost contact with the disadvantaged groups which they abandoned and simultaneously removed themselves as leaders of the struggle for the amelioration of the lot of the illiterate, impoverished masses of color.

To be sure, social aspects of colonialism cannot be divorced from the economic matrix, and the heart of that matrix in Latin America remained privilege in the form of access to property and occupation, to ownership of mines, large farms, cattle ranches, to trade, and to the bureaucracy. A stratified and hierarchical society meant that a small group closely interrelated by marriage and kinship controlled wealth and income. Failure to diversify the colonial economy meant that economic opportunity remained limited. For the masses there was no role other than that of field hands or urban proletariat. And those who labored as dependents, debt peons or chattel slaves, were stigmatized as inferior. Rationalization buttressed inferiority. Indians were ignorant, superstitious, docile, lacking intelligence and initiative, not because society made them so, but because they were Indians — so thought the elite. Similarly they rationalized the maintenance of Negro slavery on the grounds that Christianity saved the Negro from barbarism and tribal warfare. To educate such elements of congenital backwardness was an exercise in futility. The colonial legacy of social degradation and racial prejudice surfaced in the nineteenth century in the form of acute racial pessimism, in the belief that only the immigration of European Whites via colonization could supply the industrious labor force capable of effectively transforming Latin America.

Social realities have a habit, however, of proving rationalizations of the *status quo* inadequate. We are now beginning to realize that much of the social unrest of Latin America in the past century was a continuation of conflicts over access to property and occupation that the lower classes touched off in the eighteenth century, that flared up briefly in the struggles for independence and which the elite suppressed after 1824. It is in the twentieth century that the long struggle for social vindication, rooted in the colonial past, is again re-emerging.

29. The Three Centuries of Spanish Rule in America Should Not Be Characterized as a "Tyranny" or as "Oppressive"

PHILIP W. POWELL

Professor Philip W. Powell of the University of California, Santa Barbara, has long defended Spain from what he believes to be unjust attacks on her rule in America and the charge that all of the ills of Spanish America today are colonial legacies. Students who compare his interpretations with that of the Steins (Reading 28) will see how fundamentally professors of history can disagree!

The standard simplistic version of Spanish rule in America as a slavocracy, filled with tyranny, looting, bleeding taxation, and suffocating obscurantism, does not conform to the facts. Spanish rule through all this period was generally more benign than much or even most Spanish American government has been since separation from Spain. Had this not been so, Spain's rule would not have lasted as long as it did.

One of our leading authorities in such matters, Professor Lesley Byrd Simpson, writes:

> It seems to me that the average stature of the viceroys of New Spain [Mexico] was so great that no country to my knowledge was ever more fortunate in its rulers. New Spain had plenty of things the matter with it, . . . but it enjoyed a long life (three hundred years!) of relative peace, stability, and prosperity, in marked contrast to the squabbling nations of Europe. Some of the men who made this possible are worth our knowing.

And an English scholar, Ronald Syme, recently implied something similar, in broader context:

> In spite of the handicaps of geography and of distance, Spain was able to hold her wide dominions for three centuries and set upon them indelibly the stamp of her language, thought and institutions. That achievement deserves more honour than it has commonly earned — and a more searching investigation. . . .

One finds, at times, the curious paradox that taxation overseas was not as onerous as it was in some parts of the mother country. One also finds that American life was often easier, or more prosperous, than in much of the mother country, where poverty was commonplace. In food availability, for example, Spanish Americans, of whatever level, were apt to fare as well or better than their European counterparts, Spanish or otherwise. Even the lower classes of Spanish America were likely to live somewhat better than much of the European peasantry.

There were, of course, many abuses of governmental authority, and all the many and varied evils of a vast bureaucracy, cholesterol of empire. Crimes of all sorts were committed, as one might expect in an empire of such size and long life. But there was also judicial machinery and legislation for punishment of abuses. The important point is that the norm was legality and law enforcement, just as in other civilized societies. In general, Spaniards did not try to

From "Spain in America: The Real and the Unreal," in *Tree of Hate: Propaganda and Prejudices Affecting United States Relations with the Hispanic World,* by Philip Wayne Powell pp. 23–29. © Basic Books, Inc., Publishers, New York, 1970.

impose upon America something hypocritically foreign or inferior to what they lived with at home. Taxation, municipal practices, university statutes, criminal and civil legislation, judiciary, artistic endeavors, social welfare agencies, commercial practices, etc., were, *mutatis mutandis,* close approximations of Spanish usage and norms in European territories. For example, in governmental and private welfare practices alone, there is abundant testimony to the comparatively advanced concern and practices of Spaniards in the New World. Moreover, this is a subject that merits much more attention and honor than it has received. . . .

The one great innovation was, of necessity, in Indian affairs. Spain's three centuries of tutelage and official concern for the welfare of the American Indian is a record not equaled by other Europeans in overseas government of peoples of lesser, or what were considered lesser, cultures. For all the mistakes, for all the failures, for all the crimes committed, and even allowing for Crown motives of practicality and self-service, in its overall performance Spain, in relation to the American Indian, need offer no apology to any other people or nation.

Spain's Inquisition and her State-Church structure are usually blamed for an oppressive obscurantism that supposedly blighted the three centuries in America and entrenched so many of the ills that today beset Spanish American nations. Anti-Catholic prejudice in our own country makes this myth particularly attractive, and nineteenth- and twentieth-century Latin Americans are fond of reiterating it. But no scholar having acquaintance with Spanish educational and other intellectual achievement in America — e.g., Indian education, encouragement of literature, history, scientific investigations, university instruction — would subscribe to such a judgment. The Spanish record of some twenty-three colleges and universities in America, graduating 150,000 (including the poor, mestizos, and some Negroes) makes, for example, the Dutch in the East Indies in later and supposedly more enlightened times, look like obscurantists indeed. The Portuguese did not establish a single university in colonial Brazil nor in any other overseas possessions. The total of universities established by Belgium, England, Germany, France, and Italy during later Afro-Asian colonial periods assuredly suffers by any fair comparison with the pioneering record of Spain.

In this vein, let us observe a few comments by Professor John Tate Lanning, of Duke University, our leading authority on the subject of Spanish American colonial culture:

> Up until a generation ago the view that all intellectual products of Europe were excluded from America by a zealous monarch and Inquisition went almost without question. No careful scholar would now pro-

nounce upon the availability of books in America upon the exclusive basis of the estimable *Recopilación de Indias* or the *Index of Prohibited Books.* The bibliographical avenue of Enlightenment to Spanish America was at no time so thoroughly barricaded as the statutes and indexes indicate.

Again:

> An effective and relatively unhampered literary contact with the whole world of thought is implicit in the propositions defended in the [Spanish American] universities toward the end of the eighteenth century. The censorship of the Inquisition, well established though it was in law, was even more than many other somnolent colonial institutions, essentially bureaucratic and ineffectual.

He also said:

> A grandiose and tenacious injustice springing from the traditions and emotions of the early national historians [of Spanish America] is the sweeping condemnation of Spanish colonial culture as "three centuries of theocracy, obscurantism, and barbarism!"

Along the way, let us notice also that barely more than one hundred persons were executed in Spanish America as a result of Inquisition action during its some 250 years of formal existence. This would seem, I think, to compare rather favorably, as these things go, with the torture and execution of Roman Catholics in Elizabethan England (130 priests and 60 laymen, or a total of 250 killed by the state if one includes those dying in prison). And estimates of deaths for witchcraft in the German states during the sixteenth and seventeenth centuries run well into the thousands. . . .

The substantial scholarly literature on American institutional development under Spanish rule continues to increase, but this fact usually comes as a surprise to many university students and intellectuals in the United States. It seems incredible to some that achievement worthy of later intellectual consideration could have taken place in an inquisitional Spanish-Catholic environment; but, if one applies a bit of logic to the situation, there should be no such astonishment. Spain, as should be well known, was enjoying a Golden Age during most of the first two centuries of her empire-building in America, and there was no reason for the mother country to withhold this intellectual activity from her colonies. And the answer is that she did not. Spaniards in America, and their progeny, had access to Spain's great intellectual achievements, and what's more, American universities were modeled on that of Salamanca, one of the most famous in Europe. Through the mother country came the intellectual currents of the rest of Europe. This was as true of the eighteenth century as it was of the sixteenth or seventeenth.

Almost all of Spanish and Spanish American history is a testimonial to the fact that people of Spanish descent do not long acquiesce to any tyranny that the majority, or even much of a minority, finds unbearable. Spain ruled in America for more than three centuries without professional soldiery or standing military forces except in a few places where they were needed mainly to repel foreign attack or guard against frontier Indian depredations. And in all that time there was not a single rebellion that indicated widespread dissatisfaction with the Crown's rule. There were, of course, local disturbances, conspiracies, and uprisings, which made some mark on this history; but in virtually every case, except the few strictly Indian rebellions, there were apt to be Peninsulars and Americans on both sides and the circumstances were local, with little or nothing to indicate significant separatist spirit. Even when Napoleon invaded the mother country, usurped the throne, and "shook the tree of independence" by pushing Spanish Americans to extraordinary measures of self-government, most Spanish Americans did not initially aim at separation from Spain; independence from the mother country was a slow-growing idea even in that heady atmosphere of crumbling traditions. Independence was almost an accidental outcome, and there were far more important factors in this achievement than any popular rebellion against Spanish tyranny or obscurantism. The strong anti-Spanish propaganda inspired within relatively limited circles did not achieve wide popularity until years of it and abrasive fighting had crystallized dogmatic hatred into war for independence. The war period and subsequent decades spawned a literature of justification with strong hispanophobic twists.

In summary, the evidence so far presented in scholarly monographs, articles, and in documentary publications, does not allow any fair-minded observer to characterize those three centuries as a "tyranny," as uniquely "oppressive," as purposefully or generally cruel, or as "obscurantist." There is still much to be studied concerning those centuries, but it is already clear that they were too complex to fit such generalized epithets. Above all, it is completely fallacious to consider them as merely a continuation of the initial conquest patterns. . . .

30. *The Fall of the Spanish American Empire*

R. A. HUMPHREYS

Professor R. A. Humphreys almost single-handed has created a school of Latin Americanists in Great Britain during the last quarter century. As a Commonwealth Fellow he became attracted to the field while in the United States, and after his appointment to the first Chair of Latin American History in University College, London, in 1948, he steadily and systematically fostered a sound development of teaching and research. It was largely his influence that led to the establishment of several Latin American centers in British universities, the excellent *Journal of Latin American Studies,* and the Institute of Latin American Studies in London, of which he serves as Director. His publications on modern Latin American history have been distinguished for their balance and style.

At the time of the Napoleonic invasions of the Spanish peninsula in 1807–8, the Spanish empire in America stretched in unbroken line from California to Cape Horn. From Stockholm to Cape Town is less distant, and within the area ruled by Spain all western Europe from Madrid to Moscow might lie and be lost.

A hundred years earlier, at the beginning of the eighteenth century, Spain had been a major battlefield of Europe. That experience was now to be repeated, and this time foreign invasion spelt imperial destruction. The French Revolution in its Napoleonic aspect was the occasion, if not the cause, of the emancipation of Spanish America. But in the years between the war of the Spanish Succession and the wars of Napoleon, Spain herself had risen with remarkable resilience from the decrepitude into which she had fallen in the seventeenth century. Her economic decline had been first arrested and then reversed, and under Charles III and during the early years of Charles IV she enjoyed what seems in retrospect to have been an Indian summer of prosperity.

What was true of Spain was true also of her empire. Of the empire during the long years of Spain's weakness and decay we know all too little. But of its material and intellectual advance during the so-called century of enlightenment there is abundant evidence. And Spain, like Britain, undertook in the eighteenth century the task of imperial reorganization and reform. At home

From "The Fall of the Spanish American Empire" by R. A. Humphreys, *History* (October 1952), pp. 213–227, passim. Reprinted by permission.

and in the empire the administrative system was overhauled. New viceroyalties and captaincies-general were created. The establishment, in the very year of the North American Declaration of Independence, of the viceroyalty of the Río de la Plata, covering the whole, indeed more than the whole, of what is now Argentina, marked a period in the history of Spanish America. And the attempt to systematize and centralize colonial government by the division of the colonies into intendancies — "to unify the government of the great empires which God has intrusted to me," as Charles III expressed it in the Great Ordinance of Intendants for New Spain — was scarcely less important.

The reforms in the imperial economic system were equally radical. The Spanish system of colonial and commercial monopoly differed not in kind from the colonial policy of other powers, but in the extraordinary rigour with which it was applied. There were special reasons for the severity and minuteness of these economic regulations, and special reasons for the quite disastrous consequences that followed. But though the policy of colonial monopoly was never abandoned, it was, in the eighteenth century, liberalized. Slowly and cautiously the natural trade routes of the Indies were opened up. Where once Cádiz and Seville had enjoyed a monopoly within a monopoly, and the fleets and galleons had divided between them the commerce and treasure of Mexico and Perú, step by step the ports of America and the ports of Spain were opened, the age-old restrictions on inter-colonial commerce were lightened, and the tariffs and duties hampering trade revised. The so-called Decree of Free Trade of 1778, by which all the more important ports of Spain and of Central and South America were allowed to trade, if not freely at least directly, with one another, was as much a landmark in the economic history of the later empire as was the establishment of the viceroyalty of the Río de la Plata in its political history.

The reasons for these striking innovations were, in the broadest sense of the word, strategic. Efficiency in administration, the rehabilitation of colonial trade, were not so much ends in themselves as means to an end; and the end was imperial defense, the protection of the empire against foreign aggression, particularly English aggression, the elimination of foreign economic competition, and the restoration of Spanish maritime and military power in Europe. And as in British colonial policy after 1763, so in Spanish, the financial problem was paramount. Defence demanded revenue, "it being necessary," as Charles III instructed his visitor-general to New Spain,

> on account of the large sums needed in attending to the obligations of my royal crown, to exhaust all means which may appear conducive to increasing as much as possible the income from the revenues.

This was a dominant consideration both in administrative and in economic reform. And what Britain in part proposed to effect by tightening up the acts of trade, Spain in part proposed to effect by their relaxation.

The results, or the apparent results, were remarkable. The volume of imperial trade notably increased. At Buenos Aires, now the capital of the viceroyalty of Río de la Plata and no longer a dependency of Lima, the economic life of the colony was transformed. Its customs receipts, its exports, its shipping, its population, all alike rapidly increased. At Havana, Cuba, where six vessels had sufficed for the trade of Spain in 1760, two hundred were insufficient in 1778, and more than a thousand, Spanish and foreign, entered in 1801. New Spain, or Mexico, repeats the same story — a larger volume of shipping, swelling revenues, greater exports. In Perú, when the legislation of 1778 first came into effect, "speculations were multiplied to so extraordinary a degree" in the first fervour of novelty that the merchants resorted to the now familiar device of destroying their goods in order to maintain the price level. And even remote Chile experienced a new and vigorous impulse of economic change.

Whatever truth, therefore, there may be in the legend of the stagnation and decay of Spain and of the Spanish American empire in the seventeenth century, it does not hold for the eighteenth. Within Spain's transatlantic dominions the signs of an expanding economy and of a growing prosperity were everywhere, or almost everywhere, writ large. "It is just . . . to observe," wrote a competent British observer, that Perú, during the late eighteenth century

> was not only in a flourishing state both in respect to her mines and to her commerce, but also as referable to the capitals possessed by individuals, to the comparative extent of her manufactures, and to her navigation. Between the years 1790 and 1800 there existed in Lima a *commercial* capital of above 15 millions of dollars; whereas in the present year [1826] it is under one million.

Humboldt, in Venezuela, noted that "everything seemed to announce the increase of population and industry." In New Spain the public revenues increased more than sixfold in the eighteenth century, and so also did the produce of the mines. And though more than half of the world output of the precious metals still flowed from Spanish America, and though there is a lively superstition that the Spanish American colonies were made of gold and silver and nothing else, agriculture as well as mining, as the great Gálvez tells us, were the basis of their prosperity. The value of the gold and silver of the Mexican mines, says Humboldt, was less "by almost a fourth" than that of the agricultural produce. Of Venezuela and Cuba he observes that agriculture "founded more considerable fortunes" than had been accumulated by the working of the mines in Perú, and in southern South America, where the mines were few, but where Buenos Aires and even Montevideo were rapidly rising in importance, the pastoral and agricultural industries, then as now, were the economic staples.

It is reasonable to conclude, with Professor Haring, that as the eighteenth century closed the peoples of Spanish America were probably more prosperous than at any time in their history. True, in a colonial and developing area, there was no considerable growth of manufactures. Nor was there in the English colonies. But domestic manufacturing was in fact more widespread than is commonly supposed. True, also, the whole population of Spanish America was certainly not greater than that of the British Isles in 1811. But its increase in the eighteenth century was remarkable. In 1800 Mexico City was the leading city of the western hemisphere, larger than any city of Great Britain and Ireland except London and Dublin. Its rival, Lima, compared with Bristol and was itself outstripped by Havana. Even long-neglected Buenos Aires was as large as New York or Philadelphia in 1790. And the growth and embellishment of the cities (not merely the capital cities) illustrates the same expansionist trend. Here, at least, in public buildings and public display, were the marks of opulence; and it is no accident that here also, at the end of the century, there was an efflorescence of intellectual activity, in the universities and academies, in the growth of a periodical press, in literary societies and in clubs. In Santa Fé, Perú and Mexico, observed an English merchant in 1804, there was not only a greater degree of knowledge and a greater degree of progress in civilization than was commonly supposed in Europe, but, he added, though perhaps with prejudice, "much more than exists in Old Spain."

The disruption of this society by a violent cataclysm which would, within a few years, destroy much of its wealth, would seem, at first sight, an improbable event. The Conde de Aranda, one of the more far-sighted of Spanish statesmen, indeed foresaw it. "We must imagine" he wrote in 1782 "that sooner or later in [Spanish] America there will occur revolutions like those of the English colonies." And Canning's retrospective judgment, on the effect of the American Revolution, that "the operation of that example" was "sooner or later inevitable," is well known. The influences of eighteenth-century rationalism and of the French Revolution were equally powerful dissolvents. The continent, despite the censorship of the Inquisition, was not closed to ideas. Forbidden literature is always the most enticing of literature. A cultivated minority was certainly acquainted with the writings of the *philosophes,* of Rousseau, of Locke, even of Adam Smith. These were to be echoed, along with the Declarations of Independence and the Rights of Man, in the pronouncements and charters of revolutionary leaders and revolutionary governments. Yet despite the activities of an adventurer like Francisco de Miranda, who knew the "brace of Adamses" and had seen the French Revolution at first hand, despite occasional conspiracies and even outright rebellion, there was little specifically revolutionary activity in Spanish America before Spain herself fell a prey to Napoleon. The revolution, when it came, rose like a sudden tide from still, or comparatively still, waters.

Yet Spain's colonies were lost before the revolution began. The Bourbon reforms came too late, they did not go far enough, they were given insufficient time, to save the empire. And politically at least they contained no concession to the newer movement of ideas.

> "Instead of considering its colonies as a place of refuge for the idle, the profligate, and the disaffected, where they might learn to amend their lives, and, if possible, forget their errors," wrote the *Edinburgh Review* in 1806, "the Spanish Crown has watched over its foreign settlements with the solicitude of a duenna, and regulated their government as if they were to be inhabited by Carthusians."

The quotation, perhaps, is mainly interesting for the light it throws on the value placed on colonies in early nineteenth-century Britain. But it contains a solid grain of truth. The empire, from first to last, was built on paternalist and absolutist lines. It could not, in point of fact, be quite so centralized as theory might imply. The royal will was always limited by circumstance. But the price of paternalism was procrastination and inefficiency, a tradition of legalism and a disrespect for law, a class system which almost, but not quite, became a caste system, and a mounting jealousy between Spaniards born in Spain and Spaniards born in America, between, that is, the governors and the governed. "The most miserable European" wrote Humboldt "without education, and without intellectual cultivation, thinks himself superior to the whites born in the new continent." The creoles, excluded generally from the higher administrative posts, found almost their sole representation in municipal institutions. "Even in the most despotic states" says Robertson in his famous *History* "this feeble spark of liberty is not extinguished." But even here it was the local, not the representative, character of the *cabildos,* or town councils, too often closed corporations, petty oligarchies, which caused them to play so prominent a part in the events of 1808 to 1810.

There was no relaxation of this paternalistic system in the eighteenth century. On the contrary, enlightened despotism sought to rationalize and simplify the machinery of imperial administration both in Spain and in America in the interests of order, uniformity, centralization, efficiency. And though, for a time, a new life was breathed into the imperial system, the political aspirations of the creoles were forgotten, or ignored. In so far as the newly appointed intendants, invariably Spaniards, superseded minor, but creole, officials, and trespassed, moreover, on the functions of the *cabildos,* the Spanish American creoles were, in fact, still further removed from the work of government. "We were left" Bolívar was to say "in a state of permanent childhood."

And, paradoxically enough, the measures designed to secure a still closer integration between Spain and her colonies had precisely the opposite effect. In Spanish America, as in Spain, local and regional loyalties were always strong. Customs, conditions, varied enormously. Cities and squares, law and administration, might be drawn to a pattern, but the life of the colonies flowed in its own individual channels; and at a time when the Bourbon economic reforms gave to the several regions of Spanish America a new economic autonomy, the creation of new viceroyalties and captaincies-general promoted and consolidated a growing sense of regional nationalism. Colonial self-consciousness was directly stimulated. It can be no accident that the revolution, when it came, gained its first successes in those areas whose economic and political status had thus been raised. The origins of the new Spanish American nations must properly be sought in the developing life of the eighteenth century.

Apart from a small minority, an intellectual *élite,* it is possible that the rising creole middle class of lawyers, merchants, landowners and soldiers might have reconciled themselves for some time longer to their political inferiority, however much they resented their social inferiority, to the Spaniards. The loyalists, or royalists, were always far more numerous during the Spanish American revolutions than they were during the revolution for North American independence. But whatever the prosperity of Spanish America, whatever the rehabilitation of Spain, in the second half of the eighteenth century, the economic foundations of the empire had been irretrievably undermined. The recovery of Spain had failed to keep pace with the expanding economy of her colonies, and the imperial economic reforms of Charles III were no more than palliatives of a condition imperfectly understood. The trade of the empire was still a closed monopoly of Spain, but the monopoly was imposed by a country which could still not successfully apply it, a country outstripped in financial and technical resources, in facilities and skills, by its greatest colonial rival, Britain. The empire, Professor Whitaker has observed, "fell not so much because of decay within as because of pressure from without"; and from this point of view its fall was no more than a corollary of the commercial expansion of Europe and particularly of England.

What really stimulated the economic expansion of Spanish America in the eighteenth century, perhaps, were not so much the imperial economic reforms as the European search for Latin American markets and the European demand for Latin American products. And for the continued growth of European interest in Spanish America there were, apart from considerations of strategy and politics, three main reasons. First, Spanish America provided dollars, the gold and silver coin and specie which was the lubricant of international trade. The bullion supply was as interesting to the continental as it was to the British and North American merchant. Secondly, Spanish America supplied a number of raw materials, such as drugs and dyewoods, hides and skins, increasingly important for industrial and commercial purposes. Thirdly, it afforded a market for manufactured goods, particularly textiles and hardware. The market, perhaps, was not infinitely extensible as was sometimes imagined, but its potentialities were great, some English and some continental merchants knew it far better than might be supposed, and it was undoubtedly profitable.

There were, also, two ways of tapping the resources and trade of Spanish America. The first was to do so indirectly by way of Cádiz and, still more indirectly, by way of Lisbon and Rio de Janeiro. The second was the direct or contraband trade. Both had long been practiced. At the end of the seventeenth century everybody knew that the fleets and galleons at Cádiz were stocked with foreign, principally French and English, not Spanish goods, that the Spanish merchants were little more than agents or shippers, and that the returns which flowed to Spain immediately flowed out again.

> "We owe to Divine Providence," Philip V complained, "the special blessing of vast dominions in America, the centre of abundant precious metals; [yet] the Crown has always seen that . . . this is the kingdom which retains the least."

Or, in Pufendorff's phrase, which Mr. Christelow has recently quoted, "Spain kept the cow and the rest of Europe drank the milk."

Spain, in short, could not supply her colonies herself. But she maintained the pretense of so doing. What was more, she insisted that colonial products should flow only to Spain. Since the tonnage of the galleons fell by three-quarters in the seventeenth century, it is obvious that the volume of imperial trade had seriously contracted. Not only this, high duties and restrictive freights combined with the monopolistic interests of the merchant houses in Seville and Cádiz to raise the price level in America to fantastic heights. An increase of two to three hundred per cent above the prices in Spain was not uncommon. And if Spain could not herself supply her colonies with enough or cheap enough goods, neither could Europe obtain from Spain all that she wanted of colonial products. The result was an enormous contraband trade. This was the second method employed by the French, the English and the Dutch, the direct or contraband trade; and the more debilitated Spain became, the greater grew the contraband, the more the contraband, the greater Spain's debility, and the weaker her empire. . . .

The effect on Spain can partly be measured in the continuing decline in the tonnage of the fleets and galleons and in the irregularity of their sailings. When the galleons sailed for the last time in 1737 they were unable to dispose of their goods because the markets were already overstocked. Royal decree after royal decree complained of the presence of foreigners and foreign goods in the Indies. Foreigners must be expelled. Officials who connived at contraband trade should be punished with death. Even their immortal souls would be imperilled, for in 1776 the Church was recommended to teach that contraband was a mortal sin. Finally, of course, the great series of economic and commercial reforms which began in 1740 with the permission given to register ships to sail round Cape Horn and culminated in the legislation of Charles III, reflected the acute anxieties of the crown.

The reforms could alleviate, but they failed to remedy the situation. It is true that they did much to rehabilitate Spanish commerce. Though the old monopolists protested, new and more enterprising Spaniards and Spanish Americans entered trade. Shipping and revenue increased. But the contraband continued. To tap the trade of the Gulf of Mexico and the Spanish Main, the British, in 1766, established free ports in Dominica and Jamaica, extending the system, after 1787, to other strategic points in the West Indies. And there is no doubt that, despite temporary vicissitudes, the free port trade, encouraged in time of peace and specially licensed in time of war, was, as the board of trade found it, when reviewing the Free Port Acts themselves, highly "beneficial." The Spaniards might properly complain. But it was no part of British policy to enforce the Laws of the Indies. And whatever may have been the prospects that the imperial reforms of Charles III could have arrested foreign economic pressure upon the walls of the empire and that Spain herself could have been brought successfully to compete in the swelling volume of international trade, the doom of Spanish hopes was sealed by two events. The first was the death of Charles himself in 1788 and the accession of the incompetent Charles IV. The second was the entry of Spain into the French revolutionary wars.

The war of 1779 to 1783, when Spain had actively promoted the independence of England's colonies, had been costly enough. For the first time in Spanish history the crown was forced to issue paper money, soon to be inflated. The brief war with France, from 1793 to 1795, was a further blow. But when, in 1796, Spain again went to war with England, and, with a brief interval of only two and a half years, remained at war for twelve years more, the result was disaster. This was the crisis of the empire. Spain and her colonies were severed. The Spanish economy was seriously deranged. The Spanish navy was almost destroyed. And the colonies were thrown upon their own and foreign resources.

There had been occasions, in earlier years, when Spain had been compelled to tolerate the trade of friends or neutrals in Spanish America. In 1782, for example, Louisiana had been allowed to trade with France. Cuba, in 1793, was permitted to trade with the United States. In the years after 1789, moreover, the slave trade had been thrown open and foreigners allowed to engage in it. But when, on November 18, 1797, the crown opened the ports of Spanish America to neutral shipping, the measure was one of desperation. The order was indeed revoked in 1799 because it had "redounded entirely," as the decree of revocation complained, to the injury of the state and of the interests of its subjects. But what the law forbade, local regulation continued to tolerate and the crown itself to license; and though the old system was restored at the peace in 1802, with the renewal of the war once again the ports were opened.

The result, or partial result, was the rapid growth of North American trade, from Cuba to Buenos Aires and Buenos Aires to Chile. And more than one American, perhaps, like the young Richard Cleveland of Massachusetts, carried in his cargo a copy of the Federal Constitution and of the Declaration of Independence, conveniently translated into Spanish. But it was not only American trade, legitimate and illegitimate, that grew. So also did British trade. The contraband flourished at the free ports in the West Indies. It flourished at Trinidad, which alone was said to supply the Spanish colonies with goods to the value of one million pounds a year. It flourished at Vera Cruz, as Viceroy Marquina bitterly complained. It flourished at Buenos Aires. And, even on the Pacific coast, where the South Sea whalers were actively engaged in it, it extended and strengthened its hold.

There was still to be fought out in Spanish America the battle between monopoly and free enterprise, between the beneficiaries of an old order and the partisans of a new. But the issue was already resolved. It was impossible to re-enact the Laws of the Indies. The economic emancipation of Spanish America was determined before its political emancipation began.

And so far as political emancipation was concerned, the years from 1796 to 1808 were equally decisive. As Britain had formerly wavered between plundering the Spanish American colonies and trading with them, so now she hesitated between their conquest and their emancipation. In 1797 the governor of Trinidad was specifically instructed to encourage revolution on the Mainland. The invasion of Buenos Aires was prepared, and cancelled, in the same year. And there were other plans, in the mind of the British government as well as in that of Francisco de Miranda, so long plotting in England and America the emancipation of Venezuela. But fundamentally Britain was more interested in trade than territory. Her designs were commercial and strategic rather than imperial, and when, in 1806, Sir Home Popham captured Buenos Aires, it was at his own responsibility. *The Times,* indeed, rejoiced. It knew not, it said, how to express itself in terms adequate to the national advantage obtained. But the government vacillated. It did too little and that little too late. Buenos Aires was recaptured and Montevideo lost. The whole affair, said *The Times,* was "a dirty, sordid enterprise, conceived and executed in a spirit of avarice and plunder," and the chief source of the calamity was the unauthorised beginning of it.

But for Spanish America its end was all important. The viceroy of Río de la Plata had fled. It was the creoles who defeated the British, deposed the incompetent viceroy and appointed a new one. Spanish America had seen the deposition and imprisonment of the legal representative of the king. It had seen a creole militia defeat a European army. It had seen a colonial port crowded with British ships and flooded with British goods. It was not a revolution that took place at Buenos Aires as a result of the British invasions. But it was a political and economic transformation that contained the seeds of revolution.

Suddenly, however, the situation changed. Napoleon invaded Spain. The crown fell into captivity. A usurper sat upon the throne. From an enemy Britain became, overnight, the ally of Spain, and the army which Wellesley was preparing in Ireland for the liberation of Spanish America sailed, not to emancipate Spanish America from Spain, but to liberate Spain from France.

The news of the fall of the monarchy, and of the invasion of the mother country, stirred the loyalty and moved the indignation of the colonies, and, superficially, the resistance movement in Spain was almost exactly imitated in Spanish America. As juntas sprang up in Spain in the name of Ferdinand VII, so in Spanish America juntas and *cabildos* assumed the powers of viceroys, presidents and captains-general, the agents, now, of an authority which had ceased to exist. Extraordinary circumstances called for extraordinary measures. The colonists took thought for their own protection and their own future. Power reverted to the people, though by "the people" nothing more can be meant than a small but active creole minority: the revolutions in Spanish America were the work of the few, not of the many.

But that a movement which began as an assertion of independence from France should have ended as an assertion of independence from Spain was due quite as much to Spain herself as to the creole minority in her colonies whose thwarted aspirations in government and trade were thus fulfilled. For though the monarchy had collapsed, though the Peninsula was overrun, the Spaniards still clung to the principles of imperial monopoly and colonial subordination. Crown, Regency, Cortes, showed themselves equally blind, equally determined. The colonies, declared the Junta Central, in 1809, were an integral part of the Spanish monarchy, and the deduction soon followed that they owed obedience to the extraordinary authorities erected in Spain. That was not the Spanish American view. Nor had it been the Habsburg view. "Estos y esos reinos," "these and those kingdoms," was the famous phrase used to define the royal possessions in Spain and the Indies. The Indies had never belonged to Spain. They were the property of the crown of Castile, united to the kingdoms of Spain merely by a dynastic tie. The Bourbons forgot, or ignored, this Habsburg view; and so did the Spaniards. But the creoles remembered it. Just as the English colonies, in the eighteenth century, refused to accept subordination to the sovereignty of parliament, so the Spanish Americans refused to accept subordination to the people of the Peninsula. And in both cases what reason failed to arrange, force was left to decide.

THE
MODERN
AGE

*Simón Bolívar, the Liberator. New data and new perspectives are beginning
to be used to produce a new history of the early nineteenth-century revolutions
in Spanish America (Reading 31). But one cannot forget that it was the work
of a small band of revolutionaries which captured the imagination of the
people sufficiently to make a political break possible.*

*Among these figures the Venezuelan Bolívar was pre-eminent, and this
painting of The Liberator as a young officer (1819) before victory was
achieved captures effectively the romantic spirit of the time.*

SECTION VII

Did a Revolution Occur in Latin America between 1810 and 1830?

WERE THERE ANY BASIC CHANGES?

The question raised in the title of this section would have caused great surprise a generation ago, and probably would shock many in Latin America today. For their historians have almost uniformly tended to exalt the great changes wrought by their revolutionary leaders during the years when Brazil and Spanish America were breaking away from their mother countries, even though the Liberator Simón Bolívar had proclaimed on his deathbed in 1829 that he "had ploughed the sea." Historians in and out of Latin America have emphasized most often the political, biographic, and diplomatic aspects of the struggle and until recently have paid relatively scant attention to cultural, economic, and social developments. New approaches, fortunately, are now being made (Reading 31).

Did basic changes occur in the fabric of society and in institutions? At a session of the American Historical Association in 1966 much attention was paid to analyzing the continuities between the late eighteenth and early nineteenth centuries in Spanish America.[1] It was generally agreed that the independence period there should not be treated as a sharp break with the past or as merely a chronicle of *pronunciamientos,* battles, and paper constitutions full of noble sentiments on instant improvements for mankind. And at

[1] See the summary of this session in the *Hispanic American Historical Review,* 47 (1967), pp. 318–319.

an earlier meeting of the A.H.A. there was a notable presentation by Woodrow Borah, Charles Gibson, and Robert Potash in which they discussed the many relationships between colonial institutions and contemporary Latin America.[2]

It may be too soon to determine exactly what kind of revolution occurred in the various parts of the vast territory ruled by Spain in 1810, but the selections in this section are designed to be useful in studying the subject. To document some of the changes, copious literature is available in the travel accounts of the many Europeans who hastened to Latin America to find out what was happening there and in the official reports by representatives of Great Britain and the United States. Latin America aroused enormous commercial interest, particularly among British merchants and manufacturers who hoped to win great profits through joint stock companies (mines, gas, railways, insurance, docks, and canals). Cornish miners were to bring new techniques; another project aimed at joining the Pacific and Atlantic by a ship canal. There was capital enough to organize a company for almost any project:

> There were companies and plans to navigate the rivers of South America by steamboats, to fish for pearls in Colombia, to establish the "unemployed poor" of Great Britain and Ireland as agricultural colonists in the United Provinces of the Río de la Plata. There were companies to promote emigration to Chile and Colombia. There was a company which proposed to export milkmaids to Buenos Aires in order to make butter.[3]

Cultural changes were involved, too, including attempts to prepare the citizens of the new nations for the life of independence. Bolívar manifested an interest in primary education, and the Congress of Cúcuta in 1821 aimed to organize a permanent educational system. The legislators solemnly proclaimed that "Citizens cannot basically know the sacred obligations which religion and Christian morality impose upon them, or the rights and duties of man in society" unless they are educated. They then decreed the establishment of a primary school for boys in every town of one hundred or more families.[4] Girls were provided for, too, to some extent, but little could actually be spent on education for anyone anywhere. The most that can be said is that some revolutionary leaders understood the need to improve and enlarge the school

[2] Ibid., 29 (1949), pp. 170–187.

[3] R. A. Humphreys, *Liberation in South America, 1808–1827: The Career of James Paroissien* (London: The Athlone Press, University of London, 1952), p. 140.

[4] David Bushnell, *The Santander Regime in Gran Colombia* (Newark: University of Delaware Press, 1954), pp. 183–194.

system. General San Martín also understood the connection between access to books and educational advance when he established the National Library in Peru in 1822. Detailed studies on these and other topics of social history are still largely lacking, but Professor R. A. Humphreys of the University of London provides some sound general conclusions (Reading 32).

BRAZIL'S PEACEFUL BREAK WITH PORTUGAL

Brazil was different from Spanish America in the way it revolted from the mother country. It preserved its monarchy and achieved its breakaway from Portugal by peaceful means; indeed, the Prince Regent Dom João really began the independence movement when he took the unprecedented step of moving his court across the South Atlantic to escape from Napoleon's armies, which were then overrunning Portugal. It was an impressive caravan of thirty-six vessels escorted by the British Navy:

> On board were fourteen members of the Royal Family; the Counsellors of State; ministers; Justices of the Court of Appeals and the High Court; the upper echelons of the army and navy; the hierarchy of the church; a full quota of high society; a respectable contingent of the professional, scientific, literary, artistic, and business elements; a horde of bureaucrats; and as many rank and file citizens as could secure passage. Also on board were the contents of the royal treasury; the store of diamonds derived from the crown monopoly; silver plate, jewels, books, cash, and other portable assets; furnishings for a royal chapel; the royal library; a printing press; and a mass of government records. When John, the Prince Regent, set up shop in Rio de Janeiro, he had readily available the personnel and the files of a bureaucracy for the administration of a national state.[5]

On March 8, 1808, the city of Rio de Janeiro welcomed the royal flotilla sailing in under Sugarloaf Mountain. The city the court saw was incredibly primitive:

> It extended back from the beach a bare half mile and was situated on a low, flat piece of ground, surrounded in part by marshes. It had a population of possibly eighty thousand people, no sewage system, and a water system dependent on the great aqueduct built by one of the viceroys, which fed a small number of public fountains. . . .

[5] Alan K. Manchester, "The Growth of Bureaucracy in Brazil, 1808–1821," *Journal of Latin American Studies,* 4 (1972), p. 77.

The town itself was a half-awake place, with a few narrow streets paved with the granite of the surrounding mountains. The houses had one or two stories, made of stone covered with plaster and white-washed. They were roofed with semicircular tiles, the edges laid within each other to form natural channels to carry off the heavy rains. The typical dwelling had a good-sized room floored with boards laid upon beams on the ground. Behind this room were alcoves containing beds, for the colonial Brazilian guarded against any danger from the night air by making sure that there were no windows in his sleeping room. The beds were medieval in construction, and the dearth of furniture was noticeable even in houses of the well-to-do. There was usually a sofa of ceremony and some old chairs painted red and white and decorated with wreaths of flowers. The family gathering place was a verandah at the back of the house, and there the women sat, as they sat at dinner or in church, on the floor on mats, lace-making, if they were industrious, or eating sweetmeats, if they were not. At table they ate with their fingers, while the gentlemen, when they visited one another, brought along each his own knife to eat with. The kitchen was at the back of the house, with an enclosed yard. If the master of the house owned a horse, it was stabled in that yard, and quite often there was no other way to get there except through the principal room. Some English merchants who lived above their shops had their floors caulked like the deck of a ship, so that the water used to wash them would not trickle down on the goods stored below. In that hot, humid climate and marshy terrain, a smell of damp characteristically pervaded the house.

The crowds that filled the city's streets were made up largely of half-naked, sweating black slaves, who frightened and disgusted the visiting foreigners. Slaves were not only servants and unskilled laborers; they were also, in many cases, artisans and provided the only means of carrying on what public utilities existed. Frequently they hired out their services to earn money to take home at night, for the income of many a white Brazilian was entirely what his slave could earn. White women were never seen in the streets, except on their way to church, heavily veiled or shrouded in covered sedan chairs.

The lawyers and the businessmen congregated in their favorite meeting place, the corner of the Rua do Ouvidor and the Rua da Quitanda (Judge Street and Market Street). They wore rusty old black coats, ill-fitting and patched, gaily colored embroidered waistcoats with deep pockets, tight breeches fastened with square buckles of sham brilliants, stockings of homespun cotton, and enormous buckles on their shoes.

On their heads they wore powdered wigs and fantailed hats, and carried old dirks in the place of swords. Even the artisans who were not slaves dressed in this fashion. No one except a slave or a foreigner carried anything in his hand. The only vehicles for transporting merchandise were ox carts and a sort of four-wheeled truck pulled by ten or a dozen Negroes.

The numerous churches and convents and other religious buildings were the only public buildings of note. In their multiplicity and prominence and in the number and variety of religious images set up at street corners and the quantity of ex-votos hung up in the churches, was to be seen another characteristic inheritance from Portugal and of the narrow life forced upon the colony. The only community and social life the inhabitants knew was centered on religious ceremonies.[6]

The society that the Portuguese met in Brazil had been largely cut off from the ideas and practices of Europe, as shown in the backwardness of the Brazilian colonial ladies in questions of hair styles. On the voyage over, the water supply was insufficient, and fleas became so bad that the ladies, including the royal princess, were forced to cut their hair to eliminate the pests. When they disembarked in Rio de Janeiro with cropped hair, the Brazilian women were surprised to see them thus but thought short hair must be the latest court fashion, so they hurried home to cut their own! [7]

Brazilian and Portuguese historians still dispute the true nature of Dom João's rule, 1808–1821. Was the presence of the monarchy in the New World a positive force that preserved national unity and set Brazil on a peaceful road to independence, or was it a neocolonial instrument of repressive centralism and elitist control, an essentially alien regime that isolated the country from the revolutionary destinies of the New World? [8] These questions doubtless deserve further investigation, but Professor Alan K. Manchester in his recent analysis concludes that the transfer of the court to Brazil indeed exerted a significant effect on the history of Brazil (Reading 33). Dom João demonstrated a capacity for government not hitherto recognized by many historians. The bureaucrats and administrative apparatus brought from Portugal firmly established in Brazil institutions that proved to be durable and significant when the Portuguese court returned to Lisbon. And when

[6] Anyda Marchant, *Viscount Mauá and the Empire of Brazil* (Berkeley and Los Angeles: University of California Press, 1965), pp. 12–13. Reprinted by permission of the Regents of the University of California.

[7] Alan K. Manchester, *British Preeminence in Brazil: Its Rise and Decline* (Chapel Hill: University of North Carolina, 1933), p. 69.

[8] Arnold Clayton, "Interpretations of the Rule of Dom João VI in Brazil, 1808–1821" (Master's thesis, Columbia University, 1967), p. 75.

João elevated the colony in 1815 to formal and legal equality with the mother country, he struck a powerful blow for eventual Brazilian independence.

Professor Manchester recognizes that there were some points of similarity between the movements toward independence in Spanish America and Brazil. The differences were marked, too, as Professor Richard Graham brought out in his commentary on Manchester's paper. In Brazil "the marching feet of armies destroyed no crops, and no hordes were to wreck the mines or pillage the towns. The weakening of the social fabric which accompanied the political disruption in Spanish America was only dimly reflected in Brazil through the disruption of titles and, eventually, of power to Brazilian landowners." [9]

[9] Richard Graham, in "Commentary," *Conflict and Continuity in Brazilian Society,* eds. Henry H. Keith and S. F. Edwards (Columbia: University of South Carolina Press, 1969), p. 189.

31. *Only the Beginnings of a Basic Transformation Took Place*

CHARLES C. GRIFFIN

Professor Emeritus Charles C. Griffin of Vassar College has been noted for his thoughtful and balanced interpretations, particularly of the exciting and debatable revolutionary period when Spanish America was breaking away from Spain. He here discusses both the profound shock that the revolutionary wars caused in the social and economic life of the colonies and the "accelerated tempo of evolutionary transformation" that characterized those turbulent years after 1810.

The revolutions which brought about the establishment of independent governments in America differed in marked degree from the classic revolutions of modern Europe — the French and the Russian — in that their primary effect was to throw off the authority of a transatlantic empire rather than to bring about a drastic reconstruction of society. In the case of the United States, however, it has long been recognized that the revolutionary struggle did not confine itself to the political sphere, i.e., to independence and the establishment of a new federal government. Almost a generation ago the late J. Franklin Jameson published his essays on *The American Revolution Considered as a Social Movement* in which he suggested relations between the revolution and the manifold changes of the era, some already recognized, and others destined to be more fully charted by a subsequent generation of scholars. Because many of these changes were not the result of conscious revolutionary planning, but came about under the stimulus of new conditions created during and after the revolution, they had not earlier been sufficiently closely related to the revolution and to each other.

It is possible that the time may be ripe for a similar shift in emphasis in the interpretation of the revolutions for independence in Spanish America. It was natural that these movements, as starting points for new national traditions, should have been regarded at first as epic conflicts. Heroism and leadership were the main themes. When this was not enough, diplomatic and constitu-

From "Economic and Social Aspects of the Era of Spanish-American Independence" by Charles C. Griffin, *Hispanic American Historical Review*, 29 (1949), pp. 170–187, passim. Reprinted by permission of the publisher, Duke University Press.

tional history were emphasized, in consonance with the popularity of such studies in nineteenth-century European historiography. Interest in political change led eventually to the study of political theories in relation to the revolutions and hence to the broader field of the history of thought. On the one hand, the background of the revolutions has been clarified by studies of the impact of the Enlightenment on Latin America; on the other, changes closely related to the triumph of new ideologies have been charted. Of these, the new status of church-state relations and the abolition of slavery can be mentioned as examples. Until fairly recently, however, the study of economic and social history has been directed primarily to the antecedents of the revolutions rather than to the developments of the era itself. . . .

The presentation of a general view, however exploratory, is complicated by regional diversity in the character and course of the independence movement in its various centers. Differences in geography, in population, in tradition, as well as in the duration and intensity of military operations must be considered, together with variations in the extent of contact with Europe and the United States. These differentiating factors modified certain general tendencies: the destructive force of war, and the stimulation produced by free intercourse with foreign countries.

The immediate economic consequence of revolution, except in a few favored areas, was disaster. The prosperity of the later colonial economy of Spanish America was shattered by warfare which was everywhere waged with little regard for the rights of private property and the lives of non-combatants. It is only possible to suggest here the terrible destruction suffered by many regions. This reached its maximum in Venezuela, where both the human and the livestock population declined, the latter by more than one-half between 1810 and 1830. Almost as severe were the losses in the Banda Oriental and in certain parts of the Viceroyalty of New Spain. New Granada and Chile represent areas which were less continuously theatres of military action, and with a consequently lighter incidence of destruction. The extreme horrors of the *guerra a muerte* in Venezuela and the slaughter in Mexico during the early stages of revolution were not often matched in scale elsewhere, but, even where loss of life was less severe, interruption of normal economic life was serious. People were uprooted from their homes in various ways. Men were recruited, often by force, for the rival armies. Even when they escaped death they frequently never returned, taking up life again elsewhere. There were also many examples of emigration on a substantial scale. These dislocations of population had unfavorable results for agriculture and mining, removing the necessary labor force, and on business in general owing to the flight of capital along with its owners.

The interruption of normal lines of trade and communication also had serious adverse effects. Northwest Argentina suffered from the halting of trade with Peru. Montevideo, while in hands hostile to Buenos Aires, lost part of its commercial function. Guerrilla warfare in New Spain at times disrupted internal communications except by armed convoys. Wartime financial exactions, ranging from confiscation to forced loans, appropriation of goods for the use of the rival armies, forced acceptance of depreciated currency, and high and arbitrary taxation brought ruin to many. Cattle-raising countries like the Banda Oriental and the Venezuelan hinterland suffered from wholesale robbery and expropriation of the livestock on which the economy of these regions was based. Mining regions were paralyzed by flooding of the workings and destruction of equipment.

It is impossible to measure exactly the total effect of these varied consequences of war, but it is probably safe to say that from 1810 to 1820 Buenos Aires and Peru, the strongholds of the rival forces in South America, were least affected. Regions like Paraguay and, to a lesser extent, Central America suffered from isolation but were little damaged. Chile, New Granada, and Mexico underwent severe destruction at times, but were not equally affected throughout the decade. On the other hand, Venezuela and Uruguay saw no real peace during the period and their normal economic activities were totally upset.

In the second decade of revolution theatres of military operations shifted. Warfare on a large scale was over in Mexico by 1821, and in Colombia after 1822. Fighting in Chile ceased, except for guerrilla warfare in the far south. On the other hand, Peru, which had previously escaped, became the center of the fighting. Though devastation here was not so widespread nor long continued as in some other areas, the burden of supporting large armies (patriot and royalist) in the field for several years was a heavy one. The duration of military activity in what is now Ecuador was briefer, but this region gave a good deal of support to the later Peruvian campaigns. For the war as a whole, therefore, only the province of Buenos Aires and its immediate neighbors to the north and west were able to escape the direct scourge of war. Even here there were intermittent skirmishes between patriot factions especially after the year 1820.

The upheaval caused by war was not limited to destruction of life and property and the disorganization of business; it also brought changes in society which were not envisaged by the creole aristocrats and intellectuals who headed the revolts of the *cabildos* in 1809 and 1810. Except in Mexico, the revolutions had begun with efforts to dislodge the peninsular bureaucracy without otherwise changing relations among classes, but war unleashed forces that these early revolutionists were unable to harness. Race and class antagonisms flared up which could only be brought under control by the exaltation of nationalism and a parallel minimizing of class distinctions. Without any general upset in these relations, there was a blurring of lines. None of the new independent governments recognized legal disabilities for *pardos* or *mestizos*. In Mexico, the clergy no longer kept the elaborate records of caste as a part of their parochial registers.

The "career open to talents" seems to have been the rule. A mestizo general might rise to the presidency of his country; a *mulato* colonel might become a large landowner. This does not mean that an equalitarian society grew out of the wars, but it does indicate that the wars brought new blood into the ruling class and simplified the social distinctions in lower strata of the population.

The annals of revolution in Mexico and Colombia are well sprinkled with the names of prominent military officers with Indian or Negro blood in their veins, or both. Piar and Padilla in Colombia were conspicuous examples. In Mexico, Guerrero and Morelos reached even higher renown. In the lower ranks officers with similar racial antecedents were numerous. In Peru and Bolivia mestizos also held high military rank. Santa Cruz, who became president of the latter republic, was the son of an Indian woman and a Spaniard. In the naval service of Colombia a number of mulatos held commissions. The large percentage of color in the ranks of Bolívar's officers was frequently commented on by the race-conscious European officers who served in Colombia.

The tendency toward greater racial tolerance was not unchecked. White creole fear accounts in part for the severe treatment meted out to such officers as Piar and Padilla. Their insubordination might well have been condoned if it had not been for their race. If there had not been great gains for the mixed bloods, such severity as that which led to the execution of both, in spite of the brilliant military services they had rendered to the cause of independence, might not have been considered necessary.

In Río de la Plata and in Chile there do not seem to have been instances of high military commanders of recognized mixed blood. We can cite, however, the cases of politicians and journalists like Vicente Kanki Pazos (an Indian from upper Peru) and the meteoric career of Bernardo Monteagudo (a mulato from Tucumán). The strength of the creole element in the population in the Viceroyalty of Buenos Aires, except in the north, and the fact that it was not heavily depleted by the wars may be one explanation for the less conspicuous place of the mestizo in military leadership. The relatively stable agrarian economy of Chile with its strong personal ties between landowner and *inquilino* provided fewer opportunities for social change than the more elaborately stratified population of Peru, Colombia, and Mexico. In these southern regions, however, the revolution brought increasing fluidity among economic groups. "Self-made men," among them many foreigners, began to make themselves increasingly evident, beginning the process which was to ease their way into the upper social ranks of *estancieros* and merchants. This tendency was stimulated by the procedure followed by many governments in paying off officers and men with land confiscated from royalists or from the public domain. Land had been for so long a badge of social position that it proved impossible to discriminate for more than a generation against the owner of a large estate.

Another series of important social and economic changes grew out of the increasing contact with foreign lands during the course of the wars of independence. In this respect local differences are also notable. Buenos Aires, without question, developed a new economy based on foreign trade earlier than any other Spanish-American country. The accumulated demand for free trade during the later years of the viceroyalty had paved the way and the absence of Spanish power to interfere, after 1810, gave the development free rein. This ushered in the cattle boom which was to fix the character of the Argentine economy for generations. It led to expansion on the Indian frontier and to the rapid growth of the city of Buenos Aires, as population flowed in to serve the needs of an expanded commerce. Small shops and factories on a handicraft basis multiplied and the accumulation of wealth created new luxury trades. On the other hand, as Burgin has shown, free trade brought depression to Cuyo and to the northern provinces from Tucumán to Jujuy, which lost much of their market for home manufactures to foreign competition.

In Chile, with interruptions due to the wars, similar changes can be seen. Free trade meant a larger market for the grain and other food surpluses which before the revolution had been shipped almost exclusively to Peru. Valparaíso became a port of call for ships bound to the Orient and for the northwest coast of America. The export of Chilean silver and copper increased under the pressure of need to balance imported manufactures. By 1825 a number of English mining experts were planning developments in the Coquimbo region. Chilean naval activity stimulated the work of shipyards and attracted both businessmen and laborers to the port city, which soon lost its sleepy colonial aspect. Free trade, however, had a less violently stimulating effect on the economy of Chile than in Río de la Plata. The immediately available resources of Chile were less vast, and depended, for expanded exploitation, on growth of population and on a long-range development of mining equipment and transportation which could not be carried through at once.

The ports of Peru and Colombia were opened to world trade at a later time and these republics were less favorably situated than those of the far south from a commercial point of view. Trade did not develop here on a healthy basis. . . .

In Mexico free trade did not actually begin until 1823. Until that time, all but a trickle of irregular trade had continued to follow traditional colonial channels to Spain and Cuba. When commerce with Spain was suspended, great difficulty arose owing to the disappearance of Spanish commercial capital at Veracruz. It was to take time to build up a new system of credit depending on agents of European manufacturers established at Mexico City. In spite of English interest in Mexican mining, production of the precious metals, which accounted for most of Mexico's surplus, did not wholly recover in the period before 1830.

The foregoing would appear to indicate some correlation between commercial progress and a lesser degree of severity in military operations in the different regions mentioned. This factor, however, cannot have been decisive. The extent to which free trade brought economic revolution also depended on the existence of resources in demand in the world markets and on adequate transportation facilities for bringing these to the seaports. Obviously, Buenos Aires, with its easily traversed *pampa,* and Chile, with production located never very far from the sea, had a great advantage over Peru, Colombia, and Mexico. . . .

The rate and extent of trade expansion varied considerably from region to region, but the direction of change was the same. All the new republics headed toward a broader production of resources demanded by the world market and became increasingly intimately linked with the expanding economy of the nineteenth century, centered on and directed by Great Britain. This trade expansion brought other economic developments in its wake. Taxation shifted from the complex system of colonial days, with its multiple excises, monopoly franchises, and sales taxes, toward reliance on the customs duties on imports as the all-important source of revenue. Consumption of imported goods tended to outrun the ability of exports to balance them, leading to the negotiation of foreign loans on highly disadvantageous terms. Buenos Aires, Chile, Peru, Mexico, and Colombia all experienced the beginnings of their troubles with foreign creditors during this epoch. The too rapid expansion of imports may have been one cause of the financial crises which contributed to widespread political instability after the establishment of independence.

Along with the economic liberalism, of which the removal of trade barriers was concrete evidence, there developed a broader liberalism which also influenced society. The story of the abolition of slavery has often been told and need not be repeated here. It should be remembered, however, that outright abolition in some countries and gradual emancipation in others had reduced slavery to insignificant proportions in republican Spanish America before 1830. This was, of course, preceded by the manumission of slaves on a considerable scale in the course of the revolutionary wars. Freedmen formed part of San Martín's liberating forces that fought at Chacabuco and of the army of Sucre that completed the liberation of Peru at Ayacucho.

The Indian fared less well in this era. In spite of frequent references to their ancient woes in propaganda directed against the Spanish regime, the achievement of independence meant little to the native race. Though frequently involved in revolutionary fighting, Indians never wholeheartedly sided with either party in the struggle. In southern Chile they were active as royalist guerrillas. In Mexico they fought and bled with Hidalgo. In Peru and Colombia they fought on both sides, either because they were forced to do so, or because they followed some leader who had a personal reason for taking sides. The lapse of colonial protective legislation exposed them to exploitation under the increasingly individualistic republican legal codes and the war of independence ruined many of the missions which had preserved their existence, even if they did not succeed in fitting them for the competitive society they now had to face.

Perhaps the most marked social change of the era was the growth of the rift between the society of the seaports and capitals, on the one hand, and rural and provincial society, on the other. At the seats of government and in the ports upper and middle classes began to be affected by the streams of foreigners (diplomats, visiting scholars, pedagogues, merchants, soldiers, and sailors) which began to appear on the scene. Fashions began to ape the styles of London and Paris; new sports and pastimes replaced colonial recreations; even habits of food and drink changed. Provincial cities were but little affected by these newfangled notions and the countryside was largely unconscious of them. Thus, the wider, European outlook of the elite in almost every country began to show itself in minor ways long before it was enshrined in law, educational institutions, and in the arts.

The hypothesis suggested by the foregoing remarks may be summarized as follows: the revolutionary wars which led to independence were a profound shock to the society and to the economic life of the Spanish colonies. Wartime destruction left many countries less able to maintain traditional ways and opened the way for new developments. Ensuing changes were brought about, first of all, by the expansion of foreign trade, which, in turn, had repercussions on the whole economic and social structure. Nevertheless, only the beginnings of a basic transformation took place and there were many ways in which colonial attitudes and institutions carried over into the life of republican Spanish America. Liberal ideas, however, used at first to buttress the rising power of landowners and businessmen, weakened paternalistic aspects of colonialism.

The Río de la Plata region was most deeply changed by the revolution. Throughout the continent, too, the greater cities and the ports were more affected by the new than were the provinces and the countryside. There emerged, therefore, no single clearly identifiable pattern of change, and developments noted were not so much revolutionary as they were examples of an accelerated tempo of evolutionary transformation.

32. *The Great Landed Estates Remained*

R. A. HUMPHREYS

Professor R. A. Humphreys, Director of the Institute of Latin American Studies in London, has dedicated many of his writings to various aspects of the wars for independence, as will be seen from the list of suggested readings for this section. In the present selection he skillfully combines a knowledge of the variations in conditions from country to country with a realization of what institutions and ways of life had not been greatly changed by the revolutions.

The fall of the empire is the second great revolution on which modern Hispanic America is founded. Like the conquest, it was written in blood. And like the conquest, it has been shrouded in myth. "The War for Independence," declared Alberdi, "endowed us with a ridiculous and disgraceful mania for the heroic." And while, on the one hand, heroes and demigods were made to dominate the stage, on the other, the revolutions of the first quarter of the nineteenth century were seen as great popular movements leading to the triumph of the idea of liberty as against the defenders of a dark colonial past.

Heroism, of course, there was, and not on one side only. But though much was said of the sovereignty of the people, the revolutions which transformed

From *Tradition and Revolt in Latin America* by R. A. Humphreys (London: The Athlone Press, 1965), pp. 9–16, passim. Reprinted by permission.

into independent states the Hispanic-American societies that had been evolving since the conquest were "popular" revolutions only in a very restricted sense. They did not represent the sudden release of the resentments of a native people, or even of a large cross-section of a colonial population, against a European oppressor. Nor were they essentially democratic. On the contrary, most of them began, quite simply, as the revolt of one Spanish minority against another Spanish minority, of creoles, in the language of the day, against *peninsulares*. Their aim was self-government for creoles, not necessarily for the mixed races, for Indians, and for negroes, who, together, made up four-fifths of the population of Spanish America. And with the political emancipation of creoles was coupled their economic emancipation, the destruction, that is, of the commercial monopoly of Spain and the opening of the ports of the continent to the trade of the world.

But revolutions are not made in a day. Nor is it easy to control them. Conflicts of interests quickly appeared, and divergencies also of ideas and aims — between capital cities and provincial cities, for example, between conservatives and radicals, and between the reforming ideals of the "age of enlightenment" and its revolutionary ideals. Creoles fought Spaniards. But Spanish Americans also fought each other. And while rebels and royalists alike appealed to, and exploited, the illiterate masses, the struggle once begun released incalculable forces, was waged with ruthless violence, and left desolation in its wake. A few areas — Paraguay was one — escaped comparatively lightly. Coastal cities, such as Buenos Aires and Valparaiso, grew and flourished on the new currents of foreign trade. But, though the extent of the damage varied from region to region, in general, the economic life of Spanish America was disrupted and the prosperity which had marked the closing years of the colonial period destroyed. Trade routes were abandoned, mines deserted, crops and livestock laid waste. The labour supply was dislocated, capital put to flight.

As the economic life of Spanish America was disrupted, so also political stability was undermined. The Crown had been the symbol of a political control which extended to almost every aspect of colonial life. Naturally it was not always obeyed. But it supplied a unifying, cohesive force, and, in theory at least, it was invariably respected. Its disappearance left a vacuum. This the creoles had expected to fill with a new republican authority, safeguarded in written instruments of government. Instead, as Lord Acton remarked, the habits of subordination departed with the Spaniard. The wars themselves encouraged the military not the civilian virtues; and, while generals who had commanded armies aspired to govern countries, the consequences of that lack of experience in self-government which, with whatever limitations, the English colonies in North America had enjoyed became fully apparent. "Until our countrymen," wrote Bolívar, in his famous Jamaica Letter in 1815, "acquire the political talents and virtues which distinguish our brothers of the north, entirely popular systems, far from working to our advantage, will, I greatly fear, come to be our ruin." His disillusion and despair as, fifteen years later, he neared his tragic end, he summed up in a still more famous phrase: "For us America is ungovernable. He who serves a revolution ploughs the sea."

The social results of the revolutions are more difficult to estimate. This also is a field of enquiry in which much work remains to be done. But the clash of race and class was clearly marked during the wars of independence. In Mexico the great Indian and mestizo rebellions led by Hidalgo and Morelos were revolts of the dispossessed against the possessing classes. The elements of racial war were plainly visible in Venezuela, and, in what Sarmiento described as the warfare of the countryside against the town, a conflict of cultures was equally evident in Argentina. Heirs to the traditions of the eighteenth-century enlightenment, many of the revolutionary leaders, notably Bolívar and San Martín, Santander in Colombia, O'Higgins in Chile, and Rivadavia in Buenos Aires, were concerned with social and humanitarian, as well as with political and economic, reform. And though their efforts were not always successful, it is obvious that some social consequences of great importance did flow from the revolutions. Negro slavery and the slave trade were in most countries restricted or abolished, in contrast to what happened in the old Portuguese colony of Brazil. The legal disabilities affecting the mulattos and other inferior castes were removed. New men, creoles and mestizos, rose by the revolutions to enter the ranks of the ruling class. And the all-pervading influence of the Church, hitherto an arm, or at least an ally, of the State was weakened.

The relation of the social classes to one another, already changing in the late eighteenth century, was thus further modified by the revolutions. But the hierarchical structure of society remained intact. Apart from the wild Indian tribes of the interior the whole population of Spanish America in 1825 was no greater than that of England, Wales and Scotland at the time of the first Reform Bill. The Indians were by far the largest element, and after them the mestizos. But the coming of independence meant little or nothing to the Mexican peon, the Peruvian Indian or the Chilean *inquilino,* and the social and economic power of a small territorial aristocracy was in no way diminished. "The distinctively Mexican economy," Professor Woodrow Borah observes, "was already organized on the basis of latifundia and debt peonage" at the end of the seventeenth century. It was still so organized at the end of the nineteenth century. There were differences, certainly. New blood had again entered the ranks of the landed gentry. The agricultural labourer was probably still worse off at the end of the century than he was at the beginning.

And the great estates, now "little principalities," had become more numerous. In Chile O'Higgins had attempted to abolish entail. In Chile, however, it was not the entailed estates that disappeared, but O'Higgins. The *inquilinos* continued to be tied to the soil as serfs, and the great estates retained their pre-eminence until well after the middle of the century. In Venezuela, where the colonial aristocracy had been reduced both in numbers and importance, nevertheless its style of life remained, and the great estates passed into the hands of a new creole and mestizo oligarchy. As for Argentina, a neglected peripheral region of the empire till after the middle of the eighteenth century, there land had endowed its holder with social rather than economic power. It was to give both in the nineteenth century, and political power also; and it was in the nineteenth century that the great estates were built up. "We are all descendants of tradesmen or of ranchers," says a character in a well-known Argentine novel: " — this we know very well. But everyone tries to forget it, and the one who is furthest from his grandfather — who might have been a country storekeeper, a clerk, a shoemaker, or a shepherd — is the most aristocratic."

The conventional picture of Latin America in the half century after the establishment of political independence is that of a continent of disorder, in which anarchy was tempered only by despotism and despotism only by revolution. Already by 1830 the faith in the future which had animated so many of the great revolutionary leaders had been dimmed — like those visions of El Dorado which had captivated the imaginations of the British merchants. "I blush to say it," wrote Bolívar, "but independence is the sole good which we have gained at the cost of everything else." "The labour and the blood given for the independence of America," San Martín declared, twelve years later, "have been, if not wasted, at any rate unfortunately spent in most of the new states." And the opinion expressed by Hegel to his students in Berlin, that in South America "the republics depend only on military force; their whole history is a continued revolution," was to become a widespread belief in Europe.

It cannot be denied that there was much truth in this picture. But it was not the whole truth. It did not hold for Brazil, for example. Portuguese America, of course, differed markedly from Spanish America, and the differences were nowhere more strikingly illustrated than in the manner in which the two great colonial areas won their independence. What was violently achieved in Spanish America was peacefully achieved in Portuguese America. There was no sudden break with the colonial past, no prolonged and devastating civil war. The heir to the crown of Portugal himself became the Emperor of Brazil, endowed the country with its constitution, and secured its entry into

the family of nations. And the throne thus peacefully established was to survive for more than sixty-five years. Nor did this picture of chronic instability
hold for Chile. Chile, like Brazil, had its domestic disorders, most serious in
Chile in the eighteen-twenties and in Brazil in the eighteen-thirties. But Chile,
like Brazil, early succeeded in establishing stable political institutions; and
these rested, in both countries, on the support of a landed aristocracy, which
in Chile, at least, was remarkably successful in assimilating new elements.

But the empire of Brazil and the "aristocratic republic" of Chile were exceptional. In Mexico, in the thirty years before the great civil wars of the
middle century began, the executive office changed hands forty-six times.
Argentina fell under the long dictatorship of Rosas and still had to face war
between Buenos Aires and the provinces before the country could enter on
the full and natural development of its economic life in 1862. And not till the
end of the nineteenth century did Uruguay shake off its turbulent past. There
were, of course, enlightened despots and unenlightened despots, liberal revolutions and illiberal revolutions. But for many years, and over large parts of
Spanish America, it was the law of force, not the force of law, that held most
governments in power; and, since force could only be met by force, revolution
became an essential element in the political system. Venezuela is said to have
experienced fifty-two major revolutions, in all, in the first century of its independent life, and Bolivia more than sixty — by 1952, indeed, more than a
hundred and sixty.

Yet few of these nineteenth-century revolutions led to any fundamental
changes in the structure of society or the sources of social and economic
power. In Mexico the great movement of the *Reforma* in the eighteen-fifties
stripped the Church of much of its temporal power; in the name of nineteenth-
century liberalism it transferred ecclesiastical estates, often unbroken, into the
hands of lay landlords; and, in the name of nineteenth-century individualism,
it tried, without much success, to substitute private for collective ownership of
land in the Indian villages. But what other revolutionary movement resembled
this? In general, the revolutionary tradition in politics was combined with a
conservative tradition in society. What invites the attention of the historian in
Latin America, indeed, is not so much the instability of politics as the extraordinary stability of social institutions. The landed gentry, it is true, were
less successful in resisting political, personal, or military pressures in Mexico than in Chile, or in Bolivia than in Peru. As politicians they failed again
and again. But they preserved their way of life. One dictator succeeded another; in some countries a mestizo oligarchy gradually replaced a creole oligarchy; but the great estate remained at the basis of the social and economic
system.

33. The Portuguese Court Moves to Brazil, 1808

ALAN K. MANCHESTER

While Spanish America was getting ready to engage in intense political and military action to break Spain's power in America, the Portuguese monarchy moved peacefully across the South Atlantic to Brazil to escape Napoleon's armies in Portugal. As Professor Alan K. Manchester of Duke University shows, the court was moved in its entirety — demented Queen Mother, Regent Dom João, a horde of nobles and administrators, the records necessary to conduct royal business, and much more. When João in 1815 formally granted legal equality with the mother country to Brazil, he took a large and important step toward independence for Brazil.

The transfer of the Portuguese Court from Lisbon to Rio de Janeiro in 1807–1808 precipitated developments of long-term consequence. It modified radically the relationship between the Mother Country and its most prosperous colony; it shaped the course of Brazilian independence; and it contributed materially to the preservation of the union. Like Spanish America, colonial Portuguese America suffered from accentuated regionalisms of geography, economic interests, clan loyalties, and cultural development; but unlike Spanish America it emerged from the independence movement as a single political unit. Considerable spade work has yet to be done before a reasonably satisfactory answer can be formulated as to why there is only one Brazil. But it is quite clear that one of the major reasons is the fact that on the eve of the independence movement Brazil possessed the attributes of an absolutist, centralized sovereign state. . . .

As the summer and fall of 1807 wore on, Portugal came increasingly under a crossfire between France and England. After Tilsit (June 25, 1807), Napoleon was determined to close the remaining major leaks in his Continental System, namely, Denmark in the strategic Baltic-North Sea area and Portugal in the equally strategic southwest corner of Europe. The absorption of Denmark was a relatively simple operation, whereas the subjection of Portugal

"The Transfer of the Portuguese Court to Rio de Janeiro" by Alan K. Manchester, in *Conflict and Continuity in Brazilian Society*, edited by Henry H. Keith and S. F. Edwards (Columbia: University of South Carolina Press, 1969), pp. 148–173, passim. Reprinted by permission of the University of South Carolina Press. Copyright © 1969 by the University of South Carolina Press.

encountered troublesome political and military opposition and led to a totally different resolution. . . .

Life aboard the ships was deplorable. Baggage had been severely curtailed by the notice that household effects could not be accommodated and in many instances personal belongings had gone astray in the confusion of the embarkation. Some had boarded so hurriedly that there was not time to snatch up more than the most essential items — Chancellor Thomáz Antônio de Villa Nôva Portugal, for example, brought a few articles of clothing in a sack. Overloading resulted in shocking congestion. Men and children slept side-by-side on deck; women had a minimum of privacy. Cleanliness of person and linen was impossible under the circumstances. To a contemporary observer the conclusion was inescapable that the departure lacked adequate planning. The conclusion is sound if its application is restricted to the actual embarkation, and even here an exception should be made with reference to Rio Sêcco's efforts in behalf of the members of the royal family, their immediate retainers, and selected members of the Court. But to extend the application to the condition of the vessels and the adequacy of supplies is questionable. To do so ignores the readiness reports of November 28, Admiral Smith's review of the fleet on November 29, and the obvious fact that in spite of two bad storms the passage was eminently successful. One ship, the "D. João de Castro," was forced to land in Paraíba for emergency repairs and the "Medusa" put in at Pernambuco, but both were able to join the Prince Regent in Bahia. Although rationing obviously was necessary, there is no record of a critical shortage of food or water, nor is there a report of the death of anyone prominent enough to warrant notice. This was a notable achievement, particularly in view of the excessive overloading. . . .

One Christiano Muller, writing from Lisbon to Dom Domingos de Sousa Coutinho in London, reported that some months earlier he had been charged with the task of inventorying the papers, books, maps, and prints belonging to Antônio de Araújo de Azevedo, and that on the night of November 25 he had been awakened with instructions to pack up everything belonging to the Ministry of State. This he had done in thirty-seven large boxes which were sent aboard the "Medusa" during the day of November 26.

These are two examples, in different areas, of the preparation which preceded the departure. They illustrate a crucial aspect of the transfer of the Court to Rio de Janeiro. On board the fleet were the essential elements of a sovereign state: the personnel of the civil, religious, and military hierarchies; members of high society, the professions, and business; and the paraphernalia of government. The whole machinery of state was being transported, lock, stock, and barrel, to a new location overseas where it would take root and continue its accustomed ways.

The members of the royal family were distributed among three of the ships-of-the-line. . . .

There were others, less prominent but significant in the society of a sovereign state. There were José Egydio Alvares de Almeida (later Marquêz de Santo Amaro), a Brazilian by birth who was in charge of the King's Cabinet and served as confidential advisor to the Prince Regent; the brothers Lobato, Keepers of the King's Wardrobe, who were much in the confidence of the Prince Regent (later in Brazil both were made viscounts); Manoel Vieira da Silva (later Barão de Alvaiazere), also Brazilian-born, the personal physician and confidant of the Prince Regent; Theodore Ferreira Aguiar, Surgeon of the Fleet; José Correia Picanço (later Barão de Goiana), First Surgeon of the Royal Chamber and Professor of Surgery at Coimbra; Friar José Marianno da Conceição Velloso, noted botanist, member of the Academia Real das Sciências de Lisbôa and one of the literary directors of the Régia Officina Typográphica (precursor of the Imprensa Régia); João Ignacio da Cunha (later Visconde de Alcântara), judge of the affairs of orphans (*juiz dos orphões*) in Lisbon; Felisberto Caldeira Brant Pontes (later Marquêz de Barbacena), Brazilian-born graduate of the Colégio dos Nobres, Capitão de Mar e Guerra at nineteen, adjutant to the governor of Angola, holder of the badge of the Ordem de Christo, lieutenant-colonel of a regiment of the line, and owner of rich estates in Bahia and Minas Gerais; and a countless number of business men, some more, some less affluent than Pedro Gomes. And to these more useful members of society were added what Tarquínio de Sousa termed an "immense retinue of nobility, and functionaries more or less poltroons, more or less parasites."

Every minister appointed by Dom João VI in Brazil until the final two years of his residence there were on board. Members of the Council of State, justices of the Court of Appeals and the High Court, officials of the Treasury and the various juntas, the hierarchy of the Church, army and navy officers, courtiers, professional and businessmen, functionaries of the lower levels, servants, and a multitude of hangers-on were on their way to the New World, eager candidates for posts in the new, yet old bureaucracy.

The utilization of Portuguese vessels for the transfer of the Court to Rio assured possession of what in the overseas area was a sizable navy. . . .

Aboard the fleet were other essentials. The contents of the Royal Treasury and the immense store of diamonds from the Crown monopoly accompanied the Court. The royal family, nobility, businessmen, and clerics loaded silver plate, jewels, heirlooms, books, cash, and any other movable assets which were at hand. The treasury and equipment of the Royal Chapel were taken along in order to assure appropriate facilities for religious ceremonies. A printing press with type was shipped on the "Medusa"; Antônio de Araújo de Azevedo managed to salvage the collection of books, papers, maps, and prints which Christiano Muller had inventoried several months earlier; and somewhere in the fleet were the Royal Library of Ajuda and a mass of government files.

The last two items merit special mention. The primary, although by no means the sole value of the Ajuda Library lay in the Barbosa Machado Collection. Diogo Barbosa Machado, a cleric who was in his ninety-first year when he died on August 9, 1772, spent his long life in assembling printed works, most of them original editions, manuscripts, maps, prints, portraits, pamphlets, and fugitive pieces. His eclectic interests ranged through sacred and profane history, biographies of illustrious men and women, poetry, letters, geography, grammar, orations, genealogy, coats-of-arms, dictionaries, politics, and current events. The quality of his collection is suggested by his Camões items, which included a 1572 first edition and a 1597 edition of the *Lusíadas,* half a dozen commentaries dating from 1639 to 1759, and translations in Spanish, Italian, English, and Latin. In a catalogue which he himself prepared he lists thirty-four classifications with 4,301 works in 5,764 volumes. A single volume might consist of scores of items, as, for example, in the case of the fugitive pieces which were bound in some eighty-five volumes.

The fact that the Royal Library had been partially destroyed and the remainder severely damaged by the earthquake of 1755 led Barbosa Machado to donate his collection to the Crown. The transfer to the Palace of Ajuda was made between 1770 and 1773. There it was incorporated with a reconstituted Royal Library and now the whole unit was on its way to Rio de Janeiro where it was to become the basis for the Bibliotheca Pública and later for the Bibliotheca Nacional do Rio de Janeiro.

The second item, the mass of government files, is surprising in both its bulk and coverage. Three sources provide information on the amount and content. The first is a document in the Orem Papers in the Arquivo do Instituto Histórico e Geográphico Brasileiro entitled "Relação dos Officios, Notas, Tratados, Livros, e mais papeis que existem no Archivo da Secretaría de Estado dos Negócios Extrangeiros e da Guerra no Rio de Janeiro, e que ora se Remettem para Lisboa em 10 Caixões." The second is a catalogue, issued by the Ministério das Relações Exteriores, of items in the Arquivo Histórico which pre-date 1822. Pre-1808 papers are identifiable both as to date and as to whether they are originals or copies. The third source is the impressive collection entitled "Negocios de Portugal" in the Arquivo Nacional. . . .

As voluminous as the material was, it by no means exhausted the files of the Foreign Office, which were brought over in 1808 or in subsequent years. The inventory lists only those items which were taken to Lisbon in 1821. Much remained in Rio de Janeiro, as the pre-1808 papers still in the *Arquivo Histórico do Itamaraty* demonstrate. The Orem document does suggest, however, the content and the volume of the paraphernalia of government which were transferred with the Court and it provides some insight into the criteria of selection. That the Ministry of Foreign Affairs was not alone in its foresight is evident from Christiano Muller's thirty-seven large boxes of material belonging to the Ministry of State which were loaded aboard the "Medusa.". . .

From the foregoing discussion it should be obvious that the removal of the Court from Lisbon to Rio de Janeiro involved far more than the turbulent days of the embarkation, and it should also be evident that from the broader viewpoint the operation was notably successful. The personnel, the appurtenances, and the paraphernalia of the sovereign state of Portugal were safely aboard ship, well beyond the reach of Napoleon. The next step was to set up shop in the new location. . . .

During the first five weeks of his residence in Brazil, the Prince Regent was forced to operate without his usual mechanics of administration. There was no ministry through which he could channel business, no Council of State to which he could turn for advice. Instead, he used the governor of the captaincy, the Conde da Ponte, as the instrument for the dispatching of business, Dom Fernando José de Portugal as his Minister of State, and the two of them plus the Marquêz de Bellas as his principal advisers. The procedure developed, apparently, without *a priori* planning, as a means by which to carry on the affairs of state. . . .

In spite of the absence of his accustomed administrative machinery, the Prince Regent was not without advice. This he received with reference to the commercial issue from three major sources; a parecer by the Marquêz de Bellas, a *Representação* presented to him by the Conde da Ponte on behalf of the mercantile and agricultural elements of the city, and the views of José da Silva Lisbôa (later Visconde de Cairú) which were transmitted through Fernando José de Portugal. . . .

Six days after he sailed into the harbor of Bahia and four days after he went ashore, the Prince Regent issued the carta régia of January 28, 1808. It was addressed to the Conde da Ponte. In it the Prince Regent assured the Count that having considered the *Representação* which informed him of the suspension of commerce resulting from the critical developments in Europe and consequent grave damage to his vassals and to the Royal Exchequer and wishing to take prompt and effective measures to remedy the situation, he now decreed, as an interim provision, valid until a general order could be formulated, that: first, all items of whatever genre be allowed to enter the customs houses of Brazil whether in ships of friendly nations or ships belonging to his vassals, on payment of 24 percent tax, payment to be in conformity with regulations then in force, with the proviso that *molhados* (such as wine, spirits, and olive oil) pay double the current amount; second, not only his vassals but natives of friendly nations be permitted to send commodities to any port which in their opinion offered the best advantage, the permission to hold for all colonial products except brazilwood or other well-known monopolies, on payment of taxes already established in the respective captaincies; and third, all laws, edicts, and other decrees which hitherto had prohibited in Brazil reciprocal commerce and navigation between his vassals and foreigners be suspended and without force. The Conde da Ponte was to execute the decree at once, registering it in proper form and issuing the necessary orders.

From the outset the carta régia was recognized as a landmark in the transition of Brazil from colony to sovereign state. Silva Lisbôa called it the Magna Carta of Brazil and supported his statement by emphasizing the absurdity of a policy which would have continued the colonial status of the land in which the sovereign resided. Luís Gonçalves dos Santos, a contemporary, hailed the happy results of a liberal, enlightened policy which triumphed over deeply rooted practices and injurious monopolies. . . .

The period in Bahia was occupied largely in festivities with which the bemused and delirious populace welcomed the Prince Regent and his Court. Some business, much of it routine, was transacted, however, in addition to the carta régia. Utilizing the emergency administrative procedure, the Prince Regent reduced sentences and granted pardons; listened to pleas for promotions and the improvement of roads, imposts, and distilleries; determined reprisals with reference to a Dutch brig anchored in the port; ordered the sequestration of a contraband shipment of brazilwood; granted licenses for manufacturing and industry; and authorized the organization of a marine insurance company. He created a school of medicine and surgery to be located in Bahia and he granted honors and decorations with a lavish hand. But to pleas that he settle the Court in Bahia, he turned a deaf ear.

When the Prince Regent entered the bay of Rio de Janeiro on the afternoon of March 7, he still faced the task of setting up shop in the new location. The elements of the mechanism of a state were now safely in harbor. All that remained to be done, it seemed, was to provide space in which the bureaucracy could do business and to pull the trigger which would set in motion the transplanted organism. Both of these the Prince Regent did but with an additional step by which the structure of the sovereign state of Portugal was recreated in Brazil. Each major feature of the central government was specifically established by appropriate decree, with the same name (sometimes with "do Brazil" added), the same powers, the same function, the same procedures as its prototype in Portugal. Where applicable the same precedents were used to legitimize a department, a junta, or a procedure. The removal of the Court to Rio de Janeiro, thus, was not simply the transplantation of a government; it was, rather the transfer of the elements of a sovereign state which in the new location were formalized into a new, yet old and familiar system. In the process the Portuguese government in Brazil became a Brazilian government.

The Prince Regent set into motion the transplanted organization by the appointment of a ministry. . . . In the course of time, others were added. The formal institution of these branches of government did not mean necessarily that they began to function as of the date of the alvará. In some instances, as in the case of the Intendência da Polícia, this was true, but in others, such as the Royal Exchequer, the department had been in operation for some time. What it did mean was that "of Brazil" became deeply embedded in the governmental structure of Portugal.

Interspersed among these governmental decrees and a mushrooming amount of day-by-day business were items that were significant in the transition of Brazil from colony to autonomous state. On April 1, 1808, freedom of manufacturing and industry was granted to Brazil and the overseas dominions; on May 13, the Imprensa Régia was founded; on June 13, following the death of the patriarch of Lisbon, the bishop of Rio de Janeiro was appointed Court chaplain (Capellão-Mór) with "all the ranks and benefits which have gone with that post"; on June 15 the Cathedral was declared to be the Royal Chapel (Capella Real); on September 10, the official gazette began publication; on October 12 the Bank of Brazil was founded; and on November 25 ownership of land by foreigners was permitted. None of these measures would have been approved had Brazil still been viewed as a colony to be administered in accordance with the principles of the old regime.

The determination of the Prince Regent and his advisors to make Brazil over in the image of the Mother Country involved more than changes in the governmental structure. It necessitated a sharp departure from traditional practice with reference to cultural development. The old policies which had resulted in the neglect of education and public health, the suppression of literary, philosophical, and scientific academies, the disquietude inspired by libraries, the prohibition against newspapers, journals, and printing presses, and the exclusion of foreign influence were incompatible with the new status of the colony. The Prince Regent and his advisors, particularly Rodrigo de Sousa Coutinho and Antônio de Araújo de Azevedo, were aware of the fact and devoted considerable attention to it.

The Prince Regent began the reform early in his residence in Brazil. While he was still in Bahia he appointed a Physician-General (Physico-Môr) and a Surgeon-General (Cirurgião-Môr) and authorized the founding of a medical school in that city. Later in Rio de Janeiro, he founded (November 5, 1808) a School of Anatomy, Surgery and Medicine in connection with the Royal Military Hospital, appointed (July 28, 1809) a Commissioner of Public Health (Provedor-Môr da Saúde do Estado do Brasil), established (April 1, 1813) a course in surgery in connection with the Hospital de Misericórdia and (April 26, 1813) a chair of Hygiene, Pathology, and Therapeutics in the School of Surgery in Rio de Janeiro, and authorized (December 29, 1815) a full course in surgery in the city of Bahia. Still in the area of advanced education, he approved (April 23, 1811) a six-year course of mathematics, sciences, physics and natural science, and engineering in the Royal Military Academy and instituted (June 25, 1812) a course in agriculture in Bahia and a chemical laboratory in Rio. On April 7, 1808, he set up a Military Archive (Arquivo Militar do Brazil) for the preparation, collection, and verification of maps of the coastline and interior of Brazil and the overseas dominions; and on October 29, 1810, he made available to the public the Royal Library. On October 12, 1813, he inaugurated the Teatro Real de São João and in 1815 negotiated for a French mission of artists, sculptors, architects, and artisans and organized, in preparation for their coming, the Escola Real de Sciências, Artes e Offícios. He welcomed and facilitated visits by distinguished foreign scientists, artists, musicians, engineers, and curious travelers. These measures and others like them reinforced the effects of the new economic freedom. Together they exerted a profound influence on the cultural life of Brazil.

The influx of titled nobility raised the question of a comparable element in the society of the emerging state. Two factors were largely responsible for the answer. In the first place, it had long been the practice of the Portuguese Crown to utilize honors as a means by which to win the loyalty of the rural landowners. In the second place, an aristocracy of economic power and social privilege already existed in the colony. It consisted of the owners of sugar plantations, cattle ranches, and food- and commodity-producing farms, who, grouped into tightly knit clans, controlled the areas outside the major coastal towns. It was the result of an indigenous development with roots that extended far into the past, but it had not been formalized by official recognition. The answer was obvious: by utilizing his power to grant titles and to award honors the Prince Regent could establish an effective link between the Royal Person and this influential segment of Brazilian life and at the same time reinforce the nobility as an essential element in the monarchical system.

Honors (*mercês*) were of various types. The most coveted were titles of nobility. They were granted in Brazil without regard to the traditional rules. They were not hereditary and they carried no material advantage. There was always a reference to a town, a province, a river, a section of the country, a battle site, or even the name of a plantation but the relationship between the geographical terminology of the title on the one hand and reality on the other was purely honorary. To the recipient, if he accepted the award, a title meant prestige, personal satisfaction, the expense of living up to the new status in society, and a sense of obligation to the Crown. Of less prestige but nonetheless desirable was an assortment of decorations related to the five special orders, the Ordem de Christo, the Ordem de São Bento de Aviz, the Ordem de São Tiago, the Ordem da Tôrre e Espada, and the Ordem da Nôssa Senhora da Conceição, each of which had gradations of its own. One of the most highly prized honors was the Título de Conselho. Both titles and decorations were awarded to Brazilian-born colonials, continental Portuguese, and foreigners. Recipients included politicians, magistrates, professors, men of letters, and the military. Even a businessman on occasion received recognition. Awards to Brazilians were made largely but not exclusively to members of the landowning clans.

The Prince Regent was lavish in his distribution of titles and decorations. According to one estimate he created in eight years twenty-eight marquises, eight counts, sixteen viscounts, and twenty-one barons. A partial list of decorations further emphasizes the point. During his residence in Brazil, according to another estimate, João granted 4,084 knights, commanders, and grand-crosses of the Ordem de Christo, 1,422 awards of the Ordem de São Bento de Aviz, and 590 awards of the Ordem de São Tiago. The figures omit the Ordem da Tôrre e Espada, the Ordem da Nôssa Senhora da Conceição, and the Título de Conselho.

Somewhat different but closely related in its results was the practice of appointing Brazilians as officers of the militia. These appointments, also called mercês, involved more than military command. They granted certain administrative powers such as the right to convoke the people, recruit troops, collect revenue, and maintain order. The recipient, already a person of some importance in his community, became a member of the hierarchy with fidelity to the Crown.

The prodigal use of titles and honors was politically shrewd. It broke the rigidity and weakened the privileged character of the select minority of nobility but by the inclusion of Brazilians it heightened the social prestige of the segment of the population which had long enjoyed a privileged position, extended the influence of the Court to the municipalities, and won support among the great landowners of the interior. Adapted to the social conditions of the country, it became an effective means by which to mobilize the Brazilian elite in support of the Crown.

The transfer of the Court from Lisbon to Rio de Janeiro produced significant changes in the economic development, the social and cultural life, and the governmental structure of the colony. Some of these changes, particularly the economic and social aspects, penetrated to the grassroots of the interior, but politically the transformation was restricted to the central government. In setting up shop in Brazil, the Prince Regent left the administration of the captaincies intact. As Silvestre Pinheiro Ferreira reported on March 15, 1822, to a special committee of the Côrtes, nothing was done during the residence of the Court in Rio de Janeiro to modify the arbitrary, dictatorial character of the administration of the provinces. The tax system, the administration of justice, and the military organization remained colonial in point of view and practice. Additional tribunals were instituted, more districts (*comarcas*) were established, heavier taxes were imposed, and countless jobs were created, but this was done at the local level without disturbing the pattern of colonial administration. The major concern of the Prince Regent and his advisors was to perpetuate in Brazil by the transfer of the superstructure of government the centralized, absolutist system of the Portuguese monarchy, and the monarchy itself.

The course of events which was precipitated by the action of the Conselho de Estado in the Palace of Ajuda on the night of November 24, 1807, culminated in the carta de lei of December 16, 1815, which raised Brazil to the rank of kingdom, co-equal under the Crown with Portugal and the Algarves. The act constituted an official confirmation of the fact that between early 1808 and late 1815 the colony had been transformed into an autonomous state with its own political, religious, and social hierarchies, its own mechanism of government, its own social and educational amenities, and the right of self-determination in economic policy. The Mother Country and the colony were joined, and in the process the colony in effect became the Mother Country.

Domingo Faustino Sarmiento, Argentine Educator. Sarmiento usually appears as a solid, somewhat solemn figure in his pictures. And so he was in real life, for he early began the intensely active career which was to lead eventually to the presidency of Argentina (Reading 37). He had no time for games, we are told, until his doctor ordered him to play late in life. But his contributions to the educational development of his country were great, and his life stands in contrast to the dictatorship of Rosas.

SECTION VIII

Argentine Contrasts: The Dictator Rosas and the Educator Sarmiento

HOW TO EXPLAIN DICTATORS?

The rise and fall of dictators has long been a basic theme of Latin American history. Columbus was probably the first dictator, and there is no doubt that the institution still flourishes south of the Rio Grande. What permits them to develop, how they manage to maintain themselves in power, why they usually fall, and what they accomplish are highly controversial questions. It is not surprising that no magnum opus has yet been written on this complicated and debatable subject. One general volume with a valuable collection of representative selections is available. Its editor, in analyzing this puzzling and persistent phenomenon in Latin America, on which hundreds if not thousands of articles and books have been written, emphasizes "the rich variety of dictatorial types and the multitude of factors that conditioned their existence."[1]

ATTACKS ON ROSAS BY SARMIENTO

Dictators sprang up in most countries immediately following the end of European dominance. One of the most powerful and long-lasting was Juan

[1] Hugh M. Hamill, Jr., ed., *Dictatorship in Spanish America* (New York: Knopf, 1965), p. 5.

Manuel de Rosas, who ruled Argentina with an iron hand from 1815 to 1852. He has been violently attacked and stoutly defended since the time he established his power until today. Articulate exiles in neighboring Chile and Uruguay kept up a steady fire against him through newspapers, pamphlets, and books. One of the most famous of these was Domingo Faustino Sarmiento, who in 1845 wrote a classic description entitled *Facundo, o civilización i barbarie,* which is ostensibly a biography of Juan Facundo Quiroga, the provincial dictator, but actually is a profound study of what causes dictatorship. For Sarmiento, one fundamental explanation was the nature of the gauchos, the rough-riding, untutored cowboys of the immense Argentine plains (Reading 34).

Rosas began to smart under the public attacks abroad of such writers as Sarmiento and Juan Bautista Alberdi and mounted an efficient propaganda machine directed by Pedro de Angelis, which aimed at improving the dictator's image in Europe and elsewhere by publications in English, French, and Spanish.[2] Since Rosas, most dictators have followed his example of maintaining a public relations apparatus to help keep them in power.

Inside Argentina various methods were perfected to keep alive the pro-Rosas spirit, and his wife Encarnación, with other women aiding her, was a skillful manipulator in this field. One foreign visitor reported that puppet shows, theater performances, and the opera were opened with a display of public enthusiasm. The principal performers would assemble on the stage and cry out: "Long live the Confederación Argentina," to which the chorus would reply: "Viva." Then the principal characters would shout again: "Death to the savage Unitarians" (as Rosas's opponents were called), with an answering "Mueran" (May they perish!) from the chorus, after which the performance began.[3]

DIVERSE ATTITUDES TOWARD ROSAS

Foreigners visiting Argentina during the Age of Rosas reacted in diverse ways. Charles Darwin, then on his scientific voyage, was favorably impressed, at least at first, whereas Anthony King denounced Rosas as an "evil genius." [4]

After Rosas fell in 1851, he lived quietly in England as a country gentle-

[2] William S. Dudley, "Pedro de Angelis (1784–1859): Journalist, Propagandist, and Historian" (Master's thesis, Columbia University, 1966).

[3] Tom B. Jones, *South America Rediscovered* (Minneapolis: University of Minnesota Press, 1949), p. 26.

[4] Charles Darwin, *Journal of Researches into the Geology and Natural History of the Various Countries Visited by H.M.S. Beagle* (London, 1839), pp. 85–87, and John Anthony King, *Twenty-Four Years in the Argentine Republic* (New York, 1846), pp. 422–431.

man until his death in 1877, but Argentines continued to deplore his "tyranny," his personalization of power. Only toward the end of the nineteenth century did historians such as Ernesto Quesada portray Rosas as a product of his times and not as a unique monster in the annals of the Argentine nation.[5]

The debate still goes on. One writer points out that Rosas merely continued the authoritarian tradition of colonial times (Reading 35).

ROSAS REVISIONISM

After World War I, a new Rosas revisionism developed, directed by a group of bitter, antiforeign, antidemocratic writers who attracted a wide reading public: "They looked at the world about them and felt terrible doubts of Argentina's ability to continue with the social, economic, and political organization she then possessed." [6] Some of them advocated military rule and social discipline. From 1930 on, Julio Irazusta and others began to present Rosas as a hero. Biographies, novels, and political studies were published with this theme, and in 1938 this group established a historical institute and a scholarly review devoted to Rosas and his regime. They denounced the Liberals' interpretation of Argentine history. They "were part of a large sector of feeling in the country which played a part in paving the way for the military rulers of Argentina from 1943 on." [7]

The pro-Rosas spirit still lives today, in the hearts of some Argentines, as demonstrated by the decree promulgated in 1964 (Reading 36).

To balance this account of Rosas, it may be well to consider the career of Domingo Faustino Sarmiento as an educator. While Rosas was in the saddle in Argentina, Sarmiento was developing his modern educational ideas in Chile as an exile. He, too, was something of a dictator in later life as governor of his native province of San Juan and as president of Argentina; but while Rosas held sway, Sarmiento was at work evolving an educational system designed to make men free (Reading 37). His was the other face of Argentina. In contemplating Argentina today, with its curious combination of relatively advanced educational and economic development and its military rule, the contrast of Rosas and Sarmiento may help us to understand Argentina's puzzling situation.

[5] For the anti-Rosas views see José Manuel Estrada, *Lecciones sobre la República Argentina,* 2nd ed. (Buenos Aires, 1898), while Quesada presents a more favorable picture in his *La época de Rosas* (Buenos Aires, 1923).

[6] Clifton B. Kroeber, "Rosas and the Revision of Argentine History, 1880–1955," *Inter-American Review of Bibliography,* 10 (1960), pp. 3–25.

[7] Ibid.

34. *The Human Background of Dictatorship, the Gaucho*

DOMINGO FAUSTINO SARMIENTO

The life and work of Domingo Faustino Sarmiento became well known in the United States through his service here as Argentine minister (1865–1868) and through his friendship with Horace Mann, the Massachusetts educator whose wife translated his attack on dictatorship as *Life in the Argentine Republic in the Days of the Tyrants; or Civilization and Barbarism* (1868). The University of Michigan recognized his contributions to education in 1868 by awarding him the first honorary degree to be granted by an American university to a Latin American scholar.

Sarmiento's volume is a classic that is well worth reading in its entirety because it combines a vivid description of the geography and people of Argentina during a decisive period of its history with an informed analysis and poetic understanding of the basic forces at work and in conflict in his country. The *Revue des Deux Mondes* characterized the work when it was first published as

> full of attraction and novelty, instructive as history, interesting as a romançe, brilliant with imagery and coloring. "Civilization and Barbarism" is not only one of those rare testimonials which come to us of the intellectual life of South America, but it is an invaluable document. . . . This can only be done by the philosopher, the traveller, the poet, the historian, the painter of manners and customs, the publicist. Señor Sarmiento has succeeded in realizing this object in his work, which he has published in Chili, and which proves that if civilization has enemies in those regions it also has eloquent champions.*

The selection here shows how clearly Sarmiento perceived the disparity between Buenos Aires and the provinces — which still exists — and the deep-rooted influence of the gauchos in the life of Argentina.

. . . Buenos Ayres is destined to be some day the most gigantic city of either America. Under a benignant climate, mistress of the navigation of a hundred

* As quoted by Mrs. Horace Mann, in *Life in the Argentine Republic in the Days of the Tyrants* (New York, 1868), pp. x–xi.

rivers flowing past her feet, covering a vast area, and surrounded by inland provinces which know no other outlet for their products, she would ere now have become the Babylon of America, if the spirit of the Pampa had not breathed upon her, and left undeveloped the rich offerings which the rivers and provinces should unceasingly bring. She is the only city in the vast Argentine territory which is in communication with European nations; she alone can avail herself of the advantages of foreign commerce; she alone has power and revenue. Vainly have the provinces asked to receive through her, civilization, industry, and European population; a senseless colonial policy made her deaf to these cries. But the provinces had their revenge when they sent to her in Rosas the climax of their own barbarism.

The cities of Buenos Ayres and Cordova have succeeded better than the others in establishing about them subordinate towns to serve as new foci of civilization and municipal interests; a fact which deserves notice. The inhabitants of the city wear the European dress, live in a civilized manner, and possess laws, ideas of progress, means of instruction, some municipal organization, regular forms of government, etc. Beyond the precincts of the city everything assumes a new aspect; the country people wear a different dress, which I will call South American, as it is common to all districts; their habits of life are different, their wants peculiar and limited. The people composing these two distinct forms of society, do not seem to belong to the same nation. Moreover, the countryman, far from attempting to imitate the customs of the city, rejects with disdain its luxury and refinement; and it is unsafe for the costume of the city people, their coats, their cloaks, their saddles, or anything European, to show themselves in the country. Everything civilized which the city contains is blockaded there, proscribed beyond its limits; and any one who should dare to appear in the rural districts in a frock-coat, for example, or mounted on an English saddle, would bring ridicule and brutal assaults upon himself.

The whole remaining population inhabit the open country, which, whether wooded or destitute of the larger plants, is generally level, and almost everywhere occupied by pastures, in some places of such abundance and excellence, that the grass of an artificial meadow would not surpass them. . . .

Nomad tribes do not exist in the Argentine plains; the stock-raiser is a proprietor, living upon his own land; but this condition renders association impossible, and tends to scatter separate families over an immense extent of surface. Imagine an expanse of two thousand square leagues, inhabited

From *Life in the Argentine Republic in the Days of the Tyrants; or Civilization and Barbarism, from the Spanish of Domingo F. Sarmiento,* trans., with a biographic sketch, by Mrs. Horace Mann (New York, 1868), pp. 5–55, passim.

throughout, but where the dwellings are usually four or even eight leagues apart, and two leagues, at least, separate the nearest neighbors. The production of movable property is not impossible, the enjoyments of luxury are not wholly incompatible with this isolation; wealth can raise a superb edifice in the desert. But the incentive is wanting; no example is near; the inducements for making a great display which exist in a city, are not known in that isolation and solitude. Inevitable privations justify natural indolence; a dearth of all the amenities of life induces all the externals of barbarism. Society has altogether disappeared. There is but the isolated self-concentrated feudal family. Since there is no collected society, no government is possible; there is neither municipal nor executive power, and civil justice has no means of reaching criminals. I doubt if the modern world presents any other form of association so monstrous as this. . . .

Moral progress, and the cultivation of the intellect, are here not only neglected, as in the Arab or Tartar tribe, but impossible. Where can a school be placed for the instruction of children living ten leagues apart in all directions? Thus, consequently, civilization can in no way be brought about. Barbarism is the normal condition, and it is fortunate if domestic customs preserve a small germ of morality. Religion feels the consequences of this want of social organization. The offices of the pastor are nominal, the pulpit has no audience, the priest flees from the deserted chapel, or allows his character to deteriorate in inactivity and solitude. Vice, simony, and the prevalent barbarism penetrate his cell, and change his moral superiority into the means of gratifying his avarice or ambition, and he ends by becoming a party leader. . . .

In the absence of all the means of civilization and progress, which can only be developed among men collected into societies of many individuals, the education of the country people is as follows: The women look after the house, get the meals ready, shear the sheep, milk the cows, make the cheese, and weave the coarse cloth used for garments. All domestic occupations are performed by women; on them rests the burden of all the labor, and it is an exceptional favor when some of the men undertake the cultivation of a little maize, bread not being in use as an ordinary article of diet. The boys exercise their strength and amuse themselves by gaining skill in the use of the lasso and the bolas, with which they constantly harass and pursue the calves and goats. When they can ride, which is as soon as they have learned to walk, they perform some small services on horseback. When they become stronger, they race over the country, falling off their horses and getting up again, tumbling on purpose into rabbit burrows, scrambling over precipices, and practicing feats of horsemanship. On reaching puberty, they take to breaking wild colts, and death is the least penalty that awaits them if their strength or courage fails them for a moment. With early manhood comes complete independence and idleness.

Now begins the public life of the gaucho, as I may say, since his education is by this time at an end. These men, Spaniards only in their language and in the confused religious notions preserved among them, must be seen, before a right estimate can be made of the indomitable and haughty character which grows out of this struggle of isolated man with untamed nature, of the rational being with the brute. It is necessary to see their visages bristling with beards, their countenances as grave and serious as those of the Arabs of Asia, to appreciate the pitying scorn with which they look upon the sedentary denizen of the city, who may have read many books, but who cannot overthrow and slay a fierce bull, who could not provide himself with a horse from the pampas, who has never met a tiger alone, and received him with a dagger in one hand and a poncho rolled up in the other, to be thrust into the animal's mouth, while he transfixes his heart with his dagger.

This habit of triumphing over resistance, of constantly showing a superiority to Nature, of defying and subduing her, prodigiously develops the consciousness of individual consequence and superior prowess. The Argentine people of every class, civilized and ignorant alike, have a high opinion of their national importance. All the other people of South America throw this vanity of theirs in their teeth, and take offense at their presumption and arrogance. I believe the charge not to be wholly unfounded, but I do not object to the trait. Alas, for the nation without faith in itself! Great things were not made for such a people. To what extent may not the independence of that part of America be due to the arrogance of these Argentine gauchos, who have never seen anything beneath the sun superior to themselves in wisdom or in power? The European is in their eyes the most contemptible of all men, for a horse gets the better of him in a couple of plunges. . . .

Country life, then, has developed all the physical but none of the intellectual powers of the gaucho. His moral character is of the quality to be expected from his habit of triumphing over the obstacles and the forces of nature; it is strong, haughty, and energetic. Without instruction, and indeed without need of any, without means of support as without wants, he is happy in the midst of his poverty and privations, which are not such to one who never knew nor wished for greater pleasures than are his already. Thus if the disorganization of society among the gauchos deeply implants barbarism in their natures, through the impossibility and uselessness of moral and intellectual education, it has, too, its attractive side to him. The gaucho does not labor; he finds his food and raiment ready to his hand. If he is a proprietor, his own flocks yield him both; if he possesses nothing himself, he finds them in the house of a patron or a relation. The necessary care of the herds is reduced to excursions and pleasure parties; the branding, which is like the harvesting of farmers, is a festival, the arrival of which is received with transports of joy, being the occasion of the assembling of all the men for twenty leagues around, and the opportunity for displaying incredible skill with the lasso. . . .

The horse is an integral part of the Argentine rustic; it is for him what the cravat is to an inhabitant of the city. In 1841, El Chacho, a chieftain of the Llanos, emigrated to Chili. "How are you getting on, friend?" somebody asked him. "How should I be getting on?" returned he, in tones of distress and melancholy. "Bound to Chili, and on foot!" Only an Argentine gaucho can appreciate all the misfortune and distress which these two phrases express.

Here again we have the life of the Arab or Tartar. The following words of Victor Hugo might have been written in the pampas:

> He cannot fight on foot; he and his horse are but one person. He lives on horseback; he trades, buys, and sells on horseback; drinks, eats, sleeps, and dreams on horseback. — *Le Rhin.*

The men then set forth without exactly knowing where they are going. A turn around the herds, a visit to a breeding-pen or to the haunt of a favorite horse, takes up a small part of the day; the rest is consumed in a rendezvous at a tavern or grocery store. There assemble inhabitants of the neighboring parishes; there are given and received bits of information about animals that have gone astray; the traces of the cattle are described upon the ground; intelligence of the hunting ground of the tiger or of the place where the tiger's tracks have been seen, is communicated. There, in short, is the Cantor; there the men fraternize while the glass goes round at the expense of those who have the means as well as the disposition to pay for it.

In a life so void of emotion, gambling exercises the enervated mind, and liquor arouses the dormant imagination. This accidental reunion becomes by its daily repetition a society more contracted than that from which each of its individual members came; yet in this assembly, without public aim, without social interest, are first formed the elements of those characters which are to appear later on the political stage. We shall see how. The gaucho esteems skill in horsemanship and physical strength, and especially courage, above all other things, as we have said before. This meeting, this daily club, is a real Olympic circus where each man's merit is tested and assayed.

The gaucho is always armed with the knife inherited from the Spaniard. More fully even than in Spain is here realized that peninsular peculiarity, that cry, characteristic of Saragossa — *war to the knife.* The knife, besides being a weapon, is a tool used for all purposes; without it, life cannot go on. It is like the elephant's trunk, arm, hand, finger, and all. The gaucho boasts of his valor like a trooper, and every little while his knife glitters through the air in circles, upon the least provocation, or with none at all, for the simple purpose of comparing a stranger's prowess with his own; he plays at stabbing as he would play at dice. So deeply and intimately have these pugnacious habits entered the life of the Argentine gaucho that custom has created a code of honor and a fencing system which protect life. The rowdy of other lands takes to his knife for the purpose of killing, and he kills; the Argentine gaucho un-sheathes his to fight, and he only wounds. To attempt the life of his adversary he must be very drunk, or his instincts must be really wicked, or his rancor very deep. His aim is only to *mark* his opponent, to give him a slash in the face, to leave an indelible token upon him. The numerous scars to be seen upon these gauchos, accordingly, are seldom deep. A fight is begun, then, for the sake of shining, for the glory of victory, for the love of fame. A close ring is made around the combatants, and excited and eager eyes follow the glitter of the knives which do not cease to move. When blood flows in torrents the spectators feel obliged to stop the fight. If a *misfortune* has resulted, the sympathies are with the survivor; the best horse is available for his escape to a distant place where he is received with respect or pity. If the law overtakes him he often shows fight, and if he rushes through soldiers and escapes, he has from that time a wide-spread renown. Time passes, the judge in place has been succeeded by another, and he may again show himself in the township without further molestation: he has a full discharge.

Homicide is but a misfortune, unless the deed has been so often repeated that the perpetrator has gained the reputation of an assassin. The landed pro-prietor, Don Juan Manuel Rosas, before being a public man, had made his residence a sort of asylum for homicides without ever extending his protection to robbers; a preference which would easily be explained by his character of gaucho proprietor, if his subsequent conduct had not disclosed affinities with evil which have filled the world with terror. . . .

Before 1810, two distinct, rival, and incompatible forms of society, two differing kinds of civilization existed in the Argentine Republic: one being Spanish, European, and cultivated, the other barbarous, American, and al-most wholly of native growth. The revolution which occurred in the cities acted only as the cause, the impulse, which set these two distinct forms of national existence face to face, and gave occasion for a contest between them, to be ended, after lasting many years, by the absorption of one into the other.

I have pointed out the normal form of association, or want of association, of the country people, a form worse, a thousand times, than that of the nomad tribe. I have described the artificial associations formed in idleness, and the sources of fame among the gauchos — bravery, daring, violence, and opposition to regular law, to the civil law, that is, of the city. These phenomena of social organization existed in 1810, and still exist, modified in many points, slowly changing in others, and yet untouched in several more. These foci, about which were gathered the brave, ignorant, free, and unemployed peasantry, were found by thousands through the country. The revolution of 1810 carried everywhere commotion and the sound of arms. Public life, previously wanting in this Arabico-Roman society, made its appearance in all the taverns, and the revolutionary movement finally brought about provincial, warlike associations, called *montoneras,* legitimate offspring of the tavern and the field, hostile to the city and to the army of revolutionary patriots. As events succeed each other, we shall see the provincial montoneras headed by their chiefs; the final triumph, in Facundo Quiroga, of the country over the cities throughout the land; and by their subjugation in spirit, government, and civilization, the final formation of the central consolidated despotic government of the landed proprietor, Don Juan Manuel Rosas, who applied the knife of the gaucho to the culture of Buenos Ayres, and destroyed the work of centuries — of civilization, law, and liberty.

35. *Rosas Continued the Authoritarian Colonial Tradition*

JOSÉ LUIS ROMERO

José Luis Romero has played an active part in the troubled history of the University of Buenos Aires during the last generation. His study of political ideas and political events in Argentina from the colonial period onward gives him an excellent perspective from which to judge Rosas.

Juan Manuel de Rosas was a powerful *hacendado* in the province of Buenos Aires, whose political prestige grew unchecked after 1820. As an *estanciero,*

Reprinted from *A History of Argentine Political Thought* by José Luis Romero, introduction and translation by Thomas F. McGann, with the permission of the publishers, Stanford University Press. © 1963 by the Board of Trustees of the Leland Stanford Junior University.

he was able to count on great resources to gain control of the countryside; as the chief of a military force organized at his own expense — the "Colorados del Monte," or "Red Rangers" — he was able to influence decisively the events in the capital during the crisis brought on by Lavalle's seizure of power and the later execution of Dorrego. Rosas saw clearly that this was his chance to impose his authority, and he declared himself in favor of federalism. Henceforth his importance in the capital was unequalled, his power grew to near omnipotence, and at the end of 1829 he was made governor of the province.

His first government lasted until the end of 1832. In that period [General José María] Paz, who might have been his worthy rival, fell prisoner, and the League of the Interior, which Paz had organized, collapsed. At about the same time, the League of the Littoral was organized. With the disappearance of Paz, other provinces joined the new League, and they, like the original signatories of the pact, delegated to Rosas the conduct of the foreign relations of the country. Thus Rosas, on leaving power, had contributed to the establishment of a loose national regime — the Confederation — which merited the cooperation of the *caudillos* and permitted Buenos Aires to exercise a certain hegemony that did not weigh greatly on the economy of the other provinces.

From 1832 to 1834, the provincial government of Buenos Aires was in the hands of men on whom Rosas could rely, yet who were zealously watched by his followers. His authority was by now unchallengeable, and it increased — as did his wealth — thanks to the campaign he led against the Indians of the desert. The popular masses and the most reactionary anti-Rivadavian groups supported him, especially the estancieros, whose interests Rosas rigidly defended, since they were also his interests. This coalition of forces propelled him to power for a second time, despite his tactics of pretended reticence by which he succeeded in obtaining the grant of "Extraordinary Powers," which was contrary to all republican tradition.

Events favored him, but he had the cunning to create favorable conditions for his own plans. Although he sought only to exercise exceptional powers as governor of Buenos Aires, he counted on obtaining de facto authority over the entire country. To that end, he conceived the plan to leave control of the provinces in the hands of caudillos who were all-powerful in local affairs, and later to bring those leaders under his own influence. The only obstacle to this plan of action was the presence of two caudillos who exercised notorious control over vast regions: Estanislao López and Juan Facundo Quiroga. But Rosas knew how to dominate them, and with a lucid mind, marked sagacity, and, above all, long patience and invincible tenacity, he accomplished his plans.

His views on the problems of the political organization of the country were expressed in two notable documents in 1834, shortly before his second ascent to power. As a result of a conflict between the governors of Salta and Tucumán, Quiroga was given the responsibility of mediating between the two men, and from the governor of Buenos Aires he received instructions that doubtlessly had been inspired by Rosas:

> Señor Quiroga should take advantage of every opportunity to make all the people whom he will meet during his trip understand that a congress ought to be convened as soon as possible, but that at present it is useless to demand a congress and a federal constitution, since each state has not arranged its internal affairs and does not give, within a stable, permanent order, practical and positive proofs of its ability to organize a federation with the other provinces. For in this system, the general government is not united, but rather is sustained by union, and the State represents the people who comprise the republic in their relations with other nations; neither does the State resolve the disputes between the people of one province and those of another, but rather limits their activities in compliance with the general pacts of the federation — to watch over the defenses of the entire republic, and to direct their negotiations and general interests in relation to those of other States, since in cases of discord between two provinces, the constitution usually has an agreed way of deciding them, when the contenders do not arbitrate the dispute.

So expressed, this statement shows a sound and justifiable grasp of the situation. But these ideas have real significance only if one takes into account the fact that at last some of the caudillos — even Quiroga himself — were beginning to recognize the need to establish a national government, although under a federal system. Rosas' plan, therefore, was both the result of his interpretation of existing conditions and the disclosure of a scheme. His plan had been sketched out in the instructions that the mediator officially carried with him. But Rosas assumed that Quiroga was not convinced of the advantages of the plan, and tried to reinforce his arguments at a meeting; afterward he summarized his ideas in a letter he wrote to Quiroga in December 1834, at the Hacienda de Figueroa, before the two leaders separated:

> After all that experience and evidence have taught and counseled, is there anyone who believes that the remedy is to hasten the constitutional organization of the State? Permit me to make some observations in this regard, since, although we have always been in agreement on such im-

portant matters, I wish to entrust to you with bold anticipation, and for whatever service it may be to you, a small part of the many thoughts that occur to me, and about which I must speak.

No one is more persuaded than you and I of the necessity to organize a general government as being the only means of giving responsible existence to our republic.

But who can doubt that this ought to be the happy result of employing all the means suited to its accomplishment? Who may hope to reach an objective by marching in the opposite direction? Who, in order to form an organized, compact entity, does not first seek out and arrange, by thorough, permanent reforms, the elements that ought to compose it? Who organizes a disciplined army from groups of men without leaders, without officers, without obedience, without rank — an army in which not a moment passes without internal spying and fighting, and thus involves others in its disorders? How may a living, robust being be created out of members that are dead, torn, and diseased by corrupting gangrene, since the life and strength of this new, complex being can be no greater than what it receives from the elements of which it must be composed? Please observe how costly and painful experience has made us see in a practical way that the federal system is absolutely necessary for us because, among other powerful reasons, we totally lack the elements required for a unified government. Furthermore, because our country was dominated by a party that was deaf to this need, the means and resources available to sustain the State were destroyed and annulled. That party incited the people, perverted their beliefs, set private interests against each other, propagated immorality and intrigue, and split society into so many factions that they have not left even the remnants of its common bonds. They extended their fury to the point of breaking the most sacred of those bonds, the only one that could serve to re-establish the others — religion. With the country in this pitiful condition, it is necessary to create everything anew, first laboring on a small scale and piecemeal, and thereby prepare a general system that may embrace everything. You will observe that a federal republic is the most chimerical and disastrous that can be imagined in all cases when it is not composed of internally well-organized States. Since each part preserves its sovereignty and independence, the central government's authority over the interior of the republic is almost nonexistent; its principal, almost its only role, is purely representative — to be the voice of the people of the confederated states in their relations with foreign governments. Consequently, if within each individual state there are no elements of power capable of maintaining order, the creation of a general, representative government serves only to agitate the entire republic over each small disorder that may occur and to see to it that an outbreak in one state spreads to all the others. It is for this reason that the Republic of North America has not admitted to its new confederation the new people and provinces that have been formed since independence, but rather has admitted them when they have put themselves in a condition for self-rule; meanwhile, they have been left without representation as States, and have been considered as adjuncts of the Republic.

Considering the disturbed condition of our people, contaminated as they all are by Unitarians, lawmakers, seekers after political power, the secret agents of other nations, and the great secret Lodges that spread their nets over all of Europe, what hope can we have of tranquility and calm for making a federal compact, the first step a congress of federation must take? And in the impoverished state to which political agitation has driven our people, with what funds can they pay for a permanent congress and a general administration?

Steadfast in his ideas, Rosas set out to maintain the status quo of the country, and he put off every attempt to organize the State. But if that was his intent in its legal aspect, his practical plans were quite different. What he sought was that the de facto power of the caudillos be brought under his own de facto power, on which there were no legal restrictions and for which there were no predetermined forms. Quiroga's death, which occurred on his return from his mission to the North, eliminated Rosas' most important rival, one whose goal seems to have been the prompt constitutional organization of the country. A few years later, in 1838, Estanislao López also died, in Santa Fe; henceforth, there was no one in the interior who could rival the governor of Buenos Aires, who exercised his authority over the whole country and progressively brought the caudillos under his control with threats, promises, or gifts. As Domingo F. Sarmiento wrote in 1845, in *Facundo:*

At last we have our centralized republic — and all of it bent under the arbitrary rule of Rosas. The old issues debated by the political parties of Buenos Aires have been stripped of all significance; the meaning of words has been changed; the laws of the cattle ranch have been introduced into the government of the republic, which was once the most war-like and the most enthusiastic for liberty, and sacrificed most to achieve it. The death of López delivered Santa Fe to Rosas; the death of the Reinafé brothers gave him Córdoba; Facundo's death gave him the eight provinces on the slopes of the Andes. To take possession of all these, a few personal gifts, some friendly letters, and some hand-outs from the treasury sufficed.

On this basis a national State with unusual characteristics took form, founded on a system of alliances and on the authority of an all-powerful chief — principally the latter, because, since Rosas' State lacked legal form, it was merely an extension of his personal power.

An analysis of the characteristics of this situation, and of the idea of power it involved, is highly suggestive. Intelligent — more than that, supremely astute and profoundly knowledgeable in the psychology of the creoles — Rosas had succeeded in creating among the people the deep-rooted conviction of his natural right to exercise authority. Only he appeared to be capable of restoring the traditional way of life and of putting an end to civil strife; this belief, which was held by his most devoted adherents, was corroborated by the plebiscite that he had demanded be taken before he accepted the grant of total authority. In effect, this belief was generally held, and his prestige quickly turned it into idolatry, and not without magical overtones pointing to the mysterious origin of his power:

> He, with his talent and his science
> keeps the country secure,
> and that is why he gets his help
> from Divine Providence.

So the people sang, and Rosas himself tried to make them believe it, allowing his image to appear in the churches, where it received popular homage. The vague awareness of the force behind his authority facilitated the shift to autocracy, and no person or thing altered his will or succeeded in decisively influencing his resolution. "During the time I presided over the government of Buenos Aires, charged with the foreign relations of the Argentine Confederation and holding total authority, as granted to me by law" — he wrote in 1870 — "I governed according to my conscience. I am solely responsible for all my acts, good or bad, and for my errors as well as for my successes." Rosas became so powerful that years later, his nephew, Lucio V. Mansilla, could say: "There was no discussion during the time of Rosas; no criticism; no opinion." His was a personal power, independent of that granted to him by law, and he was so sure that his authority sprang from himself alone that he once hinted at the possibility of transmitting his power to his daughter, Manuelita.

Despite the broad popular basis of his support, Rosas had many influential enemies. From the outset, he was opposed by the followers of Rivadavia, against whom he had fought as a federalist; later, he had enemies among all the groups that had any sense of honor, which was an obstacle to the submission that he demanded. Rosas was implacable with all his opponents: many fled to foreign lands, and many suffered violent persecution. As Paz said: "The historian who undertakes the job of narrating these events will be hard put not to give the appearance of exaggerating what happened, and posterity will have to work as hard to persuade itself that the events we have witnessed were possible." Thanks to the use of violence, thanks to the skill with which he managed the instincts and inclinations of the creole masses, Rosas obtained apparently unanimous support. He who was not unconditionally with Rosas was his enemy — "a savage, filthy Unitarian." The fact is that Rosas succeeded in planting in the minds of the people the conviction that all their enemies — among whom were doctrinaire Federalists and many old Unitarians who had later become convinced of the advantages of federation — made up a single group, characterized by unswerving centralist beliefs and by alien, anti-creole attitudes. And these qualities were precisely the most hateful ones to the masses.

Rosas' ideology stemmed directly from a colonial inheritance that is noticeable as early as the May Revolution. As Sarmiento wrote: "Where, then, did this man learn about the innovations that he introduced into his government, in contempt of common sense, tradition, and the conscience and immemorial practices of civilized peoples? God forgive me if I am wrong, but this idea has long possessed me: he learned them from the cattle ranch, where he has spent his whole life, and from the Inquisition, in whose tradition he has been educated." The author of *Facundo* was correct: not only was Rosas the culmination of the secessionist movement that had appeared after 1810 and that was, in a strict sense, more than mere federalism; also he was the distillation of the antiliberal movement that was part of the authoritarian tradition of the colony and that retained its vigor among the rural masses.

These trends may be clearly seen if one analyzes the symbols he employed with such marked success. Defense of the Catholic faith had been the order of the day of Quiroga, whose motto was "Religion or Death," and it was seemingly one of the basic objectives of the Rosas dictatorship. The ultramontane party, represented by men like Francisco Tagle and Father Gregorio Castañeda, had struggled hard to enthrone Rosas; their faithful followers were known as the "Apostolic Party," and when the people wanted to describe their enemies, they said that they were

> mocking religion; the result:
> heretics who had blasphemed
> what is most holy, what most sacred
> of our divine cult.

Ultramontane reaction was but one aspect of the antiliberalism that followed the revolution of 1830 in France. Anything that recalled the ideas of the men of the Enlightenment, of whom the followers of Rivadavia were the direct heirs, was violently condemned by the partisans of Rosas, as is conclusively shown by General Mansilla's comment to his son, Lucio, on the day he found him reading Rousseau: "My friend, when one is the nephew of Rosas, he does not read the *Social Contract* if he intends to remain in the country, or he gets out of the country if he wishes to read the book with profit." This antiliberalism, seen clearly in the political and economic views that Rosas put into effect during his long period of rule, was intermingled with creole reaction. If he was called the "Restorer of the Laws," it was not so much because the people regarded him particularly as the defender of legal norms, but because they felt he was the guardian of the traditions of the common folk and the zealous defender of a way of life that seemed to be condemned to extinction. This explains his political xenophobia, which was, nonetheless, compatible with his alliances with the governments of countries that traded with the estancieros and with the producers of hides and salted meats. It explains the devoted support given him by the masses, who were proud of their "Americanism," and who were by tradition and by inertia opposed to progress, and infatuated with the superiority of their virtues as a pastoral people — courage and manual dexterity.

Along these lines Rosas built the indisputable popular basis for his policies, and this support allowed the all-powerful governor of Buenos Aires and proprietor of its port to impose his authority on the Confederation, which was the elementary form in which he conceived the national State. No doubt he unified the country, as Sarmiento said, but he exhausted the Confederation's possibilities during his long rule, and gradually he awakened the desire to attain unity through a solidly founded constitutional system. It cannot be denied that he fulfilled a mission, despite the overtones of barbarism that darkened his labors as governor, although it is certain that he would have been able to achieve this result by other means if such violent prejudices and rancor had not been at work within him.

36. *Rosas Still Lives in the Hearts of Some Argentines!*

This effusive tribute to Rosas demonstrates that there is still some popular support for him in Argentina, where citizens are notoriously historically-minded and patriotic. This decree was formally issued in 1964 by a municipality in the Chaco on the occasion of the naming of one of its avenues in honor of "Brigadier General Juan Manuel de Rosas."

Whereas: The naming of streets has always had as its purpose the commemoration of the attitudes, deeds, or conduct of personalities who have distinguished themselves in ways the remembrance of which should not be neglected; and

Considering: That it is therefore proper to honor the name of one of the forgers of our nationality and that this resolve is all the more fitting because the province to which this city belongs has been one of the last to be integrated as a Federal State within the vast Argentine Fatherland;

That the heroes of our National Organization effected the triumph of the Argentine Confederation already perfected and founded by Brigadier General Juan Manuel de Rosas by means of the Organic Pact of 1831;

That the said Confederation was sustained by its founder for more than two decades while he struggled against internal conspiracies and foreign coalitions under conditions that would have discouraged any other ruler or military leader;

That as governor of the province of Buenos Aires, Juan Manuel de Rosas created, by means of novel systems for the production, distribution, and commercialization of goods, useful sources of employment for the rural and proletarian workers, thereby materially improving the general welfare to which the constitution of 1853 refers;

That the rancher, businessman, and exporter Juan Manuel de Rosas founded . . . the so-called "mother industry of the country" — cattle-raising — the products of which he exported in ships flying the Argentine flag and belonging to the first Argentine National Merchant Marine, whose tonnage was surpassed only in 1943;

That he dignified the worker by assuming with national pride the name of

From Clifton B. Kroeber, *Rosas y la revisión de la historia Argentina,* trans. J. L. Muñoz Azpiri (Buenos Aires: Fondo Editor Argentino, 1965), pp. 87–90. Reprinted by permission.

"gaucho," which was used at that time to refer disdainfully to humble Argentines;

That he caused this name to be respected by the powers of the earth through the exercise of intelligence and arms;

That he initiated the first ordinance of national economic independence in the famous Customs Law of 1831, which provided financial controls and protection for our industries and crafts;

That he professed to be permanently honored "with the friendship of the poor" and to hold himself aloof from the privileges of the so-called oligarchy of Buenos Aires;

That he recovered thousands of leagues from the wilderness and founded the centers of civilization called Bahía Blanca, Junín, and 25 de Mayo;

That during twelve years of international conflict he defended Argentine sovereignty with immortal dignity, preserving it "as whole and unblemished as when it left the hands of the Almighty," and he fulfilled and for the first time brought about the true fulfillment of the oath of July 9, 1816;

That he declared the ninth of July a national holiday;

That he enjoyed the admiration of the world's leading statesmen and publicists, who considered him the champion of the rights of South American sovereignty;

That he brought dignity to the name of Argentina because of his irreproachable conduct in his personal and private life and his scrupulous management of public funds;

That he strengthened the privileges of the Church and revoked measures of persecution against Catholicism which had been dictated by previous doctrinaire governments, thereby fortifying Argentina's civil unity, one of the sources of which is the strength and solidarity of the Christian faith;

That he made the Argentine Army a specialized and technical body, providing it with industries and laboratories and establishing the bases of military manufacturing in the model barracks and workshops of Santos Lugares;

That he converted our fledgling diplomatic service into a corps of professionals and specialists in international politics and in the art of negotiation, among them Arana, Guido, Manuel Moreno, and Mariano Balcarce;

That he was the first to honor the Father of the Country by decreeing that a plaza in Buenos Aires bear the name of the Liberator during his lifetime;

That the name of Juan Manuel de Rosas survives in the bosom of this region, the latest to be recovered from the wilderness of the Argentine Chaco, as the symbol and epitome of the purest national essence;

That his heroic name, pronounced by the humble and patriotic hearts of Argentina's generous soil, will always prevent humiliations or slights to our Fatherland;

That he deserved the highest posthumous honors that any Argentine citizen has hitherto received upon setting forth on his voyage to the tomb, accompanied by the sword of San Martín and the flag of Arenales;

That the present resolution fulfills one of the desires of the Father of the Country, General José de San Martín, who in a letter to General Rosas dated on May 6, 1850, in Boulogne sur Mer expressed the hope "that upon ending his public life he would be overwhelmed by the just gratitude of every Argentine."

For all these reasons:

The Municipal Council of Roque Saenz Peña directs that:

Article 1. The name Brigadier General Juan Manuel de Rosas be given to the present Avenue of Labor along its entire length.

Article 2. The Subsecretariat of Public Works take action to put up the appropriate street signs.

37. An Argentine Educator Who Developed His Modern Ideas during the Rosas Period and Who Outlasted the Dictatorship

HAROLD BENJAMIN

Dean Emeritus Harold Benjamin of the School of Education of the University of Maryland was one of the pioneer scholars in the United States who developed an interest and competence in the history of education in Latin America. Here he shows a warm and professional appreciation of Sarmiento as an educator in a conference paper originally delivered in 1947 at the University of Texas.

Sarmiento became a teacher by the combined pressure of family tradition and of revolutionary events. When he was born in the western town of San Juan de la Frontera on February 15, 1811, the May Revolution of the Río de la Plata patriots was only nine months past. He entered the newly-established revolutionary School of the Fatherland at the age of five in 1816, the year of

From "Sarmiento the Educator" by Harold Benjamin, in *Some Educational and Anthropological Aspects of Latin America,* Latin American Studies, 5 (Austin: The University of Texas Press, 1948), pp. 7–16. Reprinted by permission.

the Declaration of Independence by the Congress of Tucumán. He taught his first class in a rural school when he was barely fifteen in 1826, a year in which liberal ideas of the kind Don Bernardino Rivadavia had fostered were being engulfed in a rising tide of barbarism. His first employment in exile in Chile at the age of twenty was as teacher of a village school. Thereafter, throughout his life, at home or in exile, in war or in peace, as professor, writer, revolutionist, and public administrator, he never ceased to pursue his true profession or forgot that he was first, last, and always a teacher.

If Sarmiento had been born a few years earlier, his desire to learn and to teach might well have led him into the service of the Church. He came from a family which, though well acquainted with poverty and illiteracy, had many distinguished sons in both the regular and the secular clergy. Two of his uncles were bishops, and another uncle was the famous friar, Justo de Santa María de Oro, delegate to the Congress of Tucumán, signer of the Declaration of Independence, and final wrecker of that Congress by his insistence that the new union's form of government should not be decided without a referendum vote of all the people in the provinces concerned.

It took a revolution and a revolutionary education to make a fighting schoolmaster of the boy who might otherwise have become a priest. Very little of his education was formal schooling, yet that schooling itself was of revolutionary character for its times.

The *Escuela de la Patria* was a progressive school established by the efforts of the energetic and liberal lieutenant governor of the province of San Juan, Don José Ignacio de la Rosa y Torres, who had been educated at Córdoba, had taken his doctorate in laws at Santiago de Chile, and who had resided in Buenos Aires for ten years. The school's first director was Don Ignacio Rodríguez who believed that his prime professional task was to be defined in terms of a certain kind of citizen for a certain kind of society and not in terms of any subject matter or other academic instruments whatever. He held that it was his duty to provide the best possible learning environment for the development of intelligent and loyal members of the new fatherland.

This creed led Rodríguez and his two brothers, who constituted the staff of the school, into various pedagogical heresies. In the first place, all the three hundred children in the school were regarded as social equals and were required to address one another accordingly. There was no exception to this rule, even for the sons of Negro slaves. Black or white, Indian or half-breed, pupil or teacher, when one citizen of the school spoke to another he addressed him as *Señor* and *Usted*.

In the second place, the Rodríguez brothers flatly rejected severe and humiliating punishments. In the class schools of the old Royalist regime, it was no doubt bad enough to break a child's spirit, but after all, if he was destined to cringe before tyrants, perhaps he had to have his spirit broken. In the *Escuela de la Patria,* however, this was unthinkable. Free men could not be developed with blows. Intelligent citizens could not learn to think for themselves in an atmosphere of intellectual servility. The coming masters of community and national destinies could not be whipped like slaves.

The doctrine of democratic equality in the Rodríguez school did not mean, however, that one citizen of the school was unable to advance beyond another. On the contrary, a spirit of healthy emulation and competition was held to be a central element of institutional and individual morale. The pupils were divided into groups in various matches and races, and individuals were rated even to the extent of designating the best scholar as *First Citizen of the Fatherland School.*

Young Domingo Sarmiento won the chair of the *First Citizen* but soon lost it in intellectual combat with another Señor. In spite of undoubtedly superior abilities, Domingo was hardly a model pupil. Suffering from occasional boredom, he engaged in sly deviltries of the age-old schoolboy variety when the teacher's back was turned. But sometimes Don Ignacio only seemed to have his back turned — he was no callow recruit to the ranks of pedagogy. Given his humane and intelligent system of discipline, moreover, he had to assign what he regarded as "natural" penalties for misbehavior. Since there was in his school an elaborate set of awards and distinctions for approved behavior, he conceived the proper penalty for disapproved acts to be a denial of awards. Thus young Domingo lost various rankings in the scholastic line-up and even sank to the depths of not being allowed to wear a silver medal of academic honor to which he was entitled by his erudition, had that quality not been unhappily tarnished by anti-social conduct.

The School of the Fatherland was destined to furnish the only formal education Domingo Sarmiento was ever to enjoy. When he was ten years old, his father decided he should be given secondary education. Hearing of a possible scholarship in the Loreto Seminary at Córdoba, he made the long trip with his son on horseback to apply for entrance only to find that there was no scholarship, at least for the son of a muleteer. When Domingo was twelve, he applied for one of the six places to be awarded to boys from the province of San Juan for study in Buenos Aires under grants from the Rivadavia government. His name was first on the list of candidates recommended by his school, but under political pressure the provincial authorities finally resorted to the drawing of lots for the final selection, and young Domingo's name remained at the bottom of the hat. A few months later four more scholarships were allotted to San Juan, but again Domingo was unlucky. Then, four years later, when the boy was sixteen years old and had already done his first teaching, there came a final chance at secondary education. A new governor, Don José Antonio Sánchez, offered to send the boy at the expense of the provincial government to the *Colegio de Ciencias Morales* in Buenos Aires. The elder Sarmiento rode into the country to get his son for this great opportunity. They had hardly reached San Juan when the lances of Facundo Quiroga appeared over the horizon from La Rioja. The Unionist government of San Juan came to a sudden end and with it the prospects of a new student for the *Colegio de Ciencias Morales*.

Thus the boy, Sarmiento, was forced into self-education, and he went at the task doggedly and brilliantly. As clerk in a store in San Juan, as soldier in the field, as laborer in the mines of Chanarcillo in Chile, and even as prisoner in jail and guardhouse, he studied and taught to the best of his ability. He read biography, history, literary criticism, natural science, whatever books he could lay hands upon. He learned French and English. He wrote voluminously. Always he tried to pass to others that which he had learned.

The foundation of the great schoolmaster's first outstanding contribution to educational theory and practice was thereby laid. Like other men of high ability who have educated themselves under the scourge of their own intellectual ambitions, he acquired very early a profound sense of the unity of all learning and a profound conviction that education could be evaluated only in terms of the total personality developed through the process of learning. From that day in his twentieth year when he lost his teaching position at the municipal school of Los Andes, Chile, on account of his radical educational ideas, to the time a half century later when as ex-president of Argentina he accepted the job of National Superintendent General of Education for the Republic, he believed in "new" methods because he felt that the traditional ones were not based on a workable educational philosophy. He had, too, the brilliant self-educated man's confidence in his own interpretation of the correctness of his methods, a confidence which carried him through a lifetime of educational innovation.

Sarmiento really began his double task of expounding and practicing his educational theories in 1839, at the age of twenty-eight, when he opened the College of Santa Rosa in his native city of San Juan. As first director of this school for young women and girls, he made his initial public statement of his theory of education as a process of growth and development, and of teaching as the provision of optimum conditions therefor. With a staff of five teachers, including three of his sisters, he proceeded to demonstrate his theory in practice. The curriculum, which included, in addition to the usual subjects of reading, writing, spelling, arithmetic, and religion, the more "advanced" studies of geography, manual arts, drawing, music, French, and Italian, and the methods of instruction, which called, in unusual manner, for the exercise of initiative and responsibility by the pupils, would probably have been sufficient in time to have excited the suspicion of the more conservative elements of the population had not Sarmiento's concurrent literary efforts excited them even sooner.

The new school had been opened on July 9. On July 20 there appeared the first issue of a new weekly journal, *El Zonda,* edited and largely written by Sarmiento. This publication had been authorized by the governor on condition that it avoid political subjects. This was something the editor could not do. Non-political articles on public education, mining, and literature were accompanied by an article of caustic criticism of various local customs which appeared to the governor to be political in object if not in form. In the resulting argument, the young schoolmaster-editor eventually landed in jail, and within a year was once more in exile in Chile.

It was in Chile that Sarmiento developed and practiced his fundamental educational ideas. He began in 1841, at the age of thirty, by publishing in *El Mercurio* of Santiago an article on the Battle of Chacabuco which attracted wide and favorable notice and earned him a steady job on that important newspaper with the assignment of writing three or four editorials each week. He began with a piece on public instruction. *El Mercurio* received a government subsidy and was the semiofficial organ of the ruling political party. One of the most prominent leaders of that party, Don Manuel Montt, was the recently-appointed Minister of Public Instruction. He was much impressed by Sarmiento's writings on educational topics and political questions and secured the Argentine emigre's appointment as editor of a new political sheet called *El Nacional* which appeared as campaign literature from April to July, 1841.

This was the beginning of a life-long friendship between two great men, the Chilean, Montt, and the Argentinian, Sarmiento. When the young Minister of Public Instruction established in January, 1842, the first Chilean Normal School which was also the first normal school in Latin America, he appointed the young schoolmaster from San Juan de la Frontera its first director.

La Escuela Normal de Preceptores de Chile was a small school with a maximum enrollment of only forty-two students in the first three years of its existence and with only one member of the faculty besides the director, but it gave Sarmiento a chance to develop his educational ideas in the training of teachers. He taught reading, grammar, geography, arithmetic, and "cosmography," demonstrating from the first his distrust of commonly accepted educational notions by refusing to use any of the standard grammars of the day and by introducing the syllabic method of teaching reading in place of the usual alphabet method.

The University of Chile, which was established by law in 1842 and which opened its doors for instruction in 1843, included Sarmiento in its Faculty of Philosophy and Humanities. At the first session of that faculty, the young schoolmaster-editor presented a paper on his ideas of a reformed spelling of the Spanish language. In this he developed the thesis which he had already expounded at length in his editorials and in his normal school classes that popular standards of pronunciation rather than etymological considerations should decide how a word should be spelled. The faculty, after a number of heated sessions, adopted his proposals in part and thus inaugurated a definite movement toward more phonetic spelling of the language.

At this time Sarmiento began the most intense educational efforts of his career. He wrote books for teachers on methods of teaching reading, grammar, and spelling. He helped found a secondary school which was so advanced in its methods for its times that parents withdrew their children at the end of two years. At the same time he redoubled his efforts in journalism which took on for him, more and more, the character of an educational instrument. He converted the press into a battering ram of continent-wide public opinion which made the tyrant, Rosas, in Buenos Aires first contemptuous, then irritated, and finally mad with rage that a scribbling schoolmaster could be so dangerous.

This period of Sarmiento's educational career culminated in 1845 with the event which made the country school teacher one of the great pioneers of comparative education. His friend, Montt, secured for him a commission to study European systems of public education for two years and a substantial grant from the Chilean government to cover his expenses.

Sarmiento's two-year journey took him to France, Spain, Italy, Germany, England, and the United States. In each of these countries he observed mainly schools and the industry, agriculture, politics, religion, and general life of the people *as they related to schools.* He seemed to be groping for measurements of national educational character, for methods of judging the worth of national systems of education, and for hallmarks of educational excellence. He found some of them in Europe, particularly in France. Whether it was because he had matured his ideas by the time he arrived in the United States, or whether it was because he was himself an American and so more disposed to understand and appreciate an American educational experiment, his enthusiasm for the educational efforts of the people of the United States was very great. Horace Mann in Massachusetts appeared to him to represent precisely the kind of educational statesmanship which a democracy had a right and a necessity to demand. The educational systems of Europe seemed to him merely to foreshadow in partial and antiquated fashion what the schools of the United States were attempting vigorously and what the schools of Chile and Argentina would be attempting as soon as Sarmiento could get back into action in his home country.

Sarmiento's first study of comparative education was his *De la Educacíon Popular* which was published in 1849. In this book he presents an interpretation and analysis of the school systems of France, Prussia, Holland, and Massachusetts, among many other general educational topics, which constituted a pioneer contribution to the then very infant (and still quite puny) subject of comparative education. Montt used it as the basis for a proposed reorganization of elementary education in Chile soon after it appeared, but the bill was defeated as being somewhat too progressive for Chile.

In 1851 there began the final revolt against Rosas, which culminated in the defeat of that tyrant at the Battle of Monte Caseros on February 3, 1852. Sarmiento, who took part in this campaign as lieutenant colonel in charge of the revolutionary army newspaper, was unable to accept the policies of the victorious general, Urquiza, and returned to Chile where his old friend, Montt, was now president. He was appointed by Montt to edit a new educational journal called *El Monitor de las Escuelas.* In this new task, Sarmiento displayed some of his best educational abilities. He was a professional schoolmaster, and like all professionally-minded men, he was intensely interested in the details of the job. He filled the pages of *El Monitor* with precise descriptions of plans, models, exercises, and devices. He discussed texts and programs of study. He reviewed theories of education. He continued his contributions to comparative education.

In 1855, Sarmiento returned to his native land, settling in Buenos Aires rather than in his home province of San Juan because of a split between the Federal government of Urquiza and the provincial government of Buenos Aires. At this point in his career, Sarmiento had done most of his educational work in Chile. He was now forty-four years old, and he had made his professional contributions as a teacher, director of single schools, educational writer, and student of comparative education. From now on, working in his native country and particularly in the provinces of Buenos Aires and San Juan, he was to be primarily a provincial and national educational administrator and educational statesman.

As senator in the Buenos Aires provincial legislature and as newspaper writer and editor, Sarmiento continued the efforts to develop an adequate system of schools which he had practiced in Chile. As director of public schools in the province of Buenos Aires, he entered upon a kind of activity which was new for him but which he carried out with energy, intelligence, and sound educational policy. No other state or provincial educational administrator of his time, whether in Spanish America or elsewhere in the world, had a clearer conception in theory and in practice of what may be called the twentieth-century view of the school administrator's function than had this fighting schoolmaster of the Andes.

What are the characteristic features of this modern view of the educational administrative task? They include, first of all, the belief that the behavior-changing forces of any society must be studied and directed as a complete pattern of action. Sarmiento was a modern educational administrator because he believed and acted upon the belief that the education of the people of San Juan, Chile, Buenos Aires, the Argentine Republic, the United States of America, any community, any nation, and the whole world constitutes a unitary phenomenon. He believed that this phenomenon must be studied, judged, understood, and administered as a whole complex of activities, ideals, and results, with no part omitted, or it will be poorly studied, inaccurately evaluated, misunderstood, and mal-administered.

Sarmiento's theory and practice of school administration also included a second great article of the modern administrator's creed. This was based on the belief in democracy as a system whereby men not only order their own ways for their own benefit but also change their own ways consciously and freely in the direction of their own ideals. Any school administrator who holds this notion to be true must engage in a comprehensive program of informing and inspiring all the people of his community, province, state, or nation with adult education, public relations, press, political, and all other available instruments of popular education. He cannot be a mere operator of schools for children and youth. He cannot set up secondary schools or colleges in intellectual and social corners. He must speak in the market place. He must be a politician. He must live with his people in good times and in bad times. When they put their hands to the plow, he must try to help direct the furrow. Even when they go to war, he has to go with them. An educational theorist, a student of comparative education, even a classroom teacher, might successfully hold himself aloof from some of these experiences, but an administrator of the Sarmiento type can never do so.

When Sarmiento was elected governor of his native province of San Juan in 1862, he continued even amid the rigors and pressures of civil war his activities as a school administrator. He founded a new secondary school and a school of agriculture. He encouraged the development of a "model" elementary school which had previously been established and named after him. He found new sources of revenue for public education by the difficult and unpopular expedient of expropriating certain Church property. He was not a democratic administrator, in the usual current meaning of that term. He was the product of a rough society where the boss spoke and acted directly, and he tended even too much for his time to administer schools in that fashion.

In 1865, Sarmiento was appointed Argentine minister to the United States. From an educational standpoint, the chief features of his three-year stay at that time in our country were his close association with national teachers' meetings and his preparation of the book called *The Schools: Foundation of the Prosperity of the Republic in the United States.* In the national educational meetings he was active in supporting the resolutions for the establishment of the United States Office of Education. He was one of the few foreign observers who have ever understood the real function of that office. In *The Schools,* he gave, among a scattering of various educational data and ideas, his last definitive statement on comparative educational matters.

This paper has treated of Sarmiento as an educator and has, therefore, omitted all mention of some of the most important acts and periods of his life. It has treated other parts of his career only very incidentally. This must be the treatment accorded to most of Sarmiento's life after his election to the presidency of the Argentine Republic in 1868. While he did retain great interest in education in the six years of his presidential term and tried in various ways to further the cause of the public schools, he was now in so high a position that his effect on education was not outstanding.

After leaving the presidency, Sarmiento continued to be active in politics and in education for the fourteen years of life remaining to him. He was again superintendent of schools for the province of Buenos Aires. He organized and headed a national council of education. He continued his educational writings.

His educational services in the period after his term as president were valuable enough to have earned him a respectable place in the history of education in Argentina even had they been his only educational contributions, but they were not of the same quality as his earlier work in Buenos Aires and in Chile. He had now occupied positions so important that it was hard for him to get down to the detailed work he had done so well in his more youthful days. He now tended to trust more to educational reform by law and decree than he had in the days when he had less to do with laws and decrees.

The old man retained his fire and much of his drive almost to the last, however. He never lost his self-confidence which his enemies called egotism and satirized by dubbing him "Master I" — *Don Yo.* "I understand that in certain quarters," he is reputed once to have said to a hushed Senate crowded with members of the opposition, "I am known as *Don Yo.* Good!

I am *Don Yo.* I am the same *Don Yo* who fought Don Juan Manuel de Rosas so long and whom Don Juan Manuel de Rosas wanted so badly to have killed. Don Juan Manuel de Rosas sleeps today under the daisies far away, and *Don Yo* is here, looking for trouble!"

Whether *Don Yo* was a great statesman, I leave to experts in statecraft to judge. Whether he was a great writer, I am glad to have scholars in the field of Latin-American letters decide. The quality of his efforts as a publicist, diplomat, and soldier can likewise be evalued much more adequately by those who know better than I the standards of excellence in such fields. Whether he was a great educator, however, is a question about which I have no slightest doubt, and I believe that my judgment of his eminence will be supported by any of my fellow students of education who will examine his life and times.

Domingo Faustino Sarmiento was so great an educator that it would be a high compliment to any European or North American schoolman of the nineteenth century to call him the Sarmiento of France, of England, or of the United States. But such a compliment would be impossible, for there was only one Sarmiento, unique product of a unique combination of intellectual and emotional, social and historical forces. He was a soldier in the never-ceasing war for the liberty of men's minds. His weapons were the weapons of his times, and the barbarism against which he fought and which he described so vividly in what is generally considered to be his greatest literary effort, *Civilización y Barbarie,* was also the barbarism of his times.

Yet those weapons and that barbarism are with us in this century all over the world as they were in San Juan and La Rioja a century ago. The war in which Sarmiento engaged must be fought and won every day. It must be fought by all of us who claim the title of educator. It must be fought in every classroom, laboratory, library, newspaper, radio station, theater, pulpit, or other spot from which men teach and learn. As we ride into this conflict, there is no spirit among those who rode before us more worthy of our salute than that of the great schoolmaster from San Juan de la Frontera.

Lucas Alamán. The life of this dominating figure in the first half of nine-teenth-century Mexican history illustrates how difficult and dangerous it is to categorize Latin American leaders. He was a conservative in politics and wrote an impressive history praising Spanish colonial rule, he was a vigorous entre-preneur who developed mining and textile industries in the new nation, and he also was a Mexican nationalist who feared and opposed American influence in Mexico.

SECTION IX

Nineteenth-Century Economic Affairs

INFLUENCE OF THE WORLD ECONOMY ON LATIN AMERICA

The late Professor Sanford A. Mosk of the University of California, Berkeley, stated a quarter of a century ago that "the economic history of Latin America has been a neglected field," and this is still true despite some recent advances. His essay on the way in which the world economy influenced the development of Latin America in the period 1850–1914 explains better than any other article the fundamental aspects of the subject (Reading 38). He was convinced that we will be handicapped in our understanding of the contemporary economic problems and trends in Latin America until we have "a better balanced and more accurate picture of Latin American history."

One way to attempt to meet the need will be by setting forth a number of case studies of particular topics in individual countries as illustrations of the broad, general lines of economic influences that Professor Mosk has analyzed in his wide-ranging exposition.

ENTREPRENEURSHIP IN BRAZIL

To begin with, let us consider Brazil where a conservative Emperor Pedro II made life difficult for an adventurous capitalist such as the Baron Mauá (Reading 39). Mauá and the other economic innovators of the years 1840–1880 at times yielded to the dangerous temptation to overextend themselves by engaging in too many enterprises simultaneously. As Richard Graham states, they had difficulty in "matching capital resources with technical com-

319

petence and administrative ability." [1] They were all influenced by Britain and British values, particularly the willingness to risk money for the sake of possible profits, which was the essence of the Victorian age. The spirit stood in direct opposition to the static agrarian life of Brazil, dominated as it was by the landed gentry who considered profits akin to usury (Reading 40). Mauá particularly was deeply influenced by the vision of an industrialized, modern society derived from an early visit to England.

INDIVIDUAL ENTERPRISE IN COLOMBIA

Recent emphasis on the problems of economic underdevelopment in Latin America in the twentieth century has obscured the spirit of enterprise that was to be found in a number of countries in the nineteenth century. Following the wars for independence, from about 1830 on, many attempts were made to bring capital and techniques to Latin America. Usually these attempts to modernize the economies have been considered the work of foreigners, but Frank Safford of Northwestern University points out in a closely reasoned essay that in Colombia "native entrepreneurs matched foreign innovators step-for-step" (Reading 41).

INDUSTRY AND RURAL LABOR IN CHILE

Chile slowly but surely strengthened its economic structure from 1830 onward, a process in which foreigners were involved in attempts to establish industries and exploit mines.[2] In the agricultural sector, the effects of the world economy so clearly explained by Professor Mosk (Reading 38) began to be seen after 1860. Until that time the colonial languor had persisted: "A few sacks of grain still moved by muleback or oxcart for export to Peru; the large estates lay in isolated neglect populated by droves of cattle and casual workers." [3] Then the world economy began to change the situation drastically. Professor Arnold J. Bauer of the University of California, Davis, describes what happened in his excellent article on Chilean rural labor:

[1] Richard Graham, *Britain and the Onset of Modernization in Brazil, 1850–1914* (Cambridge, England: Cambridge University Press, 1968), p. 206.

[2] J. Fred Rippy and Jack Pfeiffer, "Notes on the Dawn of Manufacturing in Chile," *Hispanic American Historical Review*, 28, (1948), pp. 292–296. See also Fredrick B. Pike, *Chile and the United States, 1880–1962: The Emergence of Chile's Social Crisis and the Challenge to United States Diplomacy* (Notre Dame: University of Notre Dame Press, 1963), pp. 4–8.

[3] Arnold J. Bauer, "Chilean Rural Labor in the Nineteenth Century," *American Historical Review,* 76 (1971), p. 1060.

From about 1860 on, rail and steam put European markets in reach of the peripheral zones. Chilean exports to England grew steadily while at the same time the northern mining districts and Santiago increased their demand for food. In North America, Australia, and Argentina, where no sedentary population existed, men arrived with machines in tow to produce grain for the cities of industrial Europe. Unlike these unpopulated new lands, however, central Chile contained a great many men. Whereas production in the new lands required machines, here the older farming system could be extended by including the existing population to work. Coincident with the expansion of cereal cultivation the labor systems began to change. Landowners demanded more service from the *inquilinos* and attempts were made to convert the peon into a more stable and reliable work force. Where independence and new governments scarcely had been noticed, the consequences of economic expansion were felt in the most remote corner of central Chile.[4]

The long-range effect was enormous for the future of Chilean agrarian life as well as national politics:

> Within the countries that supplied Europe's food in the nineteenth century, expansion created wholly new agrarian societies in some cases and provoked deep reform in others. In Chile expansion took place within a traditional society and the effect was to strengthen the institutions already present. The century-old system of *inquilinaje* was extended by settling new resident workers while stepping up the labor requirements of older tenants. At the same time part of the floating population was induced to settle near the central valley haciendas. During this reorganization of labor the settlement pattern of rural Chile changed from scattered and even ambulatory homesteads to small hamlets and agrarian villages. From the 1860s on, thousands of new dwarf holdings appeared in central Chile. Further fragmentation of these reduced their proprietors (or their sons) to a choice of part-time work or emigration. Some left for northern mines or railroad construction; others added to the pool of seasonal labor that, in the absence of machinery, was essential to estate agriculture.
>
> As Chile entered the twentieth century Chilean rural society was already cast in the familiar modern pattern of "minifundia-latifundia" symbiosis. On one side were the tiny privately owned plots whose owners, unable to provide subsistence for their families from their own

---

[4] Ibid., p. 1074.

land, found supplementary work on the haciendas. On the other side were the still inefficient large estates encumbered by a more abundant, stable, and desperately poor labor force. This humble mass could neither adequately feed the growing cities nor buy the products of an incipient industrial sector. Rural workers remained isolated from the new currents of Chilean life but they continued to provide the labor and votes that underlay the landowners' dominance of national politics.[5]

THE POOR IN MEXICO

No histories of poverty in nineteenth-century Mexico exist, and those interested in the seamy side of life there usually have to depend on travelers' accounts or other such impressionistic sources. However, due to the official interest of the British government we have a detailed report on the condition of the poor in 1834 that is a unique collection of data.[6] This somber picture of conditions at the beginning of Mexico's national history helps us to understand the sustained efforts of conservative Lucas Alamán to revive and strengthen the country's economy (Reading 42).

AMERICAN ENTREPRENEURS

Latin Americans for many years have had to suffer superactive Yankees eager to sell nutmegs or assist in one way or another the "development" of their countries, usually with some profit to themselves. A classic example was Edward A. Hopkins who felt called to bring various benefits to Paraguay.[7] Another such promoter was Henry Meiggs, a genial figure who knew how to ingratiate himself with Peruvians and whose remarkable exploits in building railroads in the difficult Andean terrain won for him the title "Yankee Pizarro." [8]

PEASANTS IN PERU

Railroads built by Meiggs helped to develop the country economically, but the price paid in human suffering was very high, particularly by the thousands

---

[5] Ibid., p. 1083.

[6] "The Condition of the Poor in Mexico, 1834," by N. Ray Gilmore, *Hispanic American Historical Review,* 37 (1957), pp. 213–226.

[7] "A Pioneer Promoter in Paraguay," by Harold F. Peterson, *Hispanic American Historical Review,* 22 (1942), pp. 245–261.

[8] *Latin America and the Industrial Age,* by J. Fred Rippy (New York: Putnam, 1944).

of Chinese coolies who were practically enslaved to do the dirty work.[9] And the basic economic and social problem — the debased condition of the mass of peasants who constituted the majority of the population — was not affected either by railroads or by the exploitation of guano (bird droppings) that created a boom in the middle of the nineteenth century, benefiting a few Peruvians and foreign entrepreneurs.[10]

[9] For this sad episode in Peruvian history see Watt Stewart, *Chinese Bondage in Peru: A History of the Chinese Coolie in Peru, 1849–1874* (Durham, N.C.: Duke University Press, 1951).

[10] On the guano trade and its effect on Peru, see A. J. Duffield, *The Prospects of Peru: The End of the Guano Age and a Description Thereof* (London, 1881), and Jonathan V. Levin, "Peru in the Guano Age," in *The Export Economies: Their Pattern of Development in Historical Perspective* (Cambridge, Mass.: Harvard University Press, 1960), pp. 27–123.

38. *Latin America and the World Economy, 1850–1914*

SANFORD A. MOSK

Some studies are so imaginatively conceived and soundly presented that they have a perennial value, despite the appearance of much new information on the subject. Such an article is this work by the late Professor Mosk, to whom we are indebted for his convincing guidelines for understanding the economic history of Latin America in modern times.

The fact that the Spanish colonies broke up into a large number of independent governments makes it harder to deal with the national period than with the colonial, when centralized authority gave a large degree of unity to affairs throughout the whole area. In the colonial period, too, geographic unity was matched by continuity through time. In the republican period, on the other hand, turbulence and kaleidoscopic political changes make it difficult to find a continuity in development and to appraise the long-run significance of individual events. The historian of the colonial period also enjoys an advantage in source materials. The documentary sources for colonial history are not only voluminous but they have been readily available in a few centralized archives. Materials on the national period are by no means lacking, but on the whole they have been less satisfactory for the historian, for reasons which are inherent in the political and social structure of Latin America. A sense of loyalty to political and family connections has unquestionably made its influence felt in the selection of records to be preserved and to be made available to scholars. . . .

Our understanding of the national period, therefore, in all its phases can hardly be called satisfactory. What needs to be studied in particular is the way in which institutions have been modified and reshaped since independence. It is probable that some Latin American institutions which are ordinarily viewed as a product of the colonial system will turn out on a closer inspection to bear only a superficial resemblance to institutions of colonial times and to be something very different in content. I would certainly expect such a revaluation to occur with respect to Latin American economic insti-

From "Latin America and the World Economy, 1850–1914" by Sanford A. Mosk, *Inter-American Economic Affairs*, 2 (1948), no. 3, pp. 53–82, passim. Reprinted by permission.

tutions. The commercialization of economic life in the nineteenth and twentieth centuries has not gone nearly as far in Latin America as in other parts of the world such as Western Europe and the United States. Nevertheless, it has played its part. To cite but one example, in penetrating economic life in Latin America since the middle of the nineteenth century, commercialization has brought about important changes in the heritage of colonial times with respect to land ownership and the relations between landowners and peasants.

These observations are in no sense intended to deny the importance of knowledge about the colonial period. Such knowledge — and also an understanding of pre-Columbian cultures — is basic to an understanding of Latin America. The perspective of the historian, however, has given too little weight to what has taken place since independence. Probably this deficiency has been greater in the treatment of Latin America's economic development than in any other phase of Latin American history. Certainly it has been acute in the economic field. In most of the textbooks and other general works on Latin American history there is an implicit, if not an explicit, underemphasis upon the economic development of the national period. The treatment of this subject tends to be fragmentary, sketchy, and lacking in generalizations. In all these respects, and usually too in amount of space, it falls far short of the treatment accorded the economy of colonial times.

This weakness obviously needs to be overcome if we are to have a better balanced and more accurate picture of Latin American history. Until it is overcome, too, we are handicapped in our understanding of the contemporary economic problems and trends of Latin America. Right now a number of countries in Latin America are trying to bring about significant changes in their economic structure. In doing so, it may truly be said that they are writing off the economic heritage of the colonial period. But it may be said with equal truth that they are also writing off the economic heritage of the late nineteenth and early twentieth centuries.

My purpose in writing this essay is to call attention to certain propositions about economic development since the middle of the nineteenth century which help to give meaning to the economic history of Latin America, and which thereby contribute to the understanding and analysis of today's economic problems in Latin America. It is not my intention to give a rounded sketch of Latin American economic history in this period, but rather to stress certain things which I believe have been inadequately appreciated by the historians. . . .

The opening of new areas took a variety of forms. One of the most striking and significant cases was the settlement and economic development of the interior of the United States, which made the virgin grasslands of the Mississippi

Valley a principal source of cheap food for European consumption. Other grasslands, such as those of Argentina, Australia, and Canada were also newly colonized and developed as suppliers of agricultural products for Europe in the late years of the nineteenth century and early years of the twentieth. In still other cases, areas long before settled, such as southern Russia and India, expanded their production of grain for export as the cheap and regular transportation provided by the railroad and the steamship made it possible for them to reach distant markets with ease. Even without new colonization these regions helped to bring about an expanding economic horizon.

In large part, the territorial expansion of the period 1850–1914 consisted of the opening of continental interiors outside of Europe. This process did not always involve new settlement, as we have noted above. And even where new settlement occurred, it did not always involve large numbers of persons or even permanent occupation. The exploitation of new mineral resources was often achieved by a handful of men in a mining camp or similar outpost, located in an otherwise uninhabited region and connected with markets and supply sources by a single thread of transport running to the nearest seaport. Large settlement was unnecessary. Furthermore, mining camps were often abandoned because resources played out. Such lack of permanence in settlement has been even more common in the exploitation of timber resources than in minerals.

The true significance of the territorial expansion we have been dealing with is not found in the factor of settlement, but rather in the exploitation of new and highly productive natural resources — soils, minerals, and forests. The economic resources of the world were greatly expanded. Moreover, the new additions were important because of their quality as well as their quantity. Thus, like technical improvements, they contributed to a reduction in real costs of production of basic articles of consumption — of staple items of diet, of fuel, of fabricated goods, etc.

Still another broad force making for economic advance after the middle of the nineteenth century was a great increase in population. It is estimated that in 1850 the world contained 1.2 billion inhabitants. The increase thereafter brought the total to an estimated 1.6 billion in 1900, and by 1940 it is calculated that a figure of 2.2 billion was attained. Roughly, it appears that the world's population has doubled in the last hundred years. This multiplication of consumers and of human productive power contributed to the great expansion in world output of goods and services after the middle of the nineteenth century. More people had to be fed and clothed and housed, while on the other side, more people meant more labor for productive effort. . . .

To show how the world setting of the years 1850–1914 influenced economic development in Latin America, we may refer to the economic experience of Argentina. In the middle of the nineteenth century the pulse of economic life in Argentina was faint indeed. The great pampa region was given over mainly to the hunting of wild cattle, as it had been in earlier times, an activity that cannot properly be called stockraising. No effort was made to improve the breeds of stock. Cattle were hunted and slaughtered mostly for their hides, the principal product which could be shipped to export markets. Some tallow was also exported, and a certain amount of salt beef was shipped to the West Indies and Brazil. Economically and technically the sheepraising industry was more advanced than cattle production, and wool exports were on the increase. Corn and wheat were raised, but for domestic consumption rather than for export. Actually Argentina found it necessary to import wheat and flour regularly to meet her requirements. The economy of Argentina around the middle of the nineteenth century was picturesque, but it was hardly productive.

About 1880, however, the pace of economic life began to quicken, and thereafter Argentina underwent a rapid economic transition. Within a generation the economy of Argentina was completely transformed. Possibly the most striking feature of this change was an expansion in grain production and the emergence of Argentina as a major supplier of grain for world markets. In 1870 the total cultivated acreage in Argentina amounted to only about one million acres. By 1895 over 12 million acres were under cultivation, and by 1914 an additional fivefold increase had brought the total to approximately 63 million. Lands formerly idle or used as pasturage were converted to the tillage of wheat, corn, alfalfa, and flax.

Argentina's exports reflected these new trends in crop acreage and production. In the 1880's wheat exports averaged less than 100,000 tons per year, but in the following decade the annual average was in the neighborhood of 1,000,000 tons. When the First World War broke out, Argentina was exporting approximately 2,500,000 tons of wheat each year. In the exportation of corn even greater gains were made in the years just prior to the war. The increased production of flax led to an expansion in linseed exports which rivaled that of corn in percentage terms. Alfalfa, of course, was exported in the form of livestock products.

In the same period Argentina's livestock industry assumed an entirely new character. Successful experiments with refrigerated shipping in the last quarter of the nineteenth century led to the establishment of freezing plants (*frigoríficos*) in Argentina to prepare meat for shipment to expanding overseas markets. A demand was thus created for better grades of meat than could be provided by the wild and semi-wild cattle of the pampas. Improved breeds were imported, such as Shorthorns and Herefords from Great Britain, and mixed with the native stock. A true stockraising industry was developed. To maintain the new improved breeds called for care and vigilance, and thus it became common to fence in ranches rather than to graze cattle on the open range. Further enclosures were made necessary by an intermingling of crop lands and grazing lands, such as arose in connection with the raising of alfalfa on the cattle ranches (*estancias*). Much of the cultivation of crop lands on the ranch was carried out by tenants. Tenancy had been known earlier in Argentina, but it was unimportant until the high tide of immigration began to run in the late years of the nineteenth century. Immigrants and their descendants became the nucleus of a permanent class of tenant farmers, and new types of sharecropping and other rental arrangements were worked out. In scope and nature, tenancy in Argentina in 1914 was a very different institution from the tenancy of 60 years earlier.

Perhaps all these changes in cattle-raising can be summed up by saying that a new industry was created, new types of land use appeared, and new kinds of landowner-tenant relations were fashioned.

We have already observed that a new meat-processing industry was also created in Argentina with the advent of the frigoríficos. This industry expanded rapidly after 1900. Exports of frozen beef rose from about 25,000 tons in 1900 to over 365,000 tons (frozen and chilled beef combined) in 1914. Although the number of frigoríficos was not increased greatly, the plants were expanded in size and capacity, and production was rationalized and standardized. In the year just prior to 1914, also, the frigoríficos were diversifying their output by expanding the production and exportation of canned meat.

Of strategic importance in the expansion of crop and livestock production, and in the development of the meat-processing industry, was the building of railways. In 1860 Argentina had only about 25 miles of railroads. Annual increases occurred thereafter, but it was not until about 1885 that construction was undertaken actively. Between 1885 and 1914 Argentina increased its railway mileage from 2,800 to 21,000. By 1914 most of the trunk lines across the pampa had been completed and a true network of feeder and branch lines had been created. In reaching into the interior, the railroads were typically built when settlement was still sparse, and thus they were a vital force in stimulating internal colonization. Obviously, too, the expanded production of wheat, corn, and meat for overseas markets would have been impossible without the development of a railroad network to haul these products to Rosario, Buenos Aires, and other seaports.

The preceding paragraphs have brought out the main lines of development in Argentina in the generation prior to the First World War. Figures could be cited to show advances in other branches of the economy, such as internal trade, banking operations, and public finance, but we need not pause to do so here. For our purpose it is sufficient to point out that levels of performance all through the economy were raised as Argentina became a vital factor in the world's trade in food products.

What needs to be stressed is that the true historical perspective for Argentina's economic transformation is the pattern of world economic development after the middle of the nineteenth century. It is no exaggeration to say that the new Argentine economy was a product of (1) technical advances in manufacture and in transportation which originated in the industrialized countries, and (2) a workable international economy characterized by relatively great freedom for trade, extensive migrations of people, and a large volume of international investment.

On the technical side, one of the most decisive developments for Argentina was the invention of barbed wire in the United States in the early 1870's. Imported into the pampa country, barbed wire provided an effective fencing material for enclosing improved breeds of livestock. It was important, therefore, in grading up the quality of Argentine beef. Also, the barbed wire fence made it possible to combine crop-raising with grazing in the pampa region, and thus it played its part in the expansion of output of wheat, corn, and alfalfa. In the meat-processing industry, the critically important methods of refrigeration were introduced from abroad, and other technical improvements of substantial influence came in with the American companies that started to operate in 1908. In transportation, the railroad, the steamship, and refrigerated shipping were technical developments of strategic importance for revolutionizing the Argentine economy.

These technical developments, and others which might be mentioned, could not have exerted the influence they did had it not been for the existence of an international economy. The great agricultural production of Argentina — wheat, corn, linseed, and meat — was destined for export markets in the United Kingdom and other industrialized countries of western Europe. Only a small fraction of the output of meat was consumed in Argentina itself. In 1914, for example, about one-eighth of the meat slaughtered was used for domestic consumption. For linseed, the Argentine market was negligible, and almost the whole output was shipped abroad. For wheat and corn the home market was relatively larger, but it hardly took over a third of the annual production in the years prior to 1914. Clearly the bulk of Argentina's productive effort, especially if one takes account of transport and other services connected with exportation, was directed toward foreign markets. Thus the Argentine economy was part of the larger framework of international trade.

The Argentine economy also benefited from immigration. Apart from the United States, which was in a class by itself, Argentina was one of the principal absorbers of European emigrants before the First World War. Immigration began to reach significant proportions in the 1880's, building up to a peak of 260,000 in the year 1889. This was followed by a sharp drop, but by 1896 immigration had recovered to the average levels of the 80's. The upward trend continued, and by 1906 the peak of 1889 had been surpassed. In 1912 almost 380,000 immigrants were recorded.

It is true that not all of these immigrants settled permanently in Argentina. On the basis of emigration figures compiled by the Argentine government it is estimated that roughly 45 per cent of the immigrants returned to their native lands. But even the temporary immigrants made their contribution to Argentina's economic expansion. Indeed, many of the Italians, who together with Spaniards comprised the majority of the immigrants, were seasonal workers who came each year to Argentina to do harvesting. They met a peak requirement without putting a strain on the Argentine economy during the remainder of the year. The movements of these immigrants, who were known as *golondrinas* (swallows), are a striking illustration of the interconnections and flexibility of the international economic order of pre-1914 times.

The annual cycle of migration began in October and November, when the seasonal laborers left their homes in Italy. Cheap steerage transportation brought them to Argentina where most of them first found employment in harvesting flax and wheat in the northern part of the pampa country. Thereafter they followed the course of harvesting to the south, moving much of the time on foot. By February they had begun to work in the harvesting of corn. When this task was finished in April the golondrinas returned to Italy in time to participate in the spring planting. It is, of course, impossible to know how much expansion of crop acreage in Argentina was made possible by these migratory workers. Nevertheless, those who have studied Argentine agricultural development are unanimous in saying that the expansion of acreage and output would have been much less rapid than it was prior to the First World War if the golondrinas had not been available.

Foreign capital also played a prominent part in the economic development of pre-1914 Argentina. Most of the railroads were built by British capital and operated by British companies. In 1914 over 70 per cent of the railway mileage in Argentina was owned and operated by British concerns. Other public utilities, such as streetcar systems and gas plants, were also largely British-owned, although appreciable amounts of German, French, and Italian capital were invested in such enterprises. The Argentine government, and provincial and municipal governments as well, were large borrowers of foreign funds. Here, again, Great Britain was the principal source. Not all of this borrowing, of course, was used for purposes directly relating to Argentina's economic development, but some of it went into the construction of public works which contributed to an expansion in production.

Foreign capital was also a major factor in the development of Argentina's meat-processing industry. The first frigoríficos were established by British capital with a certain amount of Argentine participation. British investment was dominant in this industry until 1908, when one of the larger American packing houses entered the Argentine industry. Three other American packers soon followed suit, and by 1914 American investment was an important feature in the meat-processing industry. This was the only sphere in which American capital was significant in Argentina before the First World War.

Precise estimates of international investment for the period before World War I are hard to come by. All such estimates, however, must be considered subject to a wide margin of error. Nevertheless, some idea of the order of magnitude involved can be gained from the following figures reported by American consular representatives in Buenos Aires. By 1913, British investments in Argentina were valued at $1,551 million; French, $771 million; German, $298 million; Belgian, $180 million; Spanish, $80 million; American, $20 million. These foreign investments in Argentina at the time, aggregated $2.9 billion. Without the inflow of this foreign capital during the preceding 25 to 30 years, Argentina could not possibly have attained the economy it had at the time of the First World War.

The influence of the pre-1914 world economy in shaping economic development in Latin America is probably shown more clearly in Argentina than in any of the other republics. The influence, however, was pervasive, and in most countries it was strongly felt. The pattern of economic specialization in Latin America in 1914 (and, therefore, today) was very different from that of 1850. Some of the differences were clear-cut differences in kind. Others represented changes in degree, but of such large degree that they also amounted to changes in kind.

To illustrate this last proposition we may refer to copper production. Numerous copper deposits in Latin America were worked in the colonial period, and even in pre-Columbian times. Some expansion took place after 1800, but it was not until the latter part of the nineteenth century that the output of copper reached substantial amounts. The decisive factor was the growth of the electrical industry. Prior to the development of this industry, copper was used principally for ornamentation, kitchen utensils, and ships' bottoms. The widespread use of electricity created new, large demands for copper in power transmission, telegraph and telephone lines, electric motors, etc. All over the world new levels of production were attained after the middle of the nineteenth century. The world as a whole produced five times more copper in the last 25 years of the century than it had in the first 50. In South America, Chile and the other copper-producing countries produced about ten times as much copper in the last half of the century as they had in the first half.

It should also be observed that the exploitation of Latin American copper resources since the middle of the nineteenth century has been carried out mostly by foreign capital. Most of the copper mines of Latin America have been operated by American companies. Much American capital, too, has gone into silver-mining in Latin America during the same period. Thus, although silver-mining was an important industry in earlier times, it has assumed new characteristics in the last 100 years. Moreover, the amount of silver production has been carried to entirely new levels. Mexico, the world's leader in silver production, is estimated to have produced about 2 billion ounces from the beginning of the colonial period to 1850, a span of more than 300 years. In the 65 years from 1851 to 1915 Mexico produced 2.2 billion ounces of silver.

In agricultural production, as in mining, new kinds of specialization emerged in Latin America in the late nineteenth and early twentieth centuries. The commercial production of bananas in Middle America did not begin to assume importance until about 1870. Shortly after 1900 the introduction of refrigerated shipping into the banana trade provided a great stimulus to the industry. The principal market for bananas was the United States, and the capital which developed the production and traffic in bananas was almost exclusively American.

The cultivation of coffee in the Caribbean region began as early as the first part of the eighteenth century, but it was not until the late years of the nineteenth that it assumed importance. After 1875, too, a shift occurred in the center of coffee production within the region. Leadership passed from the islands to the north coast of South America and the Pacific Coast of Central America, the two areas where it has remained to the present day.

The world's greatest coffee-producing country is Brazil. Here, again, we find a development mainly of the period after 1875. Not that coffee production was unknown in Brazil before that time. Actually, production and exports were increasing steadily before 1875, and Brazil had come to account for about one-half of world coffee production in that year, whereas 50 years before she had produced less than one-fifth of the world's supply. But it was in the last quarter of the nineteenth century that the industry mushroomed. By 1900 Brazil's exports of coffee were about three times as large as they had been in 1875, and they continued to mount in the early years of this century. Brazil also improved her relative position in world coffee production after 1875. In the years 1895–1899 Brazil produced two-thirds of the world's coffee supply, and in the following five-year period she accounted for as much as three-fourths of the world total.

The great expansion in Brazilian coffee acreage and production took place in the province of Sao Paulo. To this province came large numbers of immigrants, especially from Italy. By 1875 Negro slavery was dying out in Brazil, and it was finally abolished in 1888. Italian immigrants became a principal source of labor for the coffee growers, who, through their own associations and through the provincial government, did much to encourage immigration. Advertising campaigns were conducted in Italy, and free transportation was provided from Italy to Sao Paulo. In 1875 there were very few Italians in Sao Paulo. From 1875 to 1886 about 21,000 arrived, and in the years which followed the flow of Italian immigrants became even larger. From 1887 to 1906 more than 800,000 entered the province of Sao Paulo. Although these Italian immigrants were not the sole source of labor for coffee-raising, they were in a majority and it is extremely unlikely that Brazil could have achieved its great expansion in coffee production without their work.

The foregoing observations on certain Latin American mineral and agricultural products have been offered as illustrations of the importance of the changes which took place after the middle of the nineteenth century — changes which originated mainly in the world economy of the period. Although pertinent data are not always easy to come by, similar patterns of development can be traced for commodities other than those which have been cited. The development of petroleum production in Latin America, as elsewhere, has been essentially confined to the present century. The commercial production of sugar and cotton in Peru, two important items in Peruvian exports nowadays, goes back only to the end of the nineteenth century. The same dating applies to tin-mining in Bolivia. Nitrate production in South America has a somewhat longer commercial history, but it, too, must be regarded as a development of the period since 1880. . . .

This essay has dealt with the world economy of the period 1850–1914 and with its effects on the economic development of Latin America. These effects were in many ways salutary. Certainly the world economy provided the main stimulus for commercial production. However, it should not be inferred that the economic picture in Latin America was a wholly benign one in that period. . . .

Furthermore, the exports of the colonial economies represented by far the major part of their commercial production. In some countries production of food for local consumption may have been larger than production for export, but always a large percentage of the food raised was for subsistence purposes. It did not enter commercial channels. As a general rule, the colonial economies were but small consumers of their own commercial output. Their own consumption tended to be a negligible fraction of their total production. Thus their export markets — viz., the advanced industrial nations — were of the utmost importance to the colonial economies.

Before 1914 this dependence upon export markets did not give rise to acute problems. The consumption of primary materials by the manufacturing countries was an expanding one, and it was little affected by cyclical disturbances in business conditions. Also, the international economic factor functioned smoothly in that period, as we have seen, thus helping to maximize the advantages of international trade for all participating countries.

Nevertheless, it must be recognized that the colonial economies did not share equally with the industrialized nations the fruits of world economic development. The great improvements in technology and the opening up of new, highly productive resources brought about a decrease in real costs of production. Looked at from the standpoint of the consumer, this meant that a given amount of money could buy a larger amount of goods and services. On the average, therefore, people were able to consume more, to live better. In other words, average standards of living were raised.

The gains in standards of living, however, were largely confined to the industrialized countries. . . .

The lag of the colonial economies in standards of living was due to complex causes. In some cases, a deficiency in natural resources, or some other physical condition such as a difficult climate in which to work, played an important part by restricting the total productivity of the whole economy. As a general rule, however, the lag was inherent in the social and political structures of the non-industrialized regions. These conditions were not the same everywhere, but they were similar in fostering a high degree of inequality in income distribution. A large fraction of the national income in the colonial economies went to a handful of persons, while the average income for the bulk of the people was very low. The average person in such areas, therefore, was prevented from increasing his consumption of goods and services by internal social and political conditions.

The economic specialization of the colonial economies, which was a part of the international economic order of pre-1914 days, also bore a share of the responsibility, although probably a small one, for the lower living standards prevailing in such areas. Economic specialization in the form of raw-material production for export fitted in with and strengthened the existing social order in the colonial economies. Economic diversification, on the other hand, tends to weaken such a social order by creating opposing forces — as, for example, in the historical case of the rise of a middle class. The existence of a workable world economy, by creating conditions favorable to the maintenance of one-sided economies in the non-industrialized areas, tended to fortify those very qualities of social and political organization which prevented a wide distribution of national income and thus prevented the enjoyment of higher standards of living by the mass of the people in those areas.

The main causes of the relatively lower standards of living in the colonial economies were internal. But the international economy also operated in the same direction. It is true that in other ways the international economy worked in the direction of spreading higher average standards of living in the colonial economies, but this effect was clearly insufficient to offset the results of internal social and political conditions.

The most expansive, flexible, and workable international economy the world has ever known, therefore, could not insure reasonably high standards of living in Latin America and the other colonial economies. Moreover, in gearing themselves to export markets and to external sources of capital, the Latin American countries became extremely dependent upon the smooth functioning of the world economy. The First World War dealt a blow to the international economy from which it never recovered. Attempts to reconstruct it during the 1920's were only partly successful, and what was reconstructed began to break down again toward the end of that decade. In the depression of the 1930's the remainder of the international economy collapsed completely. It is beyond the scope of this essay to deal with the period subsequent to World War I, but I do want to stress, in concluding, that the economic history of Latin America in the last 30 years is in large part a reflection of the breakdown and collapse of the world economy of the preceding generation.

39. Emperor Pedro II Gave the Banker
Baron Mauá a Hard Time

ANYDA MARCHANT

Miss Marchant is a member of the bar of Virginia and of the Supreme Court who has an abiding interest in the history of Brazil. In 1965 she published the standard work *Viscount Mauá and the Empire of Brazil: A Biography of Irenêo Evangelista de Souza (1813–1889)*. The present selection comes from an earlier statement.

Brazilian historians have never paid much attention to the economic history of Brazil, and, indeed, have generally maintained a deprecatory attitude toward the businessman and his effect on the country. Involved in this neglect is the figure of Irenêo Evangelista de Souza, Baron and Viscount Mauá (1813–1889), still an almost unknown and little-studied man, even though he was Brazil's pioneer railroad builder and industrialist, an imaginative entrepreneur, and a daring innovator in investment banking.

Mauá's business life began when he was an orphan at the age of nine, in the shop of a Portuguese merchant in Rio de Janeiro in 1822. By the time he was sixteen, he had become the confidential clerk of Richard Carruthers, an English merchant and importer of English manufactured goods. Carruthers taught him the English language and English business methods, and introduced him to the variety of industry and the concepts of credit that were commonplace then in England but unknown in Brazil. When Carruthers retired to England in the late 1830's, he left his favorite clerk as managing partner of his business in Rio. By 1840, Irenêo was an important member of the business community of Rio — "Senhor Iréneo," as his English acquaintances seem characteristically to have mispronounced his name. By 1850, he was an industrialist as well as a merchant and ready to embark on investment banking in a large way.

One of the things that the boy Irenêo had learned in Carruther's firm was the idea of financial credit as a basis for industrial expansion. The most important practical result of his first trip to England in 1840 had undoubtedly

From "A New Portrait of Mauá the Banker: A Man of Business in Nineteenth-Century Brazil" by Anyda Marchant, *Hispanic American Historical Review*, 30 (1950), pp. 411–431, passim. Reprinted by permission of the publisher, Duke University Press.

been the founding, in Manchester, of the firm of Carruthers, De Castro and Company, because Carruthers' name was invaluable when his protegé needed to raise capital in England to float many of his early enterprises. Mauá's banking career was based on Carruthers' international connections, for Carruthers had his own web of international credit: his firm in London, a branch of the Manchester house; Carruthers, Souza and Company in Buenos Aires; Carruthers, Dixon and Company in New York. As the old man withdrew more and more from an active part in these businesses, Joseph Reynell de Castro, who was linked to Irenêo by boyhood friendship as well as by business partnership, took over the direction of these English affairs.

Mauá's financial network in Brazil grew so quickly that when he had decided by 1850 to have his own banking house in Rio he easily connected it intimately with the Manchester firm. In July, 1851, he founded the Banco Mauá e Companhia with a capital of ten thousand *contos*. It did not have the power to issue notes, but in heated debates over its charter in the Chamber of Deputies it had won the right to issue drafts and bills of exchange. These drafts and bills were for a term of five days with a value of not less than two hundred *milreis* (about $100 or £25) and their total at any time could not be more than one third of the bank's actual funds.

Mauá had not hesitated after he had the head office going and the business sprang at once into busy life. In 1853, he established branches in São Paulo and in Rio Grande do Sul. In 1851, the bank's deposits had been valued at 214 contos, and by March, 1854, had grown to 950 contos. In 1851, it had held discounted bills for over one thousand contos; in 1854, for over nine thousand. Only the Banco Commercial, with a total sum of over ten thousand contos in discounted bills in 1853 could equal it in volume of business.

Indeed, this very prosperity precipitated Mauá's first conflict with the Emperor and those who advised him on the financial policy of the Empire. . . .

In the period between 1851 and 1856, Brazil was enjoying exceptional prosperity. There was plenty of gold in the country. But the businessmen complained of only one unfavorable element: there was not enough paper money to keep pace with the demands of business. Caught up in the rapidly developing modern methods of business, they were fast leaving behind the idea that the only real money was specie or cash in hand.

The Minister of the Treasury in 1853, however, was more conservative. The political life of Joaquim José Rodrigues Torres, Viscount Itaboraí, dated from the days of the Regency, and he was therefore a man who carried considerable weight with the Emperor, whose favorite financial adviser he was until his death in 1872. He believed that paper money was a snare and a delusion and that real money was specie. It took much persuasion to make him concede that a bank with the right to issue paper money was a boon to the country, and he certainly did not believe that such a bank should be a private concern.

The result of the constant pressure from businessmen was the reluctant giving of his approval to the creation of the third Bank of Brazil as a bank of issue, to be formed from the forced merger of the Banco Commercial with Mauá's bank. Eighty thousand shares were distributed to the shareholders of the two banks. Thirty thousand were offered for public sale in Rio itself, and when more than three thousand eager buyers presented themselves for this lot, offering 10 per cent above the nominal price, the Treasury made a profit of six hundred contos. The new bank finally began operations on August 10, 1854, under the direction of Viscount Paraná.

The fifty thousand shares that Mauá and his shareholders received for their share in the merger did not reconcile Mauá to the high-handed destruction of his house. At first he could not believe that the government really intended to drive his bank out of business, or, rather, absorb it, but Itaboraí soon made it plain that such was the case. . . .

In the late 1850's and early 1860's, as a man in his forties, Mauá was in his prime. He was a man of average height, with brown hair, a fair skin, penetrating dark eyes under straight eyebrows, a long nose and a firmly closed mouth. His very attitude in standing for his portrait distinguished him from the typical Brazilian public man of his day, the inheritor and perpetuator of traditional gestures. He stood straight, energy apparent in every line of his figure, as if he had only paused for a moment to interrupt his all-absorbing affairs, with a trace of preoccupation still in his expressive yet reserved glance.

In private life, he was a family man of very simple tastes, a devoted husband and father. He never went on his frequent long journeys without taking his wife and some of the older children with him. When he was in Rio and came home in the evening preoccupied with financial affairs, he would walk up and down in his wife's sitting room, thinking aloud in English, for one result of his early training was that English had become his personal language, the language in which he thought, preferred to write his letters and, on provocation, swore.

His working day ended late, in the office he kept next to his bedroom, where he sat and wrote letters for half the night. He began a new day sharp at nine o'clock, reaching his downtown office before the clerks, and often in the press of business he forgot to eat. Especially on the days when the steam packets left for Europe, when he had long letters, full of detailed instructions and advice, to prepare for his partners, MacGregor in London and De Castro in Manchester, he stayed at his desk and the porter brought him food from the nearest hotel.

His memory was prodigious, for he could carry in his head the balance sheets and business details of all his enterprises, which at one time numbered twenty or more. He paid good wages and was liberal with bonuses. The old business habits he had learned with Carruthers remained with him, with the concept that a well-paid employee was worth the money in the loyalty and willingness thus obtained. His manner with his employees was a part of his art of managing his affairs. He never shouted at them, even when work was badly done, but instead questioned and advised, and, if he gave orders, gave them in a low voice. If he was dealing with a man expert in some technical field, like metallurgy or shipbuilding, in which he had only his own practical genius to guide him, he never presumed to give orders. In a subject in which he was really a master, like accountancy, he always had a reasonable explanation and the patience to present it in persuading those who worked under him to do as he said. But in spite of these soft manners, there was never any doubt when he had made up his mind.

A delicate, cheerful courtesy was a part of his nature, and he made no distinction between high and low concerning whom should receive such treatment from him. Intrigue, bad faith, personal attack could make him angry and even violent and abusive, but mistakes and a lack of understanding in those under his orders never awoke in him anything but a tolerant patience. His confidence in himself gave him a steadiness and optimism in dealing with other people that overcame all but his most implacable enemies. Unlike the typical public man of his day, raised in the enervating climate of slavery and a society of manners and privilege, he was not touchy, arrogant, autocratic. He was vain of only one thing: his own abilities to solve financial and economic problems. . . . His views were based on a simple idea: one does not develop a vast, wild country, full of natural resources but needing an immense amount of initial outlay, with gold that one carries about in one's pocket. . . .

But if the fortunes of the house remained bright, the general economic scene became darker. Three great international firms with important Brazilian holdings — Baring Brothers, Peabody and Company, and Brown, Shipley and Company — were badly affected by the approaching Civil War in the United States. The Brazilian government also felt the repercussions of bad news nearer at hand. To the south, across the border in the old Banda Oriental, trouble was brewing that was to culminate in 1865 in the Paraguayan War. But, despite every sign of approaching danger, most people in Brazil who had put their money in banks were caught without warning by the sudden financial collapse of 1864 — the "September crisis." It was the most extraordinary monetary crisis, said William Scully, the editor of the *Anglo-Brazilian Times,* that had occurred since the days of Law and the South Sea Bubble. The great firm of Souto and Company closed its doors on September 10, 1864. Its bankruptcy was a signal for runs on all the banking houses. The streets were full of people trying to withdraw their money. The police was called out to control the mobs. So great was the effect of the panic that the Bank of Brazil lost its right to issue paper money, which henceforth became a function exclusively of the Treasury.

Mauá, MacGregor and Company was not spared from the run on the banks, yet, with other houses crashing all around, it weathered the storm. In fact, the firm flourished. Perhaps Mauá saw a grim retribution in the panic, for, as he wrote to Ribeiro, unhappily there "did not exist a public spirit sufficiently energetic, on the part of the governed, to require the governors to march in accordance with public opinion." The governors could therefore go on with their own ideas until the results, which were sometimes catastrophic, as in the case of the September Crisis, convinced them of their mistakes.

Ribeiro was in a position to know how Mauá regarded the inflexible and anachronistic financial policy of "the governors," because as early as 1860 Mauá had thus written to him:

> In place of the ranch-owner, the husbandman, the landowner, the lawyer, and all others keeping what they own unproductively in money in their houses, we must induce them to bring these sums, great and little, and deposit them in the Mauá firm and its branches. When the masses understand the immense advantage of drawing credit from their money, what great sums may accumulate in our branches, to be newly employed with advantage, aiding labor and industry, producing conditions of prosperity in different localities, and what benefits will result from this impetus, and how much faster will march the creation of wealth in our country! In the United States there is a branch bank or agency in all localities where more than fifty houses are built. In England, despite the small size of the country and because of the denser population, there are three thousand seven hundred banks, banking houses and their agencies! which occupy themselves exclusively in concentrating the money capital for useful employment, and from this fact arises the amazing creation of wealth that thus operates to transform these countries day by day. . . .

Optimist as he often appeared to be, he never deceived himself about his Brazil or his place in it. His financial successes in the 1850's and 1860's left him little to desire, but he knew that money alone and the power it gave him were not enough to make for him a comfortable place in the Empire. In Dom Pedro II's Brazil, there was really no place for the combination of gifts and disadvantages that he possessed. To the Emperor himself, Mauá was always a suspect person, a dangerous man because he was powerful and not thoroughly subordinate to the dictates of the Emperor's court. Dom Pedro did not care for moneyed men whose wealth was not tied up in *fazendas* and slaves and who had sources of influence and strength outside the Emperor's sphere of control. Mauá could at times be irritated at the Emperor's coldness and indirectly expressed distrust, but to him the main complaint was the time and energy he had to spend in managing public men, from the Emperor down, whose grasp of finance and whose theories of economic development he thought both rudimentary and out of key with the times and the needs of the country. . . .

With such an attitude, it is not surprising that his greatest successes in creating a banking system based on the deposits of middle-class people were achieved outside Brazil. In Brazil, such a success was necessarily limited, for the middle class was still negligible. In the River Plate countries, however, free of the incubus of slavery, there was more opportunity, and the House of Mauá had never neglected opportunity.

Though doing business in Brazil in spite of the Emperor was a problem large enough to try the patience and exercise the ingenuity of the cleverest banker. Mauá never lacked boldness in looking for money from people who wished speculative profits from what he considered first-rate securities. He wanted capital for investment and he raised it in banking transactions. The loans for his railroads were particularly involved and difficult to manage. The money had to be raised in London for such enterprises; there was not nearly enough capital to be found in Brazil, or at least it was unwilling to come forward. But English investors, putting money into South American railways, were speculating. They did not consider such uses for their money as sound long-term investment and they naturally expected speculative profits. Seen from the other side of the Atlantic, Brazil was a place to make a fortune quickly. Mauá, on the other hand, his head full of the immense economic possibilities of the New World, insisted that such investment could be first-rate and comparable to the best to be found anywhere else in the world. He was aware of the problems presented by slavery, governmental inertia, and a sparse, thinly spread population, but he was also aware of the dangers to sound credit that arose from too much of the get-rich-quick mentality among many of his shareholders.

The wish that he had expressed to Carruthers for leisure for recreation and

European travel could not be fulfilled for several years. His manifold interests in the River Plate and, indeed, all his financial affairs were now gradually being drawn into the involvement of the Empire and the whole River Plate region in the preliminaries of the Paraguayan War. In 1864, he apparently saw no fruitful continuation of the existing situation, and, no longer postponing action every few months as each new crisis arose, broke off his affairs abruptly. He had a new scheme in mind — the merger of his house with the London and Brazilian Bank.

Much to the surprise of the international money market, he arranged the merger in London to create a new company to be known as the London, Brazilian and Mauá Bank. It was to be an international house, with branches in Portugal, Argentina, and Uruguay. For Mauá, the merger with one of the most solid banking houses of the period would have consolidated all his banking operations in Argentina, Uruguay, and Brazil. Each of the countries except Brazil approved the charter within a few days, but for effectiveness in Brazil approval by the Emperor's government was also needed.

Perhaps it was the very fact of the merger's concentrating tremendous power in the River Plate countries in Mauá's hands that frightened the Emperor's government. And that government was easily alarmed at this period as it found itself with fewer and fewer ways of escape from the events that were leading it into its first foreign war. The Emperor's Council of State thought about the matter for two months. In the end, the Council, ignoring the considerable strength that the new company would have given the Empire at a time when it needed aid in international affairs, rejected the charter.

It was the final triumph of the men of conservative beliefs in regard to banking who were in the Emperor's government. The subsequent history of Mauá's banking schemes, especially in the River Plate, merely emphasized this rejection by the Brazilian government of his theories of banking practice. Yet his banking house, in spite of consistent official disfavor and because of the vigor and ingenuity that he brought to its management, only collapsed, in 1875, after a long struggle and as a result of the disastrous effects on the Empire itself of the Paraguayan War and the disintegration of the slave-based economy. When that collapse came, there was then left, not merely the debris of Mauá's financial structure but of an epoch in the history of Brazil.

40. *Brazilian Entrepreneurs Adopt the British Habit of Work*

RICHARD GRAHAM

Mauá and the other Brazilians who were determined to modernize their country realized that more was needed than capital and technology. Constant labor and a belief in the value of toil were just as important. They saw that Britain exemplified this spirit. The British "served them as their model," as Professor Richard Graham of the University of Texas states in his wide-ranging and detailed account of how the Brazilian Empire was started on the path of modernization by a few vigorous entrepreneurs despite the opposition and lethargy of Pedro II and the traditional society there based on land.

In another study, Professor Graham shows that the influence of advanced countries on underdeveloped countries has a contemporary relevance, particularly for Americans whether they realize it or not: "Especially noticeable is an inability to understand the degree to which people in underdeveloped countries are constantly barraged with American attitudes, beliefs, and values that are alien to their culture and tend to rend the fabric of their societies. . . . The initiation of satellite communication systems will tend to exacerbate this condition still further, yet most Americans remain unaware of this dimension of their expansive force. . . . While the landing of United States Marines or other exertion of overt political power over recalcitrant regions has always attracted attention, much more pervasive and much more significant has been the degree to which the United States exerts control through modern sepoys who rule their countries in behalf of the United States.*

The ideas and attitudes of these British-influenced entrepreneurs are a final aspect of this inquiry. They were caught up by the idea of capitalism, by the belief in industrialization, and by a faith in work and practicality. Once again, it is not suggested here that Britain was the only place to which entrepreneurs could turn for these concepts. Rather, the point is that these men, whom we have chosen to examine because of their British connexions, were dominated

From *Britain and the Onset of Modernization of Brazil, 1850–1914* by Richard Graham (Cambridge, England: Cambridge University Press, 1968), pp. 207–215, *passim.* Reprinted by permission.
* Richard Graham, "Sepoys and Imperialists: Techniques of British Power in Nineteenth-Century Brazil," *Inter-American Economic Affairs,* 23 (1969), no. 1, pp. 23–24.

by these beliefs. Having said this, the fact remains that they often did turn to Britain for reinforcement of their guiding principles.

Attitudes regarding "risk-taking" and "profit-making" are evidently of key importance to development. We have noted how the willingness to risk money for the sake of possible profits lay at the root of the dynamic and creative aspects of the Victorian age. This spirit stood in direct opposition to the static agrarian life of Brazil, where profits were still considered akin to usury. As Mauá complained, it was generally thought that the state would be defrauded if the recipient of a government contract did not lose on his venture. He believed that, on the contrary, profit was the driving force of all progress: "The powerful cooperation of labor and capital for the creation of wealth can only be obtained with the indispensable condition of finding corresponding remuneration."

Industrialization was the goal toward which capitalism would impel the nation. Few things made André Rebouças angrier than the oft-repeated statement that Brazil must not industrialize because it was an "essentially agricultural" nation. If there were any really agricultural country, he said, it was England, "where they love rural life above everything else." Since real agricultural development was obviously unlikely in Brazil under the then existing system, it was ridiculous to oppose industry. Similarly, the *barão* do Penedo, despite his connexions with the more traditional sectors in Brazil, was sufficiently influenced by his long residence in London as Brazilian minister and his close connexions with the British financial and business community to believe in industrialization and oppose the idea that Brazil was "destined to have an exclusively agricultural setup." He maintained that "nothing can deny" Brazil's "legitimate ambitions to enter the area of manufacturing." Industry, he felt, was the road to perfection: it was the "agent of man's productive power" and would link Brazil to "the immense chain of civilization's achievements." It was for this reason that he insisted that his country should take a full part in the International Exposition of 1862, for he maintained the Brazilian government should imitate England by taking a more direct interest in the nation's industrial development.

The best evidence of their belief in industrialization and capitalism, of course, was precisely the fact that these men were entrepreneurs. Mauá, as we have seen, adopted the basic principles of capitalistic economic organization. He used money to make profits and he understood the nature of credit. He saw the superiority of industry as an economic activity both for the investor and for the nation. He welcomed the use of new technological processes, casting traditional methods aside. Finally, he took risks where necessary and undertook projects without assurance of success. As Joaquim Nabuco later said, his "great breadth of interests and industrial courage" made him "a powerful factor in the opening up and progress of our country."

André and Antônio Rebouças also felt that the nation would be better served by profit-making entrepreneurs than by publicly owned establishments. Furthermore, although they concentrated on railroads, dock companies, and timberlands development, a belief in industrialization was implicit in most of their activities. André campaigned for the creation of central sugar factories as a move in this direction: his ideal was for Brazil to export nothing but manufactured goods, and the first step toward this goal, he argued, would be domestic processing of Brazil's raw materials, whether refined sugar, woven cloth, finished cigars and cigarettes, or chocolate. Furthermore, he actively considered organizing a company to reopen an abandoned iron works, thus laying the basis for further industrial growth. As a teacher at the engineering school from the 1860s until the end of the empire — a position through which he influenced a whole generation of young "doers" with whom he kept in touch for years afterwards — he was recognized as the "representative of new ideas" and a spokesman for the belief in capitalism and industrialism. . . .

Another quality which characterized these entrepreneurs was their belief in the value of work. The traditional society which they sought to destroy had not inculcated the value of constant toil. In the slave society of mid-nineteenth-century Brazil, work was equated with demeaned status, and not even poverty could drive respectable people to it. To suggest to them the possibility of employment in commerce or industry was to insult them, and one foreign observer noted that "Labor is [considered] degrading and . . . custom, instead of honoring useful toil, withholds all stimulus to exertion." The society as a whole considered inner dignity, social pleasure, intellectual exercise, or spiritual rewards a greater good than hard, disciplined work. Although a cynical observer on Copacabana beach may today object that the ideal of work has still made little progress in Brazil, the fact is that the urban-industrial complexes there would have been impossible if the attitudes of the planter and slave had not been significantly altered in the last one hundred years.

The elevation of work into a positive good is one of the distinctive qualities of modernizing groups: there is so much to do, and still so few ready to do it. And not only does work contribute to modernization, but, with the increasing mobility modernization brings on, it can now lead to tangible rewards on earth. The belief in the virtue of work thus acquires a peculiarly middle-class ring. Those who hope for further upward movement or fear slippage downward must engage in unrelieved effort; yet, to assert their distinctive position and justify their single-minded concentration, the means becomes the end and it is work itself that seems to make life worth living. Simultaneously, no idea can be more conveniently preached to their employees than that the latter should toil hard and constantly. Entrepreneurs believed industrious qualities would help forge a modern nation, and the British served them as a model. André Rebouças recorded with great pride that a British engineer had said he "works like an Englishman."

The gospel of work was a characteristic theme of the Victorian era. It was said in England that "the duty of work is universal. . . . No man on God's earth has a right to be idle." Diligence was linked to the idea of Christian vocation, the love of neighbor, and the workmanship of God. Typical were the books of Samuel Smiles, who extolled the virtue of work and urged its adoption by everyone as a guiding principle of life. His most famous work, published in 1859, was entitled *Self-Help,* and its "chief object," he wrote, was "to stimulate youths to apply themselves diligently to right pursuits." He told them that "fortune is usually on the side of the industrious," and that great results were to be expected from "sheer industry and perseverance." He saw that "the men who have most moved the world have not been so much men of genius, strictly so called, as men of . . . untiring perseverance; not so often the gifted . . . as those who have applied themselves diligently to their work. . . . It is indeed marvellous what continuous application will effect in the commonest of things." Besides other titles such as *Character* (1871), *Thrift* (1875), and *Duty* (1880), there was one significantly entitled *Life and Labour* (1887). It began with the statement that "Every man worth calling a man should be willing and able to work."

In Brazil Smiles and his countrymen filled the same pulpit. J. J. Aubertin, the popular superintendent of the São Paulo Railway, announced that "the man who has too much pride to work, should also be too proud to live," adding that "he who works enjoys happiness and health; poverty and misfortune are the natural attribute of the lazy man." The books of Samuel Smiles were translated into Portuguese and were being sold in Rio de Janeiro in the 1880s. A questionnaire sent out by a Brazilian writer to persons who grew up during the last quarter of the nineteenth century turned up several who had read Smiles in that era. One of them stated that as a boy he had read "all the books of Samuel Smiles" and another said he had even been taught to admire Smiles in school.

Brazilian entrepreneurs and innovators — especially those influenced by the British — continued the task of proselytizing. Mauá asserted that *"work* is the perennial fountain of public prosperity, and is not only worthy of . . . protection, but even of high honor." His coat of arms expressed his idea by the legend, *Labor improbus omnia vincis.* Tavares Bastos criticized the first settlers in Brazil because they were "anxious for wealth earned without the hallowed sweat of toil," and a merchant insisted that "labor is ennobling" and the basis of all manly independence. André Rebouças put it this way: "When

God created the world He said to the world: move; when God created man He said to him: work."

These entrepreneurs saw that one of the obstacles to the success of their vision was the concept of work as degrading. The lower classes must learn that work was a privilege to be performed joyfully — no belief could be more helpful to the industrialist. Luís Tarqüínio leveled his guns at those "unfortunates, ignorant of the true meaning of labor, who prefer to suffer the greatest deprivations . . . rather than engage in work which they consider proper only for Negroes. . . . They forget that only ability entitles a person to choose his work." Another Anglophile felt São Paulo was a land of promise, since the poor there did not hesitate to encourage their children toward the mechanical arts, "thus instilling in their spirit a love of honest work." In fact, work was good for the poor and contributed to their moral improvement. Even the victims of a drought in Brazil's northeast needed not alms, but work, said André Rebouças. Another writer held up the end-of-century British poor laws as an example for post-abolition Brazil: "Who would be helped must work"; therefore, England had "work houses" instead of "poor houses." The gospel of work served the same needs in Brazil as it had in Britain.

The importance of practical, technical education was a direct corollary of the gospel of work. The aversion to manual labor had been reinforced by the purely literary and classical nature of colonial education and the similar alienation of the nineteenth-century law academies from the practical necessities of the country. André Rebouças put forward the idea that "We must educate the growing generation . . . for work. . . . Up to now education has been merely political: from the academy of law to the electoral colleges . . . to national parliament. Therefore [we have] this general repugnance for productive work." He attacked the law schools and their rhetorical training, which robbed Brazil of its best elements, teaching the planters' sons nothing of value. Another industrialist, Antônio Felício dos Santos, echoed this view saying that "Brazil's plight is to have been always governed by the Academies, from which one goes to the Privy Council without any interval spent in the practice and experience of business."

In contrast, André Rebouças pointed to the "eminently practical and industrious quality which constitutes the incontestable superiority of the Anglo-Saxon race." The *barão* de Jaceguai pointed with approval to the useful instruction given British naval officers. Having spent some time as naval attaché in London, he observed "the traditional English system of trusting more in practice than in theory" and felt that this was "one more proof of the incomparable practical sense of the English." He eventually became director of the Brazilian naval academy and tried to modify its curriculum in this direction.

The essentially pragmatic spirit of the British — which Nabuco described as the "realistic, practical, positive attitude" impelling their "spirit of progress" — was also felt through the various English secondary schools set up in Brazil. Although many of them were for girls, others were for boys and exercised a great influence. One of them was the Ginásio Anglo-Brasileiro founded in 1899 in São Paulo by Charles W. Armstrong. By 1910 the school had opened a branch in Rio de Janeiro which advertised that it followed "the example of the best schools of England.". . . Entrepreneurs believed in concrete results and measurable effectiveness, and the English schools in São Paulo and Rio worked to develop these qualities. These men preached the gospel of work to themselves and to their employees and so were led not only to read Samuel Smiles but to sound like him. They believed in industrial-capitalism by definition, and close contact with the British strengthened their conviction that this was the way to progress. Although this contact cannot explain why they were entrepreneurs nor be considered the cause of their failure or success, the British exerted a large influence upon these Brazilians.

Whether their principal interest was in railway lines, shipping companies, harbor works, iron foundries, food processing, timberlands, urban improvements, or banking institutions, their contact with the British helped shape the direction of their work. The British impact upon these restless and creative innovators may be considered one of the most intriguing aspects of the British role within the process of modernization in Brazil.

41. *There Was No Lack of Individual Enterprise among the Colombian Upper Class*

FRANK SAFFORD

Professor Frank Safford of Northwestern University is one of the growing group of historians who have explored Colombian archives and libraries for new facts and insights. Here is part of his larger treatment of the general economic history centering on the nineteenth century.

Most English language writings on Latin American economy in the nineteenth century have tended to stress the role of foreign and particularly British and

From "Foreign and National Enterprise in Nineteenth-Century Colombia" by Frank Safford, *Business History Review,* 39 (1965), pp. 503–526, passim. Reprinted by permission.

American innovators. British bankers and mining companies and American engineers and *empresarios* figure strongly in the literature. The native upper class generally is pictured as the passive recipient of Anglo-American technical and organizational advances.

There can be no doubt that foreign investors and innovators did play an important role in many of the Latin American countries, and particularly in Argentina, Brazil, Peru, and Mexico. British capital and technology rejuvenated the mining industries of Mexico, Peru, and Bolivia. A British company took control of and organized the guano fertilizer industry in Peru. British banks, railways, and utilities dominated Argentina, Brazil, and Mexico. In Peru and Chile, the figure of the American railroad empresario Henry Meiggs clearly stands out.

Nevertheless, investigation of one case, that of Colombia, indicates that native entrepreneurs matched foreign innovators step-for-step. Secondly, it appears that native entrepreneurial leadership came almost entirely from the established landed upper class. There is no clear evidence that a struggling minority group — whether foreign-born or native — took business leadership because of deprivation of status within Colombian society or for any other emotional reasons.

In comparing the activities of foreign and native entrepreneurs in Colombia, this article will discuss their respective roles in new enterprises, evaluate their relative strengths and weaknesses, and examine the nature of their relations. The article also suggests explanations of the differing economic roles of some of the various regional groups within the Colombian society.

In the nineteenth century, Colombia stood in the middle rank of Latin American countries. Her population, through most of the nineteenth century, was the third largest in Latin America — rising from slightly over 1,600,000 in the 1830's to more than 2,200,000 at mid-century, to more than 4,100,000 in 1895. Only in the 1890's did the population of Argentina begin to surpass that of Colombia. Aside from being large in absolute size, Colombia's population was also relatively dense by New World standards. . . . On the other hand, Colombia was not distinguished by impressive urban centers. The capital at Bogotá had by far the largest urban population, growing from 20,000 to 100,000 during the nineteenth century. But at no time was Bogotá more than half the size of Mexico City, Havana, Rio, or Buenos Aires. Even in the most densely populated regions the Colombian population was markedly rural.

Despite her relatively large and dense population, Colombia was commercially poor. In value of foreign trade between 1821 and 1880 she usually ranked no higher than seventh or eighth among Latin American countries. . . .

Weakness in foreign trade meant that Colombia lacked capital, both public and private, as the export economy in most of Latin America provided the greatest increments of capital and credit in the nineteenth century. Colombia's national revenues, tied like those of other Latin American countries to customs collections, stood at about the same rank as her foreign trade. . . .

The private sector was almost equally poor. By the standards of Rio, or Mexico, or Lima, the Colombian upper class was an indigent lot indeed. Upper-class incomes in Bogotá in the first half of the nineteenth century frequently amounted to no more than $5,000 per annum, and the number of individuals in Bogotá with a capital of more than $100,000 could be counted on the fingers of one hand. Incomes of the middle and lower classes were correspondingly small. The small middle class, composed of lower army officers, small tradesmen, and artisans, earned between $150 and $700 per year. The great mass of agricultural labor, as well as domestic servants and unskilled urban labor, earned between $70 and $75 per year. . . .

Colombia's poverty can be explained largely as a consequence of the country's geographical situation. Colombia lies entirely within the tropics, from the equator to 13 degrees north latitude; the country below 3,000 feet tends to be hot and uncomfortable. In the nineteenth century, the "hot country" presented a constant danger of death by fever and dysentery. The great bulk of Colombia's population for this reason chose to live in the cooler climate created by the three branches of the Andes running on a southwest-to-northeast axis from the Ecuadorean border to the Caribbean. . . .

On the other hand, the three mountain chains badly divided the country. Each of the three principal chains breaks into many subbranches, each of which rises sharply above deep-running mountain gorges or rivers. Most of the country's main-traveled roads pitched off down the sides of steep mountain ranges, taking gradients which only mules could negotiate. Tropical rain storms, occurring at various times in the year but in seasons covering half the year, frequently washed out whatever trails had been cut through mountainous regions. In many places, mules sank to their girths in mudholes. . . .

The condition of the mountain roads also affected transportation over relatively level territory. As the most important roads could be used only by mules, Colombians tended to send goods by muleback even in the occasional places where the terrain made the use of carts possible. Only slowly did wheeled vehicles come into use in the few places where this was practicable. As a result, land transportation costs remained high even in level places, generally above 25 cents per ton mile in the middle of the nineteenth century.

Such transportation conditions naturally inhibited the development of a national market. . . . The existence of a national market, at least for some manufactures, was made possible by the fact that until the end of the 1840's, the various provinces of New Granada were as isolated from the outside world as from each other. The interior provinces' one route for foreign trade was the Magdalena River. Until 1849, the 600 miles from the Caribbean coast to the interior port of Honda were served primarily by keelboats poled by boatmen against a current which in many places was both strong and treacherous. Using the poled boats, it cost about twice as much to bring goods to Honda up the river from the Caribbean as down the trail from Bogotá. This fact effectively eliminated Cartagena and other towns of the Caribbean coast from the national market. But it also made it possible for entrepreneurs to conceive of competing with European manufactures in the interior provinces, poor and rugged as these were.

On the assumption that the traditional interior market would remain more or less intact, the government of New Granada up to the 1840's attempted to encourage national manufacturing. Between 1821 and 1845, tariffs were moderately protective. Enterprises considered particularly meritorious were conceded loans from the government's exiguous treasury. Entrepreneurs attempting to develop internal communications and manufacturing were granted limited monopoly privileges, of ten to twenty-five years in duration. Those granted the privileges were given sole right to produce a commodity by a modern factory process; traditional cottage manufactures were not barred, nor were imported goods.

The more or less nationalist bent of the earlier period gave way during the 1840's to free trade policies which prevailed for most of the rest of the century. The free trade current was encouraged by the mediocre showing of local manufacturers, the growing efficiency of overseas competitors, the expanding European market for tropical products, and the influence of English policy. But an important factor was the breakdown of the interior's geographical protection with the definitive establishment of steamboats on the Magdalena River and in ocean transportation in the middle of the nineteenth century. These improvements in marine transportation made it cheaper to bring goods to the western provinces from Liverpool than from Bogotá. Thus, New Granada's national market became fragmented, and each segment of the interior carried on its principal economic dealing with Europe.

Colombian businessmen naturally responded to these changing conditions. Before 1845, their energies were directed to a notable extent toward domestic agriculture and manufacturing; after 1845 they tended to focus more on the production and export of tropical products and on the importation of foreign manufactures. The interior provinces, previously dependent upon the export of gold to earn foreign exchange, now could rely in addition on tobacco, cinchona bark, and many other minor commodities to make their payments to

Europe. Though most of the leading Colombian agricultural export commodities between 1845 and 1870 had only fleeting success in European markets, the export economy throughout this period remained a mania among the Colombian upper class. After persistent experimentation with various commodities, Colombian exporters finally found a winner in coffee in the years after 1865. The focus of entrepreneurial activity, therefore, changed radically during the nineteenth century, moving from an emphasis on internal development in the early decades to virtually single-minded devotion to the export economy in the second half of the century.

FOREIGN ENTERPRISE

From the first moments of Colombian independence, the government made efforts to promote the immigration of Europeans. Upper-class politicians, against the opposition of the church, legislated a species of religious toleration; naturalization was permitted after only two years' residence; land was granted to immigrants on easy terms. Despite these measures, Europeans migrated to Colombia in relatively small numbers during the nineteenth century. At mid-century, there were fewer than 850 Europeans and North Americans in Colombia. Nevertheless, these few immigrants had an influence disproportionate to their numbers because most of them were more-or-less skilled. . . .

Thus, while the number of foreigners in Colombia was not large, they were almost all well-endowed either with capital or skills, and therefore played an important part in local enterprise.

Foreign enterprisers were particularly prominent in Colombia at the beginning of the republican period. During the 1820's English adventurers in particular flocked in great numbers, each apparently expecting to find his own El Dorado. In the Wars of Independence some 4,000 soldiers from the British Isles had come to fight for the patriots; a number of their officers stayed in Colombia to undertake various enterprises. Even more important in economic activities, however, were the many merchants who came from England, Jamaica, and the United States, and established themselves in most of Colombia's ports, some of them arriving well before the Spanish armies had been driven from the field. After Colombian independence was assured, significant British and other foreign investments were made in mining, manufacturing, and communications. . . .

With the exception of ventures in agriculture and the export-import trade, most of the early British enterprises failed. In some cases they were afflicted by political problems. Colombia's nineteenth century was characterized by almost continuously acrid political disputes between the Liberal and Conservative parties. These erupted in major civil disturbances or in civil war. . . .

The early wars, particularly during the 1820's and 1830's, appear to have caused some direct losses to foreign businessmen, through forced contributions or seizure of property. But after 1841, foreigners generally were free from arbitrary exactions. This was in part because of the latent threat of gunboat diplomacy on the part of the British and United States governments, but even more because of Colombia's desire to attract foreign capital. . . .

Foreign businessmen did occasionally suffer from discrimination. . . . It appears that discrimination against foreign empresarios lessened as the early spirit of economic nationalism subsided and Manchesterian liberalism came to the fore. In steamboat navigation on the Magdalena River, for example, the Colombian government in the early period proved sporadically jealous of the rights of nationals. Juan Bernardo Elbers, after having invested more than $250,000 in his steamboat enterprise between 1823 and 1827, was suddenly stripped of his monopoly privilege in 1829. Though the privilege was restored to Elbers in 1831, it was again abrogated in 1837, in part because he had not provided the service stipulated, but also because a competing Colombian enterprise was being organized. Later, between 1846 and 1852, Colombian law forbade the navigation of foreign-owned vessels on national waters. During the 1850's, however, a complete reversal of policy occurred, and between 1855 and 1864 a large proportion of the river steamboats were foreign-owned and operated. Generally speaking, both government policy and public opinion were highly receptive to foreign enterprise, particularly between 1850 and 1880.

Perhaps as important as political discrimination in deterring foreign enterprise was the difficulty of adjusting to a Spanish, Roman Catholic cultural environment. Some American businessmen found it hard to abide the rigid Roman Catholicism which characterized Bogotá and many other towns in the Colombian interior. Hostility was occasionally quite marked among the priesthood and the masses over which they held sway.

But foreign businessmen were generally well received by Bogotá's upper class. Because of their cultural equipment, many foreigners who arrived in Colombia with little capital quickly became important in economic activities and consequently members of the upper class. Clerk or artisan to capitalist within a decade was a familiar story for those European fortune-seekers who came to Colombia in the nineteenth century. Those who had the wit to adjust sufficiently to the Colombian style were among the most respected people in the country, and precisely because of their economic acumen.

The most troublesome cultural problem for foreign businessmen was presented by traditional Spanish catch-as-catch-can economic relations. Anglo-

American businessmen who were accustomed to prompt payment of obligations found Colombian casualness on this point somewhat wearing.

Some foreign entrepreneurs also had difficulty in handling native labor. One of the British managers of the salt mines of Zipaquirá was murdered, allegedly because he had refused to permit workers to steal salt. John Steuart, who attempted to establish a hat factory in Bogotá in 1837, complained that Colombian workers were dilatory, did not follow instructions, lied and stole, and could not be won over by fair treatment.

Many other foreign observers, however, testified that Colombian labor, properly trained, promptly paid, and patiently treated, could be loyal, hardworking, and quite productive. The supposed indolence of the lower class often was attributed to a tradition of mistreatment at the hands of employers or to wages which were too low to offer an incentive for work. Charles Biddle stated that he had never known a "more hard-working and industrious people . . . whilst they have a prospect of reward to stimulate them . . . but like the inhabitants of all other countries they are not fond of working for amusement." North American workmen, he noted, would not perform half the labor of a Granadan worker for double the pay. J. D. Powles, an English merchant of long experience in New Granada, declared that Colombian workers would do anything that could reasonably be expected of them, as long as they were paid regularly, "a point of great interest to them.". . .

Most of the early foreign enterprises failed not so much for cultural or political reasons as for purely economic ones. Foreign investors and managers, in the spirit of inflated optimism which characterized most British investments in newly independent Latin America as a whole, had greatly overestimated Colombia's immediate economic potential during the 1820's. . . . Others failed simply because the market and the volume of trade in Colombia were so small. . . .

NATIONAL ENTERPRISE

Just as the flow of European businessmen slowed to a trickle, so did that of European capital. At the same time, in periods of political disturbance the larger Colombian capitalists transferred their capital from Bogotá to foreign parts or to regions of the country which were not affected by civil wars. As a result, the area with the greatest population, around Bogotá, fell into a deep depression during the 1830's. In this region, prices fell to half their levels of the 1820's, and interest rates in Bogotá rose to between 2 and 5 per cent per month.

It was in this period of acute depression, just as the interest of foreign capitalists was flagging, that the Colombian upper class took up the burden of entrepreneurial leadership. After 1830, foreigners, particularly Englishmen, Germans, and Americans, continued to supply technical skills. But the Colombian elite provided most of the capital and business organization. It is worth emphasizing that these entrepreneurial Colombians were distinctly upper class — of traditionally respected landed and commercial families. There is no evidence whatsoever of a pariah, or deprived minority, group within Colombian society assuming entrepreneurial leadership. Whether they came from Bogotá or from Medellín, Popayán, or other provincial towns, Colombia's business leaders until at least 1890 were almost entirely members of families whose upper-class position had been established before the end of the colonial period and was recognized throughout New Granada.

Early examples of elite entrepreneurial leadership can be found in efforts to establish modern factory manufacturing in the Bogotá area between 1830 and 1845. The participants in the local manufacturing movement of this period were predominantly large landowners in the Bogotá region and descendants of colonial administrators. . . .

In retrospect, some of these ventures appear suicidal — particularly given the poor state of Colombian communications and the rapid improvements being made in transportation systems and in manufacturing technique in England. At the time, however, Bogotá's upper-class enterprisers undoubtedly found encouragement in the protection afforded by high transportation costs up the Magdalena River. The motive of economic patriotism also entered in, many Colombian leaders believing that the country should remain behind in no type of economic activity. There was also a strong element of *noblesse oblige* — the establishment of factories would provide useful employment to the many beggars and vagrants in the capital, and thus serve to "moralize" the society. The elite expected, however, to make a profit while doing their moralizing. In the latter part of the 1830's, all of Bogotá's industrialists joined in asking the Colombian Congress to pass a law establishing forced apprenticeship in factories, child labor being cheaper than adult. . . .

It is not entirely clear what reasoning went into the selection of the various types of manufacture tried by the Bogotá elite. In many cases raw materials were readily available: coal and iron ore for the ironworks, high quality clay and feldspar for china, abundant wool for the woolen mill, and rags and forests for paper. Cotton yarn, on the other hand, was not obtainable by local mill-owners in the quality or at the low cost possible for English competitors. The glass factory lacked an adequate supply of potash, sodium, and lead oxide, and most of these materials had to be imported.

Market conditions were not especially favorable for the manufacturers.

Iron had a potential market in all types of agriculture, but it had to be developed, as the high cost of imported iron in the colonial period had conditioned Colombians to the use of wooden substitutes. Glassware, similarly, had not yet come into general use; and the upper classes which might use it represented only a tiny proportion of the population. China and woolen textiles, though more generally consumed, had to compete with the prestige of goods manufactured in Europe. The crude cotton textiles manufactured in Bogotá had a broad potential market among the large peasant class. But cottons faced devastating competition from lower-priced British cloth. In addition, cottage weavers in the province of El Socorro already supplied most of the domestic market with crude cottons. As cotton was grown in El Socorro, while it had to be carried some 200 miles to Bogotá, the cottage weavers could hold their own with the small mill in the capital.

The factories established in Bogotá between 1821 and 1860 were modest by comparison with European and North American establishments. Capital in the larger plants amounted to no more than $50,000. This investment, measured in dollars, was smaller than that found in contemporary mills in the United States. In addition, this amount of capital would buy much less equipment in Bogotá because of the high cost of transporting machinery by mule (or by teams of Indian bearers in the case of pieces over 250 pounds) up the steep mountain road from Honda to Bogotá. One of the largest plants, a water-powered cotton mill, had only fifteen looms. . . .

Though the Bogotá elite assumed clear leadership in early manufacturing enterprises, none of them was completely free from foreign participation. The first industrial venture of the Colombians was to buy out and reorganize an ironworks established by a French physician, Bernard Daste, after its first years of failure in the 1820's. The ironworks was finally made profitable during the 1830's through the efforts of an English merchant, Robert Bunch. The bulk of the capital, and the organization of distribution, however, were supplied by the Bogotá upper class. The china factory established in the 1830's also featured English technical aid in cooperation with Colombian capital. First experiments in firing were made with foreign help, but the enterprise was carried to success through the perseverance of a single Bogotá aristocrat, Nicolás Leiva. The Bogotá firm of Sánchez, Ponce initially used foreign technical assistance, particularly in purchasing machinery, in founding their woolen mill in 1856. Some other enterprises involving foreign technicians and local capital did not work out well. A glass factory in Bogotá failed in part for lack of a sufficient market, but also because French glassworkers imported for the purpose proved completely ungovernable.

While it is true that in most areas Colombians relied heavily on foreigners for technical advice, they also showed considerable interest in undertaking their own mechanical innovations. Beginning in 1841, annual industrial fairs were held in Bogotá, in which prizes were given for new inventions and productions. It cannot be claimed that any of the inventions submitted were of world-shaking importance, but the interest and the activity were there.

Though practically all Colombian economic innovation involved borrowing and adapting European techniques, not all new developments required the intervention of foreign personnel. Banking, for example, was largely home-grown. One of the first important experiments with banking was the establishment in Bogotá between 1839 and 1841 of a "house of exchange and discount." This rather primitive commercial bank was founded by Judas Tadeo Land-ínez, a businessman-politician from the backward interior provincial town of Tunja. It is not clear how Landínez happened to conceive of this project. . . . Aided by a loan of $450,000 from Antioquia, Landínez' operations took on considerable scale. During the year of 1841, Landínez carried on transactions involving a great proportion of the real property surrounding Bogotá in a radius of a hundred miles — buying haciendas, houses, shares in factories or other companies at inflated prices and interest rates, and then selling them again. Landínez' speculation soon whirled out of control, and he went into bankruptcy with $2,000,000 in obligations and only $500,000 in assets. In the process he brought most of the Bogotá elite to temporary ruin; property not lost directly in Landínez' crash was wasted in dozens of prolonged and complicated lawsuits. Perhaps Bogotá's bitter experience with Landínez' brief but heady speculations was one factor in delaying the establishment of other commercial banks.

After the Landínez episode, Bogotá's next experiment with credit institutions was the creation of a savings bank. . . . The Bogotá savings bank was founded as an institution to be administered by the upper class on behalf of the lower. The bank was to encourage the saving habit among the poor, who otherwise would dribble away their few reals in the consumption of aguardiente. In theory the bank's funds were to go to worthy, but small, enterprises — no loan could exceed 1,000 pesos.

The Bogotá elite gave the bank strong administrative support. The first junta of administrators was composed of sixteen of the most prestigious politicians, hacendados, and merchant-capitalists in the capital; the director was the Minister of Finance, Lino de Pombo, and his assistants included the Archbishop of Bogotá. The aristocratic administrators devoted their Sundays, by turns, to receiving deposits. The upper class at first also gave the bank financial support, with merchants and other elite types making some relatively large deposits. By the end of the 1850's, however, few large merchants were contributing, and the bulk of the fund was provided by the middle artisan class. In 1859, its fourteenth year, the savings bank had capital amounting to only a little more than $200,000.

Throughout the period from 1821 to 1870, Colombian merchants and politicians sporadically discussed the desirability of forming national banks of issue, mortgage banks, and other commercial banks. These innovations were believed to be of pressing importance because much of the interior chronically suffered from a shortage of circulating media, as well as of credit. All of the projects before 1870 failed, however, because civil wars stripped the national government and many private citizens of the capital or foreign credit needed to establish an initial fund. . . .

The first commercial banks in Bogotá which survived the nineteenth century were established in the 1870's, under the leadership of native Bogotanos, and without notable foreign assistance. In the first of these banks, the Banco de Bogotá, founded in 1870, only 9 of the 93 original shares appear to have been held by men of foreign birth. The first Colombian insurance company, the Compañía Colombiana de Seguros, was founded in 1874 by Pedro Navas Azuero, a native Bogotano, with the support of most of the notable local merchant-capitalists.

While the manufacturing and banking enterprises attempted in Bogotá between 1821 and 1870 were either failures or only modest successes, in the gold-rich region of Antioquia a number of mining enterprises were proving quite lucrative. As in the case of manufacturing in Bogotá, developments in mining in Antioquia were the joint work of native capitalist-entrepreneurs and foreign technicians. In the period between 1800 and 1820 the yield of many mines in Antioquia had fallen and local miners lacked the technique required to exploit relatively low-grade ore. In the 1820's, Francisco Montoya and four other leading citizens of the Antioquia town of Rionegro, formed a mining company for the purpose of introducing the best European techniques into the mines of Santa Rosa. They procured the services of an English engineer, Tyrell Moore, who brought new ore mills which permitted use of lower-grade ores. The increased productivity permitted by Moore's innovations was responsible for the great prosperity which characterized Antioquia in the 1830's, when most other regions of the country were deep in depression.

Wealth accrued from the mines of Antioquia between 1830 and 1860 played a dominant role in the founding of many new enterprises in other areas of the country, most notably the development of steam navigation on the Magdalena and of tobacco exporting. Leadership in both of the latter developments was provided, more than by any other single man, by Francisco Montoya, one of the five developers of the mines of Santa Rosa. Member of a distinguished Rionegro family, Montoya had fought in the patriot armies in 1815–1816, attaining the rank of colonel. During the period of Spanish repression between 1816 and 1819, he lived in Jamaica, where he carried on commercial activities. In 1824, already a rich man, he negotiated a loan of £4,750,000 in London for the Colombian government, for which service he and an Antioqueño associate, Manuel Antonio Arrubla, received a commission of more than $200,000. After forming the mining company in Antioquia, he assumed leadership of many enterprises in Bogotá, where he resided from the middle 1820's to his death in 1862. In 1836 he led the group of Colombian capitalists who obtained a franchise to construct a transit line across the Isthmus of Panama by road, rail, or water. Montoya also headed a firm (composed mostly of fellow Antioqueños) which practically monopolized keelboat transportation on the Magdalena, at the same time building roads and engaging in land freighting between the Magdalena River and Bogotá. Between 1837 and 1839 he formed a company to place a steamboat on the Magdalena; the company provided service between 1839 and 1841, when its lone steamboat was seized and destroyed during civil war. After this setback, Montoya and other Antioqueños who worked with him again turned to keelboat service on the river. In 1847, when a group of forwarding merchants in Santa Marta founded the first successful river steamer company, they found it necessary to buy Montoya's keelboats, giving him a large share of the steam company stock.

An important factor in the success of steam navigation was the development of tobacco exports from the region of Ambalema, on the banks of the Upper Magdalena. Tobacco had been cultivated in this region since at least the middle of the eighteenth century. But the amount of production had been controlled by a government monopoly, both in the colonial period and under the republic. Beginning in the 1830's, the government of New Granada adopted the policy of encouraging the export of this tobacco. Particularly after 1845, production for export increased markedly. The export of tobacco provided increased downstream freight for steamboats, and brought new exchange which permitted the expansion of imports, and thus upstream traffic.

The development of tobacco production for export was the work of both British and Colombian entrepreneurs. William Wills played an important role in the early stages. In the early 1830's, as representative of the English house of Powles, Illingworth, he began systematic testing of Granadan tobacco in European markets. In this period Wills accumulated important information on European requirements for curing and packing, which guided the industry for the next four decades.

The second important step in developing the tobacco industry was executed by Francisco Montoya and his family, five members of which composed the firm of Montoya, Sáenz. In 1845, the government of New Granada contracted out production of tobacco for the monopoly to Montoya, Sáenz, in the belief that a private businessman with credit resources superior to those of the government could expand production more efficiently and effectively. As producer of tobacco for the government monopoly between 1845 and 1849, Montoya, Sáenz established a system of centralized curing, inspection, and packing, and insisted on the most careful selection and quality control. Contemporaries generally credited Montoya and family with developing the reputation of Ambalema tobacco as being second only to Cuban leaf for cigar wrappers.

Most Colombian export commodities were developed by Colombians without noteworthy foreign assistance. Bogotanos took the lead in the cultivation of indigo in the 1860's. Colombians from the eastern provinces were also entirely responsible for the production and export of straw hats, principally to the Caribbean islands and to the southern United States. Bogotanos also made efforts, with varying success, to develop exports of cowhides and of such forest products as vegetable ivory, medicinals (sarsaparilla, ipecacuanha, ratan root), and assorted dyewoods. . . .

COMPARISON

In many respects, the performance of foreign businessmen in Colombia differed very little from that of native Colombians. The main difference between them lay in the fact that the foreigners generally had superior technical knowledge. In almost any activity requiring new types of machinery, foreign technicians played a vital role. Foreigners played a critical part in improving the mechanics of mining and manufacturing. Until the 1860's, river steamboats were almost exclusively built and captained by foreigners. But in all of these activities Colombians provided entrepreneurial initiative, business organization, and capital.

In other respects, foreign and national businessmen were very much alike. As manufacturers, they both tended to overestimate the domestic market. Foreigners, in fact, erred more than natives in this respect, for the Colombians generally attempted to produce staple goods, while foreign enterprisers tended to gravitate to luxury products having a very limited consumer base.

As exporters, English and Colombian merchants also operated similarly. English and Colombian tobacco exporters both failed to maintain quality control in Ambalema. After the collapse of Montoya, Sáenz in 1857, Ambalema was dominated by the British house of Frühling and Goschen. It was precisely during the period when the English house was the biggest exporter that Ambalema tobacco became discredited in the Bremen market. As exporters of cinchona bark and other commodities, English merchants proved themselves not a whit more adept than their Colombian counterparts.

It does not appear that foreign businessmen in Colombia showed any markedly greater genius for successful economic calculation than did native merchants. A great many foreign ventures in Colombia were marked by a tendency to over-extension. This was true of the British-owned Colombian Mining Association. It was true of Juan Bernardo Elbers' early efforts in steamboating. It was true of the American manufacturers of combs and beaver hats. It was true of the activities of the Bank of London, Mexico, and South America.

It is possible, of course, to view the foreigners' recklessness as evidence of entrepreneurial dash, contrasting it with Colombian caution and lack of interest in innovation. On the other hand, it can also be said that the Colombians appraised economic conditions more realistically and were thus less likely to be drawn into quixotic adventures. Colombian merchants were cautious because experience had revealed to them the limitations of the local market. Experience also had taught them the danger of committing capital to new enterprises in an environment of political strife. They could anticipate that during civil wars materials or markets might be cut off, or that workers or products might be seized for use by contending factions. Finally, many Colombian businessmen were cautious simply because they lacked capital and it was more difficult for them to borrow than it was for European entrepreneurs with connections in London. . . .

Distinctive cultural characteristics probably played some role in English and Antioqueño leadership. Bogotanos and other Colombians respected both groups as especially enterprising. The English were thought to be distinguished for their persistence in the face of adversity, the Antioqueños for their general industriousness. Nevertheless, other investment groups displayed many of the same characteristics. The inhabitants of the province of Santander shared with the Antioqueños a restless energy which carried them to distant parts of the country in search of new economic opportunities. The merchants of Santa Marta were the equal of the Antioqueños in shrewdness and business skill and in the ability to cooperate imaginatively in major community enterprises. Colombians from these poorer regions were constantly engaging in new endeavors, whether in manufacturing, exporting, or transportation. But their activities generally were carried out on a smaller scale and, therefore, have attracted less notice than those of the Antioqueños or of foreign investors.

Within the limits imposed by their capital resources, by the domestic market, and by the political environment, merchant-capitalists in many regions of Colombia gave a good account of themselves. The fact that their country failed to develop in any significant way during the nineteenth century can be ascribed primarily to geographical and political factors. In some areas, cultural factors, such as a weak associative spirit, played a role in inhibiting development. But among the upper class in many parts of Colombia, there was no lack of individual enterprise.

42. Lucas Alamán: Mexican Conservative and Economic Entrepreneur

CHARLES A. HALE

The greatest single economic statesman of the first fifty years in the history of independent Mexico — perhaps of all Latin America, with the possible exception of Bernardino Rivadavia of Buenos Aires — was Lucas Alamán. Professor Charles A. Hale of the State University of Iowa, in his standard work on Mexican liberalism, necessarily treats Mexican conservatism as well. Indeed, his remarks on Alamán constitute the best account in English of this key figure in both conservative thought and economic development.

Note, too, Professor Hale's illuminating analysis of the changes in Alamán's thinking, and of the supposed relationship between economics and politics in developing nations.

The chief conservative spokesman was Lucas Alamán, undoubtedly the major political and intellectual figure of independent Mexico until his death in 1853. A man of indefatigable energy and diverse talents, Alamán was not only a prolific writer, whose works fill twelve stout volumes, but also the guiding force in several administrations and an active promoter of economic development.

One can follow a rough pattern in Lucas Alamán's life that runs from activist to writer, from statesman and entrepreneur to *pensador*. It is impor-

From *Mexican Liberalism in the Age of Mora, 1821–1853* by Charles A. Hale (New Haven: Yale University Press, 1968), pp. 16–21, 212–214, 263–289, passim. Copyright © 1968 by Yale University. Reprinted by permission.

tant to note that his conservatism hardened only in the 1840s, particularly after 1846. The great bulk of Alamán's writing was done in his later years. Besides his histories, he was generally acknowledged to be the editor of *El Tiempo* and of *El Universal*. History was Alamán's principal weapon and the cornerstone of what could be called conservative political philosophy in Mexico. *El Tiempo* announced its appearance in Burkean terms by explaining that its title signified a search in the past (*tiempo pasado*) for lessons to guide in the present (*tiempo presente*), which in turn contains the seeds of the future (*tiempo por venir*). Destructive natural phenomena, such as earthquakes and volcanic eruptions, it added, cannot be a model for human development. "We thus reject from our ideas of progress all violent and revolutionary means."

On September 16, 1849, *El Universal* opened its attack on Mexico's accepted revolutionary tradition by asserting that Miguel Hidalgo's Grito de Dolores should no longer be considered Independence Day. Instead, there appeared on September 27 an article entitled "The Great Day of the Nation," commemorating Agustín de Iturbide's entry into Mexico City in 1821. The liberal newspapers *El Siglo* and *El Monitor* rose immediately to the defense of Hidalgo and of September 16, and a fierce debate ensued. It was symbolic of the broader conflict of ideas over the social and political bases of independent Mexico and the country's relation to its colonial and Hispanic past.

Alamán announced on several occasions that the purpose of his historical writing was to combat popular disrespect for Mexico's Spanish heritage and the idea that independence constituted a necessary break from it. He set out to demonstrate through history that Hernán Cortés was the founder of the Mexican nation, that three centuries of colonial rule had been on the whole beneficial and progressive, and that Mexico's only road to salvation in the present crisis was to reject liberal and disruptive doctrines and return to time-honored practices. By 1851 Alamán was claiming success for his efforts and pointed to recent patriotic orations as evidence. Alamán's conservative appeal through history had begun on February 18, 1844, when he proposed to the Ateneo Mexicano, a group of scholars and men of letters, that he prepare ten "dissertations" covering "our national history from the epoch of the Conquest to our day." He completed this effort nine years and eight volumes later, a few months before his death in June 1853. . . .

Alamán made most effective use of history as a weapon in his interpretation of the Revolution for Independence. The force of his argument was not based on mere polemic but rather on the documentation and detail of his five large volumes. His *Historia de Méjico* remains the standard treatment of the 1810–21 period, and it has never been equaled by a "liberal" version. This fact may reflect the durability of Creole conservatism in the Mexican tradition. The interpretation embedded in Alamán's narrative is clear and un-equivocal: there was not one revolution; there were two. The first was led by Miguel Hidalgo in 1810 and lasted ten years till it disintegrated in 1820; the second took place briefly in 1821 under Agustín de Iturbide. In no way, as-serted Alamán, could the first revolution be considered a war of "nation against nation," nor was it "a heroic effort of a people struggling for their liberty," trying to "shake off the yoke of an oppressor power." Hidalgo's insurrection was rather a "rising of the proletarian class against property and civilization," led by many "lost souls or ex-criminals noted for their vices." This first revolution caused a "reaction of the respectable segment of society in defense of its property and its families," which "stifled [by 1820] the gen-eral desire for independence." Moreover, "the triumph of the insurrection would have been the greatest calamity that could have befallen the country."

Lucas Alamán grew up in a wealthy and distinguished family in the pros-perous mining city of Guanajuato, which was the first target of the Revolution of 1810. As a youth of seventeen he experienced siege by Hidalgo's Indian hordes and saw the death of the enlightened Spanish intendant Riaño, a fam-ily friend. Alamán escaped with his family to Mexico City, but, he wrote in 1849, the "shout of death and destruction . . . still resounds in my ears with a terrible echo." His memories of 1810 were revived by the entry of the American army into Mexico City in September 1847. Though his house es-caped sacking, he noted that some of his neighbors were not so fortunate. Alamán concluded that Father Hidalgo was merely a demagogue, appealing to mob anarchy and the exaggerated democratic doctrines of the French Revolu-tion. His use of the Virgin of Guadalupe as an emblem was a blasphemous linking of religion and violence. After disorder had been unleashed by Hidalgo, it was impossible for more disciplined leaders like José María Morelos and Ramón López Rayón to control its fury. Alamán found ad-mirable qualities in several of the later insurgent leaders, but the movement as a whole could be termed a disaster.

The second revolution was the climax of Alamán's *Historia*. It was a frankly conservative movement directed against the anticlerical and demo-cratic principles of the Spanish cortes (assembly) and the Constitution of 1812, both of which had been reactivated in 1820. Independence was achieved as a mere breaking of political ties with Spain. Iturbide was correct, maintained Alamán, in refusing to recognize a connection between the 1810 insurrection (against which he had fought as a royalist commander) and his harmonious movement. Independence was thus "brought about by the same people who until then had been opposing it." Alamán was explicit in denying the "vulgar error" current in 1821 that independence was a resurgence of the pre-Conquest nation of Anahuac after three centuries of Spanish oppression. The nation that emerged in 1821 was for Alamán the product of sixteenth-century conquest, guided by Hispanic principles of authority, religion, and property. Alamán summed up his position in words his friend Manuel Terán had used in 1824: "I have never considered myself other than a rebellious Spaniard.". . . [Alamán became a leader of conservative thought, which increasingly opposed the United States. His views and actions on economic matters became of prime importance to independent Mexico.]

In his first report as minister of relations in 1823, Lucas Alamán began the section on mining as follows:

> It is an established principle among the economists that the most direct stimulus that can be given to agriculture and industry is to facilitate the consumption of its products and the sale of its artifacts. If we were to consider our mines from this point of view, we would find that nothing contributes as much as they to the prosperity of those [other] essential branches of public wealth.

Thus Alamán, under the influence of the new liberal economics, sought to continue the revival of mining begun by Charles III. Alamán's promotion of the Mexican mining industry had roots in his personal background and interests. After serving in the Spanish cortes, he left for Paris and London in search of funds to rehabilitate the Cata mine of Guanajuato. Its "great bonanza" in the early eighteenth century had "made my grandparents rich." When his family fled Guanajuato in 1810, the young Alamán naturally enough began his studies at the Colegio de Minería. In 1814 he departed for a six-year grand tour of Europe, highlighted by the study of mineralogy and mining technology at Paris and Freiburg. He became close to Francisco Fagoaga, descendant of another rich mining family which had been prominent in the Mining Tribunal. In the company of the Fagoagas, Alamán left Paris for Mexico in November 1822, eager to recoup his family fortune as well as to reinstate Mexico's leading industry after the disastrous years of revolution.

Between 1822 and 1824, the revival of mining became a topic of prime economic concern in Mexico, second only to the question of the tariff. There were in Alamán's view two obstacles to be overcome. One was the taxes which burdened production and the export of ore. The other was the colonial laws restricting foreigners from acquiring interests in mining. Alamán could report by 1823 that the first barrier had been cleared. An 1821 decree of the Spanish cortes, instituting a single tax of 3 percent on gold and silver (in place of the former *quinto,* seigniorage, and other taxes) was confirmed by the Mexican provisional junta in November of the same year.

The second obstacle was attacked by Alamán in a vigorous speech on September 5, 1823, supporting a proposal of the congressional mining commission. Alamán argued the need for allowing the free entry of foreign capital. Citing Adam Smith, he said that the Mexican mines should take advantage of the "natural tendency" of foreigners to seek profitable areas of investment abroad. "They will direct their investment here without needing further encouragement." Mexican capital is lacking, he insisted. Either it has left the country or it is not invested out of fear of political instability. He refuted the contention that Mexico might become dominated by foreigners. Alamán argued optimistically that once attracted to its shores, foreigners would see its good government and its "delightful" climate and would "seek spontaneously the naturalization papers which in a certain sense we are now wanting to force them to take out."

The result of Alamán's persuasion was the law of October 7, 1823, suspending colonial legislation that restricted mining contracts with foreigners. From an eclectic blend of personal economic interests, respect for past experience, and liberal economic theory, Alamán had urged successfully that the door be opened to private foreign capital. Still, he did not exclude government investment out of hand. . . .

Alamán's promotional efforts, first in Europe in 1822 and later in Mexico, led to the creation of the United Mexican Mining Association, underwritten by British capital in 1824. Alamán was its chief agent. The venture initiated a frenzied period of speculation, which saw the formation of numerous mining companies, the importation of much machinery, and even an ill-fated migration of Cornish miners. The great mining revival, which Alamán foresaw as the basis of general economic development, achieved only limited success. The foreign venture was poorly planned and managed. Alamán himself came into conflict with British agents and in 1828 resigned from the company. He reported officially in 1830 that the mines "are already on a footing to subsist by themselves, production sufficing to cover costs." Though he still referred to mining as "our peculiar industry," his tone had changed, reflecting new economic concerns.

Alamán's ideas of the 1820s, infused with economic liberalism, resembled those of the doctrinaires. Like them he spoke of the rehabilitation of mining and of its primacy in the country's economy. He welcomed foreign capital and argued against colonial restrictions, much as did Mora and Zavala. Mora's discussion of mining in 1830 indicated that he was sympathetic to Alamán's efforts of the previous decade. The difference between Alamán and the doctrinaire liberals lay in the use Alamán made of economic theory. As an entrepreneur, continuing in the ways of his ancestors, Alamán adapted the new economic doctrines to his concrete and pragmatic plans for restoring Mexico's leading industry. Funds were no longer available from the colonial banco de avíos of the Mining Tribunal, so he turned to private foreign investment, first for his personal interests, later for the industry in general. Through educational exposure to European advances, Alamán was receptive to improved technology. He wanted to modernize the industry, just as did Fausto de Elhuyar a generation earlier.

Alamán's positive and nondoctrinaire conception of development embraced more than mining. In 1823 he mentioned briefly that it was necessary to encourage manufacturing through protective (but not prohibitive) tariffs, while allowing the free entry of machines from abroad. The goal would be cheaper manufactures to compete with foreign goods. Francisco Arrillaga, the minister of finance, even made some specific proposals for mechanizing the textile industry. In short, there were differences between Alamán and the economic liberals during the 1820s, but they remained subtle. . . .

Between 1825 and 1830, Alamán remained outside government and turned his immense creative energy to private interests. He purchased property in Celaya, and had visions of developing that city of small workshops into a factory center for woolens. In doing so, he gradually liquidated his Guanajuato mines. He also purchased the rundown Hacienda de Trojes and attempted to turn it into a profitable enterprise with financial support from his father-in-law and from several chaplaincies. Valadés gives us an engaging portrait of the Alamán of these early entrepreneurial years, striking out with great energy in mining, agriculture, and textiles. In the elegant mansion of the Count of Santiago in Mexico City, he lived *"como un gran señor."* Entrepreneur, hacendado, and austere Hispanic nobleman; this was the man who in January 7, 1830, again became minister of relations.

A month after taking office Alamán reported to the congress that manufacturing "is reduced almost to nullity" because it had been promoted by the wrong methods. He went on to attack "the purely prohibitive system" and said that abundant population, capital, and adequate machinery were also prerequisites for industry. Alamán was announcing a plan for government promotion of modern industry in selected areas, to be implemented by a series of laws and orders over the next two years. Factory production was to be limited to cheap fabrics of cotton, wool, and linen, "necessary to clothe the most numerous class of our population." Mexico should continue to import luxury products from more industrialized nations. Alamán's plan for industry drew from both the free trade and the protectionist. . . . Yet in announcing positive governmental efforts to modernize industry, it was a departure from both.

A law of October 16, 1830, provided for "the establishment of a Banco de

Avío to promote national industry." Its capital was to be formed from one-fifth of the revenue received from import duties on crude cotton cloth. The 1829 prohibition on cotton cloth was to be lifted "for the time necessary, and no more," until an investment fund of one million pesos could be accumulated. The junta of the Banco, composed of the minister of relations and two others, was to import machinery and to distribute it at cost on easy terms to worthy enterprises. Special consideration would be given to those in wool, cotton, and silk. The Banco de Avío was intended as a government investment bank to develop industry on a modern basis.

How can we account for Alamán's change from mining to manufacturing, and from laissez-faire to direct government intervention? The explanation lies partly in the shift of Alamán's personal entrepreneurial interests between 1825 and 1830. It lies also in the little-studied history of capital in Mexico during the 1820s. There was a sizable withdrawal of British funds, following the frenzied speculation of 1824–26 and the subsequent panic. Whatever Spanish merchant capital remained after independence was put to flight with the expulsion decrees of 1827 and 1829. The church traditionally invested in land. Alamán had turned to foreigners to finance the mines in the absence of private domestic funds and because the Mining Tribunal was bankrupt. Disillusioned by the absence of investment from other sources, Alamán now turned to the state. . . .

The Banco de Avío was inspired by Bourbon economic institutions of the 1770s. Alamán's bank was none other than a recreation of the banco de avíos of the Mining Tribunal, now applied primarily to manufacturing. The method of funding the two investment institutions was similar. In each case a portion of government revenue derived from the particular industry in question was to be diverted into promotional purposes. Beyond the specific parallel with the mining fund of the 1770s, Alamán's conception of development in 1830 bears strong resemblance to the general policy of peninsular economic rejuvenation under Charles III. . . .

The Banco de Avío faced difficulties from the start. Despite his leadership in founding the Banco, Alamán hoped that its governing junta would be an administrative entity not totally dependent on the particular government in power. This, of course, was impossible in the period of extreme political instability between 1832 and 1835. Imported machinery for Banco-financed enterprises rusted on the docks at Veracruz. Customs duties earmarked for the Banco were appropriated by rebellious generals. The Gómez Farías regime on several occasions diverted Banco funds to other purposes. Except under one minister, Francisco Lombardo (December 1833), relations between the junta and the government were strained. Besides political obstacles, the Banco was plagued with poor investment decisions. Most of the potential enterprises were unrealistic. Lending was often determined by personal favoritism. The junta took on too many projects. The result was that by 1835 all Banco-financed ventures had ended in failure, with one notable exception — the cotton factory of Estevan de Antuñano in Puebla. . . . [Antuñano's economic ideas are described at length. He referred to the Banco de Avío as "the greatest idea to come forth since Mexico became a nation," but he regarded himself as "the founder of Mexican industry."]

It was Lucas Alamán, however, who remained the statesman of economic development in Mexico. After the fall of the Bustamante regime, he returned to his own enterprises, which included the establishment of a spinning mill at Cocolapam near Orizaba in 1836. The Banco de Avío was strengthened by further capitalization in 1835 and lent money lavishly during the next two years. Alamán, incidentally, was one of the beneficiaries, receiving 60,000 pesos for his mill. The earlier problems of the Banco returned to plague it, and by 1840 its funds were exhausted. Moreover, there was increasing sentiment that it be replaced by an organization more directly controlled by the new industrialists themselves and less dependent on the government. The result was the Junta General de la Industria Mexicana, a corporate entity modeled on the Mining Guild of the 1770s. Regional *juntas de industria* were to send representatives to Mexico City to meet every two years as the General Junta. Authority was lodged in a board (*dirección*), the director of which was to be named by the President of the Republic, just as the director of the Mining Tribunal had been named by the Crown. Lucas Alamán served as director during its four years of existence.

By 1844 Alamán had abandoned his earlier view that mining was "our proper activity"; he was now urging development on several fronts. He sought means to reconcile the interests of agriculture and manufacturing, including an attempt to expand cotton growing. Alamán's plan for development, which was also advocated by Antuñano, was a reenactment of Bourbon peninsular fomento, adapted to the circumstances of a politically independent Mexico. The objective was to advance the cause of national regeneration through an independent, balanced, and modernized economy. Government stimulus in selected areas through direct investment, special tax concessions, manipulation of the tariff, importation of machinery, and foreign technology — these Bourbon policies of a "liberalized mercantilism" were reborn in post-1830 Mexico. The eclectic and pragmatic approach to development allowed special privilege, even monopoly, to coexist with the search for a utilitarian spirit of enterprise. The plan was riddled with doctrinal inconsistencies, as had been Bourbon policies in Spain, but such inconsistencies were its very essence.

In identifying this Bourbon-inspired conception of development shared by Alamán and Antuñano, we must note again its tie to land. Antuñano and Alamán were both large landholders. As men of enterprise they were closer to the continental type of the aristocratic entrepreneur, in contrast to the English industrialist who typically formed part of a new social class, having few ties to land, family traditions, or to older activities like mining. . . .

In conclusion, let us return to the problem posed at the beginning of this chapter — the relationship between economic development and political liberalism. I have tried to demonstrate that the terms "liberal" and "conservative" cannot profitably be used to designate concepts of development. The looser categories, "doctrinaire" and "pragmatic," are more appropriate. Lucas Alamán, the chief architect of economic development through modern industry, was also the ranking political conservative of the pre-Reforma era. His political conservatism, however, developed slowly and became a hardened ideology only after 1846. His earlier approach to both political and economic problems revealed some responsiveness to liberal theory.

Estevan de Antuñano, the other principal advocate of modern industry, was largely oblivious to politics. His comments on political and social issues were few, and before 1846 they tended to be conservative. In 1834, probably in reaction to the anticlericalism of the Gómez Farías regime, he expressed respect for the church and opposed curtailing its temporal powers. He defended tithes, but said they should be paid by the consumer rather than by the producer. He opposed small landholdings, except in "very civilized countries where the sciences and useful arts have augmented population, wealth, and good taste." In Mexico, however, subdividing land to stimulate agriculture would be profitless. In 1839 Antuñano expressed preference for centralism as an antidote to anarchy, but also admitted that the centralist-federalist arguments of his day had not been profound. His general position seemed to be that the best government was one that fostered the creation of wealth through industry. He deplored the constant revolutions of his time and the general preoccupation with ephemeral political matters rather than with economic development.

Antuñano's final publication revealed a conversion to political liberalism. In 1846, he announced a "political rudiment (*embrión*) of social regeneration, or a platonic plan to make Mexico content under the federal regime." His suggested reforms included closing the colegios of theology and jurisprudence for twenty years, suppressing male religious communities, reducing the secular clergy by one-third, and instituting freedom of worship and colonization. Finally, he proposed disentailing mortmain property to underwrite a banco de avío in each state, for the purpose of promoting manufacturing and agriculture.

Thus Antuñano became a political liberal at the very time that Lucas Alamán's conservatism hardened into an ideology. Did these political positions, now crystallized, have any effect on economic ideas? Antuñano died in 1847, but his earlier economic arguments were expressed forcefully by the moderate-reformist *El Siglo* in 1850. Yet they were *also* presented by *El Universal,* perhaps even by Alamán himself. At first glance, then, the answer to the question appears negative.

This nineteenth-century tangle of political and economic views is part of the same one encountered in the all-embracing present-day concept of "revolution." What is confused are two kinds of change, two kinds of revolutionary transformation, rooted in distinct though intersecting historic models. The one revolution was political. Its model was France, but it embraced the entire Atlantic world. Identifying the principles of that revolution in the context of Mexico has been the main concern of this book. The other, the Industrial Revolution, coincided roughly in time with the political revolution. It entailed ideally, however, a process that bore little relation to politics — the change from an agrarian and rural society to one that was industrial and urban. Industrialization can coincide with political liberalization; it can be guided by liberal economic doctrine, as in England and the United States. Yet we have now learned from twentieth-century experience that economic development through industrialization can take place within a variety of political systems, guided by differing ideologies.

It is thus futile to force nineteenth-century approaches to the economic development of Mexico into the categories of political debate. Alamán and Antuñano, however imperfectly, introduced into Mexico the idea and the reality of modern industry. They drew from the doctrines of economic liberalism, but they drew even more from Bourbon mercantilist policies of the eighteenth century. There was, of course, more consistency between political and economic views by those who advocated the doctrinaire approach to development. Mora, Zavala, and Manuel Ortiz de la Torre saw economic development as a spontaneous, or natural process, resting on the actions of the free individual. The effort to free the individual from corporate and monopolistic restrictions could be pursued in the economic as in the political sphere. In postindependence Mexico, however, this approach could be discredited as not leading to development at all, but rather to the perpetuation of a colonial economy, rural and agricultural at its base. Alamán and Antuñano by no means envisioned a modern urban, industrial society; but their ideas, rooted in eighteenth-century Spain, did initiate the "style" of economic development that has emerged in our time.

There remains one final problem. Though *ideally* independent of political categories, in reality the debate over economic development was inevitably drawn into politics. The crucial element in this entanglement was the church. Several observers have pointed to the principal defect of Alamán's approach to development — that it attempted to ignore the entailed capital of the church. Alamán was even less anticlerical than were the architects of Spanish development, who at least had disentailed Jesuit property. This, of course, is one of the reasons why Jesús Reyes Heroles calls Lucas Alamán an "integral conservative," conservative in economics as well as in politics. Alamán may have hoped that the church would invest voluntarily in industry, and indeed there is evidence that it did. Still, the vast temporal power of the church was incompatible with the "spirit of enterprise" and with the modern industry that Alamán wanted to implant. It was the doctrinaire liberals, led by José María Luis Mora, who advanced a solution to this critical problem.

The inconsistencies of Alamán's position did not become apparent, however, until 1846, when the liberal-conservative debate burst forth. This may possibly explain Antuñano's final call for anticlerical reforms as a prerequisite to economic development. Except for the El Universal articles, which may or may not have been Alamán's, economic development figured little in the latter's postwar writings. His defense of the church, his attack upon liberal doctrines and the utilitarian spirit, his evocation of Hispanic values and traditions against the threat of the new society of the United States — all would logically close the door on economic modernization by any means. The debate over economic development thus became enmeshed in the ideological struggle which emerged after 1846, a struggle that was not resolved for two decades.

Punishment of Slaves in Brazil. Historians have devoted much attention in recent years to the question whether slaves were better treated in Brazil than in the United States or elsewhere. Though no simple or general answer may be given, for punishment often depended on the individual master and other circumstances, it is clear that slaves were punished in Brazil as available sources show, including this scene from the Illustrated London News *of 1845.*

SECTION X

Negro Slavery in Brazil

Slavery hangs like a dark cloud over the history of Brazil from the sixteenth century until today. Historians contemplating this system of forced labor have concluded that its establishment in America was one of the great ironies: "By the sixteenth and seventeenth centuries Europeans had arrived at the greatest dualism of them all — the momentous division between an increasing devotion to liberty in Europe and an expanding mercantile system based on Negro labor in America." [1]

The fundamental importance of Negro slavery in the history of Brazil did not diminish with the passage of time. Many of the most important movements and events of the nineteenth century — immigration, the growth of republicanism, the onset of modernization, the War of the Triple Alliance, the fall of the monarchy — were directly or indirectly related to the fate of "the peculiar institution."

Today more attention than ever is devoted to assessments of the true nature of slavery and its continuing influence in the life of Latin America's largest and most populous nation. A sophisticated school of social anthropologists and historians in Brazil is producing a large and interesting literature on many diverse aspects of slavery, and so much attention is being paid to the comparison of Negro slavery in Brazil with the institution in other parts of the Americas that it is a flourishing growth industry.

The intense desire to learn about slavery and Brazilian society began in the early years of the nineteenth century. The many travelers from Europe and the United States who visited this huge country almost always discoursed

---

[1] David Brion Davis, *The Problem of Slavery in Western Culture* (Ithaca, N.Y.: Cornell University Press, 1970), p. 108.

upon Negro slavery, in much the same way that visitors to our antebellum South did. No Latin American country has a richer travel literature for the nineteenth century than Brazil (Reading 43). However, travelers see only a part of the reality they attempt to describe, and they are often affected in their judgments by their personal convictions; it remains for the historian to sift all essential sources to present a more comprehensive and evaluative view of the past (Reading 44).

Slavery was finally abolished in 1888 by imperial decree. This act freed three-quarters of a million slaves, brought ruin to some landowners, and was one of the reasons usually given for the fall of the monarchy in 1889. The late Percy Alvin Martin of Stanford University, a pioneer in Brazilian history in the United States, addressed himself thirty years ago to the question of why the venerable and popular Emperor Pedro II was forced to abdicate.[2] Since then many explanations have been advanced; now one of the leaders in the new school of Brazilianists, Richard Graham, considers the same subject (Reading 45). Another valuable review article on the fall of the monarchy, more general in scope, was prepared by the late George C. A. Boehrer of the University of Kansas whose early death deprived us of one of the best prepared scholars in the field.[3]

Consideration of the fate of Negro slaves in Brazil has frequently led to a comparison with slavery in the United States and elsewhere in the Americas. Gilberto Freyre, Frank Tannenbaum, and others have maintained that slavery in Brazil was relatively mild. Robert Conrad has argued that this position is not supported by the facts,[4] and others have reached similar conclusions. During recent years the University of São Paulo has produced a vigorous school of sociologists and historians whose researches have laid the basis for a new approach to the complicated study of Negro slavery. One of these scholars, Emília Viotti da Costa, has concluded that the real emancipation of

[2] Percy Alvin Martin, "Causes of the Collapse of the Brazilian Empire", *Hispanic American Historical Review*, 4 (1921), pp. 4–48.

[3] "The Brazilian Republican Revolutions: Old and New Views," *Luso-Brazilian Review*, Winter 1967. For an older interpretation, see Vicente Licinio Cardoso, "A margem do Segundo Reinado," *Revista do Instituto Histórico Geográfico Brasileiro*, 98 (1925), pp. 1039–1087. A recent interpretation by Luís Martins considers the revolution as a revolt against, and a slaying of, a father by his sons. See his *O Patriarca e o bacharel* (São Paulo: Martins, 1953). See also Charles Willis Simmons, *Marshal Deodoro and the Fall of Dom Pedro II* (Durham, N.C.: Duke University Press, 1966).

[4] For more detailed information on this and other aspects of this complicated subject, see his monograph, *The Destruction of Brazilian Slavery 1850–1888* (Berkeley: University of California Press, 1973). See also Robert Brent Toplin, *The Abolition of Slavery in Brazil* (New York: Atheneum, 1972).

Negroes from their slave status is "a process still under way," a view that is shared by many other Brazilian scholars.[5]

Foreign students have also been drawn to this great topic in the history of the Americas, and they have emphasized the comparative aspects of race relations. To close this section we have the interpretations of a white, American professor of history (Reading 46). This debate will doubtless grow in intensity, and may well lead to a reevaluation of the history of the Western hemisphere.

[5] See her detailed exposition in "O escravo na grande lavoura," in *História geral da Civilização Brasileira*, vol. 2, *O Brasil Monarquico*, ed. Sérgio Buarque de Holanda, (São Paulo: Difusão Européia do Livro, 1967), pp. 135–188.

43. *Slavery Is a Curse for Both Negroes and Whites*

HERBERT H. SMITH

Herbert H. Smith, the American naturalist who saw all the major regions of Brazil during 1874–1868, was one of the many scientists who have been attracted to Brazil by the tremendous variety of flora and fauna. He also observed slavery, and he emphasized the harm it did to the masters by influencing them toward "indolence and pride and sensuality and selfishness."

I came to Brazil, with an honest desire to study this question of slavery in a spirit of fairness, without running to emotional extremes. Now, after four years, I am convinced that all other evils with which the country is cursed, taken together, will not compare with this one; I could almost say that all other evils have arisen from it, or been strengthened by it. And yet, I cannot unduly blame men who have inherited the curse, and had no part in the making of it. I can honor masters who treat their slaves kindly, albeit they are owners of stolen property.

In mere animal matters, of food and clothing, no doubt many of the negroes are better off than they were in Africa; no doubt, also, they have learned some lessons of peace and civility; even a groping outline of Christianity. But it would be hard to prove that the plantation slave, dependent, like a child, on his master, and utterly unused to thinking for himself, is better, mentally, than the savage who has his faculties sharpened by continual battling with the savage nature around him. Slavery is weakening to the brain; the slave is worse material for civilization than the savage is, and worse still with every generation of slavery.

That is not the main evil, however. The harm that slavery has done to the black race is as nothing to the evils it has heaped upon the white one, the masters. If every slave and free negro could be carried away to Africa, if every drop of cursed mixed blood could be divided, the evils would be there yet, and go down to the children's children with a blight upon humanity.

Indolence and pride and sensuality and selfishness, these are the outgrowths of slavery that have enslaved the slavemakers and their children. Do you

From *Brazil: The Amazons and the Coast* by Herbert H. Smith (New York: Charles Scribner's Sons, 1879), pp. 466–470.

imagine that they are all rich men's sons, these daintily clad, delicate young men on the Ouvidor? The most of them are poor, but they will lead their vegetable lives, God knows how, parasites on their friends, or on the government, or on the tailor and grocer, because they will not soil their hands with tools. "Laborers!" cries Brazil. "We must have labor!" and where will she get honest workmen, if honest work is a degradation? Slavery has made it so. For generations the upper classes had no work to do, and they came to look upon it as the part of an inferior race. So they have kept their hands folded, and the muscle has gone from their bones, and indolence has become a part of their nature. Still, they will be sham lords, if they cannot be real ones; so their money — what they have of it — goes for broadcloth coats and silk hats, and sensuality; a grade below that, they are yet shabby-genteel figures, with an eye to friendly invitations to dinner; and below that, they sink out of sight altogether, from mere inanition.

The rich men's sons are not parasites; sharp enough; many of them are, to keep the money they have, and double it. But from their cradle, the curse of slavery is on them. The black nurse is an inferior, and the child knows it, and tyrannizes over her as only a child can. The mother is an inferior, by her social station, and she does not often venture to thwart the child. The father, with whom authority rests, shirks it back on the irresponsible ones, who may not venture to lay sacrilegious hands on the heir of power. The amount of it is, that a child's training here consists in letting it have its own way as much as possible; and the small naughtinesses and prides develop into consuming vanity and haughtiness. It is characteristic of the Brazilians, this vanity; it may come out in snobbism, or over-confidence, or merely a fiery sensitiveness; but there it is plainly; in the best of them. Slavery is to blame for it; black slavery, and woman slavery that gives the mother no authority.

Of the sensuality that comes from slavery, the mixed races that overrun Brazil are a sufficient witness, as they are in our Southern States. But in Brazil, the proportion of these mixed races is vastly greater; I am safe in saying that not a third of the population is pure-blooded; social distinctions of color are never very finely drawn, though they are by no means abolished, as some writers would have us believe.

People who talk of "amalgamation," as a blessing to be hoped for, should study its effects here, where it is almost an accomplished fact. The mixed races are invariably bad; they seem to combine all the worst characteristics of the two parent stocks, with none of the good ones; and the evil is most apparent where the "amalgamation" is most complete. A light mulatto, or an almost black one, may be a very decent kind of a fellow; but the brown half-and-half is nearly always lazy and stupid and vain. So with the whites and Indians, or the Indians and blacks; the *mamelucos* are treacherous, and passionate, and indolent; the *mestiços* are worse yet; but a dash of mixed blood may not spoil the man that has it.

The treatment of slaves in Brazil depends, of course, on the master; largely, too, on the district. In the provinces north of the São Francisco, I am bound to say that they are treated with great kindness; on the Amazons, they would be, from necessity, if not from choice, for every ill-used slave would run off to the woods, as many have done, out of mere laziness; freedom, considered abstractly, is not likely to have much influence on the negro mind. But around Rio and Bahia, where the vast majority of the slaves are now owned, there are masters who treat their servants with a severity that is nothing short of barbarism. We shall see something of this, when we come to study the coffee-plantations.

Yet Brazil should have a certain credit above other slave-holding countries, present and past; for she alone has voluntarily set herself to getting rid of her shame. Other nations have done it by revolutions, or because they were forced to by a stronger power, or because the system died out of itself. But Brazil, among all, has had nerve to cut away the sore flesh with her own hand; to cut it away while it was yet strong, while it seemed her best vitality. Would to God that she could cut away the scar as well! But the scar will be there, long after emancipation has done its work.

By the present law, slavery will cease to exist in 1892; essentially, I think, the northern provinces will free their slaves before that time. At Pernambuco, especially, the emancipation-spirit is very strong; it has come out in the form of an abolition society, which embraces nearly every prominent man in the place; many slaves have been freed by subscription, at the meetings of this society; there, and elsewhere, the masters frequently celebrate days of public rejoicing, by releasing some old servant. Sometimes a rich man frees his entire household, by testament.

The slaves have been drained into the southern provinces for years. It is common to find three or four hundred of them on the Rio coffee-plantations; rarely, there will be as many score on the sugar-estates of Pernambuco or Pará. Now mark the result. At Rio there is a constant cry for workmen; the slaves are not sufficient, yet free laborers cannot compete with the forced ones; the planters work their negroes as they would never work their mules, yet complain that they reap no profits. In the northern provinces, there is free labor, enough and to spare; poor men have a chance in the world; rich ones are content with the fair returns that their money brings them; society is far more evenly balanced, and the level of private character is far higher than in the south. Of course, there are humane masters at Rio also; the city, in this instance, is better than the country around. Many of the negro porters are slaves; great, brawny fellows, who run in gangs through the streets, each one with a hundred and thirty pounds of coffee on his head. Sometimes we see five or six of them, trotting together, with a piano; the weight evenly distributed on the woolly craniums; the men erect, moving in time to the leader's rattle, and to a plaintive chant. The porters pay their masters a certain sum per day; what they earn over this, is their own. The best of them sometimes buy their freedom from their savings.

44. *Patterns of Living on the Vassouras Plantation*

STANLEY J. STEIN

Professor Stanley J. Stein of Princeton produced two fundamental works on the economy of Brazil: the volume on coffee from which this analysis is taken, and *The Brazilian Cotton Manufacture* (1957) a pioneering analysis of labor problems.

Slave life on the average Vassouras plantation of approximately eighty to one hundred slaves was regulated by the needs of coffee agriculture, the maintenance of *sede* [the plantation buildings] and *senzallas* [slave quarters], and the processing of coffee and subsistence foodstuffs. Since the supply of slaves was never adequate for the needs of the plantation either in its period of growth, prosperity, or decline, the slaves' work day was a long one begun before dawn and often ending many hours after the abrupt sunset of the Parahyba plateau.

Cooks arose before sunup to light fires beneath iron cauldrons; soon the smell of coffee, molasses, and boiled corn meal floated from the outdoor shed. The sun had not yet appeared when the overseer or one of his Negro drivers strode to a corner of the *terreiro* [coffee drying terraces] and reached for the tongue of a wide-mouthed bell. The tolling of the cast-iron bell, or sometimes a blast from a cowhorn or the beat of a drum, reverberated across the terreiro and entered the tiny cubicles of slave couples and the separated, crowded *tarimbas,* or dormitories, of unmarried slaves. Awakening from their five- to

Reprinted by permission of the publishers from Stanley J. Stein, *Vassouras: A Brazilian Coffee County, 1850–1900.* Cambridge, Mass.: Harvard University Press. Copyright, 1957, by the President and Fellows of Harvard College.

eight-hour slumber, they dragged themselves from beds of planks softened with woven fiber mats; field hands reached for hoes and billhooks lying under the eaves. At the large faucet near the senzallas, they splashed water over their heads and faces, moistening and rubbing arms, legs, and ankles. Tardy slaves might appear at the door of senzallas muttering the slave-composed *jongo* [slave work song] which mocked the overseer ringing the bell:

> That devil of a *bembo* taunted me
> No time to button my shirt, that devil of a bembo.

Now, as the terreiro slowly filled with slaves, some standing in line and others squatting, awaiting the morning *reza* or prayer, the senhor appeared on the veranda of the main house. "One slave recited the reza which the others repeated," recalled an ex-slave. Hats were removed and there was heard a "Praised-be-Our-Master-Jesus-Christ" to which some slaves repeated a blurred "Our-Master-Jesus-Christ," others an abbreviated "Kist." From the master on the veranda came the reply: "May-He-always-be-praised." The overseer called the roll; if a slave did not respond after two calls, the overseer hustled into the senzallas to get him or her. When orders for the day had been given, directing the various gangs to work on certain coffee-covered hills, slaves and drivers shuffled to the nearby slave kitchen for coffee and corn bread.

The first signs of dawn brightened the sky as slaves separated to their work. A few went into the main house; most merely placed the long hoe handles on their shoulders and, old and young, men and women, moved off to the almost year-round job of weeding with drivers following to check stragglers. Mothers bore nursing youngsters in small woven baskets (*jacás*) on their backs or carried them astraddle one hip. Those from four to seven trudged with their mothers, those from nine to fifteen close by. If coffee hills to be worked were far from the main buildings, food for the two meals furnished in the field went along — either in a two-team ox-cart which slaves called a *maxambomba,* or in iron kettles swinging on long sticks, or in wicker baskets or two-eared wooden pans (*gamellas*) on long boards carried on male slaves' shoulders. A few slaves carried their own supplementary articles of food in small cloth bags.

Scattered throughout the field were shelters of four posts and a grass roof. Here, at the foot of the hills where coffee trees marched up steep slopes, the field slaves split into smaller gangs. Old men and women formed a gang working close to the rancho; women formed another; the men or young bucks (*rapaziada nova*), a third. Leaving the *moleques* [Negro or mulatto male children] and little girls to play near the cook and assistants in the rancho, they began the day's work. As the sun grew stronger, men removed their shirts;

hoes rose and fell slowly as slaves inched up the steep slopes. Under the gang labor system of *corte e beirada* used in weeding, the best hands were spread out on the flanks, *cortador* and *contra-cortador* on one, *beirador* and *contra-beirador* on the other. These four lead-row men were faster working pace-setters, serving as examples for slower workers sandwiched between them. When a coffee row (*carreira*) ended abruptly due to a fold in the slope, the slave now without a row shouted to his overseer "Throw another row for the middle" or "We need another row"; a *feitor* [plantation overseer] passed on the information to the flanking lead-row man who moved into the next row giving the slave who had first shouted a new row to hoe. Thus lead-row men always boxed-in the weeding gang.

Slave gangs often worked within singing distance of each other and to give rhythm to their hoe strokes and pass comment on the circumscribed world in which they lived and worked — their own foibles, and those of their master, overseers, and slave drivers — the master-singer (*mestre cantor*) of one gang would break into the first "verse" of a song in riddle form, a *jongo*. His gang would chorus the second line of the verse, then weed rhythmically while the master-singer of the nearby gang tried to decipher (*desafiar*) the riddle presented. An ex-slave, still known for his skill at making jongos, informed that "Mestre tapped the ground with his hoe, others listened while he sang. Then they replied." He added that if the singing was not good the day's work went badly. Jongos sung in African tongues were called *quimzumba;* those in Portuguese, more common as older Africans diminished in the labor force, *visaría*. Stopping here and there to "give a lick" (*lambada*) of the lash to slow slaves, two slave drivers usually supervised the gangs by criss-crossing the vertical coffee rows on the slope and shouting "Come on, come on"; but if surveillance slackened, gang laborers seized the chance to slow down while men and women slaves lighted pipes or leaned on their hoes momentarily to wipe sweat away. To rationalize their desire to resist the slave drivers' whips and shouts, a story developed that an older, slower slave should never be passed in his coffee row. For the aged slave could throw his belt ahead into the younger man's row and the youngster would be bitten by a snake when he reached the belt. The overseer or the master himself, in white clothes and riding boots, might ride through the groves for a quick look. Alert slaves, feigning to peer at the hot sun, "spiced their words" to comment in a loud voice "Look at that red-hot sun" or intermixed African words common to slave vocabulary with Portuguese as in *"Ngoma* is on the way" to warn their fellow slaves (*parceiros*), who quickly set to work industriously. When the driver noted the approaching planter, he commanded the gang "Give praise," to which slaves stood erect, eager for the brief respite, removed their hats or touched hands to forehead, and responded "Vas Christo." Closing the ritual greeting, the senhor too removed his hat, spoke his "May He always be praised" and rode on. Immediately the industrious pace slackened.

To shouts of "lunch, lunch" or more horn blasts coming from the rancho around 10 A.M., slave parceiros and drivers descended. At the shaded rancho they filed past the cook and his assistants, extending bowls or *cuías* of gourds split in two. On more prosperous *fazendas* [plantations], slaves might have tin plates. Into these food was piled; drivers and a respected or favored slave would eat to one side while the rest sat or sprawled on the ground. Mothers used the rest to nurse their babies. A half hour later the *turma* [work group] was ordered back to the sun-baked hillsides. At 1 P.M. came a short break for coffee to which slaves often added the second half of the corn meal cake served at lunch. On cold or wet days, small cups of *cachaça* [sugar brandy] distilled from the plantation's sugar cane replaced coffee. Some ex-slaves reported that fazendeiros often ordered drivers to deliver the cachaça to the slaves in a cup while they worked, to eliminate a break. *Fanta* or supper came at 4 P.M. and work was resumed until nightfall when to drivers' shouts of "Let's quit" (*vamos largar o serviço*) the slave gangs tramped back to the sede. Zaluar, the romantic Portuguese who visited Vassouras, wrote of the return from the fields: "The solemn evening hour. From afar, the fazenda's bell tolls Ave-Maria. (From hilltops fall the gray shadows of night while a few stars begin to flicker in the sky). . . . From the hill descend the taciturn driver and in front, the slaves, as they return home." Once more the slaves lined up for roll call on the terreiro where the field hands encountered their slave companions who worked at the plantation center (sede).

Despite the fact that the economy of the fazenda varied directly with the success of its coffee production, a high percentage of plantation slave labor, which some estimated at fully two-thirds, others at one-half of the labor force, was not engaged directly in field work. "On the plantation," Couty judged, "everything or almost everything is the product of the Black man: it is he who has built the houses; he has made the bricks, sawed the boards, channeled the water, etc.; the roads and most of the machines in the *engenho* [mill] are, along with the lands cultivated, the products of his industry. He also has raised cattle, pigs, and other animals needed on the fazenda." Many were employed in relatively unproductive tasks around the sede as waiters and waitresses, stableboys and cooks, and body servants for the free men, women, and children.

Throughout the day in front of the house could be seen the activity of the terreiro. From his shaded veranda or from a window the fazendeiro watched his slaves clean the terreiro of sprouting weeds, or at harvest time revolve the drying coffee beans with wooden hoes. Until the hot sun of midday drove them to the shade, bare-bottomed black and mulatto youngsters played under the eye of an elderly "aunt" and often with them a small white child in the care of his male body servant (*pagem*) or female "dry nurse." In a corner slaves might butcher a pig for the day's consumption while some moleques threw stones at the black turkey buzzards which hovered nearby. Outside the senzalla a decrepit slave usually performed some minor task or merely warmed himself in the sun. From the engenho came the thumping sound of the pilões [pestles — parts of the coffee processing machinery] and the splash of water cascading from the large water-wheel. In the shade of the engenho an old slave wove strips of bamboo into mats and screens. Washerwomen, beating and spreading clothes to bleach in the sun, worked rhythmically "to the tune of mournful songs."

Behind the main house, the páteo enclosed on all sides offered a shelter from outsiders' eyes, a place to be at ease. Here and in the rooms around it the lives of the free and slave women blended together. Washerwomen chatted as they dipped their arms into the granite tank in the center of the páteo or stretched wet clothes to bleach on the ground, and through the door of the kitchen slaves occupied with the unending process of food preparation could be seen at long wooden work tables. From a small porch opening on the páteo, or from the dining-room window, the mistress of the house, *sinhá* (or more informally, *nhanhá*), in a dressing gown, leaned on the railing and watched, maintaining a flow of gossip with her slaves or reprimanding some. Yet, despite the close contact between free and slave, locks on the doors of pantries and cupboards and the barred windows of both gave mute testimony to the faith of the mistress in her slaves. Life for the female house slave often seemed easier in comparison with that of a field hand; indeed, many of the *mucamas* or household female slaves were chosen from the field gangs. Yet they felt they had less liberty than the field hands since they were constantly supervised. A former pagem put the case succinctly: "Of course life in the household was always better. But many a sinhá beat her mucamas with a quince switch."

The dining room, with its close relation to kitchen, páteo, and sleeping rooms, was probably the general place of family congregation on those fazendas which did not have special sewing and sitting rooms. Bedrooms were small and sparsely furnished and, in the case of the windowless alcovas, entirely dark. In the house the younger women and maiden aunts sewed and embroidered, gossiped, and made delicacies for feast days, while the mistress of the household took a direct hand in the management of affairs. Usually an active sinhá carried the keys to pantries, which were opened twice daily to dole out food for the household's main meals, and to linen, china, and silver closets. Under her direction, slaves made beds, arranged disorder, swept, and moved dust from one point to another with feather dusters, while nursemaids took charge of the younger children and wet nurses satisfied squalling infants.

At meal times, which occupied a large part of the day, diners sat on both sides of the long extension table, the fazendeiro at its head. When guests were present talk was largely between them and their host, while the children and dependent relatives ate in silence, speaking only when addressed. The senhor tapped his plate with a spoon to remind the waiter to change plates. A demi-tasse of coffee closed the meal which was followed by the inevitable toothpick taken from a silver holder. After the noon meal, while the free retired to their nap, the household slaves ate their meal, gossiped, and yawned through the washing of dishes and silverware, and, when finished, resumed the *bate-papo* [small talk] unless the mistress or master kept them busy with small biddings.

At evening roll call (*formatura*) slaves were checked and sent to evening tasks to begin what one Vassouras planter termed the "brutal system of night tasks" (*serão*), sometimes lasting to 10 or 11 P.M. During winter months the principal evening task — the sorting of dried coffee beans on the floor of the engenho or on special tables — was continued in the light of castor-oil lamps or woven *taquara* [bamboo] torches. Preparation of food for humans and animals was the next most important job: manioc was skinned by hand, scraped on a huge grating wheel, dried, and then toasted for manioc flour. Corn cobs were thrown to pigs, while slaves beat other ears on tables (*debrulhadores*) with rods to remove kernels to be ground into corn meal. Women pounded rice in mortar and pestle to hull it. Coffee for the following day's consumption was toasted in wide pans, then ground. Slaves were sent out to gather firewood, and moleques walked to nearby abandoned groves to drive in the few foraging cows, oxen, mules, and goats. A light supper ended the serão.

In the dwelling house slaves cleared the supper table and lit castor-oil lamps or candles. The planter's family retired soon to their rooms, followed by the mucama "whose job was to carry water to wash the feet of the person retiring." She departed immediately to return after a short wait, received a "God-bless-you" and blew out the light.

And now field hands straggled from the engenho to slave senzallas where they were locked for the night. Household help too was locked in tiny rooms located in the rear of the house near the kitchen. For the slaves it was the end of a long day — unless a sudden storm blew up during the night while coffee was drying on the terreiros; then they were routed out once more by the jangling bell to pile and cover hurriedly the brown beans. Except for the patrollers (*rondantes*), moving in groups on the roads and through the coffee groves to pick up slaves out without passes (*guías* or *escriptos*) to visit nearby plantations or taverns, activity ceased.

With the arrival of Saturday evening and Sunday — awaited with much the spirit of the American South's "Come day, go day, God send Sunday" — came the only interruption of the work routine of plantation life. On Saturday the evening stint was usually omitted to give the labor force an opportunity to live without close supervision. Near a fire on the drying terrace, to the beating of two or three drums, slaves — men, women, and children — led by one of their master-singers, danced and sang until the early morning hours.

Even Sunday too was partially devoted to work. In morning chores, lasting until 9 or 10, field hands attended to the auxiliary tasks of the plantation: hauling firewood from clearings, preparing pasture by burning the grass cover, clearing brush from boundary ditches, repairing dams and roads, and killing ever-present *saúva* ants with fire and bellows. Sunday was the day for distribution of tobacco cut from a huge roll of twisted leaf smeared with honey, and of clean clothing for the following week's work. Chores completed, the master "gave permission" — permitted slaves to dispose of the remainder of the day until the line-up at nightfall. It was also common for planters to "give permission" on days other than Sunday to stagger the weekly day off and prevent slaves from meeting with friends from nearby plantations.

Many now scattered to small *roças* [small cultivated plot] near the plantation center, where they raised coffee, corn, and beans. Planters gave them these plots for various reasons: they gave the slave cultivators a sense of property which, known or unknown to Brazilian masters, continued an African tradition and softened the harsh life of slavery; they provided subsistence foodstuffs which planters failed to raise in their emphasis on one-crop agriculture; and, by offering cash for the produce, planters put into slaves' hands small change for supplementary articles not provided by the plantation. Often planters insisted that slaves sell only to them the coffee they raised. Slaves obtained cash too when the custom became widespread among planters to pay for Sunday or saints'-day labor.

Where male and female slaves cohabited, men often were accompanied to the roças by their children, while women washed, mended, and cooked, bringing the noon meal to their mates in the field. The single men brought firewood for the cook to prepare their meal, returning at eating hours. Other slaves used the free time to weave sleeping mats or cut and sew clothing for sale. With cash or corn or beans, slaves went on Sundays to trade at nearby saloons (*tabernas*) or small country stores. On a visit to a fazenda of the province of Rio, the Swiss Pradez entered a fazenda-owned *venda* [country store] run by an aging slave "aunt" of the fazendeiro's confidence where he found the typical stock: tobacco and cachaça (particularly attractive to slaves), notions including mirrors, straw hats, and clothing cut from cotton cloth (*Petrope*) of a quality slightly better than the coarse cloth furnished by the plantation. Outside the confines of the fazenda, he found a white taberna proprietor who served Negroes with cachaça at a *vintem* per glass. In friendly fashion the white man, to Pradez's surprise, discussed with a slave the weather, the crops, and his master, as though the slave were a "client to be maintained."

45. *Causes for the Abolition of Slavery in Brazil*

RICHARD GRAHAM

For a note on Professor Graham see Reading 40.

One may examine the general histories of Brazil in vain in search of satisfactory explanations for the passage of the law in 1888 which freed three quarters of a million slaves, bringing ruin to many landowners and destroying the political system they had created. Although these histories mention some of the same factors with which this article is concerned, they do so only in passing and without stressing their causative importance. One is left with the general impression that the Brazilian Parliament issued the law freeing the slaves in response to humanitarian sentiments and to the pressure of public opinion aroused by a propaganda campaign ably directed by a handful of abolitionists. Pandiá Calógeras insisted that the step "was the inevitable consequence of irresistible national opinion." Clarence H. Haring, in his summary of secondary works on Brazilian history, said that "Public meetings, articles in the daily press, and abolitionist societies . . . wore down the reluctance of a Parliament dominated by slavery interests." Brazilian textbooks, not surprisingly, place their emphasis either on this same crusading effort or on the humanitarian sentiments of the emperor and the princess rather than on the pressure applied by the slaves themselves in their own behalf. The only

"Causes for the Abolition of Negro Slavery in Brazil: An Interpretive Essay" by Richard Graham, *Hispanic American Historical Review,* 46 (1966), pp. 123–137, passim. Reprinted by permission of the publisher, Duke University Press.

English-language study of the question — an article published in 1933 by Percy Alvin Martin — points to the abolitionist campaign, to parliamentary activity, and to voluntary action on the part of some slave owners and refers only in passing to the failure of the army to pursue runaway slaves.

It is true that Parliament passed the law outlawing slavery by an over-whelming majority. We know, however, that this Parliament represented the large landowners of the country, groups which depended for their income and way of life on the labor of slaves. Is it possible to maintain that the representatives of the slave owners — in many cases slave owners themselves — abandoned their clearest and most vital economic interests as a result of brilliant speeches and the outcry of the press? If the answer to this question is "no," then other answers must be found. The purpose of this article is to suggest an alternative explanation based primarily on an informed reading of the secondary literature. Although full substantiation will require careful research in primary sources, this interpretation has the initial advantage of avoiding the contradictions inherent in the conventional accounts.

The thesis of this article is that the ideas propagated by the abolitionists did in fact play a decisive role in bringing about the end of slavery but not in the way generally depicted. The abolitionists appealed to the needs of new urban groups which had emerged in Brazil after the Paraguayan War (1865–1870). These groups, stimulated by this propaganda, encouraged and abetted the virtual revolt of the slaves through mass flights from the plantations. The planters, faced with a *fait accompli,* preferred to legalize it in order to prevent the further decay of their position. In many cases a chronic shortage of slaves had already hurt them severely. Foreign influences and even pressures were largely responsible for this shortage and for the measures taken in behalf of the slaves before 1871. When the Rio Branco Law was passed, though the new urban groups were still weak, the planters had already begun to feel the labor shortage.

In order to understand the interplay of forces which led to the abolition of slavery in Brazil, it is necessary to understand two major changes in Brazilian economic and social life. One was the rise of coffee exports and the expansion of new coffee producing regions; the other was the increasing size and importance of the cities.

During the latter half of the nineteenth century Brazil was swept into the European economic vortex. The increasing momentum of the industrial revolution in Europe and the United States meant not only a rising urban population in the "developed" world and an increasing leisure with which to enjoy luxury items such as coffee, but also the application of new technology to sea and land transport, significantly lowering the cost of commodities shipped to and from Brazil. As a result, Brazilian coffee exports increased so markedly as to disturb the established economic and social relationships. At first the bulk of this production centered in the valley of the Paraíba do Sul, but coffee exportation stimulated new interest in railroad-building. In 1868 new lines were opened from the port of Santos to the rich west-central lands in the state of São Paulo, whence other railroads spread throughout the new area. By the mid-1880s the province of São Paulo was producing more coffee than Rio de Janeiro.

With the railroads went the advancing economic frontier, and west-central São Paulo was incorporated for the first time into Brazil's money economy. Where the railroad reached, there appeared the large, modern coffee plantation; neat rows of glistening bushes up and down the rolling countryside replaced the haphazard patches of subsistence crops which had formerly been grown in the virgin forest. No longer dependent on mule trains to carry their produce to waiting ships in Santos, the planters could now move more easily to ever better lands. Meanwhile, the Paraíba valley entered a period of economic decline with decaying mansions bespeaking a grander past.

The boisterous prosperity of the São Paulo coffee area brought to the fore a new group of men. The great coffee planters here were not dominated by the traditions of a seignorial past but were drawn from a previously unfavored group of small landowners and merchants. With the enthusiasm of men on their way up they threw themselves at the land, driving their insufficient slaves, borrowing money, engaging in battles over land, acquiring more, and pushing ever westward. They looked upon their land as capital rather than as a mark of status. They acquired it to produce wealth, and if old methods did not succeed, they would try new ones. As landed entrepreneurs they showed their innovating spirit by adopting a new crop, by using novel techniques to process it, and by enthusiastically supporting railroads, which they often built themselves, and they demanded a more plentiful and flexible source of labor than the institution of slavery could provide.

The increasing export trade also helped to bring about the rise of new urban groups and general commercial growth in Brazil. No longer did only foreigners become merchants. New establishments such as banks, transport companies, insurance corporations, and urban services rapidly appeared to serve the rising demands of coffee commerce. These businesses hired a growing number of urban dwellers in white-collar jobs. The expanding coffee revenues also financed a proliferating bureaucracy in the capitals to deal with the increasingly complex problems of administering a prosperous country. Smaller towns such as Itú, Sorocaba, and Campinas became more important as distributing centers for foodstuffs and supplies in a monocultural area that had previously been self-sufficient. Smaller port cities like Santos and Niteroi shared in the new prosperity. Urban growth became characteristic.

Simultaneously new attitudes appeared, divorced from the land and skeptical of aristocratic values. These were men of modern attitudes. Personal relations began to lose their importance in the cities, and men were soon talking nostalgically about the good old days in contrast to the "mercenary instinct of our time." The idea that men should be rewarded according to their ability began to receive wider acceptance. The growth of an export economy created a distinctive culture, oriented towards Europe. Port cities became the beachheads of European civilization. Fashions of clothes, eating habits, architectural styles, and opinions all reflected the new influences of Europe. . . .

The urban centers, then, were filled not only with an expanding number of merchants and bureaucrats directly related to the export economy, but also with industrial entrepreneurs, engineers, military officers, and the sons of the older aristocracy who absorbed the values of these new groups. They shared an interest in change and "progress," a belief in a society characterized by social mobility and individualism, and an economy dominated by the profit motive.

They were also almost invariably opposed to slavery. This was especially true of those men associated with industry. Their whole way of life demanded the freedom of all men to be freely contracted, freely fired, freely sold to, freely moved — units to be joined and disjoined where and how economic imperatives might require. Brazilian entrepreneurs were generally committed to the abolition of slavery. They complained that slavery slowed down capital formation and tied it up in immovable labor. An industrialist in Bahia said that the best protection that government could give industry was to end slavery. . . . Industrialists believed that the substitution of a free work force for the slave one was the solution to Brazil's labor problem. The leading São Paulo coffee-planters-turned-railroad-builders were active in importing European laborers to take the place of the slave.

The increasing demand for labor in an expanding coffee economy and the rise of urban groups dissatisfied with slavery as a system made abolition a necessity. Why then, we may ask, were the first steps toward abolition taken in the late 1860s and early 1870s, before either of these forces could be considered very strong? And why was the African slave trade prohibited as early as 1850? The answer to both these questions is to be found in the pressure applied by the British.

British efforts to destroy the slave trade have been much discussed and need not detain us here. A long succession of treaties, antislave-trade legislation, and finally, the actual invasion of Brazilian ports by British ships are clear evidence of the British commitment to this goal. Nor do we need to assess the British responsibility for the end of the slave trade. Probably both nations deserve some credit. Britain applied pressure at a time when the Brazilian government was proud of its newly established control over the entire nation and was worried about impending diplomatic and military difficulties in the Río de la Plata. At the same time a momentary surfeit of new slaves helped to bring about the passage and rigorous application of the anti-slave-trade law. Thus the energetic British actions combined with propitious circumstances in Brazil itself to end the slave trade.

It is less well known that Britain continued to put pressure on the government of Pedro II in the 1850s and 1860s until Brazil itself gave evidence of a firm commitment to end slavery. Whereas the law freeing those children of slaves born after September 28, 1871, is usually considered the first evidence of an abolitionist campaign, it was really the conclusion of the British phase of the story which had begun forty years earlier. . . . It is clear that British pressure was responsible for this law, inasmuch as neither the coffee planters of São Paulo nor the new urban groups had yet emerged to exert political influence in this direction.

Some historians have suggested that British influence toward abolition sprang less from humanitarianism than from a desire to increase the buying power of the Brazilian market for British goods. In fact people are rarely that farsighted. The results of abolition were uncertain; it might have plunged Brazil into a period of chaos and economic decline. British merchants in Rio and textile manufacturers in Manchester protested loudly against Christie's forceful actions, and he did not hesitate to say that they were aiding Brazilian slavery. A much more defensible and sophisticated explanation is that middle-class values tended to dominate the entire British nation and that slavery and the slave trade contradicted those values. The right to be master of one's own being was the most basic of all individual rights and a threat to that right anywhere in the world was a threat to the validity of all those rights that the British middle class considered essential. For the Britisher at that time it was no longer a matter of weighing pros and cons and measuring the economic advantages or disadvantages of slavery. A principle essential to their way of life was now at stake. By the same token slavery aroused opposition in those Brazilian sectors which were attacking a traditional, preindustrial and nonindividualistic society.

By the end of the 1870s the setting was favorable for the abolitionist movement. An expanding export economy was demanding more labor. It was obvious that slavery would end sooner or later and that no new slaves would be available either from Africa or from procreation. Finally new urban groups were finding slavery an impediment not only to their own financial success but to the spread of their world-view. How these general forces were translated into concrete action is of crucial importance to an understanding of this period in Brazilian history. For the sake of clarity, it is best to jump ahead, to begin with the direct causes of parliamentary action freeing the slaves, and then move backward to show the importance of these broader trends.

The most important immediate cause of abolition was the flight of the slaves from the coffee plantations of São Paulo and Rio. In the two years before the abolition law was passed in May 1888 an enormous number of slaves revolted against authority with their feet, running away from the plantations, at first secretly, one by one, and later in mass and almost publicly. The planters could do nothing by themselves against this sort of direct action, and the dichotomy of city and country now became evident for the first time, for in the system of escape the cities played an essential part, as agents of the forces of change. Rio, Niteroi, Petrópolis, Campos, Santos, São Paulo, and minor cities of the coffee region became virtually free cities to the slave, for measures were adopted to help him on to the state of Ceará, where slavery had been abolished as early as 1884, or undertook legal action to prove that he was illegally held, or gave him permanent asylum.

In São Paulo Antonio Bento de Souza e Castro organized a system whereby slaves were lured away from the plantations, put on trains or shepherded on foot to Santos, and installed in shanty-towns. He also had the temerity to offer runaway slaves to plantation owners as hired hands during the peak harvest season. The very railways that had made possible the extension of coffee agriculture now served the slave. As one historian put it: "There was not a passenger or freight train on which a runaway slave might not find means of hiding himself, and there was not a station where someone would not discreetly receive him and help him." Almost all railroad employees were said to be abolitionists, and not the least enthusiastic were the managers. In Santos where all local slaves had been freed in 1886 by public subscription, the slaves who arrived via the "underground railroad" were immediately sheltered in the outskirts of the city. As many as ten thousand were sometimes gathered there. . . .

Why did not the government stop the mass flights of slaves? Although both the provincial and central governments took action from time to time, it soon became clear that their agents, many of whom were second-generation bureaucrats with urban backgrounds, did not have their hearts in the attempt to repress slave flights. It was in the cities that the government was located, and efforts to restrain the underground railway there met civilian opposition at every turn. It is especially significant that the armed forces were recruited from the cities, especially the officers. The military schools had for years been the site of abolitionist societies. Many are the proofs of military reluctance to act as slave hunters until finally in October 1887 the Club Militar, made up of the leading elements of the army, petitioned the princess-regent to be excused from chasing slaves. The landed aristocracy were growing ever more timid before the demands of the increasingly self-assertive officers, and the military men had their way. It has even been suggested that, if the legislature had not passed the law of abolition in 1888, the cities would have risen in revolt, and the military would not have defended the regime.

The cooperation of urban classes can be seen in a humorous incident that took place in Santos. The government of the province had sent a trainload of troops to capture runaway slaves there. When the train pulled into the station, the soldiers found themselves surrounded by the leading matrons of the town who jammed the doors of the cars, preventing them from alighting. The superintendent of the railway persuaded the half-hearted commandant of the expedition to surrender to *force majeure* and return to the provincial capital. Neither the soldiers nor these representatives of the new urban groups were interested in protecting the human property of the landowners.

Finally during the first months of 1888 the planters began to free their own slaves in order to prevent them from leaving the plantations. By May it was estimated that half the slaves who had been in the Campos area six months earlier were free, and that one third of the São Paulo plantations were being worked by recently freed slaves. Since the process then in full swing would have ended slavery to all intents and purposes within a few months, the law abolishing slavery was largely a formality. One anti-abolitionist asked: "For what, an abolition law? In fact it is done already — and revolutionarily. The terrified masters seek to stem the exodus by giving immediate freedom to their slaves."

This is not to undervalue the role of the abolitionists' ideas in bringing about the end of slavery. It took much hard work to persuade the slaves to leave the plantations. The Confederação Abolicionista in Rio hired Italian peddlers to circulate among them and distribute leaflets throughout the interior. Presumably these were read to the illiterate slaves. Slave foremen murdered some of the peddlers, but the news continued to spread. The abolitionists also made it a point to convey their message to those slaves who passed through the city with their masters. On their return, these slaves carried with them the idea of escape and the knowledge that they and their fellows would be helped and protected. . . .

It was the force and effectiveness of the abolitionist crusade which persuaded large segments of the urban population to acquiesce or contribute to the success of the movement. If it had not been for the constant abolitionist effort to drive home the anachronism of slavery in an age of "progress" it is doubtful that the military officers would have refused to cooperate in preserving the status quo. Other urban groups cooperated as well in the successful escape of the slaves.

This abolitionist campaign, which began in 1879, has been examined in some detail by others, so that little need be said about it here. Throughout the 1880s journalists and publicists carried the message into the homes of the urban middle classes. Well-financed abolitionist societies provided the direction for the many-faceted campaign. These clubs presented a series of lectures, one almost every week, and it became the fashion among would-be modernists to attend. On the flimsiest excuse a demonstration would be staged, with parades, banners, and speeches. The societies published several newspapers and used all possible means to publicize the cause. In Parliament the movement found brilliant speakers to push through the early, cautious half-measures. From 1884 to 1888 this body was involved in the slavery argument almost constantly, and opponents of abolition blamed the work of the publicists in the city and the flight of the slaves in the country for the new concern. Antônio Prado, a leading coffee planter and entrepreneur who could speak for the more enlightened country interest, took up the leadership of the parliamentary maneuvers toward abolition and pushed it through. The abolitionists had successfully marshaled the concerns of the city to push a new group of planters to take a position on the side of progress.

On May 13, 1888, the princess-regent signed the law abolishing slavery in Brazil without compensation. Month-long celebrations took place in almost all the cities of Brazil with fireworks, speeches, and parades. In the countryside, however, there was little rejoicing. The slaves themselves were disoriented, not knowing what to do with their freedom. Many flocked into the cities to find their fellows who had earlier fled the plantations. The masters, even those who had acquiesced or cooperated in the final stages of the movement, were naturally dazed by the rapidity of the transformation. A general depression in the countryside followed. Government efforts to ameliorate this situation by lending funds to the landowners only strengthened still further the urban groups of bank managers, company promoters, stock manipulators, and their employees.

The effects of abolition were far-reaching. It shifted power from the sugar zone of the northeast and the old coffee region of the Paraíba valley to the new coffee zone of São Paulo state. It increased the confidence of the new urban groups and, although their victory appeared short lived, this was a significant step along the lengthy path toward modernization. It also seriously weakened the monarchy whose ties to the landowners are well known. Even the ex-slave, now a wage-earner but deprived of the sense of victory, had taken at least one step closer to the modern world.

46. The Brazilian Dilemma

CARL N. DEGLER

Brazilians and Americans are studying, and meditating on, as never before the history of Negro slavery in their countries and its significance for the future. Mary Wilhelmine Williams and Arthur Ramos were pioneers a generation ago in comparing the different fates of Negroes in the two countries,* and today there is a growing flood of publications, as is evidenced by a recent and comprehensive reader in comparative history.†

Now that black studies have been so vigorously developed in our universities, it is not surprising that some of the historians who have previously concentrated on our own national experience have been attracted to the comparative study of Negro slavery. Professor Carl N. Degler of Stanford has published a volume of great interest comparing Brazilian and United States conditions, which deservedly won a Pulitzer Prize in 1972.

A BRAZILIAN DILEMMA

Yet as Brazil continues to industrialize and the competitive society of classes spreads, the likelihood of increasing discrimination grows, too. Racial tension and color prejudice, as we have seen, already exist in Brazil, but if the ex-

Reprinted by permission of The Macmillan Company from *Neither Black nor White: Slavery and Race Relations in Brazil and the United States* by Carl N. Degler (New York: Macmillan, 1971), pp. 281–287. Copyright © 1971 by Carl N. Degler.

* The late Professor Williams of Goucher College presented a paper in 1922 at the Congresso Internacional de História da América in Rio de Janeiro entitled "The Treatment of Negro Slaves in the Brazilian Empire: A comparison with the United States of America," which was published in the proceedings of the congress and also in the *Journal of Negro History,* 15 (1930), pp. 315–336. So far as I know, Dr. Ramos never wrote anything on the subject, but I remember discussing the subject with him in detail in the early 1940s during his stay in the United States as a distinguished visitor under a program of the Department of State. The late Dr. Ramos was an outstanding Brazilian specialist in race relations, whose principal works are *As culturas negras no Novo Mundo* (Rio de Janeiro, 1937), a study of the acculturation of the Negro in America, and *The Negro in Brazil* (Washington, D.C., 1939).

† *Slavery in the New World: A Reader in Comparative History,* ed. Laura Foner and Eugene D. Genovese (Englewood Cliffs, N.J.: Prentice-Hall, 1969).

perience of Negroes in São Paulo tells us anything, it is that a competitive society encourages discrimination and tension. In part at least, therefore, the history of race relations in the United States may well be in the future of Brazil. For as the social system of Brazil approaches the competitive model of the United States, as the example of São Paulo in this century suggests it is, then antagonisms between black and white can be expected to rise. Florestan Fernandes points out that in 1950 Negroes and mulattoes made up 70 per cent of the population in Bahia and that about 11 per cent of the nation's diplomas from secondary schools were accounted for by them. In São Paulo state, where blacks and mulattoes constitute only 11 per cent of the population, they provided 7 per cent of the country's total number of secondary school graduates. The difference Fernandes rightly attributes to the growth of and therefore the opportunities provided by the *paulista* economy as compared with the Bahian. An expanding economy encourages Negroes and mulattoes "to fight for equality of opportunities and for equality of treatment." A similar experience can be expected, he predicts, as other regions of Brazil develop economically. In 1960 the London *Times* was quoted on the subject of discrimination in Brazil. The Brazilians, the newspaper observed, explain particular examples of discrimination by reference to the low level of Negro education. But the *Times* writer did not wholly accept that nonracial explanation. "A Negro waiter is a rare thing in a high class hotel or restaurant and the big shops never have them as salespeople," the paper accurately noted. "What concerns a great number of Latin Americans, primarily Brazilians, is that, with industrialization and the gradual raising of the level of incomes and consequent educational facilities, the occasion will soon come in which the Negroes will want to go beyond these limited positions. They ask — what will be the attitude of the whites who have to face that fact?"

More recently, an article on race relations in Brazil carried in the prestigious *Jornal do Brasil* commented that although some Brazilians expect to see race antagonisms decline in the future, others foresee social and racial tensions rising as Negroes compete more and more with whites. Then, the writer pointed out, the antagonism "which today is directed at social class" will be directed against color. Even a student of Brazilian race relations like Edison Carneiro, who deplores appeals to "negritude," or even the formation of Negro organizations, recognizes that the trend in his country is toward greater prejudice against color. At the conference on the Negro since abolition, held in 1968 and already referred to, Carneiro said, "I have the impression that we are entering a bad future, that is, a growing increase in prejudice in Brazil. The facts told here [examples of discrimination] are naturally a little old, but we are a type of society which promotes prejudice; we are in a period of Brazilian life also in which economic development itself, the development of the country, and social development can be as much ahead as behind; the fact is the country is growing, is experimenting with its powers in various fields and all of this will create much more prejudice than we have today. To the extent that the Negro educates himself, that the Negro gains money and notoriety, becomes more visible, there will be more prejudice than before. Only recently has the Negro competed with the white, it has been what Abdias [do Nascimento] remembers: he [the Negro] knew his place. Today the Negro knows more and in a manner that begins to compete with the white. To the extent that such occurs, which is inevitable, in view of Brazilian development, to that extent prejudice will increase."

Someone as understanding of and sympathetic to Brazil in its history of race relations as Charles Wagley, the North American anthropologist, also has some doubts that the future will be as smooth as the past in this regard. "There are indications both in the present studies and in reports from the great metropolitan centers of the country," he writes at the end of his *Race and Class in Rural Brazil,* "that discrimination, tensions, and prejudices based on race are appearing." As more and more Negroes rise socially, challenging those above, he goes on, race will become increasingly important.

Insofar as young Negroes become increasingly conscious of their position in Brazilian society, the antagonism between the colors will be accentuated. Some Brazilian sociologists like Florestan Fernandes and Oracy Nogueira point to evidence of young blacks and mulattoes breaking out of the old traditional patterns, but there is not much evidence that the kind of uprising that erupted among young Negroes in the United States in the early 1960's is in the offing in Brazil. Roger Bastide, however, asserts that Brazilian Negroes will be less timid as time goes on. And Abdias do Nascimento pays tribute to the example of the North American Negroes "whose brave struggle is a most important lesson not only there, but here, in our country." He also suggests that the example of the new African states will not be lost on the Brazilian Negroes. "The very presence of their diplomatic representatives functions as an implicit supervision and criticism of white and black relations in our racial democracy." L. A. Costa Pinto, too, notes that the stage is set for rapid change. He observes that most Negroes are barred from educational opportunities in Brazil; "it is that more profound and structural matter that is at issue. On that day in which the masses of color become conscious of that, then will commence the most acute and decisive problem in the race relations of this country." Finally, it is worth quoting a recent conclusion of a long time student of race relations in Brazil. "The social ascension of the Negroes in a class society," writes F. H. Cardoso, "contrary to what one supposed in the past, far from signifying the end to prejudice, can indicate, in fact, the beginning in Brazil of a 'Negro problem' in the same terms as it exists, for example, in the United States."

The implication or outright prediction that Brazil may be going the way of the United States ought not to be misunderstood. It is certainly not meant that Brazilians will move to the kind of racial situation from which the United States has just emerged — that is, to one in which segregation is legal and a racial defense of Negro inferiority is commonplace and the basis of the laws. History does not run backwards; moreover, the existence of the mulatto escape hatch would certainly prevent it from happening. Nor is lynching, often recognized as a peculiarly American practice, likely to come to Brazil. What does seem in the offing is that Brazil will see more, rather than less, racial friction, but that the friction will be on a low level of violence and that Negroes will remain at the bottom of the social and economic pyramid.

If the United States continues to follow a policy of compensatory assistance to Negroes, the material lot of blacks will probably continue to be better in the United States than in Brazil. For one lesson seems inescapable from the Brazilian and United States experiences: in the absence of positive aid to Negroes newly emerged from slavery, full social and economic integration into society is difficult, if not impossible to achieve. In fact, over a century after emancipation in the United States and eighty years after abolition in Brazil, Negroes in both societies are still at the bottom of the economic and social pyramids. "In the next year 1968," writes Abdias do Nascimento, "we will complete 80 years of legal abolition. Analyzing today's reality we could almost say that the Golden Law was signed yesterday. The situation of the free Negro is changed little in the 80 years since abolition: low social, educational, economic, political, and sanitary status, and the list of frustrations transformed into a strong potentiality of just resentments by the race." Nascimento goes on to observe that John F. Kennedy, in his famous speech in behalf of the Civil Rights bill in 1963, noted that the average Negro's opportunities lagged far behind those of the average white. But, Nascimento goes on, if in the United States a Negro had only half the chance of a white child to finish secondary school, in Brazil a Negro had only one-third the chance of a white; if a Negro child in the United States enjoys only a third of a white child's chance to complete college, a black in Brazil has less than a tenth of a white child's. And it seems likely that the opportunities for blacks in Brazil will not improve appreciably unless positive efforts are made to draw them into the mainstream of economic and social life. The positive efforts recently made in the United States to expand opportunities for blacks have certainly not yet met the need, but they have undoubtedly been in the right direction. Unless Brazil recognizes a similar need for positive help for blacks, the pattern of race relations there will not improve and probably will worsen as competition spreads throughout the economy and society.

Indeed, in this development it might be said lies the Brazilian dilemma to place beside the American dilemma about which Gunnar Myrdal wrote twenty-five years ago. The alternatives for Brazilians are not as sharp or obvious as they were then for Americans; Brazilians have not brazenly denied equality through legal segregation and outright public assertions of Negro inferiority. Nevertheless, there is a contradiction between their professed racial democracy and the social facts of life as we have reviewed them and Brazilian Negroes perceive them. Brazilians have the choice of continuing to insist upon their racial democracy in the face of the social facts or else they must admit that the society does not live up to its ideals. Either choice, as in any dilemma, is unpalatable for many whites. But in Brazil, as in the United States, the question is one for the whites to decide. It is they who have created the present situation. As one Negro in São Paulo rightly said, "If the problem of the Negro comes to assume in Brazil the proportions that it has acquired in the United States there will be only one group to blame: the whites." Besides, as Fernandes has pointed out, there is no social group with power in Brazilian society which also has a stake in making the ideal of a racial democracy work. The blacks who are poor and without the vote therefore lack the necessary economic and political means for effecting change, whereas the colored elite "either does not feel the necessity of this defense or does not consider it advantageous to compromise themselves for such objectives, which concern the future of the community rather than their own personal situation." Hence he calls for a conscious policy of racial integration by the Brazilian government because no longer can Brazil "continue to maintain, without grave injustice, the Negro on the margin of the development of a civilization that he helped to build. As Nabuco wrote, 'We have to reconstruct Brazil under free labor and the union of the races in liberty.' As long as we have not reached that objective, we do not have a *racial democracy,* nor a *democracy.* By a paradox of history, the Negro has become, in our era, the touchstone of our capacity to forge in the tropics this foundation of modern civilization."

The Revolutions of the Early Nineteenth Century Did Not Abolish the Colonial Heritage. In the first edition of Life in Mexico *by Fanny Calderón de la Barca, which was published by Little Brown in Boston in 1843, only one illustration was included: the imposing structure shown above, the* Tribunal de Minería, *built in the late colonial period to house the Mining Guild which had been established in 1770. The Guild drew up the important mining Ordinances of 1787, opened a School of Mines which represented a distinct achievement in scientific education, and the Guild was also notable in that its business was conducted principally by Creoles.*

From the School came many political and intellectual leaders of the Republic, and the experience gained in handling mining problems proved to be useful during the difficult years of the nineteenth century in Mexico. It is not surprising, therefore, to find the famous commentator on Mexican life, Fanny Calderón de la Barca, including this illustration in her popular work (Reading 49).

SECTION XI

The Social Life
of Nineteenth-Century
Latin America

The social history of modern Latin America is largely in its infancy, but encouraging beginnings have been made. Argentina is often studied with the capital Buenos Aires as the center of action, but the nation was built up in the nineteenth century largely by the labor of immigrants. Many of these humble workers grew wheat out on the enormous pampa, where they lived a lonely and circumscribed existence. These unsung workers made possible a prosperous wheat production (Reading 47).

The social history of Brazil has been to a great extent invented by Gilberto Freyre, the gifted Pernambucan writer who has almost single-handedly revolutionized the writing of history there in the years since 1930. One of his earliest publications was an imaginative recreation of life in Brazil in the 1850s (Reading 48).

For Mexico we have the classic description of Mexican people, customs, and the land by Fanny Calderón de la Barca, who presents an unsurpassed view of life in the 1840s (Reading 49). This sensitive Scottish woman was interested in all aspects of society. She wrote perceptively about nuns and Indians, but she moved in diplomatic circles and tended to spend a lot of time at balls, receptions, and formal affairs with a consequent emphasis on upper-class affairs.

None of these selections gives a comprehensive description of social life; that is not the purpose of their authors. But they do reveal partial aspects of nineteenth-century development and demonstrate how rich and varied social history can be.

THE FUTURE OF SOCIAL HISTORY

The period of Latin American history from 1830 until the end of the century is just beginning to be studied seriously by historians, and our knowledge of social developments during these important decades is correspondingly deficient. We do have many valuable travel accounts, but no matter how intelligent and sophisticated the traveler may be, he is likely to provide an impressionistic view of the foreign society he is describing. Moreover, it is an "outside" view.

To achieve a solid social history the local archives must be ransacked, and all too often they are poorly organized if they exist at all. Church records on births, deaths, and marriages are basic, but only a beginning has been made to exploit them. Quantitatively minded historians tend to focus on the twentieth century, for obvious reasons, though a few bold spirits are tackling nineteenth-century topics. Even newspapers, so fundamental for social historians, are sometimes hard to locate in series, though the late Dr. Howard F. Cline and other library-minded scholars have made significant advances in this difficult field.

Private papers are a weak reed to lean upon so far as nineteenth-century figures are concerned. Whether personal and family records are saved and made available for researchers seems to depend largely upon chance. There are some honorable exceptions, but the kind of intimate historical documentation represented by the 1200 Civil War letters edited by Robert Manson Myers (*The Children of Pride: A True Story of Georgia and the Civil War,* 1972) is almost inconceivable for Latin America in the nineteenth century — or the twentieth century for that matter. But changes are occurring in the way historians are looking at the past, and there is some ground for a hope that improvement is on the way.

47. The Life of the Immigrant Wheat Growers on the Pampa

JAMES R. SCOBIE

Professor James R. Scobie of Indiana University has established himself as one of the outstanding Argentine specialists in the United States, with a special flair for social history. His *Argentina: A City and a Nation* (2nd ed., 1971) has become a standard work, and the volume from which the present selection comes is one of the few solid works in English on Latin American social history. The picture given here helps us to understand why Professor Carl Solberg terms the Argentine immigration policy a tragedy: "The ruling elites valued immigration primarily as a source of cheap agricultural labor and failed to enact land distribution policies that would have encouraged immigrant farmers to settle the nation's vast and empty interior. . . . Partly as a result of the elite's tragically shortsighted land policies, after a quarter century of massive immigration, the Argentine interior remained sparsely populated and the nation's enormous agricultural potential had not developed to its capacity." *

The wheatgrower . . . was first a colonist and then, as the nineteenth century drew to a close, increasingly a tenant farmer. The distinction between the small independent-farmer class and the tenant-farmer class was important for Argentina's agricultural and social future. But in terms of origin and way of life, the colonist, the tenant farmer and, at times, even the migrant laborer were one.

They shared certain basic characteristics. Although there were sprinklings of people from all the regions of Europe, Italians from the northern agricultural districts of Lombardy and Piedmont predominated. Their overpopulated homelands provided little opportunity for advancement. They were poor, but as a general rule they were not in a state of starvation or abject misery. It was partly a push and partly a pull that started them across the Atlantic: the impossibility of advance at home, the hope that they could

From *Revolution on the Pampas: A Social History of Argentina Wheat, 1860–1910* by James R. Scobie (Austin: University of Texas Press, 1964), pp. 55–70, passim. Reprinted by permission.

* Carl Solberg, *Immigration and Nationalism: Argentina and Chile, 1890–1914* (Austin: University of Texas Press, 1970), pp. 169–170.

accumulate some small capital in America and return to Italy, Spain, or France to enjoy it. There were city boys in their midst, but the majority had some link to the land in Europe, either as farmers or rural laborers. They knew farming; but they knew it on tiny plots, on soil that had been tilled for hundreds of years. Sharecropping and high tenant rents were part of their life. They were conservative and illiterate. Neither new techniques nor scientific farming made any impression on them. Extremely materialistic in hoarding away their gains, they cared, at the same time, little about material comforts. Ambitious in the sense of wanting to accumulate a small store of capital, they nonetheless had few desires beyond that of being left alone. They were hard workers but lacked the foresight and vision to organize and diversify their rural labors. When no pressing job presented itself, they found complete idleness their only relaxation. They were a fatalistic and humble people, respectful and fearful of authority — of those who were powerful, or wealthy, or educated.

The Swiss started the rural colonization of Argentina. Most of the Swiss who came to Argentina before 1870 became farmers, and the majority of colonists as of that date were Swiss. . . . Leadership in agricultural labor, however, soon passed to Italy. . . .

The majority of these immigrants, in fact all of those with whom we are concerned here, traveled steerage or third-class. This meant an uncomfortable and crowded two to four weeks below decks, with no baths, inadequate toilets, poor food, monotony, and seasickness. But it was cheap. Argentina is twice as far as the United States from European ports, yet in the 1890's the *golondrina* could pay for his round-trip passage with two weeks' labor in Argentina.

Buenos Aires was the port into which this mass of humanity poured. In the days when contracted settlers were brought from Europe, river steamer and jolting cart immediately carried the colonists off to some remote section of the pampas. This type of immigration, however, was short-lived, and ship captains thereafter merely dumped their human cargo — immigrants who had already paid their passage — on the shore. . . .

Until 1900 the methods of handling this influx of Europeans were extremely rudimentary. Although there were immigrant commissions and even an immigrants' hotel, by and large the newcomers merely piled in on top of their countrymen in the city's slums. The era of the *conventillos* dates from the 1880's and 1890's. Hunger, dirt, and poverty were nothing new to these immigrants, and in the crowded slums they found conviviality, people who spoke their dialect or tongue, even old acquaintances and friends. In boom times at least, there was no lack of occupations in the rapidly growing city.

Immigrants, regardless of origins, appeared as bricklayers, porters, stevedores, masons, housemaids, cooks, grocers, cartmen, peddlers, and beggars. Little wonder that of these arrivals only the migrant rural laborer and those with contracts or determination pressed on through Buenos Aires to the frightening, treeless waste of the pampas.

Those who wanted to get on the land were offered several economic alternatives. The first, chronologically if not in ultimate importance to wheat growing, was the chance to become a colonist. We have already had a glimpse of the development of official, railroad, and private colonization. A company, occasionally provincial or municipal but most often private, offered land to the agriculturist; at first it was a unit of eighty acres, but as wheat growing became more and more extensive the units increased in size to two hundred fifty and eventually to five hundred acres. The ultimate aim of the company was to sell its subdivisions to the colonist; that of the colonist was ownership. The most common procedure, at least after the initial colonizing ventures, was the outright sale of property in cash installments. Under this arrangement the colonist provided his own equipment and seed, assumed all risks, and if successful, gradually paid off his mortgage. Occasionally companies made advances of machinery, seeds, and food to colonists and accepted payments in percentages of the crop, but these terms represented undesirable risks to the company. Actual title to the land was never transferred to the colonist until he had completed all his payments and had canceled all his debts with the company.

Some of the early colonies achieved a sort of linguistic or ethnic unity, and companies usually tried to fill subdivisions consecutively in order to maintain contiguous settlement. The size of a colony ranged from twenty to two hundred families, and in some cases, such as in the province of Santa Fe, colonies became the basis for cities like Esperanza or Casilda. The company frequently provided stores and rented out threshers. A school and church were also added, but the colonists paid for building costs and maintenance. The structure of the colony might have been oriented toward the community. However, since the vast majority of the settlements were commercial ventures, little encouragement was given to any project which did not promise to bring an immediate financial return. Even the practice of model or experimental farms to teach new techniques was largely ignored. Unless the director took a personal interest in his settlers or there were strong ethnic or religious bonds uniting the community, a colony tended to be little more than individual farms scattered over several square miles of pampas.

The tenant farmer did not have even this vague sense of community, fixed location, or possible hope of landownership. His life, nevertheless, was not very different from that of the colonist. Landowners were eager for his labor, especially after 1890. If he truly had nothing except a strong back and the labor of his wife and children to offer, he might start as a *medianero* — a sharecropper who received implements and seed from the landowner and turned over half his harvest in payment. He was at the bottom of the tenant-farmer class. His contract with the landowner limited cultivation of a particular plot to a year or two; then he moved to a new location. His advantage, however, was that he had little to lose. He had no capital and no equipment. If the harvest was bad, he had no rent or mortgage to pay. The landlord shouldered the major portion of the risk and the *medianero* merely provided the labor. If crops were good for several successive years, the *medianero* was able to raise himself into the *arrendatario,* or tenant, category — or if truly wise he would return to the city with his small hoard of capital. For that reason and because of the unwelcome investment and risk incurred by the landowner, the number of *medianeros* tended to decline as wheat growing expanded.

The *arrendatario* was a rural capitalist. His most typical feature was that he had a personal investment in equipment, oxen, and horses in addition to his strong back. Sometimes he might be a man of considerable means who rented large extensions from a landowner and then sublet sections to other *arrendatarios* or *medianeros.* Frequently he was a person of more modest position, yet possessing sufficient funds to purchase a small lot of land. The hope of increasing his capital by extensive agriculture made him a tenant of five hundred acres rather than the owner of fifty. More often, however, he was a former *medianero* or even a migrant laborer who had saved enough money to buy a plow, a harrow, a team of horses, and some bags of seed. For the landowner this type of tenant farming was the most desirable since the whole risk and investment were assumed by the tenant. The owner contributed only the use of his land, which probably had been paying no income before and stood to be improved by cultivation. If a fixed charge could be levied per acre, so much the better, for then the owner collected whether or not there was a harvest. A more usual procedure was to hand over a percentage of the crop, ranging from 10 to 30 per cent according to the value of the land, the distance from transportation facilities, or the particular stage of wheat-growing history. Through a contract, usually oral, an area of from two hundred to five hundred acres was turned over to the tenant for a term of from three to six years. He had to build his own home and, if he chose, shelters for implements, animals, or grain. If there was no stream or waterhole nearby, he had to dig a well for his own use and that of his animals. Yet he received no allowance for improvements when he left, since, for the stock raiser, a house and a shed were obstructions rather than improvements. The tenant was hardly master of his rented land. The contract sometimes allowed him a small portion for pasturage, but only enough for necessary work animals. The rest he was obliged to cultivate, usually with the crop which the landowner designated. If his landlord was a cattleman it was almost certain that he would have to leave the land sown to alfalfa after his last harvest. As tenant farming spread, so did obligations become more onerous, such as having to use the owner's threshing machines, buy bags from him, sell the crop to him, or secure provisions from a specified store. . . .

A final economic alternative open to the agricultural immigrant was that chosen by thousands of Italians and Spaniards: to become rural migrant laborers or *golondrinas*. The *golondrina*'s objectives were different from those of the ownership-minded colonist or the small rural capitalist, the tenant farmer. He had come to earn wages. He either was single or had left his family behind in his homeland. His employer gave him food. He slept where he could, in sheds or in the fields — something not impossible during Argentine summers. His only expense, therefore, was the transatlantic voyage. Four to five months' labor in the wheat-corn harvest could bring him from forty to fifty pounds sterling — five to ten times what he could earn in his homeland — and this represented a net profit to take back to Italy or Spain in May. By the 1900's one hundred thousand such laborers a year entered Argentina, twice the average of the previous decade. . . .

These *golondrinas* were a necessary part of Argentina's expanding cereal economy. Employed by colonists, tenant farmers, and *estancieros,* they provided the manpower which Argentina lacked to harvest the record wheat crops. Their social impact on the countryside, however, cannot be compared to that of the colonist or tenant farmer. They were true swallows, men whose cultural significance was hardly greater than that of the machinery used to reap and thresh the grain. When they remained in Argentina, as many did, married, or sent for their families, they ceased to be *golondrinas*.

The colonist and the tenant farmer were, therefore, the principals in the social formation of the wheat-growing zone. In addition to economic motivations, they shared certain similarities in environment, psychology, and way of life.

Isolation was the predominating characteristic of the Argentine rural scene. This was only natural in a pastoral society where few humans were needed in the countryside. But it remained true even after cereal culture had invaded the pampas. Roads had not been necessary before the day of wheat; products moved on the hoof or, as with goods to and from the interior provinces, by oxcart. For this, mere trails across the pampas sufficed. Railroad construction in the 1870's and 1880's leaped over the intermediate stage of road building. British companies, building the railroads as investments, were guaranteed a minimum return on their capital by the Argentine government, and agricultural development insured their profits. Isolation was apparently broken down. Farm and seaport were linked by the railways, but the links were not among the farms themselves nor with rural communities or villages. The railroads were mere feelers which probed into the zones of cereal, cattle, and sheep to gather in freight for the ports. They fulfilled the immediate transport needs of the countryside and at the same time inhibited the construction of roads. The railroads did not want competition, and so for decades the only roads permitted in Argentina were the mud ruts radiating from the railroad stations.

The agriculturist was submerged in this isolation. The transportation system took his products to market but did nothing to break down the remoteness between him and his fellow men. Roads remained as they had for three centuries — dusty shallow troughs or long canals, according to the season. . . .

The country store — the *pulpería* in Buenos Aires or the general store in Santa Fe — was rural Argentina's only social institution. Its economic aspects will be studied in a later chapter, for it served as provider of merchandise, purchaser of products, banker, and sole dispenser of credit. In the isolation of a lonely countryside, its role as a place of conviviality and a source of information and news was perhaps as vital as its economic functions. In many ways, it took the place of the church, the school, the club, and the plaza, which were conspicuously absent on the pampas.

The origins of the country store were colonial. It had emerged within the pastoral economy. The *pulpería* of Buenos Aires or of the northwestern provinces was, in the original meaning of the term, a bar, a store, and a social club for gauchos. With the development of agriculture, a railway station or a colony became its preferred locations, and its commercial and merchandising interests increased. Rather than glasses of raw cane alcohol, it now dispensed cheap red wine to Italian farmers, and rather than salt and the dried leaves of *yerba mate,* it sold meat, beans, and biscuits. Here, on a Sunday or in the idle season between harvest and planting, the agriculturist could blunt his loneliness, secure the latest wheat prices and harvest rumors, and exchange news with neighbors he never visited. Yet many a farmer was not within reach of a country store; and even when he was, it hardly fulfilled his social needs.

Churches, schools, and clubs did not penetrate into rural Argentina for the simple reason that settlement was dispersed and often temporary. The colonies of Russian Jews in Entre Ríos and Santa Fe and, to a lesser degree, some of the older Swiss colonies of Santa Fe possessed strong religious and cultural unity. But these were rare exceptions. Agriculturists in Argentina, colonists and tenant farmers alike, did not as a rule live in villages and go out each day to cultivate the surrounding fields. Because of extensive agriculture where a great deal of land was superficially tilled, farm homes were spread out at considerable distances from each other. When eighty acres was the basic unit of wheat cultivation, it nevertheless required much walking or riding to reach a neighbor; with five hundred acres, the distance was nearly tripled, and the possibility of social institutions reaching the farm decreased in proportion. Weddings, funerals, and special church holidays might warrant the long trip to town or city. But the priest, clergyman, or rabbi could not minister to widely scattered families that lacked the resources or interest to form a congregation.

Education likewise faced insurmountable problems. The children were needed to work. And even if they could have been spared, where could schools have been built to reach this dispersed population? As soon as one left Buenos Aires and the coastal cities, educational facilities declined sharply in quality and number. In large areas of the wheat zone, they were nonexistent.

The Germans, the Swiss, and the Italians had their singing clubs, their shooting clubs, and their mutual-aid societies. But these were urban institutions. They throve in the towns of the wheat zone, many of which had been former colonies, such as Esperanza, San Carlos, Roldán, and Carcarañá, but not in the countryside. . . . If the farmer's hut seemed remote from the rural town, it must be realized that the town itself was just as remote, in a cultural and social sense, from the metropolis of Buenos Aires, the bustling ports of Rosario and Bahía Blanca, or the colonial-style city of Córdoba. . . .

The average rural town had a population between 2,000–6,000; an unpaved main street, a bare plaza, a few stores, several squares of mud-brick houses, the more pretentious of which were plastered or whitewashed on the outside; occasionally a church, a school, some storage sheds, and a railroad station. If it was the seat of a political subdivision, or *partido,* there was probably some sort of town hall on the plaza. The inhabitants were people of modest means and culture. The priest, the police chief, or *comisario,* the justice of the peace, and the schoolteacher represented the aristocracy and authority of the town. Here was no doctor; the apothecary attended any serious ills. No cattleman, no lawyers, no politicians, no bankers resided in it. In short, the average town had little to recommend it. After a visit to Rafaela in 1891, an understanding and usually sympathetic observer of the Argentine scene wrote: "All I can say, however, is that, if ever a man wishes to know what it is to have an inclination to commit suicide, let him spend a week in a camp town in the Argentine." In essence, the town was a small nucleus destined to handle the barest needs of the countryside and to expedite the transportation of products to the coast. Its economic role was perfectly caricatured by the local bakery: located in the heart of the wheat zone, the baker invariably received flour from the mills of Rosario or Buenos Aires. . . .

To see how the wheatgrower actually lived, we must strike an average, as we have already done with the transportation system and the town. There were always the scenes of neat brick homes, sheds, milch cows, poultry, garden plots, small orchards of plum and peach trees, and varied crops of some Swiss colony which the propagandist loved to hold up to European immigrants. Unfortunately such pictures were the exception. It is also well to remember that the realities which served as the foundation of such lures had been developed on lands of little value, by people who nevertheless had had the opportunity to sink their roots in that land, and who in all likelihood had put in thirty years of hard labor to achieve such an idyllic agricultural life.

If isolation ruled the Argentine countryside, transiency dominated the life of the wheatgrower, molding his psyche and his way of life. He was already predisposed to look upon his occupation as an interval in which to amass a reserve that could be enjoyed in his homeland. The difficulty, at least after 1895, of securing ownership of the land and the parallel demand for tenant farmers stimulated this sense of impermanence. The idea of "home," therefore, had little meaning for the farmer. His culture placed no value on physical conveniences and his poverty had inured him to discomfort.

"Home" for the colonist or tenant farmer evoked a few of the overtones that the word had in its Anglo-Saxon origins. Home was merely a cheap, temporary shelter from the elements. Rare was the farmer who, before he secured final title to his land and sometimes not even then, spent more than a few days on the construction of his house.

The most common structure in the cereal zone was the mud-and-straw rancho. A rectangle was measured out on the ground and the soil was tamped down. At the four corners, posts were sunk and the dirt was tightly packed around them. Saplings were tied or wired to these posts to form a framework. A roof of straw thatch was added next. Nearby a pit had been dug where dirt, water, and manure had been thoroughly mixed. Bundles of straw were now plastered with this mixture and woven into the framework to form walls. Around the lower edges of these walls, dirt was piled and packed down. The completed rancho contained probably from one hundred to one hundred fifty square feet of living space, a doorway closed by a sheepskin or piece of canvas, and perhaps one or two openings or "windows" in the walls. Occasionally the interior might be divided into two rooms. If cooking was done inside, there was a hole near the ridgepole under the eaves for the smoke. Usually, however, a lean-to, attached to one side of the rancho, sheltered a small adobe baking oven as well as the open fire for cooking. . . .

The interior of the agriculturist's home further reflected his transient life and his lack of concern with physical comforts. Early travelers in Argentina used to be astonished at the furnishings of the gaucho's adobe, limited to a few ox skulls on the dirt floor. The farmer's furniture, not so picturesque, was hardly more plentiful. It is true that, as in the pastoral society, much of the day-to-day life went on outdoors or under the kitchen lean-to, and during the summer the family ate, relaxed, and slept outside. A few handmade chairs or benches served as seats, and usually the house boasted a table. Bedding was a pile of sheepskins and ponchos rolled in a corner and sometimes, as a luxury, a bed for the farmer and his wife. Despite the cold and humidity of the winter season, a fireplace or heating was unknown. Fuel, often packed sun-dried dung, was dear enough just for cooking. Lighting was almost as rare. Daylight governed rural hours; candles and kerosene were expensive, and few had the knowledge or desire to read. Clothing likewise was limited to essentials. Cheap cotton fabrics predominated despite winter temperatures which frequently dipped below freezing. Many an adult as well as the children went barefoot the whole year. Sunday clothes were reserved for the special occasion of a visit to town. Everyday trousers and shirts, skirts and blouses, were worn until they were in shreds, then mended and remended.

It can easily be believed that the wheatgrower and his family were oblivious to the habits or even the possibility of cleanliness and hygiene. Sanitary facilities were unknown. Surrounded by the broad expanse of the pampas, it would have been hard to explain to an Italian peasant the reason for an outhouse. Modesty or sanitation was hardly his concern. To his mind, bathing was equally unnecessary. Neither his culture nor his surroundings made personal cleanliness essential. In contrast with tropical northeastern Brazil, where disease had promptly wiped out unwashed German settlers, dirtiness in temperate coastal Argentina imposed no serious penalties.

Their cultural background, transient existence, and ignorance robbed these farmers of the most elementary conveniences. No one who had seen an entire Italian family, from the toddlers up, at work plowing, sowing, reaping, or threshing, would ever have called them lazy. All writers on the wheat zone praised the sober and industrious Piedmontese and Lombards as the best laborers rural Argentina had ever had. An eighteen-hour day of back-breaking labor was routine during the planting and harvest seasons. But almost as a reaction to this, they lapsed into total lethargy during the other seven months of the year. It is true that often there was little else to do, especially when a tenant farmer's contract dictated a single crop, prevented him from keeping hogs or cattle, and forced him to move on after a few years. Certainly the lack of ownership discouraged any effort to plant trees to shelter his rancho from the burning summer sun or to provide fruit for his diet. But around the wheat-grower's house, vegetable plots, chickens, even a few humble pumpkins or squash, were equally rare. Drought, locusts, and tenancy would hardly have been sufficient deterrents had desire, imagination, or knowledge driven the farmer to improve this aspect of his daily life and diet. It was simpler, how-ever, to exist on the standard diet of grease-flavored beans and corn. Even that universal staple of pastoral Argentina — beef — appeared at the wheat-grower's table only in the harvest season, to give strength for the hot, dusty threshing operations. And then it was bought, already slaughtered, from the butcher's cart or shop. Modest in his food, the farmer was equally temperate in his drink. Red wine was the sign of a special social event, a feast day, a visit to town, the arrival of an honored guest. As with beef, hard liquor or cane alcohol made its appearance at harvest time for stimulation rather than for sociability. . . .

The psychology of extensive farming is quite different from its economics and was so ingrained in the minds of the wheatgrowers that it deserves ex-amination. Studies by the Ministry of Agriculture and the Sociedad Rural indicated that the only way for the small farmer to succeed in Argentina was to diversify. The ideal farm consisted of 160 acres. It was recommended that the agriculturist put 150 of these acres to five distinct uses: pasturage, beans, clover, wheat, and a mixture of clover and wheat, and rotate these among different lots. He should also raise a few pigs, 100 sheep, and 30 milch cows. Such a farm could be handled without any outside labor. In bad years losses would be kept at a minimum and in good years there would be no wage ex-pense to eat into profits. Diversification would spread work over the twelve months of the year, would guard against total loss of a harvest, and would permit more intensive and scientific use of the soil. The Argentine agricul-turists could not grasp the importance of such practices, and it must be added that the pastoral and landed interests saw little value in intensive agricul-ture. . . .

Rather than warding off a possible total loss by spreading the risk over sev-eral crops and by investing in livestock, the farmer, with a tremendous surge of work, planted the entire area to a single crop. Then he sat back and al-lowed nature to decide his fate. Only too frequently the gamble went against him. If the myriad dangers of nature — a too-mild winter, untimely frosts, drought, locusts, or rain during the short harvest season — did not overtake him and he reaped a bumper crop, the market would catch him in its impersonal grasp and reward him with lowered wheat prices, higher railroad freights, or increased equipment costs. To his limited mental and psychological horizon, there was nothing left to do but start the same cycle over again the next year and hope that somehow a profit would miraculously emerge.

At the same time, extensive one-crop agriculture suited the pastoral and landed interests. Even the least enlightened landowner realized that the Argentine rural scene was changing and that immigrant labor was essential to that change. European peasants were accepted — as were thoroughbred bulls, improved pasture, and fences — but with the expectation that these immigrants would continue as laborers, planting alfalfa for the stockman or providing rent for the landowner. . . .

Success in the wheat zone was a relative matter. Despite hardships, the first arrivals in each new wheat zone, be it Santa Fe, Córdoba, Buenos Aires, or La Pampa, often made profits and sometimes became owners of their farms. The region of the colonies in Santa Fe became the one area of the pampas with small diversified farms. The *golondrinas* carried back to their homelands a substantial hoard in wages. The tenant farmer probably endured no worse conditions than he would have borne in Italy, Spain, or France and often substantially improved his financial position. A very few, such as Giuseppe Guazzone, who became the largest single producer of wheat in the world, made their fortunes by starting at the bottom as farmers. The expanding wheat area and extensive agriculture, however, worked against small-farm ownership, improved roads, rural social institutions, or better housing. The cultivated acreage increased, but the cultivators did not sink their roots in the pampas. On the contrary, the story of success was most frequently told by those who left the soil after a few lucky harvests and invested their savings in a shop or piece of land in some town or city.

Argentina's greatness as a wheat producer was not made by the few fortunate ones. As Bernard W. Snow, a United States statistician and commercial expert who visited Argentina shortly after the turn of the century, concluded: "The whole secret of Argentine ability to produce grains cheaply lies in the low scale of living of those connected with agriculture." The fact that there were those who would live under such conditions and still consider themselves fortunate permitted Argentina to prosper from wheat production, despite backward techniques, a lopsided land-tenure system, governmental apathy, and the indifference of the landowner.

48. *The Majority of the Brazilians in the 1850s Were Living in the Middle Ages*

GILBERTO FREYRE

Gilberto Freyre became interested in social history while a graduate student at Columbia University. There he fell under the spell of Franz Boas, the grand old man of American anthropology, and other teachers in the social sciences who were stimulating interest in cultural history. His thesis for the Master's degree, "Social Life in Brazil in the Middle of the Nineteenth Century," was such a well-written study and so firmly based on an impressive variety of primary sources that it was promptly published in the *Hispanic American Historical Review*.

On his return to Brazil he quickly developed an individual style and personal approach to the study of the history of his country. His stimulating generalizations on the peaceful intermingling of races in Brazil have not been wholly accepted by everyone, but few writers on the history of Brazil during the last forty years have been uninfluenced by his ideas.

In their material environment and, to a certain extent, in their social life, the majority of Brazilians of the fifties were in the Middle Ages: the élite only was living in the eighteenth century. Only a few men, such as the emperor himself, and a few women, such as Nisia Floresta, were conscious of the Europe of John Stuart Mill, hoop-skirts, Sir Charles Lyell, George Sand, four-wheeled English carriages, and Pius IX. Politically the English type of government was the model after which a sensible, and even sophisticated, oligarchy, in whose power the stern emperor often intruded like a big moral policeman, governed the country. Among some of those oligarchs such subtleties and nuances of political theory as "what is the nature and what are the limits of the moderating power in a parliamentary monarchy?" were often discussed. But more practical subjects occupied their attention: the better administration of civil justice, the building of railways, the relations with the boisterous republics to the south, the slave trade. They were studious and took their responsibilities seriously. The imperial senate was, during the fifties and early sixties, an assembly of brilliant minds. Machado de Assis has left us a graphic description

From "Social Life in Brazil in the Middle of the Nineteenth Century" by Gilberto Freyre, *Hispanic American Historical Review*, 5 (1922), pp. 599–627, passim. Reprinted by permission of the publisher, Duke University Press.

of the senate he knew in 1860 — the senate of the old Marquis of Itanhaem, of Rio Branco, Nabuco de Araujo, Zacarias de Goes — a place where public affairs were discussed in an able, entertaining, sometimes caustic, but always dignified, way. . . .

In an examination of the economic structure of Brazilian society in the middle of the nineteenth century we find on one side a class of landowners and slaveholders; on the other, the mass of slaves, and between the two a few "petits bourgeois" and small farmers, not counting the bureaucracy and leaving out the mercantile interests — the bulk of which was foreign. A sort of medieval landlordism prevailed. Land was owned by coffee planters in the south, cattle-proprietors in the inland provinces and Rio Grande do Sul, by *senhores de engenho* (sugar planters) in the Northeast, especially in Pernambuco. Along the coast and in scattered points of the interior were extensive monastic estates. The class of small farmers were the *"roceiros,"* not a few of whom were colored freedmen. Most of the *petit bourgeoisie* was composed of *marinheiros,* or newly arrived Portuguese. Some of these were able to rise, by their perseverance, from being keepers of kiosks or small grocershops, and *mascates,* or peddlers, to the comfortable merchant class — the fathers of future statesmen, diplomats, and judges. The liberalism of the empire, so eager to recognize individual merit, was favorable to newcomers.

By the middle of the nineteenth century the population of Brazil was, roughly speaking, seven millions. . . . Of these he [F. Nunes de Souza] classed 2,120,000 as whites: 1,100,000 as free colored, 3,120,000 as negro slaves, 180,000 as free native African, and 800,000 as Indians. Miscegenation was going on freely. As early as 1818 or 1819 the French naturalist Auguste de Saint-Hilaire found such a mixture of races in São Paulo that he described it as an "étrange bigarrure d'où resultent des complications également embarrassantes pour l'administration et dangereuses pour la morale publique." Alfred R. Wallace found in Para "a most varied and interesting mixture of races."

"There is" he writes, 'the fresh-colored Englishman, who seems to thrive as well here as in the cooler climates of his country, the sallow American, the swarthy Portuguese, the more corpulent Brazilian, the merry Negro and the apathetic but finely formed Indian; and between these a hundred shades and mixtures which it requires an experienced eye to detect." The American, C. S. Stewart, U.S.N., who visited Brazil in the early fifties, was surprised at "the fearfully mongrel aspect of the population.". . .

It was in the fifties that the first railways were built in Brazil but only in the seventies did they become a serious factor in the economic and social life of the country. . . . Steam navigation made notable progress in Brazil during the fifties. It was followed by improvements in the towns it touched. Para, for instance, gained much from the line of regular steamers on the Amazon, inaugurated in 1854. Such luxuries as camphene lights and macadam generally followed steam-navigation. Hence the progress noted by foreign observers in coast and riverside towns. The others were hardly affected by any touch of progress until railways penetrated the country. They remained truly medieval — no public lighting, no street cleaning, no macadam. And medieval they were in their customs and in their relations to the great landowners around whose estates the towns and villages were scattered.

The power of the great planters was indeed feudalistic, their patriarchalism being hardly restricted by civil laws. Fletcher, who traveled through the interior of Brazil, wrote: "The proprietor of a sugar or cattle estate is, practically, an absolute lord." And he adds: "The community that lives in the shadow of so great a man is his feudal retinue: and, by the conspiracy of a few such men, who are thus able to bring scores of lieges and partisans into the field, the quiet of the province was formerly more than disturbed by revolts which gave the government much trouble." Oliveira Lima says that those communities living in the shadow of the great planters were very heterogeneous: he compares them to the army of lieges that the Portuguese nobles of the eighteenth century kept in their states: *bravi* or rascals, bull fighters, friars, guitarrists, etc. The large Brazilian estate was a self-sustaining unit — economically and socially — depending little on the world outside its large wood gates. It had its cane-fields or its coffee-plantations, and plantations of mandioc, black beans, and other produce, for its own consumption. Its population included, besides the owner and his family, *feitores,* or overseers, *vaqueiros,* or shepherds, sometimes a chaplain and a tutor, carpenters, smiths, masons, and a multitude of slaves. Fletcher visited a coffee estate in Minas Geraes which contained an area of sixty-four square miles. Besides the rows of coffee trees he noticed large tracts of mandioc, cotton and sugar, an abundance of cattle, and one hundred and fifty hives with bees. . . .

The work people of the plantations were well-fed, and attended to by their master and mistress as a "large family of children." They had three meals a day and a little rum (*caxaca*) in the morning. Their breakfast consisted of farina or *pirão,* with fruits and rum; at midday they were given a very substantial meal of meat or fish; in the evening, black beans, rice, and vegetables. On holidays it was customary on certain estates to have an ox killed for the slaves and a quantity of rum was given to make them merry. Then they would dance the sensuous measures of the *batuque* or other African dances or sing or play the *marimba.*

As a rule the slaves were not overworked in the households either in the plantations or in the city. It is true that much was being said in the fifties, of cruel treatment of slaves in Brazil, by the British anti-slavery propaganda. Later on the British dark account of conditions was to be repeated in Brazil by Brazilian anti-slavery orators such as the young Nabuco and Sr. Ruy Barbosa — men inflamed by the bourgeois idealism of Wilberforce as well as by a very human desire for personal glory — and they did it in so emphatic a language that the average Brazilian believes today that slavery was really cruel in his country. The powerful fancy won over reality. For, as a matter of fact, slavery in Brazil was anything but cruel. The Brazilian slave lived the life of a cherub if we contrast his lot with that of the English and other European factory-workers in the middle of the last century. Alfred R.· Wallace — an abolitionist — found the slaves in a sugar plantation he visited in North Brazil "as happy as children.". . . But it is an English clergyman — the Reverend Hamlet Clark, M.A., who strikes the most radical note: "Nay indeed, we need not go far to find in free England the absolute counterpart of slavery: Manighew's London Labour, and London Poor, Dicken's Oliver Twist, Hood's Song of the Shirt and many other revelations tell of a grinding, flinty-hearted despotism that Brazilian slaveowners never can approach." As Professor Hayes points out, in England, "audiences wept at hearing how cruel masters licked their cowering slaves in Jamaica: but in their own England little Englishmen and Englishwomen ten years old were being whipped to their work," sometimes "in the factories of some of the anti-slavery orators."

At sunset the whistle of the sugar-mill closed the day's work on the Brazilian plantation. The workpeople came then for their last meal, after which they went to bed. But first they came to ask their master's and mistress' blessing: "Bênção, nhonho!" Bênção Nhanha!" holding out their right hand. Then the master and the mistress would say: "Deus te abençoe" (God bless you), making at the same time the sign of the cross.

In a typical Brazilian city-home of the higher class — say, the home of a custom-house officer — slaves numbered on the average fifteen or twenty. Since slaves were plentiful, certain necessities, and even luxuries, were produced at home, under the careful oversight of the mistress; cloth was cut and made into dresses, towels and undergarments; wine was distilled; lace and crivo (a sort of embroidery) were manufactured. Besides this the housewife superintended the cooking, the preserving, the baking of cakes, the care of the sick; taught her children and their black playmates the Lord's Prayer, the Apostles' Creed, and the Ave Maria. . . .

Slaves were plentiful. The staff of a large city-house included cooks, those trained to serve in the dining room, wet-nurses, water carriers, footmen, chambermaids — the latter sleeping in their mistresses' rooms and assisting them in the minutest details of their toilette, such as picking lice, for instance. Sometimes there were too many slaves. A lady told Doctor Fletcher that she "had nine lazy servants at home for whom there was not employment" and another one that she could not find enough work to keep her slaves out of idleness and mischief. It is easy to imagine how some housewives became pampered idlers, spending their days languidly in gossiping, or at the balcony, or reading some new novel of Macedo or Alencar. . . .

It is true that the Brazilian lady of the fifties did not go out for her shopping. She was a house prisoner. Moorish prejudices kept her from those pretty shops of fancy goods, bonnets, jewelry, *bijouterie,* which travelers admired so much in Rio de Janeiro, the Italian naval officer Eugenio Rodriguez describing them as "elegantissimi magazini." But at home she did not stay in her hammock. In a typical home works of all kinds went on during the day. Linen, silk, millinery, fancy goods, were bought from samples and pattern-books, after much running of negro boys from shop to the house: or, in many cases, from the peddler who came once or twice a week, making a noise with his yardstick. It was not necessary to go to the market to buy vegetables, fruit, or eggs since venders of these rural products, as well as of milk, meat, and fish, came to the home. There were itinerant coppersmiths who announced themselves by hitting some old stewpan with a hammer. Even novels were sold at the door. Paulo Barreto tells that Alencar and Macedo — "the best sellers" of the period — had negroes go from house to house, selling their novels in baskets. Therefore, the fact that the Brazilian woman did not go to the shops does not mean that she was too lazy to do her own shopping. She did it. And after the shopping was done in the morning it was she who superintended the various kinds of work going on in the household. . . . Fletcher who, though a Protestant clergyman, enjoyed the intimacy of many a home in Brazil, thought that the Brazilian housewife answered to the description of the "good woman" in the last chapter of Proverbs: "she looketh well to the ways of her household and eateth not the bread of idleness." Carlos de Laet — the last brilliant mind of a departed order — tells us that "to accuse a lady of not knowing how to manage her household was then the most unpleasant offence to her." Oliveira Lima characterizes the Brazilian housewife of this period as possessing "ability to manage" (*capacidade administrativa*), without which it was impossible to keep such large households going. Others might be quoted to show that in this matter the weighing of evidences reveals an active, rather than an idle woman, as the typical Brazilian housewife in slavery days.

The double standard of morality prevailed in the fifties: the lily-like woman was idolized while incontinence in the man was slightly regarded. It is true that the Emperor Dom Pedro II. made the standards of sexual morality stricter for those who were around him or who aspired to political eminence. He was a sort of Queen Victoria in breeches — only more powerful — and watched the statesmen like a moral detective. It is commonplace that he refused to appoint men to eminent positions on account of irregularities in their private life — a tradition which the Republican leaders found too foolish to maintain. But the emperor's influence was only felt in the high spheres of officialdom. In the large country estates irregularities went on freely, the colored girls constituting a disguised harem where either the master or his sons satisfied their exotic sexual tastes. . . .

In his attitude towards his wife the Brazilian of the fifties was a true patriarch of the Roman type. She was given authority in the household, but not outside. Outside she was to be, legally and socially, the shadow of her husband. "A promenade below, with the chance of a flirtation, is denied her," the American C. S. Stewart remarks in his book. Pointing out the virtues of the Brazilian matron in the *ancien régime,* of which he is the most eminent survivor, the Count Carlos de Laet says that "she knew how to obey her husband." Monsieur Expilly, a French feminist who visited Brazil in the fifties, was indignant at what he calls "le despotisme paternel" and "la politique conjugale.". . .

While the woman spent most of her time indoors, the man — the city man — spent most of his, out — in the street, in the plaza, at the door of some French hotel or in his office or warehouse. The condition was much like that in ancient Greece where people thought, with the wise old Xenophon, that "it is not so good for a woman to be out-of-doors as in, and it is more dishonourable for a man to stay in than to attend to his affairs outside." Brazilian men, like the Greeks, enjoyed the easy fellowship of the street and the plaza — and in the street and the plaza they discussed politics, Donizetti, the Aberdeen Bill, and transacted business. We are told by Sampaio Ferraz, in his excellent work "O Molhe de Olinda," that in Pernambuco, during the last half of the nineteenth century, the most important business was transacted outdoors, under the trees of Lingoeta. Lithogravures of the period, which I examined in Oliveira Lima's collection, show the streets — Rua Direita and Largo da Alfandega in Rio, Lingoeta in Pernambuco, and so on — full of groups of men, talking, smoking, taking snuff, while coffee or sugar carriers run with their cargoes, their half-naked bodies shining with oily sweat. The sentiment of home was not strong among the Brazilian men when the patriarchal family was in its full vigor. Nor did they have mundane clubs — unless if we accept as such the Masonic lodges. The street was their club.

This may serve as an explanation of the fact that the city Brazilians of the fifties did not seem to have attractive homes. Twenty years before a French traveler, Louis De Freycinet, had observed that the Brazilians spent most of their time sleeping, or outdoors, or, sometimes, receiving their friends: there-fore they only needed — the Frenchman thought — a reception room and the bedrooms. . . .

At eight or nine the girl was sent to a religious boarding school and kept there until she was thirteen or fourteen. There her training, begun at home, was continued. She was trained in that fine art — the art of being a woman. Music, dancing, embroidery, prayers, French, and sometimes English, a thin layer of literature — such were the elements of a girl's education in the board-ing school. She came back a very romantic, and sometimes bewitching, little creature, reading Sue, Dumas, and George Sand, besides the gossiping *paco-tilhas* such as *A Marmota* and Alencar's saccharine, but often erotic, *folhetins*. And how she could pray! And how she could dance! The dances of the period were the quadrille, the lanciers, and the polka; to dance them well, to be light as a feather and tiny as a piece of lace, was the highest ideal of a girl — I was told by a lady who took dancing lessons from the same teacher as Princess Isabel.

Ladies bloomed early. The years of giddy childhood were short. At four-teen or fifteen the girl dressed like a lady. Docility, and even timidity, was considered a grace. The girl was trained to be timid or, at least, to look timid before people — as timid as a little boy before the circus elephant. The Brazilian girl of the fifties was everything that the so called "very modern" girl is not. "Perhaps they were too timid" — Carlos de Laet writes of the girls of that period — "but they were adorable in the timidity." Those very timid girls were playful and talkative when given a chance. Max Radiguet tells of the custom of the Brazilian society girls going to the imperial chapel in Rio de Janeiro, where an excellent orchestra assisted by a choir of Italian soprani played every Friday evening. There "pendant toute la durée de ce concert re-ligieux les femmes accroupées sur leur caire de tapisserie prenaient sans scruple des sorbets et des glaces avec les jeunes gens qui venaient converser avec elles dans le lieu saint." When such merry rendezvous, in the shadow of the church, were not possible — and the custom was discontinued just as dances in the churches were discontinued — love-making had to be even more platonic. There was, for instance, love-making by means of a fan — that is, girls could make their fans speak a particular language of love which all lovers were supposed to understand. "It all depended on how the fan was held," an old lady explained to me while her tapering, white fingers handled a delicate fan in a thousand and one ways.

But as a rule marriage did not result from romantic lovemaking. The man whom the girl married in her early teens was seldom her own choice. He was

her parents', or her father's, choice. An English traveler describes how be-
trothals were made: "Some day the father walks into the drawing room, accompanied by a strange gentleman, elderly or otherwise. 'Minha Filha,' he
remarks, 'this is your future husband.' " Sometimes the "future husband" was
a pleasant surprise — a pale youth of twenty-three or twenty-five, a ruby or
an emerald sparkling from his forefinger, his moustaches perfumed, his hair
smooth, oily . . . a hero who had escaped from some bright German
oleogravure or from the pages of a novel. And romantic love developed between the contracting parties. But other times the "future husband" was some
fat, solid, newly-rich Portuguese, middle-aged, his neck short and his hands
coarse. Perhaps a very fine person — inside; but what a death-blow for a sentimental girl of the fifties. And yet she often accepted him — the potbellied
one — such a marriage being nothing more than a business partnership. Unfortunate marriages of the latter type became a favorite theme with Brazilian
writers of fiction in the sixties and seventies, Guimaraes' *Historia de Uma
Moça Rica* being typical of that literature. But one should be discriminating
in the matter: some marriages arranged by the girl's parents were as happy
as marriages ordinarily are.

Early marriages meant early procreation. At fifteen a girl was generally a
mother. Sometimes she was a mother at fourteen and even thirteen. The Reverend Walter Colton wrote in his diary: "A Brazilian lady was pointed out
to me to-day who is but twelve years of age, and who has two children, who
were frolicking around her steps. . . ." And he adds ". . . ladies here marry
extremely young. They have hardly done with their fictitious babies, when
they have the smiles and tears of real ones." As a consequence, girls faded
early, having tasted in a hurry the joy of careless youth.

The boy, too, was born middle-aged. Dom Pedro's prematurity may be
taken as typical. He was made an emperor at fifteen, and he was then very
thoughtful and serious; at twenty he was an old man. Youth flew from him in
a gallop. Brazilian education favored then, more than in a later day, the prematurity of the boy. Very early he was sent to the *collegio,* where he lived and
boarded. Though his home might be a street or two off, very seldom —
usually once a month — was he allowed to go there. He often got from home
boxes of cakes and bon-bons, but no such things as toys. Toys were for little
boys; he was nine or ten, nearly a man. As a rule he studied hard his Latin
grammar, his rhetoric, his French classics, his sacred history, his geography.
When that big occasion — the final examinations — came, he shone, answering well all that Padre So-and-So asked about Horace, Noah, Rebecca, rules
of punctuation, the verb *amare;* and all that some other teacher asked about
Racine, Vesuvius, and what not.

At fifteen or sixteen the boy finished his studies in the *collegio.* It was time to go to the professional school. Here, as in the girls' betrothal, it was the father's or family's choice that generally prevailed. The tendency was to scatter the boys in different schools, so that the family would be represented in different professions. One was picked to go to Pernambuco or São Paulo to study law or diplomacy; another to enter the medical school; a third to be a cadet in the military school; a fourth to go to the seminary. Among the most pious families it was considered a social, as well as a moral, failure not to have a son studying for the priesthood. Sometimes the youngest son, though of no churchly turn of mind, was the scapegoat. The family simply had to have a *padre*. As to the stupid son, who could not make good anywhere, the sensible parents sent him to business, which was looked down upon by gentlemen.

The flower of the family was picked for the law school — the law school being the training-ground, not for magistracy only, but for the parliament and the cabinet also, and for diplomacy. There were two law schools — that of Olinda, in Pernambuco, and that of São Paulo. Writing from São Paulo in 1855 Doctor Kidder said of its law school: "It is here and at the Pernambuco Law School (which contains three hundred students in the regular course) that the statesmen of Brazil receive that education which so much better fits them for the Imperial Parliament and the various legislative assemblies of their land than any preparatories that exist in the Spanish-American countries."

The "regular course," to which Doctor Kidder refers, came after a sort of pre-law course which included Latin, geometry, rational and moral philosophy, and other subjects. The "regular course" extended over a period of five years, the following subjects being studied: philosophy of law, public law, analysis of the imperial constitution, Roman law, diplomacy, ecclesiastical law, civil law, mercantile and maritime law, political economy, and theory and practice of general law. . . .

But this churchly atmosphere in the day time did not prevent most of the students from being merry, boisterous, and even wicked, after sunset. They did not care a rap for rowing or any ball game — not even for cockfighting, which some of their elders enjoyed. Making love to actresses was their favorite sport. There were generally two rival actresses, like Candiani and Delmatro, in São Paulo, and Eugenia Camara and Adelaide do Amaral, in Pernambuco, and surrounding each, a fervent group of admirers — some platonic, some not. Each group had a "poet" instead of a "cheer leader," and oratorical duels were fought in the theaters. . . . It was in the shadow of the theater that the young men enjoyed themselves, writing verses to actresses, fighting for actresses, spending money on merry suppers with actresses. . . .

It is amazing how the Brazilians of the fifties managed to live in such miserable conditions of dirt and bad smell as they did. There was practically no public hygiene to speak of. It is in a semi-official outline of the history of public health services in Brazil that the following description appears, of Rio de Janeiro in the middle of the nineteenth century: "A filthy city, in which, it may be said, there was no air, no light, no sewers, no street cleaning; a city built upon bogs where mosquitoes freely multiplied." Mme. Ida Pfeiffer saw, as she walked through the streets of Rio, carcasses of dogs, cats, and even a mule, rotting. She also refers to "le manque complet d'égouts" — the complete lack of sewers. This condition was common to the other cities of the empire — even to Pernambuco, where the Dutch had left a touch of their cleanliness. Charles Darwin, who was there in the thirties, writes of its filthy streets and offensive smells, comparing it to oriental towns. In all the towns of the empire the removal of garbage, ashes, decaying matter, and vegetables, and human excrements was made in the crudest and also the most picturesque way. Those wastes were put in pipes or barrels, nicknamed *tigres,* and carried on the heads of slaves who dumped them into rivers, the seashore, and alleys. Sometimes as a witness referred to a later-day Brazilian hygienist, "the bottom of the barrel would cast off, the contents soiling both the carrier and the streets." The decaying material was left near the bridges or on the seashores, flocks of carrion crows being depended upon to do the work of scavengers. The removal of the garbage and human waste was generally made after the church bells rang "ten o'clock." In Pernambuco the *tigres* were emptied from the bridges into the rivers Capibaribe and Beberibe: in Rio they were taken on the heads of slaves to be emptied "into certain parts of the bay every night, so that walking in the streets after 10 o'clock is neither safe nor pleasant." This quotation is from Ewbanks who adds: "In this matter Rio is what Lisbon is and what Edinburg used to be."

As there were no sewers to carry off the drainage there was no plumbing in the houses. The system of water supply was that of the *chafariz,* or public fountain. There was a constant dashing to and fro of big negro water carriers, taking water for the houses, sometimes to the third or fourth floor, where the kitchen was located. Those water carriers worked harder, perhaps, than any other class of slaves; for Brazilians made free use of water, thus making up in personal cleanliness what was lacking so painfully in public hygiene. Next to his hot coffee and his snuff, a Brazilian loved a hot bath best of all. Everywhere — in cities and in the great as well as the humble houses of the interior — water, soap, and a large clean towel welcomed a guest. On examining statistics of the period, I found that more than one third of the seventy-two factories then existing in the empire were soap factories.

Though there was no plumbing in the houses and bathtubs were unknown, rich and poor took a sheer joy in bathing. Poor people bathed in rivers, under the public eye. Landing in Para, the American, John Esaias Warren, was attracted to the freedom with which people bathed and swam in the river. "The first spectacle which arrested our attention," he writes, "was that of a number of persons of both sexes and all ages, bathing indiscriminately together in the waters of the river, in a state of entire nudity." And his comment is: "The natives of Para are very cleanly and indulge in daily ablutions; nor do they confine their baths to the dusky hours of the evening but may be seen swimming about the public wharfs at all hours of the day." While the well-to-do in the cities used "gamellas" or large wooden bowls for their ablutions those in the country states — gentlemen and ladies alike — went to the nearest stream where they could also enjoy a good swim. The suburban *chacaras* in Pernambuco, along the Capibaribe river, had crude bathhouses made of coconut palms. There the ladies undressed and then dipt into the water in free, white, nakedness, like happy mermaids.

It was customary to wash one's hands before and after a meal, the slaves bringing bowls with beautifully embroidered towels. Doctor Fletcher noticed this in Rio as well as in the interior of Minas, where he traveled in an oxcart. Not many years before Saint-Hilaire had been delighted at the apostolic simplicity with which the small farmers in Minas Geraes came themselves with a basin and a towel to wash their guest's feet before he went to bed. Children had their feet washed by their mothers or negro nurses before going to bed. On this occasion their feet were also examined, so that *bichos de pe* might be extracted with a pin, if found. . . .

49. *Life in Mexico in the 1840s as Seen by a Scottish Lady*

FANNY CALDERÓN DE LA BARCA

As the Boston Brahmin and historian William H. Prescott remarked in the preface to the first edition in 1843 of *Life in Mexico:* "The present work is the result of observations made during a two years' residence in Mexico, by a lady, whose position there made her intimately acquainted with its society, and opened to her the best sources of information in whatever could interest an enlightened foreigner. It consists of letters, written to members of her own family, and, *really,* not intended originally — however incredible the assertion — for publication."

The author, Frances Erskine Inglis, was born in Edinburgh in 1806 and married Ángel Calderón de la Barca, a Spanish diplomat, in Boston where she came to know Prescott and another famous Hispanist, George Ticknor. When her husband was appointed the first Spanish minister to Mexico, she lived in Mexico from 1840 to 1842, and there had the experiences and adventures that formed the base of her classic account. The selections here given represent well her sparkle and style.

"THE MELANCHOLY EFFECTS PRODUCED BY YEARS OF CIVIL WAR AND UNSETTLED GOVERNMENT"

Accompanied by the —— minister, we spent yesterday in visiting the Mineria, the Botanic Garden, the Museum, etc., all which leave a certain disagreeable impression on the mind, since, without having the dignity of ruins, they are fine buildings neglected. The Mineria, or School of Mines, the work of the famous architect and sculptor Tolsa, is a magnificent building, a palace whose fine proportions would render it remarkable amongst the finest edifices of any European country. All is on a great scale, its noble rows of pillars, great staircases, large apartments and lofty roofs, but it reminds one of a golden aviary, containing a few common sparrows. Several rich Spaniards contributed more than six hundred thousand dollars to its construction. We were shown through the whole of this admirable building by the director, who occupies a very handsome house attached to it. But however learned the professors may be, — and amongst them is the scientific Señor del Rio, now very old, but a man of great learning and research — the collection of minerals, the instruments and models, are all miserable and ill kept.

The Botanic Garden, within the palace, is a small ill-kept enclosure, where there still remain some rare plants of the immense collection made in the time of the Spanish government, when great progress was made in all the natural sciences, four hundred thousand dollars having been expended in botanical expeditions alone. Courses of botanical lectures were then given annually by the most learned professors, and the taste for natural history was universal.

El Arbol de las Manitas (the tree of the small hands) was the most curious which we saw in the garden. The flower is of a bright scarlet, in the form of a hand, with five fingers and a thumb; and it is said that there are only three of these trees in the republic. The gardener is an old Italian, who came over with one of the viceroys, and though now one hundred and ten years old, and

From *Life in Mexico* by Madame Calderón de la Barca, 2 vols. (Boston, 1843).

nearly bent double, possesses all his faculties. The garden is pretty from the age of the trees, and luxuriance of the flowers, but melancholy as a proof of the decay of the science in Mexico. The palace itself, now occupied by the president, formerly belonged to Cortes, and was ceded by his descendants to the government. In exchange they received the ground formerly occupied by the palace of the Aztec kings, and built on it a very splendid edifice, where the state archives are kept, and where the *Monte Pio* (the office where money is lent on plate, jewels, etc.) now is, the director of which is Don Francisco Tagle, whose apartments within the building are very elegant and spacious.

The Museum within the University, and opposite the palace, in the plaza called del Volador, contains many rare and valuable works, many curious Indian antiquities, but they are ill arranged. On the walls are the portraits of the vice-kings, beginning with Hernan Cortes. We spent a long while here examining these antiquities; but we have seen nothing in Mexico to equal the beauty of the colossal equestrian statue in bronze of Charles IV, placed on a pedestal of Mexican marble, which stands in the court of the University, but formerly adorned the middle of the square. It is a magnificent picture of sculpture, the masterpiece of Tolosa, remarkable for the noble simplicity and purity of its style, and was made at the expense of an ex-viceroy, the Marquis of Branciforte. We also saw the goddess of war lying in a corner of the court, beside the stone of sacrifices, which we had already been shown.

To-day we have been visiting the Academy of painting and sculpture, called the Academy of Fine Arts, of which I unfortunately recollected having read Humboldt's brilliant account, in my forcibly prolonged studies on board the Jason, and that he mentions its having had the most favourable influence in forming the national taste. He tells us that every night, in these spacious halls, well illumined by Argand lamps, hundreds of young men were assembled, some sketching from the plaster-casts, or from life, and others copying designs of furniture, candelabras and other bronze ornaments; and that here all classes, colours, and races, were mingled together; the Indian beside the white boy, and the son of the poorest mechanic beside that of the richest lord. Teaching was gratis, and not limited to landscape and figures, one of the principal objects being to propagate amongst the artists a general taste for elegance and beauty of form, and to enliven the national industry. Plaster-casts, to the amount of forty thousand dollars, were sent out by the King of Spain, and as they possess in the academy various colossal statues of basalt and porphyry, with Aztec hieroglyphics, it would have been curious, as the same learned traveller remarks, to have collected these monuments in the courtyard of the Academy, and compared the remains of Mexican sculpture, monuments of a semi-barbarous people, with the graceful creations of Greece and Rome.

Let no one visit the Academy with these recollections or anticipations in his mind. . . . That the simple and noble taste which distinguishes the Mexican buildings, their perfection in the cutting and working of their stones, the chaste ornaments of the capitals and relievoes, are owing to the progress they made in this very Academy is no doubt the case. The remains of these beautiful but mutilated plaster-casts, the splendid engravings which still exist, would alone make it probable; but the present disorder, the abandoned state of the building, the nonexistence of these excellent classes of sculpture and painting, and, above all, the low state of the fine arts in Mexico, at the present day, are amongst the sad proofs, if any were waiting, of the melancholy effects produced by years of civil war and unsettled government. . . .

HOLY WEEK IN MEXICO CITY

Of all the churches we entered that night, the cathedral was the most magnificent, but the most beautiful and tasteful was San Francisco. The crowd there was so dense, that we were almost carried off our feet, and were obliged, in defiance of all rule, to take the arms of our *caballeros*. Still it was worth the trouble of making our way through it to see such a superbly illuminated altar. It was now eleven o'clock, and the crowd were breaking up as the churches are shut before midnight. In one corner of the middle aisle, near the door, was the representation of a prison from which issued a stream of soft music, and at the window was a figure of Christ in chains, his eyes bandaged, and a Jew on each side; the chains hanging from his hands, and clanking as if with the motion of his arms. The rush here was immense. Numbers of people were kneeling before the window of the prison, and kissing the chains and beating their breasts with every appearance of contrition and devotion. This was the night before the Crucifixion, and the last scene of the Holy Thursday.

We reached home hardly able to stand. I never felt more dazzled, bewildered, and sleepy; but I was wakened by finding a packet of letters from home, which brought back my thoughts, or rather carried them away to very different lands.

On Good Friday, a day of sorrow and humiliation, the scene in the morning is very different. The great sacrifice is complete — the Immortal has died a mortal death. The ladies all issue forth in mourning, and the churches look sad and wan after their last night's brilliancy. The heat was intense. We went to San Francisco, again to the Tribuna of the Countess de Santiago, to see the Adoration and Procession of the Cross, which was very fine.

But the most beautiful and original scene was presented towards sunset in the great square, and it is doubtful whether any other city in the world could present a *coup-d'œil* of equal brilliancy. Having been offered the *entrée* to some apartments in the palace, we took our seats on the balconies, which commanded a view of the whole. The Plaza itself, even on ordinary days, is a noble square, and but for its one fault, a row of shops called the Parian, which breaks its uniformity, would be nearly unrivalled. Every object is interesting. The eye wanders from the cathedral to the house of Cortes (the Monte Pio), and from thence to a range of fine buildings with lofty arcades to the west. From our elevated situation, we could see all the different streets that branch out from the square, covered with gay crowds pouring in that direction to see another great procession, which was expected to pass in front of the palace. Booths filled with refreshments, and covered with green branches and garlands of flowers, were to be seen in all directions, surrounded by a crowd who were quenching their thirst with orgeat, *chia,* lemonade, or pulque. The whole square, from the cathedral to the Portales, and from the Monte Pio to the palace, was covered with thousands and tens of thousands of figures, all in their gayest dresses, and as the sun poured his rays down upon their gaudy colours, they looked like armies of living tulips. Here was to be seen a group of ladies, some with black gowns and mantillas; others, now that their church-going duty was over, equipped in velvet or satin, with their hair dressed, — and beautiful hair they have; some leading their children by the hand, dressed . . . alas! how they were dressed! Long velvet gowns trimmed with blonde, diamond earrings, high French caps befurbelowed with lace and flowers, or turbans with plumes of feathers. Now and then the head of a little thing that could hardly waddle alone, might have belonged to an English dowager-duchess in her opera-box. Some had extraordinary bonnets, also with flowers and feathers, and as they toddled along, top heavy, one would have thought they were little old women, till a glimpse was caught of their lovely little brown faces and black eyes. Now and then a little girl, simply dressed with a short frock, and long black hair plaited down and uncovered, would trip along, a very model of grace amongst the small caricatures. The children here are generally beautiful, their features only too perfect and regular for the face "to fulfill the promise of its spring." They have little colour, with swimming black or hazel eyes, and long lashes resting on the clear pale cheek, and a perfect mass of fine dark hair of the straight Spanish or Indian kind plaited down behind.

As a contrast to the Señoras, with their over-dressed beauties, were the poor Indian women, trotting across the square, their black hair plaited with dirty red ribbon, a piece of woollen cloth wrapped about them, and a little mahogany baby hanging behind, its face upturned to the sky, and its head going jerking along, somehow without its neck being dislocated. The most resigned expression on earth is that of an Indian baby. All the groups we had seen promenading the streets the day before were here collected by hundreds;

the women of the shopkeeper class, or it may be lower, in their smart white embroidered gowns, with their white satin shoes, and neat feet and ankles, and rebosos or bright shawls thrown over their heads; the peasants and country-women, with their short petticoats of two colours, generally scarlet and yellow (for they are most anti-quakerish in their attire), thin satin shoes and lace-trimmed chemises, or bronze-coloured damsels, all crowned with flowers, strolling along with their admirers, and tingling their light guitars. And above all, here and there a flashing Poblana, with a dress of real value and much taste, and often with a face and figure of extraordinary beauty, especially the figure; large and yet *élancée,* with a bold coquettish eye, and a beautiful little brown foot, shown off by the white satin shoe; the petticoat of her dress fre-quently fringed and embroidered in real massive gold, and a reboso either shot with gold, or a bright-coloured China crape shawl, coquettishly thrown over her head. We saw several whose dresses could not have cost less than five hundred dollars.

Add to this motley crowd, men dressed *à la Mexicaine,* with their large ornamented hats and sarapes, or embroidered jackets, sauntering along, smok-ing their cigars, *léperos* in rags, Indians in blankets, officers in uniform, priests in their shovel hats, monks of every order; Frenchmen exercising their wit upon the passers-by; Englishmen looking cold and philosophical; Germans gazing through their spectacles, mild and mystical; Spaniards seeming pretty much at home, and abstaining from remarks; and it may be conceived that the scene at least presented variety. Sometimes the tinkling of the bell an-nounced the approach of *Nuestro Amo.* Instantly the whole crowd are on their knees, crossing themselves devoutly. Two men who were fighting below the window suddenly dropped down side by side. Disputes were hushed, flirtations arrested, and to the busy hum of voices succeeded a profound silence. Only the rolling of the coach-wheels and the sound of the little bell were heard.

No sooner had it passed than the talkers and the criers recommenced with fresh vigour. The vendors of hot chestnuts and cooling beverages plied their trade more briskly than ever. A military band struck up an air from Semira-mis: and the noise of the innumerable *matracas* (rattles), some of wood and some of silver, with which every one is armed during the last days of the holy week, broke forth again as if by magic, while again commenced the sale of the *Judases,* fireworks in the form of that arch-traitor, which are sold on the evening of Good Friday, and let off on Saturday morning. Hundreds of these hideous figures were held above the crowd, by men who carried them tied together on long poles. An ugly misshapen monster they represent the be-trayer to have been. When he sold his master for thirty pieces of silver, did he dream that in the lapse of ages his effigies should be held up to the execration of a Mexican mob, of an unknown people in undiscovered countries beyond the seas? — A secret bargain, perhaps made whisperingly in a darkened chamber with the fierce Jewish rulers; but now shouted forth in the ears of the descendants of Montezuma and Cortes!

But the sound of a distant hymn rose on the air, and shortly after there appeared, advancing towards the square, a long and pompous retinue of mitred priests, with banners and crucifixes and gorgeous imagery, conducting a procession in which figures representing scenes concerning the death of our Saviour, were carried by on platforms, as they were the preceding evening. There was the Virgin in mourning at the foot of the cross — the Virgin in glory — and more saints and more angels — St. Michael and the dragon, etc., etc., a glittering and innumerable train. Not a sound was heard as the figures were carried slowly onwards in their splendid robes, lighted by thousands of tapers, which mingled their unnatural glare with the fading light of day.

As the *Miserere* was to be performed in the cathedral late in the evening, we went there, though with small hopes of making our way through the tremendous crowd. Having at length been admitted through a private entrance, *per favour,* we made our way into the body of the church; but the crowd was so intolerable, that we thought of abandoning our position, when we were seen and recognised by some of the priests, and conducted to a railed-off enclosure near the shrine of the Virgin, with the luxury of a Turkey carpet. Here, separated from the crowd, we sat down in peace on the ground. The gentlemen were accommodated with high-backed chairs, beside some ecclesiastics; for men may sit on chairs or benches in church, but women must kneel or sit on the ground. Why? *"Quien sabe?"* (Who knows?) is all the satisfaction I have ever obtained on that point. . . .

A VISIT TO THE ENCARNACIÓN CONVENT

The Archbishop has not only granted me permission to visit the convents, but permits me to take two ladies along with me, of which I have been informed by the Minister, Señor C——o, in a very amiable note just received, enclosing one from Señor Posada, which I translate for your edification.

> *To His Excellency, Señor Don J. de D. C——o.*
> *April 24th, 1842.*

My dear Friend and Companion:

The Abbess and Nuns of the Convent of the Encarnacion are now prepared to receive the visit of our three pilgrims, next Sunday, at half-past four in the afternoon, and should that day not suit them, let them mention what day will be convenient.

Afterwards we shall arrange their visit to the Concepcion, Enseñanza Antigua, and Jesus Maria, which are the best, and I shall let you know, and we shall agree upon the days and hours most suitable. I remain your affectionate friend and *Capellan,*

MANUEL POSADA.

27th. — Accordingly, on Sunday afternoon, we drove to the *Encarnacion,* the most splendid and richest convent in Mexico, excepting perhaps la Concepcion. If it were in any other country, I might mention the surpassing beauty of the evening, but as except in the rainy season, which has not yet begun, the evenings are always beautiful, the weather leaves no room for description. The sky always blue, the air always soft, the flowers always blossoming, the birds always singing: Thomson never could have written his "Seasons" here. We descended at the convent gate, were admitted by the portress, and received by several nuns, their faces closely covered with a double crape veil. We were then led into a spacious hall, hung with handsome lustres, and adorned with various Virgins and Saints magnificently dressed; and here the eldest, a very dignified old lady, lifted her veil, the others following her example, and introduced herself as the *Madre Vicaria;* bringing us many excuses from the old abbess, who having an inflammation in her eyes, was confined to her cell. She and another reverend mother, and a group of elderly dames, tall, thin, and stately, then proceeded to inform us, that the archbishop had, in person, given orders for our reception, and that they were prepared to show us the whole establishment.

The dress is a long robe of very fine white casimere, a thick black crape veil, and long rosary. The dress of the novices is the same, only that the veil is white. For the first half-hour or so, I fancied, that along with their politeness, was mingled a good deal of restraint, caused perhaps by the presence of a foreigner, and especially of an Englishwoman. My companions they knew well; the Señorita having even passed some months there. However this may have been, the feeling seemed gradually to wear away. Kindness or curiosity triumphed; their questions became unceasing; and before the visit was concluded, I was addressed as *"mi vida"* (my life), by the whole establishment. Where was I born? Where had I lived? What convents had I seen? Which did I prefer, the convents in France, or those in Mexico? Which were largest? Which had the best garden? etc., etc. Fortunately, I could, with truth, give the preference to their convent, as to spaciousness and magnificence, over any I ever saw.

The Mexican style of building is peculiarly advantageous for recluses; the great galleries and courts affording them a constant supply of fresh air, while the fountains sound so cheerfully, and the garden in this climate of perpetual spring affords them such a constant source of enjoyment all the year round, that one pities their secluded state much less here than in any other country.

This convent is in fact a palace. The garden, into which they led us first, is kept in good order, with its stone walks, stone benches, and an ever-playing and sparkling fountain. The trees were bending with fruit, and they pulled quantities of the most beautiful flowers for us; sweet-peas and roses, with which all gardens here abound, carnations, jasmine, and heliotrope. It was a pretty picture to see them wandering about, or standing in groups in this high-walled garden, while the sun was setting behind the hills, and the noise of the city was completely excluded, everything breathing repose and contentment. Most of the halls in the convent are noble rooms. We visited the whole, from the refectory to the *botica,* and admired the extreme cleanness of everything, especially of the immense kitchen, which seems hallowed from the approach even of a particle of dust; this circumstance is partly accounted for by the fact that each nun has a servant, and some have two; for this is not one of the strictest orders. The convent is rich; each novice at her entrance pays five thousand dollars into the common stock. There are about thirty nuns and ten novices.

The prevailing sin in a convent generally seems to be pride;

"The pride that apes humility;"

and it is perhaps nearly inseparable from the conventual state. Set apart from the rest of the world, they, from their little world, are too apt to look down with contempt which may be mingled with envy, or modified by pity, but must be unsuited to a true Christian spirit.

The novices were presented to us — poor little entrapped things! who really believe they will be let out at the end of the year if they should grow tired, as if they would ever be permitted to grow tired! The two eldest and most reverend ladies are sisters, thin, tall, and stately, with high noses, and remains of beauty. They have been in the convent since they were eight years old (which is remarkable, as sisters are rarely allowed to profess in the same establishment), and consider *La Encarnacion* as a small piece of heaven upon earth. There were some handsome faces amongst them, and one whose expression and eyes were singularly lovely, but truth to say, these were rather exceptions to the general rule.

Having visited the whole building, and admired one virgin's blue satin and pearls, and another's black velvet and diamonds, sleeping holy infants, saints, paintings, shrines, and confessionals, — having even climbed up the Azotea, which commands a magnificent view, we came at length to a large hall, decorated with paintings and furnished with antique high-backed arm-chairs, where a very elegant supper, lighted up and ornamented, greeted our astonished eyes; cakes, chocolate, ices, creams, custards, tarts, jellies, blancmangers, orange and lemonade, and other profane dainties, ornamented with gilt paper cut into little flags, etc. I was placed in a chair that might have served for a pope under a holy family; the Señora —— and the Señorita —— on either side. The elder nuns in stately array, occupied the young arm-chairs, and looked like statues carved in stone. A young girl, a sort of *pensionnaire,* brought in a little harp without pedals, and while we discussed cakes and ices, sung different ballads with a good deal of taste. The elder nuns helped us to everything, but tasted nothing themselves. The younger nuns and the novices were grouped upon a mat *à la Turque,* and a more picturesque scene altogether one could scarcely see.

The young novices in their white robes, white veils, and black eyes, the severe and dignified *madres* with their long dresses and mournful-looking black veils and rosaries, the veiled figures occasionally flitting along the corridor; — ourselves in contrast, with our *worldly* dresses and coloured ribbons; and the great hall lighted by one immense lamp that hung from the ceiling — I felt transported three centuries back, and half afraid that the whole would flit away, and prove a mere vision, a waking dream.

A gossiping old nun, who hospitably filled my plate with everything, gave me the enclosed *flag* cut in gilt paper, which, together with her custards and jellies, looked less unreal. They asked many questions in regard to Spanish affairs, and were not to be consoled for the defeat of Don Carlos, which they feared would be an end of the true religion in Spain.

After supper we proceeded upstairs to the choir (where the nuns attend public worship, and which looks down upon the handsome convent church) to try the organ. I was set down to a Sonata of Mozart's, the servants blowing the bellows. It seems to me that I made more noise than music, for the organ is very old, perhaps as old as the convent, which dates three centuries back. However, the nuns were pleased, and after they had sung a hymn, we returned below. I was rather sorry to leave them, and I felt as if I could have passed some time there very contentedly; but it was near nine o'clock, and we were obliged to take our departure; so having been embraced very cordially by the whole community, we left the hospitable walls of the Encarnacion. . . .

INDIAN MEDICINES AND REMEDIES

We went this evening to visit the Countess del —— , who has a house in the village. Found her in bed, feverish, and making use of simple remedies, such as herbs, the knowledge and use of which have descended from the ancient Indians to the present lords of the soil. The Spanish historians who have written upon the conquest of Mexico, all mention the knowledge which the Mexican physicians had of herbs. It was supposed by these last, that for every infirmity there was a remedy in the herbs of the field; and to apply them according to the nature of the malady, was the chief science of these primitive professors of medicine. Much which is now used in European pharmacy is due to the research of Mexican doctors; such as sarsaparilla, jalap, friars' rhubarb, *mechoacan,* etc.; also various emetics, antidotes to poison, remedies against fever, and an infinite number of plants, minerals, gums, and simple medicines. As for their infusions, decoctions, ointments, plasters, oils, etc., Cortes himself mentions the wonderful number of these which he saw in the Mexican market for sale. From certain trees they distilled balsams; and drew a balsamic liquid both from a decoction of the branches, and from the bark steeped in water. Bleeding and bathing were their other favourite remedies. The country-people breathed a vein with a maguey-point, and when they could not find leeches, substituted the prickles of the American hedgehog.

Besides bathing in the rivers, lakes, tanks, and fountains, they used a bath which is still to be seen in many Indian villages, and which they call the temezcalli. It is made of unbaked bricks; its form is that of a baker's oven, about eight feet wide and six high; the pavement rather convex, and lower than the surface of the soil. A person can enter this bath only on his knees. Opposite the entry is a stone or brick stove, its opening towards the exterior of the bath, with a hole to let out the smoke. Before the bath is prepared, the floor inside is covered with a mat, on which is placed a jar of water, some herbs and leaves of corn. The stove is then heated until the stones which unite it with the bath become red-hot. When the bather enters the entry is closed, and the only opening left is a hole at the top of the vault, which, when the smoke of the oven has passed through, is also shut. They then pour water upon the red-hot stones, from which a thick vapour arises, which fills the temezcalli. The bather then throws himself on the mat, and drawing down the steam with the herbs and maize, wets them in the tepid water of the jar, and if he has any pain, applies them to the part affected. This having produced perspiration, the door is opened and the well-baked patient comes out and dresses. For fevers, for bad colds, for the bite of a poisonous animal, this is said to be a certain cure; also for acute rheumatism.

For the cure of wounds, the Spaniards found the Mexican remedies most efficacious. Cortes himself was cured by one of their doctors of a severe wound in the head, received at Otumba, through which we lately passed. For fractures, for humours, for everything they had their remedy; sometimes pulverizing the seeds of plants, and attributing much of their efficacy to the superstitious ceremonies and prayers which they used while applying them, especially those which they offered up to *Tzapotlatenan,* the goddess of medicine.

A great deal of this knowledge is still preserved amongst their descendants, and considered efficacious. For every illness there is an herb, for every accident a remedy. Baths are in constant use, although these temezcallis are confined to the Indians. In every family there is some knowledge of simple medicine, very necessary, in *haciendas* especially, where no physician can possibly be procured. . . .

THE EDUCATION OF MEXICAN WOMEN

You ask me how Mexican women are educated. In answering you, I must put aside a few brilliant exceptions, and speak *en masse,* the most difficult thing in the world, for these exceptions are always rising up before me like accusing angels, and I begin to think of individuals, when I should keep to generalities. Generally speaking, then, the Mexican Señoras and Señoritas write, read, and play a little, sew, and take care of their houses and children. When I say they read, I mean they know how to read; when I say they write, I do not mean that they can always spell; and when I say they play, I do not assert that they have generally a knowledge of music. If we compare their education with that of girls in England, or in the United States, it is not a comparison, but a contrast. Compare it with that of Spanish women, and we shall be less severe upon their *far niente* descendants. In the first place, the climate inclines every one to indolence, both physically and morally. One cannot pore over a book when the blue sky is constantly smiling in at the open windows; then, out of doors after ten o'clock, the sun gives us due warning of our tropical latitude, and even though the breeze is so fresh and pleasant, one has no inclination to walk or ride far. Whatever be the cause, I am convinced that it is impossible to take the same exercise with the mind or with the body in this country, as in Europe or in the northern states. Then as to schools, there are none that can deserve the name, and no governesses. Young girls can have no emulation, for they never meet. They have no public diversion, and no private amusement. There are a few good foreign masters, most of whom have come to Mexico for the purpose of making their fortune, by teaching, or marriage, or both, and whose object, naturally, is to make the most money in the shortest possible time, that they may return home and enjoy it. The children generally appear to have an extraordinary disposition for music and drawing, yet there are few girls who are proficient in either.

When very young, they occasionally attend the schools, where boys and girls learn to read in common, or any other accomplishment that the old women can teach them; but at twelve they are already considered too old to attend these promiscuous assemblages, and masters are got for drawing and music to finish their education. I asked a lady the other day if her daughter went to school. "Good heavens!" said she, quite shocked, "she is past eleven years old!" It frequently happens that the least well-informed girls are the children of the cleverest men, who, keeping to the customs of their fore-fathers, are content if they confess regularly, attend church constantly, and can embroider and sing a little. Where there are more extended ideas, it is chiefly amongst families who have travelled in Europe, and have seen the different education of women in foreign countries. Of these the fathers occa-sionally devote a short portion of their time to the instruction of their daugh-ters, perhaps during their leisure evening moments, but it may easily be supposed that this desultory system has little real influence on the minds of the children. I do not think there are above half-a-dozen married women, or as many girls above fourteen, who, with the exception of the mass-book, read any one book through in the whole course of the year. They thus greatly sim-plify the system of education in the United States, where parties are frequently divided between the advocates for solid learning and those for superficial accomplishments; and according to whom it is difficult to amalgamate the solid beef of science with the sweet sauce of *les beaux arts.*

But if a Mexican girl is ignorant, she rarely shows it. They have generally the greatest possible tact; never by any chance wandering out of their depth, or betraying by word or sign that they are not well informed of the subject under discussion. Though seldom graceful, they are never awkward. and always self-possessed. They have plenty of natural talent, and where it has been thoroughly cultivated, no women can surpass them. Of what is called literary society, there is of course none —

> *"No bustling Botherbys have they to show 'em*
> *That charming passage in the last new poem."*

There is a little annual lying beside me called *"Calendario de las Señoritas Mejicanas,"* of which the preface, by Galvan, the editor, is very amusing.

"To none," he says, "better than to Mexican ladies, can I dedicate this mark of attention — (*obsequio*). Their graceful attractions well deserve any trouble that may have been taken to please them. Their bodies are graceful as the palms of the desert; their hair black as ebony, or golden as the rays of the sun, gracefully waves over their delicate shoulders; their glances are like the peaceful light of the moon. The Mexican ladies are not so white as the Europeans, but their whiteness is more agreeable to our eyes. Their words are soft, leading our hearts by gentleness, in the same manner as in their moments of just indignation they appal and confound us. Who can resist the magic of their song, always sweet, always gentle, and always natural? Let us leave to foreign ladies (*las ultramarinas*) these affected and scientific manners of singing; here nature surpasses art, as happens in everything, notwithstanding the cavillings of the learned.

"And what shall I say of their souls? I shall say that in Europe the minds are more cultivated, but in Mexico the hearts are more amiable. Here they are not only sentimental, but tender; not only soft, but virtuous; the body of a child is not more sensitive (*no es mas sensible el cuerpo de un niño*), nor a rose-bud softer. I have seen souls as beautiful as the borders of the rainbow, and purer than the drops of dew. Their passions are seldom tempestuous, and even then they are kindled and extinguished easily; but generally they emit a peaceful light, like the morning star, Venus. Modesty is painted in their eyes, and modesty is the greatest and most irresistible fascination of their souls. In short, the Mexican ladies, by their manifold virtues, are destined to serve as our support whilst we travel through the sad desert of life.

"Well do these attractions merit that we should try to please them; and in effect a new form, new lustre, and new graces have been given to the 'Almanac of the Mexican Ladies,' whom the editor submissively entreats to receive with benevolence this small tribute due to their enchantments and their virtues!"

There are in Mexico a few families of the old school, people of high rank, but who mingle very little in society; who are little known to the generality of foreigners, and who keep their daughters entirely at home, that they may not be contaminated by bad example. These select few, rich without ostentation, are certainly doing everything that is in their power to remedy the evils occasioned by the want of proper schools, or of competent instructresses for their daughters. Being nearly all allied by birth, or connected by marriage, they form a sort of *clan;* and it is sufficient to belong to one or other of these families, to be hospitably received by all. They meet together frequently, without ceremony, and whatever elements of good exist in Mexico, are to be found amongst them. The fathers are generally more of talent and learning, and the mothers, women of the highest respectability, to whose name no suspicion can be attached. . . .

CONTRASTS BETWEEN VILLAGES IN
NEW ENGLAND AND IN MEXICO

If any one wishes to try the effect of strong contrast, let him come direct from the United States to this country; but it is in the villages especially that the contrast is most striking. Travelling in New England, for example, we arrive at a small and flourishing village. We see four new churches, proclaiming four different sects; religion suited to all customers. These wooden churches or meeting-houses are all new, all painted white, or perhaps a bright red. Hard by is a tavern with a green paling, as clean and as new as the churches, and there are also various smart *stores* and neat dwelling-houses; all new, all wooden, all clean, and all ornamented with slight Grecian pillars. The whole has a cheerful, trim, and flourishing aspect. Houses, churches, stores, and taverns, all are of a piece. They are suited to the present emergency, whatever that may be, though they will never make fine ruins. Everything proclaims prosperity, equality, consistency; the past forgotten, the present all in all, and the future taking care of itself. No delicate attentions to posterity, who can never pay its debts. No beggars. If a man has even a hole in his coat, he must be lately from the Emerald Isle.

Transport yourself in imagination from this New England village to that of —— , it matters not which, not far from Mexico. "Look on this picture, and on that." The Indian huts, with their half-naked inmates, and little gardens full of flowers; the huts themselves either built of clay, or the half-ruined *beaux restes* of some stone building. At a little distance an hacienda, like a deserted palace, built of solid masonry, with its inner *patio* surrounded by thick stone pillars, with great walls and iron-barred windows that might stand a siege. Here a ruined arch and cross, so solidly built, that one cannot but wonder how the stones ever crumbled away. There, rising in the midst of old faithful-looking trees, the church, gray and ancient, but strong as if designed for eternity; with its saints and virgins, and martyrs and relics, its gold and silver and precious stones, whose value would buy up all the spare lots in the New England village; the lépero with scarce a rag to cover him, kneeling on that marble pavement. Leave the enclosure of the church, observe the stone wall that bounds the road for more than a mile; the fruit trees overtopping it, high though it be, with their loaded branches. This is the convent orchard. And that great Gothic pile of building, that stands in hoary majesty, surmounted by the lofty mountains, whose cloud-enveloped summits, tinged by the evening sun, rise behind it; what could so noble a building be but the monastery, perhaps of the Carmelites, because of its exceeding rich garden, and well-chosen site, for they, of all monks, are richest in this world's goods. Also we may see the reverend old prior riding slowly from under the arched gate up the village lanes, the Indians coming from their huts to do him lowly reverence as he passes. Here, everything reminds us of the past; of the conquering Spaniards, who seemed to build for eternity; impressing each work with their own solid, grave, and religious character; of the triumphs of catholicism; and of the Indians when Cortes first startled them from their repose, and stood before them like the fulfilment of a half-forgotten prophecy. It is the present that seems like a dream, a pale reflection of the past. All is decaying and growing fainter, and men seem trusting to some unknown future which they may never see. One government has been abandoned, and there is none in its place. One revolution follows another, yet the remedy is not found. Let them beware lest half a century later, they be awakened from their delusion, and find the cathedral turned into a meetinghouse, and all painted white; the *railing* melted down; the silver transformed into dollars; the Virgin's jewels sold to the highest bidder; the floor washed (which would do it no harm), and round the whole, a nice new wooden paling, freshly done in green — and all this performed by some of the artists from the *wide-awake* republic farther north. . . .

INDIANS AND CASTES IN MEXICO

25th. — We have just returned from a ride to San Bartolo, an Indian village, four leagues from this, where we went with a large party, some on horses, some on asses, others on mules, and one adventurous Jehu driving himself in a four-wheeled carriage, with a pair of horses, over a road formed of ruts, stones, holes, and rocks, where, I will venture to say, no carriage ever made its appearance before. Even the horses and asses got along with difficulty. In spite of large straw hats and green veils, we were burnt the colour of red Indians. In the middle of the day we find the sun intolerable at present, and, owing to the badness of the roads, we did not reach our destination until twelve or one o'clock.

San Bartolo is a small, scattered Indian village, with a church, and is remarkable for a beautiful spring of water, that jets cold and clear from the hard rock, as if Moses had but just smote it; for its superb tall pine-trees; for the good looks and cleanness of the Indian women, who are for ever washing their long hair in the innumerable clear streamlets formed by the spring; and for a view of Mexico, which is particularly favourable, owing to the thick, dark screen of pine wood in the foreground, and the distinct view of the

Laguna. Our dinner was carried by Indians, who had trotted off with it at day-dawn; but who had taken the wrong road, and did not arrive till long after us. We dined under the pine-trees by the side of the stream, but surrounded by crowds of gaping Indians, in too close vicinity to be agreeable. Some of the young women were remarkably handsome, with the most beautiful teeth imaginable, laughing and talking in their native tongue at a great rate, as they were washing in the brooks, some their hair and others their clothes. The men looked as dirty as Indians generally do, and by no means on a level with these handsome damsels, who are so much superior to the common race of Indians near Mexico, that one would think they had some intermixture of Spanish blood in their veins. A sister of the woman who takes charge of the hacienda where we live, is one of the most beautiful creatures I ever beheld. Large eyes, with long dark lashes, black hair nearly touching the ground, teeth like snow, a dark but glowing complexion, a superb figure, with fine arms and hands, and small beautifully-formed feet. All that is best of Indian and Spanish, "of dark and bright," seems united in her. C——n says he has seen peasant women in Andalusia on the same style of beauty, and quite as handsome. She is only nineteen. Such beauties as these startle one every now and then in some remote village. She belongs, no doubt, to the *mestizos* — the descendants of whites and Indians, the handsomest race in Mexico.

You ask if the castes in Mexico are distinct. There are seven supposed to be so. 1st, the Gachupinos, or Spaniards born in Europe; 2nd, the Creoles, that is, whites of European family born in America; 3rd, the Mestizos; 4th, the Mulattoes, descendants of whites and negroes, of whom there are few; 5th, the Zambos, descendants of negroes and Indians, the ugliest race in Mexico; 6th, the Indians; and 7th, the remains of the African negroes.

Of pure Indians, Humboldt in his day calculated that there existed two millions and a half in New Spain (without counting mestizos), and they are, probably, very little altered from the inferior Indians, as Cortes found them. The principal families perished at the time of the conquest. The priests, sole depositaries of knowledge, were put to death; the manuscripts and hieroglyphical paintings were burnt, and the remaining Indians fell into that state of ignorance and degradation, from which they have never emerged. The rich Indian women preferred marrying their Spanish conquerors to allying themselves with the degraded remnant of their countrymen; poor artisans, workmen, porters, etc., of whom Cortes speaks as filling the streets of the great cities, and as being considered little better than beasts of burden; nearly naked in *tierra caliente,* dressed pretty much as they now are in the temperate parts of the country; and everywhere with nearly the same manners, and habits, and customs, as they now have, but especially in the more distant villages where they have little intercourse with the other classes. Even in their religion, Christianity, as I observed before, seems to be formed of the ruins of their mythology; and all these festivities of the church, these fireworks, and images, and gay dresses, harmonize completely with their childish love of show, and are, in fact, their greatest source of delight. To buy these they save up all their money, and when you give a penny to an Indian child, it trots off to buy crackers, as another would to buy candy. Attempts have been made by their curates to persuade them to omit the celebration of certain days, and to expend less in the ceremonies of others, but the indignation and discontent which such proposals have caused, have induced them to desist in their endeavours.

Under an appearance of stupid apathy they veil a great depth of cunning. They are grave and gentle and rather sad in their appearance, when not under the influence of pulque; but when they return to their villages in the evening, and have taken a drop of comfort, their white teeth light up their bronze countenances like lamps, and the girls especially make the air ring with their laughter, which is very musical. I think it is Humboldt who says that their smile is extremely gentle, and the expression of their eyes very severe. As they have no beard, if it were not for a little moustache, which they frequently wear on the upper lip, there would be scarcely any difference between the faces of men and women.

The Indians in and near the capital are, according to Humboldt, either the descendants of the former labourers, or are remains of noble Indian families, who, disdaining to intermarry with their Spanish conquerors, preferred themselves to till the ground which their vassals formerly cultivated for them. It is said that these Indians of noble race, though to the vulgar eye undistinguishable from their fellows, are held in great respect by their inferior countrymen. In Cholula, particularly, there are still caciques with long Indian names; also in Tlascala — and though barefoot and ragged, they are said to possess great hidden wealth. But it is neither in or near the capital that we can see the Indians to perfection in their original state. It is only by travelling through the provinces that we can accomplish this; and should the lateness of the season oblige us to remain here any time after another minister arrives, we may probably take a longer journey in some different direction from *tierra caliente,* where we may see some tribes of the indigenous Mexicans. Certainly no visible improvement has taken place in their condition since the independence. They are quite as poor and quite as ignorant, and quite as degraded as they were in 1808, and if they do raise a little grain of their own, they are so hardly taxed that the privilege is as nought. . . .

SOCIETY PROMENADES IN CARRIAGES IN MEXICO CITY

Yesterday being a fête-day, the *Paséo* was very full of carriages, and consequently more brilliant and amusing than usual. This Paséo is the Mexican Prado or Hyde Park, while the *Viga* may be reckoned the Kensington Gardens of the metropolis, only however as succeeding to the other, for there is no walking, which in Mexico is considered wholly unfashionable; and though a few ladies in black gowns and mantillas do occasionally venture forth on foot very early to shop or to attend mass, the streets are so ill kept, the pavements so narrow, the crowd so great, and the multitude of *léperos* in rags and blankets so annoying, that all these inconveniences, added to the heat of the sun in the middle of the day, form a perfect excuse for their non-appearance in the streets of Mexico.

In the Alameda, however, which is so pretty and shady, it is very agreeable to walk; but though I have gone there frequently in the morning, I have met but three ladies on foot, and of these two were foreigners. After all, every one has feet, but ladies alone have carriages, and it may be a mixture of aristocracy and indolence which prevents the Mexican Doñas from profaning the soles of their feet by a contact with their mother earth.

The Paséo called *de Bucarelli,* after a viceroy of that name, is a long and broad avenue bounded by the trees which he planted, and where there is a large stone fountain, whose sparkling waters look cool and pleasant, ornamented by a gilded statue of Victory. Here, every evening, but more especially on Sundays and fête-days, which last are nearly innumerable, may be seen two long rows of carriages filled with ladies, crowds of gentlemen on horseback riding down the middle between these carriages, soldiers at intervals attending to the preservation of public order, and multitudes of common people and *léperos,* mingled with some well-dressed gentlemen on foot. The carriages are for the most part extremely handsome — European coaches with fine horses and odd liveries, mingled with carriages made in the country, some in the old Mexican fashion, heavy and covered with gilding, or a modern imitation of an English carriage, strong, but somewhat clumsy and ill-finished. Various hackney-coaches, drawn by mules, are seen among the finer equipages, some very tolerable, and others of extraordinary form and dimensions, which bear tokens of having belonged in former days to some noble Don.

Horses, as being more showy, are more fashionable in these public promenades than mules; but the latter animal requires less care, and is capable of undergoing more fatigue than the horse. Most families have both mules and horses in their stable, and for those who visit much this is necessary. The carriages, of which the most fashionable seems to be the *carratela,* open at the sides, with glass windows, are filled with ladies in full toilet, without mantillas, their heads uncovered, and, generally, *coiffées* with flowers or jewels; but the generality being close coaches, afford but an indistinct view of the inmates, as they pass along saluting each other with their fingers or fan. The whole scene, on the evening of a fête, is exceedingly brilliant, but very monotonous. The equestrians, with their fine horses and handsome Mexican dresses, apparently take no notice of the ladies as they pass, rarely salute them, and never venture to enter into conversation with them. But they are well aware to whom each carriage belongs, and consequently when it behoves them to make their horses curvet, and otherwise show off their horsemanship to advantage. Black eyes are upon them, and they know it. When the carriages have made two or three turns, they draw up at different stations in a semicircle a little off the road, and there the inmates sit and view the passers-by. Occasional streams of smoke may be seen issuing from the carriages, but chiefly, it must be confessed, from the most old-fashioned equipages, and from the hackney-coaches. Smoking amongst ladies in the higher classes is going very much out of fashion, and is rarely practised openly except by elderly, or at least by married ladies. In a secondary class, indeed, young and old inhale the smoke of their cigaritos without hesitation, and when a custom begins to be considered *vulgar,* it will hardly subsist another generation. Unfeminine as it is, I do not think it looks ungraceful to see a pretty woman smoke.

Porfirio Díaz, Dictator of Mexico. Heads of state like to have their pictures widely disseminated, whether they be Presidents or Kings or Dictators, and Porfirio Díaz was no exception. This painting was executed by the prominent Spanish artist Joaquín Sorolla y Bastida, who had been commissioned to paint a number of portraits of Spaniards and Spanish Americans by Archer Milton Huntington for the Hispanic Society of America in New York City.

The Society was founded by Mr. Huntington in 1905, and has become one of the great collections of the world of art, books, and manuscripts on Hispanic American culture.

Porfirio Díaz:
Dictator of Mexico

No nineteenth-century caudillo has been so much written about as Porfirio Díaz, who first became provisional president of Mexico in 1876 by revolting with the cry "No re-election" and then by 1884 had the country so thoroughly dominated that he was able to get himself "elected" term after term until the Mexican Revolution overthrew him in 1911. The *Porfiriato,* as this long period is called, produced peace and some economic progress, but these were achieved only at a great price.

The intellectuals did not go into exile as they had when Juan Manuel de Rosas held sway over Argentina, and in fact General Díaz received strong support from the positivists. As one Mexican historian explains:

> His figure came to symbolize the order and peace for which the men trained in positivism had clamored. Materialism and dehumanization were converted into models of life for the generation which developed during his regime: industry, money, railroads, and always more money. Progress definitely seemed to triumph. The social evolution seemed to be moving forward with gigantic steps, but . . . freedom was forgotten, the very thing for which it was said that order had been established.[1]

The fault was by no means his alone, but in his long years of power the people as a whole did not advance and remained illiterate. While the celebrants of the centenary of Mexican independence and of the dictator's eightieth birthday drank twenty carloads of champagne and consumed many

---

[1] Leopoldo Zea, *The Latin-American Mind,* trans. James H. Abbott and Lowell Dunham (Norman: University of Oklahoma Press, 1963), p. 284.

delicacies, the masses verged on starvation, for they had suffered a steady reduction in their incredibly low living standards during the long Porfiriato. Yet in many ways Díaz was a great man; one of his severest United States critics concludes:

> He accomplished what none of his countrymen had been able to do before him — to maintain a generation of peace. . . . But the over-shadowing fact — to remember — is that the Mexico he left in 1911 had all its problems, the problems of four centuries, still to solve.[2]

During the Porfiriato, Americans began to go to Mexico in ever-increasing numbers — to invest money, to build railroads, to buy ranches, to write books, to report for newspapers, or just to pay a tourist visit. It was during this period that the moving picture camera began to record the living scenes of Mexican history. Salvador Toscano produced enough film on a French machine that a remarkable documentary could be made, the "Memorias de un Mexicano," which is now being seen by many students at American universities thanks to the initiative of the Committee on Mexican History of the Conference on Latin American History. Newspaper photographers also began to arrive in the last years of the Porfiriato and the early years of the Revolution, so that the documentation is both varied and rich.

The accounts written by visitors from the United States are particularly revealing. One reporter, James Creelman, made the long journey from New York to Mexico City for the sole purpose of interviewing the aged dictator, who unexpectedly remarked that he would be retiring in a couple of years and hence welcomed an opposition (Reading 50). This was the beginning of the end for Díaz. But two years later he was still in the saddle, and another American, John Kenneth Turner, attacked his harsh and high-handed rule that resulted in his complete control of Mexico (Reading 51).

Another visitor was a young Harvard student from Minneapolis, Charles Flandrau, who went to Mexico to visit a brother for some months and whose delightful record of experiences there, entitled *Viva Mexico!,* constitutes an amusing and interesting view of Mexican life but also includes some sharp criticism of the Church there which helps to explain the anticlerical spirit of the Revolution when it broke out a few years later. Flandrau learned "of a powerful bishop whose 'wife' and large family of sons and daughters are complacently taken for granted by the entire diocese," and was "warned by a devout Catholic never under any circumstances to allow one's American maid servants to converse with a priest or to enter his home on any

---

[2] Ernest Gruening, *Mexico and Its Heritage* (New York: Century, 1928), p. 65.

pretext whatever." [3] Flandrau himself experienced clerical commercialism when he described a village confirmation ceremony in 1908, when the bishop arrived in Mizantla because many children were unconfirmed since his last visit there "five or eight" years ago:

> The bishop, with three priests behind him was standing at the top of the altar steps. He was wearing his mitre, and the tips of his fingers lightly touched one another, as a bishop's fingers should, on the apex of his stomach. It was a thrilling moment.
>
> Then combining, in a quite wonderful fashion, extreme rapidity with an air of ecclesiastical calm, he made his confirmatory way down one side of the nave, across the end, and up the other, preceded by one priest and followed by two. The first gathered up the certificates (no laying on of hands unless one has paid one's twenty-five centavos) and read the name of the child next in line to the bishop, who murmured the appropriate formula, made a tiny sign of the cross on a tiny forehead with the end of a dirty thumb and moved on. The second, with a bit of absorbent cotton, dipped in oil, swabbed the spot on which the cross had been signed, while the third, taking advantage of the general rapture, gently relieved everyone of his blessed candle (it had never been lighted) and carried it away to be sold again. But by the time the first priest reached my family party he had grown tired and careless. Instead of collecting the certificates singly, he began to take them in twos and threes with the result that they became mixed, and Gerónimo was confirmed, not as Gerónimo, but as "Saturnina," which happened to be the name of the little snub-nosed Totonac girl standing next to him. When I realized this had happened, I protested. Whereupon his grace and I proceeded to have "words." With exceeding bitterness he then reperformed the rite, and if the eyes of the first priest could have killed, I should have withered on my slender stalk. The priest with the cotton sought to annihilate me with an undertoned remark to the effect that my conduct was a *barbaridad,* but the third was not only *simpático* — he was farther away from the bishop: As, with much tenderness, he disengaged Gerónimo's reluctant fingers from the candle, he severely looked at me and winked. [4]

Flandrau also noted the widespread intoxication of the villagers and marveled "not, like the tourist of a week, that they are dirty, but that under the

[3] Ibid., p. 270.
[4] Ibid., pp. 258–259.

circumstances they are as clean as they are; not that so many of them are continually sick, but that any of them are ever well; not that they love to get drunk, but they can bear to remain sober." [5]

Knowledge of Mexican history has greatly increased in recent years under the impetus supplied by Daniel Cosío Villegas, who has provided a discerning evaluation of the Porfiriato (Reading 53).

The Porfiriato had its defenders and two apologists for the regime, Toribio Esquivel Obregón and Emilio Rabasa, who argued that the Revolution was unjustified because Mexico did not have a land problem: the rural, largely Indian population owned more than enough land to support itself. Professor William B. Taylor, whose recent researches have demonstrated that in fact the Oaxaca land distribution was radically different from the large hacienda type holdings in northern Mexico, points out that these apologists for the Porfiriato used examples from Oaxaca to support their argument.[6] Here again we have an example of the dangers of generalizing on Latin America!

[5] Ibid., p. 540.

[6] William B. Taylor, *Landlord and Peasant in Colonial Oaxaca* (Stanford: Stanford University Press, 1972), p. 199.

50. *President Díaz: Hero of the Americas*

JAMES CREELMAN

James Creelman represented that breed of American journalists who go abroad on their restless search for a "newsworthy" story. When his interview with President Díaz appeared in the March 1908 issue of *Pearson's Magazine,* it created a commotion in Mexico, for Díaz announced the end of his rule. As Ernest Gruening stated, in his solid volume of enduring value on Mexico: "An earthquake would have caused far less commotion. Mexico was accustomed to earthquakes. But such sentiments from the lips of Don Porfirio were startling, unprecedented, incredible. Many Mexicans refused to believe them. But no denial was forthcoming and the political ferment began." *

Did Díaz seriously intend to retire, or was this interview a clever ruse to test the loyalty of his henchmen? Gruening believed that "in the light of subsequent events the interview appears as a typical piece of Díaz duplicity, designed to test out his entourage. It was wholly in keeping with Porfirian policy that matters of such transcendent importance were revealed to an American journalist, while Mexican newspapermen were denied even a further interview on the same subject." †

The obsequious praise lavished on the dictator in the Creelman article was typical of the times: "Apart from the subsidized press and countless books, and the paeans of the beneficiaries, much of this enthusiasm was genuine." ‡ Nor was Creelman unusual. Here is one dedication of a book by an American writer: "To Señor General Don Porfirio Díaz, The Illustrious President Of Mexico, Whose Intrepid Moral Character, Distinguished Statesmanship, And Devoted Patriotism Make Him The Pride And Glory Of His Country, Is Dedicated This Volume, Describing A Beautiful And Prosperous Land, Whose Free Flag Never Waved Over A Slave, And Whose Importance As A Nation Is Due To The Patriot Under Whose Administration Mexico Now Flourishes And Holds Its Proud Position Among The Republics Of The World." §

From the heights of Chapultepec Castle President Diaz looked down upon the venerable capital of his country, spread out on a vast plain, with a ring of mountains flung up grandly about it, and I, who had come nearly four thousand miles from New York to see the master and hero of modern Mexico — the inscrutable leader in whose veins is blended the blood of the primitive

---

* Gruening, *Mexico and Its Heritage* (New York: Century, 1928), p. 91.
† Ibid., p. 92.
‡ Ibid., p. 62.
§ Marie Robinson Wright, *Picturesque Mexico* (Philadelphia: Lippincott, 1897).

Mixtecs with that of the invading Spaniards — watched the slender, erect form, the strong, soldierly head and commanding, but sensitive, countenance with an interest beyond words to express.

A high, wide forehead that slopes up to crisp white hair and overhangs deep-set, dark brown eyes that search your soul, soften into inexpressible kindliness and then dart quick side looks — terrible eyes, threatening eyes, loving, confiding, humorous eyes — a straight, powerful, broad and somewhat fleshy nose, whose curved nostrils lift and dilate with every emotion; huge, virile jaws that sweep from large, flat, fine ears, set close to the head, to the tremendous, square, fighting chin; a wide, firm mouth shaded by a white mustache; a full, short, muscular neck; wide shoulders, deep chest; a curiously tense and rigid carriage that gives great distinction to a personality suggestive of singular power and dignity — that is Porfirio Diaz in his seventy-eighth year, as I saw him a few weeks ago on the spot where, forty years before, he stood — with his besieging army surrounding the City of Mexico, and the young Emperor Maximilian being shot to death in Querétaro, beyond those blue mountains to the north — waiting grimly for the thrilling end of the last interference of European monarchy with the republics of America.

It is the intense, magnetic something in the wide-open, fearless, dark eyes and the sense of nervous challenge in the sensitive, spread nostrils, that seem to connect the man with the immensity of the landscape, as some elemental force.

There is not a more romantic or heroic figure in all the world, nor one more intensely watched by both the friends and foes of democracy, than the soldier-statesman, whose adventurous youth pales the pages of Dumas, and whose iron rule has converted the warring, ignorant, superstitious and impoverished masses of Mexico, oppressed by centuries of Spanish cruelty and greed, into a strong, steady, peaceful, debt-paying and progressive nation.

For twenty-seven years he has governed the Mexican Republic with such power that national elections have become mere formalities. He might easily have set a crown upon his head.

Yet to-day, in the supremacy of his career, this astonishing man — foremost figure of the American hemisphere and unreadable mystery to students of human government — announces that he will insist on retiring from the Presidency at the end of his present term, so that he may see his successor

From "President Diaz: Hero of the Americas" by James Creelman, *Pearson's Magazine*, 19, March 1908, pp. 231–277. A facsimile reproduction of the interview, together with a Spanish translation, appears in *Entrevista Díaz-Creelman*, Cuadernos del Instituto de Historia, Serie Documental, no. 2 (Mexico: Universidad Nacional Autónoma de México, 1963).

peacefully established and that, with his assistance, the people of the Mexican Republic may show the world that they have entered serenely and preparedly upon the last complete phase of their liberties, that the nation is emerging from ignorance and revolutionary passion, and that it can choose and change presidents without weakness or war.

It is something to come from the money-mad gambling congeries of Wall Street and in the same week to stand on the rock of Chapultepec, in surroundings of almost unreal grandeur and loveliness, beside one who is said to have transformed a republic into an autocracy by the absolute compulsion of courage and character, and to hear him speak of democracy as the hope of mankind.

This, too, at a time when the American soul shudders at the mere thought of a third term for any President.

The President surveyed the majestic, sunlit scene below the ancient castle and turned away with a smile, brushing a curtain of scarlet trumpet-flowers and vine-like pink geraniums as he moved along the terrace toward the inner garden, where a fountain set among palms and flowers sparkled with water from the spring at which Montezuma used to drink, under the mighty cypresses that still rear their branches about the rock on which we stood.

"It is a mistake to suppose that the future of democracy in Mexico has been endangered by the long continuance in office of one President," he said quietly. "I can say sincerely that office has not corrupted my political ideals and that I believe democracy to be the one true, just principle of government, although in practice it is possible only to highly developed peoples."

For a moment the straight figure paused and the brown eyes looked over the great valley to where snow-covered Popocatapetl lifted its volcanic peak nearly eighteen thousand feet among the clouds beside the snowy craters of Ixtaccihuatl — a land of dead volcanoes, human and otherwise.

"I can lay down the Presidency of Mexico without a pang of regret, but I cannot cease to serve this country while I live," he added.

The sun shown full in the President's face but his eyes did not shrink from the ordeal. The green landscape, the smoking city, the blue tumult of mountains, the thin, exhilarating, scented air, seemed to stir him, and the color came to his cheeks as he clasped his hands behind him and threw his head backward. His nostrils opened wide.

"You know that in the United States we are troubled about the question of electing a President for three terms?"

He smiled and then looked grave, nodding his head gently and pursing his lips. It is hard to describe the look of concentrated interest that suddenly came into his strong, intelligent countenance.

"Yes, yes, I know," he replied. "It is a natural sentiment of democratic peoples that their officials should be often changed. I agree with that sentiment."

It seemed hard to realize that I was listening to a soldier who had ruled a republic continuously for more than a quarter of a century with a personal authority unknown to most kings. Yet he spoke with a simple and convincing manner, as one whose place was great and secure beyond the need of hypocrisy.

"It is quite true that when a man has occupied a powerful office for a very long time he is likely to begin to look upon it as his personal property, and it is well that a free people should guard themselves against the tendencies of individual ambition.

"Yet the abstract theories of democracy and the practical, effective application of them are often necessarily different — that is when you are seeking for the substance rather than the mere form.

"I can see no good reason why President Roosevelt should not be elected again if a majority of the American people desire to have him continue in office. I believe that he has thought more of his country than of himself. He has done and is doing a great work for the United States, a work that will cause him, whether he serves again or not, to be remembered in history as one of the great Presidents. I look upon the trusts as a great and real power in the United States, and President Roosevelt has had the patriotism and courage to defy them. Mankind understands the meaning of his attitude and its bearing upon the future. He stands before the world as a statesman whose victories have been moral victories. . . .

"Here in Mexico we have had different conditions. I received this Government from the hands of a victorious army at a time when the people were divided and unprepared for the exercise of the extreme principles of democratic government. To have thrown upon the masses the whole responsibility of government at once would have produced conditions that might have discredited the cause of free government.

"Yet, although I got power at first from the army, an election was held as soon as possible and then my authority came from the people. I have tried to leave the Presidency several times, but it has been pressed upon me and I remained in office for the sake of the nation which trusted me. The fact that the price of Mexican securities dropped eleven points when I was ill at Cuernavaca indicates the kind of evidence that persuaded me to overcome my personal inclination to retire to private life.

"We preserved the republican and democratic form of government. We defended the theory and kept it intact. Yet we adopted a patriarchal policy in the actual administration of the nation's affairs, guiding and restraining popular tendencies, with full faith that an enforced peace would allow education, industry and commerce to develop elements of stability and unity in a naturally intelligent, gentle and affectionate people.

"I have waited patiently for the day when the people of the Mexican Republic would be prepared to choose and change their government at every election without danger of armed revolutions and without injury to the national credit or interference with national progress. I believe that day has come. . . .

"In the old days we had no middle class in Mexico because the minds of the people and their energies were wholly absorbed in politics and war. Spanish tyranny and misgovernment had disorganized society. The productive activities of the nation were abandoned in successive struggles. There was general confusion. Neither life nor property was safe. A middle class could not appear under such conditions."

"General Diaz," I interrupted, "you have had an unprecedented experience in the history of republics. For thirty years the destinies of this nation have been in your hands, to mold them as you will; but men die, while nations must continue to live. Do you believe that Mexico can continue to exist in peace as a republic? Are you satisfied that its future is assured under free institutions?"

It was worth while to have come from New York to Chapultepec Castle to see the hero's face at that moment. Strength, patriotism, warriorship, prophethood seemed suddenly to shine in his brown eyes.

"The future of Mexico is assured," he said in a clear voice. "The principles of democracy have not been planted very deep in our people, I fear. But the nation has grown and it loves liberty. Our difficulty has been that the people do not concern themselves enough about public matters for a democracy. The individual Mexican as a rule thinks much about his own rights and is always ready to assert them. But he does not think so much about the rights of others. He thinks of his privileges, but not of his duties. Capacity for self-restraint is the basis of democratic government, and self-restraint is possible only to those who recognize the rights of their neighbors.

"The Indians, who are more than half of our population, care little for politics. They are accustomed to look to those in authority for leadership instead of thinking for themselves. That is a tendency they inherited from the Spaniards, who taught them to refrain from meddling in public affairs and rely on the Government for guidance.

"Yet I firmly believe that the principles of democracy have grown and will grow in Mexico."

"But you have no opposition party in the Republic, Mr. President. How can free institutions flourish when there is no opposition to keep the majority, or governing party, in check?"

"It is true there is no opposition party. I have so many friends in the republic that my enemies seem unwilling to identify themselves with so small a minority. I appreciate the kindness of my friends and the confidence of my country; but such absolute confidence imposes responsibilities and duties that tire me more and more.

"No matter what my friends and supporters say, I retire when my present term of office ends, and I shall not serve again. I shall be eighty years old then.

"My country has relied on me and it has been kind to me. My friends have praised my merits and overlooked my faults. But they may not be willing to deal so generously with my successor and he may need my advice and support; therefore I desire to be alive when he assumes office so that I may help him."

He folded his arms over his deep chest and spoke with great emphasis.

"I welcome an opposition party in the Mexican Republic," he said. "If it appears, I will regard it as a blessing, not as an evil. And if it can develop power, not to exploit but to govern, I will stand by it, support it, advise it and forget myself in the successful inauguration of complete democratic government in the country.

"It is enough for me that I have seen Mexico rise among the peaceful and useful nations. I have no desire to continue in the Presidency. This nation is ready for her ultimate life of freedom. At the age of seventy-seven years I am satisfied with robust health. That is one thing which neither law nor force can create. I would not exchange it for all the millions of your American oil king."

His ruddy skin, sparkling eyes and light, elastic step went well with his words. For one who has endured the privations of war and imprisonment, and who to-day rises at six o'clock in the morning, working until late at night at the full of his powers, the physical condition of President Diaz, who is even now a notable hunter and who usually ascends the palace stairway two steps at a time, is almost unbelievable.

"The railway has played a great part in the peace of Mexico," he continued. "When I became President at first there were only two small lines, one connecting the capital with Vera Cruz, the other connecting it with Querétaro. Now we have more than nineteen thousand miles of railways. Then we had a slow and costly mail service, carried on by stage coaches, and the mail coach between the capital and Puebla would be stopped by highwaymen two or three times in a trip, the last robbers to attack it generally finding nothing

left to steal. Now we have a cheap, safe and fairly rapid mail service throughout the country with more than twenty-two hundred post-offices. Telegraphing
was a difficult thing in those times. To-day we have more than forty-five
thousand miles of telegraph wires in operation.

"We began by making robbery punishable by death and compelling the
execution of offenders within a few hours after they were caught and condemned. We ordered that wherever telegraph wires were cut and the chief
officer of the district did not catch the criminal, he should himself suffer; and
in case the cutting occurred on a plantation the proprietor who failed to
prevent it should be hanged to the nearest telegraph pole. These were military orders, remember.

"We were harsh. Sometimes we were harsh to the point of cruelty. But it
was all necessary then to the life and progress of the nation. If there was
cruelty, results have justified it."

The nostrils dilated and quivered. The mouth was a straight line.

"It was better that a little blood should be shed that much blood should be
saved. The blood that was shed was bad blood; the blood that was saved was
good blood.

"Peace was necessary, even an enforced peace, that the nation might have
time to think and work. Education and industry have carried on the task begun by the army.". . .

"And which do you regard as the greatest force for peace, the army or the
schoolhouse?" I asked.

The soldier's face flushed slightly and the splendid white head was held a
little higher.

"You speak of the present time?"

"Yes."

"The schoolhouse. There can be no doubt of that. I want to see education
throughout the Republic carried on by the national Government. I hope to see
it before I die. It is important that all citizens of a republic should receive the
same training, so that their ideals and methods may be harmonized and the
national unity intensified. When men read alike and think alike they are more
likely to act alike."

"And you believe that the vast Indian population of Mexico is capable of
high development?"

"I do. The Indians are gentle and they are grateful, all except the Yacquis
and some of the Mayas. They have the traditions of an ancient civilization of
their own. They are to be found among the lawyers, engineers, physicians,
army officers and other professional men."

Over the city drifted the smoke of many factories.

"It is better than common smoke," I said.

"Yes," he replied, "and yet there are times when common smoke is not such a bad thing. The toiling poor of my country have risen up to support me, but I cannot forget what my comrades in arms and their children have been to me in my severest ordeals."

There were actually tears in the veteran's eyes.

"That," I said, pointing to a hideously modern bull-ring near the castle, "is the only surviving Spanish institution to be seen in this landscape."

"You have not noticed the pawnshops," he exclaimed. "Spain brought to us her pawn-shops, as well as her bull-rings.". . .

There are nineteen thousand miles of railways operated in Mexico, nearly all with American managers, engineers and conductors, and one has only to ride on the Mexican Central system or to enjoy the trains de luxe of the National Line to realize the high transportation standards of the country.

So determined is President Diaz to prevent his country from falling into the hands of the trusts that the Government is taking over and merging in one corporation, with the majority stock in the Nation's hands, the Mexican Central, National and Inter-oceanic lines — so that, with this mighty trunk system of transportation beyond the reach of private control, industry, agriculture, commerce and passenger traffic will be safe from oppression.

This merger of ten thousand miles of railways into a single company, with $113,000,000 of the stock, a clear majority, in the Government's hands, is the answer of President Diaz and his brilliant Secretary of Finances to the prediction that Mexico may some day find herself helplessly in the grip of a railway trust.

Curiously enough, the leading American railway officials representing the lines which are to be merged and controlled by the Government spoke to me with great enthusiasm of the plan as a distinct forward step, desirable alike for shippers and passengers and for private investors in the roads.

Two-thirds of the railways of Mexico are owned by Americans, who have invested about $300,000,000 in them profitably.

As it is, freight and passenger rates are fixed by the Government, and not a time table can be made or changed without official approval.

It may surprise a few Americans to know that the first-class passenger rate in Mexico is only two and two-fifths cents a mile, while the second-class rate, which covers at least one-half of the whole passenger traffic of the country, is only one cent and one-fifth a mile — these figures being in terms of gold, to afford a comparison with American rates.

I have been privately assured by the principal American officers and investors of the larger lines that railway enterprises in Mexico are encouraged, dealt with on their merits and are wholly free from blackmail, direct or indirect. . . .

More than $1,200,000,000 of foreign capital has been invested in Mexico since President Diaz put system and stability into the nation. Capital for railways, mines, factories and plantations has been pouring in at the rate of $200,000,000 a year. In six months the Government sold more than a million acres of land.

In spite of what has already been done, there is still room for the investment of billions of dollars in the mines and industries of the Republic.

Americans and other foreigners interested in mines, real estate, factories, railways and other enterprises have privately assured me, not once, but many times, that, under Diaz, conditions for investment in Mexico are fairer and quite as reliable as in the most highly developed European countries. The President declares that these conditions will continue after his death or retirement.

Since Diaz assumed power, the revenues of the Government have increased from about $15,000,000 to more than $115,000,000, and yet taxes have been steadily reduced.

When the price of silver was cut in two, President Diaz was advised that his country could never pay its national debt, which was doubled by the change in values. He was urged to repudiate a part of the debt. The President denounced the advice as foolishness as well as dishonesty, and it is a fact that some of the greatest officers of the government went for years without their salaries that Mexico might be able to meet her financial obligations dollar for dollar.

The cities shine with electric lights and are noisy with electric trolley cars; English is taught in the public schools of the great Federal District; the public treasury is full and overflowing and the national debt decreasing; there are nearly seventy thousand foreigners living contentedly and prosperously in the Republic — more Americans than Spaniards; Mexico has three times as large a population to the square mile as Canada; public affairs have developed strong men like José Yves Limantour, the great Secretary of Finances, one of the most distinguished of living financiers; Vice-president Corral, who is also Secretary of the Interior; Ignacio Mariscal, the Minister of Foreign Affairs, and Enrique Creel, the brilliant Ambassador at Washington.

And it is a land of beauty beyond compare. Its mountains and valleys, its great plateaus, its indescribably rich and varied foliage, its ever blooming and abundant flowers, its fruits, its skies, its marvelous climate, its old villages, cathedrals, churches, convents — there is nothing quite like Mexico in the world for variety and loveliness. But it is the gentle, trustful, grateful

Indian, with his unbelievable hat and many-colored blanket, the eldest child of America, that wins the heart out of you. After traveling all over the world, the American who visits Mexico for the first time wonders how it happened that he never understood what a fascinating country of romance he left at his own door.

It is the hour of growth, strength and peace which convinces Porfirio Diaz that he has almost finished his task on the American continent.

Yet you see no man in a priest's attire in this Catholic country. You see no religious processions. The Church is silent save within her own walls. This is a land where I have seen the most profound religious emotion, the most solemn religious spectacles — from the blanketed peons kneeling for hours in cathedrals, the men carrying their household goods, the women suckling their babies, to that indescribable host of Indians on their knees at the shrine of the Virgin of Guadalupe.

I asked President Diaz about it while we paced the terrace of Chapultepec Castle.

He bowed his white head for a moment and then lifted it high, his dark eyes looking straight into mine.

"We allow no priest to vote, we allow no priest to hold public office, we allow no priest to wear a distinctive dress in public, we allow no religious processions in the streets," he said. "When we made those laws we were not fighting against religion, but against idolatry. We intend that the humblest Mexican shall be so far freed from the past that he can stand upright and unafraid in the presence of any human being. I have no hostility to religion; on the contrary, in spite of all past experience, I firmly believe that there can be no true national progress in any country or any time without real religion."

Such is Porfirio Díaz, the foremost man of the American hemisphere. What he has done, almost alone and in such a few years, for a people disorganized and degraded by war, lawlessness and comic-opera politics, is the great inspiration of Pan-Americanism, the hope of the Latin-American republics,

Whether you see him at Chapultepec Castle, or in his office in the National Palace, or in the exquisite drawing-room of his modest home in the city, with his young, beautiful wife and his children and grandchildren by his first wife about him, or surrounded by troops, his breast covered with decorations conferred by great nations, he is always the same — simple, direct and full of the dignity of conscious power.

In spite of the iron government he has given to Mexico, in spite of a continuance in office that has caused men to say that he has converted a republic into an autocracy, it is impossible to look into his face when he speaks of the principle of popular sovereignty without believing that even now he would take up arms and shed his blood in defense of it.

Only a few weeks ago Secretary of State Root summed up President Diaz when he said:

> It has seemed to me that all of the men now living, General Porfirio Diaz, of Mexico, was best worth seeing. Whether one considers the adventurous, daring, chivalric incidents of his early career; whether one considers the vast work of government which his wisdom and courage and commanding character accomplished; whether one considers his singularly attractive personality, no one lives to-day that I would rather see than President Diaz. If I were a poet I would write poetic eulogies. If I were a musician I would compose triumphal marches. If I were a Mexican I should feel that the steadfast loyalty of a lifetime could not be too much in return for the blessings that he had brought to my country. As I am neither poet, musician nor Mexican, but only an American who loves justice and liberty and hopes to see their reign among mankind progress and strengthen and become perpetual, I look to Porfirio Diaz, the President of Mexico, as one of the great men to be held up for the hero-worship of mankind.

51. *The Díaz System*

JOHN KENNETH TURNER

John Kenneth Turner had an entirely different approach from that of Creelman, for he had seen with his own eyes the conditions suffered by the Indians in Yucatán and the Valle Nacional.

The slavery and peonage of Mexico, the poverty and illiteracy, the general prostration of the people, are due, in my humble judgment, to the financial and political organization that at present rules that country — in a word, to what I shall call the "system" of General Porfirio Diaz.

That these conditions can be traced in a measure to the history of Mexico

From *Barbarous Mexico* by John Kenneth Turner (Chicago: Charles H. Kerr & Company, 1910), pp. 120–137, passim.

during past generations, is true. I do not wish to be unfair to General Diaz in the least degree. The Spanish Dons made slaves and peons of the Mexican people. Yet never did they grind the people as they are ground today. In Spanish times the peon at least had his own little patch of ground, his own humble shelter; today he has nothing. Moreover, the Declaration of Independence, proclaimed just one hundred years ago, in 1810, proclaimed also the abolition of chattel slavery. Slavery was abolished, though not entirely. Succeeding Mexican governments of class and of church and of the individual held the people in bondage little less severe. But finally came a democratic movement which broke the back of the church, which overthrew the rule of caste, which adopted a form of government as modern as our own, which freed the slave in fact as well as in name, which gave the lands of the people back to the people, which wiped the slate clean of the blood of the past. . . .

It was under Porfirio Diaz that slavery and peonage were re-established in Mexico, and on a more merciless basis than they had existed even under the Spanish Dons. Therefore, I can see no injustice in charging at least a preponderance of the blame for these conditions upon the system of Diaz.

I say the "system of Diaz" rather than Diaz personally because, though he is the keystone of the arch, though he is the government of Mexico more completely than is any other individual the government of any large country on the planet, yet no one man can stand alone in his iniquity. Diaz is the central prop of the slavery, but there are other props without which the system could not continue upright for a single day. For example, there is the collection of commercial interests which profit by the Diaz system of slavery and autocracy, and which puts no insignificant part of its tremendous powers to holding the central prop upright in exchange for the special privileges that it receives. Not the least among these commercial interests are American, which, I blush to say, are quite as aggressive defenders of the Diaz citadel as any. Indeed . . . these American interests undoubtedly form the determining force of the continuation of Mexican slavery. Thus does Mexican slavery come home to us in the full sense of the term. . . .

In order that the reader may understand the Diaz system and its responsibility in the degradation of the Mexican people, it will be well to go back and trace briefly the beginnings of that system. Mexico is spoken of throughout the world as a Republic. That is because it was once a Republic and still pretends to be one. Mexico has a constitution which has never been repealed, a constitution said to be modeled after our own, and one which is, indeed, like ours in the main. Like ours, it provides for a national congress, state legislatures and municipal aldermen to make the laws, federal, state, and local judges to interpret them, and a president, governors and local executives to administer them. Like ours, it provides for manhood suffrage, freedom of the press and of speech, equality before the law, and the other guarantees of life, liberty and the pursuit of happiness which we ourselves enjoy, in a degree, as a matter of course.

Such was Mexico forty years ago. Forty years ago Mexico was at peace with the world. She had just overthrown, after a heroic war, the foreign prince, Maximilian, who had been seated as emperor by the armies of Napoleon Third of France. Her president, Benito Juarez, is today recognized in Mexico and out of Mexico as one of the most able as well as unselfish patriots of Mexican history. Never since Cortez fired his ships there on the gulf coast had Mexico enjoyed such prospects of political freedom, industrial prosperity and general advancement.

But in spite of these facts, and the additional fact that he was deeply indebted to Juarez, all his military promotions having been received at the hands of the latter, General Porfirio Diaz stirred up a series of rebellions for the purpose of securing for himself the supreme power of the land. Diaz not only led one armed rebellion against a peaceable, constitutional and popularly approved government, but he led three of them. For nine years he plotted as a common rebel. The support that he received came chiefly from bandits, criminals and professional soldiers who were disgruntled at the antimilitarist policy which Juarez had inaugurated and which, if he could have carried it out a little farther, would have been effective in preventing military revolutions in the future — and from the Catholic church. . . .

In defiance of the will of the majority of the people of Mexico, General Diaz, thirty-four years ago, came to the head of government. In defiance of the will of the majority of the people he has remained there ever since — except for four years, from 1880 to 1884, when he turned the palace over to an intimate friend, Manuel Gonzalez, on the distinct understanding that at the end of the four years Gonzalez would turn it back to him again.

Since no man can rule an unwilling people without taking away the liberties of that people, it can be very easily understood what sort of regime General Diaz found it necessary to establish in order to make his power secure. By the use of the army and the police powers generally, he controlled elections, the press and public speech and made of popular government a farce. By distributing the public offices among his generals and granting them free rein to plunder at will, he assured himself of the continued use of the army. By making political combinations with men high in the esteem of the Catholic church and permitting it to be whispered about that the church was to regain some of its former powers, he gained the silent support of the priests and the Pope. By promising full payment of all foreign debts and launching at once upon a policy of distributing favors among citizens of other countries, he made his peace with the world at large. . . .

Take, for example, Diaz's method of rewarding his military chiefs, the men who helped him overthrow the government of Lerdo. As quickly as possible after assuming the power, he installed his generals as governors of the various states and organized them and other influential figures in the nation into a national plunderbund. Thus he assured himself of the continued loyalty of the generals, on the one hand, and put them where he could most effectively use them for keeping down the people, on the other. One variety of rich plum which he handed out in those early days to his governors came in the form of charters giving his governors the right, as individuals, to organize companies and build railroads, each charter carrying with it a huge sum as a railroad subsidy.

The national government paid for the road and then the governor and his most influential friends owned it. Usually the railroads were ridiculous affairs, were of narrow-gauge and of the very cheapest materials, but the subsidy was very large, sufficient to build the road and probably equip it besides. During his first term of four years in office Diaz passed sixty-one railroad acts containing appropriations aggregating $40,000,000, and all but two or three of these acts were in favor of governors of states. In a number of cases not a mile of railroad was actually built, but the subsidies are supposed to have been paid, anyhow. In nearly every case the subsidy was the same, $12,880 per mile in Mexican silver, and in those days Mexican silver was nearly on a par with gold.

This huge sum was taken out of the national treasury and was supposedly paid to the governors, although Mexican politicians of the old times have assured me that it was divided, a part going out as actual subsidies and a part going directly into the hands of Diaz to be used in building up his machine in other quarters.

Certainly something more than mere loyalty, however invaluable it was, was required of the governors in exchange for such rich financial plums. It is a well authenticated fact that governors were required to pay a fixed sum annually for the privilege of exploiting to the limit the graft possibilities of their offices. For a long time Manuel Romero Rubio, father-in-law of Diaz, was the collector of these perquisites, the offices bringing in anywhere from $10,000 to $50,000 per year.

The largest single perquisite whereby Diaz enriched himself, the members of his immediate family, his friends, his governors, his financial ring and his foreign favorites, was found for a long time in the confiscation of the lands of the common people — a confiscation, in fact, which is going on to this day.

Note that this land robbery was the first direct step in the path of the Mexican people back to their bondage as slaves and peons.

. . . The lands of the Yaquis of Sonora were taken from them and given to political favorites of the ruler. The lands of the Mayas of Yucatan, now enslaved by the *henequen* planters, were taken from them in almost the same manner. The final act in this confiscation was accomplished in the year 1904, when the national government set aside the last of their lands into a territory called Quintana Roo. This territory contains 43,000 square kilometers or 27,000 square miles. It is larger than the present state of Yucatan by 8,000 square kilometers, and moreover is the most promising land of the entire peninsula. Separated from the island of Cuba by a narrow strait, its soil and climate are strikingly similar to those of Cuba and experts have declared that there is no reason why Quintana Roo should not one day become as great a tobacco-growing country as Cuba. Further than that, its hillsides are thickly covered with the most valuable cabinet and dyewoods in the world. It is this magnificent country which, as the last chapter in the life of the Mayas as a nation, the Diaz government took and handed over to eight Mexican politicians.

In like manner have the Mayos of Sonora, the Papagos, the Tomosachics — in fact, practically all the native peoples of Mexico — been reduced to peonage, if not to slavery. Small holders of every tribe and nation have gradually been expropriated until today their number as property holders is almost down to zero. Their lands are in the hands of members of the governmental machine, or persons to whom the members of the machine have sold for profit — or in the hands of foreigners.

This is why the typical Mexican farm is the million-acre farm, why it has been so easy for such Americans as William Randolph Hearst, Harrison Gray Otis, E. H. Harriman, the Rockefellers, the Guggenheims and numerous others each to have obtained possession of millions of Mexican acres. This is why Secretary of Fomento Molina holds more than 15,000,000 acres of the soil of Mexico, why ex-Governor Terrazas, of Chihuahua, owns 15,000,000 acres of the soil of that state, why Finance Minister Limantour, Mrs. Porfirio Diaz, Vice-President Corral, Governor Pimentel of Chiapas, Governor Landa y Escandon of the Federal District, Governor Pablo Escandon of Morelos, Governor Ahumada of Jalisco, Governor Cosio of Queretaro, Governor Mercado of Michoacan, Governor Canedo of Sinaloa, Governor Cahuantzi of Tlaxcala, and many other members of the Diaz machine are not only millionaires, but they are millionaires in Mexican real estate.

Chief among the methods used in getting the lands away from the people in general was through a land registration law which Diaz fathered. This law permitted any person to go out and claim any lands to which the possessor could not prove a recorded title. Since up to the time the law was enacted it was not the custom to record titles, this meant all the lands of Mexico. When a man possessed a home which his father had possessed before him, and which his grandfather had possessed, which his great-grandfather had possessed, and which had been in the family as far back as history knew; then he considered that he owned that home, all of his neighbors considered that he owned it, and all governments up to that of Diaz recognized his right to that home.

Supposing that a strict registration law became necessary in the course of evolution, had this law been enacted for the purpose of protecting the land owners instead of plundering them the government would, naturally, have sent agents through the country to apprise the people of the new law and to help them register their property and keep their homes. But this was not done and the conclusion is inevitable that the law was passed for the purpose of plundering.

At all events, the result of the law was a plundering. No sooner had it been passed than the aforesaid members of the governmental machine, headed by the father-in-law of Diaz, and Diaz himself, formed land companies and sent out agents, not to help the people keep their lands, but to select the most desirable lands in the country, register them, and evict the owners. This they did on a most tremendous scale. Thus hundreds of thousands of small farmers lost their property. Thus small farmers are still losing their property. . . .

Another favorite means of confiscating the homes of small owners is found in the juggling of state taxes. State taxes in Mexico are fearfully and wonderfully made. Especially in the less populous districts owners are taxed inversely as they stand in favor with the personality who represents the government in their particular district. No court, board or other responsible body sits to review unjust assessments. The *jefe politico* may charge one farmer five times as much per acre as he charges the farmer across the fence, and yet Farmer No. 1 has no redress unless he is rich and powerful. He must pay, and if he cannot, the farm is a little later listed among the properties of the jefe politico, or one of the members of his family, or among the properties of the governor of the state or one of the members of his family. But if he is rich and powerful he is often not taxed at all. American promoters in Mexico escape taxation so nearly invariably that the impression has got abroad in this country that land pays no taxes in Mexico. Even Frederick Palmer made a statement to this effect in his recent writings about that country.

Of course such bandit methods as were employed and are still employed were certain to meet with resistance, and so we find numerous instances of regiments of soldiers being called out to enforce collection of taxes or the eviction of time-honored landholders. . . .

. . . Hardly a month passes today without there being one or more reports in Mexican papers of disturbances, the result of confiscation of homes, either through the denunciation method or the excuse of nonpayment of taxes. . . .

Graft is an established institution in the public offices of Mexico. It is a right vested in the office itself, is recognized as such, and is respectable. There are two main functions attached to each public office, one a privilege, the other a duty. The privilege is that of using the special powers of the office for the amassing of a personal fortune; the duty is that of preventing the people from entering into any activities that may endanger the stability of the existing regime. Theoretically, the fulfillment of the duty is judged as balancing the harvest of the privilege, but with all offices and all places this is not so, and so we find offices of particularly rosy possibilities selling for a fixed price. Examples are those of the jefes politicos in districts where the slave trade is peculiarly remunerative, as at Pachuca, Oaxaca, Veracruz, Orizaba, Cordoba and Rio Blanco; of the districts in which the drafting of soldiers for the army is especially let to the jefes politicos; of the towns in which the gambling privileges are let as a monopoly to the mayors thereof; of the states in which there exist opportunities extraordinary for governors to graft off the army supply contracts.

Monopolies called "concessions," which are nothing more nor less than trusts created by governmental decree, are dealt in openly by the Mexican government. Some of these concessions are sold for cash, but the rule is to give them away gratis or for a nominal price, the real price being collected in political support. The public domain is sold in huge tracts for a nominal price or for nothing at all, the money price, when paid at all, averaging about fifty Mexican *centavos* an acre. But never does the government sell to any individual or company not of its own special choice; that is, the public domain is by no means open to all comers on equal terms. Public concessions worth millions of dollars — to use the water of a river for irrigation purposes, or for power, to engage in this or that monopoly, have been given away, but not indiscriminately. These things are the coin with which political support is bought and as such are grafts, pure and simple.

Public action of any sort is never taken for the sake of improving the condition of the common people. It is taken with a view to making the government more secure in its position. Mexico is a land of special privileges extraordinary, though frequently special privileges are provided for in the name of the common people. An instance is that of the "Agricultural Bank," which was created in 1908. To read the press reports concerning the purpose of this bank one would imagine that the government had launched into a gigantic and benevolent scheme to re-establish its expropriated people in agriculture. The purpose, it was said, was to loan money to needy farmers. But nothing coud be farther from the truth, for the purpose is to help out the rich farmer, and only the richest in the land. The bank has now been loaning money for two years, but so far not a single case has been recorded in which aid was given to help a farm that comprised less than thousands of acres. Millions have been loaned on private irrigation projects, but never in lumps of less than several tens of thousands. In the United States the farmer class is an humble class indeed; in Mexico the typical farmer is the king of millionaires, a little potentate. In Mexico, because of the special privileges given by the government, medievalism still prevails outside the cities. The barons are richer and more powerful than were the landed aristocrats before the French Revolution, and the canaille poorer, more miserable.

And the special financial privileges centering in the cities are no less remarkable than the special privileges given to the exploiters of the *hacienda* slave. There is a financial ring consisting of members of the Diaz machine and their close associates, who pluck all the financial plums of the "republic," who get the contracts, the franchises and the concessions, and whom the large aggregations of foreign capital which secure a footing in the country find it necessary to take as coupon-clipping partners. The "Banco Nacional," an institution having some fifty-four branches and which has been compared flatteringly to the Bank of England, is the special financial vehicle of the government camarilla. It monopolizes the major portion of the banking business of the country and is a convenient cloak for the larger grafts, such as the railway merger, the true significance of which I shall present in a future chapter.

Diaz encourages foreign capital, for foreign capital means the support of foreign governments. American capital has a smoother time with Diaz than it has even with its own government, which is very fine from the point of view of American capital, but not so good from the point of view of the Mexican people. Diaz has even entered into direct partnership with certain aggregations of foreign capital, granting these aggregations special privileges in some lines which he has refused to his own millionaires. These foreign partnerships which Diaz has formed has made his government international insofar as the props which support his system are concerned. The certainty of foreign intervention in his favor has been one of the powerful forces which have prevented the Mexican people from using arms to remove a ruler who imposed himself upon them by the use of arms.

When I come to deal with the American partners of Diaz I mention those of no other nationality in the same breath, but it will be well to bear in mind that England, especially, is nearly as heavily as interested in Mexico as is the United States. While this country has $900,000,000 (these are the figures given by Consul General Shanklin about the first of the year 1910) invested in Mexico, England (according to the South American Journal) has $750,000,000. However, these figures by no means represent the ratio between the degree of political influence exerted by the two countries. There the United States bests all the other countries combined. . . .

In this chapter I have attempted to give the reader an idea of the means which General Diaz employed to attract support to his government. To sum up, by means of a careful placing of public offices, public contracts and special privileges of multitudinous sorts, Diaz absorbed all of the more powerful men and interests within his sphere and made them a part of his machine. Gradually the country passed into the hands of his officeholders, their friends, and foreigners. And for this the people paid, not only with their lands, but with their flesh and blood. They paid in peonage and slavery. For this they forfeited liberty, democracy and the blessings of progress.

52. The Díaz Regime Was Unconcerned with the Needs of the Masses and Ignorant of Their Potential Power

CHARLES C. CUMBERLAND

The late Professor Charles C. Cumberland of Michigan State University was one of the many students who developed their capacity for understanding Mexican history under Professor Charles W. Hackett at the University of Texas. Professor Cumberland's competent analysis of the beginnings of the Revolution demonstrates how closely connected were the years of the dictatorship and the violent period of the Revolution.

When in September, 1910, Mexico played host to the embassies of the world at the magnificent spectacle celebrating a century of Mexican independence, the special delegates vied with one another in extolling the virtues and strength of the Díaz regime. General Porfirio Díaz was completing his seventh term as constitutional president of Mexico, having been the dictator of his country for

From *Mexican Revolution: Genesis under Madero* by Charles C. Cumberland (Austin: University of Texas Press, 1952), pp. 3–28, passim. Reprinted by permission.

thirty-four years, and was then about to embark upon his eighth term. His nation was honored and respected; as a head of state Díaz had been phenomenally successful in stabilizing Mexico and bringing her material prosperity. The power and prestige of the aged dictator, who appeared to be hale and vigorous in spite of his eighty years, had never been greater; his government was believed to be impervious to attack, his power unassailable, his country assured of a peaceful future. And yet, within the space of eight months the Díaz government crumbled, the dictator and most of his chief advisors fled into exile, and a revolution of tremendous force began.

That the Díaz government was a dictatorship no one denied. Even its strongest supporters freely admitted that the Constitution of 1857 had been perverted, that the branches of government were nonexistent inasmuch as Díaz was the final arbiter in all questions, and that "democracy" was merely a term used indiscriminately. As Francisco Bulnes expressed it, the question was not whether Díaz was a dictator, since the Mexicans in the past had possessed neither liberty nor democracy, but whether he was a good or a bad dictator. His task, on assuming control in 1876, had been to weld the Mexican people into a peaceful unit, to stabilize the government and pacify the country, and to bring material gain and prosperity to the nation. Each part of the task impinged on the other; failure in one would have meant almost inevitable failure in the other two. . . .

Within a relatively short time after coming to power, Díaz managed to obtain the active or tacit support of the great majority of the Mexican people of all classes by attempting to meet the special interests of each class. Through this practice, supplemented by a policy of harsh repression against revolutionaries and bandits, he brought peace to Mexico, the first peace the nation had known since the colonial period, and laid the foundation for an amazing material development. Railway lines, which in 1876 had been negligible, totaled more than fifteen thousand miles in 1910. During the same period, exports and imports increased nearly tenfold, with a favorable balance of trade in most years. Smelting of precious and semiprecious metals increased fourfold, petroleum production became a major industry, textile mills were built by the hundreds, sugar mills sprang up in the southern states, and numerous smaller but important industries began. The prosperity of the epoch was reflected in the favorable relationship between national debt and national income, and in the foreign-credit standing. Mexican bonds on foreign markets sold at a premium, the national debt declined until in the early 1900's it was the smallest in the country's history, revenues increased more than tenfold, and reserves accumulated annually. The domestic and foreign financial standing of the Mexican government, under the direction of the dictatorship, was very sound. . . .

It was the economic advances and their by-products . . . that served as a stimulus for most of the support of, and much of the opposition to, the dictatorship. In view of the general financial condition of Mexico and her people when Díaz came to power — the government was heavily in debt and the people had little cash reserve for new investment — it was absolutely necessary to encourage a flow of foreign capital to Mexico if there was to be material development. From the beginning of his administration, Díaz deliberately fostered foreign investment on terms highly advantageous to the investor. The policy brought money to Mexico, but the zealous regard for the interests of the foreigner created another class in Mexican society and added to the already prejudicial social and economic stratification. The foreigner, particularly the American, was now considered the most important element in society, with much of the economic legislation framed to favor his group. The concessions made to foreigners, especially in the changes in the mining code, worked to the grave disadvantage of the nation, inasmuch as the government's proportion of income from the mines was lessened and speculation in mining properties was encouraged. The preference granted to foreigners was constantly humiliating to the nationals and was one of the most irritating facets of the dictatorship. On the other hand, often the robber was robbed, for the majority of foreigners who invested in Mexico were victimized by ignorance and sharp dealing, even though many of those who came to the country did amass fortunes.

The emphasis on industrialization had other evil effects as well, for with the development of monopolies the already clearly defined difference between rich and poor became even more marked. Mexico's economy was largely controlled by a small group of businessmen and financiers who completely dominated money and credit, controlled the most lucrative concessions, and soon became the "arbiters of the prosperity of the Mexicans." For example, of the sixty-six financial, transportation, insurance, and industrial corporations listed in the 1908 report of the Banco Central Mexicano, thirty-six had common directors from a group of thirteen men; and nineteen of the corporations had more than one of the thirteen. One of the thirteen men was on the boards of nine banks, one railroad, one insurance company, and four industrial concerns. This tight control by a small group led to many of the economic and social abuses of which the Díaz government was accused, and brought into being what a Díaz opponent called "mercantilism." "It was this 'mercantilism,'" he said, "which overwhelmed the nation, increased despotism, despoiled the people, implanted degrading speculation, and sustained infamous and depraved governors." As the monopolists became more opulent, they were blinded by their own prosperity and became less able than ever to see the needs of the less fortunate. Their own prosperity, too, bolstered by the statistics of production, foreign trade, and finances, convinced them that Mexico as a nation was prosperous and that their own interests were synonymous with national interests.

In the last decade of the nineteenth century, a few men representing the new moneyed class banded together under Díaz' father-in-law, Manuel Romero Rubio, into a group which soon came to be called the Científicos. Hardly a political party at its inception, the organization was nonetheless allied closely with a political party formed in 1892 and came to exercise all the functions of a party. The group soon determined that the most effective means of guaranteeing a continuation of the economic system that had developed would be to control the government in so far as possible during Díaz' life and absolutely after his death. Until the formation of the Científicos, Díaz had maintained his early policy of meeting the demands of the mestizos; but as the Científicos grew in power, they successfully drew him away from the mestizos and convinced him of the necessity for supporting the creoles. Looked upon by many in the nineties and in the early years of the new century as the hope for a regenerated Mexico, the Científicos came to be feared and hated, even by men who had previously been their ardent supporters. . . .

There were many evidences, tenuous to be sure, of economic instability after 1904, even in [Minister of Hacienda José Ives] Limantour's own special province — banking. Adoption of the gold standard in 1905, followed by the 1907 money panic in the United States and an export price decline, brought shrinking national revenues, which necessitated foreign borrowing, and at the same time placed a heavy strain on domestic financial institutions. The banks, although outwardly prosperous, demonstrated symptoms of instability which endangered the entire Mexican financial structure. Limantour himself recognized the symptoms and called a national conference of bankers early in 1908 for the purpose of studying the situation and proposing new laws to rectify the existing weaknesses. The banks had obviously been indulging in speculation, lending enormous sums on poor security; institutions authorized to issue bank notes were particularly at fault, engaging in practices which sometimes brought large returns but which were generally unsound. As a consequence of the conference and Limantour's recommendations, a new banking law to correct some of the dangerous policies and to encourage the establishment of investment and mortgage banks was passed in the summer of 1908.

The new regulations, however, did not correct all the evils. Less than a year later the Banco Central Mexicano, the central reserve institution, was in a condition that approached the critical. The weakness of the bank was largely the responsibility of the government itself, which at various times had "suggested" to the bank that loans be made to administration friends. When the public learned that the central bank had absorbed enough worthless paper to impair its capital, confidence in all credit and financial institutions was seriously undermined. . . .

As might be expected in such a financial situation, inflation was rampant during most of the latter part of the Díaz regime. The cost of most items, particularly the staples on which the mass of the population depended, increased enormously; there was not a corresponding increase in the wages of agricultural and industrial workers. The wage earners were therefore forced into a constantly deteriorating position. What was happening to corn, a basic part of the diet of 85 per cent of the population, indicates the trend. Between 1893 and 1906 the value of corn per unit increased on the average by 50 per cent, and after 1906 the increase was more rapid. Occasionally the government would sell corn at "much lower prices than those established by the speculators," to use Díaz' words, but these sales were temporary expedients only and were usually confined to the capital itself. Somewhat the same trend was noted in other staples. Even more destructive of the well-being of the masses was the violent fluctuation in the price of staples from day to day and from place to place; a change of 400 per cent in a matter of days was not unusual. The government, in spite of the obvious need for price stabilization, did nothing permanently constructive. . . .

While basic commodity prices were on the increase, there was no ascertainable rise in salaries. In the early nineteenth century Baron Alexander von Humboldt had estimated the average daily wage to be approximately twenty-five centavos; in 1891 the prevailing wage was between twenty-five and fifty centavos, with the average nearer the lower figure; in 1908 the daily wage was almost exactly what it had been one hundred years earlier. In sum total, the static wage and the increasing cost of commodities meant a drastic decline in real wages. . . .

In the face of his rapidly deteriorating economic position, the laborer was helpless. Not only were there no labor laws to aid the worker but as Díaz became more closely allied with the creoles and their interests he became less sympathetic to the predicament of the mestizos and Indians, who composed the working class. A cheap labor supply being one of the principal assets which Mexico could offer to foreign investors and Mexican industrialists, and the general standard of work among the laborers being rather poor, the government never considered that protection of the laborer was either necessary or desirable. In vain did some intellectuals demand an improvement of conditions; in vain did Wistano Luis Orozco, scholar and humanitarian, insist that the lower classes were the brothers of the remainder of society and had a right to demand improvement, "morally and physically." The alliance between gov-

ernment and special privilege was too strong. Labor organizations were practically unknown before 1900; and even if the workers had been organized,
they would have found it almost impossible to act in their own behalf. In most
states and territories the laws forbade strikes; in the Federal District heavy
fines and imprisonment could be imposed on any person attempting to use
physical or moral force for the purpose of increasing salaries or wages. Even
in areas where no specific law applied to striking, various means were used,
often with the aid of public officials, to defeat the aims of the workers.

But these industrially idyllic conditions, in which the laborer worked for a
pittance without question, could not continue indefinitely. The syndicalist and
anarchist concepts, though late in penetrating into Mexico, became known
after the turn of the century through the work and writing of Spaniards and
Mexicans, the most important of whom was the Mexican Ricardo Flores
Magón. Accordingly, the workers, "better taught than before to look out for
their own interests, resented . . . oppression and resolutely aspired to improve their condition." Beginning in 1906, the laborers insisted that wages be
raised and hours shortened; as a result of the industrialists' adamant refusal
to meet these demands, a period of unrest developed. Although the strikes
were defeated in most cases through government intercession, most industrial
centers saw strife of varying intensity, and the workers were at last beginning
to realize their potential strength, even though industrial labor constituted only
a small proportion of the country's total labor force. . . .

The poor condition in which the industrial worker found himself had its
counterpart, perhaps exaggerated to a degree, in the situation of the vast
number of Indians whose primary source of livelihood was the land. The
rural inhabitants, largely Indian, had been at the mercy of the Spaniard and
the creole during the colonial epoch and continued in that state after independence. But many Indian villages had been allowed to retain the community holdings which were in their possession prior to the Conquest, and
many more had been granted land by the Spanish crown. These areas, called
ejidos though actually divided into five distinct classifications, served as a
guarantee of partial independence for members of the community, but in the
immediate postindependence period considerable difference of opinion arose
among liberals over the question of the Indian and his relation to the land.
Some, arguing that the Indian did not have a European concept of ownership,
insisted that the village ejidos be left undisturbed; others, convinced that communal holding was evidence of backwardness and was not conducive to
progress, favored a distribution of village land among the inhabitants of the
village, with the individuals holding the parcels in fee simple. It was this last
contention which prevailed when the triumphant liberals, after defeating

Santa Anna and his conservative supporters in the Revolution of Ayutla, drafted the Constitution of 1857. The Ley Lerdo, which had been passed the previous year and which prohibited civil or religious corporations from owning real property not directly necessary for the functioning of the corporations, was written into the constitution. The village lands were therefore open to distribution among the members of the communities.

In the meantime the haciendas, enormous holdings of land often poorly and incompletely cultivated, were becoming increasingly important as an institution — economic, social, and political — in the rural areas. Many haciendas dated from the colonial period, but with the application of the Ley Lerdo and the Reform Laws effectuated a few years later, and with the confiscation, during both the War of Reform and the French Intervention, of much of the property belonging to the losing factions, the hacienda system was extended and a new hacienda class developed. . . .

It was on this foundation that the Díaz land system developed, and it was in the agrarian field that the Díaz government recorded one of its greatest failures. In a nation which depended heavily on agriculture, the Díaz government made no attempt to improve agricultural production through education or experimentation. Although much of the country was arid or semiarid and needed irrigation planning on a national scale, the government did practically nothing. It did not attempt to relieve the critical food shortage by encouraging increased production of cereals or other items consumed by the masses; although statistics indicate an annual increase in agricultural production, the increase was largely in items for export and gave little aid to the mass of the population. These were errors of omission; much more serious were the errors of commission in land legislation.

Díaz was not completely responsible for the development which robbed the villages of their land and forced the major portion of the Indian population into economic slavery; previous legal and constitutional provisions had set the pattern. The first interpretations of the constitutional provision had stipulated that the *suertes,* or *terrenos de común repartimiento* — agricultural lands attached to the villages at the time of the Conquest — were not subject to parceling, and as long as that interpretation prevailed many villages in the heart of the agricultural districts would retain their independence. By successive decrees in 1889 and 1890, however, Díaz brought all village lands within the categories to be parceled, and from that time forward the laws were more stringently applied. The new owner, unaccustomed to thinking in terms of private ownership and not given proper protection by the government, was easily victimized by unscrupulous officials and by individuals who legally or illegally gained control of the land. In the final analysis, the Indian villager too often found that as a result of the distribution he no longer had access to any land of his own and was forced to seek employment at the nearest hacienda.

Not all the Indian villages, however, lost their land through the instrumentality of the distribution law; many were victimized outright by a variety of other means. In some cases grasping government officials, charged with the responsibility of parceling the land and dispensing justice to the villagers, merely sold all village property to a company or an individual; such sales were irregular and illegal, of course, but the despoliation was effectuated nevertheless. In many cases the village was destroyed when an outsider gained control of the water supply and forced the village to sell. But the most disastrous practice, in so far as the loss of village lands was concerned, resulted from a series of surveying laws passed in 1863, 1883, 1894. Under these laws, each more advantageous than the last to the surveying companies and demanding fewer responsibilities from them, national lands were surveyed by individuals and companies and the surveyors allowed to gain control of enormous amounts of land. Under the 1894 law any parcel to which a legal title could not be produced could be declared *terrenos baldíos,* or untilled national lands, and any individual could file a claim to purchase the property at a set cash price. . . . Through the operation of the laws, and through official or quasi-official chicanery, enormous quantities of land came under the control of a small group of men or companies. One estimate indicates that over two and one-quarter million acres of good land, representing the means of livelihood of tens of thousands of Indians, passed from the Indian communities to the *hacendados;* this was in addition to the untold millions of acres of bona fide national lands which were alienated.

A combination of the above forces and practices meant disaster to the Indian village, and tremendous growth to the haciendas. The free agricultural village — one in which the majority of the residents had access to sufficient lands to make a living — was disappearing, and concentration of land ownership was intensifying. Between 1881 and 1889, 14 per cent of the arable land was concentrated in twenty-nine companies or individuals; by 1894, more than 20 per cent was controlled by fewer than fifty holders; and by 1910, less than 1 per cent of the families owned or controlled about 85 per cent of the land. . . .

Had the land acquired by the haciendas been profitably used, and had the villagers now forced to work for the haciendas been properly treated, the situation would not have been so disastrous. But the haciendas were not economically successful: they left too much arable land uncultivated, and they were not so productive, proportionally, as the smaller holdings. The rapid development of the hacienda system under Díaz constituted a burden on, and a retrogression of, the agricultural economy, rather than, as its proponents insisted, an improvement. . . .

Díaz' attitude toward rural and industrial labor is indicative of his loss of political perception. In contrast to his remarkable acumen in recognizing the paramount interest of each important group and in catering to those interests before 1900, after the turn of the century he was no longer able to see the forces or to adjust his policies accordingly. Labor was rapidly becoming a factor to consider in national politics, and yet Díaz and his advisors could think of nothing more constructive than suppression. When confronted with somewhat the same condition in 1876 with respect to bandits, Díaz had adroitly obtained the support of a sufficient number to counterbalance those who were recalcitrant. To labor he made no concession at all, and after 1900 labor constituted a greater potential force than had the bandits in 1876. . . .

Díaz was also unconcerned with the nationalism which had been developing rapidly in the latter part of the nineteenth century. The constant condescension displayed by the President and his government to everything Mexican, and the near adulation for everything foreign, were irritating to the younger generation. The foreigner was treated with the deference of an invited guest, the mining laws governing concessions and subsoil rights were reframed to conform with foreign concepts and practices, enormous areas of land were sold or practically given to foreigners, and foreigners were regularly favored in Mexican courts. Since citizens of the United States were the most numerous among the foreigners, one bitter critic summed it up by saying that the regime "destroyed national honor in the face of Yankee demands." Díaz was not alone in his preference for foreigners; most of the social elite were prejudiced in favor of foreign goods, foreign literature, and foreign ideas. Industrial concerns, whether under the control of Mexicans or aliens, regularly paid higher wages to foreign employees than to natives; the policy was probably justified by the foreigners' greater technical skill, but it did not endear the government or the industrialists to the laborers. All those who were proud to be Mexicans resented the rank favoritism which seemed to be common.

Even the upper classes were mixed in their support of the government after 1900. Díaz, consistently refusing to allow widespread political participation to the social and economic plutocracy, destroyed the public spirit of the class and weakened it as a bulwark of the regime. To be sure, the moneyed groups gave unstinting praise to Díaz' government, but they were without organization and without leadership other than that formed by the government. In his anxiety to protect himself against the political ambitions of this group, Díaz had enervated a potentially powerful support.

Without quite realizing what had happened, Díaz gradually lost the active support of most elements in Mexican society. Many mestizos were alienated by his gradual orientation toward creoles and foreigners, as well as by the treatment accorded labor and small proprietors. The proprietors, allied with the labor leaders, became a solid core of opposition before the end of the regime. The Indians, while not openly hostile except in rare instances, generally were becoming more and more restive as a result of agrarian developments which either threatened their independent existence or left them destitute. Members of the upper class not directly connected with the regime were either not allowed to render public service or were driven into partial opposition by the government's bland assumption that all able men served the government and that all who questioned the policies were either knaves or fools. Added to the insult was the economic injury which seemed to be impending; the rather precarious economic situation after 1905 forced many men who previously had been staunch Díaz supporters to question the safety of the Mexican economy under Díaz' continued administration. The group whose economic interests were in danger did not always actively oppose the administration; but when the revolution came, the plutocracy gave Díaz little help.

Díaz still had strong support, particularly among those who profited directly, or hoped to profit, from his government. More important to the future of the nation, and more widespread, than the support to Díaz himself was the belief in his philosophy of government. Many of those who turned against the Díaz administration, or who no longer supported it, did so because they detected weaknesses in his government rather than because they opposed the principles upon which he acted. These men, including many of the great hacendados and financiers, were quite willing to see Díaz removed from office, even though they looked with horror upon fundamental changes in the governmental or social structure. They were the men who made possible a successful revolution against Díaz, but at the same time their attitude would make it difficult for a reform government to function. As a class they foresaw a revolution, but they did not foresee the nature of the struggle; they believed it would take place after Díaz' death and would be nothing more than a quarrel over political power among the upper class. They did not recognize the symptoms of a social revolution developing in Morelos, for example, where "ragged plebeians, with their thin veneer of rudimentary civilization, were acting like savage gluttons of human carrion" during the 1908 gubernatorial election. They were unconcerned with the needs of the masses, and being unconcerned they were ignorant of the potential of those masses.

53. *The Porfiriato: Legend and Reality*

DANIEL COSÍO VILLEGAS

Licenciado Daniel Cosío Villegas is something of a phenomenon even in Mexico, where many independent and intelligent spirits flourish. Trained as an economist, he has served as a professor, ambassador, publisher, and more recently as a historian and columnist. He has been more responsible than anyone else for opening up in a decisive and stimulating way the study of the history of modern Mexico. Thanks to his investigations and to his stimulus, we now begin to see the true Porfirio Díaz; a dictator, yes, but also a patriot who defended well some of the national interests of Mexico.*

The Porfiriato must have been, as the legend has it, an era of consolidation. The tranquility of the period suggests that divisions or differences were neither so violent nor so irreconcilable as to lead to war. It was, moreover, an era in which means of communication improved significantly, thereby increasing opportunities for Mexicans to become acquainted and have contact with one another. Finally, one suspects that consolidation was also furthered by the undeniably authoritarian character of the regime, for extraordinary power makes itself felt on everything and everyone, impressing a uniform cast on the entire society.

Such must have been the Porfiriato. To be certain, however, one would have to ask whether the process of consolidation was general or selective. According to the legend, the regime was notably successful in promoting the consolidation of two areas at least: Mexican nationality and institutions. . . .

The consolidation of the Mexican nation has been the result of a very long process. Perhaps it dates from the incipient imperialism of the Aztecs, which . . . imposed some unity on the political and cultural diversity of the numerous Indian groups of the period. The conquest and domination of the Spaniards, despite the elements of profound disparity which they introduced, gave to the native civilizations elements of community, language, religion, and government which they had hitherto lacked. The consequences did not take long to appear, for the first clear manifestations of a spiritual nationalism were

From "El porfiriato, era de consolidación" by Daniel Cosío Villegas, *Historia Mexicana,* 13 (1963), pp. 76–87, passim. Reprinted by permission.
* For a judicious evaluation of past and present interpretations of Díaz, see Martín Quirarte, *Historia Mexicana,* 15 (1965–1966), no. 2–3, pp. 416–422.

evident in the eighteenth century. But it was above all during that calumniated first half of the nineteenth century that the process of national formation was accelerated, precisely because of the misfortunes that befell the newly born nation. . . . The war with the United States and the very loss of territory helped, like few other events, to consolidate our nationality, first through the sensation of danger and the feeling of hatred for the aggressor — sentiments which constitute a negative force but a tremendously effective one when a weak people is involved. Secondly, no matter how unjust and painful the loss of half of our national territory was, it is undeniable that it drastically reduced the material and spiritual task of forging the nation, as well as the time that would be needed to accomplish this task. Finally, this unhappy war also taught us that when our internal struggles passed certain limits of rancor and persistence, the danger of aggression and the irreparable loss of the nation would become real and substantial.

It does not seem that the country made use of this sad but beneficial lesson, for in a very short time, during the wars of the Reform and Intervention, the two contenders, blinded by immediate partisan interests, appealed for foreign aid. But this occurred for the last time because it became apparent that with the aid came the foreign soldier, that is, the flesh-and-blood enemy of Mexican nationhood. These two wars [were] fought so bitterly that, by way of a reaction, they created a conciliatory climate that bore fruit throughout the entire period of the Restored Republic. . . .

[By 1876], then, Mexico, as a result of so many painful and seemingly sterile struggles, was beginning to gather the positive fruits of its misfortunes; it had gone a long way toward placing general interests before partial interests.

Does all this mean that the Porfiriato did not contribute in any way to the task of consolidating the Mexican nation? By no means. It merely means that the process was lengthy, that it was initiated a long time before 1876, and that the principal direct contributions had been made previously. The contribution of the Porfiriato, while it was very important, seems to me to have had an indirect character. With the railroads, telegraph, and telephone, with the general improvement of communications and transportation, particularly of the press, the circulation of Mexicans, as well as of their wealth, ideas, and sentiments, also improved.

It is less easy to define and very difficult to assess another factor in the consolidation of the nation which appeared in a singularly active manner during the Porfirian age. Mexico had always lived under the thumb of regional caciques; accordingly, federalism had a reality that was political, social, and economic, as well as geographic and ethnic. Only Juárez emerged in 1867 as a great national figure; but the impossibility of preserving the unity of the liberal party and Juárez' need to lead his own faction in order to defend himself and prevail over the factions of Lerdo and Díaz made him lose to a large extent the general and superior character of a national figure. Díaz, on the other hand, less scrupulous in his political practices and born of a revolutionary coup and not of lawful elections, had far more liberty of action. Finding the field already sowed and blessed with better luck, he at length succeeded in putting an end to the regional caudillos and in transforming himself into the sole caudillo, that is, into the national caudillo. To this must be added the popular aura that Díaz always had, the memory of his glorious campaigns against the foreign invader, his very age, his granite-like physical appearance, and his conscious effort to acquire and exhibit the air of a man who was superior to petty and fleeting passion; his was the air of the guardian of the permanent interests of the country, the air of a monarch who receives homage not only from his own subjects but also from the outside world, the civilized world.

But Porfirio Díaz did not become merely a decorative national symbol, like the flag or anthems which evoke and exalt patriotic sentiments upon reaching the eyes or ears, not even in the more intellectual sense of serving as a symbol of national unity, like the English monarch. He was also authority, and in many respects the sole authority; he was power, and in many respects the sole power. Family disputes were laid before him, as well as disputes involving towns, authorities, or interests. All the organs of public power depended on him: legislatures, courts, judges, governors, political and military chiefs. Not only was he seen everywhere, like God, but he also made himself felt everywhere. . . .

There can be no doubt that, as the legend claims, juridical, economic, and social institutions were consolidated to some extent. One merely has to consider the peacefulness, prosperity, and longevity of the regime to admit this; when there is peace, wealth, and time, there are opportunities and resources for the undertaking of projects that in turbulent periods are left for "better times." Unfortunately, history requires more than generalities; it requires analysis and a body of facts.

With respect to juridical institutions, the work had already begun. The first great bodies of law antedated the Porfiriato: the constitution itself, the organic law of public instruction (1867), the law governing juries in criminal cases (1869), the organic law on the recourse of *amparo* (1869), the penal code (1871), the civil code (1871), the code of civil procedure (1872), the code pertaining to aliens (1876), etc. But these were few in number and limited in influence, in part because most of them could be applied only in the Federal District and in part because the conditions of the country were not sufficiently normal for their beneficial influence to be felt. During the Porfiriato, these same codes were revised, made more consistent, and complemented with new ones . . . while important legislation, such as the law on credit institutions, was also enacted. To this body of true juridical creation, there ought to be added the regulatory and administrative achievement. These gains placed the country on the path to a normal, regular existence, which in many respects became ideally impersonal. In addition, the law in general appeared to attain a respectability, a stature, that made it impervious to human negation or threats.

All this is very well, but how can one forget that political institutions are a part of juridical institutions? Can it be sustained that political institutions were consolidated during the Porfiriato? They simply disappeared, and something that does not exist is not susceptible of consolidation or dispersion.

In this matter there is no defense or qualification. No Porfirista — not even the most passionate, nor the most timid, nor the most shameful, nor the most cynical — has ever dared to affirm that Mexico progressed politically during the Díaz regime. This is the explanation of [Rafael de] Zayas Enríquez: the people of Mexico voluntarily ceded their political rights to Porfirio Díaz so that he might return them little by little as the Mexicans learned how to be free. This is the opinion of [Francisco] Bulnes: "it passes the limits of stupidity to assail General Díaz for not having done the impossible — to be a democratic president in a nation of slaves.". . .

According to Emilio Rabasa, one of the few Mexican political writers of true talent, "the dictatorship of Díaz was characterized, *above all,* by respect for *legal forms,* which he always preserved in order to keep alive in the people the sentiment that their laws were respected even though they were not enforced, and that they remained on the books so that they might recover their ascendancy in the not-too-distant future." This is the point that truly deserves investigation, for on it depends the answer to the question of whether political institutions were consolidated during the Porfiriato.

Is it possible to respect a law that is not enforced? Can a law which is not enforced remain in force? Can a law which is not enforced someday recover its ascendancy? To me, it is as clear as daylight that a law which is not enforced provokes mockery, compassion, but never respect; a law which is not enforced is a dead law, and what is dead can never remain in force; a law which is not enforced has no power and in consequence can never recover what it never had. Finally, to describe as the "not-too-distant future" an era which, like that of Díaz, lasted for thirty-five years is to forget that in so long a time a whole generation was born and raised in the delightful atmosphere of the law that is not enforced but is respected. I would say exactly the opposite of Rabasa: that nothing degrades and demoralizes a people so much as the constant, repeated, daily spectacle of the non-enforcement of the law. . . .

It is this attitude toward the law, especially the political laws, that indicates the gulf between Porfirio Díaz and the great liberals of the Reform. The latter had a blind faith in the law as a pick-axe to strike down old and noxious institutions and in the law as a cherished mould for shaping new ones. For this reason they respected the law, and to preserve or change it, they were capable of risking their lives or their futures. . . .

Porfirio Díaz, who fought for the liberal cause from his boyhood, who once accused Juárez of conservatism, did not have that respect and veneration for the law which was the very essence of Mexican liberalism. For Díaz, the law was a dead letter and consequently lacked spirit. For him, the *fact* was the instrument of change, and the fact, of course, was power and might. Because he despised the law, he did not change it or trouble himself about it; he simply forgot it and sought power in the invincible fact of being stronger than everyone else. . . .

The conclusion of all this seems obvious to me, as well as logical. Some juridical institutions were consolidated during the Porfiriato, and some were not. Those that were consolidated were the secondary ones, while the major ones — the political institutions — simply disappeared.

Abrazos for Dictators? Dictators in Latin America often have been eager to have their picture taken with high political or military officials of the United States. The late Generalissimo Rafael L. Trujillo of the Dominican Republic was particularly successful, which roused much criticism in both the United States and Latin America. This photograph shows him with the late Senator Theodore Francis Green, at that time (1939) Chairman of the Senate Foreign Relations Committee, enjoying a drink in the Senate dining room. In 1955, Vice-President Nixon visited the Dominican Republic and was photographed in a warm abrazo with the durable dictator. The next year President Eisenhower sent his brother Milton on a "fact-finding" visit to Latin America, who on his return strongly advocated that the United States treat dictators with cold correctness, and reserve warm abrazos for democratic leaders.

SECTION XIII

Imperialism, Intervention, and Communism in the Caribbean

The Caribbean area up to about 1900 was the cockpit of the Americas, where competing nations sought for power and plunder. At the end of the Spanish American War the United States assumed new responsibilities toward Cuba and Puerto Rico. The construction of the Panama Canal brought a powerful strategic consideration into United States policy. William Graham Sumner, the Yale University sociologist, was not far wrong when he delivered a Phi Beta Kappa address in 1899 on "The Conquest of the United States by Spain," in which he set forth the startling proposition that although Spain had lost the war, she had given over to the United States her imperial ambitions and burdens.

The twentieth-century history of the Caribbean remains to be written, but it is obvious that the United States' actions and its conception of its role there will be a dominant theme. The United States has supervised elections, sent in the Marines, installed customs offices, conducted health campaigns, moved in whole teams of experts to provide a variety of programs, trained constabulary forces, organized invasions such as the Bay of Pigs fiasco, and in many other ways tried to maintain stability or defend what a particular government in Washington conceived to be in the national interest.

The conception of United States national interest has varied. President Calvin Coolidge announced in April 1925 that "the person and property of a citizen are part of the general domain of the nation, even when abroad. . . . There is a distinct and binding obligation on the part of self-respecting governments to afford protection to the persons and property of their citizens, wherever they may be." [1] This was no idle threat or new doctrine, since in 1910 the United States minister to Cuba had been instructed to inform the Cuban government that if it was unable or failed to protect the lives or property of American citizens, "the Government of the U.S., pursuant to its usual custom in such cases, would land its own forces for this purpose." [2]

The subject of the United States in the Caribbean is so large and complicated that only a few of the major aspects may be touched upon here. To understand United States action, the exuberant and complacent mood of many Americans from 1900 onward must be seen as an essential part of the story. Even so outspoken an antiimperialist as Professor Sumner believed that the creation of empires was the inevitable "penalty of greatness" that obliged "the ascendant nation to extend law and order for the benefit of everybody." [3] Scott Nearing and Joseph Freeman, whose work *Dollar Diplomacy* attempted a generalized explanation for the causes and symptoms of "American imperialism," seemed to consider it an "inexorable" stage of American history. They listed all the symptoms of "dollar diplomacy" that they believed to be best illustrated in the relations between the United States and the Caribbean countries:

> Determination of boundaries; prevention of or assistance to filibustering as required by American financial interests; administration of customs houses; financial protectorates; armed intervention; overthrow of independent governments; fomenting of revolutions; building of the Panama Canal; interference with elections; controlled use of recognition policy; acquisition of naval bases; creation of local constabularies under American officers; economic interpretation of the Monroe Doctrine to freeze out European investors; solicitation of loan business for New York banks; campaign in behalf of oil interests against nationalization of Mexican natural resources. [4]

A bias against colored people was also involved, and many in the Caribbean are colored. The remarks by the American businessman George W.

---

[1] As quoted by Herbert Feis, *The Diplomacy of the Dollar: First Era, 1919–1932* (Stamford, Conn.: Archon Books, 1965), p. 29.

[2] Milton Offut, *The Protection of Citizens Abroad by the Armed Forces of the United States* (Baltimore: The Johns Hopkins Press, 1928), p. 160.

[3] James P. Shenton, "Imperialism and Racism," in *Essays in American Historiography: Papers Presented in Honor of Allan Nevins,* ed. Donald Sheehan and Harold C. Syrett (New York: Columbia University Press, 1960), p. 230.

[4] Richard M. Morse, "The Caribbean: Geopolitics and Geohistory", in *Caribbean Integration,* ed. Sybil Thomas and Thomas G. Mathews (Río Piedras: University of Puerto Rico, Institute of Caribbean Studies, 1967), p. 168. The Nearing-Freeman book was *Dollar Diplomacy: A Study in American Imperialism* (New York, 1925).

Crichfield in his popular work of 1908, appropriately entitled *American Supremacy,* convey effectively the feeling of superiority toward Latin Americans and the determination to do something for them whether they like it or not (Reading 54). This paternalistic attitude, which included elements of both dominance and responsibility, was well illustrated by the following colloquy that took place in London between British Foreign Secretary Lord Grey and United States Ambassador to Britain Walter Hines Page. This represents an unpleasant mixture of both attitudes expressed in the moralizing tone of a high official of Woodrow Wilson's administration:

Grey: Suppose you have to intervene, what then?

Page: Make 'em vote and live by their decisions.

Grey: But suppose they will not so live?

Page: We'll go in again and make 'em vote again.

Grey: And keep this up for 200 years?

Page: Yes. The United States will be here for 200 years and it can continue to shoot men for that little space till they learn to vote and rule themselves.[5]

Nor has this attitude wholly disappeared. On the eve of World War II another American ambassador to Great Britain, Joseph P. Kennedy, appealed to his countrymen to keep the hemisphere out of the war: "If any of the Latin Americans act up, kick them in the teeth." [6]

Such actions and attitudes roused opposition in the United States, especially in academic circles, and in many parts of the world were condemned as "dollar diplomacy." Professor Harry Elmer Barnes directed a series of studies on American financial imperialism,[7] and Professor Lawrence F. Hill denounced what he called the protectorate system in these words:

In its mature form, the system demanded governmental setups in Cuba, Santo Domingo, Haiti, Panama, Nicaragua and elsewhere amenable to orders from Washington. If the natives of these countries were unable or indisposed to carry out dictation from Washington, they were displaced by "expert" administrators from the United States — which had an excess of them. These "expert" administrators from the fields of

[5] As quoted by William Franklin Sands, *Our Jungle Diplomacy* (Chapel Hill: University of North Carolina Press, 1944), p. 121.

[6] Louis M. Lyons, *Newspaper Story* (Cambridge, Mass.: Harvard University Press, 1971), p. 292.

[7] Leland Hamilton Jenks, *Our Cuban Colony: A Study in Sugar* (New York: Vanguard Press, 1928); Melvin M. Knight, *The Americans in Santo Domingo* (New York: Vanguard Press, 1928); and Margaret Alexander Marsh, *The Bankers in Bolivia: A Study in American Foreign Investment* (New York: Vanguard Press, 1928).

government, military science, finance, education, and many others, were all politicians willing to execute mandates from the Potomac, and occasionally to execute Latin American natives as well. In its worst manifestations, the system led to brutal military intervention, complete obliteration of native customs and institutions, and selfish financial control by New York bankers. In all cases, the European investors were paid off or choked off and the Yankees assured a monopoly. This was the system allegedly established to fend off Old World dangers: this was the system allegedly invoked in defense of the Monroe Doctrine. And sad to relate, this was the system that brought to the United States the ill will of two thirds of the Western Hemisphere.[8]

Whatever our motives may have been, it is clear that the United States policy that supported free elections as a prime method of promoting democracy in the Caribbean failed. As one political scientist stated, "Americans have pursued this particular policy for that goal because they have mistakenly assumed that fraudulent and coerced elections are the cause of revolutions in countries which already have democratic constitutions." [9]

Cuba and the Dominican Republic represent the most serious challenges to United States policy in the Caribbean. Many nations have sought to dominate Cuba, but after 1900 United States influence became increasingly powerful. How Fidel Castro managed to triumph in 1959 and escape from the orbit of Uncle Sam remains one of the great stories of the twentieth century, some of it still shrouded in mystery. Hugh Thomas, the British writer who produced one of the best books on the Spanish civil war, has drawn up a carefully argued explanation of the coming of Castro (Reading 55). For a fair and informed evaluation of the results of Castro's revolution, we turn to a veteran Cuba-watcher, Lowry Nelson (Reading 56).

Generalíssimo Rafael Trujillo represents the nadir of all Caribbean dictators. Nevertheless, President Franklin D. Roosevelt supported him; the resulting "stability" was won, however, according to Raymond H. Pulley of the University of Virginia, only at a very high price: "The question arises as to why the United States persisted in supporting a bloody tyrant in the Dominican Republic while condemning similar regimes in Europe and while a large portion of vocal opinion disapproved of Trujillo and his methods. . . . During the period 1933–1940 the Trujillo dictatorship was the com-

[8] Lawrence F. Hill, "Our Present Peril," in *Hispanic American Essays: A Memorial to James Alexander Robertson*, ed. A. Curtis Wilgus (Chapel Hill: University of North Carolina Press, 1942), pp. 375–376.

[9] Theodore Paul Wright, Jr., *American Support of Free Elections Abroad* (Washington: Public Affairs Press, 1964), pp. 137–157.

plete antithesis of what the United States claimed itself to be — the bastion of democracy." [10]

Professor Jerome Slater describes the problems faced by the United States governments since the end of World War II and analyzes their options: They "have had to decide whether United States interests dictated support for the forces of order and stability — i.e., the status quo — or identification with the populist groups, with all the potential for violence, chaos, and radicalism that they entail." [11]

When President Lyndon B. Johnson landed Marines in the Dominican Republic in April 1965, he did so without reference to the Organization of American States. The action was a clear violation of the OAS Charter, specifically of Articles 15 (forbidding intervention "for any reason whatever") and 17 (forbidding even temporary military occupation "on any grounds whatever"). The background for this much-discussed intervention is set forth by Professor Abraham F. Lowenthal (Reading 57).

The meaning of the intervention for future United States policy is much debated. The Dominican revolution and civil war of 1965 and the American intervention "were far more complex events than either Administration advocates or critics apparently realize," concludes Professor Howard J. Wiarda. He has studied society and politics in the Dominican Republic in depth and has this to say on the causes of the outbreak of the bloody and chaotic revolution:

> There existed deep and perhaps irreconcilable divisions within the social structure and the politics which rendered the development of a functioning viable political system all but impossible. These sharp conflicts and tensions within the system were ultimately and in long-range terms more responsible for the tragic events which followed than any more immediate causes.[12]

Professor Wiarda has prepared a thoughtful note on "The Dominican Revolution in Perspective" (Reading 58). In another study he has drawn up this somber assessment of the results of the crisis:

> Whatever terms are used, it seems clear that the Dominican Revolution, civil war, U.S. intervention, and many subsequent events resulted in the near-total disintegration of the social and political infrastructure

---

[10] Raymond H. Pulley, "The United States and the Trujillo Dictatorship, 1933–1940," *Caribbean Studies,* 5 (1965), p. 31.

[11] Jerome Slater, "Democracy versus Stability: The Recent Latin American Policy of the United States," *Yale Review,* 4 (1966), no. 2, pp. 169–181.

[12] Howard J. Wiarda, "From Fragmentation to Disintegration: The Social and Political Effects of the Dominican Revolution," *América Latina* (Rio de Janeiro), año 10, no. 2 (April–June 1967) p. 55.

of the nation. The thin threads that hold it together are weak and probably overly-stretched and overly-extended. . . . The larger issues which the Revolution tragically but unmistakably brought to the surface — the role of the military, enormous gaps between rich and poor, dictatorship versus democracy, etc. — have not been resolved; and the relatively simple expedients of the withdrawal of foreign troops and the holding of elections should not serve to disguise the severe, long-term damage which the socio-political fabric has incurred. It is unlikely that the full disintegrative effects of the Dominican Revolution will shortly or easily permit the development of a viable, functioning, pluralist system.[13]

However one may view the causes and results of United States intervention, the key question posed by this tragic event, "costly to the Dominican Republic, to the United States, and to inter-American relations," [14] remains that of the United States attitude toward revolutionary change. One political scientist has stated what should be done in this way:

Several steps are essential. Public opinion must be re-educated, but before that can be done American policy makers must reeducate themselves. . . . Such a reexamination, I believe, would point to the need for two major actions: first, the United States in its public pronouncements and rhetoric must clearly de-couple genuine revolutions from "international aggression." Second, the Monroe Doctrine, which latterly has been interpreted to require the exclusion of hostile or undemocratic political ideologies from the Western Hemisphere, must be jettisoned, or at least drastically modified.[15]

A British student of inter-American relations has reached much the same conclusion: "The immediate future of the inter-American system depends mainly upon what lessons the United States learns from her current Dominican experience. If she is going to treat all revolts against military juntas or other Latin American dictatorships as 'wars of liberation' and part of a world-wide communist conspiracy the prospects for the inter-American system are gloomy indeed." [16]

[13] Ibid., p. 70.
[14] Abraham F. Lowenthal, "The Dominican Intervention of 1965: A Study of United States Policy" (Ph.D. dissertation, Harvard University, 1970), p. i. See also Dr. Lowenthal's assessment, "The Dominican Intervention in Retrospect," *Public Policy*, September 1969, pp. 133–148.
[15] Jerome Slater, *Intervention and Negotiation: The United States and the Dominican Revolution* (New York, 1970), p. 215.
[16] Gordon Connell-Smith, *The Inter-American System* (London: Oxford University Press, 1966), p. 345.

54. The United States Is Honor Bound to Maintain Law and Order in South America

GEORGE W. CRICHFIELD

Mr. Crichfield expressed in what may seem to be an exaggerated way the feeling of those who looked upon Latin Americans as "a lesser breed" who must be kept in order for their own good. If only the United States would take charge of those countries, the trains would run on time!

Our people believe in justice, and in the liberty which carries the torch of civilization over the earth. They have always earnestly desired to see stable republics established in South America. They do not believe in monarchies. They believe in "a government of the people, by the people, and for the people." Our people enthusiastically upheld President Monroe when he declared that European monarchies should not extend their territory on American soil, and each succeeding administration, without exception, has striven to aid in the establishment, maintenance, and development of decent republican governments in these countries.

When our State Department has seen revolutions, anarchy, and crime rampant in South America, foreigners being looted, robbed, and murdered (Americans suffering worse than any other class), infamy, perfidy, intrigue, and scoundrelism covering Spanish America as with a pall — it has not shut its eyes to the facts. On the contrary, no father ever watched over his wayward offspring with more care, sorrow, and anxiety than has the beneficent government of the United States observed these countries, studying by what means it could bring order out of chaos, decency out of crime.

For three quarters of a century this has been our policy, followed with patience and a spirit of philanthropy to which history affords no parallel. As one bandit government after another has appeared on the horizon of South America, our government has counselled it to exercise moderation, to walk in the paths of civilization, to respect the lives and property of foreigners; and

From *American Supremacy: The Rise and Progress of the Latin American Republics and Their Relations to the United States under the Monroe Doctrine* by George W. Crichfield (New York: Brentano's, 1908), 1, pp. 7–544; 2, pp. 635–644, passim.

we have stood between these so-called "governments" and the civilized powers of Europe.

In spite of all that our country has done for them, the incontestable fact remains that Venezuela, Colombia, Ecuador, Bolivia, Santo Domingo, Hayti, and practically all of Central America are in a worse condition to-day, politically, socially, commercially, and deeper in barbarism, than they were three quarters of a century ago. Dilettante philosophers, reactionists who are against every policy which has made the United States the peerless giant which it is, will go on shouting in behalf of our "poor oppressed Sister Republics." On such people the facts stated in the following pages will have no effect. But Americans — the hardy, brainy, practical race which has founded the Great Republic, before the tremendous power of whose solemn and deliberate judgment governments must stand or fall — that innumerable army of men who have made and who constitute "God's country" — men who hate brigand governments (all the more if they assume the name of Republics), who love justice and truth, and hate wickedness whatever may be its form — should know these Spanish-Indian-Negro countries as they actually are. If they could see Americans and American enterprises wiped off the face of the earth by the aggregations calling themselves Republics, it would not be long before the machinery of the government of the United States would be diverted towards bringing about a most thorough renovation in their conditions.

To many people it may seem impossible that in this day and age, and in the Western hemisphere, there could exist such conditions of semi-barbarism in Colombia, Venezuela, Santo Domingo, and Central America as are here disclosed. To know a country thoroughly one must have lived in it and done business in it. Distinguished writers have written admirable descriptive works of South America — of landscapes, of cities and rivers and lakes, of mountains and llanos, with a coloring of individual incident and interesting anecdote; they are admirable productions of scholarly men. One may describe a landscape from the window of a Pullman car, but one cannot in such a manner apprehend the social and political problems of the peoples through whose country the railroad passes. However brilliant a traveller may be, however acute his power of observation, it is not possible that he can probe into the depths and analyze the character and capabilities of a people, except by long and varied intercourse with them. . . .

It will be found that practically all Latin Americans exhibit the following peculiarities to a degree greater than that possessed by any other people with which I am familiar: (1) a lack of thoroughness, exactness, definiteness of aim; (2) inability to apply themselves persistently and continually to the mastery of a subject; (3) carelessness and lack of foresight; (4) contempt for the drudgery of ordinary work and a disposition to shirk it; (5) a desire to make a great display, to pretend to be what in fact they are not; (6) satisfaction with the outward appearance of knowledge, with no real desire to get at the heart of any proposition; (7) lack of initiative, invention, creative energy; (8) possession of a multitude of impracticable theories and ideas which are a nuisance, but of which it is impossible to rid them; (9) complete absence of a sense of responsibility; (10) ignorance of the most elementary methods of doing things; (11) a disposition to talk, rather than to act; (12) a disposition to do work in the showiest manner possible, but to produce what is really shoddy and worthless; (13) a disposition to make money by intrigue rather than in legitimate business; (14) a very scant respect for the property or personal rights of others, particularly foreigners; (15) absolute indolence and lack of genuine ambition, and opposition to progress.

All of these will be recognized as characteristics of large sections of our own country; and indeed they cannot be set down as the exclusive peculiarities of any people, or as all of them applying to any one section of any people. Yet in their entirety they come nearer applying to the Latin Americans than to any European race. . . .

NATIONAL INGRATITUDE

The United States has befriended the Latin-American countries in ten thousand ways; it has defended them against civilized powers for eighty years; it has submitted to outrages committed on its flag and on the persons and property of its citizens, outwardly without protest; it has declared in the presence of the world, untruthfully, but nevertheless declared it, that these countries are civilized republics, and their courts worthy the same consideration as are the courts of England or our own; it has called them "Sister Republics," and stood with its army and navy ready to defend them, at the grave risk, on more than one occasion, of having a war on its hands with the whole civilized world. In view of all this, it might reasonably be inferred that Americans are popular in South America; but it is not so. Americans are robbed more than are either Germans or Englishmen; more outrages are committed against Americans than against any other class of foreigners.

If ingratitude is the index of a criminal, then these fighting, quarrelling, intriguing, murdering communities should be classed as criminals. . . .

LATIN AMERICAN TYPES

The military Jefe is the most noted Latin-American type which impresses itself upon a visitor. The Jefe may be colonel, general, comandante, or any of the other numerous military grades. As a rule, he is a man without conscience, of unbridled ambition, cruel and relentless, and a dangerous citizen generally.

Closely allied with the military Jefe is the civil politician. This man can write pronunciamentoes, and hair-raising essays on liberty and patriotism. He also fixes up the decretas for the military Jefe to sign. A considerable portion of the graft is allotted to this type of politician. He is merely a schemer for the Jefe with his army of macheteros.

The doctors of Latin America are as numerous as the generals. They are a much more amiable class of men. While their pretensions to learning are exaggerated and amusing, nevertheless, they are a respectable element of society. Ignoring their idiosyncracies and pretensions of refinement and culture, we may sincerely like and admire these men, most of whom are very decent fellows and a large number of whom are first-class gentlemen of a high type.

Throughout Mexico, Argentina, and Chili there are enormous plantations or tracts of land called *haciendas,* the owner of which is known as a *hacendado.* This man is easily, in my opinion, the highest type of Latin-American gentleman. He has not the literary ability or the refinement and culture of the doctors, but he is an all-round man of affairs, a good business man, and really forms the backbone of the nation. It is the hacendado who gives to Mexico, Chili, and Argentina their stability and higher governmental excellence. The hacendado is usually the supporter of the government, unless it be in fact very vicious, because it is to his interest to maintain the established order of things. He does not want his property overrun by revolutionary hordes, and he knows that it is better to submit to the exactions of a corrupt government than to run the risk of losing all by siding with anarchy. These great plantations are not cultivated thoroughly, and enormous tracts of land lie fallow or in their primeval condition. No opportunity is afforded to the small man to become a landed proprietor, and this constitutes the real element of weakness in the hacienda system. The inconceivable strength of the United States is due to the fact that we have millions of home owners. A comparatively poor man with us can own his own house and farm. Not so in the countries mentioned. A landed proprietor there is necessarily a man of wealth. The coffee plantations of Venezuela and Colombia afford a somewhat similar system to that of the great landed estates in the other countries mentioned, but owing to the frequent uprisings and the despoliation by predatory bands, these plantations are usually run down and neglected.

There are many special types in Central and South America which are very interesting to a foreign observer. They may be briefly mentioned. The *arierro,* or mule-driver, is a picturesque fellow. He directs the burros in their never-ending work of transporting the products of Latin America. These burro trains by the hundreds can be found in all parts of Latin America, each animal carrying loads of two hundred or two hundred and fifty pounds, over mountains and valleys, wading rivers, climbing where it would seem to be impossible for an animal to step, going on journeys for days or even weeks. The arierro is utterly oblivious to the suffering of his beasts. He is ordinarily not a bad fellow, but is entirely indifferent to pain, and ignorant with regard to every subject except the matter in hand. The *gaucho,* or cow-boy, of the great interior plains of Argentina, Brazil, and Southern Venezuela is a most daring rider, an excellent shot, and makes one of the hardiest soldiers in the world. He loves ornaments in dress, is disposed to drink a great deal of bad liquor and indulge in gambling, and is generally a citizen with whom one must be careful in dealing. . . . The beggar is another distinctive type in Latin America which impresses itself upon the visitor with a vividness and distinctiveness which can never be obliterated. One day a week, usually Saturday, is set apart particularly for the beggars, in which they make their rounds of all the houses and streets, soliciting alms. The utter hopelessness of this type is pitiable and pathetic. They live in indescribable squalor and misery, diseased, deformed, helpless, and hopeless. There are hundreds of thousands of all ages and both sexes belonging to this type in Latin America. The enormous percentage of dire helplessness is one of the saddest features which an observer encounters in every Latin-American country. . . .

PROTECTION OF CIVILIZED MEN IN AMERICA

The United States is in honor bound to maintain law and order in South America, and we may just as well take complete control of several of the countries, and establish decent governments while we are about it. Peru, Chili, and Argentina are already fairly responsible governments. We ought not to interfere with them so long as they conduct themselves in a reasonably satisfactory manner. Mexico is an excellent government, and worthy of our best friendship. A stricter surveillance should be exercised over Costa Rica, Brazil, Uruguay, and Paraguay. These governments are not as advanced or as worthy of recognition as those named, but they are not wholly bad. There are evidences of genuine efforts at improvement, and some regard for the amenities of civilization and international rights, and a rather more decent spirit towards foreigners. Whether they will ever amount to anything or not, time alone will tell. They should be kept under the strictest friendly supervision by the United States. No marked internal or external policy should be permitted without our consent. They should be held under a quasi-protectorate, yet with such a minimum of interference with their affairs as would secure perfect security for life and property, and a reasonable measure of material and intellectual progress. . . .

THE DICTATORSHIPS SHOULD BE PLACED
UNDER A CIVILIZED GOVERNMENT

Now, what shall be said of Venezuela, Colombia, Ecuador, Bolivia, Santo Domingo, and Haiti, and the rest of Central America?

They have sinned away their day of grace. They are semibarbarous centres of rapine in an age which boasts of enlightenment. They are a reproach to the civilization of the twentieth century.

It is a waste of time to argue in connection with these States about sovereign rights. The United States should take immediate possession and jurisdiction of each and every one of them, without waiting for a pretext. It should govern them precisely the same way as it governs other territory of the United States. The century of intrigue and bloodshed and bad faith in these countries should be brought to a close, and a new era ushered in more in harmony with the sentiments of the age. With the United States in control of South America, I venture to predict that within ten years we could take a Pullman car at Maracaibo and go straight through to Buenos Ayres without change, and in ten years longer it might be that we could step into another car and go to New York. Under the present régime such conditions would not be brought about in ten thousand years.

There are doubtless many persons who would concede that this ought to be done and yet hesitate to commit the United States to such a policy on account of the apparent magnitude of the task. Our people have not yet got over the idea that the taking of Porto Rico and the Philippines under our wing was a mighty feat, and the ravings of the "antis" have rather accentuated that belief. As a matter of fact, the Philippines and Porto Rico are only specks in the ocean in comparison with the immensity of England's colonial possessions.

If the United States were to take possession of the whole of the Western Hemisphere, from the Rio Grande to Cape Horn, the total area of its territory would be only about equal to that of the British Empire, and its population not more than one third as great.

What Englishmen can do Americans can do. The United States, with vastly greater territory and population, is as truly a breeding-place of creative energy, of originating and productive enterprise, as England or any other country. . . .

No very great argument should be required to show the incomparable benefit to the United States as a nation in controlling these great territories.

It is a curious thing that the English, who are in all ordinary business matters extremely slow and conservative in comparison with Americans, should in this one matter so completely outstrip us in foresight and in a true apprehension of the right policy to pursue. If we are to become a great manufacturing nation, we must have outlets for our goods, and those outlets must be in countries where there is money to pay for them and the disposition to buy them. To develop the continent of South America properly will require twice as many tons of steel rails as it has required to develop the United States, for it is twice as large. It will require as much mining machinery, for the natural mineral resources of South America are unquestionably as great and as valuable as those of North America. The people who are now scantily clothed would, under proper conditions, be large consumers of our manufactured products. The manufactured production of the United States is now running parallel with the domestic consumption, and in a short time will overleap it. We must have markets, vast markets; for our productive capacity is great. If our workingmen are to be kept employed, if the prosperity of the United States is to continue, we must look ahead, and provide ourselves for outlets of our products. It has been truly said that when we export a million dollars' worth of goods, at least $800,000 of money has been paid to our own people for the labor of their production. I am aware that every effort of far-seeing statesmen to establish our future commercial prosperity on a sound basis calls forth protest from a certain class of mugwumps, who join the words "commercialism," "militarism," and "imperialism" as though they constitute a trinity of horrors. . . .

IMPORTANCE OF CIVILIZED CONTROL

It seems unnecessary to emphasize the beneficent effects upon the people of those South American countries which would result from placing them under the American flag. One immediate and very important consequence would be that a man could go to sleep at night without fear of being assassinated. No one, unless he has slept for some years with one eye open and an automatic revolver within reach, can appreciate the delight of unmolested sleep.

Another blessing scarcely less appreciable would be the privilege of working and reaping the results of one's efforts. To-day, in South America, military Jefes will not work, nor will they let any one else work. The enormity of this wrong can be only partially appreciated by those people in the United States who have personally observed the tyranny of the labor boss as displayed in its unvarnished ugliness in certain localities.

As fully explained in another chapter, the great majority of the people of

South America are good people — incapable of self-government, but fully capable of marvellous development under decent conditions. To those who wish to live in peace and accumulate a little property against old age or death, the American flag would be a beacon of hope. Rascals, intriguers, and the semi-bandit governing class are the only people whose liberties would in any wise be curtailed by the control of the United States.

Do I need to multiply examples in order to prove my contention? Is there any American so blind that he cannot to some extent perceive the blessings that have accrued to each successive territory which has come under the beneficent control of the United States? Look at that magnificent State, Texas, and that incomparable garden of the world, rich and beautiful California, and the rest of the splendid commonwealths which have been created out of the territory wrested from Mexico.

Suppose that territory had remained in the exclusive control of Mexico and Mexicans, and that the enterprise and capital of Americans had never entered it. Does any sane man believe it would ever have attained a fraction of its present prosperity? Even the progress of Mexico itself is due mainly not to internal activity, but to the stimulus of external enterprise exercised within its borders. Nor can any fault-finder truthfully assert that the rule of the United States in Porto Rico and the Philippines is any less promising. The mediæval systems of a century are not to be swept away in a moment, and the complete regeneration of a people is a question of time; but already much has been accomplished in both those colonies. Never before were they so well governed, never were they so clean, never was education so well looked after, public improvements so actively pushed, happiness and security of the people so thoroughly safeguarded, or such contentment and evidences of future prosperity as at the present time.

Size, distance, or inaccessibility of these countries constitutes no valid objection against this program. The world is apparently destined to be divided up among five or six great powers. The time has passed when we can permit the famines and pestilences and revolutions which grow out of barbaric or semi-barbaric conditions to destroy millions. With the world under the control of half a dozen civilized powers, wars would be unknown, and the chief function of the military would be its police duties. On this hemisphere the power which controls should be the United States. . . .

What shall be the final destiny of these countries no man can tell. What part of the United States is to take in the mighty onward march of affairs is likewise shrouded in the future. But any reasonable man must see clearly that the present condition of anarchy cannot continue indefinitely in Spanish America. It is not they alone who suffer, but the whole world; and not they alone, but the whole world, would be benefited by the United States taking possession of them.

55. The Castro Revolution Was the Culmination of a Long Series of Thwarted Revolutions

HUGH THOMAS

Professor Hugh Thomas, the British historian at the University of Reading, here gives a carefully argued explanation of the coming of Castro.

The present Cuban explanation of events is that Cuba, previously a semi-colonialist society, was so severely exploited by U.S. and Cuban capitalists that the condition of the working class eventually became intolerable, the tension being especially sharpened under the tyrant Batista (1952–58); Castro's 26th of July Movement and the Communist Party therefore formed the elite which led the masses towards a coherent realization of their misery and the country towards the "objective conditions" for revolution. Yet this explanation is also inadequate. Cuba, although a poor country in many respects, was certainly among the richer countries of Latin America. Per capita income reached a figure of $341 at its highest level in 1947. The average daily salary about the same time for the best-paid sugar worker was $3.25, which probably would have given him an annual wage (with a six-day week for the five-month sugar harvest) of nearly $500. This is a small wage, but in many countries in Latin America it would be considered high. Wages apart, however, the general availability of consumer goods, the social services per head, the labour laws, the communications system, literacy rates, all normal criteria indicate that Cuba was among the leading nations of Latin America — to be ranked in terms of development below only Argentina and Uruguay, and perhaps on a level with Chile. Certainly, Cuba had had for two generations before the revolution the highest standard of living of any tropical area in the world. It does not therefore seem to be poverty, any more than North American foolishness, that caused the revolution to take the turn it did.

From "The Origins of the Cuban Revolution" by Hugh Thomas, *The World Today,* 19 (October 1963), pp. 448–460, passim. Reprinted by permission of the author and the Royal Institute of International Affairs.

The difficulty of explaining what happened in Cuba in Marxist terms has led some people to another extreme: they have seen the whole series of events as dictated by the whims of one man. The trouble with this argument is that it really credits Castro with greater powers than any man can singly possess. Instead of describing a monster, this argument creates a god.

The origins of the revolution seem more likely to be found in the fact that Cuban society was not so much underdeveloped as stagnant: semideveloped perhaps, with some of the characteristics of advanced countries when they enter decline. Cuba was not a country in the depths of poverty, but one extraordinarily frustrated, where opportunities existed for economic and social progress but where these were wasted — and the fact of the waste was evident. The undoubted advances whetted the imagination of the working class, but did not satisfy it. The case of the well-paid sugar worker symbolizes the situation; getting $3.25 a day for the five months of the harvest, afterwards he could expect to earn nothing. Unused to saving, and perhaps incapable of doing so since he had to pay off debts incurred during the previous dead season, his life collapsed. For half the year he was comparatively well off, able to choose between a quite wide selection of consumer goods; for the rest of the year he lived in resentment, possibly more extreme than if he had been unemployed all the time, as a large fraction (around one-fifth) of his colleagues in the trade were. About 500,000 persons were in this frustrating position, nearly one-third of the total labour force of about 1.7 million. Nearly all of them were in debt throughout their lives — being disposed for that reason alone to hope for a violent upturn in society, which might declare a moratorium on, or even an annulment of, debts. The key to Cuban society before the revolution is, in fact, the sugar industry. . . .

In addition to being the world's largest producer of sugar, Cuba was, for about a century, the major single source of sugar for the United States, and for a time after the Civil War her sole source of sugar. For most of this century up to 1960, Cuba supplied between 40 and 60 per cent of U.S. sugar, with a drop towards 30 per cent and for a time 25 per cent during the 1930's depression. After this unstable period, Cuba secured a part of the U.S. market by a specific quota, allocated annually according to the U.S. Secretary for Agriculture's estimate of U.S. sugar needs. . . . The quota was a great advantage but also a great bondage, and therefore there is a certain logic in the Cuban Revolutionary Government's criticism of its existence in early 1960 and denunciation of its disappearance in August of the same year. The tragedy of the Cuban sugar industry in the years before the revolution is that it was hard to see how, even with the most effective methods of production, it could expand its share of the world market, or its own production. Both U.S. and world markets were quota-controlled and tariff-protected to the point where expansion was almost forbidden.

One should note, however, that a large percentage of Cuban sugar mills were in fact U.S.-owned. . . . Of course, it was natural for Cubans to denounce the high percentage of foreign ownership, throughout this long period, of the staple product of the country, especially when other sections of the commanding heights of industry were also U.S.-owned; these included almost all public utilities in Havana, railways, and banks, which had been largely U.S.- and Canadian-owned since the bank crash in the 1920's. However, there were some advantages in this: foreign ownership could help to keep the door open to new ideas in technology and research; some of the best schools in Cuba seem to have been run by Americans, some being financed as a public obligation, others privately; American firms were also probably less given to tax evasion than Cuban. The overall effect of U.S. ownership of such prosperity as there was in Cuba was that Americans could not avoid being blamed when things went wrong with the economy; and the economy had been in crisis for as long as anyone could remember.

In fact, Cuban sugar before the revolution was going through the classic experience of a great industry in decline. Cuban sugar-growers never sought to make the best use of their ground, the yield per acre, for instance, being far below that of Puerto Rico or Hawaii. Irrigation was not only rare but not apparently even planned, though it was obvious that it gave a higher yield. There was very little research as to the type of cane best suited for Cuban conditions: the agricultural research center at Sagua la Grande was hardly able to carry on, since even the meagre ear-marked funds often "disappeared" before they got there. Further, the industry was hamstrung by bureaucratic control. . . .

The country was also at the mercy of world sugar demand. Changes of a percentage of a cent in the world market price of sugar not only meant the creation or ruin of fortunes in Cuba, but also indicated whether ordinary life was intolerable or acceptable. . . . For example, in 1950 under the impact of post-Korean rearmament, the whole of Cuba's molasses from the 1951 harvest was sold at 20 cents a gallon, instead of 5 cents a gallon a year earlier. . . .

Credit was almost impossible to obtain unless the proposed project was in some way connected with sugar, yet investment in new industries (perhaps making use of sugar by-products) and diversification of agriculture were the only way forward. This blockage could be observed throughout the economy. Education, health, social services of all kinds, public services, commerce, departments of agriculture other than sugar, trade unions, all gave the impression of being not only incapable of development, but also afraid of it. The

Cuban educational system had deteriorated between 1925 and 1959. A smaller proportion of school-age children were enrolled in Cuban schools in 1950 than in 1925. . . .

Other Latin American economies were, and are, as unstable and as unbalanced as that of Cuba: and the central cause of the trouble, the monocrop, appears elsewhere. At the same time, none of the countries whose economies are to a lesser or greater extent monocultures actually depends on sugar, whose price has always been highly volatile. . . .

The institutions of Cuba in 1958–59 were amazingly weak. The large middle and upper class had failed to create any effective defence against the demands of what may be taken to be the majority when those demands came at last to be clearly expressed, as they did in January 1959, by a group self-confessedly middle class in origin. Perhaps the first and strongest factor working in favour of the revolution was the absence of any regionally based obstacles. . . .

To the absence of a regional restraining force was added the weakness of two other traditional conservative forces — the Church and the regular army. The Cuban Church has never really found an identity. Churches are few in Cuba. The Church played no part in the development of the Cuban spirit of independence, which instead was nurtured by freemasonry and rationalism. Few priests before 1898 were Cuban born, and even after 1900 the majority continued to come from Spain. Church and State had been separated in the Constitution of 1901, State subsidies also disappearing. Later on, the Church made something of a comeback, a large number of Catholic schools being founded in the 1930's; in 1946 a Catholic university was also founded. In the 1950's this educational emphasis led to the appearance of almost radical Catholic groups which opposed Batista. In Oriente, there was, in the early stages, some degree of relationship between the 26th of July Movement and the Church — chiefly since it was widely known that the intervention of the Archbishop of Santiago had helped save Castro's life after the Moncada attack in 1953. The leading Catholic and conservative newspaper, the *Diario de la Marina,* was, on the other hand, among the first to suggest that the 26th of July Movement was communist.

After Castro got to power, the Church made no serious move to gather middle-class opposition, and it was only in 1960, when it was too late, that a series of sporadic pastoral letters appeared denouncing communism. All church schools and convents were closed by the end of 1961, and most foreign priests and secular clergy (i.e., the majority) were expelled. Since then there has been a surprising calm in the relations between Church and State, presumably by mutual consent; the Church in Cuba has, in short, never been a serious factor in the situation.

The regular army, the second traditional opponent of revolutionary regimes, was even less of an obstacle. By early 1959 it had in fact ceased to exist — not simply due to its demoralization in 1957 and 1958, when fighting Castro in the Sierra, but also to the repeated divisions which had weakened its esprit de corps during preceding years. . . .

The trade unions also could offer no serious opposition to the revolution; yet the revolution destroyed them, or anyway converted them into departments of the Ministry of Labour. Cuban labour began to be effectively organized under the shadow of the depression and the Machado dictatorship. Batista enabled the communists to form and dominate a congress of unions in the late 1930's — in return for communist electoral support for himself. Between 1938 and 1947 the unions were, if not structurally, at least in effect a section of the Ministry of Labour. The rather cynical alliance of Batista and the communists (till 1944) was responsible for some enlightened labour legislation: a minimum wage; minimum vacation of one month; 44-hour week and 48-hour-week pay; nine days of annual sick leave; security of tenure except on proof of one of fourteen specific causes of dismissal, and so on — all admirable measures in themselves, enshrined in the 1940 Constitution, and all in effect till 1959. These measures were in fact so favourable to labour in the 1940's and early 1950's as undeniably to hinder the economic development of Cuba; labour opposition to mechanization, for example, seems to have been a serious handicap. The general impression to be gained from the labour scene just before Batista's second coup was less that of solid benefits won by a progressive working class than of a number of isolated redoubts, held with great difficulty and with continuous casualties, in a predominantly hostile territory. . . .

It was equally hopeless to expect the civil service to be a restraining factor in the revolution, although, with nearly 200,000 employees, it was the second largest source of employment, ranking after the sugar workers. Despite the passage of numerous laws, starting in 1908 under the Magoon administration, no Government was able to depend on a reliable civil service. With the exception of the National Bank, during the short period from its inception in 1949 to the Batista coup, all departments of state were regarded as the legitimate spoils of political victors. Of course, in this Cuba was no different from other countries. But in few countries of a comparable degree of wealth was the absence of an administrative career in government so conspicuous. In some Ministries, employees never seem to have appeared except to collect pay; the absence of responsibility was possibly most marked in the Ministry of Education. Also, since the salary scale was low, there was every incentive for employees of all grades to dip their hands in the government till, as their political masters did. Since governmental and nongovernmental pension funds, which were lodged in the Treasury, had been used by the Grau Government to help pay other lavish but unspecified government expenses, it was very difficult after 1947 to allow any employee to retire. Many people thought that in fact 30,000 to 40,000 government employees were really pensioners. Thus government employment was a kind of social assistance.

The scandal of the old bureaucracy is certainly a reason why, after the victory of the 26th of July Movement in 1959, the idea of a total break with the past seemed so attractive. The word government had been debased for so long; not only the old bureaucracy but the old political parties were widely and with justice regarded as organizations for the private distribution of public funds. Who in 1959, even after seven years of Batista, had really forgotten the scandal of Grau's schoolteachers; or of Grau's Minister of Education, Alemán, who had arrived suddenly one day in Miami with, was it $10 million, or was it $20 million in cash in a suitcase? In what way was Batista's cheating in the State lottery worse than Prío's? It was all very well to return to the Constitution of 1940: but how far had it worked between 1940 and 1952? It had in many instances merely laid down general principles; the subsequent legislation had never been carried out to implement it. . . .

Some of the best-intentioned sections of the Constitution were in fact a little absurd, such as the provision in Article 52 that the annual salary of a primary schoolteacher should never be less than a millionth part of the national budget. At the same time, not many people, even sincere democrats, could summon up enthusiasm for the 1940 Constitution, since it had been established with the backing of Batista and the communists. And at a deeper level, there was a genuine doubt among many in Cuba in 1958–59 about the structure of previous Cuban Constitutions ever since independence. Batista's police were certainly bloody, but the old days of gangsterism under the democratic rule of Grau were hardly better. There was a time, for instance, in 1947, when three separate political gangster groups were fighting each other in the streets of Havana, each being separately backed by different divisions of the police, whose chiefs had been specifically appointed by the President to balance them off.

Although Castro did not come to power with a real party organization, or even a real political plan, he nevertheless did have behind him a real revolutionary tradition, a tradition which was firmly rooted in the previous sixty years of Cuban politics, almost the whole of which had been passed in perpetual crisis. . . . All the time between 1902 and 1959, Cubans were trying to prove themselves worthy of the heroic figures of the War of Independence — Martí, Gómez, or Maceo. Efforts were made, understandably, necessarily perhaps, by Castro to make himself, Camilo Cienfuegos, and others the equals of the past. The men of 1959 were undoubtedly in many cases the real sons of the men who made the revolution in 1933. Castro was to do the things that many people had been talking about before. Many moderately middle-class Cubans suspected, without much economic knowledge, that the only way out of the chronic sugar crisis, the only way to diversify agriculture, was to embark on very radical measures; to nationalize American property and to force a break in commercial relations with the United States.

Amateur Marxism was a strong force on the left wing of the *Ortodoxo* Party in the early 1950's, though it is now proving an illusion to suppose that even Marxist-Leninism can bring a swift diversification of agriculture. One can see how the illusion nevertheless became widespread, how anyone who seemed likely to realize it was certain of backing, regardless of whether he trampled on formal democracy. There can be only one reason why the moderates in the Cuban Cabinet of 1959 — the admirable professional and liberal persons who now perhaps back Manuel Ray and argue that Castro has betrayed the revolution — failed to unite and resist Castro, backed by the considerable strength of the Cuban middle class: the reason is surely that they half felt all the time that, given the betrayal of so many previous revolutions, Castro was right. Many moderates after all did stay in Cuba, and many are still there.

What of the communists? They have never dictated events, but merely profited from opportunities offered to them. . . . The communists got 117,000 votes in the presidential elections of 1944, but they were by that time in a curious position, being less a party of revolution than one which had a great deal to lose, almost conservative in their reactions in fact. Thereafter their influence waned, throughout the intermediate period between then and the Castro civil war, until mid-1958 when, after some difficulty, they established a working alliance with Castro, whom they had previously dismissed as a *putschista*. Since then, they have, of course, come into their own in many respects, if not quite absolutely; but their role in the origins of the Cuban revolution seems to have been small.

To sum up: the origins of the Cuban revolution must be sought in the state of the Cuban sugar industry. Similar conditions may exist in other countries of Latin America, in respect of other crops; these have hitherto been less pronounced. Even though other revolutions in the area may in fact be equally due, they have been hindered by the strength of institutions or regional habits, which in Cuba, for historical reasons, were especially weak. Finally, the Cuban revolution of 1959, far from being an isolated event, was the culmination of a long series of thwarted revolutions.

56. *"It Was an Effort to Create Utopia"*

LOWRY NELSON

One of the fundamental volumes on pre-Castro Cuba was Lowry Nelson's *Rural Cuba* (1950). This veteran sociologist of the University of Minnesota naturally wanted to compare present-day Cuban society with his previous studies, but his request for a visa was rejected by the Cuban government so that he had to base his volume on the considerable material available in the United States. Apparently, "the revolutionary government is wary of studies that may reflect unfavorably on it."

Professor Nelson recognizes that there is no substitute for field studies, but his assessment of the pluses and minuses of the Castro revolution is worth careful study.

One undertakes an evaluation of the Cuban Revolution in full realization of the difficulties involved. Yet in the thirteenth year of its administration of the island, the revolutionary government is inevitably subject to such an assessment. It is in fact being judged, and rather harshly, by some of its most enthusiastic friends of earlier years. Writers of Marxist orientation, including the Americans Huberman and Sweezy, the French agronomist René Dumont, and the Polish-Russian-Parisian K. S. Karol, have passed judgment. All of them have enjoyed the privilege of several visits to the country and, in Karol's case, lengthy interviews with the prime minister. These privileges were denied the present author but, unlike the writers mentioned, he did come to know the old Cuba during a year's study. Most of the early enthusiasts for the revolution had never been in Cuba and did not know it first hand.

All revolutions are matters of controversy; their achievements and even their justification are debated for generations after they happen. The Cuban Revolution, as the first socialist-communist one in the hemisphere, has been up to now more controversial than most for several reasons, but chiefly because of the relation the island holds to the two major powers of the world, the one capitalist, the other communist. The revolution is controversial also because of the extremes to which it went in abolishing private property and suppressing individual initiative. It was, indeed, an effort to create utopia;

From *Cuba: The Measure of a Revolution* by Lowry Nelson (University of Minnesota Press, Minneapolis © 1972, University of Minnesota), pp. 184–206, passim. Reprinted by permission.

this sets it apart from other so-called socialist revolutions, which with the possible exception of China could more properly be termed mixed socialist-capitalist.

The preceding chapters have presented the factual information that is available in regard to various aspects of the country. Numerous statements of Fidel Castro have been quoted to indicate the goals of the revolution. The kind of society that is to be established is one without any capitalistic taint, where everyone will work for the good of the whole society, where selfishness will be replaced with altruism, and where the abundance that will result from the enthusiastic hard labor of the producing masses will be shared equally by all and be free to all. Money, "that vile intermediary," will disappear. These are the major goals, but the underlying necessity for their attainment is the *formación* of the new man. Our tentative appraisal of the revolution will be presented under rubrics which cover its moral, social economic, and political aspects.

THE MORAL REFORMS

The revolution has taken a puritanical attitude in the matter of morals. The logic is that immorality such as existed in the old Cuba was associated with capitalism, even caused by capitalism. Capitalism was the main target for destruction and with it all its evil concomitants. Besides, the necessity for economic survival made indulgence in time-wasting and energy-consuming vices, along with idleness and laziness, a kind of behavior to be forbidden.

Thus one of the early acts of the Castro government was to abolish prostitution. Practitioners of the oldest profession were taught new skills that would enable them to support themselves in a life of rectitude. Many societies have tried to suppress or control prostitution, with indifferent results, and reports from Cuba suggest that the effort has not been completely successful there. Lee Lockwood, in his interview with Castro in 1965, noted the continuation of the "Cuban institution of the *posada,*" a slang word for a "motel-like place where couples go to make love, no questions asked." While this is not prostitution, it is nevertheless sexual relations outside marriage. Other visitors to the country have noted the persistence of prostitution and Castro himself chastized some young people for engaging in this practice in his address of September 28, 1968. Notwithstanding the failure to achieve complete suppression, the regime must be given credit for its effort.

Gambling was likewise associated with capitalism, and because Americans were the major patrons as well as operators of the casinos, this evil was doubly contemptible to the regime. Another reason for abolishing gambling was the part it had played in the corruption of government officials, a practice which the new leaders were also determined to wipe out. Most people will agree that the elimination of gambling was a highly desirable action. It was condoned and approved as a tourist attraction, and tourism was a major source of income, yet its immoral concomitants, as well as gambling itself, are degrading to society.

The old Cuban institution of the lottery was also abolished. It had a history of dishonest administration and was used by politicians to enrich themselves. Thousands of poor people made a few pesos by selling lottery tickets, while other thousands purchased them by scraping together pesos and centavos which should have gone for more useful ends. It was not a social asset to the nation, and when the government decided to use the purchase of lottery tickets as a means of personal savings, instead of distributing the money in the form of winnings, most people again would applaud the action. Nevertheless Cubans soon lost interest in the project and it was scrapped. Cockfighting was also forbidden. This sport had long been a favorite recreation of the peasants, and previous regimes, under pressure from groups concerned about cruelty to animals, had tried to suppress it without much success.

But the most important moral reform occurred in the public offices when stealing from the government was made a capital offense. Much has been said and written about maladministration of public monies in Cuba by government officials. The practice has been condoned on the theory that Cuba lacked sufficient experience in self-government to develop standards of political integrity. Moreover, the existence of sinecures was often justified because the widespread unemployment in private industry made the government the only source of support for many persons. However, such arguments do not justify the excesses of most of the republican governments since the presidency of Tomás Estrada Palma.

While nobody at all acquainted with Cuba is naïve enough to think that political integrity has been universally achieved, overnight as it were, the regime must be given high marks for effort. Although honesty in government had been given high priority by reform groups for many decades, Castro is the first leader since Estrada Palma to attempt to establish it as a norm.

SOCIAL ACHIEVEMENTS

EDUCATION.   The accomplishments of the Castro regime in providing schooling for the population must be considered as a major achievement. No other aspect of the revolutionary program has attained and merited such wide acclaim. The literacy campaign of 1961 was a spectacular event, though it was more important as a socializing process than in actually ridding the country of illiteracy. The regime itself maintained that the persons involved were brought only to the first-grade level and that only continuous study beyond that level could prevent a lapse into illiteracy again. It is to the credit of the regime that opportunities for adult education were provided by means of classwork at the labor centers, correspondence courses, and special scholarships for full-time attendance at regular schools for former illiterates.

Assuredly few would question the desirability of universal literacy among citizens of modern societies. But one may question the advantage of reading skills to Cubans whose reading matter is completely censored. The newspapers are now little more than propaganda leaflets, concerned chiefly with the glorious achievements of the revolution, the evil machinations of Yankee imperialism, and internal difficulties in the United States. Beyond the dreary press, Cubans are restricted to the works of Marx and Lenin and writers of similar persuasion.

The educational system is similarly geared to the production of a generation inculcated with the revolutionary point of view. This applies not only in political matters, where no criticism of the government is tolerated, but also in the choice of a career. An emphasis on technology and science pervades the curriculum. In his speech on September 28, 1968, Castro predicted that "in twelve years the number of intermediate-level technicians in our country will not be below 800,000. Some people will say, 'Is everybody to become a technician?' Yes, everybody will have to become a technician, because there will not be a single activity in the future which will not require solid training. . . ."

In regard to higher education, a knowledgeable commentator who visited the island in late 1969 summarized the future as follows:

> The régime contemplates nothing less than universal education up to and including university level. The three existing universities have been condemned as citadels of privilege and are to be abolished as such. They will be converted into institutes of advanced research while facilities for university-level studies, heavily slanted toward science and technology, will be provided at the main centers of work throughout the country — a system of apprenticeship on a national scale combining study with productive work. How this is to be achieved in terms of teachers, buildings and equipment has not been made clear, but nothing could be more egalitarian than the intention. The entire population is to pass through the same educational mill.

The regime is able to regulate the number of students in any specialty through entrance examinations and the awarding of scholarships. A student who was in his fifth year at the University of Havana before he went into exile states that "government control of university affairs is complete. The Department of State Security (state police) has numerous agents in the University. . . . All students are encouraged to join the Union of Young Communists. . . . Many students were expelled from the university when the UJC held public assemblies accusing groups of students of being counter-revolutionaries or homosexuals." The government's extremely harsh treatment of homosexuals, it should be mentioned, is a demerit in the area of moral reform.

HEALTH AND MEDICAL FACILITIES.   The revolution has less to show for its efforts in the field of health care than in that of education, and for these reasons: (1) in 1958 Cuba already had a good program; (2) the revolution, by its policies, in effect encouraged the emigration of about a third of its physicians, thus setting back the program which was already under way; (3) serious questions can be raised about the efficacy of the rural hospital construction program.

It must be admitted that rural people in the more remote areas of prerevolutionary Cuba were poorly provided with, or completely lacked ready access to, medical help. Cuban medical personnel, along with hospitals and other facilities, were highly concentrated in urban centers. Moreover, many of the rural population were too poor to afford medical care or even to get to centers where free care was available. Bad roads in remote areas also made it difficult to obtain medical attention. It is impossible, however, to estimate how much of the population was truly deprived of needed medical care because of poverty or isolation.

In 1958 Cuba had a rather complex system for providing health care. Physicians in private practice charged patients on a fee-for-service basis. But there were many doctors employed on salary by the widespread mutual associations. These cooperatives have had a long history in the island. In the late colonial period Spanish immigrants from various provinces of the homeland organized clubs for various purposes, including recreation, children's education, and the provision of medical care on a prepaid monthly basis. Before long, the membership requirement was changed so that practically any person could be admitted regardless of the province of origin in Spain. By the late 1920's so many residents of Havana were receiving medical service through these associations that there was little opportunity for private practice. The doctors finally organized a strike. . . .

Since the conquest of yellow fever, typhoid, and certain other contagious diseases, Cuba has had a remarkably low death rate. Indeed, it is among the lowest in the world. And while other statistics on vital rates have been subject to serious question in the past, those regarding deaths are relatively reliable, because bodies cannot be interred without a death certificate. The general and infant mortality rates are shown in the table. Even though these rates have increased significantly since 1958, they are still very low in comparison with other countries of the world. The mortality rate in the United States, for example, was 9.5 in 1958 and the infant mortality rate 26.9 per thousand live births.

The revolutionary government claims that the general health of the people has improved. . . . There has been an apparent decline in the incidence of malaria and in deaths from gastroenteritis since 1964, but diptheria, hepatitis, leprosy, measles, syphilis, and tuberculosis are still problems. . . .

THE REAL HEALTH PROBLEM. As the International Bank mission reported in 1951, "Cuba is relatively free from diseases. One foreign official of long experience pointed out, no disease has reached epidemic proportions in the past twenty years and he could not remember even having to issue an unclean bill of health. . . . Plants managers, too, and others concerned with industry expressed the opinion that health was not a major problem *in industry,* except that the statutory nine days sick leave a year adds to the cost of labor."

However, the report went on to point out that a problem of general health existed because of inadequate diets, poor sanitation, and parasites. The author, on the basis of his own observations in 1945–46, can bear witness to this fact.

General and Infant Mortality Rates in Cuba [a]

Year	Total Mortality Rate	Infant Mortality Rate	Infant Deaths as Percentage of All Deaths
1953	5.8	37.6	. . .
1958	4.9	33.7	13.9
1959	6.6	34.5	15.1
1960	6.3	35.4	. . .
1961	6.6	37.2	19.6
1962	7.3	39.6	20.5
1963	6.8	37.6	20.1
1964	6.4	37.8	21.0
1965	6.5	37.7	20.3
1966	6.5	37.6	. . .
1967	6.4	. . .	. . .

[a] The general mortality rate is per thousand inhabitants, while the infant rate is the number per thousand live births.

The remedy is not necessarily hospitals, however, but improvement of the diet (which is based too much on starchy foods) and education in sanitation. There is, of course, great need for better housing, which would go far toward improving health generally.

THE REVOLUTION AND THE ECONOMY

On July 20, 1969, Castro asserted: "The greatness of . . . the ten years that have passed lies mainly in the fact that it was necessary to start practically from zero, that it was necessary to do everything." Other observers, both Cubans and Americans, have made similar statements. In previous chapters we have given the answer to these unfounded claims. Yet the progress of the revolution in the field of economic activity must be evaluated by what it had to begin with. Indeed, to be quite fair, the revolution should be measured by what development would have taken place without it. This factor is, of course, unknowable, but it should not be forgotten that an important pace of development was under way in the late 1950's.

While Cuba was not a fully developed economy, it was by no means the economic wasteland which the propaganda of the revolution tries to paint. On at least one commonly used index, Cuba in 1957 ranked 32 among 127 countries of the world, that is, in the upper quarter. It will be useful to summarize the economic position of prerevolutionary Cuba.

In 1958 the island possessed the largest cane-sugar-producing complex in the world, efficiently operated under trained and experienced managerial and technical personnel. It was rapidly becoming Cuban-owned. Of 161 centrals, 121 were owned by Cubans. The growers of sugarcane — the colonos and the owner-operators of farms — enjoyed relative security. The colonos paid a nominal rent, but enjoyed a security of occupancy practically equivalent to ownership. The major human problem in sugar production was the large unemployment of farm workers during half or more of the year.

Outside the sugar economy, other aspects of agriculture were advancing. Most notable in increased production was rice. From 1940, when imports amounted to 95 percent of consumption, production grew by 1956 to a point where only 44 percent was imported. Increase had been steady and doubtless would have continued. Livestock, notably cattle herds, supplied the nation with a per capital annual yield of around 75 pounds. Herds and pastures were rapidly undergoing improvement. Estimates of the number of cattle in 1958 vary, but there appear to have been around six million head. . . .

On January 1, 1959, Cuba's rather substantial economic resources were taken over by a group of young men and women who had little previous experience in any form of management and who were especially ignorant about agriculture, the nation's basic industry; a group of young people full of utopian dreams, enamored of political power, animated by excessive hatred for the entrepreneurs whose leadership had brought the country to its present state of economic development, and with a patronizing attitude toward the workers and peasants who had furnished the brawn and skills in constructing the economy.

The consequence to Cuba has been an almost unmitigated economic disaster. "Almost" because there have been important, but often wasteful, investments in irrigation, roads, and other parts of the infrastructure. But aside from fishing, there was not a single item in the range of agricultural and livestock products which after twelve years equaled or surpassed the per capita production of 1958. Even in sugar, after a year-long focus of effort of the whole population, production failed by a considerable amount to equal the per capita production of 1952. (In 1952 the estimated population was 5,300,000 and sugar production was 7,298,000 tons; the 1970 census showed a population of 8,553,395 and the sugar production was 8,500,000 tons.) The wreckage of the early years of the regime set back Cuba's economic development for years. It is a sad story, an unhappy story — unhappy for the more than 600,000 Cubans who left the country, were imprisoned, or served in labor camps. It is an unhappy story too for the people of the islands who have endured a decade of privation and hard labor and who have been fed on promises delayed of fulfillment.

The available evidence reveals that Fidel Castro's leadership in economic matters has been the major impediment to progress. He made three major mistakes and each time survived politically to continue making unwise decisions. The first mistake was his provocative behavior during the 1959–1960 controversy with the United States which led to the break in diplomatic relations. As noted earlier, not all the blame was Castro's, but to him belongs the major part.

The second error of major magnitude was the attempt at instant industrialization and diversification, with its consequent wastage of labor and capital resources. The third major misjudgment was the drive for the ten-million-ton sugar crop in 1970. All these mistakes have either explicitly or implicitly been acknowledged.

Beyond these misadventures, the prime minister makes day-to-day decisions without submitting them to his advisers for discussion. Castro's ego-involvement with the revolution is so intense that he feels he must make all major decisions and even many minor ones, and he cannot bring himself to delegate responsibility to others. This means that there are no opportunities for others around him to gain experience in managing the country. Castro's intense psychological need to be the sole decision-maker, whether the decision involves social, political, economic, or scientific matters, encourages sycophancy; only yes-men are tolerable. Castro's own judgment at this state of the revolution is that the economy is in a precarious condition, that austerity will continue, and that there is no hope of improvement until after 1975.

THE LEADER AND THE MASSES

The political system created in Cuba does not allow the citizenry an effective voice in policy determination. Decisions are made at the top and communicated downward to the workers and peasants. Once policy decisions have been announced by Castro and sent down through the political channels, it is up to the representatives of government and party at the base levels to see that they are implemented. The workers and peasants are simply told what has to be done; they have no part in the original decision.

This is undoubtedly a major reason why the performance of the workers has been less than the regime had hoped for. Only after the failure of 1970 did the prime minister seem to realize what had gone wrong. In his speech of September 28, 1970, he spoke of "democratization," and there followed the almost interminable series of meetings to discuss the law against loafing. It was a comparatively trivial matter to justify such elaborate "participation" by the population. More significant was the permission granted to local labor centers to nominate and elect their officers. It would seem to most observers that much more is needed. Even in 1965 Lee Lockwood raised with Castro questions about some orderly structure, such as a constitution, which would provide a mechanism of a formal character. Rather vaguely, the prime minister indicated that something might be ready by 1970 to provide for a "continuous participation of the masses in the political apparatus." "The working masses," he said, "will be the members of the Party. The Party will be something like a combined parliament of the workers and interpreters of their will." Castro appears to have lost interest in bringing this idea to realization.

"The building of socialism," warns Karol, "cannot be the business of one man or of a single group of men, however well-intentioned. If the socialist ship is to come safely into harbor, everyone alike must take to his oars — a few men rowing up in front are not enough." Otherwise, the "result is bound to be apathy and a general flagging of political interest." Castro seems to have taken heed of this advice in the modest gestures made toward labor in late 1970 and continuing in 1971. There has also been a proposal to reform the judicial structure which will allow the election of judges to serve on the people's courts.

However, it seems likely that the development of democratic structures to permit others to participate in policy formation will be difficult for a man of Castro's character. Matthews makes the comment that Castro "had no concept of the true meaning of freedom and democracy and was never to have one . . . that he had a complete blind spot in his mentality. He still does not realize it himself. It took a gradual unfolding of Cuban developments to make it clear that so long as Fidel Castro remains in power there will not be and cannot be democracy and freedom in Cuba." Karol makes a somewhat different diagnosis of the Castro personality: "All his arguments betray an aristocratic spirit, a faith in the role of the elite," rather than trust "in the fruitful exchange of ideas between the rank and file and the leaders." This analysis of Castro's temperament may be different, but the consequences are much the same as the ones stated by Matthews.

THE FOREIGN TRADE PREDICAMENT

It is axiomatic that unless production can be increased in all phases of the national economic life, the revolution is on a shaky foundation. A major difficulty stems from the change in trading partners. To be dependent on trade with Soviet Russia, several thousand miles away, instead of the United States, ninety miles distant, is patently absurd. Soviet oil tankers, after coming from the Black Sea, through the Mediterranean, and across the Atlantic, arrive every two to three days in a Cuban port. This bridge of tankers, spread over 6,000 miles of water, is the lifeline for the country since there is no other source of fuel. A tanker from Venezuela travels about 750 miles.

The growing dependence upon Soviet financial and military support is the consequence of the mistakes made by the Cuban leadership, including among others the doctrinaire insistence on moral incentives for labor to which the workers have failed to respond. The flagging morale of the Cuban people, however, cannot be cured by any resort to material rewards, since there are no longer any desirable objects which increased money income could buy. The resort to a form of coercion is the only means now open to the leadership.

How deeply in debt is Cuba? Figures for the years after 1967 are not available. A summation of the annual values of exports and imports from 1959 through 1967 shows imports of 7,327.1 million pesos and exports of 5,647.4 million pesos, leaving a cumulative trade imbalance for these years of 1,679.7 million pesos. For the preceding comparable nine years, 1950 through 1958, there was a favorable balance of trade amounting to 539.3 million pesos. . . .

From 1966 to 1970 sugar commitments to Russia totaled 22 million tons. But Cuban production during these five years was only 28.9 million tons, and obviously the USSR has had to forgo much of the sugar promised by its

Western partner. René Dumont estimated in 1969 that Cuba was 8 million tons short on its commitment to the Soviets. At 6.11 cents per pound, which the prime minister said in his address of May 20, 1970, was the rate paid by the USSR, the dollar value of the shortage would be $972 million.

These various sources indicate that the debt of Cuba to the USSR is not less than $1 billion and may be in excess of $2 billion. Indeed an estimate of $2 billion may be too conservative. In testimony before the Subcommittee on Inter-American Affairs of the House of Representatives on July 8, 1970, Robert A. Hurwitch of the state department said that "we estimate that Cuba has received $3.2 billion in economic assistance from the Soviet Union." He also said the estimated daily cost to the USSR was $1.4 million, which amounts to $511 million per year. Whatever the true amounts of Cuba's trade may be, there is sufficient evidence to show that the country is in serious economic trouble.

In 1969 the prime minister told a graduating class: "We have known the bitterness of having to depend on others and how this can be turned into a weapon against us." He referred, of course, to the United States, but the Cuban people now know what it is to be dependent upon the USSR. It is clear that the Soviets have a very expensive welfare client, and only they can decide whether the political dividends are worth the economic losses.

It is obvious, though, that Cuba's protector has begun to pay much closer attention to its client. The new trade agreement with the Soviet Union negotiated in late 1970 called for the creation of a joint Soviet-Cuban economic commission. This follows a pattern of relationships which the USSR has with other aid recipients. It most likely means a larger role of the Soviets in Cuban affairs.

Observers have also noted that the star of the old Communist Carlos Rafael Rodríguez appears to be rising. It was he who negotiated the new agreement for economic cooperation and he is chairman of the Cuban side of the new commission. Officials of very high level, along with numerous technicians and advisers, pour into Cuba as never before. The technicians are no longer limiting themselves to advising their counterparts in Havana, but are spreading over the countryside as well. . . .

BEYOND CASTRO

Difficult as it is to imagine the Cuban Revolution without Fidel Castro, such a condition must be faced eventually. Not that he is in any immediate danger, as far as anyone outside can know. Indeed, the security measures invoked especially since 1967 against enemies, real or potential, provide a reasonable guarantee of the safety of the regime in general and of the prime minister in particular. Still all men are mortal, and dictatorships in Latin America have all been of limited duration. Granted that Castro's tenure has been one of the longest and that his particular regime is different from any others that have existed in the hemisphere, it is certain to finally terminate.

What might be the situation in Cuba without Fidel Castro, the man who made and has led the revolution for thirteen years? First of all, the naming of his successor may be critical. There are two considerations on this point: Castro has already designated his brother Raúl to succeed him, and there is no constitutional alternative procedure providing for succession. Since Raúl is minister of the armed forces, his chances of making good his succession should be favorable. Yet Raúl lacks the charisma and other personal qualities which have made his brother so effective. How popular Raúl is with the officers over whom he has command and how he is regarded by his associates in the Politburo and the Central Committee of the party are not known.

There are thus many imponderables. One of them is the extent to which loyalty that the armed forces personnel and particularly the officers have sworn to Fidel can be transferred to Raúl. The same consideration applies to party officials. The leadership potential in the military and the party is not known, but in case of a power struggle any latent leaders may well surface and challenge the Castro group. It can generally be assumed that a totalitarian leader who gains and maintains power by violence builds up a reservoir of hatred in the process. The Castros are unlikely to be exceptions.

In regard to the military, it should be kept in mind that both personnel and equipment have been improved recently; specialized cadet schools were established in 1968 and Russia has been providing new armaments since that year. In addition, the police force has been enlarged and given extra training and more equipment. It is in itself a power to be reckoned with. Again, the loyalty of these groups to the regime in general is an important element.

Finally, should a power struggle develop, another major factor may prove to be the workers. The older ones have long since become disillusioned with the labor policies of the revolution. Any concerted action on their part to shut down operations might cause chaos in an already shaky economy.

Casting a shadow over any development in the future is the Soviet Union, with its vast economic and political investment in Cuba. Cuba's dependence upon it could give it veto power over any change, including the naming of Fidel Castro's successor.

In regard to post-Castro policies, we may venture two possibilities: first, a continuation of the Castro program, and second, some constrained adaptation in the economic area in the form of material incentives for labor in order to

achieve greater productivity. On the first proposition, it is arguable that who-
ever the successor, and whatever the circumstances of his coming to power,
there will be at first few if any changes in economic or political policies. It
will be a waiting period, during which everyone identified closely with the
revolution will be concerned above all with its preservation. There remains
in Cuba a latent remnant of the old republican democracy which would like
to see a return to representative government. Its strength is unknown, but it
remains a threat of consequence to the regime. With their vested interests in
the revolution, the present leaders must prevent a successful uprising of the
old democracy, since they would in all probability suffer the same consequences that they inflicted on the ones they overthrew. There will be a period
when, in spite of differences among them, the leaders will follow the admoni-
tion of Benjamin Franklin to another group of revolutionaries: "We must
indeed all hang together, or, most assuredly, we shall all hang separately."

If there has been no improvement in the economic situation when the
crisis comes — and Castro promises none before 1975 — the people will be
as restless as ever and possibly even more ready to join in a complete overthrow. This is another reason for the successors to hold a tight rein.

On the other hand, a continuation of unrest and low productivity should
suggest some changes in the direction of gradual relaxation of policy in favor
of individual initiative. One would think small enterprises might be permitted,
particularly in the service area. For despite the government's announced determination in 1968 to root out capitalism, Castro admitted the existence of a
blackmarket on May 1, 1971. Peasants would be more enthusiastic producers
if they were allowed — as they were in the early years — to market some of
their goods privately. Labor would be stimulated if there were less emphasis
on moral and more on material incentives. The USSR would hardly be likely
to oppose such moves, since they are in harmony with its own practices.

No general uprising is to be anticipated, given the measures of control that
exist. Civil war would not be possible, short of a major split in the armed
forces, which is unlikely. Barring a complete overturn, another revolution, the
more than 600,000 refugees face the likelihood of permanent exile. About one
thousand acknowledge this probability monthly by becoming United States
citizens. Nevertheless, if Cuba were "liberated" anew, as it were, and there
was a return to a constitutional democracy, the call of the homeland would be
strong. Moreover, those who have done well abroad because of their special
talents and enterprise would be able to make an enormous contribution to the
rehabilitation of Cuba. The erosion of time on the fortunes of the refugees is
one of the most pathetic aspects of the revolution.

But to leave the rarefied air of speculation and return to the *tierra firme* of reality, Cubans must face the prospect in the immediate years ahead of continued hardship without hope of improvement. Unrest and discontent cannot fail to continue and increase. This leaves us with the uncertainty that anything can happen where there is deprivation, disillusionment, and increasing suppression.

57. *United States Relations with the Dominican Republic, Indeed with the Caribbean Generally, Are a Tale of Mutual Frustration*

ABRAHAM F. LOWENTHAL

Abraham F. Lowenthal has studied intensively the tangled questions involved in the 1965 intervention in his book, *The Dominican Intervention* (Cambridge, Mass.: Harvard University Press, 1972), and in a number of articles. The following excerpts provide an illuminating background for this unfortunate episode.

The history of U.S. relations with the Dominican Republic, indeed with the Caribbean region generally, is a tale of mutual frustration. Perhaps in no other country has the influence of the United States been so long and so continuously exerted as in the Dominican Republic, yet in few places have the limits of America's power to transform foreign realities been more evident. Three times within sixty years — in 1905, in 1916, and in 1965 — the United States sent the Marines to Santo Domingo, but these military interventions are only the most dramatic episodes in a record of extraordinary American involvement in Dominican affairs, involvement which preceded the first intervention and survives the third.

Events in the Dominican Republic, for instance, occasioned the "Roosevelt corollary" to the Monroe Doctrine, the initial U.S. interest in customs receivership, and undisguised American efforts to dictate public policies of the Dominican government — all before the U.S. military occupation of 1916–24.

Abraham F. Lowenthal, "The United States and the Dominican Republic to 1965: Background to Intervention," *Caribbean Studies*, 10 (1970), no. 2 (July 1970): 30–55. Reprinted by permission of the author and The Institute of Caribbean Studies. Copyright 1970 by The Institute of Caribbean Studies, University of Puerto Rico.

More recently, in the five years before the 1965 intervention, the U.S. Government undertook a wide variety of activities in the Dominican Republic, among them: implementing OAS-approved sanctions against the brutal Trujillo dictatorship; using the threat of military force to stabilize a volatile situation after the dictatorship's sudden end; expending foreign aid for immediate political purposes; helping to organize and assure free elections under OAS supervision; assisting the elected government through the Alliance for Progress; strengthening some groups through political development programs and reinforcing others through military assistance and training; attempting to deter and then to reverse an unconstitutional change of government by threatening to withhold recognition and suspend aid and then by doing so; pressuring for a return to constitutional procedure through national elections; and eventually aiding the unconstitutional regime in many ways — funding its development programs, training its police, even providing it tactical political advice — although the promised elections were not held.

Review of this troubled history suggests that the United States has long been deeply, pervasively, but somewhat reluctantly involved in Dominican affairs. The extent of American involvement in the Dominican Republic has almost always been extraordinarily great. Its nature has been mainly preemptive and its principal motivation has been the protection of U.S. security.

Although the landing of American troops at Santo Domingo in 1965 shocked even knowledgeable observers of U.S. policy in Latin America, it should not really have been so surprising if seen in the context of previous American relations with the Dominican Republic and the rest of the Caribbean. Earlier American involvements in the area did not make inevitable the 1965 military intervention, but they did help shape the attitudes of American officials and thus made the Dominican episode more likely. An analysis of this history and its effects on American attitudes and assumptions will make the events of 1965 easier to comprehend.

Although nominally sovereign and independent since 1844, the Dominican Republic has never been able to exclude the predominant influence of the United States. As early as 1849 one Dominican president approached Washington to request that the Dominican Republic be annexed. This particular overture was rejected, but the American government's special interest in conditions on the island of Hispaniola (which the Dominican Republic shares with Haiti) due to the "proximity of that island to the United States" was noted by President Millard Fillmore in his Annual Message to Congress a year later.

Several times during the rest of the nineteenth century, American officials negotiated with Dominicans on proposed annexation agreements. Even more often, U.S. and Dominican representatives discussed proposals to grant the U.S. government special rights and concessions, particularly for use of Samaná Bay. None of these discussions ever produced lasting agreement, but one annexation proposal — strenuously backed by President U. S. Grant — did reach the floor of the Senate in 1870; half of the fifty-six senators present at the vote supported the plan.

Four scholarly analyses of successive periods in Dominican-American relations reveal the deepening U.S. involvement in Dominican affairs from 1870 to 1915. During the last quarter of the nineteenth century, "relations were necessarily of an intimate nature," and American engagement increased as U.S. private interests expanded and U.S. strategic horizons broadened. At the turn of the century, the establishment of the San Domingo Improvement Company — organized to collect the Dominican government's debts to foreign bond-holders — climaxed "two decades of steady advance toward American commercial and economic dominance of the Dominican Republic." The U.S. government's support for the San Domingo Company, another analyst concludes, "marked the beginning of a more active participation by the United States in the Dominican Republic — leading to closer control of the country's economy" as the twentieth century opened. During the first two decades of this century, a fourth scholar notes, "in no Latin American country were the economic and political intervention by the United States more in evidence nor carried farther towards their logical conclusion than in the Dominican Republic."

Step by step the U.S. government involved itself ever more deeply in Dominican affairs. Having supported the claims of the San Domingo Improvement Company on the Dominican government's resources, the U.S. government next — under President Theodore Roosevelt — asserted the right to collect customs charges at Santo Domingo and other Dominican ports in order to guarantee that the Dominican government would pay its debts. Once established, U.S. control of Dominican customs' collection paved the way for American demands to exercise final authority on the Dominican government's expenditure of revenue collected by the customs' receivership. Soon the United States government demanded, as well, the right to dictate specific policies to the Dominican government. American officials were particularly eager that the Dominicans disband their armies and establish a national constabulary under U.S. supervision, and also that Dominican factions agree to hold U.S.-supervised elections and pledge to respect the results. When the Dominican government balked at these and similar demands, the stage was set in 1916 for President Woodrow Wilson to send in the Marines.

Once the Marines landed, U.S. officials thought it necessary to establish an outright military government in the Dominican Republic. For eight years American military and civilian personnel ruled the Dominican Republic directly, taking over every branch of public administration. American troops attempted to impose order, American officers trained and commanded a Dominican constabulary, American revenue agents collected taxes, American engineers built roads and bridges, American bureaucrats set up a civil service system and reformed the post office, and American educators revamped the Dominican Republic's schools.

The occupation period marked the height of American intervention in Dominican affairs, but strong U.S. influence was assured even after the Marines withdrew and an elected Dominican regime took office in 1924. The United States–Dominican Republic Convention of that year reserved several rights to the U.S. government, and it appears that American officials considered the threat of renewed military intervention a legitimate means of assuring that these rights would be respected. Even after the Franklin Roosevelt administration formally renounced unilateral intervention as a policy instrument, the U.S. maintained its customs receivership officially until 1941 and retained other fiscal controls over the Dominican government until 1947.

U.S. entanglement in Dominican affairs decreased somewhat during the long Trujillo period, from 1930 to 1961. The last years of the Trujillo era, however, brought renewed American involvement. The U.S. government's decision in 1960 to go beyond the diplomatic and economic sanctions the OAS had voted against Trujillo by imposing a special fee on the purchase of Dominican sugar served to strengthen the will of Dominicans opposed to Trujillo and thus brought the U.S. government back into Dominican politics as a key actor. American officials in Santo Domingo identified and encouraged a group of anti-Trujillo Dominicans, assuring them that the United States government would cooperate with them should they gain power. According to some reports, U.S. agents may even have materially aided the Dominican plot which culminated with Trujillo's assassination on May 30, 1961.

Whatever the accuracy of the rumors about American complicity in Trujillo's death, it is clear that by the time Trujillo died the U.S. government was prepared once again to participate actively and directly in Dominican affairs. The extent of American involvement soon became extraordinary; from mid-1960 through 1962, writes Jerome Slater, the "United States in the Dominican Republic engaged in the most massive intervention in the affairs of a Latin American state since the inauguration of the Good Neighbor Policy." Employing a wide variety of instruments, American officials sought to help the

Dominican Republic move through the difficult transition from tyranny through disorder to constitutional democracy. . . .

Although deep and pervasive, the U.S. government's involvement in the Dominican Republic, and in the Caribbean area generally, has rarely, if ever, been positive and whole-hearted. The tension in Dominican history between the desire for protection, even for annexation, and the demand for full sovereignty has been mirrored in the United States by the conflicting pull between the urge to control foreign events and the ideal of national self-determination. Strong currents of opinion favoring respect for Dominican sovereignty have influenced U.S. policy time and again.

In the 19th century, the U.S. government several times resisted proposals put forth by Dominican politicians that the U.S. should annex the Dominican Republic. When President Grant finally sought to win the Senate's approval of annexation, vigorous opposition led by Senator Charles Sumner defeated the plan. More recently, the U.S. military interventions of 1916 and 1965 offended many American opinion leaders almost as much as they inflamed Dominican passions; both interventions were affected by domestic American opposition. All through the history of American relations with the Caribbean, indeed, runs a thread of unwanted engagement. The U.S. government has been much more concerned about how to withdraw and decrease its involvement in the Caribbean than with how to intervene there. Periods of especially intense American participation in the Caribbean (and in the Dominican Republic specifically) have characteristically been followed by years in which American officials attempted to abstain from overt involvement.

If the United States has not sought to annex the Dominican Republic, has rejected several obvious opportunities to do so, and even has sought periodically to reduce its involvement in Dominican and Caribbean affairs, why then has it continuously become so engaged in Dominican politics? What explains the U.S. government's persistent entanglement in the Dominican Republic over the years?

Many discussions of American involvement in the Caribbean stress the supposed importance of positive U.S. interests in the area, primarily economic. The whole record of American involvement in the area, however, suggests that the main interest of the U.S. government has not been economic. Security concerns and traditional axioms, not simple conquest or profit, have motivated American involvement in the Dominican Republic and the rest of the Caribbean for many decades.

Private economic interests — mainly of dubious adventurers at first, later of banks and investment houses, and in this century mainly of sugar and fruit producers — have been important in drawing the U.S. government's attention to the Dominican Republic. Undoubtedly they have influenced American policy on occasion, especially through personal relations with U.S. diplomatic representatives in Santo Domingo. But by and large, the pressure of existing business interests on American policy towards the Dominican Republic does not appear to have been substantial or effective, particularly in recent years; the U.S. government has increasingly tended to resist overt business pressures when they have been exerted.

Nor does it seem that prospective trade and investment opportunities have importantly affected American involvement in the Dominican Republic, for the country's size and resources simply have not been sufficient to attract significant U.S. commercial interests. Far from being embroiled in Dominican affairs to protect existing or proposed U.S. private interests there, the U.S. government has actually sought to spur American investment in the Dominican Republic in support of government policy. The initiative for much recent U.S. investment, like that of the "dollar diplomacy" of another era, has come from Washington, not from the business community.

Elsewhere in the Caribbean, where the United States has established and maintained important military facilities, these have undoubtedly been a cause of continuing American interest. The military advantages the Dominican Republic could offer to the United States have never been of major significance, however. The U.S. has never established a permanent military base in the Dominican Republic. The missile tracking station set up there in 1951 was never of vital importance and was abandoned by 1962. It is true that American authorities were interested a century ago in the possibilities of using Samaná and Manzanillo Bays for coaling stations or naval bases, and that some interest in Samaná continued into this century, but the main reason for continuing American concern about Samaná seems to have been to assure that the bay would not be used by Germany nor any other European power. . . .

Positive economic and military interests, then, do not account for the history of intense American involvement in Dominican affairs. The chief goal of U.S. policy, rather, has been pre-emptive. The means used by the U.S. government have varied, but the fundamental U.S. aim in the Dominican Republic and the entire Caribbean has always been the same: to assure that no situation actually or even potentially damaging to U.S. security has a chance to develop. The main concern has been to prevent the introduction into the Caribbean of any new foreign influence which might oppose the United States. Proclaimed as policy by President James Monroe in 1823, the U.S. aim to keep new foreign influence out of the Caribbean has ever since been considered "doctrine" with the force of axiom, if not of international law.

Ever since the Dominican Republic achieved formal independence in 1844, the U.S. government has aimed to prevent any external power from gaining influence there. President Polk in 1846, for example, expressed his fear that a European power might exert control over Santo Domingo, and from that time on for several decades one of the chief concerns of "successive Secretaries of State was that some foreign nation might secure Samaná Bay as a naval base." Later in the century, increased U.S. participation in Dominican affairs was "motivated at least in part by the fear of foreign intervention, especially German, in the Caribbean area." Measures taken to assure the payment of bondholders were intended less to satisfy private American claims than to preclude European intervention to obtain repayment; the U.S. sought to stem the Dominican Republic's economic deterioration and "to prevent this weakness from becoming a threat to American security" by opening the way for the introduction of European influence. "Far from being an attempt to enslave the Dominican economy," another scholar argues, the 1907 Customs Convention was "designed to set it free from foreign shackles," that is, to minimize European influence.

At the turn of the century, after the local superiority of the U.S. force over any European power had been established by the Spanish-American War, U.S. concern in the Caribbean came to focus on the possibility that political turbulence among or within the countries of the region might somehow permit the quick introduction there of extracontinental power. To prevent this eventuality, the U.S. government undertook both to promote mechanisms for settling intra-regional disputes and to foster political stability within the countries of the region. The means chosen by the United States to promote internal stability, as well as the intensity of American interest in this aim, have varied as the actual possibilities of extracontinental exploitation of local turbulence have ebbed and flowed, and as the presumed causes of instability have been analyzed and re-examined. But the basic aim — to assure local political stability in order to exclude possible opportunities for the introduction of extracontinental power — has been the keystone of U.S. policy in the Dominican Republic and the rest of the Caribbean throughout this century. . . .

American concern with the Dominican Republic's stability, and with the over-riding aim of precluding the introduction into the Caribbean of extracontinental power, continued during the thirty-one years of Trujillo's regime. During the late 1920's and the 1930's, when no European power was capable of threatening the United States, the U.S. instituted toward Latin America what came to be known as the Good Neighbor Policy, under which the United

States renounced the practice of military intervention and announced its intent to refrain from participation in the internal politics of nations in the hemisphere. Consistent with this general policy, and later with the policy of supporting Latin American allies in World War II and then the Cold War, the United States maintained normal diplomatic relations with the Dominican Republic under Trujillo for three decades and even extended some economic and military assistance throughout the period. Given the continuing American aims, the U.S. stance was understandable, despite Trujillo's flagrant departures from the principles of the Atlantic Charter, the Act of Chapultepec, and the Charter of the United Nations. However illiberal, Trujillo did bring a temporary end to Dominican turmoil and to the immediate possibility that foreign powers could be introduced into the Dominican Republic, and his continuing opposition to the Axis powers (and then to the Communist bloc) seemed to be assured. As President Roosevelt is said to have remarked, Trujillo may have been an S.O.B., but "at least he's our S.O.B."

Only when events elsewhere made Trujillo seem more a threat than a source of stability in the Caribbean did American support for Trujillo end. The U.S. government's belated realization that Castro's easy displacement of Batista in Cuba might augur ill for Trujillo and other Caribbean strongmen, together with mounting evidence that Trujillo's inter-Caribbean enmities might exacerbate the region's problems and even some indications that Trujillo was trying to court the Soviet Union, induced the U.S. government in 1959 to re-examine its policy toward the Dominican Republic. Spurred also by pressures from Venezuela and Costa Rica to oppose right-wing dictatorships as a prelude to possible actions against Castro, the United States began then to disassociate itself from Trujillo and even to press for changes within the Dominican Republic.

Dropping its previously unreserved support for the non-intervention doctrine, the U.S. government began in 1960 actively to support proposals in the OAS aimed at inducing liberalization in the Dominican political structure. Both in concert with OAS members and on its own, the U.S. government undertook measures designed to bring an end to the Trujillo regime and to facilitate a transition to a new government with a better prospect of providing lasting stability. To head off a Castro-type movement in the Dominican Republic — with its potential for introducing extracontinental power into the Caribbean — the U.S. sought out and began to aid moderate anti-Communist opponents of Trujillo. Among those in the group which assassinated Trujillo in May, 1961, were men whom the U.S. government had encouraged to organize.

The objectives of American policy during the period of transition after

Trujillo's death were mixed. The newly-installed Kennedy Administration was committing itself in 1961 to encouraging economic development, social reform, and political democracy throughout the hemisphere. President Kennedy, in presenting the Alliance for Progress proposal in March, specifically mentioned his hope that the Dominican Republic — then still under Trujillo — could soon be included. Some in the Administration — particularly the Puerto Rican group to whom Kennedy had turned for help in formulating and implementing his Alliance program — hoped to transform the Dominican Republic into a special "showcase of democracy," a demonstration of the efficacy of development under democratic auspices.

But the primary emphasis of U.S. policy towards the Dominican Republic, even in the early Kennedy Administration, was the traditional aim to prevent any security threat from arising there, now cast with new urgency in terms of the need to prevent a "second Cuba." Part of the reason for regarding the Dominican Republic as a potential "second Cuba," no doubt, was Castro's announced interest in extending his revolution to Hispaniola, evidenced concretely by his support for the June, 1959, invasion of the Dominican Republic by anti-Trujillo Dominicans. More important, probably, was the simple fact of perceived analogy, however faulty. The Dominican Republic, like Cuba, was a sugar-producing island nation in the Caribbean ruled for many years by a corrupt praetorian dictator. Differences between the two islands, at very different levels of economic and political development and with very different histories, were obscured as American officials focused their attention on the supposed similarities. Unprepared to analyze Santo Domingo in terms of its own past, American observers attempted to interpret the complicated swirl of Dominican events by referring to the experience of neighboring Cuba, with which they were more familiar and which was salient in their minds.

Whatever the reasons, it is clear that by 1961 American officials regarded the Dominican Republic as a potential "second Cuba." Just days after the Bay of Pigs, President Kennedy personally approved a contingency plan for landing troops in the Dominican Republic which stressed as the principal policy guideline that the United States could not afford and would not permit the imposition in the Dominican Republic of a pro-Castro or pro-Communist government. This theme was repeated time and again in presidential instructions to U.S. officials concerned with the Dominican Republic. President Kennedy reportedly felt that his first year in office would be successful if neither the Dominican Republic nor the Congo were lost to international Communism. He is said to have believed that there were three possibilities in the Dominican Republic "in descending order of preference: a decent democratic regime, a continuation of the Trujillo regime, or a Castro regime." "We ought to aim at the first," Kennedy reportedly concluded, "but we can't really renounce the second until we are sure we can avoid the third."

The aim of preventing a "second Cuba" shaped American policy toward the Dominican Republic at every stage after Trujillo's death in May, 1961. The dispatch of a Navy Task Force to the vicinity of Santo Domingo in June, immediately after Trujillo's assassination, was meant specifically to preclude any possible pro-Communist movement and to prevent possible Cuban involvement. President Kennedy's instructions to Consul General John Calvin Hill in July emphasized his keen interest in the progress of anti-Communist laws and other measures designed to exclude Communists and Castroist exiles from the Dominican Republic and to oust Dominican Communists already there. The ambiguous stance the U.S. government adopted later that year with respect to the Balaguer regime reflected conflict between the desire to prevent immediate Communist subversion by strengthening Balaguer's hold and the belief that Communist prospects over a longer period might better be countered by providing the Dominican people an early opportunity to choose a new government through national elections. The eventual decisions to press for the removal, first of the Trujillo family and then of General Rodríguez Echavarría and of Balaguer himself, stemmed from the U.S. view that these steps would best foster stability and thus make it easier to exclude Communist influence. And throughout this period, and those that followed, conscious American efforts were made to strengthen the Dominican Armed Forces as a bulwark against possible Communist encroachments. . . .

This focus on precluding a possible "Communist take-over" continued after Juan Bosch took office on February 27, 1963. During the very week Bosch was inaugurated, Ambassador Martin found himself preoccupied by the reported presence in the Dominican Republic of eight Communist agents. The Ambassador's first duty after Bosch became President was to ask him to accept U.S. assistance to strengthen the Dominican government's security apparatus. Fron then on, Martin continuously stressed to Bosch the need to protect the Dominican Republic from "Castro-Communist" subversion. Among the specific measures Martin recommended to Bosch were to close a supposedly Communist school, to ban travel to Cuba, to propose a law permitting deportations, and even to "enact something like our Smith Act.". . .

Since the fundamental American objective in the Dominican Republic was never really to help Bosch or even his country but rather to prevent a "second Cuba," the U.S. government's reaction when Bosch was overthrown was not surprising. When Ambassador Martin asked the State Department late in September whether Washington would send an aircraft carrier to the Dominican Republic to show U.S. support for the badly-faltering Bosch regime, the Department refused unless a Communist takeover was threatened. Bosch's fall was thus assured.

The over-riding American concern for anti-Communist stability in the Dominican Republic continued after the 1963 coup. Despite President Kennedy's strong statement condemning the coup, the break in diplomatic relations, and the suspension of all American aid, it soon turned out that the U.S. government's support for the principle of "constitutionality" was somewhat ambiguous. American officials were much more interested in keeping Communists out of office than with helping Bosch or a constitutional successor get in. . . .

The U.S. government's involvement in the Dominican Republic in 1964–1965 was in many ways less active than it had been during the period of very intense American participation from 1961 to 1963. Just as the occupation period in the Dominican Republic and elsewhere in the Caribbean in the early 1920's brought about a period of American restraint in the area, so the extraordinary activity of Martin's tenure in the Dominican Republic (and of the dynamic activism of the early Kennedy Administration) was followed by an attempt to reduce the scope and depth of American involvement in Dominican affairs. Ambassador Bennett's personal attempt to limit his participation in Dominican politics, the reduced level of AID expenditures in the Dominican Republic, and Washington's support for an IMF-recommended economic austerity program were all aspects of a conscious attempt by American officials to deal with the Dominican Republic less intensely. The U.S. government was now trying to treat the Dominican Republic as one of very many nations with economic and political problems, which would not become a matter for priority attention in Washington unless American security appeared directly to be threatened.

American policy towards the Dominican Republic in 1965, as almost always before, was keyed not to opportunity but to threat. The Dominican Republic was approached, no longer as a possible "show-case for democracy," but still as a target of "Castro-Communist" subversion. American concern was focused on preventing a Communist takeover, on precluding a "second Cuba," and events were seen through this lens. Juan Bosch and the PRD [Democratic Revolutionary Party] were viewed, not as possible partners in the Alliance for Progress but as ineffectual reformers and politicians and, even worse, as likely dupes of Communist organizers. Dominican Communists, in turn, were seen not as weak and fragmented groups of dissidents, but as potential agents of extracontinental power. The Dominican Armed Forces were conceived, not primarily as rival bands of plunder, but as an institution opposed to instability and to Communist advance.

As for the overall role of the United States, positive commitments to assist desired Dominican changes were publicized, but the emphasis of American officials was on avoiding renewed entanglement in Dominican politics and on keeping the Dominican Republic "off the front burner." Largely because of all these attitudes and assumptions, events in Santo Domingo in 1965 which might otherwise have passed almost unnoticed — by the U.S. government, at least — had they occurred in some other area or era, were to become instead the background to intervention.

58. *The Dominican Revolution in Perspective*

HOWARD J. WIARDA

Professor Howard J. Wiarda of the University of Massachusetts, Amherst, has had a long-time research interest in Dominican political affairs. Here he meditates on the basic problems involved, raises some difficult questions, and describes the sources available for a study of this much-criticized intervention that apparently was an "important turning point" in United States relations with Latin America.

On April 24, 1965, a barracks revolt was launched in the Dominican Republic by military and civilian elements favoring the restoration of constitutional government in the country and the return of Juan Bosch, a social reformer with a large popular following, to the presidency. Overnight, what had begun as a palace coup turned into a bitter, bloody and hate-filled civil war which soon took on many aspects of a genuine social revolution. As the status quo-oriented Dominican military forces disintegrated and the popular "constitutionalist" forces appeared to be gaining the upper hand, the United States, on April 28, militarily intervened.

For a brief time in the Spring of 1965, the Dominican revolution and United States intervention were the subject of worldwide speculation; a large

"The Dominican Revolution in Perspective: A Research Note" by Howard J. Wiarda, *Polity*, 1 (1968), no. 1, pp. 114–124, passim. Reprinted by permission.

number of articles, speeches, newspaper headlines, books, and discussions at the highest levels resulted. For many, the Dominican actions of the United States were considered to signal a return to "gunboat diplomacy," an indication that the United States had reverted to the policy of siding with conservative oligarchies against the popular forces favoring radical societal change and revolutionary nationalism. Military intervention in the Dominican Republic was thought to represent a sharp reversal in United States foreign policy, and a variety of groups and individuals called for a reappraisal. Popular sentiment in the United States backed the government's action, but informed opinion makers here and abroad severely questioned the foreign policy orientation of the administration.

A number of indicators seemed to support the contention that the Dominican intervention was in fact an important turning point. It meant the end of the harmonious working arrangement between the Administration and the Congress, especially the Senate Foreign Relations Committee. Influential newspapers and periodicals roundly condemned the action of the President and his Latin America advisers. Most of the Latin American nations reacted strongly against the facile abandonment by the United States of the nonintervention principle, and throughout the world peoples and governments of various persuasions — including friends and allies of the United States — vigorously criticized the armed occupation of Santo Domingo. The United States posture toward the Dominican revolution led many to question whether American statements concerning liberty, social justice, democracy, self-determinacy, and sympathy toward nationalistic movements and assertions with regard to the just aspirations of the peoples of the emerging nations were anything more than empty rhetoric.

Escalation of the war in Vietnam — especially the acceleration of the bombing in the North during the summer and fall of 1965 — pushed the Dominican Republic, its revolution, and the United States intervention there out of the headlines. The world's attention shifted to the larger conflict in Southeast Asia, and the lingering crisis in the Caribbean was all but forgotten. The concerns of scholars, at least to a certain extent, also tend to follow the headlines, and since by this time the Dominican Republic and its revolution had been relegated to the back pages, protest as well as scholarly interest came to be concentrated more on Vietnam.

The shift in attention from Santo Domingo to Vietnam has helped breed in official Washington circles and among the public at large a complacency about the Dominican intervention. Indeed, among many high-ranking officials, the 1965 Dominican policy of the United States is now frequently cited as a successful action which had many beneficial results. Support for this view is lent by the seemingly easy and honorable way the United States extricated itself from the Dominican situation in contrast to the seeming impossibility of arriving at a satisfactory solution to the Vietnam imbroglio. Among policy makers, whatever review of the Dominican intervention takes place seems to be confined to the peripheral matters — issues of timing, coordination and consultation, emphasis, and public relations — while the more fundamental questions are ignored.

The positive overall interpretation by government officials of the role of the United States in the Dominican revolution revolves around a number of disparate themes. Thus, it has been argued that the United States was able to accomplish all of its stated goals: American and other nationals were successfully evacuated from the Dominican Republic without the loss of a single life; a bloody fight to the finish among the Dominican combatants in the civil war was avoided; the Communists, who had allegedly gained the upper hand in the revolution, were prevented from coming to power; and the Dominicans were enabled to choose their leaders in an election. The O.A.S., under its new secretary general Galo Plaza, appears not to have suffered irreparable harm; the Alliance for Progress and the movement toward Latin American economic integration seem to be going forward; strident anti-Americanism, which alarmists felt would result from the United States action, has not openly manifested itself on a large scale; and criticism of the Administration's policy has been diverted. On a different level, the United States ambassador at the time of the intervention has stated that the defeat of Juan Bosch in the 1966 elections "proves" the correctness of intervention; while another high-ranking State Department official, who was extremely close to Dominican political events in recent years, has said that, given the conditions, he did not see what other options the United States might have pursued.

The complacency with which government officials — including, reportedly, the President and his closest advisers — view the actions of the United States during the Dominican revolution or interpret it as a positive achievement, and the ease with which this important crisis has been conveniently ignored or forgotten may be disturbing to those concerned with the direction of American foreign policy. Equally disturbing to the scholar, however, is the large body of literature dealing with Dominican revolution and the United States intervention produced by the many ideologues of both left and right who, with little knowledge of the Dominican Republic, of the conflicts and discontinuities often characteristic of transitional political systems, or of the complexities of the foreign policy-making process, have written a variety of more or less polemical pieces which shed little light on these events or their implications. The Dominican upheaval and the United States posture toward it *did* raise some fundamental issues the implications of which may conceivably be as important in long-range terms as those stemming from the war in Vietnam, but our understanding of these crucial events has not been greatly enhanced by the discussion that has thus far ensued or by the literature so far published. It may therefore be appropriate at this point to raise some of the issues and mention some of the literature that might profitably be explored.

Disenchantment with the Johnson Administration on the part of informed opinion makers both in the United States and elsewhere, it may be recalled, was prompted initially as much by the Dominican intervention as by the growing Vietnam involvement. In the wake of the President's impressive record in the realm of domestic legislation and his recent victory over Goldwater, 1965 had begun rather auspiciously. The Dominican intervention, however, destroyed this hopeful projection. It gave rise to the "credibility gap" and brought into question the adequacy of intelligence data gathering and analysis and the ability of the government to function rationally and effectively in a crisis situation. To many observers, the action of the United States vis-à-vis the Dominican Republic signaled the abandonment of the early Kennedy goal of assisting a democratic social revolution in Latin America, the conversion of the Alliance for Progress into just another economic giveaway, and the reversion to a policy of the "big stick" and support for narrowly-based dictators and oligarchies because they provide order, stability, and anticommunism. Questions were asked as to whether the O.A.S. was anything more than a means to institutionalize the *pax americana,* whether the United States was able to comprehend and cope with the rising tide of revolutionary nationalism and aspirations for a better life on the part of the peoples of the developing countries, and whether military solutions to essentially political problems were appropriate. Fundamental issues concerning American interests and power were raised but not often discussed in a comprehensible, meaningful way and certainly not resolved.

If any or all of the charges concerning United States policy in the Dominican crisis are even partially true, they merit more serious study than they have received up to now. Further, the polemical, one-sided tone in which the Dominican revolution and United States policy toward that country have been discussed guarantees that these events will not receive the attention in official circles they deserve. Surely it is now time for a serious and scholarly study of the Dominican crisis and its implications.

At the time of the 1965 upheaval, first of all, there was little reliable background information available concerning the Dominican Republic. No adequate historical account existed; the long (1930–1961) dictatorship of Trujillo was not well understood; and the post-Trujillo developments had been too fast, frenetic, and recent for a comprehensive treatment to have appeared. The three best books about the Dominican Republic, significantly, were all published *after* the revolution.[1] It may be suggested, for example, that had there been available an adequate and up-to-date account of Communism and the Communists in the country, the Dominican crisis might well have ended quite differently.

The literature on the revolution and intervention itself is vast, but it is not always accurate or very enlightening, and there has thus far been no account which fully covers the diverse themes and events or places them in perspective. There are at least 19 books that have been put together about the revolution and the United States action. Space considerations preclude detailed comment; but the list includes journalistic accounts of varying degrees of accuracy and sophistication. . . . None of these volumes, however, provide a clear and balanced picture of the revolution; they were poorly researched, hastily written, and badly edited, and contain many errors of fact and interpretation. Nonetheless, they do provide some primary, first-hand information and include a variety of documents unavailable elsewhere.

A second category of books are those which touch peripherally or in a single chapter on the revolution and intervention. Most of these are concerned with American policy and the decision-making process generally, and use the Dominican events for illustrations or case study purposes. These volumes based on secondary sources, tend to be popular and journalistic, but they have the merit of placing the intervention in a broader perspective.

There is a vast body of periodical literature, the preponderance of which is critical of United States policy. Relatively little of this literature is enlightening, however, except in so far as it reveals the prejudices of the writer. The popular, most often polemical, articles have not contributed a great deal to a better understanding of Dominican events and the United States response to them — except in those few cases where the author had some firsthand information or specialized knowledge. Too many of these articles were dashed off hurriedly in the "white heat" of the intervention and were frequently based on questionable assumptions and often a fundamental lack of understanding concerning the Dominican Republic and the series of events that led up to the revolution and intervention. Even the best of the periodical literature, with a more scholarly bent or in some serious essay form, does not provide a great deal that is new or revealing. The results of basic research into

---

[1] Robert D. Crassweller, *Trujillo* (New York, 1966); John B. Martin, *Overtaken by Events* (New York, 1966); and U.S. Army, *Area Handbook for the Dominican Republic* (Washington: Foreign Area Studies, American University, 1966). [Footnote in original — Ed.]

practically all the questions raised by the revolution and United States policy during this period have yet to appear in print.

Perhaps the best — and certainly most influential — of the periodical literature critical of the action of the United States is represented by Theodore Draper's writings.[2] Draper's concern is in direct contrast to official complacency, and his viewpoint deserves separate treatment. It is worth noting in this connection that, whereas at the time of the revolution American officials in Santo Domingo referred to the pro-Bosch forces as the "rebels," the new group of embassy personnel, influenced by Draper's criticisms, refer to them by the more dignified title, "Constitutionalists." Draper is surely an able and articulate critic and much of his argument of how United States policy makers prejudged the revolution is probably sound, but it is not by any means the complete or definitive analysis. Even Draper's writing smacks of a kind of "devil theory" of events, glosses over facts that are incompatible with his analysis, and at times allows ideological and value considerations to get in the way of impartial analysis. Most importantly, he has not explained how the United States was drawn into the intervention. One may sympathize with Draper's fervor and involvement, but a more balanced assessment would likely conclude that the intervention did not happen exactly the way he describes.

Indispensable sources for anyone doing research on the Dominican revolution are the public documents, notes, memoranda, and communiques filed by participants in the conflict. These would include the primary materials published by the United States, the Organization of American States, and the United Nations. Both sides in the Dominican civil strife put out a variety of newspapers, bulletins, and periodicals. Practically every organized interest in the Dominican Republic published its position on the various issues of the conflict in these periodicals. Both the Dominican press and the dispatches of the American correspondents who covered the crisis must be consulted.

There are a variety of other sources that should be examined. The United States Congress held hearings on various aspects of the revolution, and some of these are available. A number of senatorial speeches — particularly those by Fulbright, Clark, Morse, McCarthy, Kennedy, Dodd — have been published in the *Congressional Record* and in other forums. Unfortunately for the scholar, an apparent *quid pro quo* has prevented the release of either the Administration's "White Paper" supporting its stand or the Senate Foreign

[2] Especially "The Roots of the Dominican Crisis," *New Leader* (May 24, 1965); "The Dominican Crisis," *Commentary* (December, 1965); "A Case of Defamation: U.S. Intelligence vs. Juan Bosch," *New Republic* (February 19 and 26, 1966); "A Case of Political Obscenity," *New Leader* (May 9, 1966); "The New Dominican Crisis," *New Leader* (January 31, 1966). [Footnote in original.—Ed.]

Relations Committee's hearings reported to contain information damaging to the Administration position — even though there have been numerous "leaks" and semihedgings on the agreement. The diligent researcher should also trace the large number of unpublished studies now in preparation — chiefly M.A. and Ph.D. theses — which were inspired by the 1965 events. Finally, interviewing of participants would be extremely valuable to any analysis of the Dominican revolution.

This brief survey barely scratches the surface of a wealth of materials which have not as yet been tapped fully or in a systematic, scholarly way. Neither the complacency with which United States officials now appear to view these events nor the frequently shrill polemical literature seems satisfying. There is a great deal to learn from the 1965 Dominican crisis, but little of this has up to now been expressed in published form. Since neither the Administration's position nor those of its most vocal critics are fully adequate, a careful and well-researched study is now called for.

The crisis in Vietnam has overshadowed and obscured the events of 1965 in the Dominican Republic. This is in some ways unfortunate because the Dominican crisis seems to have been in fact a crucial turning point, the full implications of which will probably not be seen until some time later. There are a large number of questions, it is worth reiterating, which stem from the crisis and to which students of comparative politics and international affairs may wish to address themselves. How fully do scholars or public officials comprehend the processes of political modernization (or decay) in nations like the Dominican Republic? What are the component parts of the Dominican system and how do they relate, interact, and change? How well do we understand the role of the military, the wealthy elites, the Communists, and the emerging forces in Latin America generally? What role did each of these groups play in the Dominican revolution? What kinds of inputs go into the foreign policy decision-making process, and how are decisions then made and implemented? What alternatives might have been open at different points in the crisis? What are the implications of this crisis for the Dominican Republic; for the O.A.S. and the peoples and governments of the hemisphere; for those who are allied with, neutral toward, or hostile to the United States; for the United States itself? Was this, as some have argued, an extremely costly error which created more problems, more enemies, probably more Communists, and more deep and irreconcilable division than had previously existed in the already fragmented Dominican system? Is it true that United States interests not just in Santo Domingo but throughout the hemisphere and the world suffered a severe setback as a result of these events? Or, conversely, was this a positive and successful action on the part of the United States?

The Dominican revolution and civil war of 1965 and the American intervention are not lacking in source materials or in important questions to explore. The answers to these questions should not be predetermined but carefully and systematically investigated, for the revolution and the intervention were far more complex events than either Administration advocates or critics apparently realize. If some of the younger scholars are searching for a more relevant political science or, more simply, for a variety of interesting themes and issues to research, few subject matters of recent years would seem to be so significant or so worthy of examination.

Getúlio Vargas, Strong Man and President of Brazil. Most of the second quarter of twentieth-century Brazilian history was dominated by this astute político, *and his influence is still felt. Here we see him taking his ease in a hammock, dressed in the typical* gaúcho (*cowboy*) *dress of his native state, Rio Grande do Sol.*

SECTION XIV

The Age of Getúlio Vargas in Brazil (1930-1954) and the Coming of the Military Regime

The seizure of power by Getúlio Vargas in 1930 marked a watershed in Brazilian history. The economic and social changes which characterize the contemporary period of turmoil in Latin America's largest nation began in the second half of the nineteenth century, but the powerful impetus toward modernity came with Vargas. A consummate politician who well understood the needs of his country, Vargas proved to be a very Brazilian kind of dictator who set up no concentration camps for opponents, and who was always referred to familiarly as Getúlio by foe and friend alike. Although unimpressive physically, with no intellectual pretensions, he managed to ride out the storm of Brazilian politics in the turbulent years from 1930 to 1945, during which he put Brazil on the continental and world map as never before. He encouraged the nation's push toward industrialization, which in turn stimulated interstate migration, interregional communication and transportation, and the search for domestic instead of transatlantic markets. He aided the university system to develop rapidly, he brought the urban workers into unions and provided them with a measure of social security, and he helped to create a politically and culturally throbbing nation. Yet when the army told him to leave in 1945 he attempted no resistance. Nor did he flee to the comfortable sanctuary of Miami or Switzerland to enjoy the fruits of a bank account prudently built up in advance, as so many Spanish-American dictators have done.

He stayed in Brazil, campaigned for the senate and won. And in 1950 he made a real comeback by getting himself elected president.

His suicide in 1954, not yet fully explained, closed the career of the greatest Brazilian since the nineteenth-century emperor, Pedro II. A careful study of his life and achievements has just begun, and only a tentative assessment is possible today. But it is already clear that the important changes that occurred during the Vargas years were carefully planned and administered by the dictator. As Professor Robert M. Levine has emphasized in his meticulous study:

> Those who viewed Vargas as a tool of his political and military advisers failed to understand the manipulative skill of the man who had preserved national unity, isolated and crushed his potential enemies, and presided over the Brazilian recovery in the face of economic dislocation, rising nationalism, and clashing aspirations. A product of the violent environment of Rio Grande do Sul, Vargas cultivated his image of blandness and taciturnity, and thus belied his ability to act with swift bluntness, even when he was forced to turn against his friends. . . .
>
> The political history of the Vargas years through the end of the 1930s reveals carefully applied forces of restraint: elitism, paternalism, police repression, and government-imposed nationalism. As chief of state, Vargas skillfully dominated threats from the left, the right, and surviving spokesmen for the old pre-1930 order. He supervised the deliberate expansion of the social and geographic base of political influence and thereby set the stage for the events of postwar Brazil. He assumed dictatorial powers at a time when dictatorships controlled seventeen of the twenty-seven countries of Europe and most Latin American states. But the impact of accelerated industrialization, military growth, and the consequences of urbanization transformed Brazil under Vargas and anticipated his removal in late 1945 in the face of a new threat to the political elite, this time from below.[1]

Contemporary analyses of Vargas help us to appreciate the difficult conditions prevailing during his early years, and some of the basic problems that he later struggled with (Readings 59 and 60). Corruption and crisis, no new phenomena in Brazilian politics, marked the final years of his rule and the final act is his death in 1954, a dramatic event that shook the nation. The origin and purpose of the suicide note (Reading 61) continue to be the subject of controversy.

The history of the last quarter of a century of Brazilian history is still being

---

[1] Robert M. Levine, *The Vargas Regime: The Critical Years, 1934–1938* (New York: Columbia University Press, 1970), pp. 176, 183.

written. Certain events stand out in this turbulent period. The capital was moved inland to Brasília in 1960, but the government is just now being fully installed there. Jânio Quadros was elected president in 1961 and resigned six months later, creating another mystery. Then João Goulart came in as president, but the military deposed him in 1964 and steadily assumed more and more power until a military coup in 1968 gave General Artur da Costa e Silva dictatorial power. After he was incapacitated in 1969, a military junta assumed power, bypassing the civilian vice-president, and the death penalty was restored for acts of violence and subversion. Subsequently General Emílio Garrastazú Médici was named president by the junta and the new constitution was promulgated. The economic growth rate and population increase remain among the highest in Latin America, if not the world.

For those interested in the political maneuvering during the years since Vargas, detailed guides exist,[2] and the role of the military has recently received sophisticated treatment.[3] But we need to penetrate beneath these political affairs if we are to see some of the fundamental aspects and emotions. Therefore this section will close with a poem and a challenging view of the future of Brazil (Readings 62 and 63).

An important fact about Brazilians, no matter what their political views, is their optimism in face of their country's urgent problems. Brazil throbs with plans and bounding predictions of future growth and future power, and has done so for a long time. Yet Brazilians, more than any people in Latin America except the Mexicans, have analyzed their own national characteristics frankly and variously. One geographer has drawn up a list of "27 unfavorable realities of Brazil"; Paulo Prado began his interpretation, *Retrato do Brasil,* with the declaration: "In a radiant land lives a sad people." A historian, Sérgio Buarque de Holanda, considers the special contribution of Brazilians to civilization to be the "cordial man" who easily establishes a sense of intimacy with other people.[4] Still another famous Brazilian writer, Alceu Amoroso Lima, states:

> We are naturally pessimistic. We always see the dark side of affairs. We exaggerate our defeats. We do not believe in our victories. We only de-

[2] Such as E. Bradford Burns, *A History of Brazil* (New York: Columbia University Press, 1970), and Thomas E. Skidmore, *Politics in Brazil, 1930–1964* (New York: Oxford University Press, 1967).

[3] Alfred Stepan, *The Military in Politics: Changing Patterns in Brazil* (Princeton, N.J.: Princeton University Press, 1971), and Frederick M. Nunn, "Military Professionalism and Professional Militarism in Brazil, 1870–1970: Historical Perspectives and Political Implications," *Journal of Latin American Studies* (London), 4 (1972), no. 1, pp. 29–54.

[4] For these and other opinions see Fernando de Azevedo, *Brazilian Culture* (New York: Macmillan, 1950), pp. 115–136.

fend our own in front of foreigners. And then we throw ourselves into a facile pride which is merely another type of pessimism. . . .

At the same time our pessimism leaves us an inheritance of inconstancy. We are much more active as creators than as maintainers. We have more courage for beginnings than for endings, or, as José Bonifacio said, "We undertake much and complete little." We enjoy innovation, renovation, reformation, but not repetition, conservation, continuation. We build roads, but we do not maintain them. We raise buildings, but we willingly permit the facilities to get out of order.[5]

But Brazilians are a complex people, and one of their essential characteristics is their confidence, which, as the veteran geographer Preston James has pointed out, "is just as real a factor of the Brazilian environment as are the hills and streams and forests."[6]

One of the questions every student of Brazilian history must ask is: how much change is possible, given the basic nature of Brazilian society and politics? One historian has concluded that "the Brazilian elite has managed to survive crisis after crisis, often yielding the forms of its power but rarely its substance."[7] When the First Republic was established in 1889 one of Brazil's wisest statesmen, Joaquim Nabuco, declared in the Chamber of Deputies of the Brazilian Congress: "within the Republic there is no place for illiterates, for the small ones, for the poor."[8] Yet today, after the passage of over three quarters of a century and many political changes, the overriding characteristic of Brazil is that her enormous and growing population is still made up to a large extent of "illiterates," "small ones," and "the poor."

[5] Alceu Amorosa Lima, *A realidade americana: Ensaio de interpretação dos Estados Unidos,* 2nd ed. (Rio de Janeiro: Agir, 1955), pp. 229–230.

[6] Preston James, "The Cultural Regions of Brazil," in *Brazil: Portrait of Half a Continent,* ed. T. Lynn Smith and Alexander Marchant (New York: Dryden Press, 1951), p. 99.

[7] Richard Graham, "Landowners and the Overthrow of the Empire," *Luso-Brazilian Review,* 7 (1970), no. 2, p. 44.

[8] Ibid., p. 56.

59. Vargas Faced Many Serious Problems When He Seized Power in 1930

HORACE B. DAVIS

Horace B. Davis, an American sociologist who taught in São Paulo, described and analyzed the difficult economic and political conditions with which Vargas had to cope in the early years of his rule.

When the domination of São Paulo in Brazil's affairs was abruptly terminated in 1930 and Getulio Vargas of Rio Grande do Sul was installed as dictator in October of that year, it looked as if a new chapter might open in Brazilian history. American observers were curious to see whether the 1930 "revolution" was merely a case of the "outs" coming "in," or whether the new government would proceed to a fundamental reorganization of governmental practices and of the Brazilian social system. A number of Americans have a practical as well as a theoretical interest in Brazil's internal affairs. Brazil takes between 1 and 2 per cent of the total exports of the United States. American capital invested in Brazil totals over half a billion dollars, and has been increasing rapidly in the post-war period. Brazil, moreover, ships a billion pounds of coffee per year to the United States, which is its best customer.

The group which seized the government in 1930 did not represent a new or different social class. Few of its promises of democratic reform have been fulfilled. The government's attention has been occupied with measures, only partly successful, to stave off the effects of the world economic depression and to weather a series of political crises both within and without the Vargas group.

Brazil is primarily an agricultural country. Most of its products and nearly all of its exports come from its plantations, orchards, and ranches. Over 70 per cent of the occupied males listed in the last federal census (1920) were engaged in agriculture.

Manufacturing has developed rapidly in the fifteen years since the 1920 census was taken. In 1920 the men engaged in industry, mining and transport were 13.8 per cent of the total; the proportion is higher now, but Brazil has no heavy industry. Its light industry exists only by virtue of a protective tariff.

From "Brazil's Political and Economic Problems" by Horace B. Davis, *Foreign Policy Reports,* 11, no. 1 (March 13, 1935), pp. 2–12, passim. Reprinted by permission.

The standard of living of the urban proletariat is distinctly lower than in northern Europe; wretched as it is, however, it contrasts favorably with the miserable degradation which characterizes the bulk of the rural population.

The agricultural regions of Brazil are for the most part organized in large tracts (*latifundia*) controlled by a family or a single individual. These big ranchers and planters constitute the old Brazilian aristocracy. Their tenants are for the most part illiterate. Getulio Vargas told the Constituent Assembly in 1933 that "out of 1,000 Brazilians who should properly receive elementary school education, 513 do not enter school, and of the remaining 487, some 110 register but do not come to classes; 178 attend the first year without learning to read well; 85 finish the second year and become superficially literate; 84 go a little further but do not manage to conclude their studies; and barely 30 get the full common elementary instruction, which is of very unequal value and admittedly deficient as to the thoroughness of the teaching, and which usually does not extend over more than three years, with all the pedagogical gaps which characterize the great majority of the schools in the interior." Since those who have opportunities for education outside of school are few, the children of the new generation are growing up only 37.7 per cent "literate." The diet of the rural workers is poor and inadequate, their clothing cheap and scanty, their health appallingly bad. Referring primarily to the rural population, Director of Public Health Belisario Penna declared not long ago: "Thirty million human beings without any earthly possessions are dying slowly in Brazil from hunger, syphilis and malarial diseases." Brazil's outstanding problem is to rescue these agricultural workers, the mass of the population, from their misery, and furnish them with a decent livelihood — a task which the excellent natural resources of the country render by no means impossible.

MONOCULTURE AND ITS EFFECTS.   Brazil's agricultural system at present retards the development of higher living standards. Monoculture, or concentration on a single money-crop, characterizes the richest agricultural districts. Brazil's most important product is coffee, which constitutes 70 per cent of its exports. Two-thirds of the coffee comes from the state of São Paulo, where whole counties are devoted exclusively to this product. Other zones of monoculture are the sugar zone in Pernambuco, the cacao zone in Bahía, the herva matte (Paraná tea) zone in Paraná, the banana zone on the coast north and south of Santos, and the rubber zone in the interior of Pará.

Monoculture exhausts the soil and degrades labor. To monoculture is largely attributable the monotonous and unhealthful diet of the rural population. Landlords competing on a world market find it necessary to cut labor costs to a minimum and are confronted by the problem of obtaining and holding on their large estates a sufficient force of workers to harvest the crop. This problem was solved in the early history of the country by slavery, which lasted until 1888. Since then peonage has developed on a large scale.

Monoculture has been favored by foreign interests, which have considered the production of crops saleable on the world market the only adequate safeguard for their loans to Brazilian planters, and the means by which government borrowings might be repaid. Yet monoculture exposes the finances of both planters and government to the effects of uncontrolled and uncontrollable fluctuations in prices.

The economic crisis has focused attention on these defects in Brazil's traditional system. Sir Otto Niemeyer, British banker who headed an advisory mission to Brazil in 1931, strongly advised the country to terminate its exclusive dependence on coffee. The great drop in the price of coffee after 1929 caused many old coffee plantations to be turned over to different forms of agriculture. This "rush to polyculture" was hailed by informed Brazilian opinion as a progressive step.

In São Paulo, especially in the old coffee zone, a class of small farmers had begun to develop. But even there, it is estimated that the *latifundia* (mostly coffee plantations) still make up half of the cultivated area.

Brazil's social system is unstable. Neither the rural workers nor the urban workers, many of whom are class-conscious European emigrants, have any strong interest in maintaining it. The army is proletarian in origin and has not always sided with the ruling class in a crisis. The minor officers in the army, of the rank of lieutenant and below, have a standing grievance in that the higher ranks are in effect reserved to sons of the ruling class. The famous bandit Lampeão (The Lantern), whose roaming bands have for years defied the police from Bahía to Maranhão and have sacked many a large estate, could hardly have maintained himself so long without a considerable measure of popular support, and the phenomenon which he typifies is a kind of inchoate social revolt.

INFLUENCE OF FOREIGN IMPERIALISM.   Brazil has never ceased to depend on foreign capitalists for new capital and other services. The intervention of foreign capitalists in Brazil's political life has been exercised sometimes directly, through the grant and withdrawal of favors and the consequent exercise of influence on individual politicians; and sometimes indirectly through the diplomatic intervention of foreign governments.

Foreign capitalists are interested in Brazil for five principal reasons: shippers who serve its ports and other middlemen are interested in developing

Brazilian trade; importers of goods produced in Brazil are interested in the country as a source of supplies; foreign exporters are interested in Brazil as a market; investors attempt to place capital in remunerative enterprises or safe securities and then endeavor to protect their investments; bankers are interested in the commissions they receive for handling Brazil's financial transactions.

During the nineteenth century Great Britain exercised a preponderant influence on Brazilian affairs, and British influence is still strong. British ships handle nearly twice as much Brazilian tonnage as the ships of any other non-Brazilian nation; 19.2 per cent of Brazil's imports come from Great Britain and 7 per cent of its exports go to that country; British investments in Brazil far overshadow those of the nationals of any other country; and Brazilian federal and state governments usually approach some London banking house first when they wish to float an important loan.

The only two countries which are at all comparable with Great Britain in the importance of their economic relations with Brazil are France and the United States. Until the World War, French capital invested in Brazil nearly equalled British; and France is somewhat more important than Britain as a market for Brazil's exports, although Brazil imports comparatively little from France. A number of Brazilian government loans have been floated in Paris.

Americans have always been great consumers of coffee; per capita consumption is greater only in the Scandinavian countries. The United States is consequently Brazil's best customer; in 1932, 45.8 per cent of all Brazil's exports went to this country. The United States also supplies 30.2 per cent of Brazil's imports, or half as much again as Britain, the nearest competitor for Brazil's trade. The coffee export trade in Brazil is dominated by two or three American firms. Even before the war New York shared with London and Paris the business of floating Brazilian loans, and since 1918 the importance of the United States as a capital market has greatly increased. It is in the field of investment that economic ties between Brazil and the United States have been most strengthened during the last fifteen years. In 1918 investments by United States capitalists in Brazil amounted to barely $50,000,000; by the end of 1930 the total had grown to $557 million. At that time the United States investment in Brazil was probably greater than investment by any other country except Great Britain, and was growing at a more rapid rate than British investment. Italians, Portuguese and Germans have important investments in Brazil. Japanese capitalists, supported by their government, have recently invested heavily in São Paulo state and in Amazonas. Japanese manufacturers are making vigorous efforts to expand their South American markets.

While there are certain areas where American, or alternatively British,

French or Japanese, influence is particularly strong, it would be a mistake to speak of "spheres of influence" in Brazil, as for example in China. But struggles between groups of capitalists from different foreign countries have sometimes shaped the course of Brazilian history, and are assuming ever greater proportions.

Brazil's public finance and currency history has been influenced by the country's continued dependence on foreign capital markets. The budgets of the national government and of the states, and even of some of the larger counties, have been chronically unbalanced, and the difference has been made up by a succession of government loans contracted abroad. At the same time the real budgetary position has been concealed by an involved system of government bookkeeping. From time to time internal inflation, both open and concealed, has resulted in a depreciating foreign exchange. Government funds raised internally have come for the most part from the middle and working classes, through a system of indirect taxes. The wealthier classes have largely escaped taxation. Sir Otto Niemeyer recommended that Brazil terminate its dependence on foreign capital, diversify its agriculture, revise its budgetary system, make greater use of the neglected income and inheritance taxes, and emit paper money only through one central bank of issue.

Dependence on foreigners for services in floating loans has proved expensive for Brazil. The foreign bankers have received large commissions. But, further, their practices have on occasion imposed additional burdens on Brazil. For example, early in 1926 the state of São Paulo negotiated a loan of £10,000,000 in Britain. It was arranged that payments on this loan might be received in Brazil, although the holders of the bonds were in England. The British bankers through whom the loan had been floated — Lazard Brothers & Co. — foresaw that a transfer problem might arise if foreign exchange should run short, as it did in the fall of 1931. By ingenious manipulation, they succeeded in shifting to the state government the burden of transferring to England a large part of the principal and interest payments. The government had to resort to the illegal or "black" exchange market, and thereby lost some hundreds of thousands of dollars.

It should be pointed out that, despite the extensive foreign interests in Brazil, much domestic Brazilian capital has also been invested in trade, industry and agriculture. The most important single financial interest in Brazil is believed to be the Matarazzo chain of factories, comprising something like eighty-five establishments.

The ruling group in each of the Brazilian states is a coalition of the large landowners with the upper urban bourgeoisie, supported sometimes by foreign capitalists. Since there are no large national parties, the ruling groups in the several states form alliances to govern Brazil as a whole.

POLITICAL REVOLTS, 1922–1932

From 1889 to 1930 there had been no successful revolt against this domination, although the so-called Copacabana revolt in 1922 and especially the more extended uprising of 1924 were symptomatic of growing unrest. Some troops which participated in the 1924 uprising continued in opposition to the government for two years before it was finally forced across the border and disbanded. This group was headed by Colonel Luiz Carlos Prestes, and became known as the "Prestes Column." Its program included the breaking up of the large estates, democratization of the electoral machinery, and opposition to foreign imperialist rule. It continued in existence as a political force even after its military resistance had ceased.

THE "REVOLUTION" OF 1930.   The uprising of 1930 represented a revolt against São Paulo's domination of the national government. Ever since the 1880's, when the great expansion of coffee planting in São Paulo began, coffee production had perennially tended to outrun consumption. On three occasions — in 1906, in 1917, and in 1921 — the government had intervened to acquire surpluses or regulate new production, or both. The first intervention had been crowned with success, and the second had proved vastly profitable. Since 1921 the government has made a continuous effort to regulate coffee production. At first the policy was merely to market the crop evenly, but it soon became an effort to maintain artificially high prices. In 1929 this program could no longer be continued and the price of coffee dropped from its high point.

The federal presidency was then in the hands of a Paulista, Washington Luis. It had become customary for the presidency to be rotated, no state holding the office for more than one consecutive four-year term. When Washington Luis supported another Paulista, Julio Prestes, for the presidency, politicians from other states took the view that the Paulistas had determined to dip deeply into the federal treasury in order to save again Paulista coffee-growers from threatened bankruptcy. The *Aliança Liberal* was formed for the purpose of forestalling this possibility. The platform of the *Aliança* did not propose the withdrawal of all government support from the coffee industry — coffee was far too important an element in the national economy for such action — but it did include a plank promising "aid to agriculture, not only to coffee." Other planks called for greater independence of the judiciary and democratization of the electoral machinery. The working class was promised social legislation.

The Prestes Column supported the *Alliança Liberal* in the elections of 1930. After the elections, Prestes himself broke with the *Alliança*. He has since joined the Communist party. However, a number of other exiled leaders of the Column — including João Alberto, Miguel Costa, Juarez Tavora and Isidoro Lopez — continued to support the *Alliança,* and returned from exile in order to participate in the military uprising in October 1930. The support lent by these democratic leaders gave to the successful revolt of 1930 the appearance of a semi-popular uprising. The controlling group in the *Alliança* centered around Flores de Cunha, Oswaldo Aranha, General Goes Monteiro and Getulio Vargas, all of Rio Grande do Sul, supported by political leaders in Minas Geraes, Rio de Janeiro and other states.

THE SÃO PAULO REVOLT OF 1932.   On first assuming office as dictator, Getulio Vargas offered the task of organizing a government in São Paulo to the Democratic party. This party, founded in São Paulo only a short time before the 1930 revolt by the venerable Antonio Prado, was the official opposition to the *Partido Republicano Paulista* (PRP) which had held the power for many years in both state and nation. The Democratic party declined the assignment and soon after disappeared. Vargas then turned to the leaders of the Prestes Column. But these, after eighteen turbulent months, proved unable to reconcile the conflicting interests in the state. On June 9, 1932 an insurgent movement enlisted the support even of the federal interventor, and the whole of the state of São Paulo, together with parts of the neighboring states of Minas Geraes and Matto Grosso, fell immediately into the hands of the rebels.

The underlying causes of this revolt were economic. They may be summarized as follows:

1. The Paulistas hoped to have the federal government and the other states carry a larger share of the burden involved in the coffee control program.

2. The coffee growers of São Paulo sought greater assistance in the crisis from the Bank of Brazil which, they pointed out, was granting credits to the cattle-raisers of Rio Grande do Sul.

3. The manufacturers of São Paulo feared a return of lower protective duties.

4. The São Paulo state government depended largely on the coffee export tax. Paulistas feared that the federal government would assume the right to tax exports.

5. The powerful and influential British interests in São Paulo feared the growing rapprochement between the Vargas government and the

United States of America. They pointed to the conversations held at a crucial period of the 1930 revolt between Paul V. McKee, president of the American-controlled *Emprezas Electricas Brasileiras,* and leaders of the *Alliança Liberal,* and demanded to know what favors were to be granted American concessionaires.

The Paulista leaders were almost certainly misled as to the amount of support they could expect from the other states. In Rio Grande do Sul, Flores da Cunha had just gone into opposition to the Vargas government. Vargas made his peace with Flores da Cunha, however, and the only help the Paulista constitutionalists received from their *gaucho* allies was an expression of good-will.

Fifty to sixty thousand men were in arms in São Paulo, and about as many took the field for the federal government. The civil war which ensued was the most extensive, though not the longest, that the country had ever known. The casualties, dead and wounded, have been estimated at 15,000.

The Paulistas had inadequate access to modern implements of warfare. They did succeed in obtaining ten Curtiss-Wright airplanes, which reached them from Chile by way of Paraguay, but the machines arrived too late to influence the outcome. Hostilities ended on September 29, 1932. The Paulista defeat was due, according to one of their officers, to "absolute lack of artillery and aviation, as well as a deficiency of automatic arms."

By the peace terms, the Vargas government permitted the leaders of the revolt to leave for Europe, agreed to grant São Paulo greater independence in its own affairs, and promised to reconsider the coffee question. It even underwrote the expenses of the revolt by guaranteeing the 400,000 contos of bonds which the state government had issued — this in spite of the fact that the federal government was engaged in an unsuccessful effort to balance its own budget. Such generosity surprised even the Paulistas. Finally, the Vargas government set about at once to summon a constituent assembly.

It is sometimes said that the leaders of the São Paulo revolt of 1932 desired complete independence from the rest of Brazil, which would have meant independence also for other states and the disappearance of Brazil as a nation. This opinion is contradicted both by all public utterances of the responsible leaders and by the logic of the situation. Most of the inflammatory propaganda against the federal government which circulated during and after the 1932 movement advocated confederation. Separation has been favored by only a few of the minor leaders.

60. *Brazil Made Tremendous Advances under Vargas*

KARL LOEWENSTEIN

Professor Emeritus Karl Loewenstein of Amherst College was an experienced European political scientist at the time he went to Brazil to observe firsthand the Estado Novo proclaimed by Vargas. Loewenstein shrewdly estimated the sources and extent of the dictator's strength, and was probably right in believing that he had maintained a reasonable objectivity during his visit, being "neither corrupted by the courtesy of the government in Brazil, nor prejudiced by the protestations of the opponents."

CHANGE OF PROFILE

Perhaps one way to evaluate the impact of the Vargas regime on the Brazilian people is the dialectic process; that is, to compare the general profile of the country as it presents itself now, with what it was before the regime took over. All observers — those actuated by hostility to the Vargas government no less than its supporters — are unanimously agreed that Brazil since 1930 has made tremendous strides forward. Shedding its nineteenth-century attire the country became modernized — as some old-timers say ruefully — beyond recognition. Under the onslaught of pick and shovel much of the "Austrian" charm has fallen a victim of streamlining. Rio's delightful feudal mansions and aristocratic gardens are rapidly giving way to pretentious skyscrapers and hyper-modern apartment houses. The old-world atmosphere of the streets and squares will be lost in a few years. Regulations for the protection of artistically valuable national patrimony exist, but they are no match for the soaring prices of real estate. Downtown Rio will soon be as dully monumentalized as the business districts of our newer cities. São Paulo, busily sacrificing old quarters for wide new boulevards, vast park developments, and bold bridges swinging over the asphalt canyons, is in the throes of a large-scale transformation, outdoing Chicago. The building boom in Brazil, more often than not on a brittle financial basis, spreads to the remote sections of the land. To many it appears as a heavy mortgage on a high-living standard which is not attainable in the near future. Town planning has become almost

Reprinted with permission of the author and Russell & Russell, Publishers, from *Brazil under Vargas* by Karl Loewenstein, pp. 330–367, passim (© Copyright The Macmillan Company, 1942; New York: Russell & Russell, 1973).

an obsession. But judged by Belo Horizonte, which succeeded Ouro Preto in 1891 as the capital of Minas Geraes, the Brazilians know the business of modernizing their cities. It was planned on the blueprint to the last stone and the last tree before the first stone was set and the first tree was planted. It is one of the most fortunate examples of rational urbanization.

ECONOMIC FACTORS

Such outward changes, striking as they are, may mean very little. They may not even be symptomatic. Moreover, to credit them exclusively to the regime is probably more than unfair to the past. Nor can economic progress in general since 1930 be ascribed to the policies of the Vargas regime alone. Similarly, as the technical capacity of the Hitler machine is indebted to a large extent to the groundwork laid by the republic which overhauled Germany's industrial equipment, in many respects the Vargas regime has harvested what has been sown economically by the liberal era. Industrialization was bound to come to a country which scarcely one generation ago had begun to emerge from semifeudalism grounded in agriculture and slave work, once it had become conscious of the riches of its land and the abundance in subsoil wealth and minerals. Vargas rode into power on the crest of the depression wave of 1929–1930 which had depleted the purchasing and consuming power of Brazil's European market. Nonetheless imports of finished goods soared in inordinate proportion as compared with the export of raw materials. Brazil was compelled to bridge the gap in its balance of trade by increasing the purchasing power of the masses at home as well as by building up its own industrial capacity. Here lie the intrinsic reasons for the rapid industrialization of a heretofore mainly agricultural economy. Factories were created mainly in São Paulo, in the Federal District and in Rio Grande do Sul for manufacturing consumption goods otherwise imported from Europe. With British trade declining and the American imports restricted to capital goods and high-class specialties, Brazil's economy became for some time hooked to that of Nazi Germany. Since Hitler's economists twisted the bartering noose around his neck at will, the Brazilian merchant and businessman was none too happy about the rapidly rising figures of exports to and imports from Germany.

The second push forward to a better integrated economic equilibrium between agriculture and industry came with the second World War when European trade was sharply reduced by the British blockade and the lack of shipping room. We in the United States began to realize that the Good Neighbor Policy is reciprocal. Brazil turned to the United States for goods no longer obtainable from Europe, with some reluctance because American business methods are less elastic than those of the German, Italian, Czech, and Swiss manufacturer and less adapted to the individualized tastes of the Brazilian bourgeois classes. By 1941 the United States had forged ahead to the first place (about 60 per cent) of Brazilian imports and exports. Simultaneously the industrialization drive was intensified, this time, however, with more Brazilian than foreign capital, and it began to extend also to the production of capital goods. During 1941 the establishment of a steel industry on a vast scale got under way, centered on the largest single high-grade iron ore deposit in the world, the Itabira "mountain" in Minas Geraes. . . .

Whatever may be the merits of the Vargas government in promoting national economic life — and at times the policies adopted amounted to a rough handling of the foreign creditors — the facts and figures imply that Brazil has moved into the position of the ranking economic power south of the Rio Grande and that it is about to pass Argentina, in the past South America's recognized political and economic leader. In the last decade Brazilian mineral production has increased at least eight times even without considering the potentialities of the Itabira development. The industrial capacity has tripled, the textile output has risen threefold. The value of industrial production surpasses that of agriculture by 20 per cent and thus another predominantly agrarian country is being converted into an industrialized economy. Agriculture — although at present not more than 3 per cent of the arable land is cultivated — gives the world's largest supply of coffee, the second largest crop of cocoa, the third largest crop of corn; Brazil is fifth in cotton and in sugar, seventh in meat, and ninth in rice; and all this, if one believes the experts, is only the beginning. For a protracted war Brazilian mineral and agricultural resources may become invaluable to the United Nations; while these same riches, in addition to Brazil's strategical position, might tempt the Axis to invasion and conquest.

THE ATTITUDE OF THE VARIOUS SOCIAL CLASSES TOWARD THE REGIME

A detailed description of the economic situation under the regime is beyond the scope of this study. The preceding remarks — based rather upon a field of observation than upon the strength of statistics (government-made statistics anyway) — are to serve only as the background for attempting to present this writer's impression as to how the various social classes react toward the regime. After all, it is the attitude of the people who live under a political society, their contentedness or dissatisfaction, which establishes the record and, in the long run, decides the fate of a government. No objective device to measure the happiness of the people exists. What conclusions are submitted here are at best reasoned generalizations.

The regime has pursued successfully two seemingly conflicting or overlapping policies. One is the vigorous encouragement of national capitalization and the promotion of national enterprises, unfettered by state regimentation. The other is the fortunate co-ordination of the free play of private capitalism, with a progressive paternalism in social policies for the benefit of the laboring classes. To present these achievements in a nutshell: the economically most important groups, capital and labor, are, on the whole, satisfied with the existing social and political order; they are not desirous of any fundamental change. This is no mean accomplishment of a government in this period of violent social transformation.

THE REGIME AND THE WEALTHY: THE BUSINESSMAN AND THE ENTREPRENEUR

During its first years the Vargas regime was inclined to steer a more anticapitalistic course; but soon the wise policy was adopted of leaving business alone and not harassing it with nationalization or collectivization schemes. The hands-off attitude contributed to reconciling the economically most potent state of São Paulo to the regime more than might have been expected after the bitterness left by the defeat of 1932. Vargas himself is said to understand little of economics and personally he is not committed to any specific economic doctrine. What the well-oiled editorials of some papers write about a "directed economy" is ideological window dressing. The businessman can work in peace. The government does what capital and business — not altogether identical because of wealth derived from landed property — want it to do, provided the policies do not run counter to that other prominent trend of the regime, solicitude for the laboring masses. In spite of much speculation about eventual "nationalization" relatively little large-scale experimentation in government ownership of national resources or their utilization by the government has materialized to date. There is also much less talk about "corporativism" than is habitual in other authoritarian states which use "corporative" ideologies as soporifics for the discarded political rights of the people. The manifold boards, councils, committees, commissions can scarcely be considered as significant demonstrations of an incipient corporative trend in economic life; their functions are mainly advisory and only to a small extent regulatory. The Brazilians are realists who do not believe in the mirage of state capitalism camouflaged as corporativism. Brazil under Vargas is one of the few lands remaining on the globe where a genuinely liberal climate of economic life prevails. The profit margin in both industrial and agricultural production is relatively large, partly because of the still very cheap living conditions, partly because of the deterioration of the currency which began with the National Revolution and showed no sign of abatement until very recently. Businessmen like to complain about the costs of the social services, which amount to about 10 per cent of the annual employees wage sheet. But evidently they are bearable because of the profits in exports derived from the currency depreciation and because of the slowly rising purchasing power of the masses of consumers at home. The other complaint frequently ventilated in no uncertain terms refers to the appalling amount of bureaucratization and government control — "fiscalization" — through which a greedy state squeezes money from various and sundry victims. But the Administrative State whose advent in Brazil is so loudly heralded sails in the wake of an inflation in government personnel. The hordes of technically superfluous petty officials are a sort of substitute for the lacking government party; the more people the government keeps on its pay roll the more have a stake in the perpetuation of the existing political and social order.

Traditionally, the wealthy class of Brazil derives its income from agricultural sources. There are still huge *latifundia,* not unlike semifeudal duchies in size and administration; particularly in the less opened spaces of the vast country the owner of the *fazenda* is a political as well as a social and economic power. But the coffee and cotton aristocracy invested their profits in industry, and the men successful in business — the Crespi, Mattarazzo, Guinle, Simonsen — control today large tracts of land managed on a rationalized basis like industrial enterprises. The old landed nobility and the new aristocracy of entrepreneurs have merged. In spite of the battering which landed wealth took in a predominantly one-crop economy, the landowners still form a disproportionately large group in the governing class; and they see to it that the regime abstains from taxing away the foundations of their power as has happened in Britain. They are part and parcel of the regime; Vargas has nothing to fear from them.

By economic liberalism prevailing within, Brazil benefits also foreign capital. But foreign business is not favored by the government. Under the nationalization drive its position has become more and more precarious. Economic nationalism under the slogan "Brazil for the Brazilians" is very popular among all classes. But for the time being it is tempered by political expediency because Brazil still needs foreign capital and foreign technical experience. The resentment is directed mainly against British capital — unjustified as these complaints about British economic dominance are, because the British helped greatly to develop the country and, on the whole, did not draw inordinately high returns from their enterprise and investment. Today it is American capital which flows freely into Brazil in the form of official and private loans. The interdependence of Brazilian and American economic interests will prevent, at least as long as we are copartners against the Axis, an intensification of the nationalization efforts. Had war not come, the restriction of foreign economic activity might, in the end, not be distinguishable from outright expropriation.

THE REGIME AND THE MASSES: LABOR AND FARMER

THE URGENCY OF SOCIAL REFORM.   As a rule it is none too difficult for an authoritarian regime to find support among the well-to-do classes by protecting their vested property rights. Mussolini, Franco, and even Hitler in his early years of rule are cases in point. A much more arduous task is that of winning the sympathy of the nameless masses of the toilers in the workshops and on the farms. For this reason all modern dictators enter the stage as the friends of the forgotten man, as the protector of the underdog. Perhaps the most striking feature of present-day Brazil — and one that is universally admitted — is that Vargas personally and the regime in general are extremely popular among the laboring masses. Vargas has won the soul of the common man. Himself stemming politically from the liberal left and not belonging to the old ruling class, he succeeded in squaring the circle by keeping the wealthy in good humor and improving the lot of the poor. He accomplished this task not by *circenses* alone; the Brazilians are too realistic and he is far from being a spectacular showman. He offered them *panis*. Already in the early thirties a vast program of social reform was inaugurated; it was carried on, without the impediments of a bourgeois-minded parliament, after the inception of the *Estado Novo*. Responsible observers doubt whether Brazil, having scarcely emerged from a semifeudal economy, is ripe for the advanced social services which are uniformly superimposed upon an unevenly developed economic structure. The labor standards proclaimed by the regime are decidedly too high for the actual social level of the laboring masses. For the time being the garment of social paternalism is much too wide for the undersized body economic. Frequently, progressive social policies and economic liberalism seem incongruous. Be that as it may Vargas, by anticipating a situation in which private capitalism would have to yield to increasing pressure from the masses, took the wind out of the sails of a potential Communist movement and forestalled an eventual social revolution.

The trend toward social — or, some observers say, socialistic — reform is in line with what one observer aptly describes as "an easy receptivity on the part of law students who represent the majority of the governing class of the country, for all modern laws observed in more advanced world centers." One may add that such an ambitious eclecticism, emanating from the reform-minded ministerial bureaucracy, is discernible also in other fields of governmental activities, with a resultant cleavage between the professed aims of official policy and their inadequate realization in daily life. Any casual visitor who, strolling away from the marble hotels, casinos, glittering show windows and race courses, chances into the appalling quarters of the poor on the hills in Rio de Janeiro or into the slums of São Paulo, will encounter such misery that not even the tropical sun can romanticize it for him, let alone for the people who have to live in tin-can shacks and mud hovels. Living conditions in the interior are so primitive that the foreigner, with the glamor of the sophisticated residential sections of the big cities on the seashore still before his eyes, is prone to saddle the governing class of the present no less than of the past regimes with the gross neglect of the masses of a fine and decent people. In the rural districts shoes are commonly not available for the families of the agricultural laborer; clothes are of the cheapest cotton; dirt floors in the roughly made houses, nonexistent sanitary commodities, the scantiest and poorest furniture (if it is more than some pots and pans, wooden dishes, and a few pieces of miserable bedding), demonstrate that the most advanced social legislation, enacted in the faraway capital by well-meaning officials, is utterly unable to raise the living standard of the poor. Brazil is about to embark on a drugstore civilization. What is needed, however, is one which is firmly grounded in the little red schoolhouse. . . .

THOSE WHO ARE DISCONTENTED.   A generalizing statement on the adhesion of the people to the regime is at best hazardous. Yet presumptuous as it may be on the part of a foreigner whose personal knowledge and powers of observation are necessarily limited, he cannot but come to the conclusion that the bulk of the people are in favor of the regime. Perhaps by way of a modification one may say that obviously no class as a whole is basically averse to it. Most of all the common people feel little if any political pressure. They live on as before, their personal life is affected by the government only in that they have a little more money to earn and to spend, that somewhat better opportunities for educating their children exist, that they partake of tangible social advances. That Brazil under Vargas does not live up to the postulate of government by the people does not cause them deep grief. During the liberal era his participation in politics through the polls and otherwise, meager as it was, did not help much the man in the street personally. Now he is told to keep out of politics and he does not seem to miss them. Support of the regime is wholly unemotional; its existence, achievements, and failures are accepted as a matter of fact and with a good deal of common sense. There is no state mysticism as in Germany or in the early days of Fascism in Italy. Nor can it be said that, considering the general climate of optimism which prevails anyway in Brazil, the regime has noticeably galvanized the mind and soul of its people. Fanaticism does not go well with Brazilian irony and tolerance. To sum up: the regime rests on a broad, a very broad basis of popular acceptance, perhaps as broad as in most democracies where the opposition is bitter against the group in power for the sake of opposition. Brazil under Vargas is indeed Vargas's Brazil.

Yet there is ample evidence of dissatisfaction, of unspecified grumbling as well as of very definite complaints. There is no use denying that a political malaise is widespread among many intellectuals and in the bourgeois layers. Exception is taken to specific measures of the regime and to its atmosphere in general. Such complaints when vented by businessmen refer to the over-bureaucratization and to certain economic policies; others rail against nepotism, current inefficiency, and venality of government personnel. Discontent is most outspoken in São Paulo, traditional stronghold of liberal constitutionalism, but it is encountered also in Minas Geraes and notably in the south. In general the popularity of the regime decreases in proportion to the distance from the capital. Dissatisfaction with general political conditions is latent even among otherwise loyal officials and members of the governing class. In fact most of them are at heart liberal and democratic. An authoritarian regime which disdains rigid regimentation of public opinion leaves room for dialectics. The terms "disciplined democracy" and "Administrative State" so much in use by official propaganda, are a dialectic camouflage of the profoundly liberal current underneath. The nostalgic desire for the return to genuinely democratic forms of government persists. This applies to internal as well as to foreign policy. Deeply affected by the fall of France, the intellectuals and the bourgeoisie were unswervingly faithful to the cause of the Democracies, even in the dark days of one-sided neutrality in 1940 and 1941 when the pro-Axis wing of the government strove hard to line up Brazil with the Axis.

What the liberals complain of is that they cannot partake in their government except on conditions set by the regime. They resent the self-ordained infallibility of the governing group whose shortcomings are a public secret. They object to being barred from their legitimate share in the responsibility if not in the spoils. To many independent minds even a benevolent dictatorship is a *capitis diminutio,* undignified for a country so proud of its unbroken tradition of constitutionalism in the past. As one informant, a prominent man in the service of the regime and thoroughly loyal to it, phrased it neatly, "We have won order and tranquillity but we have lost liberty." Few are those who, by changing the sequence of values in this phrase, prefer the former to the latter. What weighs heavily on the minds of the responsible people is the unpredictability of a political order not firmly grounded in the rule of law. The oblique notion of the "interest of the state" as interpreted by an irresponsible bureaucracy casts its dark shadow over the entire realm of the "Administrative State." For a liberal lawyer — and Brazil is sociologically a lawyer's land as our civilization is typified by the businessman — the manner in which the regime deals with the courts and molds the law in accordance with political expediency is frankly exasperating. All this does not imply hostility let alone active opposition to the regime. But it contributes to the climate of political uneasiness which one cannot fail to encounter once the thin veneer of "All quiet on the internal front" has been rubbed off. Perhaps Oswaldo Aranha — himself a *ci-devant* liberal and a genuine democrat — gave an apt estimate of the situation to this writer when he declared that nations today are confronted by the choice between liberty and equality, and that the regime has chosen equality. Equality the regime has successfully striven to achieve. Among the Brazilians personality and human values count for more than money or social distinction, and the regime has given a chance of collaboration to everybody who is willing to do so. To a foreigner this sounds rather cryptic considering that Brazil is after all still an oligarchy though one rooted in a solidly democratic foundation. The gist of it is that the dictatorship cannot obliterate liberal tradition. In view of a future world order it is comforting to know that a nation which in the past has enjoyed liberal constitutionalism will not easily forget it. . . .

PORTRAIT OF A LEADER

It may sound a truism, but the greatest asset of the regime is Getulio Vargas himself. The decisive impression the foreign visitor gains in Brazil is how unequivocally well-disposed the Brazilians in all layers of the population are toward the man who Atlaslike carries the regime on his shoulders. As in most South American states, the dictatorship is personalistic in character. In that, it is altogether different from the European totalitarian pattern. No government party protects it, no coercive ideology supports it. The regime rests on no visible props, except the army; it is based on the popularity of one man alone.

It is true that the armed forces helped him into the saddle. Nor could he hold power without their continued support. Brazil is a Latin-American state in which *pronunciamentos* and military juntas flourish. He did all in his power to keep the army and navy leaders in good humor, by increased salaries for the officers and men, by heaping prestige on the military establishment, and by acceding to the political influence it was able to exact. Much more than in other South American states the Brazilian army is a separate caste, not dissimilar to the position of the military in France. It is a sort of professional nobility which jealously guards its privileged position and does not easily brook interference even by the powerful head of the government. Frequently enough the generals took matters into their own hands, at times forcing his hand. But after what probably was the most difficult task of his career, Vargas overcame the political ascendancy of the army forces. When he appointed, in January, 1941, a civilian, J. P. Salgado Filho, to head the newly established Ministry of Air, it was the symbol of the victory of civilian government over the military caste. But the armed forces are anything but democratic. They are certainly ardent patriots — at least many of them; but military success holds an understandable spell for them and military successes of the Axis close to Brazil might well spell Vargas's doom. When, at the Rio de Janeiro Conference, he cast Brazil's lot with the United Nations, it was a leap in the dark. Nobody can foretell what the hidden totalitarians among the generals will do in case of a successful landing of the Axis on Brazilian soil; it is perhaps better not to harbor too many illusions about the loyalty of some of the Brazilian leaders to the cause of democracy, who may pay lip service now but do not feel the beat of the heart for it.

On Vargas's personal vocation as a leader not a single dissenting voice can be heard. Knowing Latin-American habits one need not make much of the fact that everybody calls him by his first name. The members of the opposition no less than the horde on the bandwagon praise his quickly grasping intelligence, his common sense in evaluating realities, his administrative ability — he is a hard working bureaucrat with extremely methodical organizing habits. They admire his silent tenacity, his devotion to and knowledge of administrative technique; for these are rare qualities among modern statesmen, and in no wise conform to the melodramatic pattern of the present-day dictator. It was the great Swiss prophet of the coming cataclysm, Jakob Burckhardt, who predicted two generations ago the age of the *"simplificateurs terribles."* Vargas is not one of them: his formulas are no emotional simplification and he realizes that visionary speculation never can supplant the honest devotion to administrative routine. That he is the shrewdest of politicians, with a Machiavellian touch, goes without saying. It is the heritage of his Latin descent and environment. His favorite technique consists in quietly letting conflicting opinions come to a deadlock and then solving it by an unchallengeable decision. He is an opportunist, equally remote from preconceived doctrinairism and from nebulous political ideologies. The regime has no theory except that of eclectic realism. This explains sufficiently why some interviewers — with whom this writer does not agree — call him enigmatic; an opportunist does not readily commit himself.

Vargas does not evoke strong emotional responses in his people. He has little mystical appeal or *"charisma."* He has given ample proof of cold-blooded personal courage. But Vargas and the Brazilian people do not lend themselves to heroworship. Vargas is neither a vegetarian mystic with voices nor a cynical *braggadocio* with vices; he is a bourgeois person with bourgeois tastes and some very human failings which are no secret to many people. The personalist dictatorship in South America has few if any irrational ingredients. As is customary in authoritarian states he has been made an object of lionization by the official propaganda. It is not known whether he enjoys it much; at least he does not show it and it evidently has not gone to his head. But adulation has its definite limits. He refrains from posing as a superman. For the man on horseback he has scarcely the stature. He knows the intellectual irony of his Brazilians and especially the sharp tongues of the *Cariocans* too well to allow the propaganda machine to play up his personality into something mystical or heroic. He knows that ridicule has killed many a man.

Vargas's living habits are inoffensive and conform to bourgeois standards. He is a good father of his family; he likes horseback riding and golf, he is fanatically devoted to everything which has to do with airplanes. He has no spectacular literary or artistic tastes, which is fortunate for the intellectual life of Brazil. Of his cultural propensities nothing is known from which the inference can be drawn that they are at best average. He has a sense of humor — a rare quality among dictators — and he knows a good joke when he hears it, even one which victimizes him. He shares intellectual irony with his people.

There is another point which those knowing the atmosphere in European dictatorships cannot fail to notice. Perhaps it is too much to say that Vargas has no personal enemies. No man at the helm of the state can avoid making enemies. But there are not many who either fear or hate him. It is inconceivable that he should evoke that devouring hatred and that abject fear which European dictators instil into opponents or into their subjects. Many times he has shown his tolerance and a complete absence of political vindictiveness. His popularity today — as he has sided with public opinion against the Axis and with the United Nations — is perhaps greater than at any time in his career. This is no mean achievement for a man who has wielded power for more than a decade with practically no constitutional limitations. For once power has not corrupted a man.

With reference to Napoleon it has been said that the essential qualities of the great statesman are idealism and moderation. Vargas certainly has moderation, but he seems devoid of idealism. If idealism is equivalent to vision some concepts of the future of his country may underlie the rank opportunism of his conduct of government. However later historians may judge him as a statesman, one thing can already be stated with certainty after more than ten years of uncontested rule: in the history of Brazil he can claim a rank next to Dom Pedro. No higher praise can be bestowed on a Brazilian.

61. *Suicide Note, 1954*

GETÚLIO VARGAS

When Vargas won the presidency by the election of 1950, he found himself surrounded by problems but with less strength to handle them than before. As Professor E. Bradford Burns stated: "Congress was uncooperative and the political parties querulous. The troubled economy tended to diminish his popularity with the workers. The army watched attentively to prevent him from resorting to his old *caudilho* tactics." * When the assassination attempt against the critical journalist Carlos Lecerda seemed to implicate Vargas himself, the army asked him to step down. Instead he committed suicide on August 25, 1954. The farewell note he left stunned the nation, and led to conjecture concerning its authenticity. But "by his final act of sacrifice Vargas neutralized the political and psychological advantage his opponents had accumulated. In death, as in life, Vargas' action was well designed to yield maximum political effect." †

Once more, the forces and interests which work against the people have organized themselves afresh and break out against me.

They do not accuse me, they insult me; they do not fight me, they vilify and do not allow me the right to defend myself. They must silence my voice and impede my actions so that I shall not continue to defend, as I have always defended, the people and especially the humble. I follow my destiny. After decades of domination and plunder on the part of international economic and

From *Vargas of Brazil: A Political Biography* by John W. F. Dulles (Austin: University of Texas Press, 1967), pp. 334–335, passim. Reprinted by permission.

    * E. Bradford Burns, *A Documentary History of Brazil* (New York: Knopf, 1966), p. 369.

    † Thomas E. Skidmore, *Politics in Brazil, 1930–1964* (New York: Oxford University Press, 1967), p. 142.

financial groups, I placed myself at the head of a revolution and won. I began the work of liberation and I installed a regime of social freedom. I had to resign. I returned to the government on the arms of the people. The underground campaign of international groups joined that of the national groups which were working against the regime of assuring employment. The excess-profits law was held up by Congress. Hatreds were unleashed against the just revision of minimum wages. I wished to bring about national freedom in the utilization of our resources by means of Petrobrás; this had hardly begun to operate when the wave of agitation swelled. Electrobrás was obstructed to the point of despair. They do not want the worker to be free. They do not want the people to be independent.

I assumed the government in the midst of an inflationary spiral which was destroying the rewards of work. Profits of foreign companies were reaching as much as 500 per cent per annum. In declarations of import values, frauds of more than $100 million per year were proved. Came the coffee crisis and the value of our main product rose. We tried to defend its price and the reply was such violent pressure on our economy that we were forced to give in.

I have fought month after month, day after day, hour after hour, resisting constant, incessant pressure, suffering everything in silence, forgetting everything, giving myself in order to defend the people who now are left deserted. There is nothing more I can give you except my blood. If the birds of prey want someone's blood, if they want to go on draining the Brazilian people, I offer my life as a holocaust. I choose this means of being always with you. When they humiliate you, you will feel my soul suffering at your side. When hunger knocks at your door, you will feel in your breast the energy to struggle for yourselves and your children. When you are scorned, my memory will give you the strength to react. My sacrifice will keep you united and my name will be your battle standard.

Each drop of my blood will be an immortal flame in your conscience and will uphold the sacred will to resist. To hatred, I answer with pardon. And to those who think they have defeated me, I reply with my victory. I was a slave of the people, and today I am freeing myself for eternal life. But this people whose slave I was will no longer be slave to anyone. My sacrifice will remain forever in their souls and my blood will be the price of their ransom.

I fought against the spoliation of Brazil. I fought against the spoliation of the people. I have fought with my whole heart. Hatred, infamy, and slander have not conquered my spirit. I have given you my life. Now I offer you my death. I fear nothing. Serenely I take my first step toward eternity and leave life to enter history.

62. *"Brazil"*

RONALD DE CARVALHO

This Brazilian poet expresses well the lyrical, optimistic spirit which many Brazilians feel, in spite of all the unpleasant realities set forth in the next selection as seen by a non-Brazilian.

I hear the vast song of Brazil!

I hear the thundering steeds of Iguassú pounding the naked rocks, prancing in the wet air, trampling with watery feet the morning of spume and green trills;

I hear thy solemn melody, thy barbaric and solemn melody, Amazon, the melody of thy lazy flood, heavy as oil, that swells greater and ever greater, licking the mud of banks, gnawing roots, dragging along islands, goring the listless ocean like a bull infuriated with rods, darts, branches and leaves;

I hear the earth crackling in the hot northeast wind, earth that heaves beneath the bare bronze foot of the outlaw, earth that turns to dust and whirls in silent clouds through the streets of Joazeiro and falls to powder on the dry plains of Crato;

I hear the chirping of jungles — trills, pipings, peepings, quavers, whistles, whirrings, tapping of beaks, deep tones that hum like taut wires, clearly vibrating drums, throats that creak, wings that click and flicker, cries like the cricket's whispers, dreamy calls, long languid calls — jungles beneath the sky! . . .

I hear the millstones grinding sugar cane, the gurgle of sweet juice flowing into vats, the clank of pails among rubber trees;

and axes opening paths,

and saws cutting timber, . . .

and mangroves leafing in the sun,

and peccaries snapping their jaws at alligators asleep in the tepid mud of bayous . . .

I hear all Brazil singing, humming, calling,

shouting! . . .

From *Anthology of Contemporary Latin American Poetry*, Dudley Fitts, ed., Dudley Poore, trans. Copyright 1942 by New Directions Publishing Corporation. Reprinted by permission of New Directions Publishing Corporation.

factories grinding, pounding, panting, screaming, howling and snoring,
cylinders exploding,
cranes revolving,
wheels turning,
rails trembling,
noises of foothills and plateaux, cattlebells, neighings, cowboy songs, and
    lowings,
chiming of bells, bursting of rockets, Ouro-Preto, Baía, Congonhas, Sabará,
clamor of stock-exchanges shrieking numbers like parrots,
tumult of streets that seethe beneath skyscrapers,
voices of all the races that the wind of the seaports tosses into the jun-
    gle! . . .
But what I hear, above all, in this hour of pure sunlight . . . is the song of
    thy cradles, Brazil, of all thy cradles in which there sleeps, mouth dripping
    with milk, dusky, trusting,
the man of tomorrow!

63. *Whether Brazil Succeeds in Her Quest for Power or Not, the Passage Will Not Be Smooth*

FRANCES M. FOLAND

Frances M. Foland is a fellow of the Institute of Current World Affairs of
New York City, which sends the fellows to various countries of the world to
observe and report. Their monthly letters are usually fresh and informative
examinations, with both journalistic sparkle and scholarly depth. Some
Brazilians may wince at her frank diagnosis of Brazil's problems and prospects. But they will find it difficult to challenge her facts, even though they
may draw different conclusions.

For another challenging perspective, see the anthropologist David H. P.
Maybury-Lewis's article whose theme is "that there has been considerable
growth in Brazil since 1930 but comparatively little change."*

* "Growth and Change in Brazil since 1930: An Anthropological View," in *Portugal
and Brazil in Transition,* ed. Raymond S. Sayers (Minneapolis: University of Minnesota
Press, 1968), pp. 159–172.

INTRODUCTION: SOME INDICATORS

1. Fifth largest country in the world with 3,296,000 square miles of territory, Brazil occupies 47% of the South American land mass and borders on every nation of the continent except Ecuador and Chile.
2. Brazil's population of 95 million is by far the largest in Latin America (Mexico is second with 49 million) and is seventh in the world. At the present growth rate, 3.1%, the population will reach 230 million by the year 2000 and will surpass the United States before 2030.
3. Brazil now has five cities with over one million population: São Paulo (approximately six million), Rio de Janeiro (approximately five million) and Belo Horizonte, Recife and Porto Alegre (each with over one million). The cities are growing at 6.1% a year, doubling every ten years, and by 2000 both São Paulo and Rio de Janeiro will have approximately 12 million and will be components of a megalopolis stretching 1000 miles along the Atlantic Coast and containing 100 million people.
4. Brazil's Gross National Product, $32.4 billion in 1969, is currently increasing at about 8% and should approach $120 billion in 2000, comparable to West Germany, Japan and Great Britain today.
5. Brazil's hydroelectric potential is estimated at 150 million kilowatts, one of the highest in the world (surpassed only by Congo, China and the Soviet Union). This year (1970) Brazil's installed electric power capacity will reach 11 million kilowatts. Urubupungá power center on the Paraná River, now nearing completion, will be the largest in the world except for three complexes under construction in the U.S.S.R.
6. Brazil contains sufficient reserves of thorium and uranium to mount a major nuclear energy base. Ample deposits of other minerals include bauxite, magnesium, nickel, zinc, tungsten, beryllum, tantalum, lignite, gold, tin, iron and manganese.
7. As one of the biggest farming countries in the world, Brazil's cropland totals some 80 million acres and another 700 million is used for pasture, woodlots, wild crops or fallow reserves. Brazil feeds itself, except for wheat, and sells well over $1 billion worth of farm products abroad. About two-thirds of Brazil's area is still uncultivated; thus the country is perhaps the greatest remaining geographical frontier for farming and livestock-raising in the world. . . .

"Whither Brazil?" by Frances M. Foland, *Inter-American Economic Affairs,* 24 (1970), no. 3, pp. 43–68, passim. Reprinted by permission.

SOME FUTURIST VIEWS.   According to Herman Kahn and Anthony J. Weiner, Brazil — with a 1965 average per capita income of $280 — will need 130 years to reach the current U.S. per capita of $3,600. India with a much lower 1965 per capita of $99 will reach the goal sooner, in 117 years. This discrepancy apparently results from Brazil's high population growth. . . .

THE MATRIX.   Brazil's paragon of Foreign Ministers, the Baron of Rio Branco (1902–1912), fulfilled the nation's territorial ambitions, delineating a border of nearly nine thousand miles while asserting hegemony over a land mass larger than France along the Uruguay-Paraguay-Bolivia frontiers. It was, in a sense, a realization of a deep-felt manifest destiny, and Brazilians could rest content in their conviction that theirs was a great nation.

The sociologist Gilberto Freyre boasts that there is a distinctive Brazilian culture. From one end of the country to the other there is a certain Brazilian homogeneity and a style that sets the people apart from Spanish-Americans. Accents may vary and regional gripes may surface but, underlying Brazil's considerable diversity, is a sense of national unity and a sort of ebullient belief in the grandeur of the country. . . .

Events largely of external or coincidental origin have inflicted a welter of proddings in the last decades: not exactly of its own calculation, Brazil was forced to industrialize to compensate for shortages caused by the Depression and World War II; not exactly through its own health program, mortality rates have been reduced bringing on a population onslaught; rising expectations have challenged the passive acceptance of the status quo by the masses; around the world unheard-of nations gained independence and the concept of the Third World came into being, posing an alternative to Brazil's traditional foreign policy; and the burgeoning of science and technology has eliminated the option to "do-it-later" and dictated the imperative to "make-it-now-or-never."

All of these divisive forces converged in Brazil during the 1950's and 1960's. President Juscelino Kubitschek's (1955–1960) impetuous program of industrialization led to an unbridled inflation; President Janio Quadros (1961) initiated a precedent-breaking démarche in Brazil's foreign policy, turning toward a course independent of U.S. leadership; and President João Goulart (1961–1964) threatened real socio-economic reforms for the first time in the country's history and fell into the hands of the so-called "negative left."

Their three terms composed a heady decade, and conservatives believed that the country was reeling out of control. Strongly supported by entrepreneurs, middle class and urban workers, the military ousted Goulart and came to power on 1 April 1964, determined to eradicate the evils it felt had recently beset the country due to incompetent civilian rule: fiscal irresponsibility, international adventurism and communism.

The Brazilian military has traditionally bestowed upon itself a certain responsibility as guardian of the nation. When President Castelo Branco and his colleagues took over in 1964, they probably foresaw a brief interregnum leading to renewed civilian rule. Their political orthodoxy was affronted each time they tenuously liberalized the system, however; their Cold-War psychology and U.S. orientation conjured up a Communist behind every plea for reform; and a positivist trait confirmed their belief that only they as technocrats, immune to the vagaries of civilian politics, could discipline the economy and the populace so as to achieve the essential economic development.

Furthermore, there is "an ominous shift in the focus of thinking about Latin American development among economists . . . namely that development is not solely, or even principally, an economic problem. Rather, they find that the formal, superficial forms of democracy serve only to impede true economic growth."

Among the more influential "technocrats" articulating this view is Roberto Campos, Brazil's Minister of Planning under President Castelo Branco. It is his observation that:

> The attempt to preserve the delicate minuet of consulting the voters at short intervals and maintaining delicate checks and balances may preclude decisive and coherent action and may, in the end, hopelessly weaken the real substance of democracy in an effort to preserve its ritual trimmings. . . .

Brazil's future should be viewed with the expectation that the decision-makers who will guide it will be the military — the present clique, their rivals and their successors. Therefore, some consideration of the formation of the Brazilian military mind follows.

THE METHOD

> The technology of this century makes it possible to anticipate the irresistible realization of Brazil's destiny of greatness because she is a country that has, within her frontiers, all the resources necessary to the promotion of her humanized development.

These words from a 1969 speech by Gen. Emílio Garrastazú Médici, now President of Brazil, could well have been those of either of his two military predecessors, Gen. Arthur da Costa e Silva and Gen. Humberto Castelo Branco, both deceased. With similar backgrounds and values, the actions and goals of the three were highly congruent. Almost exactly the same age (Garrastazú Médici is nearly 65), all were born in provincial towns to modest middle-class parents of Portuguese, Basque and Italian heritage. All were members of the so-called "Sorbonne" faction within the military, closely associated with the War College.

Only 20 years old, the Escola da Guerra (ESG), the Superior War College, has had a profound role in the shaping of military intellectuals. Perhaps even more important for an analysis of Brazil's future is the civilian-military symbiosis forged by the College. As students in its standard one-year political course, mid-careers leaders are drawn from business, industry, banking and communications, as well as from the military; in the course, 51% of the graduates are civilians, and by 1969 all generals on active duty had passed through the College.

Current studies include politics, socio-psychology, economics, military affairs, doctrine and coordination, scientific intelligence and counter-intelligence. The curriculum takes into account, as input factors, such diverse phenomena as Papal encyclicals, the Cuban missile crisis, the desirability of population expansion in Brazil, and the internal problems of the United States.

The political course is oriented to a series of theories on national power, national potential, national strategy, national objectives and national policy, all of which are related to the mystique of security and development. The doctrines have in turn pervaded the Ministry of Planning and General Coordination, the National Security Council and the National Development Council of Brazil.

Courses are conducted by means of group methods and Socratic dialogue (techniques seldom encountered in Brazil). Teams work on problems and travel together throughout the country to research projects. At the end of the year the class visits the United States, inspecting military and industrial installations. Civilian graduates — given the rank of colonel and certain paramilitary responsibilities — normally join alumni associations. The whole program, therefore, is a powerful welder of camaraderie and of mutual concern and understanding among military and civilian leaders.

The Brazilian War College represents leadership training on a grand scale. On a lesser but perhaps even more important level are the many local or regional political courses organized by the local chapters of civilian graduates' associations of the ESG. These courses last from two to four months and are maintained by fees charged to the participants; over two hundred such courses have been held in Brazil in the last two years. ESG officials supervise the course content and approve the "doctrine" taught. At present their courses are attended by businessmen, bankers, university administrators and academic personnel, the clergy and others. Attendance is by invitation and is a much esteemed privilege. This is leadership training or orientation on a scale never attempted before in Brazil.

PROJECT BRAZIL.   One of the first acts of Gen. Garrastazú Médici upon being appointed President of Brazil in October 1969 was to establish an organization called "Project Brazil"; although this initiative received little notice in the national and international press, the composition and purpose of the group suggest major significance. Said to be the "brains" behind the administration, the Project personnel are civilian technocrats and majors and colonels who previously served as intelligence officers under Gen. Médici. Their basic objective is to transform Brazil into a great power equal to the U.S., U.S.S.R. or China.

Though strongly anti-Communist, these intellectuals have carefully studied the development of Russia, a country which in 1917 was far behind the Brazil of today. On the positive side, the two share size and mineral wealth; on the negative side, Brazil is still plagued by obstacles which have been overcome, at least in part, by the U.S.S.R.: problems of communications due to distance, vast and difficult frontier lands defying habitation and development, a large and pre-modern peasant sector slowing economic and socio-political progress, and an entrenched and traditional elite prone to obscurant and corrupt practices.

Brazilian planners believe the country can overcome these obstacles. . . . João Paulo dos Reis Velloso, argues that "there is nothing set about the future. What happens will depend upon our attitude and effort in increasing the capacity of national competition."

The explicit goals of the Médici Government are clustered in four strategic areas: (1) agriculture, food distribution and supply, (2) education and health, (3) scientific and technological development, and (4) an industry competitive in the international market. Specifically, plans aim at the agricultural exploitation of empty backlands by means of a vast migration of underemployed from the Northeast, a modernization of the food distribution system by means of the construction of marketing centers in all Brazilian cities of 500,000 population or more, an expansion of the primary school system to serve all school-age children, and increase in the training of technicians and a curbing of the exodus of trained personnel, increased efficiency in domestic industry so that protective tariffs may be removed, and a nationwide program of protective health measures.

In his traditional New Year's message for 1970, President Médici visualized "four horizons of our near future: the new year, the four-year term of my government, the decade of the 70's, and the last 30 years of the century. He observed: "In this decade of the 70's the Brazilian people will respond to the challenge of overcoming their deficiencies rather than falling behind in obscurity."

POSTSCRIPT. It should not be assumed from the above that the military is monolithic. The Navy and Army are continually at odds, and one Admiral called the closed-door selection of Garrastazú Médici as president "a cold military coup." More critical for the future political course is the division within the Army itself where the older Sorbonne group — typified by Castelo Branco-Costa e Silva-Garrastazú Médici — is barely tolerated by a faction of middle-rank officers who feel their opinions and rights have been ignored. Tending to be younger, the discontents' political and military philosophies were shaped during the height of the Cold War. They have less faith in democratic processes, less patience with civilian demands, less flexibility in their security concerns. Strongly nationalistic, they are even less willing than the "Sorbonnists" to compromise Brazil's economic development for the sake of democratic or populist demands. Time is on the side of these junior officers, and their ascent to power seems likely.

Though the Army's seizure of the government in 1964 was strongly supported by a large sector of the society at that time, enthusiasm has waned in the ensuing years as the officers entrenched but did not work the hoped-for-miracles to solve the country's problems. Many civilians now lament that the military "has been bitten by the blue fly" — that is, has become addicted to political power.

Though "Sorbonnists" have promised a return to normalcy, there are many indications that the military will run the government for quite some time. . . . Those who protest the situation have been jailed, exiled and denied their political rights. Armed underground opposition is harrassed and dissipated, its leaders allegedly tortured and assassinated. Street demonstrations have been quelled by massive mobilization of police and sophisticated anti-riot equipment. Odds are, therefore, on the side of a continuing military regime.

THE RECENT GOD: SCIENCE AND TECHNOLOGY

THE NEW-FELT URGENCY. . . . Brazilian leaders are increasingly convinced that they face a "now-or-never" challenge to consummate their country's potential greatness. Whereas industrialization was the supreme goal of Brazil in the 1950's, in the 1960's the inexorable dynamism of science and technology has sullied the apparent industrial success, revealing the extent of external dependency. In the words of Brazil's U.N. Ambassador, João Augusto de Araújo Castro:

. . . science and technology with all their progress and development are widening, not narrowing, the ominous gap between developed and developing nations. . . . The concept of Power today is far from encompassing the merely military aspects of power but extends to the whole range of economics, science and technology.

Brazil's internal and external policies are cognizant of the Technetronic Age. The new government has named science and technology as one of its four priorities for national development. . . .

Just as the railroads in the 19th century made possible the opening up and unification of the United States, so the application of nuclear power, communications satellites and imaginative air transport may facilitate an integral development of Brazil in the late 20th century. One futuristic dream held by Brazilian planners suggests exciting possibilities for the recalcitrant Northeast, plagued by drought, soil exhaustion and excess population. With giant nuclear reactors as cores, agro-industrial complexes at four sites — Recife, Natal, Fortaleza and São Luis — would produce electric power for evaporators to desalt water in sufficient quantity to turn arid lands into farmlands. The power would also feed factories and smelters for processing fertilizers, chemicals and ores. The four complexes could accommodate some 20 million people, over two-thirds of the region's total population. Whereas each of these complexes might cost $1 billion and involve gigantic transformations in the physical and human configurations, Brazil has already undertaken the feasible with the scheduling of a 1969 construction of its first nuclear-power center to produce 500,000 kilowatts.

In 1969 Brazil inaugurated a satellite system which vastly increases its message capabilities internally and internationally; this telecommunications network will soon service the whole nation. In a related field of science and technology, Brazil has the largest space program in Latin America. Its research seeks solutions for Brazilian problems in communications, education, meteorology, natural resource surveys, and technology and scientific administration. Currently one of the most ambitious projects focuses on the use of satellite communications for educational development. . . .

A SLOW START.   As Zbigniew Brzezinski suggests, however, "Given the fact that scientific development is a dynamic process, it is likely the gap will widen." The lead of the U.S. on all scientific and technological counts is awe-inspiring. In comparison, Brazil's investment of funds and manpower is infinitesimal: expenditures on research and development are only 1/15 of that of Japan ($60 million a year compared to $900 million) and 1/350 of that of the U.S. ($60 million vs. $21,075 million). In terms of qualified manpower, Brazil has approximately three scientists, engineers and technicians per 10,000 population, comparable to the U.S. in 1900.

Critical for an appreciation of Brazil's chances in the science and technology race are the educational system and the R. & D. complex. Education in Brazil has always been exclusive and, modeled on the European system, has tended to prepare for traditional and prestigious professions rather than to train for skills and disciplines needed in a developing society. Education has been viewed as an end in itself, for status, rather than as a useful instrument for practical application. The Brazilian Government has never been an avid supporter of education, and education's cut of the national budget fell from 11% in 1965 to 7.7% in 1968. The post-coup administrations have attempted to modernize the university and secondary levels, but with limited results.

Even if the quality of Brazilian education were good, which it is not, the quantity of those educated would impose a severe limitation on ambitions for scientific supremacy. The illiteracy rate averages 20% in urban areas and 63% in rural areas, but it is the figures on attendance at secondary and higher institutions which indicate the human resources available for modern advancement. In Brazil (1964) only 7.5% of those aged 10–19 were attending secondary school. The country had 38 universities in 1966, of which all but five were founded after 1946. Total university enrollment — 183,000 in 1968 — was about 1/5 of 1% of the population. Of this number only about 1/10 are graduated.

A further malady afflicting Brazil's short supply of qualified scientists and technicians is the "brain drain." Often educated in the United States, a Brazilian professional finds it tempting to accept a position abroad which offers greater salary and opportunity. In addition, the repressive measures of the military governments have driven off many intellectuals. The Government initiated a deliberate campaign to lure Brazilian scientists back to their native land but, again, with limited success.

Besides constrictions on the freedom of expression and on remuneration and prestige, the Brazilian trained in science and technology discovers that the scope of his work is circumscribed by inadequate funding for research and development and by a disarticulation among the three fundamental factors: the government, the productive structure of the economy and the scientific-technological infrastructure. Poorly coordinated, the efforts of these factors are seldom maximized and, in fact, each tends to establish external linkages rather than internal linkages. . . .

The capacity for innovation has been limited by the weakness of the scientific and technical system, the lack of coordination between this infrastructural system and the productive system, the low emphasis on management training and the limitations in the socio-economic climate. The Brazilian Government might break the vise of external dependency, limited innovative capacity if it could formulate a vigorous policy of scientific and technological development and allocate major resources to this cause. Throughout Latin America, however, there is too often a fissure between the plan and the implementation. Furthermore, the possibility of a major dedication to science and technology is compromised by the onslaught of competing demands for government attention.

THE BABY BOOM

SOCIAL OVERHEAD.   There are almost three million more Brazilians every year. The rate of population growth in the 1950's and 1960's was nearly 30% higher than the rate in the 1940's. The causes of this acceleration are not short-term but, rather, will continue to feed a rapid increase due to high birth rates and declining death rates. Brazil, therefore, will have 212 million in 2000, if the birth rate drops to 2.9% due to economic development; if the rate holds at the present 3.1%, the population will be 230 million.

The resultant demands on the system are staggering:

1. Between 1940 and 1980, the number of Brazilians in the 0–14 age range will have almost tripled from about 17.5 million to 50 million, or 40% of the total population. The dependency rate (.88 in 1960) is one of the highest in the world.
2. According to a U.N. report in 1967, the housing deficit in Brazil was seven million units and increasing. In Rio de Janeiro a third of the inhabitants are slum dwellers. A recent government campaign for new housing for medium- and low-income families is having some effect but consuming a large share of the domestic savings.
3. Of 5,118,500 Brazilian children who entered the first grade in 1963, only 49,300 reached the sixth grade. In 1960 only 275 *municipios* (counties) of a total of 2,764 had *colegios* (high schools).
4. The projected level of educational expenditures will exceed one-third of Brazil's gross capital formation, resulting in a heavy drain on domestic savings.
5. 1.2 million workers enter the labor force annually. Approximately 860,000 of these are illiterates or equipped with less than four years of schooling.

6. Between 1940 and 1960 the absolute number of agricultural workers increased by more than 2.2 million to a total of 11.7 million, posing a problem for development because agricultural productivity is low.

7. During the early 1960's, both output and income fell behind population increase with a consequent lowering of the per capita figures. (If prevailing trends should continue, the per capita income for Latin America by 2000 would be 15 times less than that of the United States; it is currently seven times less.)

In spite of these gloomy indicators, the Brazilian Government's population policy until very recently has been energetically expansionist. Although there have been some official second thoughts, Brazilians on the whole are strongly opposed to population control. Though a Catholic country, opposition is predicated not so much upon religious principles as upon an emotional anti-Americanism. The following charge from a Belo Horizonte newspaper is typical: "(population control is being) imposed upon us by a country with the dimensions of Brazil but with 300 million people, giving the impression that the American people with their land already overpopulated is concerning itself with our empty spaces and intends to occupy our territory."

A case in point is the reaction within Brazil to the Hudson Institute's proposal for the creation of an inland Amazon Sea. The Institute was simultaneously accused of attempting to internationalize the Amazon for imperialistic purposes, of intending to settle millions of Negro militants in the area, of developing the area for the United States survivors of a major thermonuclear exchange and that, under CIA and Pentagon orders, the study had the purpose of splitting Brazil into two nations.

URBANIZATION. Brazilians covet their empty lands and untapped resources and foresee that population growth will lead to their development. The burgeoning population migrates not to the hinterland, however, but, as if to lodestones, to the coast and the overcrowded cities. Over 60% lived in eight states in 1960, with 17.6% of the territory. All but two cities of 100,000 or more are along the coastal strip. Between 1950 and 1960, São Paulo increased by 74%, Curitiba by 100% and Rio de Janeiro by 43%.

Brazil's urban growth is unprecedented, the major cities doubling every ten years. A projection of present trends to the year 2000 foretells of three metropolitan centers — Rio de Janeiro with 13 million, São Paulo with 11 million and Belo Horizonte with five million — which will be integral units in one vast megalopolis stretching 1000 miles along the Atlantic Coast and containing 100 million people, almost half of the country's total population. This area will encompass a large part of South America's industrial heartland

and will sap other areas of their human and capital resources, thus aggravating the already serious regional disparity. . . .

The industrialization of Brazil has been characterized by high capital intensity and low utilization of labor. Given the trend toward labor-saving machinery, it is impossible to foresee when manufacturing, which now employs only about 1/10 of the labor force, will become a major employer.

A government projection (based on a 3.6% growth rate for secondary employment) indicates that by 1976, manufacturing and civil construction will employ only 14% of the total labor force. The service sector, however, will increase from 26% in 1950 to 45% in 1976. This lop-sided pattern of employment could retard Brazil's development.

A DANGEROUS BY-PRODUCT. In addition, rampant urbanization forebodes a subsidiary effect which could wreak havoc on the country's progress. With the creation of a huge lumpen-proletariat, the political system may be charged with dynamite.

The flood of migrants has crested since World War II, and they are, therefore, still largely first-generation city-dwellers. No matter how poor their urban situation, they can see some progress over their rural life. They have few high hopes for themselves but do expect the city to offer the schools, health facilities and job opportunities which will give their children a means to move upward.

Whereas existence in the countryside isolated them from the consumer market, the migrants are now fully exposed to the wares of the city. They are prime victims of the demonstration effect in an economy where the top 10% of the population receive 40% of the income, and the bottom 40% receive 10–14% of the total income. . . . But, projections into the 1970's indicate fewer children in schools, fewer jobs for young men, less food for the poor. . . .

LATENT DISCORDS. . . . A mulatto people, Brazilians have always adhered to the myth that they are free of racial prejudice. To doubt this quality is to commit heresy against the national doctrine. First trumpeter of "The Brazilian Miracle" is the noted sociologist, Gilberto Freyre, who says:

> With the miscegenation of the blacks and the whites and because of the climate, we created a *moreno* type which now dominates the majority of our population . . . in Brazil we are beyond the race problem. We simply created a Brazilian type . . . the concept of *morenidade* includes the gamut of Brazilian types from the white to the least white, from the mulatto to the black.

The Brazilian census has not recorded skin color since 1950. In that year 32 million called themselves white, 14 million mulatto, and 5.5 million black. One can be sure that a large number of the 32 million had some Negro blood for in Brazil to have any white blood is to become white, whereas in the U.S. to have any black blood is to become Negro. In regard to the latitude allowed as to who is white, Brazil is far more generous than the U.S.

However, there is a very considerable degree of racial prejudice in Brazil, well camouflaged so far but posing a real threat to the country's social tranquillity. Prejudice against *pretos,* those with no white blood, is absolute — even mulattos look down on them. Most middle- and upper-class parents, particularly in Southern Brazil, abhor the idea of their daughter's associating with dark-skinned boys, let alone marrying them. Those with a heavy mix of Negro blood find restaurants, hotels and clubs closed to them; when the myth somehow works to get them into one of these inner sanctums, they often are shunned and embarrassed by the others of the "in-group." One seldom finds a dark-skinned person in a high position in either private enterprise or government. Although whites and blacks live side by side in the slums, statistics would show that the darker the skin, the less the education and the lower the salary.

As urban crowding continues and social tensions increase, as the lighter-skinned men and the darker-skinned men compete for the same job, as political mobilization and participation intensify, there may soon come in Brazil a day when a deep-seated prejudice can no longer be glossed over by the myth. Miscegenation will blur the battlelines and save Brazil from a confrontation such as the U.S. is experiencing, but the real possibility of racial conflict looms in Brazil's future. . . .

Brazil adjoins ten South American countries but has managed to stabilize its borders with little effort. A major contributor to peace has been the empty interior of the continent. Several factors suggest that the vacuum may soon be filling up: the Brazilian government has initiated a deliberate policy to develop the hinterlands; minerals are being discovered in the upper reaches of the Amazon; the cattle industry is taking over vast areas for grazing; pioneering farmers are pushing into virgin lands; and, an economic plan facilitating investments is attracting enterprises into Amazônia.

The first "nation" to bear the brunt of this drive to the West is the Indian. There are some 100,000 to 120,000 Indians, largely primitive, living in the rain forests and highlands of the sparsely-populated Amazon basin. The experience of other countries corroborates that these aborigines suffer as speculators, miners and ranchers penetrate the distant areas.

Gold, diamonds, precious stones, manganese, tin, lignite, tantalite, bauxite and other minerals are drawing man into the wilderness. One example of a frontier zone lately come to life is Rondônia, adjoining Bolivia. Until recently inhabited only by primitive Indian tribes and scattered rubber-gatherers, the federal territory is now experiencing Brazil's most rapid population increase, some 200% in the last decade. The reason is in-migration; the cause is the discovery of tin. Likewise, there is geological exploration on the Bolivian side, and the two nationals intermix at the mining camps, often political exiles and criminals seeking refuge from one side to the other.

Another area of population confrontation between two nations is the Paraguay border. Brazilian laws prohibit Paraguayans from buying land within a 150 kilometer belt on the Brazilian side of the border but, on the Paraguayan side, even lands belonging to the public treasury are falling into the hands of Brazilian *latifundistas*. In this case the reason for expansionism is the coffee industry which has exhausted the soil to the east.

In addition, there is a growing concern and interest in the control of the huge drainage basin of the Rio de la Plata. Including the La Plata, Paraná, Upper Paraná and Uruguay Rivers, the network covers an area almost twice the size of Western Europe and encompasses large areas of Peru, Bolivia, Paraguay, Brazil, Argentina and Uruguay. Brazil controls some of the most important headwaters that flow as several tributaries from the Mato Grosso. The other nations fear a riverine imperialism as Brazil diverts the water for its hydroelectric works. Discussions for multi-national development have not gone well.

The days of the Portuguese *bandeirantes* (pioneers-adventurers) pushing in over the plateau are past, and Brazilian expansionism has long been dormant. Now, however, spurred by the goal of development and swollen by a population surfeit, Brazilian territorial aggressiveness forbodes a coming era of border clashes — an internecine turbulence between "The Colossus of the South" and its many neighbors.

THE HUMAN ELEMENT

Arriving in Rio de Janeiro, Herman Kahn [1] wore a dark, ready-made suit, a white shirt of ordinary cloth, a $20 raincoat, and his tie was crooked. He met Daniel Machado de Campos, president of the Commercial Association — "mustache, suit, shirt and tie impeccable."

That the Brazilian journalist covering Kahn's arrival noted these details and chose to include them in his story is significant of the national character.

[1] The American economist, staff member of the Hudson Institute, who had come to study the Brazilian economy. [Ed.]

Brazilians extol the chic (spelled "chique" in Portuguese). The beauty salon is a basic institution, frequented every three days or so by women of the middle and upper classes, just to have a comb; only poor women do not dye their greying hair. On the Rua Augusta in São Paulo — called the most elegant commercial street in Latin America — one can buy a Rolls Royce, a Christian Dior dress, a diamond necklace, or a Picasso. Brazilians buy them.

Brazilians buy almost anything — it is a rage born of a century's inflation. Money saved is worthless tomorrow. A Volkswagen bought today is sold for more cruzeiros next year. Merchandise catalogs and menus shun prices as they would too soon have to be reprinted. A consumer buys on credit, pays only the minimum, at the last minute; a retailer stalls payment to the whole-saler who, in turn, stalls the manufacturer. The ensuing devaluation profits he who tarries longest.

So it goes in a country of go-go consumerism; mores militate against thrift and accumulation. The test for Brazil's leaders bent on development is whether they can convert the consumer to a saver, transform a live-for-this-day bravado into a work-for-tomorrow resolve, change the Carnaval bac-chanal into a constructive investor.

Herman Kahn allegedly quipped in Brazil that the country had everything necessary for greatness — just one change was needed: populate it with Japanese.

Causes which move Brazilians are *fútebol* (soccer), *as misses* (beauty contests) and *os festivais* (popular music festivals). Joseph Novitski of *The New York Times* reported from Brazil that:

> Soccer is the national sport, the national pastime and the national pride; (when Pele, the soccer hero, scored his 1,000th goal), it was a moment of hoarse, happy release for Brazilians, some of whose po-litical energies, frustrated under a stern military regime have been poured into soccer. . . . Professional and amateur sociologists have asserted that cheering at a soccer game is a release for poor, hungry Brazilians and for their middle-class compatriots.

That Brazil won the 1970 World Soccer Championship, and, in addition retains the gold cup as a result of three international victories, is a boon to the Brazilian ego and an asset for the military government.

Gunnar Myrdal, Swedish economist, visited and lectured in Brazil in October 1968. As one of three causes for Brazil's underdevelopment, he named "the great apathy of the people" (the other two: the entrenched ruling groups and the high birth rate). He surprised the Brazilian press, limited in its freedom of expression, by saying that "if the people were not so apathetic, they would now govern their country," instead of allowing a military dictatorship.

Although it is difficult for a citizen and legatee of Anglo-Saxon democracies to comprehend, it is possible to pair the apathy of a people with the repression of a government to produce a compliant and stagnant populace; Brazil's mother country, Portugal, is a prime example of this. The present Brazilian Government strives for a precarious balance — it seeks economic dynamism in conjunction with political decadence. In addition, there is a severe incongruence between the goals of the leadership and the average citizenry — the former seeks national security and economic development, while the latter seeks the good life and the freedom to do his own thing.

Another consideration pertinent to Brazil's potential for greatness is that it is a tropical country. World leaders have always been temperate countries. The climate not only poses barriers to agricultural and industrial production, but it also slows man's pace and tempts him to an existence closer to nature than to office or factory. The pace of São Paulo, with a brisk climate on the Tropic of Capricorn at 2500 ft. altitude, contrasts with muggy, coastal Rio de Janeiro where, during early morning and lunch hours, business and professional men are not in their offices but on the beach. In addition, debilitating tropical and nutritional diseases plague the bulk of the population: shistosomiasis, filariasis, Chagas, intestinal parasitosis, beriberi, kwaskiorkor, malaria and typhoid.

There is no doubt that Brazil has all the elements necessary for greatness but some catalyst must prompt a reaction among the people which will motivate them to the sacrifices and hard work attendant on development. Perhaps a charismatic leader could evangelize the populace with some quasi-religious cause, such as nationalism. But, in any case, Brazilians and foreigners captured by the country's charm can rest assured that God is a Brazilian, and in the year 2000 there will still be pretty girls on Copacabana Beach and the best Carnaval in the world in Rio de Janeiro.

CLOSING NOTE

There is a saying that "Brazil is a country of the future — and always will be." It now seems that the realization of Brazil's potential hovers in the near future rather than the distant future but, if it is not grasped soon, it will always retreat as the horizon.

The high number of variables seems to cluster in three constellations: those defining the physical attributes of the land, those indicating the contradictory strengths and weaknesses of the leadership, and those describing the idiosyncracies of the Brazilian people. Some of the key tendencies which appear in the current Brazilian scene are the following:

Authoritarian government and political decay

Rigid central planning to accelerate economic development with considerable stress on science and technology

Difficulties in shifting the Brazilian economy from the role of borrower to innovator

Power ploys within the Army with factions competing for supreme authority, possibly resulting in a continuation of "coups within coups"

A continuing lag in the social infrastructure — schools, housing, urban planning, health facilities — as population outstrips it

Increasing urban chaos and unemployment

Outbreaks of discontent suppressed by strong-arm tactics

Opening up of the backlands with major gains in known natural wealth

Mounting pressures on frontier areas and confrontations with neighboring nations

Research and development leading to membership in the nuclear and space clubs

Rapid progress in science and technology relative to other Latin American nations and an enlarged role as regional leader

Ambivalent relationship with the U.S., resenting the continuing dependency but realizing the inevitability of economic and strategic partnership.

Whatever Brazil's success in the quest for Power, prevision suggests that it will not be a smooth passage.

Women in the Mexican Revolution. Women were to be found in Mexico wherever men were fighting during the revolutionary years. Soldaderas rode with their men on the tops of freight cars as they moved into battle, and served as cooks, companions, and fellow fighters under most difficult circumstances.

Sra. Gertrude Duby Blom, the veteran Swiss anthropologist and honorary Mexican citizen who presides over that unusual study center in Na-Bolom in San Cristóbal de Las Casas, photographed a number of the women who actively campaigned with General Emiliano Zapata. One of his most valuable aides is shown here, Apolinaria Flores, who was his curandera. The wounded were brought to her by night from the mountains and were returned to their camps by day to fight on.

Twentieth-Century Revolutionary Changes

WHAT IS A REVOLUTION?

Latin America over the years has experienced hundreds of "revolutions" that were simply sudden explosions of violence that determined succession in political office. The outstanding fact about some of the revolutions in the twentieth century is that they also involved rapid and comprehensive changes in social structure and values. The transformation of Cuba under Castro has already been treated (Readings 55 and 56), as well as the many developments in Brazil during the "Age of Vargas" (Readings 59–60). The readings in this section are focused on a variety of revolutionary changes in a number of countries. Each one has been written about by many students, so that the sheer amount of material is almost overwhelming.[1] A recent bibliography on Latin American studies in non-Western and East European countries runs to over eight hundred pages, and much of the interest has been concentrated on revolutions.[2] Inasmuch as revolutionary changes are an integral part of

---

[1] For an example of the types and quantity of studies, see Cole Blasier, "Studies of Social Revolution: Origins in Mexico, Bolivia, and Cuba," *Latin American Research Review,* 2 (1967), no. 3, pp. 28–64. See also Ronald H. Chilcote, *Revolution and Structural Change in Latin America: A Bibliography on Ideology, Development, and the Radical Left (1930–1965),* 2 vols. (Stanford: Hoover Institution on War, Revolution, and Peace, 1970). 10,005 items listed. Unannotated.

[2] Martin H. Sable, *Latin American Studies in the Non-Western World and Eastern Europe* (Metuchen, N.J.: Scarecrow Press, 1970). Lists 2,926 items and states (pp. 52–53) that in 1964 the Raten America Kyokai published a 175-page annotated bibliography in the Japanese language entitled *Nihon no Latin America Chosa Kenkyuso Gaisetsu.*

Latin American life, teachers will probably wish to lecture on them and to assign their students some of the excellent collections of readings already available on particular revolutions. The purpose of the selections given here is to illustrate some of the new and controversial aspects of the revolutions for students to consider in relation to their other reading.

WOMEN

One word of caution may be in order. The abundant literature on twentieth-century Latin America contains few references to the fundamental — even "revolutionary" — changes now affecting over half its population: women.[3] The thousands of doctoral dissertations prepared on Latin America in the United States alone since 1900 shed only a faint light on the distinctive role of women in the past or on their possible future in Latin American society. The intense and widespread discussions of the need for a "revolution" of the structure of Latin American life usually concern economic and political matters; almost no attention has been paid to the part women can be expected to play in it. Yet their position is definitely changing, though at somewhat different rates from country to country and region to region. In some cities we are told that many of the women who regularly attend mass use birth control methods now. Everywhere women legally have the vote. Even in such a conservative nation as Colombia, women are beginning to participate in dialogues between lay people and the church hierarchy on economic and social questions. Divorce is discussed more insistently and more publicly than ever before, with women actively engaged in this highly controversial and delicate question. To one who first visited Latin America in 1935 when none of these changes were occurring, the results seem to be revolutionary. Yet not much has been written on this subject.

MEXICO: HOW TO MEASURE SOCIAL PROGRESS?

The writer Katherine Anne Porter once told a story of her experience in the Mexican Revolution that expresses perfectly one of the questions most people ask about this turbulent period that began in 1910:

> During the Madero revolution I watched a street battle between Mader-
> istas and Federal troops from the window of a cathedral; a grape-vine

[3] I have treated this subject at greater length, with bibliographic suggestions, in my *Contemporary Latin America: A Short History* (Princeton: Van Nostrand, 1968), pp. 220–222.

heavy with tiny black grapes formed a screen, and a very old Indian woman stood near me, perfectly silent, holding my sleeve. Later she said to me, when the dead were being piled for burning in the public square, "It is all a great trouble now, but it is for the sake of happiness to come." She crossed herself, and I mistook her meaning. "In Heaven?" I asked. Her scorn was splendid. "No, on earth. Happiness for men, not for angels!" She seemed to me then to have caught the whole meaning of revolution and to have said it in a phrase.[4]

Has the Revolution brought happiness in Mexico? Perhaps for some men, but the Revolution did little for women (Reading 64). But can social progress be measured? A historian has confronted this question and attempted to construct a "poverty index." He then applied his yardstick to federal expenditures for social purposes by each administration since 1910, and he reached some startling conclusions (Reading 65).

Will the present apparent stability in Mexico continue? Will the political Revolutionary Family that has maintained itself in power for many years be able to do so in the 1970s?

Fresh approaches and new ideas on how to study history are always welcome and are one indication of the present vitality of practitioners in the field of Latin America. The Third Reunion of Mexican and North American Historians held at Oaxtepec in 1969 was particularly fruitful in this respect, with many suggestive papers being presented.[5] Another important contribution has been made by Professor James W. Wilkie and his wife Edna Monzón de Wilkie in their oral history work that records the views of articulate leaders, in contradistinction to the in-depth interviews of Oscar Lewis with the poor and inarticulate.[6] One more method is illustrated by a British scholar who has analyzed in detail the value to historians of the 1910–1917 period of literary sources.[7]

[4] Katherine Anne Porter, "Why I Write About Mexico," in *The Collected Essays and Occasional Writings of Katherine Anne Porter* (New York, 1970), p. 355.

[5] *Investigaciones contemporáneas sobre historia de México: Memorias de la Tercera Reunión de Historiadores Mexicanos y Norteamericanos* (Mexico City and Austin: Universidad Nacional Autónoma de México, El Colegio de México, and The University of Texas at Austin, 1971). See especially "Nuevos métodos y técnicas de investigación histórica" (pp. 617–648).

[6] James W. Wilkie and Edna Monzón de Wilkie, *México visto en el siglo XX: Entrevistas de historia oral* (Mexico: Instituto Mexicano de Investigaciones Económicas, 1969).

[7] John Rutherford, *Mexican Society during the Revolution: A Literary Approach* (Oxford: Clarendon Press, 1971).

ARGENTINA: A FAILED REVOLUTION?

Some may be surprised to find this relatively advanced country included in a section on revolutionary changes. There were radical improvements, insists Juan Domingo Perón, the army officer who was able to dominate Argentina with the help of his wife Evita (Reading 66). But a British scholar argues that Perón's regime was a "Revolution that failed." [8] However if we consider how women progressed during the period 1943–1955, Perón's policies were, if not revolutionary, definitely an improvement in some respects. Women's rights, for example, were increased due in considerable part to the actions and power of the dictator's wife. The history of the struggle by Argentine women for greater economic and social equality is much longer than the story of Evita Perón, however, as Professor Nancy Hollander makes clear (Reading 67). She describes the earlier associations of women in Argentina to improve their position, and points out that President Perón was also well aware of the political significance of women.

The dust has not yet settled, for Perón is still very much alive in Spain. He talks from time to time about returning to Argentina even though the army holds power there and has had little sympathy for accepting an important political role for *peronismo*. But the military do have faith in their ability to guide the country's destinies, a faith that has been explained on the basis of history,[9] while another writer explains all Argentine history by a glance at the past (Reading 68).

DID BOLIVIA HAVE A REVOLUTION?

All the textbooks tell of the victory of Victor Paz Estenssoro and his revolutionary party (MNR) in 1952, of his downfall in 1964, and of the many changes of government since then. Economic and political conditions following the end in 1935 of the Chaco War against Paraguay remained difficult, and there was great disorganization in most sectors of national life. Paz at the head of the MNR won the election in 1951, but a military junta voided the election and refused to allow Paz to assume the presidency. About a year later, tin miners, students, school teachers, the military police, and government employees fought a violent three-day battle to overthrow the junta and to install Paz as head of the duly elected MNR government.

[8] H. S. Ferns, *Argentina* (New York: Praeger, 1969), pp. 184–200.
[9] Robert A. Potash, *The Army and Politics in Argentina, 1928–1945: Yrigoyen to Perón* (Stanford: Stanford University Press, 1969), pp. 283–287.

Most observers of the confused scene in Bolivia agree that there was indeed significant change after 1952; Bolivia seemed to have turned a corner. This is the message of an eyewitness account of how the revolution broke out (Reading 69) as well as the later analyses by a historian [10] and an anthropologist (Reading 70), though much still remains to be done there.

Thus it remains a strange and hitherto not fully explained mystery that Che Guevara failed to understand that Bolivia had already experienced a revolution and thus was not really ripe for further change. The 1952 nationalization of the most important mines and the 1953 agrarian reform were crucial events whose effects are still being felt.

How could Che Guevara believe that a few non-Bolivian guerrilla fighters, unsupported by either the Bolivian Indians or the Bolivian Communist party, could bring about further revolutionary change after the nationalization of mines and agrarian reform? Was this merely ignorance of the physical terrain as well as of the political and psychological situation in Brazil? Or was it merely one more illustration of the conviction that so many foreigners have had since the sixteenth century — missionaries, American ambassadors, and international agencies alike — that they knew what was good for Bolivia, and were determined to bring about changes they judged desirable whether the Bolivians agreed with them or not? At any rate Che Guevara, master of guerrilla warfare, who had played such an important role in the Castro revolution, was killed in October 1967 in Bolivia under confusing circumstances, and his faltering movement collapsed.

A reporter for the *Chicago Daily News,* Georgie Anne Geyer, in the spring of 1968 interviewed Régis Debray to try to find an explanation for the Che Guevara fiasco in Bolivia, for she felt that "a mist of unreality hung over the entire adventure that rose so spectacularly and failed so decisively." Debray was the young French revolutionary theoretician who had served as "resident philosopher to Che's guerrillas." Here is what she concluded after long discussions with Debray in the dusty town of Camiri, the remote Bolivian post where Bolivian authorities had imprisoned him:

> The entire Debray theory — the attempted application elsewhere of the Castroite experience — proved faulty largely because it was based on an erroneous supposition.
>
> The Cubans did not understand their own revolution. They believed it was waged by only a handful of courageous men in the mountains who mounted the fight against Batista. Indeed, they were the revolu-

---

[10] Herbert S. Klein, *Parties and Political Change in Bolivia, 1880–1952* (Cambridge, England: Cambridge University Press, 1969) pp. 403–409.

tion's symbol. But the revolution was really waged in the cities — by the middle classes who came to despise Batista. Nor did the Cubans basically care about Bolivia, that funny, beautiful little Indian country where all the tables have three legs. They looked at it in the way that the United States so often has mistakenly looked upon little countries — not in terms of anything intrinsic, but strategically, manipulatively.

Perhaps, as Che lies in his secret grave and as Debray sits in his sunny courtyard pondering many things, there is still one other reason why they failed. It is not a rational reason, but few things, and particularly movements like Che's and adventures like Debray's, can be explained in totally rational terms.

The entire Bolivian tale presents the question as to how the "invaders," as the Bolivians called them, could do what they had long accused their own worst enemy, the United States, of doing. One has to wonder whether there is not perhaps something in men that causes them to hate things so much because that is what they themselves most truly are. Whether there is not something that drives men ultimately to act out in their own lives what they most hate their enemies for doing.[11]

CHILE AND PERU

After Cuba, no Latin American country has received more attention in recent years than Chile because of its duly elected socialist regime. When Dr. Salvador Allende assumed the direction of this democracy in 1970, the world waited to see how rapidly he would be able "to nudge" Chile toward a socialist state. The situation called for change, and a decade ago Professor Pike considered the gulf between the "haves" and "have nots" so deep that it invited "a devastating social revolution" (Reading 71). President Eduardo Frei Montalva's presidency under a Christian Democrat rule (1964–1970) initiated important developments in agrarian reform and the Chileanization of the copper mines upon which the national economy rests heavily. But evidently he did not proceed fast enough. It is the better part of wisdom for a historian to avoid discussing current events, especially those in such a rapidly changing area as Latin America. But often there are some basic developments worth noting, particularly when a military-dominated, semicapitalistic country such as Peru seems to be moving in somewhat the same direction, economically at least, as socialist Chile.

[11] Georgie Anne Geyer, "Why Guevara Failed: An Interview with Régis Debray," *Saturday Review*, August 24, 1968, pp. 14–18.

WHAT HAPPENED IN URUGUAY?

For a long while this small country was a "model democracy" in Latin America. It had everything: an intelligent electorate, no church-state problem, no dictators; women enjoyed an enviable economic, legal, and psychological status; and Uruguayans were noted for their very advanced social legislation. After 1950 it became evident that all was not well in the first and most famous welfare state in the continent. Now it is generally recognized as a sick welfare state, and political observers are busy diagnosing what went wrong.[12]

A FINAL OBSERVATION

Though Latin America is undergoing changes, some of which are revolutionary, their direction and their causes must be carefully examined if we are not to be led astray by facile generalizations. The development process in Latin America displays certain special characteristics, according to one experienced political scientist. Latin American society remains "in many ways a profoundly conservative and unrevolutionary society." And what changes have occurred do not follow any particular pattern: "In the past most changes have come about sporadically, not usually as the result of any 'glorious revolution' or even through much purposeful action." [13]

Yet there is one constant — the puzzling and controversial question of what should be the policy of the United States toward Latin America. Here, too, voices counseling caution and realism are being heard, at least in the groves of academe (Reading 72).

[12] See M. H. J. Finch, "Three Perspectives on the Crisis in Uruguay," *Journal of Latin American Studies,* III (November, 1971), Part 2, pp. 173–190.

[13] Howard J. Wiarda, "The Latin American Development Process and the New Developmental Alternatives: Military 'Nasserism' and 'Dictatorship with Popular Support,'" *The Western Political Quarterly,* 25 (1972), pp. 489–490.

64. *The Mexican Revolution Was No Revolution for Women*

ANNA MACÍAS

For her doctorate in Latin American history at Columbia University, Professor Anna Macías of Ohio Wesleyan University specialized in the political ideology of the Mexican revolution that began in 1810. Recently she has turned her attention to the role of women in more recent Mexican history. The present selection is part of a paper presented at the annual meeting of the American Historical Association in 1971. Her conclusions tend to confirm what the author of one of the few books on the Mexican family stated: Despite the many drastic changes brought by the revolution it "has not yet succeeded in sweeping from the feminine mind the preconceptions about her incapacity, her dependence on man, and her absolute need for resignation that traditionally have weighed her down for centuries." *

In 1959 Mrs. Parinal Dos, an Indian civil servant, said that "the greatest revolution a country can know is the one which changes the condition and way of life of its women. Whether one agrees with this judgment or not, most Mexicanists will agree that historians have paid relatively little attention to the role of Mexican women in the social revolution that began in 1910, or to the changes that upheaval wrought in their condition and way of life. The few historians who in the revolutionary era devoted any attention at all to Mexican women differed sharply in their conclusions. In 1916 M. C. Rolland, in a brief essay on "Women in Mexico" asserted that, ". . . the revolution of these later years makes evident what we might call an 'acceleration' of the vindication of women in America." But in 1928, after eleven years of the revolutionary regimes of Carranza, Obregon, and Calles, Ernest Gruening concluded that "the revolution has done little, purposefully, toward the emancipation of women. . . . Nor will it achieve a thorough-going emancipation of Mexico while one half of its population remains to be set free." But before one can examine the problem of what the Mexican revolution did or

From "Mexican Women in the Social Revolution" by Anna Macías. Published by permission of the author.
* María Elvira Bermúdez, *La vida familiar del Mexicano* (Mexico City: Robredo, 1955).

did not do to change the situation and the role of the female, one has to see what her condition and way of life were in the centuries before 1910. . . .

On the eve of the Mexican revolution attitudes toward women, the sex mores, and the role either "good" or "bad" women were expected to play in the society had changed to some degree since the colonial period but could not on the whole be said to have improved. Altogether the legal and real situation of women in Mexico in 1910, and of their sisters elsewhere in Latin America, was unenviable. Yet up to 1910 feminism had made little headway in Mexico, and as can be expected it was championed almost exclusively by female schoolteachers and the handful of other professional women who were beginning to study or practice medicine, the law, dentistry, or pharmacy. Only the bravest of these women became advocates of woman's emancipation, for hostility to feminism, even of the most moderate variety, was undisguised. In 1904 one journalist who signed himself *Pistache* identified all feminists with "bad" women. "The women who speak of feminism are not good," as asserted, "and wish to call themselves 'progressive and liberal' because that sounds better than what they really are." Other unfriendly critics accused the feminists of being un-feminine. One sociologist predicted that Mexican women would lose "100% of their charms as a result of the triumphal entrance of feminism into Mexico."

That feminism did not make a triumphal entry into Mexico with the coming of the revolution is clear when one examines the political plans and the social reforms associated with Francisco I. Madero and Venustiano Carranza. Although both men received support from a number of educated women and several feminist societies, the only reform that directly affected women in the period from 1911 to early 1915 was the divorce law. Drawn up at the very end of 1914 and first promulgated on January 25, 1915, the law provided for absolute divorce for the first time in Mexican history.

According to Carranza the law would be a powerful factor for morality among all classes in society and would reduce concubinage among the upper classes and free unions among the poor. He argued that *amasiato* or free union was universal among the poor classes in Mexico, not so much because weddings were expensive, but because legal marriage was indissoluble. He believed that poor Mexicans had an "instinctive fear of ties with irreparable consequences," and that by making divorce possible there would be fewer free unions and illegitimate children. The law would benefit upper and middle class women for whom legal separation was seldom a satisfactory remedy for an unhappy marriage. Carranza noted that because of custom and the kind of education they received, most middle and upper class married women could not support themselves. When and if a marriage failed, the wife, not being able to support herself and not being able to contract a new marriage, became the victim of her husband and was, according to Carranza, in a real status of slavery. He maintained that there would be a decline in concubinage because a wife would no longer have to tolerate her husband's adultery and could sue for divorce if he kept a mistress.

Although a few *feministas exaltadas* or advanced feminists advocated divorce in Mexico, the more numerous moderate feminists opposed it on the grounds that it would hurt rather than help most married women. It appears that Carranza's divorce law was issued, not as a result of pressure from women, but rather from men, who, if one looks closely at the law, stood to benefit from it more than women. To Mexican feminists, the new law retained the same odious double standard that was part of the 1884 law which had established legal separation in Mexico. That earlier law automatically granted legal separation to the husband whose wife committed adultery under any circumstances. The husband's adultery was grounds for legal separation only under certain conditions, that is, if he committed adultery in the home, kept a mistress, and created a public scandal by mistreating or permitting his mistress to mistreat his wife. In addition, the new law provided that while the man could remarry immediately after a divorce was granted, the woman could not remarry for 300 days after the divorce was final. This stipulation did not protect any woman. Rather, a man marrying a divorced woman was assured that she was not pregnant by the first husband.

Critics of the divorce law pointed out later that it did not spell out the penalties for failure to make alimony or child support payments. Further, the provision that "the spouse upon whom falls the obligation to pay . . . alimony may pay an amount equivalent to a flat five years of support and avoid any further payment," was a disadvantage to a divorced wife with infants or young children. This matter of alimony and child support payments is significant, for Carranza had noted in the preamble to the law that most married women were not prepared to work outside the home to support themselves and their children. It appears that Carranza did not accompany the new divorce law with a notable effort to hire more women in government posts, to improve their educational opportunities, or to initiate other measures which would help women be more self-sufficient. This may explain why the divorce law did not receive much support from feminists. The advocates of the law assumed that a divorced woman would have no difficulty remarrying, but a feminist critical of the law asserted in 1921 that a divorced woman, no matter how guiltless, was treated with scorn and contempt.

On the national level, and until 1915, only the divorce law directly affected women, which makes it clear why Ernest Gruening concluded that the revolution did not purposefully accomplish much for their emancipation. In fact, when one considers that women played a vital role in the revolution as *soldaderas,* as couriers and propaganda agents for the revolutionary forces, and as nurses on the field of battle, it appears that they gave a great deal more than they received from its national leaders.

Yet M. C. Rolland had a point when he asserted that there was an "acceleration" of the movement in favor of women's rights in Mexico as a result of the revolution. For on the regional level, and particularly in the distant state of Yucatán, a number of steps were taken to improve the socioeconomic condition of women which had an impact on national policies.

At first glance it seems odd that Yucatán, famous for its henequen plantations and infamous for the virtual enslavement of its Maya population during the Porfiriato, should be the principal locus of women's liberation. Yet Yucatán was also one of the first Mexican states to make education beyond primary school available to women. Shortly after the Republic was restored in 1867, the Instituto Literario de Niñas was established at Mérida. Its first director was the American Enriqueta Dorchester. She was succeeded by a native Yucatecan, Rita Cetina Gutiérrez, a distinguished poet as well as teacher, who devoted her life to the education of women. By 1912, the graduates of this school, which was renamed the Escuela Normal de Profesoras, were teaching in scores of schools in the peninsula of Yucatán. At Mérida in 1870 was founded one of the earliest feminist societies, *La Siempreviva.* The group edited a periodical by the same name staffed by women and dedicated to furthering the education of females. Between 1910 and 1915 at least eight pamphlets and books on the subject of the rights of women and on divorce were published in Mérida, a record which appears to have been unmatched by Mexico City, where most of the nation's publishing was centered.

The Countess Emilia Pardo Bazán, the novelist and ardent feminist, once observed that "for woman to progress, it would be necessary, in the first place, that she want to and secondly, that she find some of the terrain prepared [and] some help from men too." Considerable help came from Salvador Alvarado, who was appointed by Carranza as revolutionary governor of Yucatán early in 1915. Alvarado, who still awaits a definitive biography in Spanish or English, was an important figure in the revolution from 1909, when he first became a supporter of Madero, until his death in 1924, during the de la Huerta uprising. A northerner like most of the prominent revolutionaries, Alvarado was born in Culiacán, Sinaloa in 1880 and, as a merchant and contractor near the border, had occasion to travel in the United States where he studied and learned the English language. He joined the

military revolt against the Díaz regime in 1910, and saw action in practically every important battle fought against Díaz and then against Huerta,
when the latter deposed Madero. Known for his superb organizational and
administrative talents, and for a strict honesty in the handling of large sums
of money, Alvarado was probably chosen by Carranza as Governor of
Yucatán to insure that part of the large revenues available to that State from
the sale of henequen would find their way to Carranza's treasury in Vera
Cruz.

After defeating counter-revolutionary forces in Yucatán, Alvarado entered
Mérida on March 19, 1915, and had a tenure of three years in which he
developed his program of social and economic reform with no interference
from the outside. The price of henequen rose sharply during World War I
because Yucatán was the principal source of binder twine used by most wheat
farmers in the United States. As a result, Alvarado was able to send funds
to Carranza and have enough left over to finance a series of far-reaching
socio-economic reforms in Yucatán.

In his political orientation Alvarado was a radical rather than a liberal,
which is to say that he wanted to wipe out all the accumulated injustices of
400 years of colonial and national history at once. In three years he drew up
hundreds of legislative decrees intended to correct every evil and end every
abuse in Yucatecan society. Unlike other revolutionary intellectuals such as
Felix Palavicini and Manuel Gamio, who thought woman would soften her
brain or lose her charms by receiving a higher education or by competing
with men in the work-a-day world, Alvarado viewed the struggle for woman's emancipation as part of the general struggle in Mexico to aid her weak-
est and most oppressed people — Indians, workers, peons, and domestics.

Barely a month after he entered Mérida and on April 29, 1915, Alvarado
made clear that his Government intended to help women support themselves.
La Voz de la Revolución, an independent but pro-Alvarado newspaper
established in Mérida after the Constitutionalist forces entered the city, reported him as saying that "until now women have been solely an object of
luxury or of social dissipation." Alvarado informed the public that positions
in the state government as office workers, clerks, cashiers and accountants
were now open to qualified women, and urged them to apply for these jobs.
He also drew up a special law intended to improve the situation of female
domestic servants, who were badly paid, if they were paid at all, who had
little time to themselves, and who were locked in at night by their employers. He decreed minimum wages and maximum hours for domestics and
prohibited employers from insisting that maids live in unless the latter had
no home of their own.

Alvarado then turned his attention to an even more unfortunate group of women. By the stroke of the pen, he sought to outlaw brothels and to free prostitutes from their dependence on madames, pimps, and corrupt "vice squad" officers. He established a separate health service unconnected with the police or any other branch of the government to provide prostitutes regular examinations by doctors paid adequately for their services. Although Alvarado was generally accused of being a Utopian by skeptics, he was realistic enough to know that prostitution could not be ended by fiat but that something might nevertheless be done to end the exploitation of prostitutes and free them from the brothels.

Alvarado's main efforts to emancipate women were focused on improving their opportunities for education. Educational reform was his abiding passion, and in three years over 30% of the government revenues were expended on schools. He established a school of agriculture, founded some 1,000 rural schools and added 40 new urban primary schools, laid the foundations for a university, set up the first Montessori school for young children, created the scholar-republics as a kind of political science laboratory in the primary schools, initiated special schools for monolingual Maya children, and sponsored vocational schools for men and women.

He devoted considerable attention to the School of Domestic Arts, where 230 females studied careers ranging from home economics to telegraphy. This particular school had a large budget, and the salaries paid to the predominantly female teachers averaged $1,500 pesos a month, only about $200 pesos less than the pay of doctors in the newly formed School of Medicine. Alvarado also introduced co-education in primary schools through the third grade, deploring the fact that children grew up in ignorance of the opposite sex. He decreed co-education in the normal schools, encouraged more women to enter the professional schools, and invited all women with intellectual interests to join the Ateneo Peninsular, the previously all-male Athenaeum.

A man who was frank to the point of bluntness, Alvarado made clear at the first Pedagogical Congress in 1916 why he was interested in the woman's liberation. "The Mexican woman has no will of her own," he lamented, "and she does the bidding of her father, her lover, her husband, and her confessor." A radical anti-clerical who used Yucatan's churches as schools, meeting halls, or warehouses, Alvarado stated "we believe that while the priest continues to be the protector, counselor, and guide of women [Mexico] will be in danger and nothing will be done towards its progress or liberation." The alliance between women and the Church had to be broken, according to

Alvarado, by giving women an adequate education, a sense of their own personality and, above all, a chance to be independent human beings.

Impatient for concrete and immediate results from his reforms and anxious to involve Yucatecans in their own liberation, Alvarado called a number of congresses in Mérida to publicize his ambitious reforms and gain public support for them. Thus from late 1915 to early 1917 he called, in addition to the two feminist congresses which will be discussed below, two pedagogical congresses and at least one workers' congress. On October 28, 1915, some seven months after his government was established in Yucatán, Alvarado announced that he was convening a feminist congress to be held in Mérida before the end of the year. The pro-government *La Voz de la Revolución* reported this novel event in banner headlines the next day, and in the weeks and months following gave considerable attention in feature articles and editorials to the coming congress and to the whole question of women's rights in Mexico and the rest of the world. It was the first feminist congress held in Mexico, and apparently the second held in all of Latin America, the first having met at Buenos Aires in May 1910. Alvarado instructed organizers of the congress to deal with such basic questions as the best means of freeing women from the yoke of tradition, the role of primary education and of the State in woman's liberation, and the role women should play in public life.

Alvarado found enthusiastic support for his proposed congress and by January 1916 it was clear that over 600 women, many of them schoolteachers in Yucatan's urban and rural schools, would attend. The coming congress generated so much euphoria that one of its organizers, Consuelo Zavala, warned the public not to expect it to solve age-old problems in four days. She said that "congress" was a misnomer and that "preliminary studies on woman" was a more accurate description of the coming event. A congress implied a culmination, but Señorita Zavala stressed that the struggle for woman's liberation in Mexico was only beginning and that she and her associates involved in the congress represented only a tiny minority of Mexican women.

From the first day of the meetings it was clear that despite the homogeneity of its predominantly educated middle-class participants, there were at least three distinct and antagonistic points of view represented. One group, admittedly small, but vocal nonetheless, was patently anti-feminist and lamented that since 1867 more and more women had sought and obtained an education beyond primary school. "School teachers do not marry," wailed Señorita García Ortiz before her predominantly unmarried audience, asserting that the more education a woman received the fewer her chances for happiness, that is, for marrying and raising a family. While her remarks were resented by her auditors they were aware that few men of their acquaintance were interested in marrying a woman who was their intellectual equal or superior. Señorita García was expressing the traditional prejudice against educated women which Sor Juana had felt so keenly in the 17th century.

At the other extreme were advanced feminists. They insisted that women were intellectually and morally the equals of men and that they could and should take an active role in society by voting and running for office. Even more radical, they insisted that woman, like man, is born with a strong sexual instinct and that women could not be free human beings until they had an adequate sex education that prepared them for marriage and armed them against falling into prostitution through sheer ignorance. While Señorita García's assertion that school teachers seldom marry ruffled her audience, the assertion by Hermila Galindo, one of Mexico's most radical feminists, that women could not be free until they acknowledged and understood their own sexuality scandalized her genteel audience. . . . According to the traditional sex mores inherited from both the Aztec and Spanish colonial past, a "good" woman is not supposed to be interested in sex at all. Only "bad" women are acknowledged to have a sex drive. Sociologists studying contemporary Mexico report that this is still the case, and that Mexican men think of their mothers, sisters, wives and daughters as "good" and therefore uninterested in sex. All other women are possibly "bad," that is, potential sex objects. But even here a "bad" woman is thought of as an *object,* and as passive in the sexual relationship. The idea of a woman, good or bad, taking an interest in her own sexuality and an active role in the sexual relationship is something few Mexican men will acknowledge.

In any case, Hermila Galindo's insistence on female sexuality and her plea for a study of woman such as Simone de Beauvoir was to publish almost forty years later, aroused a storm that almost disrupted the congress.

The third point of view, and the one which predominated in the resolutions ultimately accepted by the delegates, was that of the moderate feminists. They argued that the opening of schools and teaching careers to women since the 1850s was a step forward and not merely, as the antifeminists argued, a guarantee against finding a husband. The moderates argued that universal, primary, and laical education had to be made available to all women, not just 20% of the female population. They put special emphasis on laical schools, favored a rationalistic approach to religious matters, viewing the primary school as the vehicle for ending what they characterized as religious superstition, bigotry, and intolerance. In addition they argued that in primary school and beyond women needed to receive a practical or vocational education which would enable them to support themselves when necessary and to be better wives and mothers when they remained at home. The moderates wanted women to be the intellectual companions of their husbands and the competent teachers of their children. They also argued that women should marry out of choice and not necessity, and that only women with an education and a knowledge of the world had that choice. At the same time they argued that for the present political rights should be exercised only by men but that since women were intellectually and morally equal to men they should, at some future time, vote and hold office.

The moderates agreed with the radicals on one very important matter, and that was the need to reform the Civil Code of 1884 in every sphere that discriminated against women. This included the articles on guardianship, matrimony, child custody, inheritance, and the rights of single women to leave the parental home on reaching the age of 21. This was one of the most concrete proposals to emerge from the congress, and Alvarado probably forwarded it to Carranza. The latter may have had it in mind when he issued his Law of Domestic Relations on April 9, 1917 as a complement to the 1914 divorce law. The 1917 law guaranteed the rights of married women with respect to guardianship and child custody, taking part in legal suits, and drawing up contracts. Women were to have equal authority with their husbands in the home with respect to their children's education and the expenditure of family funds. The law also permitted paternity suits and gave fathers the right to acknowledge illegitimate children.

Although the First Feminist Congress of Yucatan of January 13–16, 1916 was rather a chaotic affair, with some unpleasant personal altercations, the intellectual level of many of the papers was high and the commentaries well-reasoned and often eloquent. The male reporters of *La Voz de la Revolución* were astonished to see some 620 women dealing so expertly with ideas. One of them exclaimed: "There are many well-informed women in Yucatán. Many more than, in general, we are aware of."

Yet Governor Alvarado was disappointed with the Congress and did not attend the closing session as planned. His reasons were perhaps best expressed by the anonymous reporter of the pro-government press who observed that the Congress had demonstrated that there was still considerable prejudice against women. To be truly emancipated he felt that women needed "a little more courage" than they had displayed at the Congress. He complained that too few women defended "progressive, rationalistic" education and woman suffrage; the rest he thought had been timid and conservative.

The proposal for woman's suffrage was at first rejected by the majority on the grounds that women needed more time and training to assume civic responsibilities, even on the municipal level. At the very last session of the Congress on January 16, however, a new petition on suffrage signed by 28 of the more radical delegates was hastily submitted. It proposed that Yucatán's constitution be changed to permit women over 21 to vote in municipal elections and to hold local office. It also asked that the State government initiate an appeal that female suffrage in municipal elections be added to the country's constitution. The new petition, despite the earlier vote against suffrage by the congress members, was now approved by a unanimity of votes. It is difficult to tell from the newspaper accounts of the last meeting how this about-face was accomplished. In any case, it may have been this last minute change, as well as over-all disappointment with the First Feminist Congress, which led Alvarado to announce on June 12, 1916 that a second congress would be held at the end of November. He announced that the second meeting would be a national feminist congress and expressed the hope that women would come from as many Mexican states as possible to exchange ideas with their Yucatecan sisters.

To avoid the chaos of the first congress, only about 240 delegates from Yucatán were invited to attend, and most of them were schoolteachers. Very few representatives came from other states, and from the beginning the conference was renamed the Second Feminist Congress of Yucatán. The absence of out-of-state delegates was not due to lack of interest. It must be remembered that the trip to Yucatán from the most populous centers of Mexico was long and expensive and that in 1916 middle-class women did not usually travel unaccompanied by the husband or male relatives.

In general the Second Feminist Congress was much more conservative than the first in dealing with the general themes of how best to emancipate women, but it did approve by a vote of 147 to 87 the proposal that women be permitted to vote in municipal elections. The debate on suffrage was acrimonious, and when it came time to vote on the issue of women holding office, only 90 women were present to vote and only a third of those voted in the affirmative.

Both the first and second feminist congresses made clear that in 1916 few women in Yucatán wanted to be actively involved in politics. Only the more advanced feminists wanted to vote, and only in municipal elections.

That women were even interested in discussing their political rights in 1916 seems remarkable, however, when one considers the role and situation of Mexican women in the previous four centuries. From pre-Columbian times to well into the nineteenth century, generation after generation of Mexican mothers had taught their daughters that women must be submissive to men and have no will of their own. A stereotype developed of the self-abnegating, self-sacrificing, and long-suffering Mexican wife and mother who sought solace in religion. Since women were thought by most to be biologically, intellectually and socially inferior to men, a gifted woman lived in isolation and found few means of developing or using her talents.

With the coming of the Reform movement, with its active encouragement of education for women beyond primary school, attitudes began to change. Between 1875 and 1910 a numerically small yet significant group of educated women emerged. Most, but not all, were schoolteachers, and to end their isolation and to educate the literate public concerning woman's emancipation, they began to form feminist societies and edit journals. Very often they met with indifference, derision and hostility, but some influential men supported their efforts to improve the educational and economic situation of women.

During the Mexican revolution of 1910–1920 the efforts on behalf of women's rights by the national leadership appear inconclusive and piecemeal. The main impetus for woman's liberation came from Salvador Alvarado during his three years as revolutionary governor of Yucatán. Bent on transforming the Mexican woman from a weak, passive and inert element into a vital force for progress in Mexico, he introduced important legislation and encouraged women to study, to work outside the home, and to take part in public life. He found immediate support from hundreds of educated women in Yucatán and called the first two feminist congresses held in Mexico.

While the two congresses had few immediate results, they had more than symbolic value. For the first time in Mexican history a large group of women found a public forum for expressing their views concerning their legal rights, the kind of education females should have, the need for greater economic opportunities for women, the relationship of women and the Mexican church, and the effects of the double standard on women. It was only a beginning, not a consummation, but that is what the social revolution of 1910–1920 was: a beginning towards the goal of the social equality of all Mexicans. The end is not yet in sight.

65. *How to Measure the Mexican Revolution*

JAMES W. WILKIE

Professor James W. Wilkie of the University of California, Los Angeles, is one of the pioneers in applying quantitative methods to the study of Latin American historical problems. Here he addresses himself to the thorny question of how to measure the effects of the Mexican Revolution. As he predicted, his "analysis of social change for the masses presented here will undoubtedly be controversial," but henceforth the methods he devised and the conclusions he reached will have to be taken into account by all serious students of Mexican history since 1910.* And Wilkie's book will doubtless stimulate as he hoped, "analysis of different levels of social change."

FOUR IDEOLOGICAL PERIODS

The quantitative summaries of expenditure in the Mexican Revolution reveal four periods of ideological action. Francisco I. Madero, apostle of the Mexican Revolution of 1910, took over the presidency in 1911 with a wide base of support among the politically aware population, but he did not make a sharp break with Porfirio Díaz's budgetary policies. Madero's average projected and actual expenditures differed only slightly in percentage terms from those of the dictator he had overthrown. The man who might have reoriented drastically the role of the state set a conservative precedent of governmental action. Succeeding governments during the period from 1913 to 1920 held to this concept of government. Though there was much radical talk of aiding the masses, especially in the early 1920's, there was only a gradual shift away from a passive role for the state in social and economic affairs.

From *The Mexican Revolution: Federal and Social Change Since 1910* by James W. Wilkie, 2nd ed. rev. (1970), pp. 35–39, 204–207, 276–285, passim. Originally published by the University of California Press; reprinted by permission of the Regents of the University of California.

* For comments see the article by Thomas E. Skidmore and Peter H. Smith, "Notes on Quantitative History: Federal Expenditure and Social Change in Mexico Since 1910," *Latin American Research Review*, 5 (1970), no. 1, pp. 71–86; Wilkie's rejoinder, "New Hypotheses for Statistical Research in Recent Mexican History," ibid., 6 (1971), no. 2, pp. 3–18; and David Barkin, "Public Expenditures and Social Change in Mexico: A Methodological Critique," *Journal of Latin American Studies*, 4 (1972), no. 1, pp. 105–112. Wilkie has also applied his methods to religious data, "Statistical Indicators of the Impact of National Revolution on the Catholic Church in Mexico, 1910–1967," *Journal of Church and State*, 12 (1970), pp. 89–106.

The first actual dramatic presidential action which rejected the old concept of the administrative state came under Lázaro Cárdenas, 1934–1940. Cárdenas, who predicated his program on achieving social justice, sought and found greater funds for state action, and he used them. He increased social expenditure to a new high. This action and Cárdenas's expenditure of an average of 37.6 per cent of the federal purse in the economic sphere of national life marked the turning point of Mexico's Revolution.

Though subsequent presidents would often balk at using the resources of the state to intervene in social affairs, . . . the active state was firmly established. The implementation of the Constitution of 1917 could finally be undertaken. . . . Cárdenas's program was rooted in a consensus for state action after 1930. Ortiz Rubio, caught up in the ideological swirl of how to cope with the depression, made halting moves to achieve economic recovery and social well-being. Cárdenas became a presidential candidate in the trough of a depression, but . . . basically the economy had recovered by the time he took office. With actual pesos per capita at their predepression level in 1934, Cárdenas could effectively call upon the country's resources for radical new experiments in statecraft.

The wartime presidency of Manuel Avila Camacho projected almost exactly the same average percentage expenditure as Cárdenas had projected, but an actual shift away from social expenditure to greater economic expenditure became evident. The ideology of emphasis on economic development won a startling percentage increase under Miguel Alemán in the postwar period. Alemán projected an average economic expenditure of almost 40 per cent of the budget, but he spent 51.9 per cent of the expanded federal purse for economic development. This emphasis in the revolution lasted until López Mateos de-emphasized economic expenditure in favor of renewed social goals. López Mateos projected the ideology of a balanced revolution, and nowhere is this clearer than in his budgets which offered to spend a relatively balanced percentage of federal funds on social, economic, and administrative activities. However, in years of greatly expanding actual expenditure per capita, López Mateos emphasized the percentage share of administrative functions, especially at the expense of social development.

In sum, ideological periods of political revolution (emphasizing administrative forms of change), social revolution, economic revolution, and balanced revolution may be quantitatively seen to encompass four respective time spans: 1910–1930, 1930–1940, 1940–1959, and 1959–1963. Naturally there are many crosscurrents within these periods, for no analysis can be wholly consistent. At best the periods of ideological drive offer a way to look at the spirit of the times in Mexico. All interest groups do not necessarily approve of the trajectory of any given period, but they do operate within each period's context, and they may actively seek to change the direction of their times. Unless such dissident groups offer a plausible program which can be carried out through a consensus of society, however, they will have to resort to rebellion and rule by sheer force.

Since President Venustiano Carranza's attempt to rule by military control of Mexico from 1915 to 1920, Mexico's Revolutionary Family has based its appeal on social and economic gains in society. Ideology of Revolution has been the banner for continued power, though until the 1930's the official party did not undertake a really active role of national integration. Thus, for example, dissident Catholic and Communist groups have not appealed to enough persons to shift directly the historical path of Mexico in any given period. Certainly they have never been able to build upon any general dissatisfactions or tensions in society to overthrow the Revolutionary Family. . . .

DEFINITION OF POVERTY

Poverty can be discussed in many different meanings and contexts. In the rich nations one may speak of intellectual and spiritual poverty in addition to a poverty of monetary income which falls below an arbitrary standard of living. In underdeveloped countries, it is hard to speak of these types of poverty when large numbers of the population can not, for example, read or write, speak the national language, or obtain proper diet and medical care. If persons live in isolated villages and are ill-clothed and ill-shod, it is difficult to talk of intellectual and spiritual poverty, for day-to-day adversity is the primary fact which governs life. There are, of course, many romanticists who actually believe that the life of the Mexican peasant is an idyllic one and should not be upset for the dubious advantages of modern civilization, but these people have never lived in the Mexican countryside. All revolutionists have talked in terms of raising the standard of living of the people. None has proposed to let the masses remain stagnant in a traditional agricultural paradise where they can pluck their guitars, drink pulque or tequila, and fall into a timely siesta to accommodate the passing tourist looking for the picturesque old Mexico of Porfirio Díaz.

If Mexico is to become a modern, integrated nation, the people must lead a better life. The success of the Revolution can and must be evaluated in social as well as economic terms. It is necessary to note that this study is not proposing any method of change, or even suggesting that spiritual poverty might not result from amelioration of the hardships in the old way of life which we define. The poverty treated in this study can not begin to compare with poverty in a developed country, for it deals with some basic deprivations of life.

The characteristics of poverty chosen for the Index are the only census items for standard of living that can be traced back with historical continuity. From 1910 to 1940 only three items were gathered by census takers which would reveal the immediate social position of the populace. After a decade of social revolution in the 1930's, the 1940 census was concerned with specifically checking to see what the social conditions of the people were. Therefore, since 1940 we have seven items with which to work. In 1960, with the shift to renewed interest in the social conditions of the masses, the López Mateos government included a new item in the census which attempts to measure directly the nation's dietary pattern. The new item asks whether or not persons more than one year old eat regularly at least of the following foods yielding nonvegetable protein: meat, fish, milk, and eggs. This item is, of course, of no use here, for it will take several censuses to see what changes take place, and what the item really means.

Analysis of social change during the period 1910–1960 is based on the assumption that all of the seven items under consideration represent relative degrees of nonmodern standards of living. The items cover the persons actually stating in the census that they (1) are illiterate, (2) speak only an Indian language, (3) live in a community with less than 2500 persons, (4) go barefoot, (5) wear sandals, (6) regularly eat tortillas instead of wheat bread and (7) are without sewage disposal. These characteristics of poverty carry equal weight in the Index, since, for example, who is to say that illiteracy is more of a problem than only speaking an Indian language. In either case the individual is denied access to many benefits of modern culture.

Lest we grow indignant that the above items are based on American standards applied somehow dishonestly to Mexico in the hope of corrupting her to follow our path, we should note that Mexican anthropologists have attempted since at least as early as 1916 to modernize Mexican society while maintaining the best of traditional values. Mexico's most famous anthropologist, Manuel Gamio, has written that the Spanish language must be spread to every corner of Mexico in order to integrate the nation, and the tortilla and the sandal must give at least some ground to the progress that man has laboriously worked out to improve human health and comfort. Three of the above items (4–6) were included in the 1940 census on the assumption that an analysis of poverty would reveal the number of Indians in the populace. As we will see, these items did not have as much to do with Indian culture as with the general culture of poverty.

There are problems in developing analyses of poverty and perhaps a few should be noted before we continue our discussion. Any definition of poverty must be somewhat abstract, and it must override individual variations. It is important to recognize, however, that though an individual may exhibit one or more of the characteristics in the Poverty Index and still not be considered poor by his neighbors, the sum of poverty characteristics has a great deal to do with the collective well-being of the nation.

If we view the items included in the Poverty Index as characteristics which tend to reveal the relative health of society at a given historical time, then the Index will make sense. If we view the items on an individual level we face such inconsistencies as pointed out by Oscar Lewis in his study of *Life in a Mexican Village: Tepoztlán Restudied* (Urbana: University of Illinois, 1951, Chapter IX). Lewis's statistical calculations of standards of living showed that the eating of tortillas correlated positively with economic position: wealthy people preferred bread. On the other hand, the wearing of shoes did not correlate with wealth, but with age: the older generation desired to go barefoot or wear sandals. Nevertheless, we may note that regardless of how individuals lived in Tepoztlán in the 1940's when Lewis studied them, by 1950 the census showed that in the state of Morelos (in which Tepoztlán is located) a dramatic decline had taken place in the percentage of the population regularly eating tortillas and going barefoot. The former figure decreased spectacularly again by 1960. The percentage of the population wearing sandals went up slightly between 1940 and 1950 before falling somewhat below the 1940 figure by 1960. . . .

CONCLUSION

The president of Mexico has great power to use federal funds in almost any way he sees fit in order to carry out his programs. These programs are not generally spelled out to the public, but budgetary analysis reveals what they have been. We find, therefore, a considerable difference between the styles of presidents in the Revolution. Presidents have reflected the ideology of their time by the way they allocated the federal purse for administrative, social, and economic expenditure in order to integrate the Mexican nation.

A political concept of the state dominated Mexican governmental affairs from the fall of the dictator Porfirio Díaz to the rise of Lázaro Cárdenas during the early 1930's. Cárdenas himself seized the opportunity that the crisis in political revolution presented to undertake the social restructure of Mexico. He not only definitively reoriented the economy away from the agricultural hacienda system, he also proposed to change the educational system and swiftly to integrate the Mexican people into a nation, a program which had been delayed since Mexico's independence in 1821. We have seen that his programs had little practical effect on the life of the common man, who remained illiterate, shoeless, isolated, underfed, and without sewage disposal. A large number still could not speak Spanish by the time Cárdenas left office. Even with Cárdenas's Six-Year Plan, Mexico could not be remade in one presidential term. The social drive apparently went out of the Revolution when Cárdenas turned his office over to Manuel Avila Camacho, and many have been led to conclude that the Revolution died in 1940. We have found that social benefits for the masses as well as economic development came at a rapid rate only after 1940.

Strikes, land distribution, and Socialist Education were curtailed as Mexico entered an epoch of ideology dominated by the concept of economic revolution. In a period of industrialization, irrigation, and public works, everyone was sure that immediate benefits to the masses were being postponed until Mexico was economically developed. The group which sponsored economic revolution, led by Alemán, also believed that social benefits would have to be sacrificed in the name of progress. The Poverty Index, however, indicates that the revolution was very much alive, and that Mexico experienced its most rapid social change for the masses between 1940 and 1960. West Central and East Central Mexico benefited more in decrease of poverty from economic impetus, for example, than they ever did from the so-called immediate benefits of social revolution.

We must remember, nevertheless, that because of the reorientation of the economy under Cárdenas, money was channeled by the private sector into the business of urbanization. Whereas Cárdenas had planned to establish a rural Mexico based on the communal farm, he created *minifundios* which have not contributed to the growth of the Mexican economy. Many wealthy landholders, fearing expropriation, invested in the city, at first in real estate, then in business, and finally in light industry. The basis for a new order unintentionally grew out of the social revolution.

Though Mexican workers (who may have gained in psychological terms from land labor policies under Cárdenas) might have lost ground in "indirect benefits" between 1940 and 1960, they could take advantage of the ideology of economic revolution's new opportunities. The Poverty Index began to decline relatively rapidly after 1940. Though inflation was not caused by deliberate government policy, minimum wages were maintained at a low rate to allow for Mexican capital formation, but according to one investigator capital formation did not result from such a policy. Since a low minimum wage policy was not responsible for capital formation and consequent rapid economic development, we must look elsewhere for the drive of economic revolution.

Once the stimulus to the economy provided by World War II was gone, Alemán and Ruiz Cortines expanded state action into the economic life of Mexico to the greatest extent in national history. Agricultural credit and land distribution were ignored, since there was no guarantee that loans could be paid back by *ejidatarios,* and especially since the communal farm appeared to be holding back agricultural production due to its uneconomic organization. Money was taken from social and "unproductive" economic expenditure to be channeled into investments and subsidies of private enterprises developed in conjunction with government planning. Economic growth was the result, and a decrease in the Poverty Index was a major by-product.

Overt governmental neglect of social programs and lower level bureaucrats, however, led to struggle in the official family which resulted in the apparent rejection of the Alemán ideology by Ruiz Cortines; but since Ruiz Cortines had no program of his own, he became more *alemanista* than Alemán. Not until López Mateos did the minimum wage and social expenditure for education again become important in governmental policy.

The Revolution has been governed by the intellectual currents which have been prevalent in different periods. Madero was obsessed with the ideal of political democracy as the solution to social ills. Let each man vote, and government can not oppress him. This was a negative view of the state's role and it lasted until 1930. The goals of social redemption through government action, proposed by the Constitution of 1917, were forgotten in the rush of Mexico's return to normalcy in the 1920's after a decade of civil war. There was no need for an expanded budget, for the government was not responsible for the development of the Mexican nation. In any case, international politics represented by Ambassador Dwight W. Morrow of the United States demanded other courses of action. The budget would have to be balanced, the foreign debt paid, and foreign rights protected.

With the end of the passive state in the depression of the 1930's, the Mexican Revolution from 1910 to 1930 passed from the scene. The old guard of the revolutionists, represented by Plutarco Elías Calles did not leave the political arena without a struggle, however, for there was more than a clash of personalities at stake; there was a concept of government and organization of life which had to be fought out. The clash in policy is best represented by Calles's administrative budgets and Cárdenas's dynamic use of federal funds to bring change into Mexico. Social revolution gained ascendancy from 1934 to 1940, but it began to fade with the expropriation of the foreign-owned oil industry in 1938. The swing to the ideology of economic revolution was completed under Avila Camacho and lasted until the official party recognized in the late 1950's that a change was necessary in order to continue to lead in Mexico.

The ideology of balanced revolution proposed by López Mateos offered to bring the best of political, economic, and social periods into a unified program. López Mateos allowed opposition into the House of Representatives, for the banner of revolutionary democracy had worn unbelievably thin. In fact the only people who have found democracy in Mexico in recent years have been naïve foreign commentators who have given up assessing political democracy and turned to analyzing "social democracy." The Mexicans themselves have not been misled, however, and the lack of political democracy has been continually criticized, especially by the intellectuals. Still, the people are philosophic about the Revolutionary Family, for they have always been governed by one elite group or another. If the official party continues to sponsor national growth and cedes to the demands or desires of pressure groups, complaints will be neither loud nor effective.

The possibility of a sophisticated, balanced revolution has come in the past ten years. Mexico now has enough funds per capita to begin to undertake the massive social expenditure to complement the economic development which must be maintained. The considerable growth of the budget has resulted from increased taxation in Mexico, but it is also dependent upon credit. To this date the governmental debt apparently has been skillfully managed by the ideologists of balanced revolution, but we are back to the problems generated by the 1920's: If debt payment considerations dominate expenditure, what will happen to Mexico's national development? One may argue that devoting a large share of the budget to the public debt — as much as 36.2 per cent in 1961 — brings more credits to stimulate expanded governmental activity. We can arrive at no conclusion regarding these views, for the future is unpredictable. We can, however, point up what the government is doing, and later we will be able to evaluate the social results of the style of balanced revolution.

Historically, Obregón and Calles found governmental independence of action more and more limited as they were drawn into the web of debt payments and international finance. Obregón might have attempted to carry out the program of social expenditure which he projected in the early 1920's had he not become involved with the problems of recognition and the assumption of Mexico's pre-revolutionary debt. These presidents, like Madero, had little concept of the active state. Calles was basically an administrator, and he viewed the state's role as one of co-ordination and indirect stimulus. Thus he founded the Bank of Mexico, the National Irrigation Commission, the National Road Commission, and many more agencies to encourage national reconstruction and expansion. Obregón and Calles lived in a world of the passive state in the 1920's, and it was quite different from the world of the active state which López Mateos faced in the 1960's, for foreign capital and foreign governments were not so understanding about the use of international credits and loans.

The presidents of active state intervention have engaged in some, generally limited, deficit spending. Cárdenas inaugurated deficit spending as standard governmental policy in the late 1930's. Avila Camacho increased it during World War II, and though Alemán played it down, subsequent presidents have not worried about balancing the budget.

Alemán thought that his program of state action would be less controversial and problematic than Cárdenas's action, which set out to remake traditional society; but as one looks back on revolutionary process, it is clear that Alemán's policies revamped the basis of Mexican society as much as Cárdenas's programs. In the long run the change in the poverty level of a significant percentage of persons may well constitute a revolution which will finally effectively challenge the old order which has worked against change in the structure of social and economic power. Though Cárdenas distributed much land of Mexico, and broke the hacienda system, the people who received the land have often remained impoverished due to the small size of their holding, inability to find credit, and isolation from markets, supplies, doctors, and schools. Whatever one may think about urbanization in Mexico, it does bring people into larger units where it is more possible for them to enjoy a better standard of living. Cárdenas had come to de-emphasize the political and economic labor strike by the time his presidential period was over, and he had given up his Socialistic Education program in the face of hostile pressure from the Church. As Cárdenas's term concluded there were many protests against his social revolution. In the face of civil war, Cárdenas chose a moderate to follow him in the presidency. He gave up social revolution, perhaps because he saw that people did not live much better than before the depression. Certainly peace was more important to Cárdenas than renewed civil war.

Labor turmoil and population pressure on the land have dictated the turn to balanced revolution since 1960. The advance of the economy and decrease in the Poverty Index during the years of economic revolution led to a crisis in Mexican politics which approached the threat to the official party that arose at the end of Cárdenas's term. The crisis was not reflected directly in the presidential campaign, as it was in 1940, but it showed up in the massive labor revolt against the government and its captive unions. After years of Revolution and promises, the Revolutionary Family must now fulfill the articulate demands of labor and peasant, even if, as in the case of land distribution, the program may no longer be feasible. If the ideology of balanced revolution is to be successful, it must learn from the past which shows that the stereotypes of the Revolution do not hold up.

We have examined presidential policy in eras of political, social, and economic revolution, and it is clear from the social results of the Revolution that certain ideas held dear by different wings within the Revolutionary Family are erroneous. Political revolution destroyed the old institutional order; it did not create a democratic state. Social revolution attacked the old structure of society; it did not bring about a new one, either economically or socially. Economic revolution brought industrialization to a high point; it did not create balanced economic growth or a large internal market. As the balanced revolution undertakes to remedy the failures of earlier phases of the Revolution, the question will be whether Mexico has the resources to permit adequate growth in all sectors of the society and economy at once. Or will a hierarchy of goals again demand dramatic pushes in one direction and then another?

Madero was not a real revolutionist. He engineered an overthrow of the presidency, but planned to leave government, society, and economy to run as they always had with the exception that democracy would be introduced. The violence which followed his assassination contributed little to the social growth of Mexico and destroyed the economy. The programs of the 1920's amounted to a rejection of social change, for the politics of social redemption turned to the politics of high finance and luxury for the official party leaders throughout most of the 1920's and early 1930's. The regime of Portes Gil was an exception to this pattern.

Cárdenas did not ruin the Mexican economy and he did not materially help the masses to any great extent, as his enemies and friends have continued to claim. Though his program for the rural proletariat did not bear fruit, his policy of aiding the urban worker brought social change in the Federal District. Industrialization gained steam in the late 1930's, and consequently we need not give all credit to the post-1940 period for the process of economic advance. In practice, social revolution did not scare private capital as much as private investors have claimed. Cárdenas's legacy to the masses was not so much in material improvement, but in the psychological position of importance which he gave them. Cárdenas revivified the social ideals of the Constitution of 1917, and he brought the masses into politics in organized groups which could no longer be ignored. The urban and rural proletariat provided a counterbalance to the power of the military, and the generals lost their power during Cárdenas's term. Cárdenas was able further to limit the role of the military in national life by serving as Minister of War under Avila Camacho during World War II. The generals who might have renewed a bid for prestige were overshadowed by the fame and wisdom of an ex-president who knew how to ensure that the military would serve and not dominate government. Cárdenas was the progenitor of real active state intervention in all phases of national life. He had to fight the battle such a controversial policy raised, and he has set the standard for social and economic budgetary policy ever since. Cárdenas's specific programs were criticized by the Alemán group, but his policy of government budgeting for national economic integration was accepted.

Alemán undertook indirect social programs which did not sacrifice the masses, as his opponents have claimed. Since decrease of poverty apparently occurred more rapidly after 1940 than during the Cárdenas era, we may say that direct social benefits for the people are not the whole answer for national integration. The people must not wait around for someone to give them something to do, as Cárdenas proposed; they must themselves see that social advance comes from personal initiative to solve their problems.[1] Government action which gives benefits without a basis for opportunity and social advancement can not solve the problems of Mexico. Alemán's policies, however, provided the base for this social advance with too little direct attention to the people. Without education and public health, for example, social integration will not keep up with economic development.

In sum, the Mexican Revolution is not yet complete. Much has been done for the people, but there is still much remaining to do before Mexico is a socially integrated nation. Government policy is of primary importance in directing this work of nation-building, for it has created the climate for over-all development. Prior to 1910 there was very little social improvement. Fifty years later some regions of the country, especially the South, live in severe poverty. The results of the Revolution have been very mixed when tested regionally. With the concrete identification of different periods in the

---

[1] When talking about this with Cárdenas in the summer of 1962, he was still insistent that if the government gives the people something to do they will work. He rejected the idea that people have always waited for the government, the Church, and the military to give them work, hence they do not actively solve their own problems and this is a basic deterrent to social advance. Interview with Cárdenas, August 25, 1962, while traveling from Uruapan to Apatzingán, Michoacán.

Mexican Revolution, it is clear that social change is a long process, longer than many imagine. Theory of revolutions is often based on the violent stages of governmental change, the assumption being that if social change is to occur it will take place concomitantly with political upheaval. We have shown that the real revolution in Mexican society has come about mainly in times of political stability since 1940. In other words, it took thirty years before the official party of the Revolution was able to introduce the conditions under which relatively rapid social development could take place. This is not so surprising, for even though it took seven years of violence before a constitution was written in 1917 which projected the goals of the movement, much constructive governmental activity remained before an accumulation of favorable conditions allowed social change.

Several recommendations concerning future scholarship may be drawn from this work. Since we have shown that presidential power in Mexico is closely related to the budgetary system which gives the chief executive great flexibility of operation, the question arises as to whether or not the locus of power in other presidential systems may not stem largely from the same type of arrangement. Certainly this might be a fruitful line of inquiry in examining developing nations which have a political system that theoretically operates with checks and balances. Most foreign investigators have simply assumed that the Mexican government functions with the modicum of checks and balances which its Constitution provides. Mexican analysts have taken their system for granted, and in the process we get a great deal of talk about theory and practice of government in Mexico, but very little understanding about how the system actually works. To develop a more sophisticated analysis of quantification of ideology than is presented here, we need to have some studies of budgetary policy in other developing countries. It is hoped that the method developed in this analysis will aid scholars in carrying out and refining such undertakings.

Students of Mexican history have tended to judge the Mexican permanent revolution in terms which have ignored the people for whom the Revolution was theoretically undertaken. The analysis of social change for the masses presented here will undoubtedly be controversial. But an attempt to measure the decrease in characteristics of poverty is offered in order to understand a hitherto-neglected aspect of the revolutionary process. Due to the problems discussed at length in the last two chapters, the index must by its nature be tentative and delimited to cover levels of poverty which probably harm the Mexican in collective terms more than in individual terms. It is difficult, if not impossible, to compress a series of items into a meaningful Poverty Index; certainly the result is an abstract one which does not take into account inconsistencies or variations, but this is the problem with any conceptual tool of social analysis. It is hoped, however, that in spite of its problems, it will stimulate analysis of different levels of social change.

Finally, we may suggest that the very meaning of the word "revolution" and the very essence of the "revolutionary process" need re-evaluation. If, as we have attempted to show, the revolutionary process may have a series of stages which only begin when the violent stage of upheaval is completed, our findings about revolution in Mexico need to be tested in other societies.

66. *Juan Domingo Perón Expounds His Doctrine and Evita Perón Gives Her Views on What Place Women Should Occupy in the World*

JUAN DOMINGO PERÓN

One of the best ways to appreciate the stress and the emotions of those heady Perón years is to read what the leaders said. Here are samples of their ideas on some of the issues.

Juan Perón in items 1–5 sets forth some of his fundamental objectives in the early years (1944–1947) and in item 6, while in exile in Paraguay after his downfall in 1955, looks back on his accomplishments.

Evita Perón in the years to come will probably be considered one of the great women of modern Latin America. Certainly she aroused powerful emotions among the Argentine masses, if the demonstrations I witnessed in Buenos Aires on April 22, 1953, on the occasion of the first anniversary of her death, were any indication. One of the best ways to understand her life comes from this 1952 statement:

> That Eva should expect to succeed solely through the manipulation of others, that she should use her sex as a weapon, was not only the result of her home life and her upbringing but was natural to the culture of the society in which she now found herself. The Argentine woman had been exploited just as much as the peon and only in cases of great wealth or unusual strength of character had she been able to escape from the position of inferior dependency to which the men in the family had consigned her; in most cases such dependency seemed so usual to the women themselves that the thought of any freedom frightened and shocked them. Argentine men — and by no means only Argentine men among South Americans — regarded their women, some-times respectfully, as mothers, wives, virgin daughters, or mistresses; too seldom did they regard them as individuals as intelligent as themselves. This attitude toward women may be seen in Argentina today when many of the Opposition and the military disapprove of Eva Perón not so much

because of the corruption and illegality she has encouraged but because she is a woman in a position of great power.

The Argentine woman had, at that time, no vote; she could not get a divorce, and still cannot, unless she went abroad for it; she and her children and her property were in the hands of her husband, who had in most cases been chosen for her by her family. A married woman was expected to stay at home and raise a large family; it was a matter for boasting if a man got his wife pregnant on the honeymoon. A woman who remained single stayed at home as companion to her mother, who, because of her daughter's singleness, often regarded her as if she were mentally retarded; or she was offered the equally ungrateful position of unpaid nurse and governess to her nephews and nieces. Only among the middle classes in the city was a changing economy making it possible for a wife to go out to earn her own living. A poor man was, of course, always willing for his wife to go out to work as long as her earnings went into his own pocket. . . .

It is not surprising that the Argentine woman should so often have regarded her sex as her only marketable commodity, whether she were the daughter of an oligarch whose guaranteed virginity went down to the highest bidder in a cloud of Brussels lace and with the blessing of the Church, or the little servant girl who got herself an imitation gold watch by smuggling the butcher boy into bed or a woman of the port whose prices ranged from a peso up. And the woman who earned her own living, however determined she might be to do so respectably, could not escape the consciousness that the men with whom she had dealings valued her as much for her amorous potentialities as they did for her business ability; nor, however she resisted, could she entirely escape the temptation of using herself as barter.*

1. THE RULING CLASS

An attempt has been made to lead the public to believe that the oligarchy, that untoward lodge of demagogues, represented the ruling class in the country, its elite, and as such was made up of wise, rich and good people. We must observe that "the wise are seldom rich, and the rich seldom good."

Items 1–3 are from Juan Domingo Perón. *Perón Expounds His Doctrine* (Buenos Aires, 1948), pp. 53, 146–147, 149; items 4–5 are from Juan Domingo Perón, *The Voice of Perón* (Buenos Aires: Subsecretaría de Informaciones de la Presidencia de la Nación Argentina, 1950), pp. 131–132; item 6 is a portion of the declaration made to the United Press by Ex-President Perón in Paraguay, October 5, 1955, and later published in Juan Perón, *La fuerza es el derecho de las bestias* (Montevideo: Edicíones Cicerón, 1955), p. 15 — translation by Lewis Hanke.

* María Flores, *The Woman with the Whip: Eva Perón* (Garden City: Doubleday, 1952), pp. 36–39. Reprinted by permission of William Morris Agency, Inc. Copyright © 1952 by Mary Main. For recent interpretations, see Jeane Kirkpatrick, *Leader and Vanguard in Mass Society: A Study of Peronist Argentina* (Cambridge, Mass.: M.I.T. Press, 1971); V. S. Naipaul, "The Corpse at the Iron Door," *New York Review of Books,* XIX (August 10, 1972), pp. 3–8.

Nor must we forget that neither the wise nor the good found a place among Argentine politicians. (October 15th, 1944)

2. OBJECTIVES

From today onwards we shall industrialize the country so that our work may be done by Argentine workers and so that they may earn what foreign workers earned before. This is what industrialization means to us. To accomplish this cycle we shall complete and intensify the economic cycle of production and consumption, we shall produce more, and value that production in view of our own industrialization and commerce, avoiding exploitation and increasing the consumption. When this cycle is closed, we shall be able to provide our country with 80 or 90 per cent of our production and we shall only export 10 or 20 per cent, because it is necessary to convince ourselves that the money of a man from Catamarca or Santiago del Estero is worth as much as that of the English, Americans or Japanese. All this problem is in itself simple if one tries to solve it, but it gets complicated when one cannot or does not want to solve it. We have our orientation clearly defined and a plan of action that will take us directly to the achievement of the objectives we are looking for. (July 30th, 1947)

3. EVERYTHING SHOULD BE ARGENTINE

Foundations have already been laid for the national tin-plate factory — an article of trade which is taking too long in getting to our country — in which the containers we need to export our production in will be manufactured. Due to the lack of a factory of tin-plate containers, the Republic has lost many thousands of millions of pesos; and we have not had any tin-plate factory before because certain foreigners that negotiated with our food production, objected to it. But in the future we shall have the containers that our production requires, the ships necessary to transport it, and those who in previous times commanded here as if they were in their own land, will have to submit and receive our products canned by Argentine hands, transported by Argentine railways and taken to Europe by Argentine ships. (March 2nd, 1947)

4. ANOTHER SOCIAL SERVICE

It would never occur to anyone that the air, the sun, the light, and the water in the rivers were the exclusive heritage of a chosen few. The very idea seems absurd to us. The time will come when it will also seem absurd to us that culture and advantages of industrial civilization, petroleum, and sources of energy should be exploited by a privileged few.

In the same way, I understand that, with the passing of the years, the distribution of food supplies will become another social service, because proper nourishment is one of the most powerful sources of energy, and one which is most directly responsible for the development and perfecting of a community of human beings. (April 29th, 1949)

5. ARGENTINE RAILWAYS

We have reached our "coming of age" which enables us, to the same extent as anybody else, to estimate our true value and to govern our country by ourselves. For this reason it is of vital importance that basic industries should be national, sometimes controlled by the State and at others privately owned, but always in the hands of Argentines. In achieving this purpose and effecting this policy of recovery, it is of vital importance that the railways should be nationalized, to say nothing of reasons of sovereignty which are easy to understand. (September 17th, 1946)

6. MY ACHIEVEMENTS

When I entered the government, there were persons in my country who were paid 20 centavos a day and peons who got as little as 10 or 15 pesos per month. Workers were killed barbarously in the sugar mills and fields because of criminal working conditions. In a country which had 45 million cows the inhabitants died for lack of food. Argentina was a country of fat bulls and undernourished peons.

Social security was practically unknown, though insignificant pensions were paid to a few public employees and army officers. We established retirement pay for all workers, including the employers. We created pensions for the aged and the sick, thus banishing from the country the sad spectacle of misery in the midst of abundance.

We legalized the existence of sindical organizations previously declared illegal by Argentine law, and we fostered the organization of the General Confederation of Labor which now has six million paid members.

We made possible absolutely free education for all who wanted to study, without distinction of class, creed, or religion, and in only eight years we built 8,000 schools of all kinds.

Great dams with their power plants increased the size of Argentine farmlands and more than 35,000 public works were the result of the first governmental five-year plan alone, among them the gas pipeline 1,800 kilometers long, the Pistarini Airport, the Eva Perón oil refinery (which the rebels wished to bombard in spite of its costing 400 million dollars and ten years of labor), the coal exploitation of Río Turbo and its railroad, more than twenty great electric plants, etc., etc.

When I entered the government not even pins were made in Argentina. When I left buses, tractors, automobiles, locomotives, etc., were being manufactured. I left the railroads recovered for the nation, as well as telephones and gas. I left a merchant marine, an air fleet, etc. But why continue? All Argentines know this better than I do.

Now I hope that the People will be able to defend what has been achieved against the greed of their false liberators.

EVITA PERÓN

7. HOME OR THE FACTORY?

Every day thousands of women forsake the feminine camp and begin to live like men.

They work like them. They prefer, like them, the street to the home. They are not resigned to being either mothers or wives.

They substitute for men everywhere.

Is this "feminism"? I think, rather, that it must be the "masculinization" of our sex.

And I wonder if all this change has solved our problem.

But no. All the old ills continue rampant, and new ones, too, appear. The number of young women who look down upon the occupation of homemaking increases every day.

And yet that is what we were born for.

We feel that we are born for the home, and the home is too great a burden for our shoulders.

Then we give up the home . . . go out to find a solution . . . feel that the answer lies in obtaining economic independence and working somewhere. But that work makes us equal to men and — no! We are not like them! They can live alone; we cannot. We feel the need of company, of complete company. We feel the need of giving more than receiving. Can't we work for anything else than earning wages like men?

And, on the other hand, if we give up the work which makes us independent so as to form a home . . . we burn our boats once and for all.

Items 7–9 are from Eva Perón, *My Mission in Life* (New York: Vantage Press, 1953), pp. 189–190, 195–196, 205–206, passim. Reprinted by permission.

No profession in the world has less chance of a comeback than our profession as women.

Even if we are chosen by a good man, our home will not always be what we dreamed of when we were single.

The entire nation ends at the door of our home, and other laws and other rights begin . . . the law and the rights of man — who very often is only a master, and also, at times, a dictator.

And nobody can interfere there.

The mother of a family is left out of all security measures. She is the only worker in the world without a salary, or a guarantee, or limited working hours, or free Sundays, or holidays, or any rest, or indemnity for dismissal, or strikes of any kind. All that, we learned as girls, belongs to the sphere of love . . . but the trouble is that after marriage, love often flies out of the window, and then everything becomes "forced labor" . . . obligations without any rights! Free service in exchange for pain and sacrifice!

I do not say it is always like this. I should have no right to say anything, since *my* home is happy . . . if I did not see the suffering every day of so many women who live like that . . . with no outlook, with no rights, with no hope.

That is why every day there are fewer women to make homes.

Real homes, united and happy! And the world really needs more homes every day, and for them more women willing properly to fulfill their destiny and their mission. That is why the first objective of a feminine movement which wishes to improve things for women — which does not aim at changing them into men — should be the home.

We were born to make homes. Not for the street. Common sense shows us the answer. We must have in the home that which we go out to seek: our small economic independence — which would save us from becoming women with no outlook, with no rights and with no hope!

8. THE GREAT ABSENCE

I think the feminist movement organized as a vital force in each country and in all the world should and would do great good to all humanity.

I do not know where I once read that in this world of ours the great need is for love.

I would modify this a bit and say that rather does the world today suffer from a great absence: that of woman.

Everything, absolutely everything in this contemporary world, has been made according to man's measure.

We are absent from governments.

We are absent from parliaments.

From international organizations.

We are in neither the Vatican nor the Kremlin.

Nor in the high commands of the imperialists.

Nor in the commissions of atomic energy.

Nor in the great business combines.

Nor in Freemasonry, nor in other secret societies.

We are absent from all the great centers constituting a power in the world.

And yet we have always been present in the time of suffering, and in all humanity's bitter hours.

It would seem as though our calling were not substantially that of creating, but rather that of sacrifice.

Our symbol should be of the Mother of Christ at the foot of the Cross.

And yet our highest mission is nothing but to create.

I cannot understand, then, why we are not in those places where an attempt is being made to create man's happiness.

Haven't we, by any chance, a common destiny with man? Shouldn't we perhaps share in creating the happiness of the family?

Perhaps man has failed in his attempts thus far to make mankind happy, precisely *because* he has not invited us to join his great social organizations. . . .

9. WOMEN AND ACTION

I firmly believe that woman — contrary to the common opinion held by men — lives better in action than in inactivity.

I see them every day in my work of political service and social welfare.

The reason is very simple. Man can live exclusively for himself. Woman cannot.

If a woman lives for herself, I think she is not a woman, or else she cannot be said to live. That is why I am afraid of the "masculinization" of women.

When that occurs, women become even more egoistic than men, because we women carry things to greater extremes than men.

A man of action is one who triumphs over all the rest. A woman of action is one who triumphs *for* the rest. Isn't this a great difference?

Woman's happiness is not her own happiness, but that of others.

That is why, when I thought of my feminist movement, I did not want to take woman out of what is so much her own sphere. In politics men seek their own triumph.

Women, if they did that, would cease to be women.

I have not wanted women to look at themselves in the woman's party . . . but rather that right there they should serve others in some fraternal and generous form.

Woman's problem everywhere is always the deep and fundamental problem of the home.

It is her great destiny — her irremediable destiny.

She needs to have a home; when she cannot make one with her own flesh, she does so with her soul, or she is not a woman!

Well, for this very reason I have wanted my party to be a home . . . that each basic unit should be something like a family . . . with its great loves and its small disagreements, with its sublime fruitfulness and its interminable laboriousness.

I know that in many places I have already attained this.

Above all, where the women I have appointed are most womanly!

More than political action, the feminist movement has to develop social service. Precisely because social service is something that we women have in the blood!

Our destiny and our vocation is to serve others, and that is social service. Not that other "social life" . . . which is contrary to *all* service . . . !

67. *Women: The Forgotten Half of Argentine History*

NANCY CARO HOLLANDER

Professor Nancy Caro Hollander received her graduate training in Latin American history at the University of California, Los Angeles. During 1971–1972 she served as Chairwoman of the Women's Studies Program at San Diego State College and now is teaching Latin American history at California State College, Domínguez Hills.

The present selection is a part of the paper she delivered at the 1971 annual meeting of the American Historical Association.

The level of civilization of a people can be judged by the social position of its women.   DOMINGO FAUSTINO SARMIENTO

Although one would never know it by perusing the majority of books on Argentine history, women make up approximately one-half of that nation's population. Yet the history of Argentine women parallels the history of women in most countries to the extent that it is largely unwritten. This essay is an attempt to redress this injustice and to demonstrate the contributions of the masses of Argentine women to their country's economic and political life. . . . Within this context it evaluates the political mobilization of women within the Peronist movement of 1945–55. In order to appreciate why women became one of the major pillars of support for Peronism, it is necessary to examine the historical experience of women as the most exploited group within the Argentine working class.

Contrary to the generally accepted notion that Argentine women have never been in the mainstream of public employment, since the development of an urban, industrial base in the late nineteenth century women filled the factories and sweatshops as a source of super-exploitable labor. . . .

Employers hired women to work in hazardous, unhealthy conditions and at low wages, paying them on the average half of what male workers earned for the same job. This fact made women workers very appealing to employers, and by 1887, according to the census of Buenos Aires, 39% of the paid work force of that city was composed of women.

In 1904, Dr. Juan Bialet Masse, an investigator for the National Labor Department, traveled the entire expanse of Argentina gathering data with respect to the condition of the working class in each province. He published a three-volume study which documented that the majority of Argentine people suffered from a miserable standard of living and low paying, unsteady jobs. However, he concluded that in every province it was women who suffered from the most intense discrimination and exploitation. In Mendoza, as elsewhere, he reported that upon questioning employers about their preference for hiring women workers, they replied that besides being cheaper labor, women were more subordinate and had lower rates of absence from work than men. . . .

Official government investigations continued to detail the long hours, filthy conditions and low pay that characterized the work of women. Perhaps the most vivid description was provided in 1913 by Carolina Muzzili, a militant feminist and inspector for the National Labor Department. She visited dozens of factories and commercial establishments, issuing questionnaires to women workers which provided her with testimony as to the brutalizing effects of

Nancy Caro Hollander, "Women: The Forgotten Half of Argentine History." Published by permission of the author, and of the University of Pittsburgh Press. The paper appeared in the volume edited by Ann Pescatello, *Female and Male in Latin America: Essays* (Pittsburgh: University of Pittsburgh Press, 1973). © 1973 by the University of Pittsburgh Press.

work conditions on their minds and bodies. Muzzili's report pointed out that in the laundry industry, for example, women worked from 11 to 12 hours daily, often without any rest breaks. Her indignation led her to compute the rate of profit made by one employer who consistently overworked his female employees. She concluded that while the worker was paid only 2.60 pesos a day, the employer took 7.30 pesos a day in profits from each worker. All investigations of the National Labor Department revealed the fact that women were paid on the average of one-half the wages earned by men for the same job and that minors were paid yet one-half the wages paid to women. Moreover, most women, shortly after beginning to work, acquired the chronic diseases typical of damp and dirty conditions, such as menstrual irregularities, rheumatism, sciatica and TB.

By 1914, according to the national census of that year, there were 714,893 women working in industrial, commercial and professional positions. That figure represented 22% of the total paid work force 14 years of age and older. The director of the census commented that, "we should applaud the increasing proportion of women working because the degree of independence that women have reached in society, the various ways in which they apply their intelligence and energy and are thus surrounded by respect and consideration, are eloquent indications of the general culture and progress of our society."

This comment serves to highlight the contradiction of women's situation as of that year in Argentina. While it was true that the number of women who were wage earners increased yearly, this fact alone did not define the degree to which women were able to achieve any qualitative change from their traditional secondary status in Argentine society. Women were still subject to the control of their fathers and husbands due to their total juridical dependency on men inherited from Spanish legal tradition. Women's husbands still maintained the right to dispose of their earnings because legally the adult married woman was reduced to the status of a minor. Furthermore, women still did not have the right to vote or to be elected to public office. These restrictions on women underscored legally the idealized image of women in Argentine culture which remained that of the housewife-mother: the lovely decoration, weak, not very intelligent and totally dependent on the male for her source of identification and status. Paradoxically enough, often the very men who spoke of women as the "weaker sex" in need of male protection found no inconsistency in their positions as the owners of industry in which women of the working class were so exploited.

It was to the above inequities that the Argentine feminist movement, emerging in the early twentieth century, addressed itself. The movement was composed of a variety of organizations and ideologies, all of which dealt with the civil, economic and political rights of Argentine women. . . .

The efforts of these militant women and sympathetic individuals in Congress were responsible for changes in the laws during the 1920's regarding women. In 1924 protective legislation for working women (law 11.317) was passed, specifying that industrial and commercial establishments could employ women for only eight hours a day or 48 hours a week. Night work was forbidden, as was work in certain factories or jobs considered dangerous. Special rules regarding maternity were established, as well as the requirement that factories with more than 50 female workers provide rooms in which nursing mothers could care for their infants. A series of penal regulations was set up to enforce the law.

This legislation affected working women who during the 1920's made up approximately 18.4% of the paid work force of Buenos Aires in industry, commerce and communications. It did not affect the thousands of women working in the agricultural sector where families were generally hired as a unit and the wages paid to the husband for his own labor plus that of his wife and children. Nor did it affect the serf-like conditions of thousands of women who worked in rural and urban areas as domestic servants. The legislation, even for the women that it covered, did not address itself to the issue of unequal wages paid to women. In fact, the difference between the wages paid to women and men for the same work *increased* during the 1920's.

On September 22, 1926, the Congress passed historic legislation which potentially affected the lives of all Argentine women by substantially changing their civil status. Undoubtedly influenced by progressive legislative changes regarding women in other countries in the post World War One period, the Argentine Congress voted women their long fought for right to equal civil status with men. The legislation affected mainly the adult married woman who had traditionally been reduced to the legal status of a minor upon marriage. Now she could exercise any profession or job without permission from her husband and could dispose of her earnings at her own discretion; she could enter into any civil or commercial agreement without her husband's authorization; and she had authority over her children and their goods in case of legal separation, whether or not she remarried. Article 6 of the law, however, perpetuated the dominance of the husband in marriage because it claimed that he was the official administrator of conjugal property and income and was under no automatic obligation to share this authority unless the wife demanded it through legal process. Obviously many women continued in the same submissive position within the family due both to the force of custom and because they were unaware that the law provided them with a procedure to claim equal authority in marriage. . . .

During the thirties and early forties, women were increasingly employed in the public work force, especially in the capital city. During this period, many people migrated to Buenos Aires from the interior of Argentina in search of work opportunities, and these migrations were composed of approximately twice as many women as men. Women came to represent roughly one-quarter of the paid work force in Buenos Aires. More strikingly, they represented 33 per cent of all industrial workers in that city, and in such industries as textiles, tobacco and clothing they made up the overwhelming majority.

. . . The increasing public employment of women elicited interesting responses from political economists and intellectuals which revealed Argentine attitudes toward women in general. In an almost hysterical fashion, many viewed the process with alarm and detailed the tragic consequences for Argentina of this change in the traditional role of women. Indeed, many insisted that it was because women were working outside the home that Argentina was suffering from a series of crises such as a declining birth rate, the decreasing moral significance of the family, the increasing unemployment rate among men due to "unfair" competition of cheap female labor and the consequent decline in the dominant position of the father within the family structure. . . .

In contrast to the above arguments, one of the main feminist organizations active during the 1930's, the Argentine Association for Women's Suffrage, argued that women should be paid equal wages for equal work with men. This was necessary because of a rising cost of living and family responsibilities which weighed as heavily on the woman as on the man. It would eliminate the competition between male and female workers and thus improve the conditions for both sexes. According to its founder, Carmela Horne de Burmeister, the organization had branches in many provinces and a membership of 80,000 in 1932. The women campaigned for women's suffrage, workers' housing projects, reduced prices for prime necessities, maternity homes and benefits and day nurseries for the children of working mothers.

In the environment of the thirties and early forties, however, there was little chance that these demands would be realized. In fact, at the same time that the role of women in the work force was being attacked by the intellectuals, women's recently won equal civil rights were being attacked by the conservative Justo government. In 1935 a reform of the civil code was proposed. Article 333 aimed at revising the legislative gains made in 1926 by once again reducing the married woman to the status of a minor. At a time when a large percentage of women were earning their own wages, Article 333 proposed that the married woman would not be able to work, spend her earnings, administer her property or be a member of a commercial or civil organization without the authority of her husband.

A campaign was launched against ꞇnis reactionary measure and a feminist organization called the Argentine Union of Women was founded in 1936. Its president was Victoria Ocampo, an important figure in the literary world, and its vice president was Maria Rosa Oliver, a prominent writer and political activist. The women in the organization delivered public lectures, sponsored radio discussions and printed and distributed thousands of leaflets demanding equal political and economic rights for women, but especially urging the rejection of the proposed legislative reform. Angered by the attempts to reduce the status of women in Argentina, Victoria Ocampo delivered a speech on radio in which she argued that the feminist movement should begin to speak of "women's liberation" instead of "women's emancipation," because the term referred better to the reality of the master-slave relationship between men and women.

The anti-feminist sentiments of the regimes of the 1930's continued unabated after the GOU [Group of United Officers] army coup of 1943. General Ramírez encouraged industry, commerce and the government to stop hiring female workers; in fact, no woman was supposed to be appointed to any position in the government above the rank of clerk. He tried to halt the influence of the feminist movement and actually disbanded the Committee for Victory, a women's fund raising society working for the victory of the Allies with a membership of 50,000. When Paris was liberated from the Nazis, many Argentines celebrated with demonstrations in Buenos Aires. President Farrell not only claimed that the demonstrations involved "outside elements" of extremist ideologies, but he noted with special disapproval the leading role of women in starting some of the impromptu demonstrations.

However, at the same time that the GOU presidents were attempting to reinforce the notion that women's place was in the home, Juan Domingo Perón, who had become Secretary of the Department of Labor and Welfare, began to implement policies and to make public statements which indicated his departure from the mainstream of official attitudes toward women.

On the 3rd of October, 1944, Perón presided over the inauguration of Argentina's first special Women's Division of Labor and Assistance which he created in the Department of Labor and Welfare. He delivered a speech in which he declared that the establishment of this Division was the most agreeable task that he had yet performed because he recognized the contributions that women had made to the greatness of Argentina. Perón asserted that because "more than 900,000 Argentine women are part of the paid work force in all kinds of jobs and professions . . . it is our duty to morally and materially dignify their efforts." He went on to say that in Argentina women's participation in the paid work force was encouraged rather than restricted and that this special Division dealing with the rights and needs of women workers was a social necessity. He called for the improvement and implementation of existing protective legislation and a law establishing women's right to equal pay for equal work.

Less than one year later, on July 26, 1945, Perón, in his capacity as vice president of Argentina, delivered a speech at a Congressional meeting attended by thousands of women, in which he urged the adoption of legislation giving women the right to vote. He pledged his profound support for women's equal political rights and his intention to work increasingly toward that goal.

After his election to the presidency in 1946, Perón submitted to Congress his first five-year plan in which he included a proposal for women's suffrage.

It is not within the scope of this essay to review the various interpretations of the significance of Peronism as an historical phenomenon in Argentina. Suffice it to say that Peronism, contrary to the traditional interpretation, was not a fascist movement. It represented a bourgeois nationalist movement in an underdeveloped country with a colonial export economy. It was a coalition of class forces which included the new industrialists who had developed as a result of the depression and the Second World War and the working class, especially the previously unorganized workers who had migrated to Buenos Aires during the thirties and early forties. The populist character of the movement was reflected in the fact that its ideology stressed the equality and dignity of the working class and the necessity of industrialization to ensure that equality.

Within this context, the women's movement became more nationalistic and popularly based than the previous feminist movements described above. Any analysis of Perón's appeal to the newly arrived "cabecitas negras" from the interior of Argentina to Buenos Aires would apply especially to the women who made up a good percentage of these migrants. These women represented the most exploited and marginal group of people in society. Not only had they never before been mobilized politically, but they suffered from a sense of uprootedness, isolation, loneliness and alienation that made them most accessible to a political movement that actually improved their economic and political situation and offered them a charismatic leader — indeed, a charismatic couple — with which they could identify.

It is difficult to evaluate the factors which influenced Perón to view women as he did; and it is almost impossible to know the degree to which he sincerely wished to aid women or to appeal to them in order to gain an added organized source of political support. The point I wish to stress here is that this aspect of the Peronist movement is ignored by most historians. Moreover, the historians who stress the change in the status of women which occurred during the Perón years attribute this change to the influence and actions of Eva Perón. Even official Peronist literature, when referring to the role of women within the movement, account for their participation because of the sudden historical appearance of Eva Perón. While not denying the important role that Eva Perón would play in the Peronist feminist movement, it is my contention that the mobilization of women during the Perón years flowed organically from their objective situation in Argentine society and from Perón's awareness of their growing importance in the work force, as well as his desire to deflect the influence on women of traditional Marxist and feminist leadership.

Though by no means revolutionary, Perón's policies with respect to women were historically progressive. He came to power in Argentina supporting women's suffrage. In contrast, Mexico, which had had a social revolution in 1910, did not give women the right to vote until 1953, and Chile, which has had the longest history of stable parliamentary government in Latin America, did not legalize women's suffrage until 1949. Moreover, the Peronist movement institutionalized the political mobilization of women by establishing the Peronist Feminist Party in 1949, while official ideology eulogized women as equal partners in the struggle to build an industrialized country with a just distribution of the wealth.

Perón, because of post-war prosperity and protective measures for Argentine industry, was able to institute government social security programs which improved the standard of living for the working class in general and for working women in particular. That his policies had a direct impact on women is proven by the fact that by 1949, women, including female minors, made up 45% of the industrial workers in Buenos Aires. This figure represents a 62.5% increase over that of 1939, while for the same period the number of men employed in industry had increased only 23%. The percentage of salaried employees represented by women had risen from 13% in 1939 to 28% in 1949.

The working conditions and wages of this increasing number of working women were improved through protective legislation passed by the Department of Labor. In January of 1944, minimum wages were established for piece work done in the home. On September 28, 1945, decree 23.372 fixed the minimum wage in the food industry and gave women a minimum wage of 20% below that of men. While not giving women equal pay, the measure improved the traditional situation in which women were generally paid 40% of what male workers earned.

In 1949, women working in the textile industry were given the right to equal wages with men, a situation which affected more than 15,000 women workers. It is not possible to document whether in fact this last measure was actualized. According to a questionnaire sponsored by the International Labor Organization in 1959, women workers generally earned from 7% to 15% less than men in Argentina. While by no means equitable, the differential in wages according to sex in Argentina is one of the lowest in the non-Socialist world.

The number of women pursuing university educations and professional careers rose dramatically during the Perón years. While from 1931 to 1940 the increase in the percentage of women attending the university over the previous decade was 68.52%, from 1941 to 1950 there was a 139.51% increase and from 1951 to 1960 a 153.62% increase. At the same time, the increase in the percentage of men attending university from 1941 to 1950 was 74.04% and from 1951 to 1960, 44.27%. However, women tended to prepare for careers traditionally defined as women's professions, including medicine, philosophy, education and law.

In 1954, the Congress passed a new family code. It included the right of divorce, a reform fought for by feminist organizations for decades. In 1955, after Perón's fall, the divorce law was abolished.

The most dramatic change that women experienced during Perón's regime was the conquest of suffrage and the right to be elected to public office. Although there had been numerous attempts in previous years to win Congressional approval of women's suffrage, it was not until September 23, 1947, with pressure from the Executive and the mobilization of women by Eva Perón, that Congress approved the bill legalizing the vote for women. On that date there were mass demonstrations in Buenos Aires in celebration of the event. Women from all social classes, including workers who left their jobs to join the demonstrations, filled the streets in jubilation and listened to Eva Perón speak to them about the significance of that day for women and for Argentina. She described the struggles that they had had to wage with the representatives of the oligarchy in Congress for the passage of the law. She asserted that the vote which women had won was a new tool in their hands. "But our hands are not new in struggle, in work and in the repeated miracle of creation," she said, urging women to use the vote with the same consciousness that they had demonstrated historically in fighting and working by the sides of their men to build a great Argentina.

The election of 1951 reflected the impact that the conquest of suffrage had had on women. 90.32% of the registered female voters voted in comparison to only 86.08% of the registered male voters. In the Buenos Aires area, 93.87% of the women voted while only 91.45% of the men voted. The majority of women everywhere voted the Peronist ticket; the percentage of women's votes going to Perón ranged from 83% to 53%. Perhaps the most significant fact of all marking a new departure in Argentine history was the number of women Peronist candidates elected to the national and provincial Congresses. In the national Congress, seven female Senators and 24 female Deputies were elected. No other country in the Americas could boast of such a high number of elected female representatives.

On April 25, 1953, the Deputies of the national Congress elected Delfina Deglinomini de Parodi as its vice president, an event which symbolized the rising status of women during this period. She was the first woman in Argentina and one of the first women in the world to occupy such a high position. According to her, the change in the status of women under Perón was "the revolution in the revolution."

The political organization of the masses of women began with the campaign for women's suffrage. Women Peronists who were organizing women in the poor neighborhoods formed women's centers that eventually developed into the "unidades basicas" (literally, basic units, these centers were defined as the basic organizational structure of the Peronist movement), which were organized by women for women all over the country. Their functions, among others, were to affiliate women to the Peronist movement by way of lectures and conferences, to offer new work skills and to provide doctors and lawyers to help women with medical and legal problems. According to women involved in the establishment of these centers, they were in every neighborhood and were always open so that women had a place to be together to develop their own political thought and practice without the influence of men.

On July 26, 1949, under the leadership of Eva Perón, the Peronist Feminist Party was inaugurated. This was also a departure in Argentina with respect to the political organization of women because the forms traditionally used by other political parties were women's "committees" and women's "auxiliaries." In the case of the Peronist movement, the official interpretation was that it was composed equally of three branches: the Peronist Men's Party, the Peronist Feminist Party and the General Federation of Workers. Thus the feminist branch of the party had equal importance with the men's branch. Eva Perón, in her speech inaugurating the first national assembly of the Peronist Feminist Party, asserted that its aspirations and its program were based on the Peronist doctrine of economic liberation, political sovereignty and social justice. She congratulated women on not being mere spectators of history. In spite of having suffered double exploitation, both in the home and on the job, she said, women were joining with equal commitment the struggle of the working class. Thus she linked the women's movement ideologically to the struggle of the workers for a strong Argentina independent of the control of the oligarchy and foreign capitalist powers.

The program of the Peronist Feminist Party stated that the Peronist movement gave women full equality with men and that the Feminist Party functioned to affiliate women to struggle for the conquests of Peronism and the liberation of women. "The Peronist Feminist Party opens its doors to all women of the people, and especially to the humble women who have been forgotten by the poets and by the politicians," the program stated. And quoting Eva Perón, it asserted that women had their own separate branch in the party because "just as only the workers could wage their own struggle for liberation, so too could only women be the salvation of women."

Perhaps it is Eva Perón herself who provides the best synthesis of the progressive and conservative tendencies in Peronism with respect to the image of women. Born an illegal child to a lower class family in Los Toldos, she suffered the stigma of such status in a society dominated by bourgeois morality. In 1935, when she was in her teens, like millions of other women suffering from the depression and seeking jobs in Argentina's capital city, Eva moved to Buenos Aires. She was motivated by the desire to be an actress, one of the few supposedly glamorous alternatives to domestic or factory work available to young women. Condemned to a life of poverty and marginality, she was able to achieve some success only through her relations with prominent men in the theatre. It was through a network of such relations that she eventually met Colonel Juan Perón in the early 1940's. She was a young woman of 25, with little education and no political experience. Thus her political ideology developed mainly as a result of her relationship with Perón. However, it is generally acknowledged that Eva, for all the limitations of her political analyses, felt much more authentically in touch with the working class than did Perón. Indeed, she viewed herself as the link between Perón and the people, and she once said, "The people can be sure that between them and their government, there could never be a separation. Because in this case in order to divorce himself from his people, the President would have to first divorce his own wife!"

According to one author, Perón's approach was a paternalistic one. "Thus with all his welfare work in the balance in his favor, Perón was still part of a system through which he was trying to achieve more power. But Eva came from 'nowhere,' with no institutional ties to this system, and all resolute to destroy it." In this regard, a telling difference between the two came in 1951 when, in reaction to an attempted military coup against Perón, Eva wanted to pass out guns to the workers to defend the regime while Perón feared to do so.

Eva Perón had the dynamic energy and anger that came from being lower class and a woman in Argentine society. She once said that "I remember very well that I was sad for days when I found out that the world had both poor and rich people; and the strange thing is that it wasn't the existence of the poor people that hurt me as much as knowing that at the same time there existed the rich." This statement reflects in a sense the ambivalence of the lower class toward bourgeois society. Eva Perón's public image reflected that ambivalence. At first, as the President's wife, she wanted to be accepted by the women and men of the oligarchy, and so she dressed in elaborate, very expensive clothing and was referred to officially as Señora Doña María Eva Duarte de Perón. But as she became more directly involved in political activity and took on her own militant political identity, her image changed. She began to dress in plain, unadorned clothing and was referred to simply as Evita. In fact, she became known as "comrade Evita" throughout Argentina, and she often asserted that her name had transformed itself into "a battle cry for all the women of the world."

As the head of the Peronist Feminist Party and the Eva Perón Foundation and with her influence in the General Federation of Workers, Evita had perhaps as much power as any woman in the world, and she used it. But for all her power and strength, she constantly emphasized publicly that all of her actions were founded on her love and admiration for Perón. She praised Perón as the savior of Argentina to whom all workers and women should look for leadership in what she perceived as the revolutionary movement to make Argentina economically strong and politically sovereign. Furthermore, at the same time that she urged women to struggle autonomously for their own political development, she reinforced the traditional view of the role of women within the home as the mainstay of the society. "The home," she said, reflecting the general assumptions of Peronist ideology, "is the sanctuary of motherhood and the pivot of society. It is the appropriate sphere in which women, for the good of the country and of her own children, fulfills her patriotic duty daily. . . ."

Not only did Evita represent the progressive and conservative aspects of the Peronist movement with respect to women, but she also symbolized the contradictions of Peronism with respect to its bourgeois class content and the aspirations of the working class that supported it. "The virtues and the defects of Eva Perón," writes Juan José Sebreli, "are those of the Argentine woman of her era with its immense possibilities and its limitations, and all women of Argentina should view themselves through her mirror. Not completely class conscious, her passionate, spontaneous, anarchistic conception at once reflected and stimulated the spontaneity of the Argentine working class. The workers saw themselves reflected in Eva Perón because they lacked ideological tools . . . and because they did not have an authentic class-based party, nor a coherent, revolutionary ideology. . . ."

Because the Peronist movement did not challenge the basic socio-economic structure of Argentina which had traditionally been controlled by the oligarchy and foreign interests, no sustained economic growth could take place from the early 1950's on. Thus whatever advances women (and the working class in general) made under Perón were curtailed, especially after the 1955 coup which removed him from power. The present position of women in Argentina — increasing unemployment among female workers, lack of opportunities for women college graduates and no female representatives in Congress — must be seen within the legacy of Peronism: several decades of economic stagnation, a constant rising cost of living and continual political instability.

68. *The Past Behind the Present in Argentina*

GEORGE PENDLE

George Pendle, the British writer who has specialized in the history of the Río de la Plata countries, here provides in brief compass a bird's-eye view of Argentine history which emphasizes historical continuities.

The absence of a "stabilized and integral collective life" in Argentina is partly the consequence of the country's extraordinary geographical diversity — subtropical luxuriance in the north; Andean deserts, and oases, in the west; temperate, fertile plains in the centre; the windswept south — and the great distances that separate the chief groups of population.

Argentina has been divided by history no less than by geography. In colonial times the Spaniards, whose main base in South America was on the Pacific coast at Lima, generally approached the area now named Argentina from that side of the Andes; and they established their principal settlements in the Andean foothills and marginal mountain ranges, where they founded Salta, Tucumán, Santiago del Estero, Mendoza, Córdoba. To the east, across the vast pampa, on the muddy estuary of the Río de la Plata, Buenos Aires was no more than a sad little outpost of the Empire. Thus geographical separation was confirmed by the pattern of settlement.

When, in the second half of the eighteenth century, Buenos Aires became

From "Argentina: The Past Behind the Present," by George Pendle, *International Affairs*, 38, no. 4 (October 1962), pp. 494–500. Reprinted by permission.

the seat of administration of a new Spanish vice-royalty that stretched from the Andes to the Atlantic, the people in the east and west of the country were not united. This development merely reversed the relative importance of Buenos Aires and the Andean towns. Buenos Aires grew in prosperity, while the western towns declined. Liberation from Spanish rule in the early years of the nineteenth century, and the opening of Buenos Aires to the shipping of all nations, carried the separation further. The merchants in Buenos Aires now found it cheaper to obtain woollen *ponchos* from Yorkshire by sea than overland by ox-cart from Santiago del Estero, cheaper to get wine from France than from Mendoza, sugar from Brazil than from Tucumán. As Domingo Faustino Sarmiento wrote in his classic work on the period, *Facundo,* Argentina contained two incompatible types of society: on the one hand there was, in Buenos Aires, an urban civilization on the Spanish and European model; on the other hand, in the countryside, the wild life of the uneducated and lawless *gaucho*. Moreover Buenos Aires, being the nation's only port, received and appropriated to itself all the Customs duties, leaving the other provinces almost without public income.

For many years after the attainment of independence from Spain there was no national government, though Buenos Aires constantly fought to extend its authority westwards across the pampa. The dictator Rosas during his long rule (1835–52) ruthlessly crushed rebellious provincial *caudillos,* but he could not entirely subdue them. In 1853 the provinces set up a Confederation, which Buenos Aires refused to join, and Argentina was in fact two states until, at the battle of Pavón in 1861, the Buenos Aires army defeated the Confederate forces. Thereafter, Argentina was in organization one nation. But successive presidents of the republic, by using their constitutional powers to "intervene" in the provinces, kept alive the old resentment. Time after time, when they disapproved of the results of provincial elections, they would depose provincial governors, members of the provincial legislatures, municipal officials, and judges and install their own representative — an *interventor* — to manage provincial affairs and to "supervise" the next elections. This procedure continues today.

After the 1850s the economy of the pampa was transformed by the building of railways, the development of cattle-raising to satisfy European (chiefly British) demand, and the coming of a flood of agricultural labourers from Italy and Spain. But this extraordinary economic growth did not greatly contribute to the unification of Argentine society. The railways were not designed to draw the population together: their purpose was to carry the pastoral and agricultural produce of the interior by the shortest route to the shores of the Río de la Plata for shipment abroad. The European immigrants, arriving in such numbers, naturally did not help to form a "stabilized and integral collective life." (In 1895 the population of Argentina was about 4 million, of whom one million were foreigners.) Nor was the preponderance of Buenos Aires reduced. The landowners, enormously enriched, built extravagant mansions for themselves in the capital, while the standard of living of the rural workers was no better than before.

In 1890–1 a brief interruption occurred in the rising national prosperity. Excessive optimism and public extravagance had produced a high degree of inflation. The crisis revealed another conflict of interests, though this proved to be less fundamental than it seemed at that time.

During the period of inflation the conservative landowners — who were now in permanent control of the central government — welcomed the fall in the value of the Argentine currency because they sold their meat and grain for British pounds or French francs, and in consequence of the depreciation they received a higher peso income for their exports. On the other hand, the inflation threatened to ruin the Buenos Aires merchants, who had to pay at soaring peso rates for the British manufactures, the French wines, and the olive oil which they imported. A large proportion of the merchant and shop-keeping class were of European birth, or the sons of immigrant parents, and their outlook had little in common with that of the landowners.

This urban middle class were the main strength of a Radical Party which arose out of the crisis of 1890–1. Their principal demand was for free suffrage and honest elections — in other words, that their own class should be given an opportunity to share in the management of the country. In the second decade of the twentieth century the Radicals made their first experiment in government; but of course by then they were just as Argentine as the Conservatives, and when their leader, Hipólito Irigoyen, was elected president of the republic in 1916 he ruled just as autocratically as his predecessors. Indeed, Irigoyen outdid all previous rulers in the use — or abuse of his powers of intervention in the provinces.

Again and again liberal-minded men sincerely tried to set up representative government of the British or North American kind, but when a more or less democratic régime was established it almost invariably evolved into a dictatorship or was overthrown by a coup d'état. It would not be an exaggeration to say that the conflict between imported democratic ideas and the local tradition of personal leadership — *caudillismo* — has been the central theme of political development in Argentina, as in other South American republics. Parkinson has even suggested that "it is to South America that we must look, in the first instance, for dictatorship introduced and perpetuated as an admitted necessity; defended by thinkers of integrity and seen by historians as a positive good. . . . All modern dictatorship owes its inspiration to Simón Bolívar."

Under Irigoyen the Radicals wasted their opportunity, and they were replaced in 1930–1 by a military-Conservative alliance. In fact the Radicals — the name was a misnomer — had discovered that they did not really desire any drastic alteration in the economic system. Consequently they, almost as much as the Conservatives, failed to gain the support of the urban working class, who were rapidly growing in strength and could not indefinitely be denied participation in public affairs. Nor were the workers greatly attracted to Socialism, which they were inclined to regard as a foreign creed. When the stream of immigration was cut off after the economic crisis of 1930 the workers became more and more Argentine in outlook and ready to follow a *caudillo* who would appeal to their nationalist sentiments and who would offer to improve their standard of living — an improvement which they were unable to achieve by parliamentary means.

The army, too, was increasingly dissatisfied with the Conservatives, into whose hands the government had passed again. A group of younger officers, in particular, were determined that Argentina should be transformed into a modern industrialized state, and they realized that the conservative oligarchy were obstructing that transformation. So the military coup d'état which occurred in 1943 not only removed the Conservatives but prepared the way for a new era.

In the next two years, however, the senior officers grew alarmed by the activities of one of their colleagues, Colonel Juan Perón, who, as Secretary of Labour and Social Welfare, was gaining extraordinary popularity among the working class by promoting their interests with great zeal and publicity. In 1945, in an attempt to halt this process, Perón's military critics compelled him to resign from the government. Perón defiantly appealed to the workers for support. He was then placed under arrest. Working-class riots followed, and the trade union leaders — feverishly assisted by the young radio performer Eva Duarte who, like Perón himself, was of humble social origin — organized large-scale demonstrations. To appease the crowds, Perón was released.

As President of Argentina Perón raised the standard of living of the workers. He encouraged the expansion of urban industry — not only in Buenos Aires, but also in provincial towns such as Córdoba. He would have developed the southern oil-fields if he had remained longer in power.

In making these and other contributions to social and economic progress, however, and in his manoeuvres to maintain himself in power, Perón aggravated the fragmentation which for so many years had been characteristic of Argentine society. By playing one sector of the community against another — politicians, landowners, businessmen, workers — he weakened the opposition but increased internal disunity.

Perón's military successors likewise, by repressing and ostracizing the *Peronistas,* made it impossible for an "integral collective life" to come into being. The Aramburu government dedicated itself to the purging of the country of every trace of *Peronismo.* Those who had been connected with that régime were dismissed from the federal and provincial administrations, and from universities, law-courts, and embassies abroad. Military *interventores* were placed in charge of the trade unions, and the Peronista Party was outlawed. The workers retaliated with strikes and sabotage. Employers (as the Buenos Aires Correspondent of *The Times* wrote) now treated the workers with deliberate lack of consideration, their attitude being: "Well, you fellows: you have had your day. Now it's our turn."

As the Peronistas — comprising about one third of the electorate — were not permitted to nominate their own candidates for the general elections in 1958, they voted for the faction of the Radical Party that was headed by Dr Arturo Frondizi, who had indicated that he would give them a fair deal if he were elected. With the Peronistas' assistance Frondizi won an overwhelming victory, and in spite of the protests of some members of the military hierarchy General Aramburu allowed him to be inaugurated in the presidency.

Frondizi had declared that he would govern, not for any one party, but for the whole nation, and it was evident that he intended to bring the Peronistas back into the community. Soon after assuming office he ordered a general increase in wages, granted an amnesty to those who were in prison or exile for political offences, and enabled Peronistas to re-enter the public service. The military leaders objected to these concessions, and during the next three years they repeatedly compelled the president to dismiss from official posts those whom they suspected of having Peronista sympathies. Nevertheless, at the congressional and provincial elections in March 1962 Frondizi rather rashly allowed the Peronistas to vote for their own candidates. This was doubtless another attempt to close the rift in the community; at the same time Frondizi probably judged that the Peronistas, having been proscribed for six years, would no longer vote as a bloc. In the event, the Peronistas won more than half of the available seats in the Chamber of Deputies and the majority of the available provincial governorships. Thereupon the leaders of the armed forces, fearing that Frondizi would permit the revival of Peronismo to continue, deposed him, imprisoned him, and ordered the annulment of the elections. The generals and admirals now had no clear policy for the nation. Their one aim was to keep the Peronista workers out of politics, to drive them back to where they properly belonged — to the meat-packing plants, the textile factories, etc., whence Perón had so irresponsibly brought them forth.

In deposing Frondizi, as when overthrowing Perón, the military were serving the interests of the upper class (now consisting not only of the landowners, but also of industrialists, bankers, and merchants). It is true that the majority of the military officers today are of petit bourgeois origin, but they (and their wives) saw a career in the armed forces as means to social advancement. During the 1930s and 1940s they were pampered by military governments, and in the social upsurge of the Perón era they gained prestige and quite comfortable prosperity. After the revolution which overthrew Perón in September 1955, officers with Peronista left-wing tendencies were placed in retirement, and the disputes which subsequently occurred within the armed forces arose mainly from disagreement on the measures to be adopted for preserving order and the traditional social structure.

In Argentina, as in other Latin American countries, the desire of the present military hierarchy, as of the civilian oligarchy, is that the capitalist system shall be perpetuated, and that whatever modifications may have to be made to adjust it to modern conditions shall cause the least possible inconvenience to the privileged members of the community.

Conditions are constantly changing, but to a considerable extent we can find in the past the explanation of why the Argentines behave as they do today. During the nineteenth century, as we have observed, they acquired the habit of *not* co-operating with one another. Caudillo was against caudillo, the capital city against the provinces. Landowners who amassed vast wealth soon became (with some notable exceptions) absentee owners, inhabiting quite another world from that of their *peones*. When foreign settlers arrived, they were allowed to live their own lives in their own way; and while their children were taught at school to sing the Argentine national anthem and to honour the national heroes, they learned also to be Argentine individualists, each one of them a *"Señor Yo,"* a "Mister I." Military officers — featherbedded heirs of the soldiers who marched across the Andes with San Martín — today still pay lip service to parliamentary democracy but take it for granted that government by decree is the only practical method of preserving order.

Of course, many of the characteristics and conditions described in the present article are by no means peculiar to Argentina. A combination of *all* of them does not exist, however, in any other country. Critics — foreigners, and Argentines too — contend that the Argentine way of conducting affairs is deplorable. Nevertheless, it is in this way that Argentina became, and still manages to remain, the most highly developed nation in Latin America.

Most foreigners — and, indeed, most Argentines whom one meets abroad — know little of Argentina outside Buenos Aires and the nearby holiday resorts. But Buenos Aires is a deceptive city. In appearance, and in its way of life, it is the most European of all Latin America's major cities, so one is apt to forget that it only exists by reason of the very *un*-European hinterland, which it dominates but which, since the pastures and grainfields provide the city's wealth, does, in a sense, dominate the city in return.

Buenos Aires is swept by a wind that comes from the desolate south; a wind that has passed over the dreary adobe villages of the remote regions, and over the rich *pampa;* a wind which, meeting the warm air currents from the north, creates violent storms upon the capital. Likewise, Buenos Aires, in spite of its European aspect, is affected by powerful social and political pressures that are provincial, disturbing ànd, above all, South American. This is nothing new. It has always been so.

69. *An Eyewitness Account of the 1952 Revolution in Bolivia*

CARTER GOODRICH

The late Professor Carter Goodrich of Columbia University and the University of Pittsburgh had extensive experience in Argentina and Bolivia on various kinds of economic missions, so that he was very experienced in the mores of Latin America. Here he gives his own personal story of how the revolution broke out in 1952 and how the new government tackled its pressing problems.

The Bolivian Revolution of 1952 opened with a burst of rifle and machine-gun fire at daybreak on the Wednesday of Easter Week. The firing ceased on the afternoon of Good Friday, and a new government was in possession of the capital city of La Paz.

The Hotel Sucre Palace, in which my wife and I were living, was not touched in the three days of street fighting. The manager refused to let the revolutionary forces plant a machine gun on the roof, and he took the precaution of flying the flags of Paraguay and the United Nations, since both the Paraguayan ambassador and the UN mission of technical assistance had offices in the building. The iron gates of the hotel were kept locked except during the brief informal truce on Good Friday morning, called so that the religious could go to mass and housewives could replenish their supplies. As the fighting went on, we could see from the hotel roof ambulances and trucks carrying wounded to a Red Cross station in the next street and returning for more, their stretchers still soaked with blood. On the third day we watched the firing approach us as troops loyal to the old government fought their way uphill to a point less than a quarter of a mile away. . . .

Since I had been sent on missions to Bolivia during the governments of President Urriolagoitia and of the military junta and since I was stationed in La Paz from February 1952 until September 1953, certain of my impressions may assist in the interpretation of the revolution. . . .

On Good Friday, as has been indicated, the junta was overthrown, and Siles took possession of the Presidential Palace. When I called on him on the afternoon of Easter Sunday, he greeted me as a friend because of our earlier encounter but added that, in any case, he would have received me without malice. Moreover, since the authorities at headquarters in New York had, on the holiday weekend, taken extraordinarily rapid action on a cable sent the preceding morning, I was able to convey to the new government an offer of emergency assistance on behalf of the United Nations and the related international organizations. . . .

THE GOVERNMENT'S PROBLEMS

The most urgent preoccupations of the government were usually with matters not included in the program of technical assistance. At the beginning, indeed, the problems were to assure the survival of the regime and sometimes to determine the balance of power within it. Civil servants from the orderly countries of Western Europe found it strange to work in offices with rifles or machine guns stacked in the closets, and the experts in the ministry of mines

From "Bolivia in Time of Revolution" by Carter Goodrich, in *Beyond the Revolution: Bolivia since 1954,* ed. James M. Malloy and Richard S. Thorn, pp. 3–22, passim, by permission of the University of Pittsburgh Press. © 1971 by the University of Pittsburgh Press.

learned that the Dodge power wagon, given to the government by the United Nations to facilitate their travels to the mines, was doing double duty at night tracking down enemies of the regime. In one very minor conflict between supporters in the army and the military police, a stray bullet knocked a tile off the roof of our house and the cook rushed in shouting that it was "the Rosca revolution." Her fear was not merely that the bloodshed would begin again but that the aristocracy would come back into power.

On January 6, 1953, an attempt by part of the right wing of the MNR [National Revolutionary Movement] to secure the exclusion of Juan Lechín, the miners' leader, from the cabinet was quickly put down. The next day the trade unions celebrated in the Plaza Murillo and a number of left-wing speeches were made. But the president took the occasion to remind his supporters that Bolivia could live only by the sale of its tin to the capitalist countries:

> The people must realize that Bolivia is not an island. It is in America. It is a backward country economically and from this it follows that it cannot speak in the language employed by others who talk of tunnels towards far-off countries for the export of our minerals.

NATIONALIZATION OF THE TIN MINES. The government's first major decision was to nationalize the mines of the great tin companies. The mission had two experts in mining and, later, a third on the problem of smelting. Lechín was quicker than some of his fellow ministers in seeing how to make use of the UN personnel on technical questions. These experts were not, however, consulted by the committee which drafted the nationalization decree. The mission also had no part in the negotiations that led to the early reopening of the British and American markets for Bolivian tin to which the president's speech referred. The nationalization decree of October 31, 1952, affirmed the principle of compensation for the expropriated companies, but it also made counterclaims against them which left the final balance in doubt. The government itself, however, realized that compensation could not be avoided. Professor Blasier's chapter describes the agreement reached with the Patiño interests in June 1953, later extended to the two other large companies, by which a part of the gross proceeds was to be set aside for this purpose. It seems clear, however, that informal understandings must have been arrived at still earlier, since the United States government had already made several purchases for its Texas City smelter and the private English firm of Williams-Harvey, in which the Patiño company held a large interest, had contracted in

January 1953 to purchase more than 50 percent of the Bolivian output for the next three years. Within less than four months of expropriation, a Patiño smelter thus became once more the purchaser of the product of the ex-Patiño mines.

With characteristic MNR stage management, the nationalization decree was signed by the members of the government in the presence of a great throng of miners at the mining camp of María Barzola, in Catavi, where some of their fellows had been shot down by the military police. At sunrise the next Sunday a mass was celebrated at the top of the Cerro Rico at Potosí, the hill which in colonial times has been the world's richest source of silver and was still being mined for tin. The miners present took a vow that they would work their hardest for the good of the industry, now that it belonged to the people, and even give up the practice of "high-grading" or stealing particularly rich chunks of ore for backyard refining. On its part the government made particular efforts to retain the services of the foreigners who provided most of the operating and technical management of the industry. The miners' union and, apparently, the miners themselves had come to believe that these officials were an asset to their industry that should not be lost. At one camp, indeed, the miners held the departing manager captive until they received word from La Paz to release him. One who did decide to stay, the North American who became general manager of the Unificada mine at Potosí, was rewarded by what must have been one of the world's noisiest birthday celebrations. Wakened at 12:01 A.M. by a great blast of dynamite, he rushed to the door and found his miners and their womenfolk with two bands ready to begin a twenty-four hour fiesta. On the other hand, most managers and engineers refused to stay, either because they distrusted the new regime or because they feared possible blackballing for future employment by private companies. Perhaps a hundred remained but more than two hundred — North Americans, British, Dutch, Germans, and others — left the country. Those who left included almost every man who had been either a manager or a chief engineer of a major operation.

If the vows of Potosí had any lasting effect on labor productivity in the mines, it was more than offset by a decision that reflected the struggles of the preceding years. "All miners who had been dismissed for political reasons between 1946 and 1952 were reinstated in their jobs after the April 9 revolution, while no workers then employed were dismissed." Because of their part in the revolution and the importance of their product to the economy, the miners could claim high priority for their demands; a later chapter will discuss the effect on the national economy of overstaffing and increased labor costs.

THE INDIAN IN THE NATIONAL LIFE.   The MNR's second major concern was to "incorporate the Indian in the national life." The barriers separating the three groups of white, *cholo* ("mixed Indian and white blood"), and Indian were supposedly distinct and impenetrable, yet the census taker would almost certainly record as *blanco* ("white") the exceptional full-blooded Indian who had acquired wealth and a comfortable home. Though the distinctions were always stated in racial terms, in practice they sometimes reflected differences in life style and economic status rather than descent. At any rate, the Indians to whom the MNR slogan primarily referred were neither those who had moved to the mining camps nor the members of the small jungle tribes in the eastern lowlands but rather the mass of the Quechua and Aymara population living and working on the land for the *haciendas* or in the remaining independent indigenous communities. For these Indians, known as *campesinos* ("country dwellers"), the degree of isolation from organized Bolivian society can hardly be exaggerated. It was to them that a municipal official in Cochabamba referred when he told me that the only solution for the problems of the country was to exterminate the Indians and replace them with European immigrants. Even when far more liberal members of the upper class discussed the need to improve the condition of the campesinos, the conversation was likely to betray traces of the traditional vague fear of Indian revolt.

The cholo occupied a different position. He was typically a town dweller performing a variety of functions in the lower reaches of the urban economy. He was obviously at home in La Paz, and so, even more obviously, was the chola with her brown derby and layers of bright skirts, sitting beside a pile of oranges on the street corner or on a mound of vegetables in the central market, or perhaps keeping shop in a hole in the adobe wall surrounding the gardens of a fashionable mansion. On the other hand, whenever Indians appeared in La Paz before the revolution, they kept mainly to the back streets, dressed in extremely ragged clothing, or drove llama trains loaded with llama dung to serve as fuel in their masters' town houses. Some of them served as bearers of burdens. One of these appeared at our office in the hotel staggering under a wooden box of supplies which, according to the stenciled label, weighed well over two hundred pounds. This he had carried upstairs on his back since Indians were not allowed to use the elevator. Though the campesinos could be independent enough in their own setting, as I learned from the hilarity which greeted my efforts to buy a digging stick in the village market at Tiahuanaco, they appeared in the city as members of an alien and inferior class.

Against this background, even city-based foreigners could see something of the changes brought about by the acts of the revolutionary government. A new Ministry of Countrymen's Affairs, *Asuntos Campesinos,* was established, proclaiming its policies in posters with inscriptions like the following:

> The Indian has served us for four centuries.
> Let us devote the next fifty years to serving him.

Its offices were on the Prado a few blocks from the Hotel Sucre Palace, and before long the broad sidewalks were crowded with Indian families waiting for conferences with its officials or signing up for the campaign against illiteracy.

More spectacular were the processions of tens of thousands of campesinos from all over the country that were brought in to La Paz by truckloads to celebrate various official holidays such as the Anniversary of the Revolution on April 9. Each group carried banners bearing the slogans of the revolution and, in some cases, of the attack on *analfabetismo* ("illiteracy"), and it was usually preceded by its own band playing panpipes or native drums or other instruments. Some of the men, and even a few women, carried guns. In each unit the first rank or two of the marchers typically included the village leaders with their staffs of office and others in the native costume of their region. The procession, which formed an ethnologist's or at least a photographer's review of the indigenous population of the country, moved for hours through the main streets of the city and ended in either the Plaza Murillo or the stadium where the president rendered an account of his stewardship.

In the meanwhile the campesinos of the Cochabamba region had formed strong agrarian syndicates, and agents of the ministry had been encouraging the development of similar organizations in other regions. A campesino militia had been organized and supplied with guns, putting it on the same footing with the miners' and workers' groups, both of whom had retained their rifles since the revolution. Efforts were made to spread educational facilities to the mass of the Indian population, the literacy requirement for voting was abolished, and suffrage was made universal.

THE LAND REFORM.   The MNR began its second year in power by appointing a commission under the chairmanship of Vice-President Siles, instructed to make, within ninety days, proposals for carrying out the party's commitment to real agrarian reform. On this occasion my colleagues and I found the atmosphere quite different from that which had surrounded the earlier period of decision regarding the mines. Either because we had won more confidence or because land reform was a less sensitive issue (since this time the property to be expropriated was almost entirely Bolivian), the mission was given the opportunity to provide an expert on land reform and its administration. The man chosen was the well-known Mexican agricultural economist, Edmundo Flores. The government could be confident that, as a Mexican, he would be in sympathy with the general policy of agrarian reform; indeed, Foreign Minister Guevara had once told me that the purpose of the Bolivian revolution was to achieve the results of the Mexican revolution "without ten years of Pancho Villa." On our part, we knew that Flores was concerned that more should be done than had been done in Mexico to make the reform economically viable.

All members of the commission were agreed on abolition of the prevailing system under which the Indian typically gave three or four days of labor a week to the *patrón* ("landlord") without wages, receiving in return the right to cultivate for his own use a small parcel of land on the estate. All were further agreed that the Indian should receive land of his own. There were disagreements as to whether the expropriated landlords should be compensated, and, if so, how — and whether the new owners should pay for the land they were to receive. The main motives for reform were moral and political, to redress injustice and to redistribute power. The preamble of the decree, however, described the old system as "irrational" as well as "unjust" and listed as one of the objectives "the liberation of the forces of agricultural production." Actually, several provisions of the decree were intended to promote economic efficiency. The *latifundio,* defined as a large rural property farmed by traditional techniques with servile labor, was abolished as serving no social purpose. On the other hand, there was an attempt to preserve what was called the *empresa agrícola* ("agricultural enterprise") which invested capital, used modern techniques, and paid wages — a provision which was, as Flores pointed out, quite unique in land reform legislation. Other articles were intended to encourage reinvestment by landlords and settlement by campesinos in the underdeveloped areas of the Oriente. Elaborate attempts were made to adjust the provisions to the varying geographical conditions of the country, and in the end the decree contained no less than 176 articles. The full details are not worth recalling since many of them, as later chapters will show, were made inoperative either by subsequent inflation or by the actions of the campesinos themselves. From the beginning, it was clear that the Indians' small plots of land were now their own property and that unpaid labor was abolished. But how much land, if any, was to be kept by the patrón and how his former holdings were to be divided and worked were not, in practice, wholly determined by the text of the law.

Promulgation of the decree was again an exercise in MNR showmanship. The date chosen, August 2, was declared to be "The Day of the Indian." The place was in the Cochabamba valley whose campesinos, more strongly organized than those of other parts of Bolivia, had since the revolution already accomplished by force a land reform more drastic than that provided for by the decree. The ceremony, which I attended as one of my last official duties in the country, took place in a field outside the village of Ucureña in the presence of a throng of one hundred thousand Indians. The members of the cabinet affixed their signatures. One of them, it was said, signed away several hundred thousand acres of family property. Wálter Guevara, who, like many other educated Bolivians, had learned one of the Indian languages in childhood from the servants, made the address in Quechua. President Paz closed the proceedings with the traditional offering of chicha and coca leaf to *Pachamama* ("mother earth").

Within its first sixteen months in office, the new regime had nationalized the great tin mines, which were the nation's main source of foreign exchange, and overturned the organization of agriculture, which was the occupation of the great mass of the people. In the one case the government risked the opposition of powerful foreign and expatriate interests, and in the other it took away the basis of power from the class which had provided the principal leadership within the country. A formerly servile population, whose new prestige was symbolized by the processions in La Paz, had been given guns and the vote and, now, a right to the land and responsibility for its use. . . .

70. *The Revolution Didn't Change Everything for the Bolivian Indians*

DWIGHT B. HEATH

Professor Dwight B. Heath of the Anthropology Department, Brown University, has been one of the most assiduous and informed Bolivia-watchers during the last decade. He agrees with others who have closely observed events there that the Indians are probably a little better off than before economically. Though their lives may be just as hard as before the revolution, they have changed psychologically. They build schools, now more often possess arms, and for the first time in history they appear to believe that they can be an effective part of the nation. But Professor Heath's latest report shows that some old habits persist. It also appears from other sources that the MNR rule from 1952 to 1966 did little to provide educational opportunities for the people.*

Edmundo Flores is a brilliant Mexican economist who sometimes likes to play the role of whatever Latins would call the cracker-barrel philosopher. In the course of discussing one of my papers several years ago, he observed that "One of the slogans that fascinated Mexicans was 'Haciendas without hacendados.' Nice in theory! But of course when you take away the hacendado, you create a political vacuum, and it may well be filled by a local leader who is fully as nasty as the former landlord — and with bad table manners thrown in." Of course, Flores doesn't believe in "political vacuums" any more than did Machiavelli, but his homespun phraseology comes remarkably close to characterizing one of the most widespread and important results of Bolivia's revolutionary agrarian reform.

The campesinos [1] of Bolivia are proud beneficiaries of the only social revolution in 20th century South America. Although they took no part in the fighting that brought the Nationalist Revolutionary Movement (MNR) to power, many of them are still militant in support of that party that "gave us the conquests of the revolution, namely: agrarian reform, universal suffrage, nationalization of the mines, and educational reform." The list of "conquests of the revolution" comprises a virtual litany in which each catch-phrase is pregnant with meaning. "Agrarian reform" refers primarily to the fractionation of large haciendas and, in the highlands, abolition of the quasi-feudal *colonato* system whereby campesinos worked without pay in exchange for usufruct privileges to small plots, which have since been allotted to them. "Universal suffrage" refers to dropping the combined literacy and property-holding requirements, so that the electorate was promptly increased by more than 1200 percent, and the formerly disenfranchised campesino majority won a voice in politics.

"Nationalization of the mines" refers to the holdings of Hochschild, Aramayo, and Patiño enterprises, each of which used to have an annual budget

From "Hacendados with Bad Table Manners: Campesino Syndicates as Surrogate Landlords in Bolivia" by Dwight B. Heath, *Inter-American Economic Affairs*, 24 (1970), pp. 3–13. Reprinted by permission.

* Lambros Comitas, "Educación y estratificación social en Bolivia," *América Indígena*, 28 (1968), p. 649.

[1] "Campesino" is used in Bolivian Spanish in a dual sense — not only meaning "peasant" (as it does in Spanish elsewhere and even in English recently), but also as a post-revolutionary euphemism for "indio" (Indian), which carried an immense burden of negative connotations. [Footnote in original. — Ed.]

larger than that of the Republic of Bolivia; operation of the mines by a governmental entity has been economically disastrous but immensely popular. "Educational reform" refers to fostering of formal schooling for campesinos; as limited as it is now, it is symbolically important to people who were previously denied access to schools. Perhaps the most telling indication of the quality of change since the overthrow of the traditional quasi-feudal system is the depth of feeling with which many Indian campesinos assert that "now we are becoming human beings."

It is difficult for those affected — either as beneficiaries or "victims" — not to overestimate the pervasiveness of change in such a revolutionary setting. Nevertheless, as a social scientist who never suffered the pain and humiliation of serfdom, nor the anguish and discomfort of losing land and laborers, I think that I discern marked continuity in terms of functions, in spite of appreciable formal change, when analyzing what has become of patron-client relations on Bolivian haciendas. In many instances, campesino syndicates have come to play many of the roles that pertained previously to the landlord, especially in terms of cultural brokerage but also in many other respects.

Until the revolution in 1952, both local and national governments were content to leave management of the campesinos almost entirely in the hands of *hacendados* (owners of haciendas). In some areas, the hacendados actually lived on their property and took an active part in dealing with their peons (*colonos*) — e.g., settling disputes, administering first aid, sanctioning marriages and divorces, offering usufruct privileges in land, and so forth. When the hacendado was not in residence, a mayordomo (usually a mestizo) did these things in his name. The relative autonomy of the hacienda could be attributed in part to problems of transportation and communication, but perhaps more to the point were indifference of officials with respect to peons on the one hand, and respect for the traditional autarchy of hacendados on the other.

The hacienda comprised a community in most senses, and the peons had little recourse to domains beyond. Campesinos participated in a distinctive local sociocultural system which provided no direct access to regional or national institutions of education, government, or commerce. The rare dealings they had with the world beyond the hacienda were almost invariably mediated by the hacendado as patron and broker. The power of the hacendado was virtually absolute on his own property, and the hacendados formed a block whose wealth and political connections allowed them to effectively manipulate other levels. In retrospect, the brokerage role of the hacendado is justified by the gentry as part of their benevolent paternalism; it is roundly condemned by the campesinos as having been a systematic limitation of their horizons.

The foregoing description in very general terms applies to all of the four major zones of Bolivia: the altiplano, the temperate valleys, the yungas, and the eastern lowlands. The author has conducted research in the last two areas; the small but excellent literature on the other areas similarly reveals considerable local variation in emphases and tactics, but with striking overall similarity in precisely this respect: that the campesino syndicates have become surrogate landlords in post-revolutionary Bolivia.

THE PRE-REVOLUTIONARY SITUATION

Among the services that hacendados required of their peons in most areas was unpaid agricultural labor totaling about one man-week per household per week. In the highland areas, more feudal services were exacted: *faena,* group work projects on hacienda property, to care for roads, irrigation ditches, walls, manorhouse grounds, etc.; and *pongueaje,* periodic service rendered, by turns, in the manor house, with men as busboys and women as cook-maids. A variety of other obligations varied locally, including the provision of eggs, firewood, the care of livestock, dairying and cheese-making, drying and baling coca, etc.

The hacendados, proud of their "white" heritage, took their dominant positions to be not only "right" but even "natural," in view of the supposed inherent inferiority of Indians. A few were sadistically abusive, but most enjoyed a degree of leisure and comfort that cost only in terms of labor on the part of the colonos. Indians were considered "like children," so many hacendados provided first-aid for their colonos, rudimentary schooling for a few chosen individuals, and even spoke on their behalf on those rare occasions when a colono had to deal with anyone beyond the hacienda community (e.g., if more sophisticated medical aid were needed, the hacendado would take his colono to the government clinic or to a pharmacist in the provincial capital; if the police charged a colono, the hacendado would intermediate; and so forth). In each such instance, the hacendado would serve as patron and broker for his colono, who in turn was his client. The hacendado had power over the colono, and could choose those realms in which he wished to serve as patron. The hacendado could, of course, be restrictive as well as facilitating — in terms of obstructing as well as providing "connections" — and the colono had virtually no ways of seeking other patrons, even for limited purposes. For example, hacendados tried to keep labor organizers and other "agitators" from contacting their colonos.

Even when the social reformers of the MNR acceded to power in 1952, no one would have been so bold as to predict the degree to which the sociocultural system of the campesinos (ex-colonos) was to be opened, and the pervasiveness of change in ways of thinking and acting that have in fact occurred. It is a truism that most of this change was also felt by the ex-hacendados as well — (although the effects of such changes were obviously restricting rather than facilitating for that formerly dominant group).

POST-REVOLUTIONARY CHANGES

The cardinal purpose of this paper is to illustrate realignment of the major patronage-clientage networks involving campesinos, as old roles have been redefined and new ones created, in the aftermath of the MNR revolution.

Probably the most important changes are three that take place at the level of the individual hacienda-community. First, the colonos (tenant farmers in an almost feudal serfdom) became ex-colonos (independent freeholders). Second, the hacendados (quasi-feudal landlords) were generally forced off the land and lost all claim to the services of campesinos; most ex-hacendados are now business or professional men in cities. Third, virtually all ex-colonos joined to form a *sindicato* (peasant league), a corporate entity to represent all who had been colonos on a single hacienda.

The change in status of former colonos is the basis for the enormous psychological impact of the revolution, the campesinos cherish what they call their "liberation from slavery." They look back on their obligations to the hacendado as having been extremely burdensome, and their status as having been degrading, even in those instances where hacendados were not physically abusive or sexually exploitative.

The change of status of former hacendados has been, by contrast, a harsh deprivation which they strongly resent. They consider that their property (often household goods as well as the land) were "stolen" and that the Indians, supported by the opportunistic MNR, are unjustly and systematically persecuting them for no other reason than resentment combined with covetousness.

The formation of syndicates has been a potent force (probably the crucial one) in providing political socialization for campesinos, and, on most ex-haciendas, the syndicate provides both a sense of participatory community and a channel for brokerage with respect to nearly all of an individual ex-colono's contacts with the world beyond.

In order to effect approaching pervasive reform in a quasi-feudal system, it is necessary to create new social institutions. After the revolution of 1952, the campesinos on a given ex-hacienda were often linked to each other only as distant neighbors and as former co-workers of a dispossessed employer. The ex-hacendado and former mayordomo who had been the coordinators, decision-makers, and brokers usually left the community, so that leadership and organization were minimal until the syndicates emerged as effective institutions, based on new kinds of authority and explicitly oriented toward a new set of goals which could be subsumed under the novel rubric of campesino welfare. Although the syndicates were unlike anything seen by most campesinos before, they were not a unique social invention. Their organizational structure is very similar to that of the miners unions, on which they seem to have been consciously modeled.

Although the syndicates were constituted primarily as means of securing title to land, they gradually came to serve other functions as well. The syndicates were effective organizations for political socialization and indoctrination by a small cadre skilled in demagoguery and able to channel small-scale patronage. The clients in this relationship offered occasional support for MNR by participating in political demonstrations, both locally and in major cities.

The actual activities of the syndicates are varied, and include far more than land claims and political demonstrations. Often these activities overlap with the jurisdiction of pre-existing formal institutions. For example, it is the syndicates and not the courts that have supplanted the hacendado in resolving conflicts between campesinos. This applies not only to informal accusations of petty theft, minor assault, and so forth, but even to such institutionalized differences as divorce. It goes without saying that such conflict resolutions do not have the legal force of orthodox court procedures, but they are often respected locally nevertheless. The syndicates also mediate in some cases of inheritance, land exchange, and so forth, despite the fact that they have had no official legal jurisdiction since dissolution of the *Juntas Rurales,* short-lived rural land courts of the mid-1950's.

Another important kind of syndical activity is public works projects. For example, on many of the ex-haciendas, ex-colonos pooled their labor to build schools, and often they even went on to hire teachers paid by special assessments (*cuotas*) when the authorities declined to assign paid teachers. The self-conscious concern with education is deep and pervasive in contemporary campesino life; in the words of one articulate spokesman, "The landlords took advantage of our grandfathers, our fathers, and us because we were ignorant. Now our sons must never suffer the abuses of slavery, because they know enough. The accomplishments of the revolution of April (1952) are of the utmost importance — there are no more Indians; we are becoming human beings! But the *real* revolution — the establishment of a completely new order based on social justice — that must be based on the education of the masses."

Other public works projects include the installation of water systems, the building and maintenance of roads, bridges, and trails, the construction of football fields or of plazas, occasionally the construction of a first aid station (*puesta sanitaria*), and so forth, for which campesinos usually provide both funds and labor (although they seek technical assistance and material through high-level campesino organizations).

Syndicates are involved not only in law, education, and public works, but also in economics. One of the most popular and inaccurate myths concerning Indians in highland Latin America is their supposed predilection for communal cooperation. It appears that urban nationals have accepted this as uncritically as have foreigners, and many ambitious development plans have failed because they were based on this unfounded assumption. Contrary to the expectations — and explicit intentions — of those who fostered the syndicates, few have become cooperatives in any meaningful way, although many have become so in name, and thereby enjoy certain advantages with respect to taxation. Although they are by no means communalistic as is often assumed, this is not to say that Bolivian campesinos are totally uncooperative. The *aini,* the traditional pattern of reciprocal labor exchange that used to be restricted to the extended family, now sometimes involves most of the members of a syndicate. Similarly, cooperation of other kinds has been taught as a crucial tool in effecting the common goals of the ex-colonos, both within the local community and beyond it. They early learned, from their organizers and from the dramatic example of miners and other unionized workers, that there is power in numbers.

A variety of other nonpolitical activities occur among the campesino syndicates. Among the most widespread is soccer, with frequent inter-syndical competition which is enjoyed as a spectator sport. In a few syndicates, teachers offer night courses in Spanish and in literacy; such courses are well attended, by women as well as men. Occasionally, a first aid kit and some medicine are kept for use, at cost, by syndicate members. Although there is no formal program of social security, orphans and the aged are usually cared for by kinsmen, but in at least some instances, when there were no relatives on the ex-hacienda, such individuals were informally adopted by neighbors within the syndicate. Occasionally, an imaginative and energetic agricultural extension agent takes advantage of the syndical organization in order to reach ex-colonos more efficiently with demonstrations, films, and other educational services.

Other means by which campesino syndicates could serve their members are often discussed, more by leaders than by the rank-and-file. For example, it is not only outsiders who talk about the potential value of cooperatives. An important aspect of MNR policy was to foster cooperatives, by exhortation and by preferential taxation. Syndical leaders throughout the country generally agree that the economic situation of ex-colonos could be strengthened by the introduction of cooperatives for buying goods and necessities, and for selling agricultural produce. In no instance, however, had this ideal been translated into action.

The elected secretary-general of a syndicate clearly has power in many domains, but it is by no means unlimited. In sharp contrast with the stereotype held by townsmen, there are only a few campesino leaders who have become *caciques,* or despotic autocrats. On the contrary, major decisions are usually submitted to the rank-and-file, although, to be sure, their support is often achieved more through demagogic oratory than studied debate. The campesinos, rank-and-file as well as leaders, speak proudly of the new democratic processes exemplified in regular syndicate meetings, even though the chief official of a local syndicate (whose official title is *"secretario general"*), is often referred to, in clear personification, as *"el sindicato."* In fact, he often acts in the same global patron and broker role vis-à-vis his constituents as did the hacendado before him.

Quite apart from representing the syndicate in extra-hacienda contexts, the secretary-general also has considerable responsibility on the ex-hacienda. For example, he oversees public works projects, such as preparation of a soccer field, building a school, and so forth. Furthermore, he keeps track of those who have fulfilled their obligations (called *faena,* just as such projects before the reform) and serves as foreman throughout the work. Not only does a man in this status serve as a spokesman for his syndicate elsewhere, but he must also provide hospitality to visiting secretaries-general and to other distinguished visitors. By the same token, any outsider attempting to gain effective entree into the ex-hacienda community would be impolitic not to explain his mission to the secretary-general whose local authority — like that of the hacendado before the revolution — is so great that he is often called on to act as judge, although he has no legal power within the official judicial hierarchy.

There is no clear-cut survival of *pongueaje,* the housekeeping obligation of colonos, but the role of members' wives in cooking for and serving "visiting firemen" on syndical business is required and unremunerated as was similar work performed for the hacendado in pre-reform days.

When the secretaries-general speculate enthusiastically about the potential value of instituting buying cooperatives, they cite the very advantages that colonos used to enjoy in many hacienda commissaries.

Several secretaries with specialized functions constitute the directorate of any syndicate, but the specific list varies, and some posts are often vacant or inactive. There is little competition for syndical office at the local level, and secretaries often serve until they ask to be relieved. Sometimes elections are held annually, and reelection for several successive terms is common. Positions within the syndicate are not ranged in any particular hierarchy of prestige, and there is no standard sequence of progression. It would be inappropriate to consider the syndical organization as comparable in any significant way to the civil-religious hierarchy traditionally so important in the social organization of many highland Indian communities.

CONCLUSIONS

In short, despite sweeping reforms in the forms of social structure instituted by the MNR, there are many instances in which aspects of the *patrón-peón* relationship persist virtually unchanged, in functional terms. A new *patrón-peón* type of functional relationship has been established with a new form, the syndicate (or the secretary-general) assuming the dominant paternalistic status formerly held by the hacendado, and the campesino continuing in a relatively dependent servile status.

Only in a few instances have secretaries-general strong-armed their way into monopolizing the land, which may have been what Flores meant when he referred to some post-revolutionary Mexican *caciques*. But if we consider the hacendado role in behavioral terms, it is more crucial as patron and broker than merely as landlord. And, in this sense, the *sindicatos campesinos* in most instances have come to play the role that formerly was played by the hacendado. In those cases where a strong individual dominates rather than the corporate board of *secretarios* or the community consensus, we may well speak of them as "hacendados with bad table manners."

71. *The Background for Reform in Chile*

FREDRICK B. PIKE

The world tends to look upon Chile as a country with substantial democratic traditions, with no pattern of recurring dictatorship or domination by the military. It also has had deep social and economic problems that help to explain the background of the present socialist government there under Dr. Salvador Allende.

Professor Fredrick B. Pike of the University of Notre Dame history faculty has long been noted for his frank and independent judgments on Latin American history. The fact that his conclusions are based upon a wide variety of sources makes them worthy of careful consideration. The following selection comes from his chapter "Social Conditions in Mid-Twentieth Chile: Old Problems Acquire New Urgency."

UNITED STATES MISAPPRAISALS OF CHILEAN SOCIAL CONDITIONS

The misappraisals made by United States observers, who have erred by way of excessive optimism because they have failed to probe beneath surface appearances, have sometimes encouraged their country to proceed as if no urgent social problem existed in Chile. In 1931, for example, upon his return to New York after an extended stay in Chile, Spruille Braden reported that the communist threat to that country had virtually disappeared. He added: "In Chile there is much less difference between the rich and the poor than in any country of the world that I know . . . a tremendous leveling in life has occurred there. . . . The Chilean today confronts his hard situation with serenity."

At the time Braden made this remarkable statement, statistics revealed that the annual average income for approximately 90 per cent of the entire Chilean labor force was one thousand pesos, roughly the equivalent of eighty dollars. The million workers represented by this statistic had perhaps experienced a leveling process, but not of the sort to which Braden had alluded. Furthermore, the lower-income sectors and reform-minded elements showed that they were not, after all, serene: they established the short-lived Socialist

From *Chile and the United States, 1880–1962 by Fredrick B. Pike* (Notre Dame: University of Notre Dame Press, 1963), pp. 271–293, passim. Reprinted by permission.

Republic in 1932; they flocked to join socialist and communist organizations throughout the 1930's; and in the 1938 presidential elections they helped achieve victory for the candidate of the Radical-Socialist-Communist Party alliance.

By no means have all United States observers formulated naively optimistic appraisals concerning Chile. In 1936 George McBride in a classic study of Chilean agrarian society painted a bleak and accurate picture of the master-and-man structure and depicted the horrors of the marginal existence led by thousands who were virtually serfs. Some twenty-five years later, the *New York Times* published factual, hard-hitting editorials on Chile's appalling social conditions. But the disconcerting message for some reason has never been taken to heart, and the United States has continued largely to judge Chile by the writings and utterances of suave and distinguished upper-class writers and diplomats who constantly offer assurances of their country's progressivism. This approach is clearly demonstrated in the book *Chile through Embassy Windows,* in which Claude G. Bowers, United States ambassador in Santiago from 1939 to 1954, heaped uncritical praise upon all the superficial aspects of Chilean life and judged the country by its lustrous veneer. *The Atlantic Monthly* in one of its 1959 "Reports" found Chile a nation where major problems were being resolved. In the same year, upon returning from his Latin-American tour, President Eisenhower displayed confidence and noted that when visiting a Chilean housing project he could tell by looking into the eyes of the occupants that he was viewing a happy people. These happy-eyed people gave the majority of their votes in the 1958 presidential and in the 1961 congressional elections to the Marxist ticket.

THE SITUATION AS OTHERS HAVE SEEN IT.   Other foreign observers and many Chileans have not been so easily deceived. In 1923 the French writer André Bellesort in *La jeune amérique* noted that Chile, although appearing to be politically the best organized of the Latin-American republics, was undermined by the existence of a lower class so miserable, so bereft of hope, that it had neither sufficient energy nor class consciousness to aspire toward improvement. Nearly fifteen years later Radical Party Senator Gabriel González Videla, later to serve his country as president, implied in one of his most brilliant speeches in the upper chamber that the French writer's gloomy appraisal was still applicable. If the Chilean rightists, asserted González Videla, lost a proportion of their livestock equal to that of the annual human loss occasioned by infant mortality and abortion, they would take immediate steps to remedy the situation. But in the face of the manpower loss to the Chilean race, they assumed always a calm attitude and spoke of the inevitable balance of nature. With considerable eloquence González Videla pleaded that Chile begin to utilize the potential of all classes of the population; that it take special pains to safeguard the health of the young and to provide them with adequate schools, so that a Chilean's ability to rise in society would be limited only by his own capacity. This impassioned denunciation of Chile's social structure was timely in 1937. It would have been equally timely at the beginning of the 1960's.

THE STATISTICS OF POVERTY AND WEALTH. Statistics must be called upon to support so critical a generalization. According to figures compiled by the Chilean Development Corporation . . . the real income of all groups in Chile grew approximately 40 per cent between 1940 and 1953. Distribution of this income, however, worked to the disadvantage of lower-class manual laborers. These workers, comprising roughly 57 per cent of the active population, won an increase in effective remuneration of only 7 per cent. The real income of white-collar workers rose an estimated 46 per cent, and that of proprietors, of the self-employed and of workers in the various services soared 60 per cent. Little wonder, then, that Roberto Jadue Saba in a 1960 study affirmed: ". . . from 1940 to 1954 there has been a regressive redistribution of total income, carried out at the expense of the lower-income groups."

This conclusion, confirmed in a later study by Helio Varela, becomes all the more meaningful in the light of a reliable estimate that in 1942 — before the retrogressive redistribution process was well under way — 77 per cent of the working force did not earn sufficient income to provide a single man with a decent and respectable mode of life. Only 0.3 per cent enjoyed income adequate to provide the minimal standards of respectable living for a family of four. . . .

The grinding lower-class poverty to which these figures attest has led many to question the wisdom of President Jorge Alessandri's anti-inflation measures. In 1959 and 1960, Alessandri fought inflation essentially by calling upon workers to make the first and the greatest sacrifice — a policy that had also been urged by United States advisers in the 1955–1956 Klein-Saks mission. Workers were asked to accept wage readjustments of one third of the increase in cost of living. This outraged even the usually moderate Daniel Armanet, long-time director of the excellent monthly, *Economía y Finanzas*. Armanet asserted: "To maintain salaries almost unalterable when the level of prices has risen, is mathematically the same as to lower them when prices have remained stable. This, in a country of low living standards, is an intolerable measure."

What do some of the statistics that have been cited mean, when translated into concrete examples of human existence in Chile? What are some of the inescapable conditions of life for Chile's city-dwelling lower classes?

THE URBAN POOR.   *Illiteracy and Illegitimacy.*   National illiteracy figures and educational survey data suggest that over one fourth of the urban lower classes are either illiterate, and therefore disfranchised, or else educated only to the extent of being able to spell out laboriously the simplest words. Even more suggestive of governmental inattention to social problems is the fact that illiteracy rates have tended to remain rather constant between 1930 and 1952, amounting in both years to approximately 25 per cent of the population. The Chilean education structure has not, during the past generation, been given the funds or direction necessary to enable it to keep pace with the population increase. Much of the potential of the Chilean population, therefore, remains unrealized. This situation is all the more lamentable in view of the fact that in previous generations, Chile was one of the leaders among Latin-American nations in educational advances.

In addition to the handicap of illiteracy, many of Chile's urban lower classes suffer from the stigma of illegitimacy. The over-all rate of illegitimacy continues to hover around 30 per cent, which implies that close to 50 per cent of the lower classes are illegitimate.

Housing Conditions.   In 1941, a government housing agency estimated that 152,000 new units would have to be constructed within the next nine years to house adequately the anticipated population increment. Even if these units had been constructed, nothing would have been done for those living in overcrowded, unsanitary squalor as of 1941. But, in the nine-year period the number of units actually constructed was 50,903. Statistics for 1941 and 1942 showed that of the 6,100 children brought to court on various criminal charges, 95 per cent came from sub-standard homes, or else had no homes at all. Allocation of public funds for housing projects, nonetheless, aroused the ire of Senator Fernando Alessandri Rodríguez who argued in 1943 that private enterprise alone must be allowed to provide houses for the needy. Senator Alessandri maintained that the United States had relied exclusively upon private enterprise in its housing projects, and admonished Chileans to follow this enlightened procedure.

A government census, the results of which were published in 1955, declared that 30 per cent of the population was housed in units not meeting minimal sanitary standards. Experts, moreover, estimated that between 1953 and 1959 the number of urgently needed housing units rose from 400,000 to 500,000. Another aspect of the problem was underscored by an economist who noted in 1957 that Chilean rentals take one of the highest percentages of income of any country in the world. One consequence is the prevalence of *callampas* (literally, mushrooms), slum areas made up of shacks constructed by squatters which simply grow spontaneously without planning, authorization, or control.

Even more discouraging is the blatant disregard for human dignity which the government has sometimes shown in constructing slum-clearance projects. "Lo Valledor" in Santiago is an example. Its approximately 11,000 units are capable of providing shelter for between 50,000 and 80,000 persons. But its wooden huts of concentration-camp uniformity into which thousands can be crowded impress many viewers, be they housing experts or amateur observers, as an outrage to humanity. Unheated, lacking a sewage system and indoor water, separated by barbed wire, with an outdoor toilet boasting not the slightest semblance of privacy, they create an ambient which seems calculated to deprive their occupants of any hope for a decent existence. Nowhere else in Latin America has this writer seen such a dreary array of flimsily slapped-together wooden crates masquerading as a government housing project. The few Chilean upper- or middle-class members who have seen "Lo Valledor" typically shrug their shoulders when queried about the matter, and note that such houses are all the lower classes deserve, and are at least better than the *callampas* which they ostensibly replace. The last is a debatable contention. The *callampa* shacks at least demonstrate an originality and spontaneity in construction and design that might actually be more stimulating to the imagination and the psyche of their dwellers than the stolid sameness of the "Lo Valledor" huts.

Alcoholism and Undernourishment.   Chilean doctors and students of social conditions have long been convinced that per-capita alcohol consumption is higher in Chile than in any other Latin-American country. The striking fact of this situation is that upper and middle classes are, it is commonly agreed, reasonably temperate. This means that the lower classes must do much more than their share in driving up consumption figures. This seems in particular to be a function of the lower-class men — for their women are not noted for drinking excesses. In various urban slum areas it is estimated that from 20 per cent to 30 per cent of the men are chronic drunkards, who can be expected to spend the majority of weekends on prolonged binges. . . .

The habitual drunkenness of a large portion of lower-class workers produces notable effects on Chilean productivity. Industrial accidents occur at the highest rate on Monday, and absenteeism is also highest on that day. There is a commonplace joke in Chile that Monday is a sort of unofficial holiday, the so-called San Lunes, or Blessed Monday.

Lower-class chronic drunkenness arises in part from the fact that, given relative food and wine costs, wine is often the cheapest source of caloric energy. Therefore, many men can scarcely afford not to be drunkards. Closely connected to drunkenness, then, is the problem of undernourishment. In 1945, careful investigations revealed that only 14 per cent of the primary school students did not show evidence of long-term undernourishment. At about the same time Senator Guillermo Azócar described in the upper chamber how one could stand on any street corner of Santiago and observe the degeneration of the Chilean race in the parading files of the sick, lame, deformed, and underfed. The senator further observed that whenever he began to discuss this matter, he was soon induced to desist because of the bored and annoyed expressions of his colleagues. In the years following Azócar's gloomy appraisal, the problem of undernourishment has become more acute. Recent studies indicate that the average height of Chileans is now actually declining because of malnutrition.

Disease and Infant Mortality.   Given the background already described, it is only natural that Chile has long had one of the highest tuberculosis rates, as well as one of the shortest spans of average life expectancy, of all the Latin-American republics. In addition, it is likely that one out of every four children born to urban, lower-class parents will die before reaching the age of five. The infant mortality rate in Chile is still one of the highest in the southern hemisphere.

GENERAL OBSERVATIONS ON CHILE'S URBAN LOWER CLASSES.   Because of the conditions in which they live, urban lower classes are generally regarded by their social superiors as the dregs of humanity, incapable of contributing anything except the brute labor which makes it possible for the upper classes to pursue their "higher cultural calling." Once a year, however, the humble laborers do have a holiday dedicated to them, the day of the Chilean *roto* (literally, broken one). They are then privileged to hear on the radio or at mass gatherings flowery oratory which proclaims the virtues and superiority of the Chilean lower classes. If they could read, they might also marvel at some of the books which convey the same message. In this way, privileged-class orators and writers offer assurances that the *rotos* have not been wronged, for, as the reasoning goes, they continue to be superior to lower classes elsewhere in the world. . . .

Leading a subhuman, marginal existence, denied any likelihood that they or their children will greatly improve their lot, the Chilean *rotos* survive on the basis of their incredible stamina, patience, resignation, inward resources, and a zest for life that even the most adverse circumstances cannot totally crush. The women in this class, especially, struggle heroically to provide their children with the most essential elements of food and clothing so that they need not join the hordes of juvenile beggars roaming city streets.

It is the *roto* children who particularly arrest the attention of visitors to the poorer districts of Chilean urban centers. In the attentive and alert expressions of so many of them, promise, ability, and intelligence seem clearly revealed. . . .

ASPECTS OF RURAL CHILE. The social conditions of agrarian life are no better than those encountered in urban regions. In rural Chile there still endures an outmoded, nonproductive, semifeudalistic land and social structure that denies to the serf (*inquilino*) any right to share in the riches of society beyond what his master may paternalistically dole out to him. It is a fact, moreover, that although Chile's gross agricultural output has increased slightly since the early 1940's, per-capita productivity has notably declined. The failure of agricultural production to keep pace with rising needs in Chile has been one significant factor contributing to the post-Second World War inflation and has also forced the nation to import huge quantities of food. During the 1950's Chile, with some of the finest land resources in Latin America, capable according to most authorities not only of feeding its own population but of providing food for sister republics as well, devoted an annual average of approximately one sixth of its foreign currency expenditures to food imports. How has this incredible situation come into being? One authority asserts: "The basic reason underlying the failure of Chilean agriculture to keep up with growing needs may have to be sought in its semifeudal structure."

Chilean agricultural land is still concentrated in the hands of a few. It is estimated that 9.7 per cent of agrarian property holders own 86 per cent of the arable land, while 74.6 per cent own 5.2 per cent. In the provinces of Santiago, Valparaíso, and Aconcagua the situation is even more unbalanced, with 7 per cent of the landowners possessing 92 per cent of the land. Many of the large-estate owners are urban *nouveau riche* elements that have acquired land relatively recently. Others, though descendants of traditionally landowning families, have at some period in the twentieth century acquired urban and foreign economic interests which furnish the major portion of their income. For neither group of landowners does essential livelihood depend upon productive use of rural property. Furthermore, a sense of responsibility to the common good has never developed to the extent necessary to induce them to increase output. A study prepared by the Economic Commission for

Latin America in 1953 revealed that vast areas of land in Santiago and Valparaíso provinces, although well suited to intensive farming, were not under cultivation. The study showed further that 35 per cent of the landholders who owned arable land that was neither under cultivation nor in pasture were simply not interested in augmenting production. . . .

The large estate owners' lack of interest in productive management as a means of bringing food to the hungry is illustrated by the fact that in 1961 the number of extensive rural holdings offered for sale in Chile was considerably more than the market could absorb. Worried by the mounting pressure for legislation that would require effective utilization of land, the owners, who are not primarily dependent upon income from their agrarian operations, were trying to dispose of their farm property. They simply did not want to be bothered with introducing advanced methods of production.

The lack of concern which the landowners have shown for the basic needs of the lower classes is evident also in the type of relations which many have maintained with their serfs. The National Society of Agriculture (*Sociedad Nacional de Agricultura*), the most powerful association of landowners, has customarily exerted its full force and influence to deny to the rural worker the right to enter into agrarian syndicates or cooperatives. The power of the landowners is reflected also in the fact that the majority of rural laborers are not included in the benefits of the social security laws. Moreover, there is little desire on the part of many landowners to elevate the educational and cultural level of these laborers, to turn them into well-fed, efficient workers with incentives for greater output. Given their basic social and economic attitudes, nothing could interest these landowners less. This situation once led Gabriela Mistral to observe: "Our rural barbarism is enormous.". . .

The continuance of semifeudalism, then, has contributed to the chronic undernourishment of vast population segments, to the disrepute of manual labor in general and to the freezing of urban manual laborers in their lowly social position, and to the difficulty of erecting a modern economic structure in the cities. The plight of the urban underlings cannot be fundamentally bettered until the rural landowners are either goaded into contributing to the over-all needs of the nation, or until they are stripped of their present power and influence.

THE MIDDLE CLASS AS A CONTRIBUTING FACTOR TO THE CULTURE OF POVERTY

It is possible to blame the landowners rather directly for the deterioration of Chilean agriculture, and indirectly for the poverty and stagnation of the urban centers. It is logical to assess Chile's urban middle class — many members of which are also landowners — with a major share of the direct responsibility for the plight of the lower classes in the cities. Chile's urban middle sectors have traditionally demonstrated colossal indifference to the social problem and have dedicated themselves to defending the value-judgments of the upper classes.

The readily observable traits of the middle class have led to the introduction into the Chilean vocabulary of the word *siútico*. A *siútico* is a middle-class individual who emulates the aristocracy and its usages and hopes to be taken for one of its members. It is generally agreed that Chile's middle class abounds in *siúticos*.

Because of their desire to assume upper-class attitudes, middle group members have developed very little consciousness of themselves as members of a distinct class. It is extremely difficult to detect opinions, customs, and value-judgments in Chile that are demonstrably middle class. Almost the only clear middle-class trait has been the tendency to shun the lower mass and to embrace the aristocracy. This fact may stem in part from the fact that historically . . . the Chilean aristocracy has in general been more open to entry by middle-class elements than in other Latin-American countries. . . .

A large number of Chilean writers have turned their attention to the middle class. . . .

The number of authors who have commented upon the middle-class betrayal and exploitation of the manual laborers is legion. Not only because of their impressive number, but because of their close agreement, their charges cannot be lightly dismissed. This writer's own observations and conversations in Chile have confirmed, moreover, that the country is still to a large degree characterized by a close association between upper and middle groups which works to the disadvantage of the lower mass.

Probably the attitudes of Chile's middle class have produced an important superficial advantage for the country. Because this group has in its political, social, and economic thinking so closely reflected the attitudes of the aristocracy, there has been almost no disruption as middle sectors have won increasing power in Chilean politics. This has contributed notably to Chilean stability. The role assumed by middle sectors may also have contributed to economic and social stagnation.

Obviously, not all middle-class members uphold aristocratic values. As of 1962 there were many signs that some middle groups might sincerely be seeking an alliance with the lower classes and not (as in the past) simply trying through hypocritical promises to play the game of political opportunism. Stung by inflation and with their hopes for expanding opportunity frustrated by Chile's lack of real growth, some middle-class supporters of the Christian Democrat Party, of the activist wing of the Radical Party, and of the FRAP alliance, seemed intent upon siding with the lower masses in a genuine attempt to alter the traditional sociopolitical structure. Some of the young members of the Conservative Party seemed also to fit into this category. This was a relatively new development in Chilean politics, one that could in the years ahead prove to be of great significance.

EDUCATION AND THE CLASSES.   Since early in this century Chilean educators and intellectuals have been writing books pointing out the inadequacy and outmoded orientation of the national educational structure. One of the features most commonly criticized is the lack of attention to technical education, with the accompanying overemphasis of the philosophical approach. This not only has slowed the rate of economic progress, but has meant that the typical middle-class product of the national educational system — which is, incidentally, largely controlled by middle-class, Radical Party bureaucrats — has been taught to think like an aristocrat of the past century and to hold in disdain manual labor and those who perform it.

As early as 1910, Alejandro Venegas in *Sinceridad* charged Chilean education with turning out stuffy sycophants of the aristocracy, utterly devoid of interest in the common good and unable to contribute to the vitally needed economic progress of their country. Two years later, Francisco Antonio Encina suggested in his *Nuestra inferioridad económica* that the type of education received made it impossible for the average Chilean to respond adequately to modern economic challenges. In 1916, *El Mercurio* observed: "We have among us thousands of university graduates who are true monuments of uselessness, and at the same time a living indictment of our national educational system." The early 1920's saw several Chilean congressmen complaining that education only prepared their countrymen to become doctors, lawyers, architects, and engineers versed exclusively in theory, and did nothing to prepare a person to develop the nation's natural wealth. Many national congressmen also agreed that Chilean education helped preserve class prejudice and at the same time implanted disdain for labor and technical proficiency.

The later criticisms that have been heaped upon education are well summarized in the writings of Amanda Labarca, who for longer than she might care to recall has been one of Chile's outstanding *pensadores,* feminists, and educators. Possessing faith in the ultimate role of the middle class in moving Chile ahead, Labarca feels that a superannuated educational system has unduly delayed this class in fulfilling its destiny. Coming to the heart of the problem, another writer-educator asserted in 1950 that education must begin to emancipate itself from the social prejudices which lead 99 per cent of those entering the *liceo* — somewhat the equivalent of the United States high school, but organized around an entirely different curriculum and dedicated to a different social purpose — to want to be professionals, so as to gain access to the world of the aristocracy. Educators, it was further alleged, have passively permitted the continuing neglect of those studies that would be genuinely useful in developing the country. . . .

RACIAL CONSIDERATIONS AND THE CLASSES. The majority of Chile's lower classes display recognizable Indian features, often manifest in some degree of skin-darkness. On the other hand, the great majority of the middle and practically the entirety of the upper classes do not clearly exhibit physical characteristics attributable to Indian blood. This fact has exercised profound effects upon the nation's social structure and has contributed to the incredible slowness of the ruling classes in concerning themselves with the crushing burdens of the lower classes.

Racist interpretations are commonplace in Chile. Early in the twentieth century, Nicolás Palacios in a very popular book, *La raza chilena,* suggested that Chilean superiority to other Latin-American populations stemmed largely from the predominance of Basque or Gothic blood. In later times one of the most convinced of Chile's many racists has been the distinguished historian Francisco Antonio Encina, who basically repeats the Palacios assertions about the superiority of Gothic blood. . . .

If Chilean superiority is regarded as the consequence of Basque or Gothic blood, what place is left for the Indian and those who share his blood? It is not necessary to search far in Chilean literature for the answer. Politician and author Alberto Cabero argued that Chileans are superior to Peruvians because there are few Indians and mixed-bloods in Chile. . . .

The anti-Indian literature produced in Chile is vast. A random sampling of some of the published opinions illustrates the broad aspects of the prejudice that is an important national characteristic. One writer asserted that high infant mortality among the lower classes results from the stupidity and proneness toward uncleanliness and drunkenness bequeathed by their Indian blood; another stated that the mental inferiority of Araucanians is recognized by almost all Chileans; while from still a different source came the pronouncement that the racial superiority of the white upper classes made unavoidable the exploitation of the inferior, mixed-blood, lower classes. A prominent army general contended that Indians are lazy, dirty, irresponsible, and that southern Chile was doomed unless Indian influence was eradicated by European immigration. A noted intellectual was even more pessimistic, observing that because Chilean lower classes in general were contaminated by Indian blood, national progress was unlikely unless a veritable flood of white immigration descended upon the entire country. Echoing this pessimistic tone, another writer suggested that the Indian mentality, which could not advance beyond concepts of subsistence production, was responsible for Chile's problems. On the other hand, there have been many writers who although defending the Indian have sadly noted the prevailing tendency to hold aborigines and those sharing their blood in contempt, and to consider the Indians and mixed-bloods as an impediment to national progress. . . .

Upper-class criteria have even permeated down to the lowest social strata. Skin tone is the first feature that many of the humblest folk look to in assessing the physical qualities of a new-born child. If light, the child is beautiful (*precioso*); if dark, it is ugly (*feo*). This is a tragic indication of the psychological trauma which, in addition to material adversity, afflicts the lower classes.

The factor of Indian blood has contributed in telling manner to middle-class rejection of the lower classes. Priding itself on its whiteness, the middle class by and large believes in the inferiority of Indians and mixed bloods. Clinging to the aristocracy, it has erected a psychological barrier between itself and at least one third of the population. To a subtler but to just as deep-rooted an extent as in Peru, Ecuador, Bolivia, and Guatemala, the Indian problem, or a variant of it, is involved in Chile's social and economic ills.

THE TWO CHILES. The profound consequences of the social problem have created in Chile two distinct modes of existence separated by well-nigh unbreachable barriers. There is a Chile of the rulers and the assimilated portion of the population, a Chile noted for its stability, orderliness, sophistication, culture, and enlightened legal and political institutions. There is another Chile made up of people who can best be described (in words made famous by Arnold Toynbee) as an internal proletariat: in society but not of society. Put in other terms, it is safe to say that while Chile is a nation ostensibly with a population of over 7,000,000, considerably less than 5,000,000 actually participate or will participate upon reaching maturity in the vital currents of national existence. The other more than 2,000,000 exist in a category that is somewhat similar to serfdom or slavery. Because of their situation they are themselves demoralized, and bereft of hope and vitality. Perhaps worse, the presence of an immobile, inert mass of still docile and fatalistic workers demoralizes, corrupts, and enervates those who take advantage of them and imparts a viciously derogatory connotation to the word labor.

The gulf between the two population elements has prevented Chile from producing the consistent, dynamic, and energetic drive that is necessary to impel an underdeveloped country into the modern era. A nation that purposely prevents intercourse, communication, mobility, and cross-pollination among the social classes automatically limits its potential for progress in the sort of world that exists in the twentieth century. What is more, in the long run, it invites a devastating social revolution.

72. What Should Be United States Policy toward Latin America?

KARL M. SCHMITT

Naïve assumptions and political predispositions abound in the Good Neighborhood. Some seem to believe that the United States is responsible for every problem in Latin America, while others — usually North Americans — are convinced that if only Latin Americans would emulate us all would be well and eventually they would be prosperous and worthy too!

Professor Karl M. Schmitt of the Government Department of the University of Texas, Austin, has long pondered on how United States policy should be shaped to recognize the complexities and realities involved. He believes that the United States is "in need of a thorough review of its Latin American policies" and sets down his program *"if he were President."*

Today the United States does not have a Latin American policy; rather it has a series of policies. Some are mutually contradictory, and some are contrary to the political realities. In narrowly security matters we follow once again the Monroe Doctrine with its basic commitment to unilateral action, as evidenced in the Guatemalan case, the two Cuban affairs, and the Dominican crisis. Moreover, as in the past we seemingly can apply the Doctrine only to the Caribbean area. We still support the concept of an inter-American system and its organizational structure (the OAS and subordinate bodies), and a series of treaties; but the structure functions fitfully and the treaties are often

From "Contradictions and Conflicts in U.S. Foreign Policy: The Case of Latin America" by Karl M. Schmitt, in *American Foreign Policy and Revolutionary Change,* ed. Jack B. Gabbert (Pullman, Wash.: Washington State University Press, 1968), pp. 44–47. Reprinted by permission.

dead letters. We pay lip service to the Good Neighbor Policy, but the United States has rejected nonintervention as an unworkable concept and makes no pretense of treating the Latin American states as equal and sovereign. And, finally, the United States acts as though the Alliance for Progress as outlined by John Kennedy were a reality when in fact no alliance has been formed, progress has been uneven, and some of the basic concepts of the Alliance have been scrapped as inexpedient or unworkable.

I believe that there is no formula for a totally successful and integrated policy. It is significant to note, however, that in this world in turmoil, in this revolutionary age, the only working policy of the United States for the Western Hemisphere is the Monroe Doctrine with its assumption of unilateral action by the United States in pursuit of its security. It is not the Monroe Doctrine that is the "obsolete shibboleth" (as it was once called), but rather the Good Neighbor Policy with its nonintervention doctrine based on an assumption of collective security, the equality of states, and the pursuit of common interests. These conditions no longer exist, if they ever did. The Monroe Doctrine with its limited geographic applicability and its limited scope is obviously not enough of a policy. But I do not believe that the Alliance for Progress or the Inter-American System as presently constituted offer the basis for viable policies. They contain too many internal contradictions and reflect too many insoluble conflicts of interest between the Latin American states and the United States to provide firm foundations for tackling hemisphere problems.

What, then, can we offer in the way of a workable set of policies and programs for the United States in its relations to its Western Hemisphere neighbors? Before launching into a set of prescriptions, let me make clear that I recognize the severe limitations of any such suggestions in terms of conflicts of national interest as perceived by governments and peoples on both sides of the issues. To the United States, most Latin American governments appear too unstable to engage in meaningful bargaining; while to most Latin American states, the United States appears so overwhelmingly powerful that she must be constrained at all costs in any way possible. In economic matters severe conflicts of interest appear almost irreconcilable. Not only is there disagreement as to who should bear the burden of development in Latin America, but there is disagreement as to how to proceed. The United States has been more interested in long-range programs, while Latin Americans are interested in short-run benefits to allay immediate social unrest. There is, too, the question of private versus public capital. Obviously not everyone can be fully satisfied.

I have postulated in this paper four major policy developments of the

United States with respect to Latin America: the Monroe Doctrine, the Inter-American System, the Good Neighbor Policy, and the Alliance for Progress. I believe that none of these are totally acceptable, but that all of them contain some aspects that are usable. What I propose is an amalgamation. This would be my program *if I were President.*

I. With respect to the Monroe Doctrine — I would never use the term in the presence of Latin Americans except in an historical context.
1. I would exercise restraint as far as possible in matters of armed intervention.
2. I would recognize that at some time it might be necessary to intervene with armed force for security or humanitarian reasons, but:
a. I would intervene coldly and openly;
b. I would attempt to obtain as much support as possible from Latin American governments; and
c. If I failed to receive support I would not badger, complain, threaten, or try to punish those who refused support.
II. With respect to the Inter-American System — I have little respect for the Organization of American States, its subsidiary organizations, and its treaties and pacts. I do not think much can be done with the system. Over the long run I would try to turn it into something like the United Nations:
1. I would make it a platform for open debate on all problems; air issues; reinstate the general conferences on a regular schedule.
2. I would emphasize its study, fact-finding, and statistic-gathering functions since I find these highly useful.
3. I would cease using it as an organ of coercion or punishment.
III. With respect to the Good Neighbor Policy — I believe that the Good Neighbor Policy as conceived and operated in the 1930's and 1940's is obsolete.
1. I would abandon the concept of absolute nonintervention and try at all costs to avoid future commitments to the doctrines; I recognize I may have to concede on this issue in the light of past events and Latin American expectations.
2. I would abandon the concepts of multilateralization of the Monroe Doctrine and of mutual defense of the hemisphere.
3. I would attempt to treat all states and their governments with respect and dignity. I would recognize all regimes and I would work toward the normalization of relations with Cuba.
IV. With respect to the Alliance for Progress — I regard the Alliance as

basically a U.S. economic assistance program. I believe that it is to the best interest of the United States to have prosperous neighbors, and I believe that we can modestly assist economic development.

1. For the moment I would continue the present commitment of U.S. public funds and for the long run attempt to increase them as the political climate in the United States permits.

2. I would attempt to create the concept of an alliance by channeling virtually all funds through the Inter-American Development Bank with the final say on the dispersal of funds delegated to a panel composed primarily of Latin Americans, *e.g.,* the Inter-American Committee of the Alliance for Progress (CIAP). (I would think that the performance of these groups would have great impact for a future increase of Alliance aid.)

3. I would abandon all attempts at sanctions for failures in the areas of social reform and political freedom; I believe that we are almost totally unable to influence structural changes in Latin America. These will have to come from within, involving as they do basic cultural attitudes and values.

4. I would abandon efforts to establish any sort of guidelines for Latin American public or private investments. These are beyond our power to change in any important ways.

5. I would abandon all efforts to promote foreign investments in Latin America. Private capital will go at its own risk seeking profit and security.

6. I would continue to encourage European and Japanese governments to help promote development in Latin America, but I would have no expectation of substantial assistance.

7. I would continue a modest amount of military aid and retain the program under U.S. controls. My reasons are as follows:

   a. The Latin American states will continue to purchase armaments. I see no reason why they should not purchase them from the United States; but I would make no attempts to push sophisticated equipment on them.

   b. Over many years the United States maneuvered to remove non-hemisphere military units and training missions from the area. The virtual monopoly of U.S. military advisers in Latin America is to our interest, and arms sales to the area is one way of maintaining that hegemony.

Substantially what I have said is designed to remove the United States from the aid business except for military assistance and as a supplier of some of the resources for development. I recognize that this exclusion will not be possible in any absolute sense. Occasions will arise when certain governments or regimes, not eligible for funds from CIAP, may make claims upon the United States that our government will want to honor for various reasons, political or otherwise. Nonetheless, I will stick to my principles in the expectation that the exceptions will prove infrequent. In other words, I want to place the responsibility for development as much as possible where it belongs, with the Latin American leaders themselves. By these measures I expect to promote the interests of the United States with a minimum of friction with its Latin American neighbors. There are no expectations of "solving" the problems.